Readings in

American Government

Fourth Edition

MARY P. NICHOLS

DAVID K. NICHOLS

 KENDALL/HUNT PUBLISHING COMPANY
2460 Kerper Boulevard P.O. Box 539 Dubuque, Iowa 52004-0539

Contents

Chapter I

The Founding and the Principles of Government

The Declaration of Independence states the principles of equality and freedom which provide the basis for an American public philosophy. American politics has revolved around interpretation and applications of those principles. Abraham Lincoln provides a classic statement of the meaning of the Declaration when he argues against the institution of slavery. The equality of rights proclaimed by the Declaration, he argues, was meant to function as a goal or standard for Americans to revere and to seek to approximate in their politics.

The equal rights that legitimate governments protect, according to the Declaration, include the rights to life, liberty, and the pursuit of happiness. Men are equal in their possession of freedom. But when equality is interpreted to mean an equal right to rule, or democratic government, a conflict between equality and freedom might result. The Lincoln-Douglas exchange reveals the danger in deriving an unqualified majority rule from the principle of equality. Douglas, supporting state sovereignty on the question of slavery, argues that slavery should be permitted in a state if a majority of its people desire it. In contrast to Douglas, Lincoln maintains that no majority can legislate slavery because that institution deprives men of their inalienable rights. There are some things that are not open to majority decision. It is necessary to limit majority rule by the ends of government stated in the Declaration.

Martin Diamond argues that the Declaration actually leaves open the possibility that other forms of government besides democracy may be legitimate. The principle of equality in the Declaration, according to Diamond, demands only that governments protect the inalienable rights of men and that they be based on the consent of the governed. Majority rule is only one way to achieve the legitimate end of government. While the Declaration established both the legitimate end and foundation of government, it is the Constitution, Diamond argues, that institutes a democracy, although one that tries to check majority rule in order to safeguard the end of government—security of rights.

The Founders, then, tried to establish a government that would combine the ends given in the Declaration with majority rule. Alternate means to these ends, the Virginia and the New Jersey Plans, were presented at the Constitutional Convention. The Virginia Plan assumes that only a strong national government would protect liberty, while the New Jersey Plan reflects a concern that a strong national government operating over a large territory would eventually destroy liberty and prevent the people from governing themselves. This small republic argument is stated by the Anti-Federalist Centinel: a republic is possible only in a small territory, since only a despotism could hold a large country together. Madison, one of the authors of the Virginia Plan, gives his answer to the partisans of the small republic in his account to Jefferson of what happened at the Convention. He says that those who oppose a strong national government fearing that its distance from the people would lead to tyranny forget that majorities too can be tyrannical. They trust majorities, says Madison, because they assume that the local population is homogeneous in character, with no conflicts of interest among the parts.

Indeed, for Madison, the way to prevent majority tyranny is to establish a large republic with a flourishing commerce. Since commerce over a large territory produces many different interests, especially those based on different kinds of property, no one interest could form a majority of the whole. Majorities would be composed of a large number of smaller groups which would have to moderate their demands in order to form majorities. A tyrannical majority would therefore be less likely. Separation of powers, checks and balances, and bicameralism are institutional arrangements that work together with the extended sphere of the large republic to protect liberty. As in the formation of majorities by coalition, interest will counteract interest, in a system that necessitates compromise and mutual accommodation.

John Adams, like Madison, sought to prevent despotism and preserve liberty by the working of self-interest. And in this regard, bicameralism is a crucial part of Adam's theory of government. For Adams, however, the Senate was to represent the wealthy class of citizens, and the House to represent the poor; and since the concurrence of both was necessary to pass laws, neither class could oppress the other. Adams is perhaps too optimistic about the ability of such simple means to achieve the desired end of accommodating rich and poor to each other, and he fails to see, as did Madison, that the people of a large commercial republic would form groups not so much on the basis of the *amount* of property as on the *kind* of property they own. Indeed, Madison thought that the large commercial republic would overcome divisions between rich and poor—precisely what Adams sought to institutionalize. Because Madison understood that the two houses of Congress would *not* represent different classes, he sought to ensure their dissimilarity by institutional means.

Hamilton too is well aware of the benefits of economic self-interest, but attempts to elevate its operation in government above the mean or petty. At the Constitutional Convention he proposed life tenure for Senators in order to give the office sufficient power and prestige to interest the best citizens. He doubted that a shorter term "would induce the sacrifices of private affairs, which an acceptance of public trust would require, so as to ensure the services of the best citizens." He had written earlier that the best legislator would consider it "not more the duty, than the privilege of his office, to do good to mankind; from this commanding eminence, he would look down on any mean or interested pursuit." Intrigue for personal aggrandizement, Hamilton thought, would be inconsistent with the legislator's "dignity of pride" and "delicacy of honor."

Hamilton gives a higher tone to the notion of a commercial republic, as he did to the self-interest of a legislator. In Federalist 11, he shows how union will bring commercial prosperity. United, America could establish a navy to protect her ships, set the terms for foreign trade, "make herself the admiration and envy of the world"; divided into separate states she would suffer "poverty and disgrace." The economic strength derived from union is a condition for political strength, but should the states remain separate, Europe could confine them to merely "passive commerce" and thereby be able to "prescribe the conditions of [their] political existence." The country's ability to command respect depends on its strength. Our neutrality will be respected, Hamilton writes, only when it is defended by an adequate power; a country "despicable in its weakness" forfeits even the privilege of being neutral. While Madison favors union because it provides the large size necessary to moderate the conflict of the parts, Hamilton favors union because it overcomes the debilitating and petty conflict of the parts.

Hamilton's argument for a standing army suggests that in a commercial republic men are preoccupied by their private affairs, pursuing their own economic gain. It is for this reason we cannot rely on a militia, whose members would not wish to leave their occupations and families in peacetime. But why would such private men take delight, as Hamilton does, in America as the "admiration and envy of the world"? Would such men be the material out of which Hamilton could forge America's strength? Must not there be something more than commercialism to make Hamilton's splendid commercial republic? Tocqueville explains how men in times of equality have a passion for physical well-being, or a desire to satisfy even the least wants of the body. Men continually seek greater wealth and fear economic ruin. As Tocqueville describes him, the American is not someone who would look down on anything from "a commanding eminence." Although Hamilton thought that properly promoted commercial activity would be "the wings" enabling America to "soar to dangerous greatness," Tocqueville thought that commercial activity in times of equality produces only mediocrity.

Furthermore, although the commercial man Tocqueville describes would be a good member of the groups of which Madison hoped majorities would be formed, he might not be a good citizen of a republican or self-governing community. The Anti-Federalists, somewhat more than the Federalists, were concerned with the good character of the citizenry. When the Centinel asks how the happiness of the community can come from "jarring adverse interests," he is not asking about the efficacy of coalition majorities and checks and balances, but about the quality of life in a republic where such expedients set the tone of life. The alternative he suggests is not the aristocratic society described by Tocqueville, where only a few can attain a lofty greatness, nor Hamilton's complex, industrious society infused with pride. Rather, Centinel longs for a simple society of citizens whose liberties are preserved by their own participation in a government close to them and simple enough for them to understand. Checks and balances are not needed to prevent majority tyranny, for the people are virtuous and there are no great disparities in wealth.

The Anti-Federalists and Hamilton both have reservations against the low character of the commercial republic. Hamilton attempted to elevate the commercial spirit to great heights, and endow Americans with strength of character and breadth of vision. The Anti-Federalists, in contrast, emphasized simple or unchecked democracy, virtue in the citizens, and public spiritedness as the best means to preserve republican liberty. These reservations against the commercial republic have continued to this day in various forms, for each represent legitimate, if conflicting, aspirations. Indeed, the American regime itself is constituted by a tension or dialogue between the commercial republic and the reservations against it.

Jefferson shares with the Anti-Federalists a concern with republican liberty. He desired to divide the country into wards or "small republics" where every citizen transacted in person the public business. Because each man participated in political affairs, he would be ready to fight for his liberties and serve in the militia of his ward.

One does not have to go as far as organizing the country into wards, however, to obtain some of the benefits that the Anti-Federalists saw attached to small republics. American federalism itself institutionalizes local self-government and thus necessitates the involvement of the people in governing themselves. Federalism is a way of combining some of the advantages of a small republic with those of a national commercial republic. Federalist 39 and *McCulloch v. Maryland* present the argument for a strong national government that nevertheless maintains a sphere for independent state action.

Tocqueville shows why the community and local government that the Anti-Federalists desired is all the more important where the principle of equality prevails. Equal social conditions, Tocqueville argues, isolate or alienate men, whereas local governments serve to bring men together into communities, converting self-interested individuals into citizens who consider the interests of others as well as their own.

William A. Schambra contrasts the national community sought through the New Deal with Reagan's new federalism. He allows us to see that at the heart of the New Deal is the attempt to attain at the national level the community that the Anti-Federalists desired, with its public-spirited sacrifice and egalitarianism. The New Deal thus can be considered another critique of the commercial republic and its self-interested individualism. By combining egalitarianism with centralization, the New Deal tried to assimilate elements of the Anti-Federalist tradition into the Federalist one. Schambra points out that this idea of a national community not only is based on unreasonable expectations of human nature but also undermines the local governments, where public-spirited community may be possible. Moreover, Tocqueville's analysis of how equality on a national level leads to both alienation and homogeneity points to difficulties in the idea of a national community. Reagan's understanding of government is an alternative to New Deal liberalism. Schambra presents the case for Reagan's attempt to transfer authority to state and local governments as well as for his reliance on private sector initiatives. He claims that Reagan's program was based on various elements in the American tradition—the Anti-Federalists' concern for community and their understanding that citizenship emerges best in small communities, the Hamiltonian notion of the dignity of commerce, and the regime's emphasis on the pursuit of self-interest. Schambra provides an excellent statement of the highest purposes federalism can serve.

Schambra notes the importance of the Presidency in the theory of New Deal liberalism, for the President was supposed to promote national community through his rhetoric. While Schambra may be correct in criticizing this understanding of leadership, we should not allow his criticism to extend to statesmanship altogether. In indicating the dangers of local or state autonomy, the Lincoln-Douglas exchange suggests the need for statesmanship on a national level. Federalism, with its reliance on local majorities, although it may moderate national homogeneity or conformism, may also lead to local oppression. Lincoln's statesmanship fulfills the nation's need for statesmen to articulate the ends of the regime and to unite the various parts of the regime in a respect for those ends. Indeed, if Schambra's description of the underlying rationale of Reagan's program is correct, Reagan himself may have used his office to formulate and promote the ends implied in the American tradition. While federalism may allow a citizenship like that desired by the Anti-Federalists to enter into the commercial republic, the national institutions, particularly the Presidency, insofar as they permit or even encourage statesmanship, allow the nation to attain a Hamiltonian strength of purpose.

1

Thomas Jefferson

The Declaration of Independence (1776)

When in the Course of human events, it becomes necessary for one people
to dissolve the political bands which have connected them with another, and
to assume among the powers of the earth, the separate and equal station to
which the Laws of Nature and of Nature's God entitle them, a decent respect
to the opinions of mankind requires that they should declare the causes which
impel them to the separation. We hold these truths to be self-evident, that all
men are created equal, that they are endowed by their Creator with certain
unalienable Rights, that among these are Life, Liberty and the pursuit of
Happiness. That to secure these rights, Governments are instituted among
Men, deriving their just powers from the consent of the governed, That whenever any Form of Government becomes destructive to these ends it is the
Right of the People to alter or to abolish it, and to institute new Government,
laying its foundation on such principles and organizing its powers in such
form, as to them shall seem most likely to effect their Safety and Happiness.
Prudence, indeed, will dictate that Governments long established should not
be changed for light and transient causes; and accordingly all experience hath
shewn, that mankind are more disposed to suffer, while evils are sufferable,
than to right themselves by abolishing the forms to which they are accustomed.
But when a long train of abuses and usurpations, pursuing invariably the same
Object evinces a design to reduce them under absolute Despotism, it is their
right, it is their duty, to throw off such Government, and to provide new
Guards for their future security. Such has been the patient sufferance of these
Colonies; and such is now the necessity which constrains them to alter their
former Systems of Government. The history of the present King of Great
Britain is a history of repeated injuries and usurpations, all having in direct
object the establishment of an absolute Tyranny over these States. To prove
this, let Facts be submitted to a candid world. He has refused his Assent to
Laws, the most wholesome and necessary for the public good. He has forbidden
his Governors to pass Laws of immediate and pressing importance, unless
suspended in their operation till his Assent should be obtained; and when so

The text is reprinted here from *The Papers of Thomas Jefferson,* edited by Julian
P. Boyd (Princeton: Princeton University Press, 1950–). This is the text of the parch-
ment copy of the Declaration (now in the National Archives) which was signed on
August 2, 1776. It is generally accepted as the most authentic of various copies.

suspended, he has utterly neglected to attend to them. He has refused to pass other Laws for the accommodation of large districts of people, unless those people would relinquish the right of Representation in the Legislature, a right inestimable to them and formidable to tyrants only. He has called together legislative bodies at places unusual, uncomfortable, and distant from the depository of their public Records, for the sole purpose of fatiguing them into compliance with his measures. He has dissolved Representative Houses repeatedly, for opposing with manly firmness his invasions on the rights of the people. He has refused for a long time, after dissolutions, to cause others to be elected; whereby the Legislative powers, incapable of Annihilation, have returned to the People at large for their exercise; the State remaining in the mean time exposed to all the dangers of invasion from without, and convulsions within. He has endeavoured to prevent the population of these States; for that purpose obstructing the Laws for Naturalization of Foreigners; refusing to pass others to encourage their migrations hither, and raising the conditions of new Appropriations of Lands. He has obstructed the Administration of Justice, by refusing his Assent to Laws for establishing Judiciary powers. He has made Judges dependent on his Will alone, for the tenure of their offices, and the amount and payment of their salaries. He has erected a multitude of New Offices, and sent hither swarms of Officers to harrass our people, and eat out their substance. He has kept among us, in times of peace, standing Armies without the Consent of our legislatures. He has affected to render the Military independent of and superior to the Civil power. He has combined with others to subject us to a jurisdiction foreign to our constitution, and unacknowledged by our laws; giving his Assent to their Acts of pretended Legislation: For Quartering large bodies of armed troops among us: For protecting them, by a mock Trial, from punishment for any Murders which they should commit on the Inhabitants of these States: For cutting off our Trade with all parts of the world: For imposing Taxes on us without our Consent: For depriving us in many cases of the benefits of Trial by Jury: For transporting us beyond Seas to be tried for pretended offences: For abolishing the free System of English Laws in a neighbouring Province, establishing therein an Arbitrary government, and enlarging its Boundaries so as to render it at once an example and fit instrument for introducing the same absolute rule into these Colonies: For taking away our Charters, abolishing our most valuable Laws, and altering fundamentally the Forms of our Governments: For suspending our own Legislatures, and declaring themselves invested with power to legislate for us in all cases whatsoever. He has abdicated Government here, by declaring us out of his Protection and waging War against us. He has plundered our seas, ravaged our Coasts, burnt our towns, and destroyed the Lives of our people. He is at this time transporting large Armies of foreign Mercenaries to compleat the works of death, desolation and tyranny, already begun with circumstances of Cruelty & perfidy scarcely paralleled in the most barbarous ages, and totally unworthy the Head of a civilized nation. He has constrained our fellow Citizens taken Captive on the high Seas to bear Arms against their Country, to become the executioners of their friends and Brethren, or to fall themselves by their Hands. He has excited domestic insurrections amongst us, and has endeavoured to bring on the inhabitants of our frontiers, the merciless Indian Savages, whose known rule of warfare, is an undistinguished destruction of all ages, sexes and conditions. In every stage of these Oppressions We have Petitioned for Redress in the most humble terms: Our repeated Petitions have been answered only by repeated injury. A Prince, whose character is thus marked by every act which may define a Tyrant, is unfit to be the ruler of a free people. Nor have We been wanting in attentions to our Brittish brethren. We have warned them from time to time of attempts by their legislature to extend an unwarrantable jurisdiction over us. We have reminded them of the circumstances of our emigration and settlement here. We have appealed to their native justice and magnanimity, and we have conjured them by the ties of our common kindred to disavow these usurpations, which, would inevitably interrupt our connections and correspondence. They too have been deaf to the voice of Justice and of consanguinity. We must, therefore, acquiesce in the necessity, which denounces our Separation, and hold them, as we hold the rest of mankind, Enemies in War, in Peace Friends.

We, therefore, the Representatives of the United States of America, in General Congress, Assembled, appealing to the Supreme Judge of the world for the rectitude of our intentions, do, in the Name, and by Authority of the good People of these Colonies, solemnly publish and declare, That these United Colonies are, and of Right ought to be Free and Independent States; that they are Absolved from all Allegiance to the British Crown, and that all political connection between them and the State of Great Britain, is and ought to be totally dissolved; and that as Free and Independent States, they have full Power to levy War, conclude Peace, contract Alliances, establish Commerce, and to do all other Acts and Things which Independent States may of right do. And for the support of this Declaration, with a firm reliance on the protection of divine Providence, we mutually pledge to each other our Lives, our Fortunes and our sacred Honor.

2

Abraham Lincoln

The Meaning of
the Declaration of Independence (1857)

. . . Chief Justice Taney, in his opinion in the Dred Scott case, admits that the language of the Declaration is broad enough to include the whole human family, but he and Judge Douglas argue that the authors of that instrument did not intend to include negroes, by the fact that they did not at once, actually place them on an equality with the whites. Now this grave argument comes to just nothing at all, by the other fact, that they did not at once, *or ever afterwards,* actually place all white people on an equality with one or another. And this is the staple argument of both the Chief Justice and the Senator, for doing this obvious violence to the plain unmistakable language of the Declaration. I think the authors of that notable instrument intended to include *all* men, but they did not intend to declare all men equal *in all respects.* They did not mean to say all were equal in color, size, intellect, moral developments, or social capacity. They defined with tolerable distinctness, in what respects they did consider all men created equal—equal in "certain inalienable rights, among which are life, liberty, and the pursuit of happiness." This they said, and this meant. They did not mean to assert the obvious untruth, that all were then actually enjoying that equality, nor yet, that they were about to confer it immediately upon them. In fact they had no power to confer such a boon. They meant simply to declare the *right,* so that the *enforcement* of it might follow as fast as circumstances should permit. They meant to set up a standard maxim for free society, which should be familiar to all, and revered by all; constantly looked to, constantly labored for, and even though never perfectly attained, constantly approximated, and thereby constantly spreading and deepening its influence, and augmenting the happiness and value of life to all people of all colors everywhere. The assertion that "all men are created equal" was of no practical use in effecting our separation from Great Britain; and it was placed in the Declaration, not for that, but for future use. Its authors meant it to be, thank God, it is now proving itself, a stumbling block to those who in after times might seek to turn a free

From Speech at Springfield, Illinois, June 26, 1857, in *The Collected Works of Abraham Lincoln,* Vol. II, Rutgers University Press, 1953.

people back into the hateful paths of despotism. They knew the proneness of prosperity to breed tyrants, and they meant when such should re-appear in this fair land and commence their vocation they should find left for them at least one hard nut to crack.

I have now briefly expressed my view of the *meaning* and *objects* of that part of the Declaration of Independence which declares that "all men are created equal."

Now let us hear Judge Douglas' view of the same subject, as I find it in the printed report of his late speech. Here it is:

"No man can vindicate the character, motives and conduct of the signers of the Declaration of Independence, except upon the hypothesis that they referred to the white race alone, and not to the African, when they declared all men to have been created equal—that they were speaking of British subjects on this continent being equal to British subjects born and residing in Great Britain—that they were entitled to the same inalienable rights, and among them were enumerated life, liberty, and the pursuit of happiness. The Declaration was adopted for the purpose of justifying the colonists in the eyes of the civilized world in withdrawing their allegiance from the British crown, and dissolving their connection with the mother country."

My good friends, read that carefully over some leisure hour, and ponder well upon it—see what a mere wreck—mangled ruin—it makes of our once glorious Declaration.

"They were speaking of British subjects on this continent being equal to British subjects born and residing in Great Britain!" Why, according to this, not only negroes but white people outside of Great Britain and America are not spoken of in that instrument. The English, Irish, and Scotch, along with white Americans, were included to be sure, but the French, Germans, and other white people of the world are all gone to pot along with the Judge's inferior races.

I had thought the Declaration promised something better than the condition of British subjects; but no, it only meant that we should be *equal* to them in their own oppressed and *unequal* condition. According to that, it gave no promise that having kicked off the King and Lords of Great Britain, we should not at once be saddled with a King and Lords of our own.

I had thought the Declaration contemplated the progressive improvement in the condition of all men everywhere; but no, it merely "was adopted for the purpose of justifying the colonists in the eyes of the civilized world in withdrawing their allegiance from the British crown, and dissolving their connection with the mother country." Why, that object having been effected some eighty years ago, the Declaration is of no practical use now—mere rubbish—old wadding left to rot on the battle-field after the victory is won.

I understand you are preparing to celebrate the "Fourth," tomorrow week. What for? The doings of that day had no reference to the present; and quite half of you are not even descendants of those who were referred to at that day. But I suppose you will celebrate; and will even go so far as to read the Declaration. Suppose after you read it once in the old fashioned way, you read it once more with Judge Douglas' version. It will then run thus: "We hold these truths to be self-evident that all British subjects who were on this continent eighty-one years ago, were created equal to all British subjects born and *then* residing in Great Britain."

And now I appeal to all—to Democrats as well as others,—are you really willing that the Declaration shall be thus frittered away?—thus left no more at most, than an interesting memorial of the dead past? thus shorn of its vitality, and practical value; and left without the *germ* or even the *suggestion* of the individual rights of man in it? . . .

3

Stephen A. Douglas and Abraham Lincoln

Exchange on State Sovereignty and the Problem of Majority Rule (1858)

Senator Douglas' Speech

LADIES AND GENTLEMEN: It is now nearly four months since the canvass between Mr. Lincoln and myself commenced. On the 16th of June the Republican Convention assembled at Springfield and nominated Mr. Lincoln as their candidate for the U.S. Senate, and he, on that occasion, delivered a speech in which he laid down what he understood to be the

From the Lincoln-Douglas Debates, Oct. 15, 1858, in *The Collected Works of Abraham Lincoln,* Vol. III, Rutgers University Press, 1953.

Republican creed and the platform on which he proposed to stand during the contest. The principal points in that speech of Mr. Lincoln's were: First, that this government could not endure permanently divided into free and slave States, as our fathers made it; that they must all become free or all become slave; all become one thing or all become the other, otherwise this Union could not continue to exist. I give you his opinions almost in the identical language he used. His second proposition was a crusade against the Supreme Court of the United States because of the Dred Scott decision; urging as an especial reason for his opposition to that decision that it deprived the negroes of the rights and benefits of that clause in the Constitution of the United States which guarantees to the citizens of each State, all the rights, privileges, and immunities of the citizens of the several States. . . . In that Chicago speech [of July 11] he even went further than he had before, and uttered sentiments in regard to the negro being on an equality with the white man. (That's so.) He adopted in support of this position the argument which Lovejoy and Codding, and other Abolition lecturers had made familiar in the northern and central portions of the State, to wit: that the Declaration of Independence having declared all men free and equal, by Divine law, also that negro equality was an inalienable right, of which they could not be deprived. He insisted, in that speech, that the Declaration of Independence included the negro in the clause asserting that all men were created equal, and went so far as to say that if one man was allowed to take the position, that it did not include the negro, others might take the position that it did not include other men. He said that all these distinctions between this man and that man, this race and the other race, must be discarded, and we must all stand by the Declaration of Independence, declaring that all men were created equal. . . .

I took up Mr. Lincoln's . . . propositions in my several speeches, analyzed them, and pointed out what I believed to be the radical errors contained in them. First, in regard to his doctrine that this government was in violation of the law of God which says, that a house divided against itself cannot stand, I repudiated it as a slander upon the immortal framers of our constitution. I then said, have often repeated, and now again assert, that in my opinion this govennment can endure forever, (good) divided into free and slave States as our fathers made it,—each State having the right to prohibit, abolish or sustain slavery just as it pleases. ("Good," "right," and cheers.) This government was made upon the great basis of the sovereignty of the States, the right of each State to regulate its own domestic institutions to suit itself, and that right was conferred with understanding and expectation that inasmuch as each locality had separate interests, each locality must have different and distinct local and domestic institutions, corresponding to its wants and interests. Our fathers knew when they made the government, that the laws and institutions which were well adapted to the green mountains of Vermont, were unsuited to the rice plantations of South Carolina. They knew then, as well as we know now, that the laws and institutions which would be well adapted to the beautiful prairies of Illinois would not be suited to the mining regions of California. They knew that in a Republic as broad as this, having such a variety of soil, climate and interest, there must necessarily be a corresponding variety of local laws—the policy and institutions of each State adapted to its condition and wants. For this reason this Union was established on the right of each State to do as it pleased on the question of slavery, and every other question; and the various States were not allowed to complain of, much less interfere, with the policy of their neighbors. ("That's good doctrine," "that's the doctrine," and cheers.)

Suppose the doctrine advocated by Mr. Lincoln and the abolitionists of this day had prevailed when the Constitution was made, what would have been the result? Imagine for a moment that Mr. Lincoln had been a member of the convention that framed the Constitution of the United States, and that when its members were about to sign that wonderful document, he had arisen in that convention as he did at Springfield this summer, and addressing himself to the President, had said "a house divided against itself cannot stand: (laughter) this government divided into free and slave States cannot endure, they must all be free or all be slave, they must all be one thing or all be the other, otherwise, it is a violation of the law of God, and cannot continue to exist;"—suppose Mr. Lincoln had convinced that body of sages, that that doctrine was sound. What would have been the result? Remember that the Union was then composed of thirteen States, twelve of which were slaveholding and one free. Do you think that the one free State would have outvoted the twelve slaveholding States, and thus have secured the abolition of slavery? (No, no.) On the other hand, would not the twelve slaveholding States have outvoted the one free State, and thus have fastened slavery, by a Constitutional provision, on every foot of the American Republic forever? You see that if this abolition doctrine of Mr. Lincoln had prevailed when the government was made, it would have established slavery as a permanent institution, in all the States whether they wanted it or not, and the question for us to determine in Illinois now as one of the free States is, whether or not we are willing, having become the majority section, to enforce a doctrine on the minority, which we would have resisted with our heart's blood had it been attempted on us when we were in a minority. ("We never will," "good, good," and cheers.) How has the South lost her power as the majority section in this Union, and how have the free States gained it, except under the operation of that principle which declares the right of the people of each State and each territory to form and regulate their domestic institutions in their own way. It was under that principle that slavery was abolished in New Hampshire, Rhode Island, Connecticut, New York, New Jersey, and Pennsylvania; it was under that principle that one half of the slaveholding States became free; it was under that principle that the number of free States increased until from being one out of twelve States, we have grown to be the majority of States of the whole Union, with the power to control the House of Representatives and Senate, and the power, consequently, to elect a President by Northern votes without the aid of a Southern State. Having obtained this power under the operation of that great principle, are you now prepared to abandon the principle and declare that merely because we have the power you will wage a war against the Southern States and their institutions until you force them to abolish slavery everywhere. (No, never, and great applause.) . . .

I hold that there is no power on earth, under our system of government, which has the right to force a constitution upon an unwilling people. (That's so.) Suppose there had been a majority of ten to one in favor of slavery in Kansas, and suppose there had been an abolition President, and an abolition administration, and by some means the abolitionists succeeded in forcing an abolition constitution on those slaveholding people, would the people of the South have submitted to that act for one instant. (No, no.) Well, if you of the South would not have submitted to it a day, how can you, as fair, honorable, and honest men insist on putting a slave constitution on a people who desire a free State. ("That's so," and cheers.) Your safety and ours depend upon both of us acting in good faith, and living up to that great principle which asserts the right of every people to form and regulate their domestic institutions to suit themselves, subject only to the Constitution of the United States. ("That's the doctrine," and immense applause.) . . .

I hold that it is a violation of the fundamental principles of this government to throw the weight of federal power into the scale, either in favor of the free or the slave States. Equality among all the States of this Union is a fundamental principle in our political system. We have no more right to throw the weight of the federal government into the scale in favor of the slaveholding than the free States, and last of all should our friends in the South consent for a moment that Congress should withhold its powers either way when they know that there is a majority against them in both Houses of Congress. . . . .

The whole South are rallying to the support of the doctrine that if the people of a Territory want slavery they have a right to have it, and if they do not want it that no power on earth can force it upon them. I hold that there is no principle on earth more sacred to all the friends of freedom than that which says that no institution, no law, no constitution, should be forced on an unwilling people contrary to their wishes. . . . I say to you that there is but one hope, one safety for this country, and that is to stand immovably by that principle which declares the right of each State and each territory to decide these questions for themselves. (Hear him, hear him.) This government was founded on that principle, and must be administered in the same sense in which it was founded.

But the Abolition party really think that under the Declaration of Independence the negro is equal to the white man, and that negro equality is an inalienable right conferred by the Almighty, and hence, that all human laws in violation of it are null and void. With such men it is no use for me to argue. I hold that the signers of the Declaration of Independence had no reference to negroes at all when they declared all men to be created equal. They did not mean negro, nor the savage Indians, nor the Fejee Islanders, nor any other barbarous race. They were speaking of white men. ("It's so," "it's so," and cheers.) They alluded to men of European birth and European descent—to white men, and to none others, when they declared that doctrine. ("That's the truth.") I hold that this government was established on the white basis. It was established by white men for the benefit of white men and their posterity forever, and should be administered by white men, and none others. But it does not follow, by any means, that merely because the negro is not a citizen, and merely because he is not our equal, that, therefore, he should be a slave. On the contrary, it does follow, that we ought to extend to the negro race, and to all other dependent races all the rights, all the privileges, and all the immunities which they can exercise consistently with the safety of society. Humanity requires that we should give them all these privileges; christianity commands that we should extend those privileges to them. The question then arises what are those privileges, and what is the nature and extent of them. My answer is that that is a question which each State must answer for itself. We in Illinois have decided it for ourselves. We tried slavery, kept it up for twelve years, and finding that it was not profitable we abolished it for that reason, and became a free State. We adopted in its stead the policy that a negro in this State shall not be a slave and shall not be a citizen. We have a right to adopt that policy. For my part I think it is a wise and sound policy for us. You in Missouri must judge for yourselves whether it is a wise policy for you. If you choose to follow our example, very good; if you reject it, still well, it is your business, not ours. So with Kentucky. Let Kentucky adopt a policy to suit herself. If we do not like it we will keep away from it, and if she does not like ours let her stay at home, mind her own business and let us alone. If the people of all the States will act on that great principle, and each State mind its own business, attend to its own affairs, take care of its own negroes and not meddle with its neighbors, then there will be peace between the North and the South, and East and the West, throughout the whole Union. (Cheers.) Why can we not thus have peace? Why should we thus allow a sectional party to agitate this country, to array the North against the South, and convert us into enemies instead of friends, merely that a few ambitious men may ride into power on a sectional hobby? How long is it since these ambitious Northern men wished for a sectional organization? Did any one of them dream of a sectional party as long as the North was the weaker section and the South the stronger? Then all were opposed to sectional parties; but the moment the North obtained the majority in the House and Senate by the admission of California, and could elect a President without the aid of Southern votes, that moment ambitious Northern men formed a scheme to excite the North against the South, and make the people be governed in their votes by geographical lines, thinking that the North, being the stronger section, would outvote the South, and consequently they, the leaders, would ride into office on a sectional hobby. I am told that my hour is out. It was very short.

Mr. Lincoln's Reply

. . . I have stated upon former occasions, and I may as well state again, what I understand to be the real issue in this controversy between Judge Douglas and myself. On the point of my wanting to make war between the free and the slave States, there has been no issue between us. So, too, when he assumes that I am in favor of introducing a perfect social and political equality between the white and black races. These are false issues, upon which Judge Douglas has tried to force the controversy. There is no foundation in truth for the charge that I maintain either of these propositions. The real issue in this controversy—the one pressing upon every mind—is the sentiment on the part of one class that looks upon the institution of slavery *as a wrong,* and of another class that *does not* look upon it as a wrong. The sentiment that contemplates the institution of slavery in this country as a wrong is the sentiment of the Republican party. It is the sentiment around which all their actions—all their arguments circle—from which all their propositions radiate. They look upon it as being a moral, social and political wrong; and while they contemplate it as such, they nevertheless have due regard for its actual existence among us, and the difficulties of getting rid of it in any satisfactory way and to all the constitutional obligations thrown about it. Yet having a due regard for these, they desire a policy in regard to it that looks to its not creating any more danger. They insist that it should as far as may be, *be treated* as a wrong, and one of the methods of treating it as a wrong is to *make provision that it shall grow no larger.* [Loud applause.] They also desire a policy that looks to a peaceful end of slavery at sometime, as being wrong. These are the views they entertain in regard to it as I understand them; and all their sentiments—all their arguments and propositions are brought within this range. I have said and I repeat it here, that if there be a man amongst us who does not think that the institution of slavery is wrong in any one of the aspects of which I have spoken, he is misplaced and ought not to be with us. And if there be a man amongst us who is so impatient of it as a wrong as to disregard its actual presence among us and the difficulty of getting rid of it suddenly in a satisfactory way, and to disregard the constitutional obligations thrown about it, that man is misplaced if he is on our platform. We disclaim sympathy with him in practical action. He is not placed properly with us.

On this subject of treating it as a wrong, and limiting its spread, let me say a word. Has any thing ever threatened the existence of this Union save and except this very institution of Slavery? What is it that we hold most dear amongst us? Our own liberty and prosperity. What has ever threatened our liberty and prosperity save and except this institution of Slavery? If this is true, how do you propose to improve the condition of things by enlarging Slavery—by spreading it out and making it bigger? You may have a wen or a cancer upon your person and not be able to cut it out lest you bleed to death; but surely it is no way to cure it, to engraft it and spread it over your whole body. That is no proper way of treating what you regard a wrong. You see this peaceful way of dealing with it as a wrong—restricting the spread of it, and not allowing it to go into new countries where it has not already existed. That is the peaceful way, the old-fashioned way, the way in which the fathers themselves set us the example.

On the other hand, I have said there is a sentiment which treats it as *not* being wrong. That is the Democratic sentiment of this day. I do not mean to say that every man who stands within that range positively asserts that it is right. That class will include all who positively assert that it is right, and all who like Judge Douglas treat it as indifferent and do not say it is either right or wrong. These two classes of men fall within the general class of those who do not look upon it as a wrong. And if there be among you anybody who supposes that he as a Democrat, can consider himself "as much opposed to slavery as anybody," I would like to reason with him. You never treat it as a wrong. What other thing that you consider as a wrong, do you deal with as you deal with that? Perhaps you *say* it is wrong, *but your leader never does, and you quarrel with anybody who says it is wrong.* Although you pretend to say so yourself you can find no fit place to deal with it as a wrong. You must not say anything about it in the free States, *because it is not here.* You must not say anything about it in the slave States, *because it is there.* You must not say anything about it in the pulpit, because that is religion and has nothing to do with it. You must not say anything about it in politics, *because that will disturb the security of "my place."* [Shouts of laughter and cheers.] There is no place to talk about it as being a wrong, although you say yourself it *is* a wrong. But finally you will screw yourself up to the belief that if the people of the slave States should adopt a system of gradual emancipation on the slavery question, you would be in favor of it. You would be in favor of it. You say that is getting it in the right place, and you would be glad to see it succeed. But you are deceiving yourself. You all know that Frank Blair and Gratz Brown, down there in St. Louis, undertook to introduce that system in Missouri. They fought as valiantly as they could for the system of gradual emancipation which you pretend you would be glad to see succeed. Now I will bring you to the test. After a hard fight they were beaten, and when the news came over here you threw up your hats and *hurrahed for Democracy.* [Great applause and laughter.] More than that, take all the argument made in favor of the system you have proposed, and it carefully excludes the idea that there is anything wrong in the institution of slavery. The arguments to sustain that policy carefully excluded it. Even here to-day you heard Judge Douglas quarrel with me because I uttered a wish that it might sometime come to an end. Although Henry Clay could say he wished every slave in the United States was in the country of his ancestors, I am denounced by those pretending to respect Henry Clay for uttering a wish that it might sometime, in some peaceful way, come to an end. The Democratic policy in regard to that institution will not tolerate the merest breath, the slightest hint, of the least degree of wrong about it. Try it by some of Judge Douglas' arguments. He says he "don't care whether it is voted up or voted down" in the Territories. I do not care myself in dealing with that expression, whether it is intended to be expressive of his individual sentiments on the subject, or only of the national policy he desires to have established. It is alike valuable for my purpose. Any man can say that who does not see anything wrong in slavery, but no man can logically say it who does see a wrong in it; because no man can logically say he don't care whether a wrong is voted up or voted down. He may say he don't care whether an indifferent thing is voted up or down, but he must logically have a choice between a right thing and a wrong thing. He contends that whatever community wants slaves has a right to have them. So they have if it is not a wrong. But if it is a wrong, he cannot say people have a right to do wrong. He says that upon the score of equality, slaves should be allowed to go in a new Territory, like other property. This is strictly logical if there is no difference between it and other property. If it and other property are equal, his argument is entirely logical. But if you insist that one is wrong and the other right, there is no use to institute a comparison between right and wrong. You may turn over everything in the Democratic policy from beginning to end, whether in the shape it takes on the statute book, in the shape it takes in the Dred Scott decision, in the shape it takes in conversation or the shape it takes in short maxim-like arguments—it everywhere carefully excludes the idea that there is anything wrong in it. . . .

4

Martin Diamond

The Revolution of
Sober Expectations (1975)

. . . What wants understanding is precisely how our institutions of government sprang from the principle of the Declaration of Independence. How and to what extent were they generated by the Declaration of Independence? And what more had to be added actually to frame those institutions? . . .

We must read the Declaration closely to free ourselves from two centuries of obscuring usage. We have transformed the Declaration in our minds by reading the phrase "consent of the governed" as meaning rule by majorities, that is, democratic government. Indeed we think of the Declaration as our great democratic document, as the clarion call to and the guide to our democratic nature. But the Declaration does *not* say that consent is the means by which government is to operate. Rather, it says that consent is necessary only to institute the government, that is, to establish it.

The people need not, then, *establish* a government which *operates* by means of their consent. In fact, the Declaration says that they may organize government on "such principles" as they choose, and they may choose "any form of government" they deem appropriate to secure their rights. That is, the Declaration was not prescribing any particular form of government at all, but rather was following John Locke's contract theory, which

From Diamond, "The Revolution of Sober Expectations," in *America's Continuing Revolution: An Act of Conservation,* published by American Enterprise Institute, 1975. Reprinted by permission.

taught the right of the people, in seeking to secure their liberties, to establish *any* form of government. And by any form of government the Declaration emphatically includes—as any literate eighteenth century reader would have understood—not only the democratic form of government but also aristocratic and monarchical government as well. That is why, for example, the Declaration has to submit facts to a "candid world" to prove the British king guilty of a "long train of abuses." Tom Paine, by way of contrast, could dispose of King George more simply. Paine deemed George III unfit to rule simply because he was a *king* and kingly rule was illegitimate as such. The fact that George was a "Royal Brute" was only frosting on the cake; for Paine his being royal was sufficient warrant for deposing him. But the Declaration, on the contrary, is obliged to prove that George was indeed a brute. That is, the Declaration holds George III "unfit to be the ruler of a free people" not because he was a king, but because he was a *tyrannical* king. Had the British monarchy continued to secure to the colonists their rights, as it had prior to the long train of abuses, the colonists would not have been entitled to rebel. It was only the fact, according to the Declaration, that George had become a tyrannical king that supplied the warrant for revolution.

Thus the Declaration, strictly speaking, is neutral on the question of forms of government: *any* form is legitimate provided it secures equal freedom and is instituted by popular consent. . . .

It is to the constitution that we must ultimately turn as the completion of the American Revolution. As to those democratic institutions, the Declaration says no more than this: If you choose the democratic form of government, rather than the aristocratic or monarchic or any mixture thereof, it must be a democratic government which secures to all people their unalienable rights. But how to do that? The Declaration is silent. . . .

What was truly revolutionary in the American Revolution and its Declaration of Independence was that liberty, civil liberty—the doctrine of certain unalienable rights—was made the end of government. Not, as had been the case for millennia, whatever end power haphazardly imposed upon government; nor any longer the familiar variety of ends—not virtue, not piety, not privilege or wealth, not merely protection, and not empire and dominion; but now deliberately the principle of liberty. . . .

While modern followers of Edmund Burke may warn of the dangers of devotion to abstract principles, they cannot blink aside the revolutionary American devotion to precisely such an abstract principle. The American truth was undeniably as abstract as, say, Robespierre's tyrannizing truth or Lenin's tyrannizing truth. And yet there is indeed something moderate and nonutopian in the American devotion to liberty which warrants Burkean celebration. Whence then the difference? Wherein was the American

Revolution one of sober expectations while the Jacobin and Leninist were revolutions of unbridled expectations? The answer lies not in degrees of devotion to abstractness, but in the substantive nature of the principle each was abstractly devoted to. It is one thing to be abstractly devoted to the Reign of Virtue or to unlimited equality in all respects or to mass fraternity or to classless society or to the transformation of the human condition itself, and quite another to be devoted to the abstract principle of civil liberty. Civil liberty as a goal constrains its followers to moderation, legality, and rootedness in regular institutions. Moreover, moderate civil liberty does not require terror and tyranny for its fulfillment. Liberty is an abstract principle capable of achievement; Jacobin or Leninist equality or mass fraternity are not. Moderate civil liberty is a possible dream, utopian equality and fraternity are impossible dreams. And the recent popular song to the contrary notwithstanding, the political pursuit of impossible dreams leads to terror and tyranny in the vain effort to actualize what cannot be. . . .

[S]obriety also lies in the Founding Fathers' coolheaded and cautious acceptance of democracy. Perhaps not a single American voice was raised in unqualified, doctrinaire praise of democracy. On the contrary, there was universal recognition of the problematic character of democracy, a concern for its weaknesses and a fear of its dangers. The debate in American life during the founding decade gradually became a debate over how to create a decent democratic regime. Contrary to our too complacent modern perspective regarding democracy, which assumes that a government cannot be decent unless democratic, our Founding Fathers more skeptically, sensibly, and soberly, were concerned how to make this new government *decent even though democratic.* All the American revolutionaries, whether they were partisans of the theory that democratic republics had to be small or agrarian or only loosely confederated in order to remain free, or whether they retained the traditional idea that democracy had to be counterbalanced by nobility or wealth, or whether they subscribed to the large-republic theory implicit in the new Constitution—all the American revolutionaries knew that democracy was a problem in need of constant solution, in constant need of moderation, in constant need of institutions and measures to mitigate its defects and guard against its dangers. . . .

The half-revolution begun in 1776 reached its completion only when the peculiar American posture toward democracy received its definitive form in the framing and ratification of the Constitution a decade later. . . . [I]n contemplating that convention we would find the answer to our earlier question: how did our institutions spring from the Declaration and what had to be added to bring those institutions into being? They sprang on the one hand from the love of free government inspired by the noble *sentiments* of Jefferson's Declaration, and on the other hand from the theoretic *wisdom* of James Madison whose sober clarity regarding democracy gave the shape and thrust to our unique democratic form of government and way of life. . . .

5

Centinel

The Small Republic Argument (1787)

. . . The late Convention have submitted to your consideration a plan of a new federal government. The subject is highly interesting to your future welfare. Whether it be calculated to promote the great ends of civil society, viz., the happiness and prosperity of the community, it behoves you well to consider, uninfluenced by the authority of names. Instead of that frenzy of enthusiasm, that has actuated the citizens of Philadelphia, in their approbation of the proposed plan, before it was possible that it could be the result of a rational investigation into its principles, it ought to be dispassionately and deliberately examined on its own intrinsic merit, the only criterion of your patronage. If ever free and unbiased discussion was proper or necessary, it is on such an occasion. All the blessings of liberty and the dearest privileges of freemen are now at stake and dependent on your present conduct. . . .

The late revolution having effaced in a great measure all former habits, and the present institutions are so recent, that there exists not that great reluctance to innovation, so remarkable in old communities, and which accords with reason, for the most comprehensive mind cannot foresee the full operation of material changes on civil polity . . . .

I am fearful that the principles of government inculcated in Mr. Adams' treatise, and enforced in the numerous essays and paragraphs in the newspapers, have misled some well designing members of the late Convention. . . . He asserts that the administrators of every government, will ever

From "Centinel I" (believed to have been written by Samual Bryan), in *Pennsylvania and the Federal Constitution 1787–1788,* ed. John Bach McMaster and Frederick D. Stone, The Historical Society of Pennsylvania, 1888.

be actuated by views of private interest and ambition, to the prejudice of the public good; that therefore the only effectual method to secure the rights of the people and promote their welfare, is to create an opposition of interests . . . .

Suppose a government could be formed and supported on such principles, would it answer the great purposes of civil society? If the administrators of every government are actuated by views of private interest and ambition, how is the welfare and happiness of the community to be the result of such jarring adverse interests?

Therefore, as different orders in government will not produce the good of the whole, we must recur to other principles. I believe it will be found that the form of government, which holds those entrusted with power in the greatest responsibility to their constituents, the best calculated for freemen. A republican, or free government, can only exist where the body of the people are virtuous, and where property is pretty equally divided. In such a government the people are the sovereign and their sense or opinion is the criterion of every public measure; for when this ceases to be the case, the nature of the government is changed, and an aristocracy, monarchy or despotism will rise on its ruin. The highest responsibility is to be attained in a simple structure of government, for the great body of the people never steadily attend to the operations of government, and for want of due information are liable to be imposed on. If you complicate the plan by various orders, the people will be perplexed and divided in their sentiments about the source of abuses or misconduct; some will impute it to the senate, others to the house of representatives, and so on, that the interposition of the people may be rendered imperfect or perhaps wholly abortive. But if, imitating the constitution of Pennsylvania, you vest all the legislative power in one body of men (separating the executive and judicial) elected for a short period, and necessarily excluded by rotation from permanency, and guarded from precipitancy and surprise by delays imposed on its proceedings, you will create the most perfect responsibility; for then, whenever the people feel a grievance, they cannot mistake the authors, and will apply the remedy with certainty and effect, discarding them at the next election. This tie of responsibility will obviate all the dangers apprehended from a single legislature, and will the best secure the rights of the people. . . .

[I]f the United States are to be melted down into one empire, it becomes you to consider whether such a government, however constructed, would be eligible in so extended a territory; and whether it would be practicable, consistent with freedom? It is the opinion of the greatest writers, that a very extensive country cannot be governed on democratical principles, on any other plan than a confederation of a number of small republics, possessing all the powers of internal government, but united in the management of their foreign and general concerns.

It would not be difficult to prove, that anything short of despotism could not bind so great a country under one government; and that whatever plan you might, at the first setting out, establish, it would issue in a despotism.

If one general government could be instituted and maintained on principles of freedom, it would not be so competent to attend to the various local concerns and wants, of every particular district, as well as the peculiar governments, who are nearer the scene, and possessed of superior means of information; besides, if the business of the *whole* union is to be managed by one government, there would not be time. Do we not already see, that the inhabitants in a number of larger States, who are remote from the seat of government, are loudly complaining of the inconveniences and disadvantages they are subjected to on this account, and that, to enjoy the comforts of local government, they are separating into smaller divisions? . . .

6

Selections from the Records of the Federal Convention of 1787

a. The Virginia Plan

Mr. Randolph (then) opened the main business. He expressed his regret, that it should fall to him, rather than those, who were of longer standing in life and political experience, to open the great subject of their mission. But, as the convention had originated from Virginia, and his colleagues supposed, that some proposition was expected from them, they had imposed this task on him.

He then commented on the difficulty of the crisis, and the necessity of preventing the fulfillment of the prophecies of the American downfall. . . .

From *Records of the Federal Convention of 1787,* ed. Max Farrand.

1. In speaking of the defects of the confederation he professed a high respect for its authors, and considered them as having done all that patriots could do, in the then infancy of the science, of constitutions, & of confederacies,—when the inefficiency of requisitions was unknown—no commercial discord had arisen among any states—no rebellion had appeared as in Mass.—foreign debts had not become urgent—the havoc of paper money had not been foreseen—treaties had not been violated—and perhaps nothing better could be obtained from the jealousy of the states with regard to their sovereignty.

He then proceeded to enumerate the defects: I. that the confederation produced no security against foreign invasion; congress not being permitted to prevent a war nor to support it by their own authority—Of this he cited many examples; most of which tended to show, that they could not cause infractions of treaties or of the law of nations, to be punished: that particular states might by their conduct provoke war without control; and that neither militia nor draughts being fit for defense on such occasions, enlistments only could be successful, and these could not be executed without money.

2. that the federal government could not check the quarrels between states, nor a rebellion in any not having constitutional power nor did it have means to interpose according to the exigency.

3. that there were many advantages, which the U.S. might acquire, which were not attainable under the confederation—such as a productive impost—counteraction of the commercial regulations of other nations—pushing of commerce. . . .

4. that the federal government could not defend itself against the encroachments from the states.

5. that it was not even paramount to the state constitutions, ratified as it was in many of the states.

6. He next reviewed the danger of our situation, appealed to the sense of the best friends of the U.S.—the prospect of anarchy from the laxity of government everywhere; and to other considerations.

7. He then proceeded to the remedy; the basis of which he said, must be the republican principle.

He proposed as conformable to his ideas the following resolutions, which he explained one by one.

Resolutions proposed by Mr. Randolph in Convention.
May 29, 1787.

1. Resolved that the articles of Confederation ought to be so corrected & enlarged as to accomplish the objects proposed by their institution; namely, "common defense, security of liberty and general welfare."

2. Resd. therefore that the rights of suffrage in the National Legislature ought to be proportioned to the quotas of contribution, or to the number of free inhabitants, as the one or the other rule may seem best in different cases.

3. Resd. that the National Legislature ought to consist of two branches.

4. Resd. that the members of the first branch of the National Legislature ought to be elected by the people of the several States every   for the term of   ; to be of the age of   years at least, to receive liberal stipends by which they may be compensated for the devotion of their time to public service; to be ineligible to any office established by a particular State, or under the authority of the United States, except those peculiarly belonging to the functions of the first branch, during the term of service, and for the space of   after its expiration; to be incapable of re-election for the space of   after the expiration of their term of service, and to be subject to recall.

5. Resd. that the members of the second branch of the National Legislature ought to be elected by those of the first, out of a proper number of persons nominated by the individual Legislatures, to be of the age of   years at least; to hold their offices for a term sufficient to ensure their independency, to receive liberal stipends, by which they may be compensated for the devotion of their time to public service; and to be ineligible to any office established by a particular State, or under the authority of the United States, except those peculiarly belonging to the functions of the second branch, during the term of service, and for the space of   after the expiration thereof.

6. Resd. that each branch ought to possess the right of originating Acts; that the National Legislature ought to be impowered to enjoy the Legislative Rights vested in Congress by the Confederation & moreover to legislate in all cases to which the separate States are incompetent, or in which the harmony of the United States may be interrupted by the exercise of individual Legislation; to negative all laws passed by the several States, contravening in the opinion of the National Legislature the articles of Union; and to call forth the force of the Union against any member of the Union failing to fulfill its duty under the articles thereof.

7. Resd. that a National Executive be instituted; to be chosen by the National Legislature for the term of   years, to receive punctually at stated times, a fixed compensation for the services rendered, in which no increase or diminution shall be made so as to affect the Magistracy, existing at the time of increase or diminution, and to be ineligible a second time; and that besides a general authority to execute the National laws, it ought to enjoy the Executive rights vested in Congress by the Confederation.

8. Resd. that the Executive and a convenient number of the National Judiciary, ought to compose a council of revision with authority to examine every act of the National Legislature before it shall operate, & every act of a particular Legislature before a Negative thereon shall be final; and that the dissent of the said Council shall amount to a rejection, unless the Act of the National Legislature be again passed, or that of a particular Legislature be again negatived by   of the members of each branch.

9. Resd. that a National Judiciary be established. . . .

10. Resd. that a Republican Government & the territory of each State, except in the instance of a voluntary junction of Government & territory, ought to be guaranteed by the United States to each State. . . .

11. Resd. that the Legislative Executive & Judiciary powers within the several States ought to be bound by oath to support the articles of Union.

12. Resd. that the amendments which shall be offered to the Confederation, by the Convention ought at a proper time, or times, after the approbation of Congress to be submitted to an assembly or assemblies of Representatives, recommended by the several Legislatures to be expressly chosen by the people, to consider & decide thereon.

b. The New Jersey Plan

Mr. Patterson, laid before the Convention the plan which he said several of the deputations wished to be substituted in place of that proposed by Mr. Randolph. . . .

The propositions from N. Jersey moved by Mr. Patterson were in the words following.

1. Resd. that the articles of Confederation ought to be so revised, corrected & enlarged, as to render the federal Constitution adequate to the exigencies of Government, & the preservation of the Union.

2. Resd. that in addition to the powers vested in the U. States in Congress, by the present existing articles of Confederation, they be authorized to pass acts for raising a revenue by levying a duty or duties on all goods or merchandizes of foreign growth or manufacture, imported into any part of the U. States, by stamps on paper, vellum or parchment and by a postage on all letters or packages passing through the general post-office, to be applied to such federal purposes as they shall deem proper & expedient; to make rules & regulations for the collection thereof; and the same from time to time, to alter & amend in such manner as they shall think proper: to pass Acts for the regulation of trade & commerce as well with foreign nations as with each other provided that all punishments, fines, forfeitures & penalties to be incurred for contravening such acts rules and regulations shall be adjudged by the Common law Judiciaries of the State in which any offense

contrary to the true intent & meaning of such Acts rules & regulations shall have been committed or perpetrated, with liberty of commencing in the first instance all suits & prosecutions for that purpose in the superior common law Judiciary in such State, subject nevertheless, for the correction of all errors, both in law & fact in rendering judgment, to an appeal to the Judiciary of the U. States. . . .

3. Resd. that the U. States in Congress be authorized to elect a federal Executive to consist of   persons, to continue in office for the term of   years, to receive punctually at stated times a fixed compensation for their services, in which no increase or diminution shall be made so as to affect the persons composing the Executive at the time of such increase or diminution, to be paid out of the federal treasury; to be incapable of holding any other office or appointment during their time of service and for   years thereafter; to be ineligible a second time, & removable by Congress on application by a majority of the Executives of the several States; that the Executives besides their general authority to execute the federal acts ought to appoint all federal officers not otherwise provided for, & to direct all military operations; provided that none of the persons composing the federal Executive shall on any occasion take command of any troops, so as personally to conduct any enterprise as General, or in other capacity.

4. Resd. that a federal Judiciary be established. . . .

5. Resd. that all Acts of the U. States in Congress made by virtue & in pursuance of the powers hereby & by the articles of confederation vested in them, and all Treaties made & ratified under the authority of the U. States shall be the supreme law of the respective States so far forth as those Acts or Treaties shall relate to the said States or their Citizens, and that the Judiciary of the several States shall be bound thereby in their decisions, any thing in the respective laws of the Individual States to the contrary notwithstanding; and that if any State, or any body of men in any State, shall oppose or prevent the carrying into execution such acts or treaties, the federal Executive shall be authorized to call forth the power of the Confederated States, or so much thereof as may be necessary to enforce and compel an obedience to such Acts, or an observance of such Treaties. . . .

c. Alexander Hamilton: Proposal for a New Government

The extent of the Country to be governed, discouraged him. The expense of a general Govt. was also formidable; unless there were such a diminution of expense on the side of the State Govts. as the case would admit. If they were extinguished, he was persuaded that great economy might be obtained by substituting a general Govt. He did not mean however to shock the public opinion by proposing such a measure. On the other hand he saw no *other* necessity for declining it. They are not necessary for any of the great purposes of commerce, revenue, or agriculture. Subordinate authorities he was aware would be necessary. There must be district tribunals: corporations for local purposes. But cui bono, the vast & expensive apparatus now appertaining to the States. The only difficulty of a serious nature which occurred to him, was that of drawing representatives from the extremes to the center of the community. What inducements can be offered that will suffice? The moderate wages for the 1st. branch, would only be a bait to little demagogues. Three dollars or thereabouts he supposed would be the utmost. The Senate he feared from a similar cause, would be filled by certain undertakers who wish for particular offices under the Govt. This view of the subject almost led him to despair that a Republican Govt. could be established over so great an extent. He was sensible at the same time that it would be unwise to propose one of any other form. In his private opinion he had no scruple in declaring, supported as he was by the opinions of so many of the wise & good, that the British Govt. was the best in the world: and that he doubted much whether any thing short of it would do in America. He hoped gentlemen of different opinions would bear with him in this, and begged them to recollect the change of opinion on this subject which had taken place and was still going on. It was once thought that the power of Congress was amply sufficient to secure the end of their institution. The error was now seen by every one. The members most tenacious of republicanism, he observed, were as loud as any in declaiming against the vices of democracy. This progress of the public mind led him to anticipate the time, when others as well as himself would join in the praise bestowed by Mr. Neckar on the British Constitution, namely, that it is the only Govt. in the world "which unites public strength with individual security."—In every community where industry is encouraged, there will be a division of it into the few & the many. Hence separate interests will arise. There will be debtors & creditors &c. Give all power to the many, they will oppress the few. Give all power to the few they will oppress the many. Both therefore ought to have power, that each may defend itself against the other. To the want of this check we owe our paper money— installment laws &c. To the proper adjustment of it the British owe the excellence of their Constitution. Their house of Lords is a most noble institution. Having nothing to hope for by a change, and a sufficient interest by means of their property, in being faithful to the national interest, they form a permanent barrier against every pernicious innovation, whether attempted on the part of the Crown or of the Commons. No temporary Senate will have firmness enough to answer the purpose. . . . Gentlemen differ in their opinions concerning the necessary checks, from the different estimates they form of the human passions. They suppose seven years a sufficient period to give the Senate an adequate firmness, from not duly considering the amazing violence & turbulence of the democratic spirit. When a great object of Govt. is pursued, which seizes the popular passions, they spread like wild fire, and become irresistable. He appealed to the gentlemen from the N. England States whether experience had not there verified the remark. As to the Executive, it seemed to be admitted that no good one could be established on republican principles. Was not this giving up the merits of the question; for can there be a good govt. without a good Executive. The English model was the only good one on this subject. The hereditary interest of the King was so interwoven with that of the nation, and his personal emoluments so great, that he was placed above the danger of being corrupted from abroad—and at the same time was both sufficiently independent and sufficiently controlled, to answer the purpose of the institution at home. One of the weak sides of Republics was their being liable to foreign influence & corruption. Men of little character, acquiring great power become easily the tools of intermedling neighbors. Sweden was a striking instance. The French & English had each their parties during the late Revolution which was effected by the predominant influence of the former. What is the inference from all these observations? That we ought to go as far in order to attain stability and permanency, as republican principles will admit. Let one branch of the Legislature hold their places for life or at least during good-behavior. Let the Executive also be for life. He appealed to the feelings of the members present whether a term of seven years, would induce the sacrifices of private affairs which an acceptance of public trust would require, so as to ensure the services of the best citizens. On this plan we should have in the Senate a permanent will, a weighty interest, which would answer essential purposes. But is this a Republican Govt. it will be asked? Yes, if all the Magistrates are appointed, and vacancies are filled, by the people, or a process of election originating with the people. He was sensible that an Executive constituted as he proposed would have in fact but little of the power and independence that might be necessary. On the other plan of appointing him for 7 years, he thought the Executive ought to have but little power. He would be ambitious, with the means of making creatures; and as the object of his ambition would be to *prolong* his power, it is probable that in case of a war, he would avail himself of the emergency, to evade or refuse a degradation from his place. An Executive for life has not this motive for forgetting his fidelity, and will therefore be a safer depositary of power. It will be objected probably, that such an executive will be an *elective Monarch,* and will give birth to the tumults which characterize that form of Govt. He would reply that *Monarch* is an indefinite term. It marks not either the degree or duration of power. If this Executive Magistrate would be a monarch for life—the other proposed by the Report from the Committee of the whole, would be a monarch for seven years. The circumstance of being elective was also applicable to both. It had been observed by judicious writers that elective monarchies would be the best if they could be guarded against the *tumults* excited by the ambition and intrigues of competitors. . . .

7

James Madison

The Work of the Constitutional Convention (1787)

To Thomas Jefferson

Dear Sir:

You will herewith receive the result of the convention, which continued its session till the 17th of September. . . .

It appeared to be the sincere and unanimous wish of the convention to cherish and preserve the union of the states. No proposition was made, no suggestion was thrown out, in favor of a partition of the empire into two or more confederacies.

It was generally agreed that the objects of the Union could not be secured by any system founded on the principle of a confederation of sovereign states. A *voluntary* observance of the federal law by all the members could never be hoped for. A *compulsive* one could evidently never be reduced to practice, and if it could, involved equal calamities to the innocent & the guilty, the necessity of a military force both obnoxious & dangerous, and in general a scene resembling much more a civil war than the administration of a regular government.

From *The Writings of James Madison,* Oct. 24, 1787, Vol. V, G.P. Putnam's Sons, 1904.

Hence was embraced the alternative of a government which instead of operating, on the states, should operate without their intervention on the individuals composing them; and hence the change in the principle and proportion of representation.

This ground-work being laid, the great objects which presented themselves were (1) to unite a proper energy in the Executive, and a proper stability in the Legislative departments, with the essential characters of Republican Government. (2) to draw a line of demarkation which would give to the General Government every power requisite for general purposes, and leave to the States every power which might be most beneficially administered by them. (3) to provide for the different interests of different parts of the Union. (4) to adjust the clashing pretensions of the large and small States. Each of these objects was pregnant with difficulties. The whole of them together formed a task more difficult than can be well conceived by those who were not concerned in the execution of it. Adding to these considerations the natural diversity of human opinions on all new and complicated subjects, it is impossible to consider the degree of concord which ultimately prevailed as less than a miracle.

The first of these objects, as respects the Executive, was peculiarly embarrassing. On the question whether it should consist of a single person, or a plurality of co-ordinate members, on the mode of appointment, on the duration in office, on the degree of power, on the re-eligibility, tedious and reiterated discussions took place. The plurality of co-ordinate members had finally but few advocates. Governor Randolph was at the head of them. The modes of appointment proposed were various, as by the people at large—by electors chosen by the people—by the Executives of the States—by the Congress, some preferring a joint ballot of the two Houses—some a separate concurrent ballot, allowing to each a negative on the other house—some, a nomination of several candidates by one House, out of whom a choice should be made by the other. Several other modifications were started. The expedient at length adopted seemed to give pretty general satisfaction to the members. As to the duration in office, a few would have preferred a tenure during good behavior—a considerable number would have done so in case an easy & effectual removal by impeachment could be settled. It was much agitated whether a long term, seven years for example, with a subsequent & perpetual ineligibility, or a short term with a capacity to be re-elected, should be fixed. In favor of the first opinion were urged the danger of a gradual degeneracy of re-elections from time to time, into first a life and then a hereditary tenure, and the favorable effect of an incapacity to be reappointed on the independent exercise of the Executive authority. On the other side it was contended that the prospect of necessary degradation would discourage the most dignified characters from aspiring to the office, would take away the principal motive to the faithful discharge of its duties—the hope of being rewarded with a reappointment would stimulate ambition to violent efforts for holding over the Constitutional term—and instead of producing an independent administration, and a firmer defense of the constitutional rights of the department, would render the officer more indifferent to the importance of a place which he would soon be obliged to quit forever, and more ready to yield to the encroachments of the Legislature of which he might again be a member. The questions concerning the degree of power turned chiefly on the appointment to offices, and the control on the Legislature. An *absolute* appointment to all offices—to some offices—to no offices, formed the scale of opinions on the first point. On the second, some contended for an absolute negative, as the only possible mean of reducing to practice the theory of a free Government which forbids a mixture of the Legislative & Executive powers. Others would be content with a revisionary power, to be overruled by three fourths of both Houses. It was warmly urged that the judiciary department should be associated in the revision. The idea of some was that a separate revision should be given to the two departments—that if either objected two thirds, if both, three fourths, should be necessary to overrule.

In forming the Senate, the great anchor of the Government, the questions as they came within the first object, turned mostly on the mode of appointment, and the duration of it. The different modes proposed were (1) by the House of Representatives. (2) by the Executive. (3) by electors chosen by the people for the purpose. (4) by the State Legislature.— On the point of duration, the propositions descended from good behavior to four years, through the intermediate terms of nine, seven, six, & five years. The election of the other branch was first determined to be triennial, and afterwards reduced to biennial.

The second object, the due partition of power between the General & local Governments, was perhaps of all, the most nice and difficult. A few contended for an entire abolition of the States; some for indefinite power of Legislation in the Congress, with a negative on the laws of the States; some for such a power without a negative; some for a limited power of legislation, with such a negative; the majority finally for a limited power without the negative. The question with regard to the negative underwent repeated discussions, and was finally rejected by a bare majority. As I formerly intimated to you my opinion in favor of this ingredient, I will take this occasion of explaining myself on the subject. Such a check on the States appears to me necessary (1) to prevent encroachments on the General authority, (2) to prevent instability and injustice in the legislation of the States.

1. Without such a check in the whole over the parts, our system involves the evil of imperia in imperio. If a complete supremacy somewhere is not necessary in every Society, a controlling power at least is so, by which the general authority may be defended against encroachments of the subordinate authorities, and by which the latter may be restrained from encroachments on each other. If the supremacy of the British Parliament is not necessary as has been contended, for the harmony of that Empire; it is evident I think that without the royal negative or some equivalent control, the unity of the system would be destroyed. The want of some such provision seems to have been mortal to the ancient Confederacies, and to be the disease of the modern. Of the Lycian confederacy little is known. That of the Amphyctions is well known to have been rendered of little use whilst it lasted, and in the end to have been destroyed, by the predominance of the local over the federal authority. . . . The case of the United Netherlands is in point. The authority of a Stadtholder, the influence of a Standing Army, the common interest in the conquered possessions, the pressure of surrounding danger, the guarantee of foreign powers, are not sufficient to secure the authority and interest of the generality against the anti-federal tendency of the provincial sovereignties. . . . Still more to the purpose is our own experience both during the war and since the peace. Encroachments of the States on the general authority, sacrifices of national to local interests, interferences of the measures of different States, form a great part of the history of our political system. It may be said that the new Constitution is founded on different principles, and will have a different operation. I admit the difference to be material. It presents the aspect rather of a feudal system of republics, if such a phrase may be used, than of a Confederacy of independent States. And what has been the progress and event of the feudal Constitutions? In all of them a continual struggle between the head and the inferior members, until a final victory has been gained in some instances by one, in others, by the other of them. In one respect indeed there is a remarkable variance between the two cases. In the feudal system the sovereign, though limited, was independent; and having no particular sympathy of interests with the Great Barons, his ambition had as full play as theirs in the mutual projects of usurpation. In the American Constitution the general authority will be derived entirely from the subordinate authorities. The Senate will represent the States in their political capacity; the other House will represent the people of the States in their individual capacity. The former will be accountable to their constituents at moderate, the latter at short periods. The President also derives his appointment from the States, and is periodically accountable to them. This dependence of the General on the local authorities, seems effectually to guard the latter against any dangerous encroachments of the former; whilst the latter, within their

respective limits, will be continually sensible of the abridgement of their power, and be stimulated by ambition to resume the surrendered portion of it. We find the representatives of Counties and Corporations in the Legislatures of the States, much more disposed to sacrifice the aggregate interest, and even authority, to the local views of their constituents, than the latter to the former. I mean not by these remarks to insinuate that an esprit de corps will not exist in the National Government or that opportunities may not occur of extending its jurisdiction in some points. I mean only that the danger of encroachments is much greater from the other side, and that the impossibility of dividing powers of legislation, in such a manner, as to be free from different constructions by different interests, or even from ambiguity in the judgment of the impartial, requires some such expedient as I contend for. Many illustrations might be given of this impossibility. . . . The line of distinction between the power of regulating trade and that of drawing revenue from it, which was once considered the barrier of our liberties, was found on fair discussion, to be absolutely undefinable. . . . Even the boundaries between the Executive, Legislative, & Judiciary powers, though in general so strongly marked in themselves, consist in many instances of mere shades of difference. It may be said that the Judicial authority, under our new system will keep the States within their proper limits, and supply the place of a negative on their laws. The answer is, that it is more convenient to prevent the passage of a law than to declare it void after it is passed; that this will be particularly the case, where the law aggrieves individuals, who may be unable to support an appeal against a State to the supreme Judiciary; that a State which would violate the Legislative rights of the Union, would not be very ready to obey a Judicial decree in support of them, and that a recurrence to force, which, in the event of disobedience would be necessary, is an evil which the new Constitution meant to exclude as far as possible.

2. A constitutional negative on the laws of the States seems equally necessary to secure individuals against encroachments on their rights. The mutability of the laws of the States is found to be a serious evil. The injustice of them has been so frequent and so flagrant as to alarm the most steadfast friends of Republicanism. I am persuaded I do not err in saying that the evils issuing from these sources contributed more to that uneasiness which produced the Convention, and prepared the Public mind for a general reform, than those which accrued to our national character and interest from the inadequacy of the Confederation to its immediate objects. A reform therefore which does not make provision for private rights, must be materially defective. The restraints against paper emissions, and violations of contracts are not sufficient. Supposing them to be effectual as far as they go, they are short of the mark. Injustice may be effected by such an infinitude of legislative expedients, that where the disposition exists it

can only be controlled by some provision which reaches all cases whatsoever. The partial provision made, supposes the disposition which will evade it. It may be asked how private rights will be more secure under the Guardianship of the General Government than under the State Governments, since they are both founded on the republican principle which refers the ultimate decision to the will of the majority, and are distinguished rather by the extent within which they will operate, than by any material difference in their structure. A full discussion of this question would, if I mistake not, unfold the true Principles of Republican Government, and prove in contradiction to the concurrent opinions of the theoretical writers that this form of Government, in order to effect its purposes, must operate not within a small but an extensive sphere. I will state some of the ideas which have occurred to me on the subject. Those who contend for a simple Democracy, or a pure republic, actuated by the sense of the majority, and operating within narrow limits, assume or suppose a case which is altogether fictitious. They found their reasoning on the idea, that the people composing the Society, enjoy not only an equality of political rights; but that they have all precisely the same interests, and the same feelings in every respect. Were this in reality the case, their reasoning would be conclusive. The interest of the majority would be that of the minority also; the decisions could only turn on mere opinion concerning the good of the whole, of which the major voice would be the safest criterion; and within a small sphere, this voice could be most easily collected, and the public affairs most accurately managed. We know however that no society ever did or can consist of so homogeneous a mass of Citizens. In the savage state indeed, an approach is made towards it; but in that state little or no Government is necessary. In all civilized societies, distinctions are various and unavoidable. A distinction of property results from that very protection which a free Government gives to unequal faculties of acquiring it. There will be rich and poor; creditors and debtors; a landed interest, a monied interest, a mercantile interest, a manufacturing interest. These classes may again be subdivided according to the different productions of different situations & soils, & according to different branches of commerce and of manufactures. In addition to these natural distinctions, artificial ones will be founded, on accidental differences in political, religious, or other opinions, or an attachment to the persons of leading individuals. However erroneous or ridiculous these grounds of dissention and faction may appear to the enlightened Statesman or the benevolent philosopher, the bulk of mankind who are neither Statesmen nor Philosophers, will continue to view them in a different light. It remains then to be enquired whether a majority having any common interest, or feeling any common passion, will find sufficient motives to restrain them from oppressing the minority. An individual is never allowed to be a judge or even a witness in his own cause. If two individuals are under the bias of interest or enmity against a third, the rights of the latter could never be safely referred to the majority of the three. Will two thousand individuals be less apt to oppress one thousand, or two hundred thousand one hundred thousand? Three motives only can restrain in such cases: (1) a prudent regard to private or partial good, as essentially involved in the general and permanent good of the Whole. This ought no doubt to be sufficient of itself. Experience however shows that it has little effect on individuals, and perhaps still less on a collection of individuals, and least of all on a majority with the public authority in their hands. If the former are ready to forget that honesty is the best policy; the last do more. They often proceed on the converse of the maxim, that whatever is politic is honest. (2) respect for character. This motive is not found sufficient to restrain individuals from injustice. And loses its efficacy in proportion to the number which is to divide the pain or the blame. Besides as it has reference to public opinion, which is that of the majority, the standard is fixed by those whose conduct is to be measured by it. (3) Religion. The inefficacy of this restraint on individuals is well known. The conduct of every popular Assembly, acting on oath, the strongest of religious ties, shows that individuals join without remorse in acts against which their consciences would revolt, if proposed to them separately in their closets. When indeed Religion is kindled into enthusiasm, its force like that of other passions is increased by the sympathy of a multitude. But enthusiasm is only a temporary state of Religion, and whilst it lasts will hardly be seen with pleasure at the helm. Even in its coolest state, it has been much oftener a motive to oppression than a restraint from it. If then there must be different interests and parties in society; and a majority when united by a common interest or passion cannot be restrained from oppressing the minority, what remedy can be found in a republican Government, where the majority must ultimately decide, but that of giving such an extent to its sphere, that no common interest or passion will be likely to unite a majority of the whole number in an unjust pursuit. In a large Society, the people are broken into so many interests and parties, that a common sentiment is less likely to be felt, and the requisite concert less likely to be formed, by a majority of the whole. The same security seems requisite for the civil as for the religious rights of individuals. If the same sect form a majority and have the power, other sects will be sure to be depressed. Divide et impera, the reprobated axiom of tyranny, is under certain qualifications, the only policy, by which a republic can be administered on just principles. It must be observed however that this doctrine can only hold within a sphere of a mean extent. As in too small a sphere oppressive combinations may be too easily formed against the weaker party; so in too extensive a one, a defensive concert may be rendered too difficult against the oppression of those entrusted with the administration. The great desideratum in Government is, so to modify the sovereignty as that it may be sufficiently neutral betwen different parts of the Society to control one part from invading the rights of another, and at the same time sufficiently controlled itself, from setting up an interest adverse to that of the entire Society. In absolute monarchies, the Prince may be tolerably neutral towards different classes of his subjects but may sacrifice the happiness of all to his personal ambition or avarice. In small republics, the sovereign will is controlled from such a sacrifice of the entire Society, but is not sufficiently neutral towards the parts composing it. In the extended Republic of the United States. The General Government would hold a pretty even balance between the parties of particular States, and be at the same time sufficiently restrained by its dependence on the community, from betraying its general interests.

Begging pardon for this immoderate digression I return to the third object above mentioned, the adjustments of the different interests of different parts of the Continent. Some contended for an unlimited power over trade including exports as well as imports, and over slaves as well as other imports; some for such a power, provided the concurrence of two thirds of both Houses were required; Some for such a qualification of the power, with an exemption of exports and slaves, others for an exemption of exports only. The result is seen in the Constitution. S. Carolina & Georgia were inflexible on the point of the slaves.

The remaining object created more embarrassment, and a greater alarm for the issue of the Convention than all the rest put together. The little States insisted on retaining their equality in both branches, unless a complete abolition of the State Governments should take place; and made an equality in the Senate a sine qua non. The large States on the other hand urged that as the new Government was to be drawn principally from the people immediately and was to operate directly on them, not on the States; and consequently as the States would lose that importance which is now proportioned to the importance of their voluntary compliances with the requisitions of Congress, it was necessary that the representation in both Houses should be in proportion to their size. It ended in the compromise which you will see, but very much to the dissatisfaction of several members from the large States. . . .

8

James Madison

Federalist 10 (1787)

Among the numerous advantages promised by a well-constructed Union, none deserves to be more accurately developed than its tendency to break and control the violence of faction. The friend of popular governments never finds himself so much alarmed for their character and fate as when he contemplates their propensity to this dangerous vice. He will not fail, therefore, to set a due value on any plan which, without violating the principles to which he is attached, provides a proper cure for it. The instability, injustice, and confusion introduced into the public councils have, in truth, been the mortal diseases under which popular governments have everywhere perished, as they continue to be the favorite and fruitful topics from which the adversaries to liberty derive their most specious declamations. The valuable improvements made by the American constitutions on the popular models, both ancient and modern, cannot certainly be too much admired; but it would be an unwarrantable partiality to contend that they have as effectually obviated the danger on this side, as was wished and expected. Complaints are everywhere heard from our most considerate and virtuous citizens; equally the friends of public and private faith and of public and personal liberty, that our governments are too unstable, that the public good is disregarded in the conflicts or rival parties, and that measures are too often decided, not according to the rules of justice and the rights of the minor party, but by the superior force of an interested and overbearing majority. However anxiously we may wish that these complaints had no foundation, the evidence of known facts will not permit us to deny that they are in some degree true. It will be found, indeed, on a candid review of our situation, that some of the distresses under which we labor have been erroneously charged on the operation of our governments; but it will be found, at the same time, that other causes will not alone account for many of our heaviest misfortunes; and, particularly, for that prevailing and increasing distrust of public engagements and alarm for private rights which are echoed from one end of the continent to the other. These must be chiefly, if not wholly, effects of the unsteadiness and injustice with which a factious spirit has tainted our public administration.

From *The Federalist.*

By a faction I understand a number of citizens, whether amounting to a majority or minority of the whole, who are united and actuated by some common impulse of passion, or of interest, adverse to the rights of other citizens, or to the permanent and aggregate interests of the community.

There are two methods of curing the mischiefs of faction: the one, by removing its causes; the other, by controlling its effects.

There are again two methods of removing the causes of faction: the one, by destroying the liberty which is essential to its existence; the other, by giving to every citizen the same opinions, the same passions, and the same interests.

It could never be more truly said than of the first remedy that it was worse than the disease. Liberty is to faction what air is to fire, an aliment without which it instantly expires. But it could not be a less folly to abolish liberty, which is essential to political life, because it nourishes faction than it would be to wish the annihilation of air, which is essential to animal life, because it imparts to fire its destructive agency.

The second expedient is as impracticable as the first would be unwise. As long as the reason of man continues fallible, and he is at liberty to exercise it, different opinions will be formed. As long as the connection subsists between his reason and his self-love, his opinions and his passions will have a reciprocal influence on each other; and the former will be objects to which the latter will attach themselves. The diversity in the faculties of men, from which the rights of property originate, is not less an insuperable obstacle to a uniformity of interests. The protection of these faculties is the first object of government. From the protection of different and unequal faculties of acquiring property, the possession of different degrees and kinds of property immediately results; and from the influence of these on the sentiments and views of the respective proprietors ensues a division of the society into different interests and parties.

The latent causes of faction are thus sown in the nature of man; and we see them everywhere brought into different degrees of activity, according to the different circumstances of civil society. A zeal for different opinions concerning religion, concerning government, and many other points, as well of speculation as of practice; an attachment to different leaders ambitiously contending for pre-eminence and power; or to persons of other descriptions whose fortunes have been interesting to the human passions, have, in turn, divided mankind into parties, inflamed them with mutual animosity, and rendered them much more disposed to vex and oppress each other than to co-operate for their common good. So strong is this propensity of mankind to fall into mutual animosities that where no substantial occasion presents itself the most frivolous and fanciful distinctions have been sufficient to kindle their unfriendly passions and excite their most violent conflicts. But the most common and durable source of factions has been the various and unequal distribution of property. Those who hold and those who are without property have ever formed distinct interests in society. Those who are creditors, and those who are debtors, fall under a like discrimination. A landed interest, a manufacturing interest, a mercantile interest, a moneyed interest, with many lesser interests, grow up of necessity in civilized nations, and divide them into different classes, actuated by different sentiments and views. The regulation of these various and interfering interests forms the principal task of modern legislation and involves the spirit of party and faction in the necessary and ordinary operations of government.

No man is allowed to be a judge in his own cause, because his interest would certainly bias his judgment, and, not improbably, corrupt his integrity. With equal, nay with greater reason, a body of men are unfit to be both judges and parties at the same time; yet what are many of the most important acts of legislation but so many judicial determinations, not indeed concerning the rights of single persons, but concerning the rights of large bodies of citizens? And what are the different classes of legislators but advocates and parties to the causes which they determine? Is a law proposed concerning private debts? It is a question to which the creditors are parties on one side and the debtors on the other. Justice ought to hold the balance between them. Yet the parties are, and must be, themselves the judges; and the most numerous party, or in other words, the most powerful faction must be expected to prevail. Shall domestic manufacturers be encouraged, and in what degree, by restrictions on foreign manufacturers? are questions which would be differently decided by the landed and the manufacturing classes, and probably by neither with a sole regard to justice and the public good. The apportionment of taxes on the various descriptions of property is an act which seems to require the most exact impartiality; yet there is, perhaps, no legislative act in which greater opportunity and temptation are given to a predominant party to trample on the rules of justice. Every shilling with which they overburden the inferior number is a shilling saved to their own pockets.

It is in vain to say that enlightened statesmen will be able to adjust these clashing interests and render them all subservient to the public good. Enlightened statesmen will not always be at the helm. Nor, in many cases, can such an adjustment be made at all without taking into view indirect and remote considerations, which will rarely prevail over the immediate interest which one party may find in disregarding the rights of another or the good of the whole.

The inference to which we are brought is that the *causes* of faction cannot be removed and that relief is only to be sought in the means of controlling its *effects*.

If a faction consists of less than a majority, relief is supplied by the republican principle, which enables the majority to defeat its sinister views by regular vote. It may clog the administration, it may convulse the society; but it will be unable to execute and mask its violence under the forms of the Constitution. When a majority is included in a faction, the form of popular government, on the other hand, enables it to sacrifice to its ruling passion or interest both the public good and the rights of other citizens. To secure the public good and private rights against the danger of such a faction, and at the same time to preserve the spirit and the form of popular government, is then the great object to which our inquiries are directed. Let me add that it is the great desideratum by which alone this form of government can be rescued from the opprobrium under which it has so long labored and be recommended to the esteem and adoption of mankind.

By what means is this object attainable? Evidently by one of two only. Either the existence of the same passion or interest in a majority at the same time must be prevented, or the majority, having such coexistent passion or interest, must be rendered, by their number and local situation, unable to concert and carry into effect schemes of oppression. If the impulse and the opportunity be suffered to coincide, we well know that neither moral nor religious motives can be relied on as an adequate control. They are not found to be such on the injustice and violence of individuals, and lose their efficacy in proportion to the number combined together, that is, in proportion as their efficacy becomes needful.

From this view of the subject it may be concluded that a pure democracy, by which I mean a society consisting of a small number of citizens, who assemble and administer the government in person, can admit of no cure for the mischiefs of faction. A common passion or interest will, in almost every case, be felt by a majority of the whole; a communication and concert results from the form of government itself; and there is nothing to check the inducements to sacrifice the weaker party or an obnoxious individual. Hence it is that such democracies have ever been spectacles of turbulence and contention; have ever been found incompatible with personal security or the rights of property; and have in general been as short in their lives as they have been violent in their deaths. Theoretic politicians, who have patronized this species of government, have erroneously supposed that by reducing mankind to a perfect equality in their political rights, they would at the same time be perfectly equalized and assimilated in their possessions, their opinions, and their passions.

A republic, by which I mean a government in which the scheme of representation takes place, opens a different prospect and promises the cure for which we are seeking. Let us examine the points in which it varies from pure democracy, and we shall comprehend both the nature of the cure and the efficacy which it must derive from the Union.

The two great points of difference between a democracy and a republic are: first, the delegation of the government, in the latter, to a small number of citizens elected by the rest; secondly, the greater number of citizens and greater sphere of country over which the latter may be extended.

The effect of the first difference is, on the one hand, to refine and enlarge the public views by passing them through the medium of a chosen body of citizens, whose wisdom may best discern the true interest of their country and whose patriotism and love of justice will be least likely to sacrifice it to temporary or partial considerations. Under such a regulation it may well happen that the public voice, pronounced by the representatives of the people, will be more consonant to the public good than if pronounced by the people themselves, convened for the purpose. On the other hand, the effect may be inverted. Men of factious tempers, of local prejudices, or of sinister designs, may, by intrigue, by corruption, or by other means, first obtain the suffrages, and then betray the interests of the people. The question resulting is, whether small or extensive republics are most favorable to the election of proper guardians of the public weal; and it is clearly decided in favor of the latter by two obvious considerations.

In the first place it is to be remarked that however small the republic may be the representatives must be raised to a certain number in order to guard against the cabals of a few; and that however large it may be they must be limited to a certain number in order to guard against the confusion of a multitude. Hence, the number of representatives in the two cases not being in proportion to that of the constituents, and being proportionally greatest in the small republic, it follows that if the proportion of fit characters be not less in the large than in the small republic, the former will present a greater option, and consequently a greater probability of a fit choice.

In the next place, as each representative will be chosen by a greater number of citizens in the large than in the small republic, it will be more difficult for unworthy candidates to practice with success the vicious arts by which elections are too often carried; and the suffrages of the people being more free, will be more likely to center on men who possess the most attractive merit and the most diffusive and established characters.

It must be confessed that in this, as in most other cases, there is a mean, on both sides of which inconveniencies will be found to lie. By enlarging too much the number of electors, you render the representative too little acquainted with all their local circumstances and lesser interest; as by reducing it too much, you render him unduly attached to these, and too little fit to comprehend and pursue great and national objects. The federal Constitution forms a happy combination in this respect; the great and aggregate interests being referred to the national, the local and particular to the State legislatures.

The other point of difference is the greater number of citizens and extent of territory which may be brought within the compass of republican than of democratic government; and it is this circumstance principally which renders factious combinations less to be dreaded in the former than in the latter. The smaller the society, the fewer probably will be the distinct parties and interests composing it; the fewer the distinct parties and interests, the more frequently will a majority be found of the same party; and the smaller the number of individuals composing a majority, and the smaller the compass within which they are placed, the more easily will they concert and execute their plans of oppression. Extend the sphere and you take in a greater variety of parties and interests; you make it less probable that a majority of the whole will have a common motive to invade the rights of other citizens; or if such a common motive exists, it will be more difficult for all who feel it to discover their own strength and to act in unison with each other. Besides other impediments, it may be remarked that, where there is a consciousness of unjust or dishonorable purposes, communication is always checked by distrust in proportion to the number whose concurrence is necessary.

Hence, it clearly appears that the same advantage which a republic has over a democracy in controlling the effects of faction is enjoyed by a large over a small republic—is enjoyed by the Union over the States composing it. Does this advantage consist in the substitution of representatives whose enlightened views and virtuous sentiments render them superior to local prejudices and to schemes of injustice? It will not be denied that the representation of the Union will be most likely to possess these requisite endowments. Does it consist in the greater security afforded by a greater variety of parties, against the event of any one party being able to outnumber and oppress the rest? In an equal degree does the increased variety of parties comprised within the Union increase this security. Does it, in fine, consist in the greater obstacles opposed to the concert and accomplishment of the secret wishes of an unjust and interested majority? Here again the extent of the Union gives it the most palpable advantage.

The influence of factious leaders may kindle a flame within their particular States but will be unable to spread a general conflagration through the other States. A religious sect may degenerate into a political faction in a part of the Confederacy; but the variety of sects dispersed over the entire face of it must secure the national councils against any danger from that source. A rage for paper money, for an abolition of debts, for an equal division of property, or for any other improper or wicked project, will be less apt to pervade the whole body of the Union than a particular member of it, in the same proportion as such a malady is more likely to taint a particular county or district than an entire State.

In the extent and proper structure of the Union, therefore, we behold a republican remedy for the diseases most incident to republican government. And according to the degree of pleasure and pride we feel in being republicans ought to be our zeal in cherishing the spirit and supporting the character of federalists.

9

James Madison

Federalist 51 (1788)

To what expedient, then, shall we finally resort, for maintaining in practice the necessary partition of power among the several departments as laid down in the Constitution? The only answer that can be given is that as all these exterior provisions are found to be inadequate the defect must be supplied, by so contriving the interior structure of the government as that its several constituent parts may, by their mutual relations, be the means of keeping each other in their proper places. Without presuming to undertake a full development of this important idea I will hazard a few general observations which may perhaps place it in a clearer light, and enable us to form a more correct judgment of the principles and structure of the government planned by the convention.

In order to lay a due foundation for that separate and distinct exercise of the different powers of government, which to a certain extent is admitted on all hands to be essential to the preservation of liberty, it is evident that each department should have a will of its own; and consequently should be so constituted that the members of each should have as little agency as possible in the appointment of the members of the others. Were this principle rigorously adhered to, it would require that all the appointments for the supreme executive, legislative, and judiciary magistracies should be drawn from the same fountain of authority, the people, through channels having

From *The Federalist.*

no communication whatever with one another. Perhaps such a plan of constructing the several departments would be less difficult in practice than it may in contemplation appear. Some difficulties, however, and some additional expense would attend the execution of it. Some deviations, therefore, from the principle must be admitted. In the constitution of the judiciary department in particular, it might be inexpedient to insist rigorously on the principle: first, because peculiar qualifications being essential in the members, the primary consideration ought to be to select that mode of choice which best secures these qualifications; second, because the permanent tenure by which the appointments are held in that department must soon destroy all sense of dependence on the authority conferring them.

It is equally evident that the members of each department should be as little dependent as possible on those of the others for the emoluments annexed to their offices. Were the executive magistrate, or the judges, not independent of the legislature in this particular, their independence in every other would be merely nominal.

But the great security against a gradual concentration of the several powers in the same department consists in giving to those who administer each department the necessary constitutional means and personal motives to resist encroachments of the others. The provision for defense must in this, as in all other cases, be made commensurate to the danger of attack. Ambition must be made to counteract ambition. The interest of the man must be connected with the constitutional rights of the place. It may be a reflection on human nature that such devices should be necessary to control the abuses of government. But what is government itself but the greatest of all reflections on human nature? If men were angels, no government would be necessary. If angels were to govern men, neither external nor internal controls on government would be necessary. In framing a government which is to be administered by men over men, the great difficulty lies in this: you must first enable the government to control the governed; and in the next place oblige it to control itself. A dependence on the people is, no doubt, the primary control on the government; but experience has taught mankind the necessity of auxiliary precautions.

This policy of supplying, by opposite and rival interests, the defect of better motives, might be traced through the whole system of human affairs, private as well as public. We see it particularly displayed in all the subordinate distributions of power, where the constant aim is to divide and arrange the several offices in such a manner as that each may be a check on the other—that the private interest of every individual may be a sentinel over the public rights. These inventions of prudence cannot be less requisite in the distribution of the supreme powers of the State.

But it is not possible to give to each department an equal power of self-defense. In republican government, the legislative authority necessarily predominates. The remedy for this inconveniency is to divide the legislature into different branches; and to render them, by different modes of election and different principles of action, as little connected with each other as the nature of their common functions and their common dependence on the society will admit. It may even be necessary to guard against dangerous encroachments by still further precautions. As the weight of the legislative authority requires that it should be thus divided, the weakness of the executive may require, on the other hand, that it should be fortified. An absolute negative on the legislature appears, at first view, to be the natural defense with which the executive magistrate should be armed. But perhaps it would be neither altogether safe nor alone sufficient. On ordinary occasions it might not be exerted with the requisite firmness, and on extraordinary occasions it might be perfidiously abused. May not this defect of an absolute negative be supplied by some qualified connection between this weaker department and the weaker branch of the stronger department, by which the latter may be led to support the constitutional rights of the former, without being too much detached from the rights of its own department?

If the principles on which these observations are founded be just, as I persuade myself they are, and they be applied as a criterion to the several State constitutions, and to the federal Constitution, it will be found that if the latter does not perfectly correspond with them, the former are infinitely less able to bear such a test.

There are, moreover, two considerations particularly applicable to the federal system of America, which place that system in a very interesting point of view.

First. In a single republic, all the power surrendered by the people is submitted to the administration of a single government; and the usurpations are guarded against by a division of the government into distinct and separate departments. In the compound republic of America, the power surrendered by the people is first divided between two distinct governments, and then the portion allotted to each subdivided among distinct and separate departments. Hence a double security arises to the rights of the people. The different governments will control each other, at the same time that each will be controlled by itself.

Second. It is of great importance in a republic not only to guard the society against the oppression of its rulers, but to guard one part of the society against the injustice of the other part. Different interests necessarily exist in different classes of citizens. If a majority be united by a common interest, the rights of the minority will be insecure. There are but two methods of providing against this evil: the one by creating a will in the community independent of the majority—that is, of the society itself; the other, by comprehending in the society so many separate descriptions of citizens as will render an unjust combination of a majority of the whole very improbable, if not impracticable. The first method prevails in all governments possessing an hereditary or self-appointed authority. This, at best, is but a precarious security; because a power independent of the society may as well espouse the unjust views of the major as the rightful interests of the minor party, and may possibly be turned against both parties. The second method will be exemplified in the federal republic of the United States. Whilst all authority in it will be derived from and dependent on the society, the society itself will be broken into so many parts, interests and classes of citizens, that the rights of individuals, or of the minority, will be in little danger from interested combinations of the majority. In a free government the security for civil rights must be the same as that for religious rights. It consists in the one case in the multiplicity of interests, and in the other in the multiplicity of sects. The degree of security in both cases will depend on the number of interests and sects; and this may be presumed to depend on the extent of country and number of people comprehended under the same government. This view of the subject must particularly recommend a proper federal system to all the sincere and considerate friends of republican government, since it shows that in exact proportion as the territory of the Union may be formed into more circumscribed Confederacies, or States, oppressive combinations of a majority will be facilitated; the best security, under the republican forms, for the rights of every class of citizen, will be diminished; and consequently the stability and independence of some member of the government, the only other security, must be proportionally increased. Justice is the end of government. It is the end of civil society. It ever has been and ever will be pursued until it be obtained, or until liberty be lost in the pursuit. In a society under the forms of which the stronger faction can readily unite and oppress the weaker, anarchy may as truly be said to reign as in a state of nature, where the weaker individual is not secured against the violence of the stronger; and as, in the latter state, even the stronger individuals are prompted, by the uncertainty of their condition, to submit to a government which may protect the weak as well as themselves; so, in the former state, will the more powerful factions or parties be gradually induced, by a like motive, to wish for a government which will protect all parties, the weaker as well as the more powerful. It can be little doubted that if the State of Rhode Island was separated from the Confederacy and left to itself, the insecurity of rights under the popular form of government within such narrow limits would be displayed by such reiterated oppressions of factious majorities that some power altogether independent of the people would soon be called for by the voice of the very factions whose misrule had proved the necessity of it. In the extended republic of the

United States, and among the great variety of interests, parties, and sects
which it embraces, a coalition of a majority of the whole society could
seldom take place on any other principles than those of justice and the
general good; whilst there being thus less danger to a minor from the will of
a major party, there must be less pretext, also, to provide for the security of
the former, by introducing into the government a will not dependent on the
latter, or, in other words, a will independent of the society itself. It is no less
certain than it is important, notwithstanding the contrary opinions which
have been entertained, that the larger the society, provided it lie within a
practicable sphere, the more duly capable it will be of self-government. And
happily for the *republican cause,* the practicable sphere may be carried to a
very great extent by a judicious modification and mixture of the *federal
principle.*

10

John Adams

The Role of the Rich and the Poor
in the Legislature (1787)

. . . There can be no free government without a democratical branch
in the constitution. . . .

The rich, the well-born, and the able, acquire an influence among the
people that will soon be too much for simple honesty and plain sense, in a
house of representatives. The most illustrious of them must, therefore, be
separated from the mass, and placed by themselves in a senate; this is, to all
honest and useful intents, an ostracism. A member of a senate, of immense
wealth, the most respected birth, and transcendent abilities, has no influence in the nation, in comparison of what he would have in a single repre-

From *A Defense of the Constitutions of the Government of the United States,* in
The Life and Work of John Adams, Vol. IV and Vol. VI, Little, Brown, and Co.,
1851.

sentative assembly. When a senate exists, the most powerful man in the state may be safely admitted into the house of representatives, because the people have it in their power to remove him into the senate as soon as his influence becomes dangerous. The senate becomes the great object of ambition; and the richest and the most sagacious wish to merit an advancement to it by services to the public in the house. When he has obtained the object of his wishes, you may still hope for the benefits of his exertions, without dreading his passions; for the executive power being in other hands, he has lost much of his influence with the people, and can govern very few votes more than his own among the senators. . . .

* * * * * * * * * *

Marchamont Nedham lays it down as a fundamental principle and an undeniable rule, "that the people, (that is, such as shall be successively chosen to represent the people,) are the best keepers of their own liberties, and that for many reasons. First, because they never think of usurping over other men's rights, but mind which way to preserve their own." . . .

Would Mr. Nedham be responsible that, if all were to be decided by a vote of the majority, the eight or nine millions who have no property, would not think of usurping over the rights of the one or two millions who have? Property is surely a right of mankind as really as liberty. Perhaps, at first, prejudice, habit, shame or fear, principle or religion, would restrain the poor from attacking the rich, and the idle from usurping on the industrious; but the time would not be long before courage and enterprise would come, and pretexts be invented by degrees, to countenance the majority in dividing all the property among them, or at least, in sharing it equally with its present possessors. Debts would be abolished first; taxes laid heavy on the rich, and not at all on the others; and at last a downright equal division of every thing be demanded, and voted. What would be the consequence of this? The idle, the vicious, the intemperate, would rush into the utmost extravagance of debauchery, sell and spend all their share, and then demand a new division of those who purchased from them. The moment the idea is admitted into society, that property is not as sacred as the laws of God, and that there is not a force of law and public justice to protect it, anarchy and tyranny commence. . . .

Though we allow benevolence and generous affections to exist in the human breast, yet every moral theorist will admit the selfish passions in the generality of men to be the strongest. There are few who love the public better than themselves, though all may have some affection for the public. . . .

The only remedy is to take away the power, controlling the selfish avidity of the governor, by the senate and house; of the senate, by the governor and house; and of the house, by the governor and senate. Of all possible forms of government, a sovereignty in one assembly, successively chosen by the people, is perhaps the best calculated to facilitate the gratification of self-love, and the pursuit of the private interest of a few individuals; a few eminent conspicuous characters will be continued in their seats in the sovereign assembly, from one election to another, whatever changes are made in the seats around them, by superior art, address, and opulence, by more splendid birth, reputations, and connections, they will be able to intrigue with the people and their leaders, out of doors, until they worm out most of their opposers, and introduce their friends; to this end, they will bestow all offices, contracts, privileges in commerce, and other emoluments, on the latter and their connections, and throw every vexation and disappointment in the way of the former, until they establish such a system of hopes and fears throughout the state, as shall enable them to carry a majority in every fresh election of the house. The judges will be appointed by them and their party, and of consequence, will be obsequious enough to their inclinations. . . .

It is agreed that "the end of all government is the good and ease of the people, in a secure enjoyment of their rights, without oppression;" but it must be remembered, that the rich are *people* as well as the poor; that they have rights as well as others; that they have as clear and as *sacred* a right to their large property as others have to theirs which is smaller; that oppression to them is as possible and as wicked as to others; that stealing, robbing, cheating, are the same crimes and sins, whether committed against them or others. The rich, therefore, ought to have an effectual barrier in the constitution against being robbed, plundered, and murdered, as well as the poor; and this can never be without an independent senate. The poor should have a bulwark against the same dangers and oppressions; and this can never be without a house of representatives of the people. But neither the rich nor the poor can be defended by their respective guardians in the constitution, without an executive power, vested with a negative, equal to either, to hold the balance even between them, and decide when they cannot agree. If it is asked, When will this negative be used? it may be answered, Perhaps never. The known existence of it will prevent all occasion to exercise it; but if it has not a being, the want of it will be felt every day. . . .

11

Alexander Hamilton

On the Character of the Legislator (1778)

. . . The station of a member of Congress is the most illustrious and important of any I am able to conceive. He is to be regarded not only as a legislator, but as the founder of an empire. A man of virtue and ability, dignified with so precious a trust, would rejoice that fortune had given him birth at a time, and placed him in circumstances so favourable for promoting human happiness. He would esteem it not more the duty, than the privilege and ornament of his office, to do good to mankind; from this commanding eminence, he would look down with contempt upon every mean or interested pursuit.

To form useful alliances abroad—to establish a wise government at home—to improve the internal resources, and finances of the nation would be the generous objects of his care. He would not allow his attention to be diverted from these to intrigue for personal connections, to confirm his own influence; nor would be able to reconcile it, either to the delicacy of his honour, or to the dignity of his pride, to confound in the same person the representative of the Commonwealth, and the little member of a trading company. Anxious for the permanent power and prosperity of the State, he would labour to perpetuate the union and harmony of the several parts. He would not meanly court a temporary importance, by patronizing the narrow views of local interest, or by encouraging dissensions either among the people or in Congress. In council, or debate, he would discover the candor of a statesman, zealous for truth, and the integrity of a patriot studious of the public welfare; not the cavilling petulance of an attorney, contending for the triumph of an opinion, nor the perverse duplicity of a partisan, devoted to the service of a cabal. Despising the affectation of superior wisdom, he would prove the extent of his capacity, by foreseeing evils, and contriving expedients to prevent or remedy them. He would not expose the weak sides of the State, to find an opportunity of displaying his own discernment, by magnifying the follies and mistakes of others. In his transactions with individuals, whether foreigners or countrymen, his conduct would be guided by

From Hamilton, "Publius Letter, III," Nov. 16, 1778, in *The Papers of Alexander Hamilton,* Vol. I, Columbia University Press, 1969.

the sincerity of a man, and the politeness of a gentleman, not by the temporising flexibility of a courtier, nor the fawning complaisance of a sycophant. . . .

12

Alexander Hamilton

Federalist 11 (1787)

The importance of the Union, in a commercial light, is one of those points about which there is least room to entertain a difference of opinion. . . .

There are appearances to authorize a supposition that the adventurous spirit, which distinguishes the commercial character of America, has already excited uneasy sensations in several of the maritime powers of Europe. . . . Those of them which have colonies in America look forward to what this country is capable of becoming, with painful solicitude. . . . Impressions of this kind will naturally indicate the policy of fostering divisions among us, and of depriving us, as far as possible, of an ACTIVE COMMERCE in our own bottoms. This would answer the threefold purpose of preventing our interference in their navigation, of monopolizing the profits of our trade, and of clipping the wings by which we might soar to a dangerous greatness. Did not prudence forbid the detail, it would not be difficult to trace, by facts, the workings of this policy to the cabinets of ministers.

If we continue united, we may counteract a policy so unfriendly to our prosperity in a variety of ways. By prohibitory regulations, extending, at the same time, throughout the States, we may oblige foreign countries to bid against each other, for the privileges of our markets. . . .

A further resource for influencing the conduct of European nations towards us, in this respect, would arise from the establishment of a federal

From *The Federalist*.

navy. There can be no doubt that the continuance of the Union under an efficient government, would put it in our power, at a period not very distant, to create a navy which, if it could not vie with those of the great maritime powers, would at least be of respectable weight if thrown into the scale of either of two contending parties. This would be more peculiarly the case in relation to operations in the West Indies. A few ships of the line, sent opportunely to the reinforcement of either side, would often be sufficient to decide the fate of a campaign, on the event of which interests of the greatest magnitude were suspended. Our position is, in this respect, a most commanding one. And if to this consideration we add that of the usefulness of supplies from this country, in the prosecution of military operations in the West Indies, it will readily be perceived that a situation so favorable would enable us to bargain with great advantage for commercial privileges. A price would be set not only upon our friendship, but upon our neutrality. By a steady adherence to the Union, we may hope, erelong, to become the arbiter of Europe in America, and to be able to incline the balance of European competitions in this part of the world as our interest may dictate.

But in the reverse of this eligible situation, we shall discover that the rivalships of the parts would make them checks upon each other, and would frustrate all the tempting advantages which nature has kindly placed within our reach. In a state so insignificant our commerce would be a prey to the wanton intermeddlings of all nations at war with each other; who, having nothing to fear from us, would with little scruple or remorse supply their wants by depredations on our property as often as it fell in their way. The rights of neutrality will only be respected when they are defended by an adequate power. A nation, despicable by its weakness, forfeits even the privilege of being neutral.

Under a vigorous national government, the natural strength and resources of the country, directed to a common interest, would baffle all the combinations of European jealousy to restrain our growth. This situation would even take away the motive to such combinations, by inducing an impracticability of success. An active commerce, an extensive navigation, and a flourishing marine would then be the offspring of moral and physical necessity. We might defy the little arts of the little politicians to control or vary the irresistible and unchangeable course of nature.

But in a state of disunion, these combinations might exist and might operate with success. It would be in the power of the maritime nations, availing themselves of our universal impotence, to prescribe the conditions of our political existence; and as they have a common interest in being our carriers, and still more in preventing our becoming theirs, they would in all probability combine to embarrass our navigation in such a manner as would in effect destroy it, and confine us to a PASSIVE COMMERCE. We should then be compelled to content ourselves with the first price of our commodities, and to see the profits of our trade snatched from us to enrich our enemies and persecutors. That unequalled spirit of enterprise, which signalizes the genius of the American merchants and navigators, and which is in itself an inexhaustible mine of national wealth, would be stifled and lost, and poverty and disgrace would overspread a country which, with wisdom, might make herself the admiration and envy of the world. . . .

An unrestrained intercourse between the States themselves will advance the trade of each by an interchange of their respective productions, not only for the supply of reciprocal wants at home, but for exportation to foreign markets. The veins of commerce in every part will be replenished, and will acquire additional motion and vigor from a free circulation of the commodities of every part. Commercial enterprise will have much greater scope, from the diversity in the productions of different States. When the staple of one fails from a bad harvest or unproductive crop, it can call to its aid the staple of another. The variety, not less than the value, of products for exportation contributes to the activity of foreign commerce. It can be conducted upon much better terms with a large number of materials of a given value than with a small number of materials of the same value; arising from the competitions of trade and from the fluctuations of markets. Particular articles may be in great demand at certain periods, and unsalable at others; but if there be a variety of articles, it can scarcely happen that they should all be at one time in the latter predicament, and on this account the operations of the merchant would be less liable to any considerable obstruction or stagnation. . . .

The world may politically, as well as geographically, be divided into four parts, each having a distinct set of interests. Unhappily for the other three, Europe, by her arms and by her negotiations, by force and by fraud, has, in different degrees, extended her dominion over them all. Africa, Asia, and America, have successively felt her domination. The superiority she has long maintained has tempted her to plume herself as the Mistress of the World, and to consider the rest of mankind as created for her benefit. . . . Facts have too long supported these arrogant pretensions of the Europeans. It belongs to us to vindicate the honor of the human race, and to teach that assuming brother, moderation. Union will enable us to do it. Disunion will add another victim to his triumphs. Let Americans disdain to be the instruments of European greatness! Let the thirteen States, bound together in a strict and indissoluble Union, concur in erecting one great American system, superior to the control of all transatlantic force or influence, and able to dictate the terms of the connection between the old and the new world!

13

Alexander Hamilton

The Military in a Commercial Republic (1787)

. . . [Opponents of the Constitution would like standing armies to be prohibited.] From a close examination it will appear that restraints upon the discretion of the legislature in respect to military establishments in time of peace, would be improper to be imposed, and if imposed, from the necessities of society, would be unlikely to be observed.

Though a wide ocean separates the United States from Europe, yet there are various considerations that warn us against an excess of confidence or security. On one side of us, and stretching far into our rear, are growing settlements subject to the dominion of Britain. On the other side, and extending to meet the British settlements, are colonies and establishments subject to the dominion of Spain. This situation and the vicinity of the West India Islands, belonging to these two powers, create between them, in respect to their American possessions and in relation to us, a common interest. . . .

Previous to the Revolution, and ever since the peace, there has been a constant necessity for keeping small garrisons on our Western frontier. No person can doubt that these will continue to be indispensable, if it should only be against the ravages and depredations of the Indians. These garrisons must either be furnished by occasional detachments from the militia, or by permanent corps in the pay of the government. The first is impracticable; and if practicable, would be pernicious. The militia would not long, if at all, submit to be dragged from their occupations and families to perform that most disagreeable duty in times of profound peace. And if they could be prevailed upon or compelled to do it, the increased expense of a frequent rotation of service, and the loss of labor and disconcertion of the industrious pursuits of individuals, would form conclusive objections to the scheme. It would be as burdensome and injurious to the public as ruinous to private citizens. The latter resource of permanent corps in the pay of the government amounts to a standing army in time of peace; a small one, in-

From Federalist 8 and 24, in *The Federalist*.

deed, but not the less real for being small. Here is a simple view of the subject, that shows us at once the impropriety of a constitutional interdiction of such establishments, and the necessity of leaving the matter to the discretion and prudence of the legislature. . . .

. . . The industrious habits of the people of the present day, absorbed in the pursuits of gain, and devoted to the improvements of agriculture and commerce, are incompatible with the condition of a nation of soldiers, which was the true condition of the people of those republics. The means of revenue, which have been so greatly multiplied by the increase of gold and silver and of the arts of industry, and the science of finance, which is the offspring of modern times, concurring with the habits of nations, have produced an entire revolution in the system of war, and have rendered disciplined armies, distinct from the body of the citizens, the inseparable companions of frequent hostility. . . .

14

Alexis de Tocqueville

Equality and Commerce (1840)

In America the passion for physical well-being is not always exclusive, but it is general; and if all do not feel it in the same manner, yet it is felt by all. The effort to satisfy even the least wants of the body and to provide the little conveniences of life is uppermost in every mind. . . .

When riches are hereditarily fixed in families, a great number of men enjoy the comforts of life without feeling an exclusive taste for those comforts. The heart of man is not so much caught by the undisturbed possession of anything valuable as by the desire, as yet imperfectly satisfied, of possessing it and by the incessant dread of losing it. In aristocratic communities the wealthy, never having experienced a condition different from their own, entertain no fear of changing it; the existence of such conditions hardly occurs to them. The comforts of life are not to them the end of life, but simply a way of living; they regard them as existence itself, enjoyed but scarcely thought of. As the natural and instinctive taste that all men feel for being well off is thus satisfied without trouble and without apprehension, their faculties are turned elsewhere and applied to more arduous and lofty undertakings, which excite and engross their minds.

Hence it is that in the very midst of physical gratifications the members of an aristocracy often display a haughty contempt of these very enjoyments and exhibit singular powers of endurance under the privation of them. All the revolutions which have ever shaken or destroyed aristocracies have shown how easily men accustomed to superfluous luxuries can do without the necessaries of life; whereas men who have toiled to acquire a competency can hardly live after they have lost it.

If I turn my observation from the upper to the lower classes, I find analogous effects produced by opposite causes. Among a nation where aristocracy predominates in society and keeps it stationary, the people in the end get as much accustomed to poverty as the rich to their opulence. The latter bestow no anxiety on their physical comforts because they enjoy them without an effort; the former do not think of things which they despair of obtaining and which they hardly know enough of to desire. In communities of this kind the imagination of the poor is driven to seek another world; the miseries of real life enclose it, but it escapes from their control and flies to seek its pleasures far beyond.

When, on the contrary, the distinctions of ranks are obliterated and privileges are destroyed, when hereditary property is subdivided and education and freedom are widely diffused, the desire of acquiring the comforts of the world haunts the imagination of the poor, and the dread of losing them that of the rich. Many scanty fortunes spring up; those who possess them have a sufficient share of physical gratifications to conceive a taste for these pleasures, not enough to satisfy it. They never procure them without exertion, and they never indulge in them without apprehension. They are therefore always straining to pursue or to retain gratifications so delightful, so imperfect, so fugitive.

If I were to inquire what passion is most natural to men who are stimulated and circumscribed by the obscurity of their birth or the mediocrity of their fortune, I could discover none more peculiarly appropriate to their condition than this love of physical prosperity. The passion for physical comforts is essentially a passion of the middle classes; with those classes it grows and spreads, with them it is preponderant. From them it mounts into the higher orders of society and descends into the mass of the people.

⌐I never met in America any citizen so poor as not to cast a glance of hope and envy on the enjoyments of the rich or whose imagination did not possess itself by anticipation of those good things that fate still obstinately withheld from him.

On the other hand, I never perceived among the wealthier inhabitants of the United States that proud contempt of physical gratifications which is sometimes to be met with even in the most opulent and dissolute aristocracies.⌐Most of these wealthy persons were once poor; they have felt the sting of want; they were long a prey to adverse fortunes; and now that the victory is won, the passions which accompanied the contest have survived it; their minds are, as it were, intoxicated by the small enjoyments which they have pursued for forty years. . . .

* * * * * * * * * *

. . . It commonly happens that in the ages of privilege the practice of almost all the arts becomes a privilege, and that every profession is a separate sphere of action, into which it is not allowable for everyone to enter. Even when productive industry is free, the fixed character that belongs to aristocratic nations gradually segregates all the persons who practice the same art till they form a distinct class, always composed of the same families, whose members are all known to each other and among whom a public opinion of their own and a species of corporate pride soon spring up. In a class or guild of this kind each artisan has not only his fortune to make, but his reputation to preserve. He is not exclusively swayed by his own interest or even by that of his customer, but by that of the body to which he belongs; and the interest of that body is that each artisan should produce the best possible workmanship. In aristocratic ages the object of the arts is therefore to manufacture as well as possible, not with the greatest speed or at the lowest cost.

When, on the contrary, every profession is open to all, when a multitude of persons are constantly embracing and abandoning it, and when its several members are strangers, indifferent to and because of their numbers hardly seen by each other, the social tie is destroyed, and each workman, standing alone, endeavors simply to gain the most money at the least cost. The will of the customer is then his only limit.⌐But at the same time a corresponding change takes place in the customer also. In countries in which riches as well as power are concentrated and retained in the hands of a few, the use of the greater part of this world's goods belongs to a small number of individuals, who are always the same. Necessity, public opinion, or moderate desires exclude all others from the enjoyment of them. As this aristocratic class remains fixed at the pinnacle of greatness on which it stands, without diminution or increase, it is always acted upon by the same wants and affected by them in the same manner. The men of whom it is composed naturally derive from their superior and hereditary position a taste for what is extremely well made and lasting. This affects the general way of thinking of the nation in relation to the arts. It often occurs among such a people that even the peasant will rather go without the objects he covets than procure them in a state of imperfection. In aristocracies, then, the handicraftsmen work for only a limited number of fastidious customers; the profit they hope to make depends principally on the perfection of their workmanship.

Such is no longer the case when, all privileges being abolished, ranks are intermingled and men are forever rising or sinking in the social scale. Among a democratic people a number of citizens always exists whose patrimony is divided and decreasing. They have contracted, under more prosperous circumstances, certain wants, which remain after the means of satisfying such wants are gone; and they are anxiously looking out for some surreptitious method of providing for them. On the other hand, there is always in democracies a large number of men whose fortune is on the increase, but whose desires grow much faster than their fortunes, and who gloat upon the gifts of wealth in anticipation, long before they have means to obtain them. Such men are eager to find some short cut to these gratifications, already almost within their reach. From the combination of these two causes the result is that in democracies there is always a multitude of persons whose wants are above their means and who are very willing to take up with imperfect satisfaction rather than abandon the object of their desires altogether.

The artisan readily understands these passions, for he himself partakes in them. In an aristocracy he would seek to sell his workmanship at a high price to the few; he now conceives that the more expeditious way of getting rich is to sell them at a low price to all. But there are only two ways of lowering the price of commodities. The first is to discover some better, shorter, and more ingenious method of producing them; the second is to manufacture a larger quantity of goods, nearly similar, but of less value. Among a democratic population all the intellectual faculties of the workman are directed to these two objects: he strives to invent methods that may enable him not only to work better, but more quickly and more cheaply; or if he cannot succeed in that, to diminish the intrinsic quality of the thing he makes, without rendering it wholly unfit for the use for which it is intended. When none but the wealthy had watches, they were almost all very good ones; few are now made that are worth much, but everybody has one in his pocket. Thus the democratic principle not only tends to direct the human mind to the useful arts, but it induces the artisan to produce with great rapidity many imperfect commodities, and the consumer to content himself with these commodities. . . .

The handicraftsmen of democratic ages not only endeavor to bring their useful productions within the reach of the whole community, but strive to give to all their commodities attractive qualities that they do not in reality possess. In the confusion of all ranks everyone hopes to appear what he is not, and makes great exertions to succeed in this object. This sentiment, indeed, which is only too natural to the heart of man, does not originate in the democratic principle; but that principle applies it to material objects. The hypocrisy of virtue is of every age, but the hypocrisy of luxury belongs more particularly to the ages of democracy.

To satisfy these new cravings of human vanity the arts have recourse to every species of imposture. . . .

When I arrived for the first time at New York, by that part of the Atlantic Ocean which is called the East River, I was surprised to perceive along the shore, at some distance from the city, a number of little palaces of white marble, several of which were of classic architecture. When I went the next day to inspect more closely one which had particularly attracted my notice, I found that its walls were of whitewashed brick, and its columns of painted wood. All the edifices that I had admired the night before were of the same kind.

The social condition and the institutions of democracy impart, moreover, certain peculiar tendencies to all the imitative arts, which it is easy to point out. They frequently withdraw them from the delineation of the soul to fix them exclusively on that of the body, and they substitute the representation of motion and sensation for that of sentiment and thought; in a word, they put the real in the place of the ideal.

I doubt whether Raphael studied the minute intricacies of the mechanism of the human body as thoroughly as the draftsmen of our own time. He did not attach the same importance as they do to rigorous accuracy on this point because he aspired to surpass nature. He sought to make of man something which should be superior to man and to embellish beauty itself. David and his pupils, on the contrary, were as good anatomists as they were painters. They wonderfully depicted the models that they had before their eyes, but they rarely imagined anything beyond them; they followed nature with fidelity, while Raphael sought for something better than nature. They have left us an exact portraiture of man, but he discloses in his works a glimpse of the Divinity.

This remark as to the manner of treating a subject is no less applicable to its choice. The painters of the Renaissance generally sought far above themselves, and away from their own time, for mighty subjects, which left to their imagination an unbounded range. Our painters often employ their talents in the exact imitation of the details of private life, which they have always before their eyes; and they are forever copying trivial objects, the originals of which are only too abundant in nature. . . .

* * * * * * * * * *

. . . ⌈In Europe we are wont to look upon a restless disposition, an unbounded desire of riches, and an excessive love of independence as propensities very dangerous to society. Yet these are the very elements that ensure a long and peaceful future to the republics of America. Without these unquiet passions the population would collect in certain spots and would soon experience wants like those of the Old World, which it is difficult to satisfy; for such is the present good fortune of the New World that the vices of its inhabitants are scarcely less favorable to society than their virtues.⌋These circumstances exercise a great influence on the estimation in which human actions are held in the two hemispheres. What we should call cupidity, the Americans frequently term a laudable industry; and they blame as faintheartedness what we consider to be the virtue of moderate desires.

In France simple tastes, orderly manners, domestic affections, and the attachment that men feel to the place of their birth are looked upon as great guarantees of the tranquility and happiness of the state. But in America nothing seems to be more prejudicial to society than such virtues. The French Canadians, who have faithfully preserved the traditions of their ancient customs, are already embarrassed for room in their small territory; and this little community, which has so recently begun to exist, will shortly be a prey to the calamities incident to old nations. In Canada the most enlightened, patriotic, and humane inhabitants make extraordinary efforts to render the people dissatisfied with those simple enjoyments which still content them. There the seductions of wealth are vaunted with as much zeal as the charms of a moderate competency in the Old World; and more exertions are made to excite the passions of the citizens there than to calm them elsewhere. If we listen to their accounts, we shall hear that nothing is more praiseworthy than to exchange the pure and tranquil pleasures which even the poor man tastes in his own country for the sterile delights of prosperity under a foreign sky; to leave the patrimonial hearth and the turf beneath which one's forefathers sleep—in short, to abandon the living and the dead, in quest of fortune. . . .

In America too much knowledge cannot be diffused; for all knowledge, while it may serve him who possesses it, turns also to the advantage of those who are without it. New wants are not to be feared there, since they can be satisfied without difficulty. . . .

The American republics of the present day are like companies of [merchants], formed to explore in common the wastelands of the New World and busied in a flourishing trade.⌈The passions that agitate the Americans most deeply are not their political, but their commercial passions; or, rather, they introduce the habits of business into their political life. They love order, without which affairs do not prosper; and they set an especial value upon regular conduct, which is the foundation of a solid business. They prefer the good sense which amasses large fortunes to that enterprising genius which frequently dissipates them; general ideas alarm their minds, which are accustomed to positive calculations; and they hold practice in more honor than theory. . . .⌋

* * * * * * * * * *

In certain remote corners of the Old World you may still sometimes stumble upon a small district that seems to have been forgotten amid the general tumult, and to have remained stationary while everything around it was in motion. The inhabitants, for the most part, are extremely ignorant and poor; they take no part in the business of the country and are frequently oppressed by the government, yet their countenances are generally placid and their spirits light.

⌈In America I saw the freest and most enlightened men placed in the happiest circumstances that the world affords; it seemed to me as if a cloud habitually hung upon their brow, and I thought them serious and almost sad, even in their pleasures.

The chief reason for this contrast is that the former do not think of the ills they endure, while the latter are forever brooding over advantages they do not possess.⌋ It is strange to see with what feverish ardor the Americans pursue their own welfare, and to watch the vague dread that constantly torments them lest they should not have chosen the shortest path which may lead to it.

A native of the United States clings to this world's goods as if he were certain never to die; and he is so hasty in grasping at all within his reach that one would suppose he was constantly afraid of not living long enough to enjoy them. He clutches everything, he holds nothing fast, but soon loosens his grasp to pursue fresh gratifications.

In the United States a man builds a house in which to spend his old age, and he sells it before the roof is on; he plants a garden and lets it just as the trees are coming into bearing; he brings a field into tillage and leaves other men to gather the crops; he embraces a profession and gives it up; he settles in a place, which he soon afterwards leaves to carry his changeable longings elsewhere. If his private affairs leave him any leisure, he instantly plunges into the vortex of politics; and if at the end of a year of unremitting labor he finds he has a few days' vacation, his eager curiosity whirls him over the vast extent of the United States, and he will travel fifteen hundred miles in a few days to shake off his happiness. Death at length overtakes him, but it is before he is weary of his bootless chase of that complete felicity which forever escapes him.

At first sight there is something surprising in this strange unrest of so many happy men, restless in the midst of abundance. The spectacle itself, however, is as old as the world; the novelty is to see a whole people furnish an exemplification of it.

Their taste for physical gratifications must be regarded as the original source of that secret disquietude which the actions of the Americans betray and of that inconstancy of which they daily afford fresh examples. He who has set his heart exclusively upon the pursuit of worldly welfare is always in a hurry, for he has but a limited time at his disposal to reach, to grasp, and to enjoy it. The recollection of the shortness of life is a constant spur to him. Besides the good things that he possesses, he every instant fancies a thousand others that death will prevent him from trying if he does not try them soon. This thought fills him with anxiety, fear, and regret and keeps his mind in ceaseless trepidation, which leads him perpetually to change his plans and his abode.

If in addition to the taste for physical well-being a social condition be added in which neither laws nor customs retain any person in his place, there is a great additional stimulant to this restlessness of temper. Men will then be seen continually to change their track for fear of missing the shortest cut to happiness.

It may readily be conceived that if men passionately bent upon physical gratifications desire eagerly, they are also easily discouraged; as their ultimate object is to enjoy, the means to reach that object must be prompt and easy or the trouble of acquiring the gratification would be greater than the gratification itself. Their prevailing frame of mind, then, is at once ardent and relaxed, violent and enervated. Death is often less dreaded by them than perseverance in continuous efforts to one end. . . .

* * * * * * * * * *

. . . We must first understand what is wanted of society and its government. Do you wish to give a certain elevation to the human mind and teach it to regard the things of this world with generous feelings, to inspire men with a scorn of mere temporal advantages, to form and nourish strong convictions and keep alive the spirit of honorable devotedness? Is it your object to refine the habits, embellish the manners, and cultivate the arts, to promote the love of poetry, beauty, and glory? Would you constitute a people fitted to act powerfully upon all other nations, and prepared for those high enterprises which, whatever be their results, will leave a name forever famous in history? If you believe such to be the principal object of society, avoid the government of the democracy, for it would not lead you with certainty to the goal.

⌐But if you hold it expedient to divert the moral and intellectual activity of man to the production of comfort and the promotion of general well-being; if a clear understanding be more profitable to man than genius; if your object is not to stimulate the virtues of heroism, but the habits of peace; if you had rather witness vices than crimes, and are content to meet with fewer noble deeds, provided offenses be diminished in the same proportion; if, instead of living in the midst of a brilliant society, you are contented to have prosperity around you; if, in short, you are of the opinion that the principal object of a government is not to confer the greatest possible power and glory upon the body of the nation, but to ensure the greatest enjoyment and to avoid the most misery to each of the individuals who compose it—if such be your desire, then equalize the conditions of men and establish democratic institutions. . . .⌐

15

Thomas Jefferson

On Citizenship (1824, 1816, 1814)

. . . My own State . . . is now proposing to call a convention for amendment. Among other improvements, I hope they will adopt the subdivision of our counties into wards. The former may be estimated at an average of twenty-four miles square; the latter should be about six miles square each, and would answer to the hundreds of your Saxon Alfred. In each of these might be: 1st. an elementary school; 2nd. a company of militia with its officers; 3rd. a justice of the peace and constable; 4th. each ward should take care of their own poor; 5th. their own roads; 6th. their own police; 7th. elect within themselves one or more jurors to attend the courts of justice; and, 8th. give in at their Folkhouse their votes for all functionaries reserved to their election. Each ward would thus be a small

From *The Writings of Thomas Jefferson,* Vol. VII and VI, Taylor and Maury, 1854.

republic within itself, and every man in the State would thus become an act-ing member of the common government, transacting in person a great por-tion of its rights and duties, subordinate indeed, yet important, and entirely within his competence. The wit of man cannot devise a more solid basis for a free, durable, and well administered republic.]

* * * * * * * * * *

. . . If it is believed that these elementary schools will be better managed by the governor and council, the commissioners of the literary fund, or any other general authority of the government, than by the parents within each ward, it is a belief against all experience. Try the principle one step further and amend the bill so as to commit to the governor and council the management of all our farms, our mills, and merchants' stores. No, my friend, the way to have good and safe government is not to trust it all to one but to divide it among the many, distributing to everyone exactly the func-tions he is competent to. Let the national government be entrusted with the defense of the nation and its foreign and federal relations; the State govern-ments with the civil rights, laws, police, and administration of what con-cerns the State generally; the counties with the local concerns of the coun-ties, and each ward direct the interests within itself.] It is by dividing and subdividing these republics from the great national one down through all its subordinations until it ends in the administration of every man's farm by himself, by placing under everyone what his own eye may superintend, that all will be done for the best. What has destroyed liberty and the rights of man in every government which has ever existed under the sun? The gener-alizing and concentrating all cares and powers into one body, no matter whether of the autocrats of Russia or France, or of the aristocrats of a Venetian senate. And I do believe that if the Almighty has not decreed that man shall never be free (and it is a blasphemy to believe it), that the secret will be found to be in the making himself the depository of the powers respecting himself, so far as he is competent to them, and delegating only what is beyond his competence by a synthetical process to higher and higher orders of functionaries, so as to trust fewer and fewer powers in proportion as the trustees become more and more oligarchical. The elementary repub-lics of the wards, the county republics, the State republics, and the republic of the Union would form a gradation of authorities, standing each on the basis of law, holding every one its delegated share of powers, and con-stituting truly a system of fundamental balances and checks for the govern-ment.] Where every man is a sharer in the direction of his ward- republic, or of some of the higher ones, and feels that he is a participator in the govern-ment of affairs, not merely at an election one day in the year but every day; when there shall not be a man in the State who will not be a member of some one of its councils, great or small, he will let the heart be torn out of his body sooner than his power be wrested from him by a Caesar or a Bonaparte. How powerfully did we feel the energy of this organization in the case of embargo? . . .

* * * * * * * * * *

. . . [W]e have no paupers. . . . The great mass of our population is of laborers; our rich, who can live without labor, either manual or professional, being few, and of moderate wealth. Most of the laboring class possess property, cultivate their own lands, have families, and from the demand for their labor are enabled to exact from the rich and the competent such prices as enable them to be fed abundantly, clothed above mere decency, to labor moderately and raise their families. They are not driven to the ultimate resources of dexterity and skill, because their wares will sell although not quite so nice as those of England. The wealthy, on the other hand, and those at their ease, know nothing of what the Europeans call luxury. They have only somewhat more of the comforts and decencies of life than those who furnish them. Can any condition of society be more desirable than this? . . . In England, happiness is the lot of the aristocracy only; and the proportion they bear to the laborers and paupers, you know better than I do. Were I to guess that they are four in every hundred, then the happiness of the nation would be to its misery as one in twenty-five. In the United States it is as eight millions to zero, or as all to none. But it is said they possess the means of defense, and that we do not. How so? Are we not men? Yes; but our men are so happy at home that they will not hire themselves to be shot at for a shilling a day. Hence we can have no standing armies for defense, because we have no paupers to furnish the materials. The Greeks and Romans had no standing armies, yet they defended themselves. The Greeks by their laws, and the Romans by the spirit of their people, took care to put into the hands of their rulers no such engine of oppression as a standing army. Their system was to make every man a soldier, and oblige him to repair to the standard of his country whenever that was reared. This made them invincible; and the same remedy will make us so. In the beginning of our government we were willing to introduce the least coercion possible on the will of the citizen. Hence a system of military duty was established too indulgent to his indolence. This is the first opportunity we have had of trying it, and it has completely failed; an issue foreseen by many, and for which remedies have been proposed. That of classing the militia according to age, and allotting each age to the particular kind of service to which it was competent, was proposed to Congress in 1805, and subsequently; and, on the last trial, was lost, I believe, by a single vote only.

Had it prevailed, what has now happened would not have happened. Instead of burning our Capitol, we should have possessed theirs in Montreal and Quebec. We must now adopt it, and all will be safe.

16

James Madison

Federalist 39 (1788)

. . . The first question that offers itself is whether the general form and aspect of the government be strictly republican. It is evident that no other form would be reconcilable with the genius of the people of America; with the fundamental principles of the Revolution; or with that honorable determination which animates every votary of freedom to rest all our political experiments on the capacity of mankind for self-government. If the plan of the convention, therefore, be found to depart from the republican character, its advocates must abandon it as no longer defensible. . . .

If we resort for a criterion to the different principles on which different forms of government are established, we may define a republic to be, or at least may bestow that name on, a government which derives all its powers directly or indirectly from the great body of the people, and is administered by persons holding their offices during pleasure for a limited period, or during good behavior. It is *essential* to such a government that it be derived from the great body of the society, not from an inconsiderable proportion or a favored class of it; otherwise a handful of tyrannical nobles, exercising their oppressions by a delegation of their powers, might aspire to the rank of republicans and claim for their government the honorable title of republic. It is *sufficient* for such a government that the persons administering it be appointed, either directly or indirectly, by the people; and that they hold their appointments by either of the tenures just specified; otherwise every government in the United States, as well as every other popular government that has been or can be well organized or well executed, would be degraded from the republican character. . . .

From *The Federalist.*

On comparing the Constitution planned by the convention with the standard here fixed, we perceived at once that it is, in the most rigid sense, comformable to it. The House of Representatives, like that of one branch at least of all the State legislatures, is elected immediately by the great body of the people. The Senate, like the present Congress and the Senate of Maryland, derives its appointment indirectly from the people. The President is indirectly derived from the choice of the people, according to the example in most of the States. Even the judges, with all other officers of the Union, will, as in the several States, be the choice, though a remote choice, of the people themselves. The duration of the appointments is equally conformable to the republican standard and to the model of State constitutions.

Could any further proof be required of the republican complexion of this system, the most decisive one might be found in its absolute prohibition of titles of nobility, both under the federal and the State governments; and in its express guaranty of the republican form to each of the latter.

"But it was not sufficient," say the adversaries of the proposed Constitution, "for the convention to adhere to the republican form. They ought with equal care to have preserved the *federal* form, which regards the Union as a *Confederacy* of sovereign states; instead of which they have framed a *national* government, which regards the Union as a *consolidation* of the States." And it is asked by what authority this bold and radical innovation was undertaken. The handle which has been made of this objection requires that it should be examined with some precision.

Without inquiring into the accuracy of the distinction on which the objection is founded, it will be necessary to a just estimate of its force, first, to ascertain the real character of the government in question; secondly, to inquire how far the convention were authorized to propose such a government; and thirdly, how far the duty they owed to their country could supply any defect of regular authority.

First.—In order to ascertain the real character of the government, it may be considered in relation to the foundation on which it is to be established; to the sources from which its ordinary powers are to be drawn; to the operation of those powers; to the extent of them; and to the authority by which future changes in the government are to be introduced.

On examining the first relation, it appears, on one hand, that the Constitution is to be founded on the assent and ratification of the people of America, given by deputies elected for the special purpose; but, on the other, that this assent and ratification is to be given by the people, not as individuals composing one entire nation, but as composing the distinct and independent States to which they respectively belong. It is to be the assent and ratification of the several States, derived from the supreme authority in each State—the authority of the people themselves. The act, therefore, establishing the Constitution will not be a *national* but a *federal* act.

That it will be a federal and not a national act, as these terms are understood by the objectors—the act of the people, as forming so many independent States, not as forming one aggregate nation—is obvious from this single consideration: that it is to result neither from the decision of a *majority* of the people of the Union, nor from that of a *majority* of the States. It must result from the *unanimous* assent of the several States that are parties to it, differing not otherwise from their ordinary assent than in its being expressed, not by the legislative authority, but by that of the people themselves. Were the people regarded in this transaction as forming one nation, the will of the majority of the whole people of the United States would bind the minority, in the same manner as the majority in each State must bind the minority; and the will of the majority must be determined either by a comparison of the individual votes, or by considering the will of the majority of the States as evidence of the will of a majority of the people of the United States. Neither of these rules has been adopted. Each State, in ratifying the Constitution, is considered as a sovereign body independent of all others, and only to be bound by its own voluntary act. In this relation, then, the new Constitution will, if established, be a *federal* and not a *national* constitution.

The next relation is to the sources from which the ordinary powers of government are to be derived. The House of Representatives will derive its powers from the people of America; and the people will be represented in the same proportion and on the same principle as they are in the legislature of a particular State. So far the government is *national,* not *federal.* The Senate, on the other hand, will derive its powers from the States as political and co-equal societies; and these will be represented on the principle of equality in the Senate, as they now are in the existing Congress. So far the government is *federal,* not *national.* The executive power will be derived from a very compound source. The immediate election of the President is to be made by the States in their political characters. The votes allotted to them are in a compound ratio, which considers them partly as distinct and coequal societies, partly as unequal members of the same society. The eventual election, again, is to be made by that branch of the legislature which consists of the national representatives; but in this particular act they are to be thrown into the form of individual delegations from so many distinct and co-equal bodies politic. From this aspect of the government it appears to be of a mixed character, presenting at least as many *federal* as *national* features.

The difference between a federal and national government, as it relates to the *operation of the government,* is by the adversaries of the plan of the convention supposed to consist in this, that in the former the powers operate on the political bodies composing the confederacy in their political capacities; in the latter, on the individual citizens composing the nation in their individual capacities. On trying the Constitution by this criterion, it falls under the *national* not the *federal* character; though perhaps not so completely as has been understood. In several cases, and particularly in the trial of controversies to which States may be parties, they must be viewed and proceeded against in their collective and political capacities only. But the operation of the government on the people in their individual capacities, in its ordinary and most essential proceedings, will, in the sense of its opponents, on the whole, designate it, in this relation, a *national* government.

But if the government be national with regard to the *operation* of its powers, it changes its aspect again when we contemplate it in relation to the extent of its powers. The idea of a national government involves in it not only an authority over the individual citizens, but an indefinite supremacy over all persons and things, so far as they are objects of lawful government. Among a people consolidated into one nation, this supremacy is completely vested in the national legislature. Among communities united for particular purposes, it is vested partly in the general and partly in the municipal legislatures. In the former case, all local authorities are subordinate to the supreme; and may be controlled, directed, or abolished by it at pleasure. In the latter, the local or municipal authorities form distinct and independent portions of the supremacy, no more subject, within their respective spheres, to the general authority than the general authority is subject to them, within its own sphere. In this relation, then, the proposed government cannot be deemed a *national* one; since its jurisdiction extends to certain enumerated objects only, and leaves to the several States a residuary and inviolable sovereignty over all other objects. It is true that in controversies relating to the boundary between the two jurisdictions, the tribunal which is ultimately to decide is to be established under the general government. But this does not change the principle of the case. The decision is to be impartially made, according to the rules of the Constitution; and all the usual and most effectual precautions are taken to secure this impartiality. Some such tribunal is clearly essential to prevent an appeal to the sword and a dissolution of the compact; and that it ought to be established under the general rather than under the local governments, or, to speak more properly, that it could be safely established under the first alone, is a position not likely to be combated.

If we try the Constitution by its last relation to the authority by which amendments are to be made, we find it neither wholly *national* nor wholly *federal*. Were it wholly national, the supreme and ultimate authority would reside in the *majority* of the people of the Union; and this authority would be competent at all times, like that of a majority of every national society to alter or abolish its established government. Were it wholly federal, on the other hand, the concurrence of each State in the Union would be essential to every alteration that would be binding on all. The mode provided by the plan of the convention is not founded on either of these principles. In requiring more than a majority, and particularly in computing the proportion by *States,* not by *citizens,* it departs from the national and advances towards the *federal* character; in rendering the concurrence of less than the whole number of States sufficient, it loses again the *federal* and partakes of the *national* character.

ᒥThe proposed Constitution, therefore, even when tested by the rules laid down by its antagonists, is, in strictness, neither a national nor a federal Constitution, but a composition of both. In its foundation it is federal, not national; in the sources from which the ordinary powers of the government are drawn, it is partly federal and partly national; in the operation of these powers, it is national, not federal; in the extent of them, again, it is federal, not national; and, finally in the authoritative mode of introducing amendments, it is neither wholly federal nor wholly national.

17

McCulloch v. Maryland (1819)

Mr. Chief Justice Marshall *delivered the opinion of the Court:**

In the case now to be determined, the defendant, a sovereign state, denies the obligation of a law enacted by the legislature of the Union, and the plaintiff, on his part, contests the validity of an act which has been passed by the legislature of that state. The constitution of our country, in its most interesting and vital parts, is to be considered; the conflicting powers of the government of the Union and of its members, as marked in that constitution, are to be discussed; and an opinion given, which may essentially influence the great operations of the government. No tribunal can approach such a question without a deep sense of its importance, and of the awful responsibility involved in its decision. But it must be decided peacefully, or remain a source of hostile legislation, perhaps of hostility of a still more serious nature; and if it is to be so decided, by this tribunal alone can the decision be made. On the Supreme Court of the United States has the constitution of our country devolved this important duty.

From *McCulloch v. Maryland,* 4 Wheat. 316 (1819).

*Citations omitted throughout the Supreme Court cases in this volume.

The first question made in the cause is, has Congress power to incorporate a bank?

It has been truly said that this can scarcely be considered as an open question, entirely unprejudiced by the former proceedings of the nation respecting it. The principle now contested was introduced at a very early period of our history, has been recognized by many successive legislatures, and has been acted upon by the judicial department, in cases of peculiar delicacy, as a law of undoubted obligation.

It will not be denied that a bold and daring usurpation might be resisted, after an acquiescence still longer and more complete than this. But it is conceived that a doubtful question, one on which human reason may pause, and the human judgment be suspended, in the decision of which the great principles of liberty are not concerned, but the respective powers of those who are equally the representatives of the people, are to be adjusted; if not put at rest by the practice of the government, ought to receive a considerable impression from that practice. An exposition of the constitution, deliberately established by legislative acts, on the faith of which an immense property has been advanced, ought not to be lightly disregarded.

The power now contested was exercised by the first Congress elected under the present constitution. The bill for incorporating the bank of the United States did not steal upon an unsuspecting legislature, and pass unobserved. Its principle was completely understood, and was opposed with equal zeal and ability. After being resisted, first in the fair and open field of debate, and afterwards in the executive cabinet, with as much persevering talent as any measure has ever experienced, and being supported by arguments which convinced minds as pure and as intelligent as this country can boast, it became a law. The original act was permitted to expire; but a short experience of the embarrassments to which the refusal to revive it exposed the government, convinced those who were most prejudiced against the measure of its necessity and induced the passage of the present law. It would require no ordinary share of intrepidity to assert that a measure adopted under these circumstances was a bold and plain usurpation, to which the constitution gave no countenance. . . .

The government of the Union, then (whatever may be the influence of this fact on the case), is, emphatically, and truly, a government of the people. In form and in substance it emanates from them. Its powers are granted by them, and are to be exercised directly on them, and for their benefit.

This government is acknowledged by all to be one of enumerated powers. The principle, that it can exercise only the powers granted to it, would seem too apparent to have required to be enforced by all those arguments which its enlightened friends, while it was depending before the people, found it necessary to urge. That principle is now universally admitted. But the question respecting the extent of the powers actually granted, is perpetually arising, and will probably continue to arise, as long as our system shall exist.

In discussing these questions, the conflicting powers of the general and state governments must be brought into view, and the supremacy of their respective laws, when they are in opposition, must be settled.

If any one proposition could command the universal assent of mankind, we might expect it would be this—that the government of the Union, though limited in its powers, is supreme within its sphere of action. This would seem to result necessarily from its nature. It is the government of all; its powers are delegated by all; it represents all, and acts for all. Though any one state may be willing to control its operations, no state is willing to allow others to control them. The nation, on those subjects on which it can act, must necessarily bind its component parts. But this question is not left to mere reason; the people have, in express terms, decided it by saying, "this constitution, and the laws of the United States, which shall be made in pursuance thereof," "shall be the supreme law of the land," and by requiring that the members of the state legislatures, and the officers of the executive and judicial departments of the states shall take the oath of fidelity to it.

The government of the United States, then, though limited in its powers, is supreme; and its laws when made in pursuance of the constitution, form the supreme law of the land, "anything in the constitution or laws of any state to the contrary notwithstanding."

Among the enumerated powers, we do not find that of establishing a bank or creating a corporation. But there is no phrase in the instrument which, like the articles of confederation, excludes incidental or implied powers; and which requires that everything granted shall be expressly and minutely described. Even the 10th amendment, which was framed for the purpose of quieting the excessive jealousies which had been excited, omits the word "expressly," and declares only that the powers "not delegated to the United States, nor prohibited to the states, are reserved to the states or to the people;" thus leaving the question, whether the particular power which may become the subject of contest has been delegated to the one government, or prohibited to the other, to depend on a fair construction of the whole instrument. The men who drew and adopted this amendment had experienced the embarrassments, resulting from the insertion of this word in the articles of confederation, and probably omitted it to avoid those embarrassments. A constitution, to contain an accurate detail of all the subdivisions of which its great powers will admit, and of all the means by which they may be carried into execution, would partake of a prolixity of a legal code, and could scarcely be embraced by the human mind. It would probably never be understood by the public. Its nature, therefore, requires, that only its great outlines should be marked, its important objects designated, and the minor ingredients which compose those objects be deduced from the nature of the objects themselves. . . . In considering this question, then, we must never forget that it is a constitution we are expounding.

⌐Although, among the enumerated powers of government, we do not find the word "bank" or "incorporation," we find the great powers to lay and collect taxes; to borrow money; to regulate commerce; to declare and conduct a war; and to raise and support armies and navies. The sword and the purse, all the external relations, and no inconsiderable portion of the industry of the nation, are entrusted to its government.⌐It can never be pretended that these vast powers draw after them others of inferior importance, merely because they are inferior. Such an idea can never be advanced. But it may with great reason be contended, that a government, entrusted with such ample powers, on the due execution of which the happiness and prosperity of the nation so vitally depends, must also be entrusted with ample means for their execution. The power being given, it is the interest of the nation to facilitate its execution. It can never be their interest, and cannot be presumed to have been their intention, to clog and embarrass its execution by withholding the most appropriate means.⌐ Throughout this vast republic, from the St. Croix to the Gulf of Mexico, from the Atlantic to the Pacific, revenue is to be collected and expended, armies are to be marched and supported. The exigencies of the nation may require that the treasure raised in the north shall be transported to the south, that raised in the east conveyed to the west, or that this order should be reversed. Is that construction of the constitution to be preferred which would render these operations difficult, hazardous, and expensive? Can we adopt that construction (unless the words imperiously require it) which would impute to the framers of that instrument, when granting these powers for the public good, the intention of impeding their exercise by withholding a choice of means? If, indeed, such be the mandate of the constitution, we have only to obey; but that instrument does not profess to enumerate the means by which the powers it confers may be executed; nor does it prohibit the creation of a corporation, if the existence of such a being be essential to the beneficial exercise of those powers. It is, then, the subject of fair inquiry, how far such means may be employed. . . .

The power of creating a corporation, though appertaining to sovereignty, is not, like the power of making war, or levying taxes, or of regulating commerce, a great substantive and independent power, which cannot be implied as incidental to other powers, or used as a means of executing them. It is never the end for which other powers are exercised, but a means by which other objects are accomplished. . . .

⌐But the constitution of the United States has not left the right of Congress to employ the necessary means for the execution of the powers conferred on the government to general reasoning. To its enumeration of powers is added that of making "all laws which shall be necessary and proper, for carrying into execution the foregoing powers, and all other powers vested by this constitution, in the government of the United States, or in any department thereof."

The counsel for the State of Maryland have urged various arguments, to prove that this clause, though in terms a grant of power, is not so in effect; but is really restrictive of the general right, which might otherwise be implied of selecting means for executing the enumerated powers. . . .

[T]he argument on which most reliance is placed, is drawn from the peculiar language of this clause. Congress is not empowered by it to make all laws, which may have relation to the powers conferred on the government, but such only as may be "necessary and proper" for carrying them into execution. The word "necessary" is considered as controlling the whole sentence, and as limiting the right to pass laws for the execution of the granted powers, to such as are indispensable, and without which the power would be nugatory. That it excludes the choice of means, and leaves to Congress, in each case, that only which is most direct and simple.

Is it true that this is the sense in which the word "necessary" is always used? Does it always import an absolute physical necessity, so strong that one thing, to which another may be termed necessary, cannot exist without that other? We think it does not. If reference be had to its use, in the common affairs of the world, or in approved authors, we find that it frequently imports no more than that one thing is convenient, or useful, or essential to another. To employ the means necessary to an end, is generally understood as employing any means calculated to produce the end, and not as being confined to those single means, without which the end would be entirely unattainable. Such is the character of human language, that no word conveys to the mind, in all situations, one single definite idea; and nothing is more common than to use words in a figurative sense. Almost all compositions contain words, which, taken in their rigorous sense, would convey a meaning different from that which is obviously intended. It is essential to just construction, that many words which import something excessive should be understood in a more mitigated sense—in that sense which common usage justifies. The word "necessary" is of this description. It has not a fixed character peculiar to itself. It admits of all degree of comparison; and is often connected with other words, which increase or diminish the impression the mind receives of the urgency it imports. A thing may be necessary, very necessary, absolutely or indispensably necessary. To no mind would the same idea be conveyed by these several phrases. This comment on the word is well illustrated by the passage cited at the bar, from the 10th section of the 1st article of the constitution. It is, we think, impossible to compare the sentence which prohibits a state from laying "imposts or duties on imports or exports, except what may be absolutely necessary for executing its inspection laws," with that which authorizes Congress "to make all laws which shall be necessary and proper for carrying into execution" the powers of the general government, without feeling a conviction that the convention understood itself to change materially the meaning of the word "necessary," by prefixing the word "absolutely." This word, then, like others, is used in various senses; and, in its construction, the subject, the context, the intention of the person using them, are all to be taken into view.

Let this be done in the case under consideration. The subject is the execution of those great powers on which the welfare of a nation essentially depends. It must have been the intention of those who gave these powers, to insure, as far as human prudence could insure, their beneficial execution. This could not be done by confiding the choice of means to such narrow limits as not to leave it in the power of Congress to adopt any which might be appropriate, and which were conducive to the end. This provision is made in a constitution intended to endure for ages to come, and consequently, to be adapted to the various crises of human affairs. To have prescribed the means by which government should, in all future time, execute its powers, would have been to change entirely the character of the instrument, and give it the properties of a legal code. It would have been an unwise attempt to provide, by immutable rules, for exigencies which, if foreseen at all, must have been seen dimly, and which can be best provided for as they occur. To have declared that the best means shall not be used, but those alone without which the power given would be nugatory, would have been to deprive the legislature of the capacity to avail itself of experience, to exercise its reason, and to accommodate its legislation to circumstances. If we apply this principle of construction to any of the powers of the government, we shall find it so pernicious in its operation that we shall be compelled to discard it. . . .

Take, for example, the power "to establish post-offices and post-roads." This power is executed by the single act of making the establishment. But, from this has been inferred the power and duty of carrying the mail along the post-road, from one post-office to another. And, from this implied power, has again been inferred the right to punish those who steal letters from the post-office, or rob the mail. It may be said, with some plausibility, that the right to carry the mail, and to punish those who rob it, is not indispensably necessary to the establishment of a post-office and post-road. This right is indeed essential to the beneficial exercise of the power, but not indispensably necessary to its existence. So, of the punishment of the crimes of stealing or falsifying a record or process of a court of the United States, or of perjury in such court. To punish these offenses is certainly conducive to the due administration of justice. But courts may exist, and may decide the cause brought before them, though such crimes escape punishment. . . .

This clause, as construed by the state of Maryland, would abridge, and almost annihilate this useful and necessary right of the legislature to select its means. That this could not be intended is, we should think, had it not been already controverted, too apparent for controversy. We think so for the following reasons:

1st. The clause is placed among the powers of Congress, not among the limitations on those powers.

2d. Its terms purport to enlarge, not to diminish the powers vested in the government. It purports to be an additional power, not a restriction on those already granted. . . .

If no other motive for its insertion can be suggested, a sufficient one is found in the desire to remove all doubts respecting the right to legislate on that vast mass of incidental powers which must be involved in the constitution, if that instrument is not a splendid bauble.

We admit, as all must admit, that the powers of the government are limited, and that its limits are not to be transcended. But we think the sound construction of the constitution must allow to the national legislature that discretion, with respect to the means by which the powers it confers are to be carried into execution, which will enable that body to perform the high duties assigned to it, in the manner most beneficial to the people. Let the end be legitimate, let it be within the scope of the constitution, and all means which are appropriate, which are plainly adapted to that end, which are not prohibited, but consist with the letter and spirit of the constitution, are constitutional. . . .

Should congress, in the execution of its powers, adopt measures which are prohibited by the constitution; or should congress, under the pretext of executing its powers, pass laws for the accomplishment of objects not intrusted to the government; it would become the painful duty of this tribunal, should a case requiring such a decision come before it, to say, that such an act was not the law of the land. But where the law is not prohibited, and is really calculated to effect any of the objects intrusted to the government, to undertake here to inquire into the degree of its necessity, would be to pass the line which circumscribes the judicial department, and to tread on legislative ground. This court disclaims all pretensions to such a power. . . .

It being the opinion of the court that the act incorporating the bank is constitutional, and that the power of establishing a branch in the state of Maryland might be properly exercised by the bank itself, we proceed to inquire:

⌐2. Whether the state of Maryland may, without violating the constitution, tax that branch?⌐ . . .

[The] great principle is, that the constitution, and the laws made in pursuance thereof are supreme; that they control the constitution and laws of the respective states, and cannot be controlled by them. From this, which may be almost termed an axiom, other propositions are deduced as corollaries, on the truth or error of which, and on their application to this case, the cause has been supposed to depend. These are, 1st. that a power to create implies a power to preserve. 2d. That a power to destroy, if wielded by a different hand, is hostile to, and incompatible with these powers to create and to preserve. 3d. That where this repugnancy exists, that authority which is supreme must control, not yield to that over which it is supreme. . . .

That the power of taxing [the bank] by the states may be exercised so as to destroy it, is too obvious to be denied. . . .

All subjects over which the sovereign power of a state extends, are objects of taxation; but those over which it does not extend, are, upon the soundest principles, exempt from taxation. This proposition may almost be pronounced self-evident.

The sovereignty of a state extends to everything which exists by its own authority, or is introduced by its permission; but does it extend to those means which are employed by Congress to carry into execution—powers conferred on that body by the people of the United States? We think it demonstrable that it does not. Those powers are not given by the people of a single state. They are given by the people of the United States, to a government whose laws, made in pursuance of the constitution, are declared to be supreme. . . .

If we measure the power of taxation residing in a state, by the extent of sovereignty which the people of a single state possess, and can confer on its government, we have an intelligible standard, applicable to every case to which the power may be applied. We have a principle which leaves the power of taxing the people and property of a state unimpaired; which leaves to a state the command of all its resources, and which places beyond its reach, all those powers which are conferred by the people of the United States on the government of the Union, and all those means which are given for the purpose of carrying those powers into execution. We have a principle which is safe for the states, and safe for the Union. We are relieved, as we ought to be, from clashing sovereignty; from interfering powers; from a repugnancy between a right in one government to pull down what there is an acknowledged right in another to build up; from the incompatibility of a right in one government to destroy what there is a right in another to preserve. We are not driven to the perplexing inquiry, so unfit for the judicial department, what degree of taxation is the legitimate use, and what degree may amount to the abuse of the power. . . .

We are unanimously of opinion that the law passed by the legislature of Maryland, imposing a tax on the Bank of the United States, is unconstitutional and void. . . .

18

Alexis de Tocqueville

The Purposes Served by Local Self-government (1840)

. . . Selfishness is a vice as old as the world, which does not belong to one form of society more than to another; individualism is of democratic origin, and it threatens to spread in the same ratio as the equality of condition.

From *Democracy in America* by Alexis de Tocqueville, translated by Henry Reeve, revised by Francis Bowen, and edited by Phillips Bradley. Copyright 1945 and renewed 1973 by Alfred A. Knopf, Inc. Reprinted by permission of Alfred A. Knopf, Inc.

Among aristocratic nations, as families remain for centuries in the same condition, often on the same spot, all generations become, as it were, contemporaneous. A man almost always knows his forefathers and respects them; he thinks he already sees his remote descendants and he loves them. He willingly imposes duties on himself towards the former and the latter, and he will frequently sacrifice his personal gratifications to those who went before and to those who will come after him. Aristocratic institutions, moreover, have the effect of closely binding every man to several of his fellow citizens. As the classes of an aristocratic people are strongly marked and permanent, each of them is regarded by its own members as a sort of lesser country, more tangible and more cherished than the country at large. As in aristocratic communities all the citizens occupy fixed positions, one above another, the result is that each of them always sees a man above himself whose patronage is necessary to him, and below himself another man whose co-operation he may claim. Men living in aristocratic ages are therefore almost always closely attached to something placed out of their own sphere, and they are often disposed to forget themselves. It is true that in these ages the notion of human fellowship is faint and that men seldom think of sacrificing themselves for mankind; but they often sacrifice themselves for other men. In democratic times, on the contrary, when the duties of each individual to the race are much more clear, devoted service to any one man becomes more rare; the bond of human affection is extended, but it is relaxed.

Among democratic nations new families are constantly springing up, others are constantly falling away, and all that remain change their condition; the woof of time is every instant broken and the track of generations effaced. Those who went before are soon forgotten; of those who will come after, no one has any idea: the interest of man is confined to those in close propinquity to himself. As each class gradually approaches others and mingles with them, its members become undifferentiated and lose their class identity for each other. Aristocracy had made a chain of all the members of the community, from the peasant to the king; democracy breaks that chain and severs every link of it. . . .

Thus not only does democracy make every man forget his ancestors, but it hides his descendants and separates his contemporaries from him; it throws him back forever upon himself alone and threatens in the end to confine him entirely within the solitude of his own heart. . . .

Despotism which by its nature is suspicious, sees in the separation among men the surest guarantee of its continuance and it usually makes every effort to keep them separate. . . .

Thus the vices which despotism produces are precisely those which equality fosters. These two things perniciously complete and assist each other. Equality places men side by side, unconnected by any common tie; despotism raises barriers to keep them asunder. . . .

It is easy to see that in those same ages men stand most in need of freedom. When the members of a community are forced to attend to public affairs, they are necessarily drawn from the circle of their own interests and snatched at times from self-observation. As soon as a man begins to treat of public affairs in public, he begins to perceive that he is not so independent of his fellow men as he had at first imagined, and that in order to obtain their support he must often lend them his co-operation.

⌐When the public govern, there is no man who does not feel the value of public goodwill or who does not endeavor to court it by drawing to himself the esteem and affection of those among whom he is to live. Many of the passions which congeal and keep asunder human hearts are then obliged to retire and hide below the surface. Pride must be dissembled; disdain dares not break out; selfishness fears its own self. Under a free government, as most public offices are elective, the men whose elevated minds or aspiring hopes are too closely circumscribed in private life constantly feel that they cannot do without the people who surround them. Men learn at such times to think of their fellow men from ambitious motives; and they frequently find it, in a manner, their interest to forget themselves.⌐ . . .

The desire of being elected may lead some men for a time to violent hostility; but this same desire leads all men in the long run to support each other; and if it happens that an election accidentally severs two friends, the electoral system brings a multitude of citizens permanently together who would otherwise always have remained unknown to one another. . . .

The Americans have combated by free institutions the tendency of equality to keep men asunder, and they have subdued it. The legislators of America did not suppose that a general representation of the whole nation would suffice to ward off a disorder at once so natural to the frame of democratic society and so fatal; they also thought that it would be well to infuse political life into each portion of the territory in order to multiply to an infinite extent opportunities of acting in concert for all the members of the community and to make them constantly feel their mutual dependence. The plan was a wise one. The general affairs of a country engage the attention only of leading politicians, who assemble from time to time in the same places; and as they often lose sight of each other afterwards, no lasting ties are established between them. But if the object be to have the local affairs of a district conducted by the men who reside there, the same persons are always in contact, and they are, in a manner, forced to be acquainted and to adapt themselves to one another.

It is difficult to draw a man out of his own circle to interest him in the destiny of the state, because he does not clearly understand what influence the destiny of the state can have upon his own lot. But if it is proposed to make a road cross the end of his estate, he will see at a glance that there is a connection between this small public affair and his greatest private affairs; and he will discover, without its being shown to him, the close tie that unites private to general interest. Thus far more may be done by entrusting to the citizens the administration of minor affairs than by surrendering to them in the control of important ones, towards interesting them in the public welfare and convincing them that they constantly stand in need of one another in order to provide for it. A brilliant achievement may win for you the favor of a people at one stroke; but to earn the love and respect of the population that surrounds you, a long succession of little services rendered and of obscure good deeds, a constant habit of kindness, and an established reputation for disinterestedness will be required. Local freedom, then, which leads a great number of citizens to value the affection of their neighbors and of their kindred, perpetually brings men together and forces them to help one another in spite of the propensities that sever them. . . .

19

William A. Schambra

From Self-Interest to Social Obligation: Local Communities v. the National Community (1982)

Our recent emphasis on voluntarism, the mobilization of private groups to deal with our social ills, is designed to foster [a] spirit of individual generosity and our sense of communal values.
—President Ronald Reagan

Reagan's cutbacks of government aid reflect an abandonment of notions of social obligation, if the words "social" and "obligation" have any nuance at all.
—Michael Kinsley

The debate over President Reagan's effort to shift some social programs from the federal government to the private sector has tended to dwell, thus far, on immediate, practical questions of cost and efficiency—as most American political debates do, in their early stages. Supporters of private sector initiatives tend to argue that such initiatives will be less expensive and more effective than federal government programs. Opponents claim that the private sector cannot possibly replace all the services once performed by the federal government and that, besides, the private sector is disorganized and duplicative. Seldom does the debate touch the moral and political questions that are truly at the heart of the controversy: Which approach to social problems is an appropriate expression of our social obligation to assist others? Which set of programs nourishes and sustains that sense of obligation in the context of the American political order?

The issue of social obligation is critical for supporters of both federal government programs and private sector initiatives. Without a well-developed sense of obligation, Americans will not long support an active federal government program of social services. . . . Furthermore, unless Americans possess a sense of obligation, they will not volunteer the time and effort or contribute the funds necessary to sustain social programs within the private sector, thereby causing the failure of private sector initiatives.

When President Reagan reaches the deepest level of the debate over private sector initiatives, as in the speech from which the opening quotation is taken, he makes us aware of this fundamental question of obligation at the center of the debate—a question far more important, ultimately, than matters of cost and efficiency. The president argues, in those moments, that voluntarism is necessary to foster individual generosity and communal values; it is the means by which we will rebuild a sense of social obligation in America. President Reagan apparently believes that social obligation is taught within the small local community, where individuals encounter public responsibilities in an immediate, concrete fashion. Only by associating with his fellow citizens, according to this view—only by deliberating about, and cooperating to solve common problems—will the individual begin to develop a sense of public-spiritedness, a sense that he is part of, and obligated to, a community. This truth by itself, in the president's view, justifies the effort to return responsibility for some important social programs to the local, private, voluntary sector, where they may begin to restimulate the sense of citizenly obligation. The encouragement of private sector initiatives, according to President Reagan, is not merely a "halfhearted replacement for budget cuts," but it is, in fact, "right in its own regard" because it is "part of what we can proudly call the 'American personality.'"

Michael Kinsley and other Reagan critics are, to put it mildly, skeptical of this argument. Far from seeking to nurture social obligation, as Kinsley argues in the opening quotation, President Reagan is in fact abandoning it altogether. As for the "mobilization of private groups to deal with social ills," Reagan is said to be simply "salving people's consciences with a lot of malarky about private initiative."

Behind Kinsley's skepticism of voluntarism lies the venerable liberal view that most important social problems today are national in scope and that our social obligation to deal with them is satisfied only by national programs. . . . The social obligation expressed in national programs does, to be sure, require for its sustenance a sense of community. In the liberal view, however, the truly important community is to be found at the national—not the local—level. Indeed, the idea of the "great national community" is the central moral support of modern liberalism and its powerful central government. . . .

The lines are sharply drawn, then, between President Reagan and modern liberalism on the question: How do we nurture social obligation in America? It may not be too much of a simplification to say that the president believes this will happen only within the local community, whereas liberals maintain that it must be done at the level of the national community. As we shall see, however, liberalism attempts to build kinds of community and obligation that are inappropriate to the American regime and that are, therefore, impossible to sustain. The private sector initiatives program, by contrast, seeks to return to the American tradition of local community, best described long ago by Alexis de Tocqueville. Voluntarism nurtures and expresses a sense of obligation that is appropriate to the American regime and that is, therefore, likely to endure.

Self-Interest and Social Obligation

When we begin to search for a form of social obligation appropriate to the American regime, we quickly discover that our regime, at least in its theoretical foundations, is not particularly hospitable to notions such as social obligation, duty, compassion, or charity. The Declaration of Independence, our national credo, speaks of individual rights—to life, liberty, and the pursuit of happiness—but does not mention individual duties or obligations. Our Constitution nowhere speaks of citizenly duties or obligations to society, as do so many other constitutions in the world today. Rather, the Constitution's purpose is to "secure [those] rights" delineated in the Declaration of Independence. Our deepest political commitment has always been to liberty—to the idea that the individual, most of the time, is the best judge of what is in his own interest. Conditions have changed over two hundred years, and government has grown, but individualism remains a core principle of our regime.

Those who wish that America were more willing to fulfill its social obligations to the poor, sick, uneducated, and jobless have often complained about our national individualism—or, as it is then called, our selfishness. . . .

If advocates of social reform have been quick to perceive the harsh, ungenerous aspects of American individualism, however, they have been slower to acknowledge the tremendous benefits we have reaped from that tradition. In the political sphere, our individualism has assumed the form of a staunch defense of the rights of individuals—including the rights of the "poor, sick, uneducated and jobless," the first victims of regimes lacking a tradition of individualism. In the economic sphere, individualism has meant the unleashing of the productive and acquisitive energies of millions of people, creating in America a prosperity beyond the wildest fantasies of earlier men. The material precondition of any program of assistance (especially a generous program) to the poor, sick, uneducated, and jobless is precisely that prosperity—the product of selfish, ungenerous American individualism. . . .

It would be a gross underestimation of the American people, however, to suggest that self-interest or its exaggerated form, Social Darwinism, is the sum of our political tradition. From the nation's beginning, Americans have held that self-interest is the necessary but by no means sufficient condition for a decent republic. At a minimum, it has always been understood that in times of grave emergency Americans must put aside self-interest and rush to the defense of the nation. There are also other times when self-interest must give way to the assistance of those in need. Americans have always realized that they have citizenly duties as well as individual rights.

The sense of citizenly duty, however, does not have the same sturdy roots in human nature as does self-interest. A sense of obligation to others does not come to us as easily as concern with self. Self-interest will flourish if we simply stand out of the way; duty and obligation, on the other hand, must be assiduously cultivated. Indeed, one of the great, enduring issues of American politics—the Founders had to struggle with it, as do present-day advocates of social reform—has been: How do we nurture and preserve some sense of citizenly duty, public-spiritedness, or social obligation within the American regime of self-interest? . . .

Liberalism, Self-Interest, and Community

The problem of taming self-interest in the name of community or citizenly obligation is at the center of modern liberalism. Liberalism today stands for an extensive federal social service program on behalf of the poor and helpless and supported by heavy taxation. American individualism, however, has always posed a great problem for this program. Self-interest tells the citizen that the suffering of the poor, usually "out of sight," in remote parts of the country, is none of his concern. The taxes and the programs they finance, therefore, come to be resented and possibly repealed.

Liberalism understands this, however, and so undertakes to replace self-interested individualism with a sense of obligation felt by each citizen toward every other. The citizen must come to feel that the suffering of the poor in every part of the country, however remote, is indeed his concern. This kind of obligation comes only when the citizen belongs to a genuine community—when he feels a oneness with his fellow citizens, including the poor and helpless. Ultimately, then, the essential moral underpinning for liberalism's extensive federal social service program is the "great national community"—the citizen's sense of belonging to one nation, and the feeling of obligation to help fellow citizens by means of national programs. . . .

The catalyst of the national community, in the liberal view, is the president—the galvanizing, unifying voice of all the American people. The presidency, as Franklin D. Roosevelt noted, is "not merely an administrative office. That's the least of it. It's predominately a place of moral leadership." The progressive president, according to Michael Walzer, will use his office to "invoke the moral vision of a society whose citizens are committed to one another and willing to share the costs of commitment." . . .

The great prophet of this liberal vision for America was Herbert Croly. . . .

Croly's powerful central government was but the instrument of a far larger project: the creation of a true national community, within which Americans would transcend self-interest altogether and bind themselves to the purposes of the nation. . . .

The sense of obligation to be generated within Croly's national community was obviously an exalted one. For Croly, a "democratic scheme of moral values reaches its consummate expression in the religion of human brotherhood," and that "religion" "can be realized only through the loving-kindness which individuals feel toward . . . their fellow countrymen." . . .

The vision of the great national community, comprising citizens with a sense of neighborly obligations, became the essential moral underpinning of the New Deal. Roosevelt understood that only the moral doctrine of national oneness and neighborliness was adequate to sustain the vast expansion of national government programs undertaken by his administration. Citizens would continue to support national programs only if they possessed a truly national sense of obligation. . . .

The Problem of the National Community

The solid truth in liberalism's vision of national community is that there are, of course, times when we must and do pull together as one nation—when we must transcend self-interest, thinking first of the national good and the good of all our "neighbors." Such times were the Great Depression, the Civil War, and the two world wars. In moments of great crisis the gravity and proximity of national danger seem to transform the American people, to draw from them truly noble sacrifices. . . .

Such self-transcendent, nation-forging moments are truly extraordinary, however, requiring extraordinary circumstances (such as war), which are not often desirable, and extraordinary leaders (such as Lincoln and Roosevelt), who are not often at hand. Indeed, this is the central dilemma confronting modern liberalism: it seeks to make permanent and ordinary a kind and degree of community possible only in transitory and extraordinary circumstances. It attempts to solve this dilemma by building a powerful, dynamic presidency (a sort of institutionalized Roosevelt), and by characterizing its programs as battles, campaigns, crusades, and wars. . . .

This liberal project ultimately founders, however, because Americans cannot perpetually be kept on war footing—especially when the war being fought is but a moral stand-in for the real thing. American self-interestedness and individualism are too powerful, too rooted in our political traditions and institutions, to permit more than fleeting moments of self-transcendence and national neighborliness. . . .

Lest this seem an excessively harsh or pessimistic assessment of the prospects for national community, it should be recalled that President Carter was the preeminent spokesman for this point of view. It was, indeed, the centerpiece of his famous "malaise" speech of July 1979. The problem facing America, according to Carter in that speech, was far more than an energy problem—it was in fact the breakdown of the national community, a "loss of a unity of purpose for our Nation." In the wake of this loss, there had been a great resurgence of self-interest and petty materialism. . . .

President Carter, unhappily, had nothing to offer to remedy the situation beyond the now-tired device of a "moral equivalent of war." Energy, Carter argued, "will be the immediate test of our ability to unite this Nation". . . .

President Carter was wise to be concerned about the disintegration of the sense of community and the resurgence of self-interest, even if his solution to the problem was unimaginative and ultimately unacceptable. . . .

If Carter identified a real problem, however, what is the solution? As liberalism's national community erodes, how are we to avoid slipping into mean-spirited individualism? . . .

Local Community and Social Obligation

These concerns lead us to a consideration of President Reagan's private sector initiatives program. President Reagan denies that he is a proponent of mean-spirited individualism . . . . In his speeches the president has agreed with liberals that we have a social obligation to the poor and helpless, and he has agreed that this obligation may be cultivated only within a true community, where citizens sense their oneness with other citizens. He denies, however, that it is possible to build this sense of community or oneness on a national scale. In his view, it may be cultivated only within the small, local community. "It is . . . activity on a small, human scale that creates the fabric of community. . . . The human scale nurtures standards of right behavior, a prevailing ethic of what is right and wrong."

Returning responsibility for some social programs to the local level—through private sector initiatives and the new federalism—will reinvigorate a true sense of community, according to Reagan, and thus "foster [a] spirit of individual generosity and our sense of communal values." Social obligation may be restored, but only quietly, at the local level—not through a grand moral equivalent of war.

The Reagan position sounds radical to us, accustomed as we have become over the past fifty years to the notion that the only legitimate expression of social obligation is a national program undertaken on behalf of the national community. The private sector initiatives program is, however, a reflection of a longstanding American tradition of local community and voluntary activity that was, in fact, the undisputed basis for social welfare in this country prior to the New Deal. We cannot understand that tradition, or its resurrection in Reagan's program, until we have considered the unsurpassed theoretical treatment of it to be found in Alexi de Tocqueville's *Democracy in America*.

Central to Tocqueville's famous volume written in the 1830s is the same concern that lies at the heart of modern liberalism, and at the heart of the private sector initiatives debate: How do we cultivate a sense of obligation in naturally self-interested individuals? . . .

If there was hope for mankind in this democratic, individualistic age, according to Tocqueville, it could be found in America. . . .

Tocqueville found that America had countered the dangers of individualism by means of a series of devices—foremost among them administrative decentralization and voluntary association—that had in common a single principle. These devices all force the individual to assume responsibility for a small portion of the public business—business that affects his immediate self-interest and is therefore important to him, but that nonetheless compels him to interact with others and thus gradually to see beyond his immediate self-interest to the common good. These devices gently draw the individual out of the "solitude of his own heart" and thereby cultivate a citizen who bears some sense of public-spiritedness or social obligation.

Administrative decentralization is one of the most important tools for forging a responsible citizenry. Always a powerful tradition in America, local government had its roots in the New England town meeting. Even after the Union had been formed, however, Tocqueville notes, "the lawgivers of America did not suppose that a general representation of the whole nation would suffice" to ward off the dangerous tendencies of individualism. "They thought it also right to give each part of the land its own political life so that there should be an infinite number of occasions for the citizens to act together and so that every day they should feel that they depended on one another." Citizens acting together and depending on one another thus develop a sense of obligation and come to form a genuine community.

Citizenly obligation can grow, however, only when it is immediately, tangibly clear to the individual that public matters affect his personal well-being. According to Tocqueville, social obligation cannot be cultivated by those devices that subsequently were to be so important to liberalism, such as high-flown appeals to national unity, patriotism, or morality—"it is difficult to force a man out of himself and get him to take an interest in the affairs of the whole state, for he has little understanding of the way in which the fate of the state can influence his own lot." In the regime of self-interest, public involvement and therefore social obligation are achieved only when the citizen experiences, in a concrete way, the connection between private interest and public affairs: "If it is a question of taking a road past his property, he sees at once that this small public matter has a bearing on his greatest private interests, and there is no need to point out to him the close connection between his private profit and the general interest."

Once the individual enters the public realm to deal with the question of the "road past his property," he is forced to act together with others, and "as soon as common affairs are treated in common, each man notices that he is not as independent of his fellows as he used to suppose and that to get their help he must often offer his aid to them." Although he entered the public realm out of self-interest, gradually he is habituated into thinking of the good of others; he acquires a sense of obligation. "At first it is of necessity that men attend to the public interest, afterward by choice. What had been calculation becomes instinct. By dint of working for the good of his fellow citizens, he in the end acquires a habit and taste for serving them."

Private, voluntary associations operate in much the same way as administrative decentralization to produce a sense of citizenly obligation in the democratic individual. Americans, Tocqueville maintains, are instinctively joiners: "Americans of all ages, all stations in life, and all types of dispositions are forever forming associations." Associations are formed to meet immediate, concrete problems that have a tangible bearing on individual self-interest. "If some obstacle blocks the public road halting the circulation of traffic, the neighbors at once form a deliberative body; this improvised assembly produces an executive authority which remedies the trouble. . . ." As citizens associate, "pursuing in common the objects of common desire," they become accustomed to considering the interests of others as well as their own self-interest. "Feelings and ideas are renewed, the heart enlarged, and the understanding developed . . . by the reciprocal action of men one upon another" in associations.

Voluntary associations and administrative decentralization are, then, democratic devices for taming the great problem of democracy—individualism. . . . It must be understood, however, that these devices do not raise men far above self-interest. The kind of morality they generate is best described as "self-interest properly understood"—the principle, according to Tocqueville, by which Americans enjoy explaining almost "every act of their lives." . . .

Tocqueville's gentle, realistic strategy for moderating self-interest on behalf of community and citizenly obligation is at the heart of today's private sector initiatives program. President Reagan's effort to revitalize local government and voluntary associations is nothing less than an attempt to resuscitate Tocqueville's citizen-forging devices in the context of the twentieth century. The president believes that, by returning some social programs to the local, voluntary sector, citizens will once again be confronted immediately and concretely with public responsibility. Individuals who volunteer and associate with one another, working to solve "common problems in common," will come to feel a sense of obligation to others. Within the small local community, citizens will once again be molded from self-interested individuals.

The private sector initiatives program, then, is one answer to the question raised by President Carter in his "malaise" speech: How are we to avoid the "path . . . to fragmentation and self-interest" and reinvigorate the sense of community and obligation in modern America? Whether the program will be a sufficient answer is, of course, not known, but there are reasons for encouragement. . . .

Above all . . . Tocquevillian social obligation does not require extraordinary circumstances like war or rhetorical substitutes therefor. It in fact rests on the ordinary, everyday circumstances of local administration and citizenly participation therein. In short, we have some hope that private sector initiatives will begin to rebuild the sense of community in America, because the democratic devices described by Tocqueville seek to nurture a form of public-spiritedness or social obligation that is appropriate to the American regime. Liberalism's devices do not.

Conclusion

None of this is meant to suggest that we should abandon all, most, or even many social service programs at the federal level. Modern industrial civilization, of course, requires a far more powerful national government than the one Tocqueville saw in the America of the 1830s. The federal government, necessarily, is responsible for a much wider range of social services today. The extensive array of social services that seems to be demanded by modern circumstances, however, will not be provided by the American political system unless the American taxpayer/voter feels a sense of obligation to provide it. . . .

Private sector initiatives—far from being a mean-spirited rejection of social obligation—may in fact be the only way to rebuild that obligation in the wake of the collapse of liberalism's national community. By transferring some programs to the local, voluntary level, we may begin to reconstruct the sense of obligation ultimately required to support those programs we would leave at the federal level. . . .

Chapter II

Political Parties, Elections, and the Bureaucracy

Political parties, elections, and the bureaucracy are in some important respects extra-Constitutional features of the American political system. The Constitution did provide a detailed mechanism for presidential selection, but that mechanism was transformed very early in our nation's history by the development of political parties. Parties very quickly became the major institutional force structuring electoral politics as well as an important influence on the policy debate within government.

Whereas the Constitution was silent on the issue of political parties, it did anticipate the development of a kind of bureaucracy in the executive branch. But there is no indication that the authors of the Constitution envisioned anything approaching the size of the contemporary federal bureaucracy or the degree of independence that resulted from civil service reform. It has become commonplace to speak of the modern bureaucracy as a fourth branch of government, a branch that is outside the original separation of powers scheme set forth in the Constitution.

Thus, one must look beyond the Founding period to fully comprehend the contemporary character of elections, parties and the bureaucracy, but it would be a mistake to neglect the importance of Constitutional principles and mechanisms in their development and operation. For example, the operation of the electoral college described by Hamilton is very different than the Presidential selection process we see today. Hamilton thought the electoral college would allow for both popular opinion and the deliberate choice of a select body of citizens to operate in the election of the President. Popular opinion would determine the choice of electors, but electors operating in "circumstances favorable to deliberation" would choose the President.

The electoral college never operated in the way Hamilton envisioned. The selection of Washington was a foregone conclusion. By the time the election of 1796 occurred, the rise of political parties transformed independent electors into delegates pledged to vote for the nominee of their party. Lord Bryce claims that party nomination of candidates is one cause of the lack of great statesmen in the office of the Presidency.

Martin Diamond argues, however, that even though the electoral college does not operate in the way intended by the framers, it nonetheless promotes Constitutional principles. Electors may not exercise independent judgment, but the building of electoral majorities on a state by state basis creates a complex majority. Presidential candidates must build a coalition of competing interests on a state by state basis rather than appeal to a simple national majority based upon the lowest common denominator of national public opinion. A national direct popular election, according to Diamond, would undermine interest based politics and encourage the development of more principled, but less stable and more dangerous political parties.

Similarly, James Ceaser argues that development of political parties came to promote Constitutional principles. Under the direction of Martin Van Buren parties institutionalized the screening function for Presidential candidates that was originally to be performed by the electors. Although parties would not be likely to produce the "continental figure" intended by the Founders, Van Buren thought that they would preserve the Constitutional character of the office. Broad-based consensus parties would help to moderate popular election campaigns and to restrain the President once in office.

Ceaser goes on to explain that contemporary reforms of political parties and the electoral process are rooted in the Progressive rejection of consensus politics and of institutions designed to moderate or restrain the expression of public opinion. The Progressive conception of politics viewed elections as a plebiscite in which voters choose between different political principles formulated by party leaders. Only in such a purely democratic system can the corrupting influences of self-interest be replaced by a healthy concern for the public good. But Ceaser questions whether parties that substitute principles for interests will be either healthy or viable. He fears that a politics based exclusively on principles will be potentially demagogic and dangerously divisive.

The desire to disentangle self-interest from politics lies behind both campaign finance reform and reforms aimed at depoliticizing the bureaucracy. Campaign finance laws passed in the early 1970s sought to minimize corruption and the appearance of corruption in the electoral process. The case of *Buckley v. Valeo* illustrates that the state's interest in restricting campaign finance practices may come into conflict with the Constitutional protection of free speech. The case also raises the question of whether equal political influence can or should be guaranteed by the government. As Justice Burger points out in his dissent, limitations on contributions and federal campaign financing may not equalize influence but will more likely provide incumbents with an increased advantage. The attempt to limit the influence of private contributors may ultimately help to insulate incumbents from effective electoral challenges.

The majority opinion in *Rutan v. Republican Party of Illinois* holds up a standard of neutral bureaucracy free from corrupting political pressures of a patronage system. But Justice Scalia, in his dissent, argues that political control of the administration supports our party system, and thus is a legitimate goal of government. There may be disagreement over the proper balance between administrative competence and partisan control, but neither element should be eliminated from the conduct of administration.

Like Scalia, Herbert Storing is also critical of attempts to take political judgment out of administration. Storing, however, looks not to the partisan politics of a patronage system, but to "the special kind of practical wisdom" that can be found and nurtured in the civil service. Civil servants have a familiarity with practical details, they are concerned with proper procedure, they are characteristically modest in their expectations for change, and their view extends beyond the next election. They offer a perspective that complements or corrects that of the party politician and politically neutral technician.

Storing's ideas regarding the bureaucracy are clearly reflected in the proposals put forward by Constance Horner as the director of the Office of Personnel Management. Horner contends that the recent conflict between those who support objective civil service tests and those who see such tests as a bar to a more culturally diverse civil service can be resolved in part by considering individual character as an important element in any hiring decision. The qualities praised by Storing are not easily measured by an objective test of specialized knowledge. Good judgment is related to good character. Horner also concludes that an appreciation of Constitutional principles can provide a unifying theme for the education of civil servants. Only if civil servants share a common appreciation of the principles that animate the Constitutional system, will they be able to perform their diverse tasks in a way that serves the long-term interests of the nation.

20

Alexander Hamilton

The Electoral College (1788)

The mode of appointment of the Chief Magistrate of the United States is almost the only part of the system, of any consequence, which has escaped without severe censure, or which has received the slightest mark of approbation from its opponents. The most plausible of these, who has appeared in print, has even deigned to admit that the election of the President is pretty well guarded. I venture somewhat further, and hesitate not to affirm that if the manner of it be not perfect, it is at least excellent. It unites in an eminent degree all the advantages the union of which was to be wished for.

It was desirable that the sense of the people should operate in the choice of the person to whom so important a trust was to be confided. This end will be answered by committing the right of making it, not to any pre-established body, but to men chosen by the people for the special purpose, and at the particular conjuncture.

It was equally desirable, that the immediate election should be made by men most capable of analyzing the qualities adapted to the station, and acting under circumstances favorable to deliberation, and to a judicious combination of all the reasons and inducements which were proper to govern their choice. A small number of persons, selected by their fellow-citizens from the general mass, will be most likely to possess the information and discernment requisite to such complicated investigations.

It was also peculiarly desirable to afford as little opportunity as possible to tumult and disorder. This evil was not least to be dreaded in the election of a magistrate, who was to have so important an agency in the administration of the government as the President of the United States. But the precautions which have been so happily concerted in the system under consideration, promise an effectual security against this mischief. The choice of *several,* to form an intermediate body of electors, will be much less apt to convulse the community with any extraordinary or violent movements, than the choice of *one* who was himself to be the final object of the public

From Federalists 68, in *The Federalist.*

wishes. And as the electors, chosen in each State, are to assemble and vote in the State in which they are chosen, this detached and divided situation will expose them much less to heats and ferments, which might be communicated from them to the people, than if they were all to be convened at one time, in one place.

Nothing was more to be desired than that every practicable obstacle should be opposed to cabal, intrigue, and corruption. . . . They have not made the appointment of the President to depend on any preexisting bodies of men, who might be tampered with beforehand to prostitute their votes; but they have referred it in the first instance to an immediate act of the people of America, to be exerted in the choice of persons for the temporary and sole purpose of making the appointment. And they have excluded from eligibility to this trust, all those who from situation might be suspected of too great devotion to the President in office. No senator, representative, or other person holding a place of trust or profit under the United States, can be of the numbers of the electors. Thus without corrupting the body of the people, the immediate agents in the election will at least enter upon the task free from any sinister bias. Their transient existence, and their detached situation, already taken notice of, afford a satisfactory prospect of their continuing so, to the conclusion of it. The business of corruption, when it is to embrace so considerable a number of men, requires time as well as means. Nor would it be found easy suddenly to embark them, dispersed as they would be over thirteen States, in any combinations founded upon motives, which though they could not properly be denominated corrupt, might yet be of a nature to mislead them from their duty.

Another and no less important desideratum was, that the Executive should be independent for his continuance in the office on all but the people themselves. He might otherwise be tempted to sacrifice his duty to his complaisance for those whose favor was necessary to the duration of his official consequence. This advantage will also be secured, by making his reelection to depend on a special body of representatives, deputed by the society for the single purpose of making the important choice. . . .

The process of election affords a moral certainty, that the office of President will never fall to the lot of any man who is not in an eminent degree endowed with the requisite qualifications. Talents for low intrigue, and the little arts of popularity, may alone suffice to elevate a man to the first honors in a single State; but it will require other talents, and a different kind of merit, to establish him in the esteem and confidence of the whole Union, or of so considerable a portion of it as would be necessary to make him a successful candidate for the distinguished office of President of the United States. It will not be too strong to say, that there will be a constant probability of seeing the station filled by characters preeminent for ability and virtue. And this will be thought no inconsiderable recommendation of the Constitution, by those who are able to estimate the share which the executive in every government must necessarily have in its good or ill administration. Though we cannot acquiesce in the political heresy of the poet who says:

> "For forms of government let fools contest—That which is best administered is best,"—

yet we may safely pronounce, that the true test of a good government is its aptitude and tendency to produce a good administration. . . .

21

James Bryce

Why Great Men Are Not Chosen Presidents (1888)

Europeans often ask, and Americans do not always explain, how it happens that this great office, the greatest in the world, unless we except the Papacy, to which any man can rise by his own merits, is not more frequently filled by great and striking men? In America, which is beyond all other countries the country of a "career open to talents," a country, moreover, in which political life is unusually keen and political ambition widely diffused, it might be expected that the highest place would always be won by a man of brilliant gifts. But since the heroes of the Revolution died out with Jefferson and Adams and Madison some sixty years ago, no person except General Grant has reached the chair whose name would have been remembered had he not been President, and no President except Abraham Lincoln has displayed rare or striking qualities in the chair. Who now knows or cares to know anything about the personality of James K. Polk or Franklin Pierce? The only thing remarkable about them is that being so commonplace they should have climbed so high.

Several reasons may be suggested for the fact, which Americans are themselves the first to admit.

One is that the proportion of first-rate ability drawn into politics is smaller in America than in most European countries. This is a phenomenon whose causes must be elucidated later: in the meantime it is enough to say that in France and Italy, where half-revolutionary conditions have made public life exciting and accessible; in Germany, where an admirably-organized civil service cultivates and develops statecraft with unusual success; in England, where many persons of wealth and leisure seek to enter the political arena, while burning questions touch the interests of all classes and make men eager observers of the combatants, the total quantity of talent devoted to parliamentary or administrative work is far larger, relatively to the population, than in America, where much of the best ability, both for

From *The American Commonwealth,* Vol. I, Chapter 3.

thought and for action, for planning and for executing, rushes into a field which is comparatively narrow in Europe, the business of developing the material resources of the country.

Another is that the methods and habits of Congress, and indeed of political life generally, seem to give fewer opportunities for personal distinction, fewer modes in which a man may commend himself to his countrymen by eminent capacity in thought, in speech, or in administration, than is the case in the free countries of Europe.

A third reason is that eminent men make more enemies, and give those enemies more assailable points, than obscure men do. They are therefore in so far less desirable candidates. It is true that the eminent man has also made more friends, that his name is more widely known, and may be greeted with louder cheers. Other things being equal, the famous man is preferable. But other things never are equal. The famous man has probably attacked some leaders in his own party, has supplanted others, has expressed his dislike to the crotchet of some active section, has perhaps committed errors which are capable of being magnified into offences. No man stands long before the public and bears a part in great affairs without giving openings to censorious criticism. Fiercer far than the light which beats upon a throne is the light which beats upon a presidential candidate, searching out all the recesses of his past life. Hence, when the choice lies between a brilliant man and a safe man, the safe man is preferred. Party feeling, strong enough to carry in on its back a man without conspicuous positive merits, is not always strong enough to procure forgiveness for a man with positive faults.

A European finds that this phenomenon needs in its turn to be explained, for in the free countries of Europe brilliancy, be it eloquence in speech, or some striking achievement in war or administration, or the power through whatever means of somehow impressing the popular imagination, is what makes a leader triumphant. Why should it be otherwise in America? Because in America party loyalty and party organization have been hitherto so perfect that any one put forward by the party will get the full party vote if his character is good and his "record," as they call it, unstained. The safe candidate may not draw in quite so many votes from the moderate men of the other side as the brilliant one would, but he will not lose nearly so many from his own ranks. Even those who admit his mediocrity will vote straight when the moment for voting comes. Besides, the ordinary American voter does not object to mediocrity. He has a lower conception of the qualities requisite to make a statesman than those who direct public opinion in Europe have. He likes his candidate to be sensible, vigorous, and, above all, what he calls "magnetic," and does not value, because he sees no need for, originality or profundity, a fine culture or a wide knowledge. Candidates are selected to be run for nomination by knots of persons who, however expert as party tacticians, are usually commonplace men; and the choice between those selected for nomination is made by a very large body, an assembly of over eight hundred delegates from the local party organizations over the country, who are certainly no better than ordinary citizens. How this process works will be seen more fully when I come to speak of those Nominating Conventions which are so notable a feature in American politics.

It must also be remembered that the merits of a President are one thing and those of a candidate another thing. An eminent American is reported to have said to friends who wished to put him forward, "Gentlemen, let there be no mistake. I should make a good President, but a very bad candidate." Now to a party it is more important that its nominee should be a good candidate than that he should turn out a good President. A nearer danger is a greater danger. As Saladin says in *The Talisman,* "A wild cat in a chamber is more dangerous than a lion in a distant desert." It will be a misfortune to the party, as well as to the country, if the candidate elected should prove a bad President. But it is a greater misfortune to the party that it should be beaten in the impending election, for the evil of losing national patronage will have come four years sooner. "B" (so reason the leaders), "who is one of our possible candidates, may be an abler man than A, who is the other. But we have a better chance of winning with A than with B, while X, the candidate of our opponents, is anyhow no better than A. We must therefore run A." This reasoning is all the more forcible because the previous career of the possible candidates has generally made it easier to say who will succeed as a candidate than who will succeed as a President; and because the wire-pullers with whom the choice rests are better judges of the former question than of the latter.

After all, too, and this is a point much less obvious to Europeans than to Americans, a President need not be a man of brilliant intellectual gifts. Englishmen, imagining him as something like their prime minister, assume that he ought to be a dazzling orator, able to sway legislatures or multitudes, possessed also of the constructive powers that can devise a great policy or frame a comprehensive piece of legislation. They forget that the President does not sit in Congress, that he ought not to address meetings, except on ornamental and (usually) non-political occasions, that he cannot submit bills nor otherwise influence the action of the legislature. His main duties are to be prompt and firm in securing the due execution of the laws and maintaining the public peace, careful and upright in the choice of the executive officials of the country. Eloquence, whose value is apt to be overrated in all free countries, imagination, profundity of thought or extent of knowledge, are all in so far a gain to him that they make him a bigger man, and help him to gain a greater influence over the nation, an influence which, if he be a true patriot he may use for its good. But they are not necessary for the due discharge in ordinary times of the duties of his post. A man may lack them and yet make an excellent President. . . .

So far we have been considering personal merits. But in the selection of a candidate many considerations have to be regarded besides personal merits, whether they be the merits of a candidate, or of a possible President. The chief of these considerations is the amount of support which can be secured from different States or from different regions, or, as the Americans say, "sections," of the Union. State feeling and sectional feeling are powerful factors in a presidential election. The Northwest, including the States from Ohio to Dakota, is now the most populous region of the Union, and therefore counts for most in an election. It naturally conceives that its interests will be best protected by one who knows them from birth and residence. Hence *prima facie* a North-western man makes the best candidate. A large State casts a heavier vote in the election; and every State is of course more likely to be carried by one of its own children than by a stranger, because his fellow-citizens, while they feel honoured by the choice, gain also a substantial advantage, having a better prospect of such favours as the administration can bestow. Hence, *coeteris paribus,* a man from a large State is preferable as a candidate. . . . The problem is further complicated by the fact that some States are already safe for one or other party, while others are doubtful. The North-western and New England States are most of them certain to go Republican: the Southern States are (at present) all of them certain to go Democratic. It is more important to gratify a doubtful State than one you have got already; and hence, *coeteris paribus,* a candidate from a doubtful State, such as New York or Indiana, is to be preferred. . . .

"What shall we do with our ex-Presidents?" is a question often put in America, but never yet answered. The position of a past chief magistrate is not a happy one. He has been a species of sovereign at home. He is received—General Grant was—with almost royal honours abroad. His private income may be insufficient to enable him to live in ease, yet he cannot without loss of dignity, the country's dignity as well as his own, go back to practice at the bar or become partner in a mercantile firm. If he tries to enter the Senate, it may happen that there is no seat vacant for his own State, or that the majority in the State legislature is against him. It has been suggested that he might be given a seat in that chamber as an extra member; but to this plan there is the objection that it would give to the State from which he comes a third senator, and thus put other States at a disadvantage. In any case, however, it would seem only right to bestow such a pension as would relieve him from the necessity of re-entering business or a profession.

We may now answer the question from which we started. Great men are not chosen Presidents, firstly, because great men are rare in politics; secondly, because the method of choice does not bring them to the top; thirdly, because they are not, in quiet times, absolutely needed. I may observe that the Presidents, regarded historically, fall into three periods, the second inferior to the first, the third rather better than the second.

Down till the election of Andrew Jackson in 1828, all the Presidents had been statesmen in the European sense of the word, men of education, of administrative experience, of a certain largeness of view and dignity of character. All except the first two had served in the great office of secretary of state; all were well known to the nation from the part they had played. In the second period, from Jackson till the outbreak of the Civil War in 1861, the Presidents were either mere politicians, such as Van Buren, Polk, or Buchanan, or else successful soldiers, such as Harrison or Taylor, whom their party found useful as figure-heads. They were intellectual pigmies beside the real leaders of that generation—Clay, Calhoun, and Webster. A new series begins with Lincoln in 1861. He and General Grant his successor, who cover sixteen years between them, belong to the history of the world. The other less distinguished Presidents of this period contrast favourably with the Polks and Pierces of the days before the war, but they are not, like the early Presidents, the first men of the country. If we compare the eighteen Presidents who have been elected to office since 1789 with the nineteen English prime ministers of the same hundred years, there are but six of the latter, and at least eight of the former whom history calls personally insignificant, while only Washington, Jefferson, Lincoln, and Grant can claim to belong to a front rank represented in the English list by seven or possibly eight names. It would seem that the natural selection of the English parliamentary system, even as modified by the aristocratic habits of that country, has more tendency to bring the highest gifts to the highest place than the more artificial selection of America.

22

Martin Diamond

The Electoral College and the
American Idea of Democracy (1977)

In 1967, a distinguished commission of the American Bar Association recommended that the Electoral College be scrapped and replaced by a nationwide popular vote for the President, with provision for a runoff election between the top two candidates in the event no candidate received at least 40 percent of the popular vote. This recommendation was passed by the House in 1969, came close to passage in the Senate in 1970, and is now once again upon us. It is this proposal that has just been endorsed by President Carter and that is being pressed upon Congress under the leadership of Senator Bayh.

The theme of this attack upon the Eletoral College is well-summarized in a much-quoted sentence from the 1969 ABA Report: "The electoral college method of electing a President of the United States is archaic, undemocratic, complex, ambiguous, indirect, and dangerous." . . .

Not only is [the Electoral College] not at all archaic, [however,] but one might say that it is the very model of up-to-date constitutional flexibility. Perhaps no other feature of the Constitution has had a greater capacity for dynamic historical adaptiveness. The electors became nullities; presidential elections became dramatic national contests; the federal elements in the process became strengthened by the general-ticket practice (that is, winner-take-all); modern mass political parties developed; campaigning moved from rather rigid sectionalism to the complexities of a modern technological society—and all this occurred tranquilly and legitimately within the original constitutional framework (as modified by the Twelfth Amendment).

The Electoral College thus has experienced an immense historical evolution. But the remarkable fact is that while it now operates in historically transformed ways, in ways not at all as the Framers intended, it nonetheless still operates largely to the ends that they intended. What more could one ask of a constitutional provision?

From Diamond, "The Electoral College and the American Idea of Democracy," published by American Enterprise Institute, 1977. Reprinted by permission.

To appreciate why the original electoral provisions proved so adaptable, we have to recollect what the original intention was. . . .

The device of independent electors as a substitute for direct popular election was hit upon for three reasons, none of which supports the thesis that the intention was fundamentally undemocratic. First, and above all, the electors were not devised as an undemocratic substitute for the popular will, but rather as a nationalizing substitute for the state legislatures. In short, the Electoral College, like so much else in the Constitution, was the product of the give-and-take and the compromises between the large and the small states, or, more precisely, between the confederalists—those who sought to retain much of the Articles of Confederation—and those who advocated a large, primarily national, republic. . . .

[T]he confederalists fought hard to have the President selected by the state legislatures or by some means that retained the primacy of the states as states. It was to fend off this confederalizing threat that the leading Framers, Madison, James Wilson, and Gouverneur Morris, hit upon the Electoral College device. . . .

Second, the system of electors also had to be devised because most of the delegates to the Convention feared, not democracy itself, but only that a straightforward national election was "impracticable" in a country as large as the United States, given the poor internal communications it then had. Many reasonably feared that, in these circumstances, the people simply could not have the national information about available candidates to make any real choice, let alone an intelligent one. And small-state partisans feared that, given this lack of information, ordinary voters would vote for favorite sons, with the result that large-state candidates would always win the presidential pluralities. How seriously concerned the Framers were with this "communications gap" is shown by the famous faulty mechanism in the original provisions (the one that made possible the Jefferson-Burr deadlock in 1801). Each elector was originally to cast two votes, but without specifying which was for President and which for Vice-President. The Constitution required that at least one of these two votes be for a non-home-state candidate, the intention being to force the people and their electors to cast at least one electoral vote for a truly "continental" figure. Clearly, then, what the Framers were seeking was not an undemocratic way to substitute elite electors for the popular will; rather, as they claimed, they were trying to find a practicable way to extract from the popular will a nonparochial choice for the President.

The third reason for the electoral scheme likewise had nothing to do with frustrating democracy, but rather with the wide variety of suffrage practices in the states. Madison dealt with this problem at the Constitutional Convention on July 19, 1787. While election by "the people was in

his opinion the fittest in itself," there was a serious circumstantial difficulty. "The right of suffrage was much more diffusive in the Northern than
the Southern states; and the latter could have no influence in the election on
the score of the Negroes. The substitution of electors obviated this difficulty." That is, the electoral system would take care of the discrepancies between state voting population and total population of the states until, as
Madison hoped and expected, slavery would be eliminated and suffrage discrepancies gradually disappeared. . . .

These were the main reasons, then, why the leading Framers settled for
the electoral system instead of a national popular election, and none may
fairly be characterized as undemocratic. . . .

[T]he chief contemporary attack on the Electoral College has little to
do with the autonomous elector or, as is said, the "faithless elector." The
autonomous elector could be amended out of existence (and without doing
violence to the constitutional intention of the Electoral College), but this
would not lessen the contemporary hostility to it as undemocratic. . . .

The gravamen of the "undemocratic" indictment of the Electoral College rests on the possibility that, because votes are aggregated within the
states by the general-ticket system, in which the winner takes all, a loser in
the national popular vote may nonetheless become President by winning a
majority of the electoral votes of the states. . . . [I]t suffices to refor-
mulate the issue and get it on its proper footing.

In fact, presidential elections are already just about as democratic as
they can be. We already have one-man, one-vote—*but in the states.* Elections are as freely and democratically contested as elections can be—*but in
the states.* Victory always goes democratically to the winner of the raw
popular vote—*but in the states.* The label given to the proposed reform,
"direct popular election," is a misnomer; the elections have already become
as directly popular as they can be—*but in the states.* Despite all their
democratic rhetoric, the reformers do not propose to make our presidential
elections more directly democratic, they only propose to make them more
directly *national,* by entirely removing the states from the electoral process.
Democracy thus is not the question regarding the Electoral College, federalism is: should our presidential elections remain in part *federally* democratic, or should we make them completely *nationally* democratic?

Whatever we decide, then, democracy itself is not at stake in our decision, only the prudential question of how to channel and organize the
popular will. That makes everything easier. When the question is only
whether the federally democratic aspect of the Electoral College should be
abandoned in order to prevent the remotely possible election of a President
who had not won the national popular vote, it does not seem so hard to opt
for retaining some federalism in this homogenizing, centralizing age. When

federalism has already been weakened, perhaps inevitably in modern circumstances, why further weaken the federal elements in our political system by destroying the informal federal element that has historically evolved in our system of presidential elections? The crucial general-ticket system, adopted in the 1830s for reasons pertinent then, has become in our time a constitutionally unplanned but vital support for federalism. Also called the "unit rule" system, it provides that the state's entire electoral vote goes to the winner of the popular vote in the state. Resting entirely on the voluntary legislative action of each state, this informal historical development, combined with the formal constitutional provision, has generated a federal element in the Electoral College which sends a federalizing impulse throughout our whole political process. It makes the states as states dramatically and pervasively important in the whole presidential selection process, from the earliest strategies in the nominating campaign through the convention and final election. Defederalize the presidential election—which is what direct popular election boils down to—and a contrary nationalizing impulse will gradually work its way throughout the political process. The nominating process naturally takes its cues from the electing process; were the President to be elected in a single national election, the same cuing process would continue, but in reverse. . . .

Our consciences will be further eased when we note that the abhorrence of the federal aspect of the Electoral College—which causes the potential discrepancy between electoral and popular votes—cannot logically be limited to the Electoral College. It rests upon premises that necessitate abhorrence of any and all *district* forms of election. What is complained about in the Electoral College is endemic to all districted electoral systems, whether composed of states, or congressional districts, or parliamentary constituencies. If population is not exactly evenly distributed in all the districts (and it never can be), both in sheer numbers and in their political predispositions, then the possibility cannot be removed that the winner of a majority of the districts may not also be the winner of the raw popular vote. . . .

[T]he national popular-vote/district-vote discrepancy . . . can and does occur here regarding control of both the House and the Senate. Why is it not a loaded pistol to our democratic heads when control over our lawmaking bodies can fall, and has fallen, into the hands of the party that lost in the national popular vote? . . .

The House has largely escaped the "undemocratic" charge (especially now, after major reapportionment) despite the fact that its districted basis likewise creates a potential discrepancy between winning a majority of seats and winning the national popular vote for Congress. By the populistic reasoning and rhetoric that attacks the Electoral College, the House also fails the standard of national majoritarianism. But we quite ungrudgingly see the wisdom in departing from that standard in order to secure the many advantages of local districting. To indicate only a few: First, there is democratic responsiveness to local needs, interests, and opinions in general. Americans have always believed that there is more to democracy itself than merely maximizing national majoritarianism; our idea of democracy includes responsiveness to *local* majorities as well. Further, because of our multiplicity of interests, ethnic groups, religions, and races, we have always believed in local democratic responsiveness to geographically based minorities whose interests may otherwise be utterly neglected; such minorities secure vigorous direct representation, for example, only because of the districted basis of the House of Representatives. The state-by-state responsiveness of the Electoral College is an equally legitimate form of districted, local democratic responsiveness. There is also the security to liberty that results from the districted decentralization of the political basis of the legislature; and we cherish also the multiplication of opportunities for voluntary political participation that likewise results from that districted decentralization. Finally, we cherish the guarantee that districting provides, that power in the legislature will be nationally distributed, rather than concentrated in regional majorities, as would be possible in a nondistricted election of the House. . . .

This kind of complex reasoning is the hallmark of the American idea of democracy: a taking into account of local as well as national democratic considerations and, even more importantly, blending democratic considerations with all the other things that contribute to political well-being. . . .

[In the next place, t]o judge fairly the charge of ambiguity . . . the Electoral College must be compared in this regard with other electoral systems and, especially, with the 40 percent plus/runoff system proposed by President Carter and Senator Bayh as its replacement. . . .

The American electorate has a fundamental tendency to divide closely, with "photo finish" elections being almost the rule rather than the exception. The Electoral College almost always announces these close election outcomes with useful amplification. In purely numerical popular votes, an election outcome might be uncertain and vulnerable to challenge; but the Electoral College replaces the numerical uncertainty with an unambiguously visible constitutional majority that sustains the legitimacy of the electoral result. If this magnifying lens is removed, the "squeaker" aspect of our presidential elections will become more visible and, probably, much more troubling. For example, the problem of error and fraud, no doubt endemic in some degree to all electoral systems, could very well be aggravated under the proposed national system, because every single precinct polling place could come under bitter scrutiny as relevant to a close and disputed national outcome. In contrast, under the Electoral College, ambiguity of outcome sufficient even to warrant challenge is infrequent and is always limited to but a few states. . . .

Not only is it extremely unlikely that the proposed replacement could match this record of unambiguity, but the 40 percent plus plurality provision could very well introduce a different and graver kind of ambiguity into our political system. This would not be uncertainty as to who is the winner, but a profounder uncertainty as to whether the winner is truly the choice of the American people. . . .

The Electoral College strongly encourages the two-party system by almost always narrowing the election to a race between the two major-party candidates. Obviously, when there are only two serious competitors, the winner usually has a majority or large plurality of the total vote cast. But, as we shall shortly see, the new system would encourage minor and maverick candidacies. This multiplication of competitors would likely reduce the winning margin to the bare 40 percent plurality requirement of the new system. If so, we would have traded in a majority- or high plurality-presidency for one in which nearly 60 percent of the people might often have voted against the incumbent. How ironic it would be if a reform demanded in the name of democracy and majority rule resulted in a permanent minority presidency! . . .

[A]ll the dangers critics claim to see in the Electoral College are entirely matters of speculation. Some have never actually occurred, and others have not occurred for nearly a century. . . .

[But t]hree dangers seem seriously to threaten under the proposed reform: weakening the two-party system, weakening party politics generally, and further imperializing the presidency.

Many have warned that the 40 percent plus/runoff system would encourage minor parties and in time undermine the two-party system. The encouragement consists in the runoff provision of the proposed reform, that is, in the possibility that minor parties will get enough votes in the first election to force a runoff. Supporters of the proposed change deny this likelihood. For example, the ABA Report argues that a third party is unlikely to get the 20 percent of the popular vote necessary to force a runoff. Perhaps so, and this has been very reassuring to supporters of the reform. But why does it have to be just "a" third party? Why cannot the runoff be forced by the combined votes of a half dozen or more minor parties that enter the first election? Indeed, they are all there waiting in the wings. The most powerful single constraint on minor-party presidential candidacies has always been the "don't throw your vote away" fear that caused their support to melt as election day approached. Norman Thomas, who knew this better than anyone, was certain that a national popular election of the kind now proposed would have immensely improved the Socialist electoral results. Now this is not to say that the Electoral College alone is what prevents ideological parties like that of the Socialists from winning elections in America. Obviously, other and more powerful factors ultimately determine that. But what the electoral machinery can determine is whether such parties remain electorally irrelevant, minuscule failures, or whether they can achieve sufficient electoral success to fragment the present two-party system. . . .

Moreover, not only ideological parties would be encouraged by the proposed change, but also minor parties and minor candidacies of all sorts. Sectional third parties would not be weakened by the 40 percent plus/runoff arrangement; they would retain their sectional appeal and pick up additional votes all over the country. The threat that dissident wings might bolt from one of the two major parties would instantly become more credible and thereby more disruptive within them; sooner or later the habit of bolting would probably take hold. Would there not also be an inducement to militant wings of ethnic, racial, and religious groups to abandon the major party framework and go it alone? And, as the recent proliferation of primary candidacies suggests, would-be "charismatics" might frequently take their case to the general electorate, given the inducements of the proposed new machinery. . . .

If runoffs become the rule as is likely, . . . [t]here would be two winners in [the first election]; we would have created a valuable new electoral prize—a second place finish in the preliminary election. This would be a boon to the strong minor candidacies; needing now only to seem a "viable" alternative for second place, they could more easily make a plausible case to potential supporters. But, more important, there would be something to win for nearly everyone in the first, or preliminary, election. Minor party votes now shrink away as the election nears and practically disappear on election day. As is well known, this is because minor-party supporters desert their preferred candidates to vote for the "lesser evil" of the major candidates. But the proposed reform would remove the reason to do so. On the contrary, as in multiparty parliamentary systems, the voter could vote with his heart because that would in fact also be the calculating thing to do. There would be plenty of time to vote for the lesser evil in the eventual runoff election. The trial heat would be the time to help the preferred minor party show its strength. Even a modest showing would enable the minor party to participate in the frenetic bargaining inevitably incident to runoff elections. And even a modest showing would establish a claim to the newly available public financing that would simultaneously be an inducement to run and a means to strengthen one's candidacy. . . .

Most Americans agree that the two-party system is a valuable way of channelling democracy because that mode of democratic decision produces valuable qualities of moderation, consensus, and stability. It follows then that the proposed reform threatens a serious injury to the American political system.

Not only might the change weaken the two-party system, but it might well also have an enfeebling effect on party politics generally. The regular party politicians, which is to say, the state and local politicians, would become less important to presidential candidates. This tendency is already evident in the effect the presidential primaries are having; regular party machinery is becoming less important in the nominating process, and the individual apparatus of the candidates more important. The defederalizing of the presidential election seems likely to strengthen this tendency. No longer needing to carry states, the presidential candidates would find the regular politicians, who are most valuable for tipping the balance in a state, of diminishing importance for their free-wheeling search for popular votes. They probably would rely more and more on direct-mail and media experts, and on purely personal coteries, in conducting campaigns that would rely primarily on the mass media. The consequence would seem to be to disengage the presidential campaign from the party machinery and from the states and to isolate the presidency from their moderating effect. If "merchandising" the President has become an increasingly dangerous tendency, nationalizing and plebiscitizing the presidency would seem calculated only to intensify the danger.

This raises, finally, the question of the effect of the proposed reform on the presidency as an institution, that is, on the "imperial presidency." . . . The presidency has always derived great moral authority and political power from the claim that the President is the only representative of all the people. Why increase the force of that claim by magnifying the national and plebiscitary foundations of the presidency? . . .

23

James W. Ceaser

Political Parties and
Presidential Ambition (1978)

According to political scientists of the last generation, party competition was an essential feature of any form of popular government. How dismayed they would be, therefore, to learn from contemporary students of American politics that our parties are "decomposing" and that our national electoral process is increasingly taking on the characteristics of nonpartisan competition. While the labels of the two traditional parties continue to exist, the institutions bearing these labels have lost many of their previous functions. Parties no longer structure the voting behavior of large numbers of citizens. They have ceased to play a major role in constraining presidential decision-making, and presidents now place little reliance on them in their efforts to generate public support for policy initiatives. Perhaps most important of all, party organizations have lost their influence in determining the outcome of presidential nominations. Under the "open" nominating process that has emerged since 1968, the races have for all practical purposes become plebiscitory contests among the individual contenders. Candidates create large personal campaign organizations and devise their own programs and electoral strategies, very much as if they were establishing national parties of their own. These personalistic features of the nomination contests continue into the final election stage, as the parties become the extensions of the organizations of the victorious nominees.

What are the implications of this decline in the role of traditional parties for the presidential selection process and for the presidency itself? Is it a positive development, as many reformers argue, or does it pose a serious threat to moderate republican government, as many of their opponents contend? Addressing these questions today is of more than academic significance. The recent changes in the presidential selection process have resulted not primarily from forces beyond the control of political actors but from the decisions of practicing politicians in party commissions and state legislatures. . . .

From Ceaser, "Political Parties and Presidential Ambition," *Journal of Politics,* August, 1978. Reprinted by permission of the author and the *Journal of Politics.*

The reform theory of selection on which the current open system is based was introduced to national politics at the 1968 Democratic Convention. In its original formulation, the theory attacked the legitimacy of the influence of the regular party organizations and called for "direct democracy" in the selection of presidential nominees. As the theory evolved within the official reform commissions established by the party in 1968 and 1972, the ideal of "fairness" emerged as a single most important value for the nomination process. By fairness was meant procedural regularity and the replication in the selection of delegates of the expressed candidate preferences of the participants. While the reform commissions did not expressly call for direct democracy in the form of more primaries, the emphasis reformers placed on popular participation and the individual's right to the expression of a candidate preference certainly encouraged the subsequent adoption of presidential primaries in many states.

The reform view of presidential selection should be compared with the very different perspective of the Founders and the originators of permanent party competition. For these statesmen the concern was not so much with the procedural goal of fairness as with the substantive results of how power was sought and exercised. After satisfying themselves of the compatibility of their systems with the basic requirements of popular government, they turned their attention to regulating the behavior of presidential aspirants with a view to preventing dangerous political divisions and leadership styles that might undermine the intended character of the presidency. . . .

For the Founders, a major objective in selection was to prevent the creation of factions that form around "different leaders ambitiously contending for pre-eminence and power." By their electoral institutions the Founders sought to deflect the great force of presidential ambition from its possible manifestations in demagoguery of "image" appeals and to channel it into conduct that would promote the public good. This also was the goal of Martin Van Buren and his followers in the party school of the 1820s and 1830s. They held that the nonpartisan system that emerged in 1824 encouraged the very kind of leadership appeals that the Founders wanted to avoid. Only by instituting party competition between two parties of moderate principle could leadership be circumscribed within safe limits. The answer to personal faction for Van Buren was party, though party of a different sort from that which the Founders had feared. Whatever differences exist between the views of the Founders and Van Buren—and these, as we shall see, are not insignificant—they both accepted the premise that the electoral process should be considered as an institution that controlled candidate behavior.

This premise went unchallenged until the rise of the Populist and Progressive movements at the turn of the century. According to Woodrow Wilson, the most thoughtful spokesman of the Progressive view, the selection system should be designed to elevate a dynamic leader above the political party and make the party serve his will. In Wilson's thought, party is transformed from an institution that constrains leadership to an instrument that enhances it. "Leadership," the central theme of Wilson's proposed revision of the constitutional system, could best take root in an open nominating process in which each contender presented his program directly to the people. The winners would then earn the right to "own" their parties. Wilson accordingly proposed national primaries, making it clear that contenders might appeal beyond traditional partisan followings to form new constituencies. Wilson was satisfied that the problem of dangerous leadership appeals could be avoided in an open selection process: the wisdom of the people along with the self-restraint of the leaders obviated the need for any institutional guidance.

A balance of sorts existed throughout most of this century between institutional elements representing Van Buren's theory of selection and those representing Wilsonian ideas. This system, known sometimes as the "mixed" system because of the presence of both candidate-oriented primaries and organization-dominated selection procedures, was overthrown after 1968. Although there are some differences between the Progressive and the reform views, the reformers have accepted the crucial Progressive premise about the safety of an open nominating system. . . .

The Functions of the Presidential Selection System

To facilitate discussion of the theories of the electoral process noted above, it will be helpful first to identify four major objectives or "functions" of the selection system. By the selection system here we are referring to the nomination and the final election stages, since both are part of the same general process. . . .

First, the selection system should promote the proper character of the presidential office in respect both to its powers and to the style of presidential leadership. This implies that, at least up to a certain point, the office should be thought of as the end and the selection process the means. Many today might take exception to this assumption. Two recent defenders of reform theory, John Saloma and Frederick Sontag, argue that the goal of the selection system should be increased participation, which they see as a means of building citizen virtue. Pre-reform theorists, though no less concerned about citizen virtue, looked elsewhere for its cultivation. They focused instead on more directly related issues such as the effect of the selection system on the presidency, realizing that the way in which power is sought will have a profound influence on how it is subsequently exercised. Many of the important historical debates on the role of parties in our system have centered on this issue. The Founders and John Quincy Adams opposed party competition because they thought it would compromise the president's independence, while Woodrow Wilson sought to transform parties into candidate-centered organizations in order to increase the president's power.

Second, the selection system should ensure an accession to power that is unproblematic and widely regarded as legitimate. . . . Legitimacy refers to whether the people accept the process as being in accord with their understanding of republican principles. . . . On the other hand, since the selection system can be an important "teacher" of the meaning of democracy, there is a danger in its being changed in response to an ephemeral interpretation of republican principles backed by some candidate or faction seeking a temporary advantage. This possibility is greatest in the nominating system which is outside the sphere of direct Constitutional regulation.

Third, the selection system should help promote the choice of an able executive. What transforms this concern from a meaningless expression of hope to a legitimate institutional question is the reasonable assumption, backed by comparative research into selection in various liberal democracies, that different systems affect the type of person apt to compete and succeed. A plebiscitory nomination system would seem to place a greater premium on those qualities that appeal to a mass audience, such as vigor, appearance, and the aura of sanctimony; "closed" systems will value to a greater degree those qualities esteemed by the narrower group empowered to select, for example, "keeping one's word" in the case of American politicians or trustworthiness in the case of British parliamentarians. . . .

Finally, the selection system should prevent the harmful effects of the pursuit of office by highly ambitious contenders. Almost every major politician will at one time or another fix his attention on becoming president and adjust his behavior to improve his chances of being considered. For those who enter the select circle of legitimate contenders, the tendency will be to adopt whatever strategies are legal and acceptable—and even some that are not—if they promise results. It is reasonable to assume, therefore, that the ambition of contenders, if not properly guided, can lead to strategies and appeals that threaten the public good. . . .

The problems that presidential ambition can create may be classified under two broad headings. The first is the disruption of the proper functioning of an office or institution: office-holders, using their positions to further their presidential aspirations, may perform in a way that conflicts with their intended constitutional role. . . .

The second problem, by no means exclusive of the first, is the attempt of candidates to build a popular following by the "arts of popularity"—by empty "image" appeals, by flattery, or by the exploitation of dangerous passions. The general term for such appeals is demagoguery, although one often find the term restricted today to harsh utterances that evoke anger and fear. It is a mistake, however, to fail to recognize the demagogic character of a "soft" flattery that tells the people they can do no wrong or of seductive appeals that hide behind a veil of liberality, making promises that can never be kept or raising hopes that can never be satisfied. . . .

Institutional regulation of behavior consists in establishing certain constraints and incentives—not criminal penalities—that promote desired habits and actions and discourage unwanted behavior. The selection system, conceived in this sense, is the institution that structures the conduct of presidential aspirants and their supporters. By marking out a certain path to the presidency, it influences the behavior of the nation's leading politicians and, by their example, the style of politics in the regime as a whole. Regulation of presidential ambition is likely to work most effectively where it relies on the candidates' own strongest impulse: if matters can be arranged such that undesirable behavior will detract from the chance of success, candidates will turn "voluntarily" to other strategies. Properly channeled, ambition can be used to curb its own excesses.

The Founders

The Founders' two main objectives for presidential selection were to help secure the executive's independence from Congress and to prevent the kind of campaign that would undermine the constitutional character of the office. The first objective, which has been identified by nearly every scholar of the Founders' thought, was to be accomplished by giving the president an electoral base outside of the legislature. The second objective, which has been almost entirely overlooked in the literature on the founding, can only be understood after treating the more general question of constitutional authority and the threat posed to it by the claim to popular leadership.

One of the distinguishing features of constitutional government for the Founders was rule based on institutional authority. Office-holders, in their view, were to rest their claim to govern on the legally defined rights and prerogatives of their offices. This kind of authority was threatened by claims to rule on informal grounds, such as personal heroic standing or assertions of embodying the will of the people. The latter claim was particularly dangerous to constitutional government in a popular regime. The people were already recognized as the source of ultimate authority for the system as a whole, and it would involve but one small step for an enterprising leader to activate the principle of popular sovereignty and make it the immediate basis of political rule. . . .

The Founders' analysis of the problem of popular authority appears in *The Federalist* in the context of their discussion of the House. Here Publius warns against the danger that the House, urged on by some of its "leaders," might seek to "draw all power into its impetuous vortex." But it is crucial to observe that it is not the House itself that the Founders fear, but the claim to informal popular authority. Any institution asserting power on the basis of "its supposed influence over the people" is properly suspect on the Founders' grounds. . . .

The general name we have given to this kind of noninstitutional rule is "popular leadership." "Popular" refers to the source of the authority and "leadership" to its informal character. . . . The establishment of the Constitution, [the Founders] doubtless thought, obviated the need for leaders, as authority would henceforth rest on an institutional foundation. This foundation was also understood to protect the possibility for the exercise of statesmanship by providing the president with a margin of discretion free from the immediate constraints of public opinion. . . .

Besides serving as a claim to authority, popular leadership is a way of soliciting power. The Founders refer to it in this context as "the popular arts." Where the popular arts are employed in seeking office, the danger increases that informal authority will be claimed as the basis for governing. The popular arts accustom the people to the style of popular leadership and train aspirants to generate support and power by this means. To protect the constitutional character of the presidency, the Founders accordingly thought it essential to discourage the use of the popular arts in the selection process.

The Founders identified two basic forms of the popular arts. The first was issue arousal. From their experience with elections for state legislatures after the Revolutionary War, the Founders became deeply concerned about demagogic issue appeals directed against property and merit. . . . The other form of the popular arts was the use of appeals that played upon certain passions relating to the personal qualities of the leader, what we might call today "image" appeals. Of course the Founders wanted the voters to focus on character qualifications, but they drew a distinction between character assessments based on a calm consideration of the candidates' merits and those influenced by strong emotions or flattery. . . .

The general principle the Founders followed in attempting to discourage the use of the popular arts was to make the election turn on personal reputation, not issue appeals. Personal reputation, the Founders believed, would serve as a rough approximation for merit: those who became well-known at the national level would most likely have had to earn a reputation by distinguished service to the state. The institutional means for favoring reputation over issue appeals was sought in the first instance by creating large electoral districts. . . . The Founders reasoned that since all elections pose the problem of name recognition for the candidates, persons with established reputations begin with a decided advantage. The larger the size of the district, the more difficult it becomes for one using issue arousal to overcome this advantage—an assessment that might need to be reversed today in light of modern communications and of the extended campaign which gives a greater chance to the "outsider." . . . Applied to the case of the largest possible district, a nationwide constituency, there was all the more reason to expect a safe result. . . .

The proposal for direct election failed to gain the support of most delegates at the Convention. The opposition came from a number of quarters, including some who objected on the "practical" grounds that there would not normally be persons with a sufficient national reputation to command the votes of the people in the face of competition from strong regional candidates. This opposition obliged the direct election advocates to search for another plan, and they readily shifted their support to the proposal of an election by specially chosen electors. Along with providing the same guarantee of presidential independence, this plan increased the likelihood of selecting a continental figure, as the electors would be more knowledgeable about national affairs and could practically be given two votes for the presidential contest. The system also had the advantage of allowing for a certain degree of indirectness in the choice of the president. It therefore provided further insurance that the election would turn on reputation rather than the use of the popular arts. The electors, it was thought, would be less likely than the people to be swayed by popular appeals and might even resent them, even as—to cite an analogy that is only partly apt—convention delegates who formerly had discretion resented attempts by candidates to go over their heads to the people. By making the use of the popular arts unnecessary and perhaps counterproductive, the Founders sought to close the door to direct popular appeals and induce the ablest candidates to "campaign" by establishing a record of distinguished public service that might earn them a reputation for virtue.

From a cursory reading of the one paper in *The Federalist* that is devoted to presidential selection (#68), one might receive the impression that the Founders viewed the pursuit of the presidency as a gentlemanly affair conducted among reluctant participants. Yet nothing could be further from the truth. There was a sense, of course, in which they expected that the immediate campaign would *appear* in this light, just as it was formerly the practice for aspirants to wait for their party to confer the nomination upon them. But this kind of campaign would conceal, even as it controlled, the powerful ambitons of the candidates. No more "realistic" analysis of political motivation exists in American thought than that which Hamilton provides in *The Federalist*. Hamilton begins with politicians as we find them: high-spirited, ambitious, and in some cases committed to achieving a noble fame. Hamilton's aim is . . . to make politicians serve popular government. Ambition, the dominant force that drives most major politicians, is a neutral quality that leads them to seek out the path to success. Properly channeled it can divert politicians from destructive behavior and lead them to act for the public good, even to take risks and incur momentary displeasure for the sake of long-term glory. Hamilton's understanding of virtue admits and allows for the desire for reward: it can best be described as conduct on behalf of the public, even if that conduct is undertaken for self-interested reasons. The office of the presidency was designed by the Founders to attract persons of the highest ambition or virtue, and the selection system was meant to point their ambition in the proper direction.

Martin Van Buren

Martin Van Buren began his national political career as a senator from New York in 1821, during the Era of Good Feelings. Competition between parties had ceased at the national level, and the dominant opinion in Washington was hostile to any manifestations of partisanship. . . . Van Buren quickly became the leading opponent of this view, calling immediately on his arrival at the capitol for a "resuscitation of the old Democratic Party" and later, after the election of 1824, for a renewal of two-party competition. . . .

Van Buren developed his case for parties in response to an impending crisis in the presidential selection process. His objectives were to ensure the legitimacy of the choice of the president by keeping the election from the House of Representatives and to prevent a dangerous politics of personal factionalism caused by nonpartisan competition. . . .

The advocates of a strong, independent executive at the Constitutional Convention fought the idea of selection by Congress on the grounds that it would make the president, in Morris's words, "the tool of a faction of some leading demagogue in the Legislature." They won their main point with the adoption of the system of electors, but an auxiliary election by the House, voting by states, was also included for the purpose of breaking a tie or making the choice where no candidate received the required minimum of electoral votes.

The likelihood of an election by the House increased with the adoption of the Twelfth Amendment in 1804. Designed to eliminate intrigue between the electors of the defeated party and the vice-presidential candidate of the victorious party, the amendment also made it less likely that a final decision could be made at the electoral stage by reducing the number of presidential votes of each elector from two to one while maintaining the same requirement for election. As long as the Republican Party continued to coalesce behind one candidate, the tendency of the amendment was obscured. But with the collapse of the Republican caucus in 1824, it became evident that under nonpartisan competition a House election would be the normal result. The outcome of the election of 1824 demonstrated that at the same time that it confirmed some of the worst fears about the House system—its tendency to promote confusion and intrigue and its inability to gain full public confidence.

Van Buren and his followers argued that party competition could ensure that the election was determined at the electoral stage by providing the candidates with broad national followings. If there were no continental figures in the nation, the reputations of the parties would take their place; if there were too many continental figures, the parties would limit the field. Party competition thus offered an institutional solution to a problem that the Founders had relied on chance to resolve. . . .

Van Buren's second defense of party competition was that it was the best device under existing circumstances for controlling presidential ambition. In proposing party competition to solve a problem that the Founders had wanted to solve by nonpartisanship, Van Buren was not necessarily challenging the Founders' plan, for nonpartisan competition in the 1820s bore little resemblance to what the Founders had envisioned. Direct popular appeals by the candidates had become an accepted element of the campaign, a change that resulted from the precedent of the election of 1800 and from the transformation of the elector from the discretionary trustee to a bound agent. Given this new circumstance, a different solution to the problem of controlling the popular arts was required. If popular leadership was now legitimate, the challenge was somehow to distinguish its healthy from its unhealthy expressions and to devise some institutional means to admit the former and exclude the latter.

Nonpartisan competition, according to Van Buren, was no longer an answer to this problem. On the contrary, it was the very cause of personal factionalism and dangerous leadership appeals. It allowed a large number of candidates to enter the contest without doing anything to channel the direction of their ambition. . . .

According to Van Buren . . ., party competition would prevent candidates from devising their own appeals and compel them to adhere to the safer principles on which they planned to establish the major parties. The character of leadership appeals would be controlled by institutions rather than left subject to accident and personal candidate strategies. Nominations would be made by party leaders knowledgeable about national politics and in a position to deliberate about which candidate could best maintain a delicately balanced party coalition. Issue appeals in the name of one or another of the parties would be admitted, but appeals independent of parties would be discouraged. The system would remain formally open to challenges by new parties, as two-party competition was a doctrine founded on opinion, not law. But the bias of the electoral process was against openness in the modern sense of eliminating all institutional controls designed to discourage certain kinds of appeals. It was the task of those founding the new parties to establish their credibility and enlist public support behind them on a long-term basis. Party in this respect would be made "prior" to political leadership. Leadership would not formulate new principles or create new electoral alignments but articulate the established principles and maintain existing coalitions. If this implied a loss in the dynamic character of leadership, it also promised a greater degree of safety and moderation.

Having made the theoretical case for renewed party competition, Van Buren turned to his partisan task of creating the Democratic party. . . .

While Van Buren wanted to retain the same basic electoral alignment that existed under the first party division, he sought to establish a different kind of partisanship. The contest over first principles of the regime would be replaced by a more moderate division over the scope of federal power. Parties dividing on this question could exist together without each feeling the need to destroy a seditious rival. To go along with this more restrained partisanship, Van Buren proposed a new ethic of tolerance. The original partisans, Jefferson once wrote, "cross the streets and turn their heads the other way, lest they should be obliged to touch their hats." Van Buren offered a different model. He proclaimed his pride in not being "rancorous in my party prejudices" and in maintaining friendly personal relations with many political opponents. . . .

Van Buren acknowledged that the principles of the parties would be very general, in part so that each party could accommodate a broad coalition of interests. Moreover, Van Buren recognized the need for patronage, no doubt in the belief that with a partisan division based on secondary issues, it was necessary, in order to sustain party organizations, to supplement the motivation of purpose with that of interest. . . . Although the modern "amateur" conception of party finds the slightest touch of interest unacceptable, it remains an unanswered question whether an ideal equilibrium point can be found and maintained at which the division over principle is sufficiently serious to sustain partisan organizations yet not so great as to threaten the underlying consensus in the regime.

While there is much in Van Buren's plan for party competition that is consistent with the views of the Founders, it nonetheless served to modify the regime in some very important ways. First, party competition recognized and institutionalized a more active role for the voice of the majority in determining national policy. Elections were no longer understood merely as a way of elevating a worthy individual; they were also contests between competing groups in which the victorious party could claim authority for carrying out its program.

Second, party competition implied a different conception of executive leadership. The Founders had wanted illustrious "continental figures" whose freedom from control by any electoral group would enable them to stand above the conflict of factions. By recognizing the need for parties of a broad coalitional character under an umbrella of general principle, Van Buren was required to accept a less elevated kind of leadership. His model was what we might call the "politician," one skilled at brokering among various groups. Executive leadership would have to be partisan in character, although the broad principles on which the parties stood would still leave room for considerable discretion. Many have seen a connection between Van Buren's concept of parties and the so-called "Madisonian system" of the Founders, for in both one finds encouragement for the formation of coalitional majorities. But it is also important to observe the differences. Madison intended the system of competing factions and coalitions to take place in the House and to be balanced by an executive standing above factions. Van Buren, on the other hand, extended the influence of the "Madisonian system" to the executive by introducing a coalitional concept of leadership into the choice of a president.

Finally, in emphasizing the restraint of ambition, Van Buren, in contrast to the Founders, may not have given sufficient scope to it. One finds a continual concern in Van Buren's thought with preventing the potential abuse of power, but little appreciation of its positive uses. It was the absence of a doctrine of the positive executive power, much more than the self-interested character of the parties, that troubled Woodrow Wilson.

Woodrow Wilson

The Progressives inaugurated the modern idea of presidential selection—a plebiscitory nomination race in which the candidates build their own constituencies within the electorate and in which the victorious candidate "captures" his party label. Along with this idea came a rejection of the view that the electoral process should control presidential ambition. The new purpose of the selection process was to build a base of popular support for the victorious candidate and help establish the concept of leadership as the central feature of the regime. . . .

A number of Progressive spokesmen articulated a new conception of how to attain the public good that rejected entirely the pluralist concept of adding together various interests to make a coalitional majority. The public good, in the view of these Progressives, could only be known directly and as a whole. The connection between this conception of politics and the new institutional roles for the presidency and presidential selection is most clearly formulated in the thought of Woodrow Wilson.

Wilson began with nothing less than a full-scale attack on the old basis of constitutional government. The public good, in his view, could not be realized through the operation of formal institutions working within the confines of legally delegated and separated powers. It had to be forged in a "life" relationship between a leader and the people. . . .

The most striking aspect of this concept of leadership is its informal or noninstitutional character. Wilson called for the rule of those who would lead "not by reason of legal authority, but by reason of their contact and amenability to public opinion." . . .

[W]hile Wilson sought to give great scope to executive power—more, in many respects, than Hamilton might have countenanced—he did so by draining the office of its formal constitutional authority and by transforming the premise of statesmanship from one that was understood to require a substantial degree of freedom from public opinion to one that operated entirely on the plane of public opinion. . . .

Although Wilson is known today as the father of the party government school in America, it is necessary to understand that he conceived of party in an entirely different sense than Van Buren. A party is a body of people that forms around and serves a particular leader. . . .

Wilson makes parties appear and be strong when they can assist the leader but transforms them into empty shells where they might restrict the leader's freedom. . . .

Wilson's objective, at least while a scholar, was not to delineate the principles of a new partisan division—indeed he was always vague about what programs the parties should adopt—but to alter the traditional relationship between party and leader in order to institutionalize dynamic leadership.

Every regime, it is clear, needs to be "renewed" at moments of crisis by extraordinary acts of political leadership. Given this fact, it might be said that the constraints that the Founders and Van Buren imposed on leadership were too severe. Yet one must bear in mind that they were speaking at the level of analysis of institutional structures, and institutions operating "as usual" may not be able to meet every situation or challenge. Seen from this perspective, they might not have wanted to prevent absolutely a recourse to popular leadership, but only to erect a bias against it, such that it would have to "prove" itself in the face of institutional deterrents. A bias of this kind would normally prevent the dangers of popular leadership yet still not prevent change and renewal when needed. Wilson took the opposite view and argued that a bias in favor of change in the electoral process was desirable and that under such a system leaders of high quality would continually emerge. . . .

A fundamental question is whether in opening the selection system to continual change Wilson did not also open it to dangerous or demeaning leadership appeals. . . .

Modern Reform

The Progressives' call for a plebiscitory selection system met with only partial success. The movement for universal state primaries got off to a promising start between 1911 and 1916, but then stalled with the decline of the Progressive movement after the First World War. In some states primary laws were repealed, while in others the party organizations were able to reassert control over the primary process. What resulted was a "mixed" system that contained elements deriving from the conflicting theories of Martin Van Buren and the Progressives. . . . Its two constituent elements continued to be reflected in two alternative nomination campaigns—the inside strategy of negotiation with party leaders and the outside strategy of direct appeals to the people. The representation of the party organization served to thwart a demagogue, while the primaries enabled a popular candidate to challenge the insularity of the power-brokers. . . .

Even before the recent reform movement, a slight shift had begun to occur in the direction of a greater reliance on the outside strategy. But it was the reforms, and in particular the increase in primaries which they prompted, that decisively established the plebiscitory character of the current system. . . .

[O]ne might well ask whether the reformers did not concede too much to the populist sentiments of the moment. . . . The reliance on "closed" nominating procedures by parties in other democratic nations seems to belie the claim that direct democracy in candidate selection is a requisite of republican legitimacy. As long as the *electoral* system remains open, meaning that the right of new parties to challenge is not denied or impaired, it would seem that the legitimacy of the system could be defended. . . .

If the plebiscitory system is not required to assure the legitimacy of the selection process, neither, it seems, can it be justified in terms of its effects on the other three functions of presidential selection. . . . [T]here is no basis in theory and surely none in experience for concluding that a plebiscitory system guarantees candidates of greater competence or superior virtue. As regards the prevention of the harmful effects of the campaign, a number of serious problems have already become evident. By encouraging more candidates and an earlier start of the campaign, the new system introduces considerations of electoral politics into the process of governing at a much earlier date. Campaigns inevitably tend to drain normal legal authority and force an incumbent who is re-eligible to become absorbed, in Tocqueville's words, "in the task of defending himself [rather than] ruling in the interest of the state." Moreover, the "openness" of the campaign to many contestants excites the ambitions of a large number of politicians and influences their conduct in the performance of their official duties. Observers of the Congress have already noted the effect of the new system in contributing to a decline of the Senate as a serious deliberative body. In accord with the need under the current system to build popular constituencies, Senators having presidential aspirations have been more apt to emphasize "media coverage over legislative craftmanship.". . .

The checks on presidential power in the American system have traditionally been formal as well as informal, deriving from the Constitutional system of separated powers and from the power-brokers within the parties whose support was required by candidates and incumbent presidents seeking re-election. Under the present system, however, the successful candidate "owns" his party and need not answer to specific persons who can hold him accountable. This ownership, it must be added, has come at a high price, for the decline of parties has taken away from the executive a valuable resource that could buy support from the public and from members of Congress. The president now stands directly before the bar of public opinion, and it therefore should not be surprising if presidents become more assertive in their claims to authority and more "popular" or demagogic in their methods of appeal, if only to compensate for their loss of partisan support. In light of these difficulties, it may be asked whether we should not reconsider the wisdom of the recent reforms, even if this implies resisting "the inexorable movement . . . toward direct democracy."

24

Buckley v. Valeo (1976)

Per Curiam.*

These appeals present constitutional challenges to the key provisions of the Federal Election Campaign Act of 1971, as amended in 1974. . . . The Act, summarized in broad terms, contains the following provisions: (a) individual political contributions are limited to $1,000 to any single candidate per election, with an overall annual limitation of $25,000 by any contributor; independent expenditures by individuals and groups "relative to a clearly identified candidate" are limited to $1,000 a year; campaign spending by candidates for various federal offices and spending for national conventions by political parties are subject to prescribed limits; (b) contributions and expenditures above certain threshold levels must be reported and publicly disclosed; (c) a system for public funding of Presidential campaign activities is established by Subtitle H of the Internal Revenue Code. . . .

The Act's contribution and expenditure limitations operate in an area of the most fundamental First Amendment activities. Discussion of public issues and debate on the qualifications of candidates are integral to the operation of the system of government established by our Constitution. . . . In a republic where the people are sovereign, the ability of the citizenry to make informed choices among candidates for office is essential. . . .

The interests served by the Act include restricting the voices of people and interest groups who have money to spend and reducing the overall scope of federal election campaigns. Although the Act does not focus on the ideas expressed by persons or groups subjected to its regulations, it is aimed in part at equalizing the relative ability of all voters to affect electoral out-

---

*Only Justices Brennan, Stewart, and Powell joined all portions of the per curiam opinion. Included among the plaintiffs were a candidate for the Presidency of the United States, a United States Senator who is a candidate for reelection, a potential contributor, the Committee for a Constitutional Presidency-McCarthy '76, the Conservative Party of the State of New York, the Mississippi Republican Party, the Libertarian Party, the New York Civil Liberties Union, Inc., the American Conservative Union, the Conservative Victory Fund, and Human Events, Inc.

From *Buckley v. Valeo,* 424 U.S. 1 (1976).

comes by placing a ceiling on expenditures for political expression by citizens and groups. . . .

A restriction on the amount of money a person or group can spend on political communication during a campaign necessarily reduces the quantity of expression by restricting the number of issues discussed, the depth of their exploration, and the size of the audience reached. This is because virtually every means of communicating ideas in today's mass society requires the expenditure of money. . . .

By contrast with a limitation upon expenditures for political expression, a limitation upon the amount that any one person or group may contribute to a candidate or political committee entails only a marginal restriction upon the contributor's ability to engage in free communication. A contribution serves as a general expression of support for the candidate and his views, but does not communicate the underlying basis for the support. The quantity of communication by the contributor does not increase perceptibly with the size of his contribution, since the expression rests solely on the undifferentiated, symbolic act of contributing. . . . While contributions may result in political expression if spent by a candidate or an association to present views to the voters, the transformation of contributions into political debate involves speech by someone other than the contributor.

Given the important role of contributions in financing political campaigns, contribution restrictions could have a severe impact on political dialogue if the limitations prevented candidates and political committees from amassing the resources necessary for effective advocacy. There is no indication, however, that the contribution limitations imposed by the Act would have any dramatic adverse effect on the funding of campaigns and political associations. The overall effect of the Act's contribution ceilings is merely to require candidates and political committees to raise funds from a greater number of persons and to compel people who would otherwise contribute amounts greater than the statutory limits to expend such funds on direct political expression, rather than to reduce the total amount of money potentially available to promote political expression.

The Act's contribution and expenditure limitations also impinge on protected associational freedoms. . . . [T]he Act's contribution limitations permit associations . . . to aggregate large sums of money to promote effective advocacy. By contrast, the Act's $1,000 limitation on independent expenditures "relative to a clearly identified candidate" precludes most associations from effectively amplifying the voice of their adherents, the original basis for the recognition of First Amendment protection of the freedom of association. . . .

In sum, although the Act's contribution and expenditure limitations both implicate fundamental First Amendment interests, its expediture ceilings impose significantly more severe restrictions on protected freedoms of political expression and association than do its limitations on financial contributions. . . .

It is unnecessary to look beyond the Act's primary purpose—to limit the actuality and appearance of corruption resulting from large individual financial contributions—in order to find a constitutionally sufficient justification for the $1,000 contribution limitation. . . . To the extent that large contributions are given to secure political quid pro quos from current and potential officeholders, the integrity of our system of representative democracy is undermined. . . .

Of almost equal concern as the danger of actual quid pro quo arrangements is the impact of the appearance of corruption stemming from public awareness of the opportunities for abuse inherent in a regime of large individual financial contributions. . . . Congress could legitimately conclude that the avoidance of the appearance of improper influence "is also critical [if] confidence in the system of representative Government is not to be eroded to a disastrous extent." . . .

[However, w]e find that the governmental interest in preventing corruption and the appearance of corruption is inadequate to justify § 608(e) (1)'s ceiling on independent expenditures.

The parties defending § 608(e) (1) contend that it is necessary to prevent would-be contributors from avoiding the contribution limitations by the simple expedient of paying directly for media advertisements or for other portions of the candidate's campaign activities. . . . Yet such controlled or coordinated expenditures are treated as contributions rather than expenditures under the Act. . . . Unlike contributions, such independent expenditures may well provide little assistance to the candidate's campaign and indeed may prove counterproductive. The absence of prearrangement and coordination of an expenditure with the candidate or his agent not only undermines the value of the expenditure to the candidate, but also alleviates the danger that expenditures will be given as a quid pro quo for improper commitments from the candidate. . . .

It is argued, however, that the ancillary governmental interest in equalizing the relative ability of individuals and groups to influence the outcome of elections serves to justify [this limitation]. But the concept that government may restrict the speech of some elements of our society in order to enhance the relative voice of others is wholly foreign to the First Amendment, which was designed "to secure 'the widest possible dissemination of information from diverse and antagonistic sources,' " and " 'to assure unfettered interchange of ideas for the bringing about of political and social changes desired by the people.' " New York Times v. Sullivan. The First Amendment's protection against governmental abridgment of free expression cannot properly be made to depend on a person's financial ability to engage in public discussion. . . .

The Act also sets limits on expenditures by a candidate "from his personal funds, or the personal funds of his immediate family, in connection with his campaigns during any calander year." . . .

[These ceilings also impose] a substantial restraint on the ability of persons to engage in protected First Amendment expression. The candidate, no less than any other person, has a First Amendment right to engage in the discussion of public issues and vigorously and tirelessly to advocate his own election and the election of other candidates. . . .

The primary governmental interest served by the Act—the prevention of actual and apparent corruption of the political process—does not support the limitation on the candidate's expenditure of his own personal funds. . . .[T]he use of personal funds reduces the candidate's dependence on outside contributions and thereby counteracts the coercive pressures and attendant risks of abuse to which the Act's contribution limitations are directed.

The ancillary interest in equalizing the relative financial resources of candidates competing for elective office, therefore, provides the sole relevant rationale for Section 608(a)'s expenditure ceiling. . . . [T]he First Amendment simply cannot tolerate § 608(a)'s restriction upon the freedom of a candidate to speak without legislative limit on behalf of his own candidacy. . . .

Section 608(c) of the Act places limitations on overall campaign expenditures by candidates seeking nomination for election and election to federal office. . . .

No governmental interest that has been suggested is sufficient to justify the restriction on the quantity of political expression imposed by § 608(c)'s campaign expenditure limitations. . . . The interest in alleviating the corrupting influence of large contributions is served by the Act's contribution limitations and disclosure provisions rather than by § 608(c)'s campaign expenditure ceilings.

The interest in equalizing the financial resources of candidates competing for federal office is no more convincing a justification for restricting the scope of federal election campaigns. Given the limitation on the size of outside contributions, the financial resources available to a candidate's campaign, like the number of volunteers recruited, will normally vary with the size and intensity of the candidate's support. There is nothing invidious, improper, or unhealthy in permitting such funds to be spent to carry the candidate's message to the electorate. . . .

In sum, the [contribution limits] are constitutionally valid. These limitations along with the disclosure provisions, constitute the Act's primary weapons against the reality or appearance of improper influence stemming from the dependence of candidates on large campaign contributions. The contribution ceilings thus serve the basic governmental interest in safeguarding the integrity of the electoral process without directly impinging upon the rights of individual citizens and candidates to engage in political debate and discussion. By contrast, the First Amendment requires the invalidation of the Act's independent expenditure ceiling, its limitation on a candidate's expenditures from his own personal funds, and its ceilings on overall campaign expenditures. These provisions place substantial and direct restrictions on the ability of candidates, citizens, and associations to engage in protected political expression, restrictions that the First Amendment cannot tolerate. . . .

[The disclosure requirements of the Act] are attacked as overbroad—both in their application to minor-party and independent candidates and in their extension to contributions as small as $10 or $100. . . .

The governmental interests sought to be vindicated by the disclosure requirements . . . fall into three categories. First, disclosure provides the electorate with information "as to where political campaign money comes from and how it is spent by the candidate" in order to aid the voters in evaluating those who seek Federal office. . . .

Second, disclosure requirements deter actual corruption and avoid the appearance of corruption by exposing large contributions and expenditures to the light of publicity. . . . A public armed with information about a candidate's most generous supporters is better able to detect any post-election special favors that may be given in return. . . .

Third, and not least significant, record-keeping, reporting and disclosure requirements are an essential means of gathering the data necessary to detect violations of the contribution limitations described above.

The disclosure requirements, as a general matter, directly serve substantial governmental interests. In determining whether these interests are sufficient to justify the requirements we must look to the extent of the burden that they place on individual rights.

It is undoubtedly true that public disclosure of contributions to candidates and political parties will deter some individuals who otherwise might contribute. In some instances, disclosure may even expose contributors to harassment or retaliation. . . .

[A]ppellants primarily rely on "the clearly articulated fears of individuals, well experienced in the political process." At best they offer the testimony of several minor-party officials that one or two persons refused to make contributions because of the possibility of disclosure. On this record, the substantial public interest in disclosure identified by the legislative history of this Act outweighs the harm generally alleged. . . .

[The Court next considers public financing of Presidential campaigns.] A series of statutes for the public financing of Presidential election campaigns produced [this] scheme. . . .

A major party is defined as a party whose candidate for President in the most recent election received 25% or more of the popular vote. A minor party is defined as a party whose candidate received at least 5% but less than 25% of the vote at the most recent election. . . . Major parties are entitled to $2,000,000 to defray their national committee Presidential nominating convention expenses [and] must limit total expenditures to that amount. . . . A minor party receives a portion of the major-party entitlement determined by the ratio of the votes received by the party's candidate in the last election to the average of the votes received by the major-parties' candidates. . . . No financing is provided for [the conventions of] new parties. . . .

For expenses in the general election campaign, § 9004(a)(1) entitles each major-party candidate to $20,000,000. To be eligible for funds the candidate must pledge not to incur expenses in excess of the entitlement under § 9004(a)(1) and not to accept private contributions except to the extent that the fund is insufficient to provide the full entitlement. Minor-party candidates are also entitled to funding, again based on the ratio of the vote received by the party's candidate in the preceding election to the average of the major-party candidates. Minor-party candidates must certify that they will not incur campaign expenses in excess of the major-party entitlement and that they will accept private contributions only to the extent needed to make up the difference between that amount and the public funding grant. New-party candidates receive no money prior to the general election, but any candidate receiving 5% or more of the popular vote in the election is entitled to post-election payments according to the formula applicable to minor-party candidates. . . .

Chapter 96 establishes a third account in the Fund, the Presidential Primary Matching Payment Account. . . . The threshold eligibility requirement is that the candidate raise at least $5,000 in each of 20 States, counting only the first $250 from each person contributing to the candidate. In addition, the candidate must agree to abide by the spending limits in § 9035. Funding is provided according to a matching formula: each qualified candidate is entitled to a sum equal to the total private contributions received, disregarding contributions from any person to the extent that total contributions to the candidate by that person exceed $250. . . . .

Appellants argue that as constructed public financing invidiously discriminates. . . .

In several situations concerning the electoral process, the principle has been developed that restrictions on access to the electoral process must survive exacting scrutiny. The restriction can be sustained only if it furthers a "vital" governmental interest, that is "achieved by a means that does not unfairly or unnecessarily burden either a minority party's or an individual candidate's equally important interest in the continued availability of political opportunity.'' . . . [T]he inability, if any, of minority-party candidates to wage effective campaigns will derive not from lack of public funding but from their inability to raise private contributions. . . . Congress enacted Subtitle H in furtherance of sufficiently important governmental interests and has not unfairly or unnecessarily burdened the political opportunity of any party or candidate.

It cannot be gainsaid that public financing as a means of eliminating the improper influence of large private contributions furthers a significant governmental interest. . . . Congress' interest in not funding hopeless candidacies with large sums of public money necessarily justifies the withholding of public assistance from candidates without significant public support. . . .

Mr. Chief Justice Burger, concurring in part and dissenting in part.

. . . Disclosure is, in principle, the salutary and constitutional remedy for most of the ills Congress was seeking to alleviate. I therefore agree fully with the broad proposition that public disclosure of contributions by individuals and by entities—particularly corporations and labor unions—is an effective means of revealing the type of political support that is sometimes coupled with expectations of special favors or rewards. . . .

Disclosure is, however, subject to First Amendment limitations which are to be defined by looking to the relevant public interests. The legitimate public interest is the elimination of the appearance and reality of corrupting influences. . . .

The Court's theory, however, goes beyond permissible limits. Under the Court's view, disclosure serves broad informational purposes, enabling the public to be fully informed on matters of acute public interest. Forced disclosure of one aspect of a citizen's political activity, under this analysis, serves the public right-to-know. This open-ended approach is the only plausible justification for the otherwise irrationally low ceilings of $10 and $100 for anonymous contributions. The burdens of these low ceilings seem to me obvious, and the Court does not try to question this. With commendable candor, the Court acknowledges:

> "It is undoubtedly true that public disclosure of contributions to candidates and political parties will deter some individuals who otherwise might contribute."

Examples come readily to mind. Rank-and-file union members or rising junior executives may now think twice before making even modest contributions to a candidate who is disfavored by the union or management hierarchy. Similarly, potential contributors may well decline to take the obvious risks entailed in making a reportable contribution to the opponent of a well-entrenched incumbent. . . .

The public right-to-know ought not be absolute when its exercise reveals private political convictions. Secrecy, like privacy, is not *per se* criminal. On the contrary, secrecy and privacy as to political preferences and convictions are fundamental in a free society. . . .

Finally, no legitimate public interest has been shown in forcing the disclosure of modest contributions that are the prime support of new, unpopular or unfashionable political causes. There is no realistic possibility that such modest donations will have a corrupting influence especially on parties that enjoy only "minor" status. Major parties would not notice them; minor parties need them. . . .

I would therefore hold unconstitutional the provisions requiring reporting of contributions of $10 or more and to make a public record of the name, address, and occupation of a contributor of $100 or more.

I agree fully with that part of the Court's opinion that holds unconstitutional the limitations the Act puts on campaign expenditures which "place substantial and direct restrictions on the ability of candidates, citizens, and associations to engage in protected political expression, restrictions that the First Amendment cannot tolerate." Yet when it approves similarly stringent limitations on contributions, the Court ignores the reasons it finds so persuasive in the context of expenditures. For me contributions and expenditures are two sides of the same First Amendment coin. . . .

Limiting contributions, as a practical matter, will limit expenditures and will put an effective ceiling on the amount of political activity and debate that the Government will permit to take place. . . .

I dissent from Part III sustaining the constitutionality of the public financing provisions of the Act.

Since the turn of this century when the idea of Government subsidies for political campaigns first was broached, there has been no lack of realization that the use of funds from the public treasury to subsidize political activity of private individuals would produce substantial and profound questions about the nature of our democratic society. . . .

The Court chooses to treat this novel public financing of political activity as simply another congressional appropriation whose validity is "necessary and proper" to Congress' power to regulate and reform elections and primaries. . . .

Senator Howard Baker remarked during the debate on this legislation:

> "I think there is something politically incestuous about the Government financing and, I believe, inevitably then regulating, the day to day procedures by which the Government is selected. . . . I think it is extraordinarily important that the Government not control the machinery by which the public expresses the range of its desires, demands, and dissent."

. . . [I]n my view, the inappropriateness of subsidizing, from general revenues, the actual political dialog of the people—the process which begets the Government itself—is as basic to our national tradition as the separation of church and state . . . or the separation of civilian and military authority, neither of which is explicit in the Constitution but which have developed through case by case adjudication of express provisions of the Constitution.

Recent history shows dangerous examples of systems with a close, "incestuous" relationship between "government" and "politics." . . . [T]he Court points to no basis for predicting that the historical pattern of "varying measures of control and surveillance," which usually accompany grants from Government will not also follow in this case. . . . Up to now, this Court has scrupulously refrained, absent claims of invidious discrimination, from entering the arena of intra-party disputes concerning the seating of convention delegates. . . . But once the Government finances these national conventions by the expenditure of millions of dollars from the public treasury, we may be providing a springboard for later attempts to impose a whole range of requirements on delegate selection and convention activities. . . .

[T]he scheme approved by the Court today invidiously discriminates against minor parties. . . . [T]he present system could preclude or severely hamper access to funds before a given election by a group or an individual who might, at the time of the election, reflect the views of a major segment or even a majority of the electorate. . . .

I would also find unconstitutional the system of "matching grants" which makes a candidate's ability to amass private funds the sole criterion for eligibility for public funds. Such an arrangement can put at serious disadvantage a candidate with a potentially large, widely diffused—but poor—constituency. The ability of a candidate's supporters to help pay for his campaign cannot be equated with their willingness to cast a ballot for him.

I cannot join in the attempt to determine which parts of the Act can survive review here. The statute as it now stands is unworkable and inequitable.

I agree with the Court's holding that the Act's restrictions on expenditures made "relative to a clearly identified candidate," independent of any candidate or his committee, are unconstitutional. Paradoxically the Court upholds the limitations on individual contributions, which embrace precisely the same sort of expenditures "relative to a clearly identified candidate" if those expenditures are "authorized or requested" by the "candidate or his agents." The Act as cut back by the Court thus places intolerable pressure on the distinction between "authorized" and "unauthorized" expenditures on behalf of a candidate. . . .

Moreover, the Act—or so much as the Court leaves standing—creates significant inequities. A candidate with substantial personal resources is now given by the Court a clear advantage over his less affluent opponents, who are constrained by law in fundraising, because the Court holds that the "First Amendment cannot tolerate" any restrictions on spending. Minority parties, whose situation is difficult enough under an Act that excludes them from public funding, are prevented from accepting large single-donor contributions. At the same time the Court sustains the provision aimed at broadening the base of political support by requiring candidates to seek a greater number of small contributors, it sustains the unrealistic disclosure thresholds of $10 and $100 that I believe will deter those hoped-for small contributions. . . .

25

Rutan v. Republican Party of Illinois (1990)

Mr. Justice Brennan *delivered the opinion of the Court.*

To the victor belong only those spoils that may be constitutionally obtained. *Elrod* v. *Burns* (1976), and *Branti* v. *Finkel* (1980), decided that the First Amendment forbids government officials to discharge or threaten to discharge public employees solely for not being supporters of the political party in power, unless party affiliation is an appropriate requirement for the position involved. Today we are asked to decide the constitutionality of several related political patronage practices—whether promotion, transfer, recall, and hiring decisions involving low-level public employees may be constitutionally based on party affiliation and support. We hold that they may not.

The petition and cross-petition before us arise from a lawsuit protesting certain employment policies and practices instituted by Governor James Thompson of Illinois. On November 12, 1980, the Governor issued an executive order proclaiming a hiring freeze for every agency, bureau, board, or commission subject to his control. The order prohibits state officials from hiring any employee, filling any vacancy, creating any new position, or taking any

From *Rutan* v. *Republican Party of Illinois*, 58 LW 4872 (1990).

similar action. It affects approximately 60,000 state positions. More than 5,000 of these become available each year as a result of resignations, retirements, deaths, expansion, and reorganizations. The order proclaims that "*no* exceptions" are permitted without the Governor's "express permission after submission of appropriate requests to [his] office."

Requests for the Governor's "express permission" have allegedly become routine. Permission has been granted or withheld through an agency expressly created for this purpose, the Governor's Office of Personnel (Governor's Office). Agencies have been screening applicants under Illinois' civil service system, making their personnel choices, and submitting them as requests to be approved or disapproved by the Governor's Office. Among the employment decisions for which approvals have been required are new hires, promotions, transfers, and recalls after layoffs.

By means of the freeze, according to petitioners, the Governor has been using the Governor's Office to operate a political patronage system to limit state employment and beneficial employment-related decisions to those who are supported by the Republican Party. In reviewing an agency's request that a particular applicant be approved for a particular position, the Governor's Office has looked at whether the applicant voted in Republican primaries in past election years, whether the applicant has provided financial or other support to the Republican Party and its candidates, whether the applicant has promised to join and work for the Republican Party in the future, and whether the applicant has the support of Republican Party officials at state or local levels.

Five people (including the three petitioners) brought suit against various Illinois and Republican Party officials in the United States District Court for the Central District of Illinois. They alleged that they had suffered discrimination with respect to state employment because they had not been supporters of the State's Republican Party and that this discrimination violates the First Amendment. Cynthia B. Rutan has been working the State since 1974 as a rehabilitation counselor. She claims that since 1981 she has been repeatedly denied promotions to supervisory positions for which she was qualified because she had not worked for or supported the Republican Party. Franklin Taylor, who operates road equipment for the Illinois Department of Transportation, claims that he was denied a promotion in 1983 because he did not have the support of the local Republican Party. Taylor also maintains that he was denied a transfer to an office nearer to his home because of opposition from the Republican Party chairmen in the counties in which he worked and to which he requested a transfer. James W. Moore claims that he has been repeatedly denied state employment as a prison guard because he did not have the support of Republican Party officials.

The two other plaintiffs, before the Court as cross-respondents, allege that they were not recalled after layoffs because they lacked Republican credentials. . . .

In *Elrod,* we decided that a newly elected Democratic sheriff could not constitutionally engage in the patronage practice of replacing certain office staff with members of his own party "when the existing employees lack or fail to obtain requisite support from, or fail to affiliate with, that party." The plurality explained that conditioning public employment on the provision of support for the favored political party "unquestionably inhibits protected belief and association." It reasoned that conditioning employment on political activity pressures employees to pledge political allegiance to a party with which they prefer not to associate, to work for the election of political candidates they do not support, and to contribute money to be used to further policies with which they do not agree. The latter, the plurality noted, had been recognized by this Court as "tantamount to coerced belief." (citing *Buckley* v. *Valeo*). At the same time, employees are constrained from joining, working for or contributing to the political party and candidates of their own choice. "[P]olitical belief and association constitute the core of those activities protected by the First Amendment," the plurality emphasized. Both the plurality and the concurrence drew support from *Perry* v. *Sindermann,* (1972), in which this Court held that the State's refusal to renew a teacher's contract because he had been publicly critical of its policies imposed an unconstitutional condition on the receipt of a public benefit.

The Court then decided that the government interests generally asserted in support of patronage fail to justify this burden on First Amendment rights because patronage dismissals are not the least restrictive means for fostering those interests. The plurality acknowledged that a government has a significant interest in ensuring that it has effective and efficient employees. It expressed doubt, however, that "mere difference of political persuasion motivates poor performance" and concluded that, in any case, the government can ensure employee effectiveness and efficiency through the less drastic means of discharging staff members whose work is inadequate. The plurality also found that a government can meet its need for politically loyal employees to implement its policies by the less intrusive measure of dismissing, on political grounds, only those employees in policymaking positions. Finally, although the plurality recognized that preservation of the democratic process "may in some instances justify limitations on First Amendment freedoms," it concluded that the "process functions as well without the practice, perhaps even better." Patronage, it explained, "can result in the entrenchment of one or a few parties to the exclusion of others" and "is a very effective impediment to the associational and speech freedoms which are essential to a meaningful system of democratic government."

Four years later, in *Branti, supra,* we decided that the First Amendment prohibited a newly appointed public defender, who was a Democrat, from discharging assistant public defenders because they did not have the support of the Democratic Party. The Court rejected an attempt to distinguish the case from *Elrod,* deciding that it was immaterial whether the public defender had attempted to coerce employees to change political parties or had only dismissed them on the basis of their private political beliefs. We explained that conditioning continued public employment on an employee's having obtained support from a particular political party violates the First Amendment because of "the coercion of belief that necessarily flows from the knowledge that one must have a sponsor in the dominant party in order to retain one's job." . . .

We first address the claims of the four current or former employees. Respondents urge us to view *Elrod* and *Branti* as inapplicable because the patronage dismissals at issue in those cases are different in kind from failure to promote, failure to transfer, and failure to recall after layoff. Respondents initially contend that the employee petitioners' First Amendment rights have not been infringed because they have no entitlement to promotion, transfer, or rehire. We rejected just such an argument in *Elrod,* and *Branti,* as both cases involved state workers who were employees at will with no legal entitlement to continued employment. . . .

Respondents next argue that the employment decisions at issue here do not violate the First Amendment because the decisions are not punitive, do not in any way adversely affect the terms of employment, and therefore do not chill the exercise of protected belief and association by public employees. This is not credible. Employees who find themselves in dead-end positions due to their political backgrounds *are* adversely affected. They will feel a significant obligation to support political positions held by their superiors, and to refrain from acting on the political views they actually hold, in order to progress up the career ladder. . . .

Employees who do not compromise their beliefs stand to lose the considerable increases in pay and job satisfaction attendant to promotions, the hours and maintenance expenses that are consumed by long daily commutes, and even their jobs if they are not rehired after a "temporary" layoff. These are significant penalties and are imposed for the exercise of rights guaranteed by the First Amendment. Unless these patronage practices are narrowly tailored to further vital government interests, we must conclude that they impermissibly enroach on First Amendment freedoms.

We find, however, that our conclusions in *Elrod,* and *Branti,* are equally applicable to the patronage practices at issue here. A government's interest in securing effective employees can be met by discharging, demoting or transferring staff members whose work is deficient. A government's interest in securing employees who will loyally implement its policies can be adequately served by choosing or dismissing certain high-level employees on the basis of their political views. Likewise, the "preservation of the democratic process" is no more furthered by the patronage promotions, transfers, and rehires at issue here than it is by patronage dismissals. First, "political parties are nurtured by other, less intrusive and equally effective methods." Political parties have already survived the substantial decline in patronage employment practices in this century. . . . Second, patronage decidedly impairs the elective process by discouraging free political expression by public employees. . . .

Petitioner James W. Moore presents the closely related question whether patronage hiring violates the First Amendment. Patronage hiring places burdens on free speech and association similar to those imposed by the patronage practices discussed above. A state job is valuable. Like most employment, it provides regular paychecks, health insurance, and other benefits. In addition, there may be openings with the State when business in the private sector is slow. There are also occupations for which the government is a major (or the only) source of employment, such as social workers, elementary school teachers, and prison guards. Thus, denial of a state job is a serious privation.

Nonetheless, respondents contend that the burden imposed is not of constitutional magnitude. Decades of decisions by this Court belie such a claim. We premised *Torcaso* v. *Watkins* (1961), on our understanding that loss of a job opportunity for failure to compromise one's convictions states a constitutional claim. We held that Maryland could not refuse an appointee a commission for the position of notary public on the ground that he refused to declare his belief in God, because the required oath "unconstitutionally invades the appellant's freedom of belief and religion." . . .

We hold that the rule of *Elrod* and *Branti* extends to promotion, transfer, recall, and hiring decisions based on party affiliation and support and that all of the petitioners and cross-respondents have stated claims upon which relief may be granted. . . .

Mr. Justice Scalia, *dissenting.*

Today the Court establishes the constitutional principle that party membership is not a permissible factor in the dispensation of government jobs, except those jobs for the performance of which party affiliation is an "appropriate requirement." It is hard to say precisely (or even generally) what that exception means, but if there is any category of jobs for whose performance party affiliation is not an appropriate requirement, it is the job of being a judge, where partisanship is not only unneeded but positively undesirable. It is, however, rare that a federal administration of one party will appoint a judge from another party. And it has always been rare. Thus, the new principle that the Court today announces will be enforced by a corps of judges (the Members of this Court included) who overwhelmingly owe their office to its violation. Something must be wrong here, and I suggest it is the Court.

The merit principle for government employment is probably the most favored in modern America, having been widely adopted by civil-service legislation at both the state and federal levels. But there is another point of view, described in characteristically Jacksonian fashion by an eminent practitioner of the patronage system, George Washington Plunkitt of Tammany Hall:

> "I ain't up on sillygisms, but I can give you some arguments that nobody can answer.
> "First, this great and glorious country was built up by political parties; second, parties can't hold together if their workers don't get offices when they win; third, if the parties go to pieces, the government they built up must go to pieces, too; fourth, then there'll be hell to pay." W. Riordon, Plunkitt of Tammany Hall 13 (1963).

It may well be that the Good Government Leagues of America were right, and that Plunkitt, James Michael Curley and their ilk were wrong; but that is not entirely certain. As the merit principle has been extended and its effects increasingly felt; as the Boss Tweeds, the Tammany Halls, the Pendergast Machines, the Byrd Machines and the Daley Machines have faded into history; we find that political leaders at all levels increasingly complain of the helplessness of elected government, unprotected by "party discipline," before the demands of small and cohesive interest-groups.

The choice between patronage and the merit principle—or, to be more realistic about it, the choice between the desirable mix of merit and patronage principles in widely varying federal, state, and local political contexts—is not so clear that I would be prepared, as an original matter, to chisel a single, inflexible prescription into the Constitution. Fourteen years ago, in *Elrod* v. *Burns,* the Court did that. *Elrod* was limited however, as was the later decision of *Branti* v. *Finkel,* to patronage firings, leaving it to state and federal legislatures to determine when and where political affiliation could be taken into account in hirings and promotions. Today the Court makes its constitutional civil-service reform absolute, extending to all decisions regarding government employment. Because the First Amendment has never been thought to require this disposition, which may well have disastrous consequences for our political system, I dissent.

The restrictions that the Constitution places upon the government in its capacity as lawmaker, i.e., as the regulator of private conduct, are not the same as the restrictions that it places upon the government in its capacity as employer. We have recognized this in many contexts, with respect to many different constitutional guarantees. Private citizens perhaps cannot be prevented from wearing long hair, but policemen can. Private citizens cannot have their property searched without probable cause, but in many circumstances government employees can. Private citizens cannot be punished for refusing to provide the government information that may incriminate them, but government employees can be dismissed when the incriminating information that they refuse to provide relates to the performance of their job. With regard to freedom of speech in particular: Private citizens cannot be punished for speech of merely private concern, but government employees can be fired for that reason. Private citizens cannot be punished for partisan political activity, but federal and state employees can be dismissed and otherwise punished for that reason.

Once it is acknowledged that the Constitution's prohibition against laws "abridging the freedom of speech" does not apply to laws enacted in the government's capacity as employer the same way it does to laws enacted in the government's capacity as regulator of private conduct, it may sometimes be difficult to assess what employment practices are permissible and what are not. That seems to me not a difficult question, however, in the present context. The provisions of the Bill of Rights were designed to restrain transient majorities from impairing long-recognized personal liberties. They did not create by implication novel individual rights overturning accepted political norms. Thus, when a practice not expressly prohibited by the text of the Bill of Rights bears the endorsement of a long tradition of open, widespread, and unchallenged use that dates back to the beginning of the Republic, we have no proper basis for striking it down.[1] Such a venerable and accepted tradition is not to be laid on the examining table and scrutinized for its conformity to some abstract principle of First-Amendment adjudication devised by this Court. To the contrary, such traditions are themselves the stuff out of which the Court's principles are to be formed. They are, in these uncertain areas, the very points of reference by which the legitimacy or illegitimacy of *other* practices are to be figured out. When it appears that the latest "rule," or "three-part test," or "balancing test" devised by the Court has placed us on a collision course with such a landmark practice, it is the former that must be recalculated by us, and not the latter that must be abandoned by our citizens. I know of no other way to formulate a constitutional jurisprudence that reflects, as it should, the

---

[1]The customary invocation of *Brown v. Board of Education,* 347 U.S. 483 (1954) as demonstrating the dangerous consequences of this principle is unsupportable. I agrue for the role of tradition in giving content only to *ambiguous* constitutional text; no tradition can supersede the Constitution. In my view the Fourteenth Amendment's requirement of "equal protection of the laws," combined with the Thirteenth Amendment's abolition of the institution of black slavery, leaves no room for doubt that laws treating people differently because of their race are invalid. Moreover, even if one does not regard the Fourteenth Amendment as crystal clear on this point, a tradition of *unchallenged* validity did not exist with respect to the practice in *Brown*. To the contrary, in the 19th century the principle of "separate-but-equal" had been vigorously opposed on constitutional grounds, litigated up to this Court, and upheld only over the dissent of one of our historically most respected Justices. See *Plessy* v. *Ferguson,* (1896) (Harlan, J., dissenting).

principles adhered to, over time, by the American people, rather than those favored by the personal (and necessarily shifting) philosophical dispositions of a majority of this Court. . . .

[P]atronage was, without any thought that it could be unconstitutional, a basis for government employment from the earliest days of the Republic until *Elrod*—and has continued unabated *since Elrod,* to the extent still permitted by that unfortunate decision. Given that unbroken tradition regarding the application of an ambiguous constitutional text, there was in my view no basis for holding that patronage-based dismissals violated the First Amendment—much less for holding, as the Court does today, that even patronage hiring does so.

Even accepting the Court's own mode of analysis, however, and engaging in "balancing" a tradition that ought to be part of the scales, *Elrod, Branti,* and today's extension of them seem to me wrong.

The Court limits patronage on the ground that the individual's interest in uncoerced belief and expression outweighs the systemic interests invoked to justify the practice. The opinion indicates that the government may prevail only if it proves that the practice is "narrowly tailored to further vital government interests."

That strict-scrutiny standard finds no support in our cases. Although our decisions establish that government employees do not lose all constitutional rights, we have consistently applied a lower level of scrutiny when "the governmental function operating . . . [is] not the power to regulate or license, as lawmaker, an entire trade or profession, or to control an entire branch of private business, but, rather, as proprietor, to manage [its] internal operatio[ns] . . . ." When dealing with its own employees, the government may not act in a manner that is "patently arbitrary or discriminatory," but its regulations are valid if they bear a "rational connection" to the governmental end sought to be served.

In particular, restrictions on speech by public employees are not judged by the test applicable to similar restrictions on speech by nonemployees. We have said that "[a] governmental employer may subject its employees to such special restrictions on free expression as are reasonably necessary to promote effective government." In *Public Workers* v. *Mitchell,* upholding provisions of the Hatch Act which prohibit political activities by federal employees, we said that "it is not necessary that the act regulated be anything more than an act reasonably deemed by Congress to interfere with the efficiency of the public service." We reaffirmed *Mitchell* in *CSC* v. *Letter Carriers,* over a dissent by Justice Douglas arguing against application of a special standard to government employees, except insofar as their "job performance" is concerned. We did not say that the Hatch Act was narrowly tailored to meet the government's interest, but merely deferred to the judgment of Congress, which we were not "in any position to dispute." Indeed, we recognized that the Act was not indispensably necessary to achieve those ends, since we repeatedly noted that "Congress at some time [may] come to a different view." In *Broadrick* v. *Oklahoma* (1973), we upheld similar restrictions on state employees, though directed "at political expression which if engaged in by private persons would plainly be protected by the First and Fourteenth Amendments."

To the same effect are cases that specifically concern adverse employment action taken against public employees because of their speech. In *Pickering* v. *Board of Education of Township High School Dist.* (1968), we recognized:

> "[T]he State has interests as an employer in regulating the speech of its employees that differ significantly from those it possesses in connection with regulation of the speech of the citizenry in general. The problem in any case is to arrive at a balance between the interests of the [employee], as a citizen, in commenting upon matters of public concern and the interests of the State, as an employer, in promoting the efficiency of the public services it performs through its employees."

Because the restriction on speech is more attenuated when the government conditions employment than when it imposes criminal penalties, and because "government offices could not function if every employment decision became a constitutional matter," we have held that government employment decisions taken on the basis of an employee's speech do not "abridg[e] the freedom of speech," merely because they fail the narrow-tailoring and compelling-interest tests applicable to direct regulation of speech. We have not subjected such decisions to strict scrutiny, but have accorded "a wide degree of deference to the employer's judgment" that an employee's speech will interfere with close working relationships.

When the government takes adverse action against an employee on the basis of his political affiliation (an interest whose constitutional protection is derived from the interest in speech), the same analysis applies. That is why both the *Elrod* plurality and the opinion concurring in the judgment, as well as *Branti* and the Court today, rely on *Perry* v. *Sindermann* (1972), a case that applied the test announced in *Pickering,* not the strict-scrutiny test applied to restrictions imposed on the public at large. Since the government may dismiss an employee for political *speech* "reasonably deemed by Congress to interfere with the efficiency of the public service," it follows *a fortiori* that the government may dismiss an employee for political *affiliation* if "reasonably necessary to promote effective government."

While it is clear from the above cases that the normal "strict scrutiny" that we accord to government regulation of speech is not applicable in this field, the precise test that replaces it is not so clear; we have used various formulations. The one that appears in the case dealing with an employment practice closest in its effects to patronage is whether the practice could be "reasonably deemed" by the enacting legislature to further a legitimate goal. For purposes of my ensuing discussion, however, I will apply a less permissive standard that seems more in accord with our general "balancing" test: can the governmental advantages of this employment practice reasonably be deemed to outweigh its "coercive" effects?

Preliminarily, I may observe that the Court today not only declines, in this area replete with constitutional ambiguities, to give the clear and continuing tradition of our people the *dispositive* effect I think it deserves, but even declines to give it substantial weight in the balancing. That is contrary to what the Court has done in many other contexts. . . .

But even laying tradition entirely aside, it seems to me our balancing test is amply met. I assume, as the Court's opinion assumes, that the balancing is to be done on a generalized basis, and not case-by-case. The Court holds that the governmental benefits of patronage cannot reasonably be thought to outweigh its "coercive" effects (even the lesser "coercive" effects of patronage hiring as opposed to patronage firing) not merely in 1990 in the State of Illinois, but at any time in any of the numerous political subdivisions of this vast country. It seems to me that that categorical pronouncement reflects a naive vision of politics and an inadequate appreciation of the systemic effects of patronage in promoting political stability and facilitating the social and political integration of previously powerless groups.

The whole point of my dissent is that the desirability of patronage is a policy question to be decided by the people's representatives; I do not mean, therefore, to endorse that system. But in order to demonstrate that a legislature could reasonably determine that its benefits outweigh its "coercive" effects, I must describe those benefits as the proponents of patronage see them: As Justice Powell discussed at length in his *Elrod* dissent, patronage stabilizes political parties and prevents excessive political fragmentation—both of which are results in which States have a strong governmental interest. Party strength requires the efforts of the rank-and-file, especially in "the dull periods between elections," to perform such tasks as organizing precincts, registering new voters, and providing constituent services. Even the most enthusiastic supporter of a party's program will shrink before such drudgery, and it is folly to think that ideological conviction alone will motivate sufficient numbers to keep the party going through the off-years. "For the most part, as every politician knows, the hope of some reward generates a major portion of the local political activity supporting parties." . . .

The Court simply refuses to acknowledge the link between patronage and party discipline, and between that and party success. . . . It is unpersuasive to claim, as the Court does, that party workers are obsolete because campaigns are now conducted through media and other money-intensive means. Those techniques have supplemented but not supplanted personal contacts. Certainly they have not made personal contacts unnecessary in campaigns for the lower-level offices that are the foundations of party strength, nor have they replaced the myraid functions performed by party regulars not direcly related to campaigning. And to the extent such techniques have replaced older methods of campaigning (partly in response to the limitations the Court has placed on patronage), the political system is not clearly better off. Increased reliance on money-intensive campaign techniques tends to entrench those in power much more effectively than patronage—but without the attendant benefit of strengthening the party system. A challenger can more easily obtain the support of party-workers (who can expect to be rewarded even if the candidate loses—if not this year, then the next) than the financial support of political action committees (which will generally support incumbents, who are likely to prevail).

It is self-evident that eliminating patronage will significantly undermine party discipline; and that as party discipline wanes, so will the strength of the two-party system. But, says the Court, "[p]olitical parties have already survived the substantial decline in patronage employment practices in this century." This is almost verbatim what was said in *Elrod*. Fourteen years later it seems much less convincing. Indeed, now that we have witnessed, in 18 of the last 22 years, an Executive Branch of the Federal Government under the control of one party while the Congress is entirely or (for two years) partially within the control of the other party; now that we have undergone the most recent federal election, in which 98% of the incumbents, of whatever party, were returned to office; and now that we have seen elected officials changing their political affiliation with unprecedented readiness, Washington Post, Apr. 10, 1990, p. A1, the statement that "political parties have already survived" has a positively whistling-in-the-graveyard character to it. Parties have assuredly survived—but as what? As the forges upon which many of the essential compromises of American political life are hammered out? Or merely as convenient vehichles for the conducting of national presidential elections?

The patronage system does not, of course, merely foster political parties in general; it foster the two-party system in particular. When getting a job, as opposed to effectuating a particular substantive policy, is an available incentive for party-workers, those attracted by that incentive are likely to work for the party that has the best chance of displacing the "ins," rather than for some splinter group that has a more attractive political philosophy but little hope of success. Not only is a two-party system more likely to emerge, but the differences between those parties are more likely to be moderated, as each has a relatively greater interest in appealing to a majority of the electorate and relatively lesser interest in furthering philosophies or programs that are far from the mainstream. The stabilizing effects of such a system are obvious. . . .

Equally apparent is the relatively destabilizing nature of a system in which candidates cannot rely upon patronage-based party loyalty for their campaign support, but must attract workers and raise funds by appealing to various interest-groups. There is little doubt that our decisions in *Elrod* and *Branti,* by contributing to the decline of party strength, have also contributed to the growth of interest-group politics in the last decade. Our decision today will greatly accelerate the trend. It is not only campaigns that are affected, of course, but the subsequent behavior of politicians once they are in power. The replacement of a system firmly based in party discipline with one in which each office-holder comes to his own accommodation with competing interest groups produces "a dispersion of political influence that may inhibit a political party from enacting its programs into law."

Patronage, moreover, has been a powerful means of achieving the social and political integration of excluded groups. By supporting and ultimately dominating a particular party "machine," racial and ethnic minorities have— on the basis of their politics rather than their race or ethnicity—acquired the patronage awards the machine had power to confer. No one disputes the historical accuracy of this observation, and there is no reason to think that patronage can no longer serve that function. The abolition of patronage, however, prevents groups that have only recently obtained political power, especially blacks, from following this path to economic and social advancement. . . .

While the patronage system has the benefits argued for above, it also has undoubted disadvantages. It facilitates financial corruption, such as salary kickbacks and partisan political activity on government-paid time. It reduces the efficiency of government, because it creates incentives to hire more and less-qualified workers and because highly qualified workers are reluctant to accept jobs that may only last until the next election. And, of course, it applies some greater or lesser inducement for individuals to join and work for the party in power.

To hear the Court tell it, this last is the greatest evil. That is not my view, and it has not historically been the view of the American people. Corruption and inefficiency, rather than abridgement of liberty, have been the major criticisms leading to enactment of the civil-service laws—for the very good reason that the patronage system does not have as harsh an effect upon conscience, expression, and association as the Court suggests. As described above, it is the nature of the pragmatic, patronage-based, two-party system to build alliances and to suppress rather than foster ideological tests for participation in the division of political "spoils." What the patronage system ordinarily demands of the party worker is loyalty to, and activity on behalf of, the organization itself rather than a set of political beliefs. He is generally free to urge *within the organization* the adoption of any political position; but if that position is rejected he must vote and work for the party nonetheless. The diversity of political expression (other than expression of party loyalty) is channeled, in other words, to a different stage—to the contests for party endorsement rather than the partisan elections. It is undeniable, of course, that the patronage system entails some constraint upon the expression of views, particularly at the partisan-election stage, and considerable constraint upon the employee's right to associate with the other party. It greatly exaggerates these, however, to describe them as a general "coercion of belief". Indeed, it greatly exaggerates them to call them "coercion" at all, since we generally make a distinction between inducement and compulsion. The public offical offered a bribe is not "coerced" to violate the law, and the private citizen offered a patronage job is not "coerced" to work for the party. In sum, I do not deny that the patronage system influences or redirects, perhaps to a substantial degree, individual political expression and political association. But like the many generations of Americans that have preceded us, I do not consider that a significant impairment of free speech or free association.

In emphasizing the advantages and minimizing the disadvantages (or at least minimizing one of the disadvantages) of the patronage system, I do not mean to suggest that that system is best. It may not always be; it may never be. To oppose our *Elrod-Branti* jurisprudence, one need not believe that the patronage system is *necessarily* desirable; nor even that it is always and everywhere *arguably* desirable; but merely that it is a political arrangement that may sometimes be a reasonable choice, and should therefore be left to the judgment of the people's elected representatives. The choice in question, I emphasize, is not just between patronage and a merit-based civil service, but rather among various combinations of the two that may suit different political units and different eras: permitting patronage hiring, for example, but prohibiting patronage dismissal; permitting patronage in most municipal agencies but prohibiting it in the police department; or permitting it in the mayor's office but prohibiting it everywhere else. I find it impossible to say that, always and everywhere, all of these choices fail our "balancing" test.

The last point explains why *Elrod* and *Branti* should be overruled, rather than merely not extended. Even in the field of constitutional adjudication, where the pull of *stare decisis* is at its weakest, one is reluctant to depart from precedent. But when that precedent is not only wrong, not only recent, not only contradicted by a long prior tradition, but also has proved unworkable in practice, then all reluctance ought to disappear. In my view that is the situation here. Though unwilling to leave it to the political process to draw the line between desirable and undesirable patronage, the Court has neither been prepared to rule that no such line exists (*i.e.,* that *all* patronage is unconstitutional) nor able to design the line itself in a manner that judges, lawyers, and public employees can understand. *Elrod* allowed patronage dismissals of persons in "policymaking" or "confidential" positions. *Branti* retreated from that formulation, asking instead "whether the hiring authority can demonstrate that party affiliation is an appropriate requirement for the effective performance of the public office involved." What that means is anybody's guess. . . .

Even were I not convinced that *Elrod* and *Branti* were wrongly decided, I would hold that they should not be extended beyond their facts, viz., actual discharge of employees for their political affiliation. Those cases invalidated patronage firing in order to prevent the "restraint in places on freedoms of belief and association." The loss of one's current livelihood is an appreciably greater constraint than such other disappointments as the failure to obtain a promotion or selection for an uncongenial transfer. . . .

I would reject the alternative that the Seventh Circuit adopted in this case, which allows a cause of action if the employee can demonstrate that he was subjected to the "substantial equivalent of dismissal." The trouble with that seemingly reasonable standard is that it is so imprecise that it will multiply yet again the harmful uncertainty and litigation that *Branti* has already created. . . .

The Court's opinion, of course, not only declines to confine *Elrod* and *Branti* to dismissals in the narrow sense I have proposed, but, unlike the Seventh Circuit, even extends those opinions beyond "constructive" dismissals—indeed, even beyond adverse treatment of current employees—to all hiring decisions. In the long run there may be cause to rejoice in that extension. When the courts are flooded with litigation under that most unmanageable of standards (*Branti*) brought by that most persistent and tenacious of suitors (the disappointed office-seeker) we may be moved to reconsider our intrusion into this entire field.

In the meantime, I dissent.

26

Herbert J. Storing

Political Parties and the Bureaucracy (1964)

. . . [The] exclusion of the political party from the vast majority of federal offices has not, of course, come about by accident or thoughtless adaptation

From Storing, "Political Parties and the Bureaucracy," in *Political Parties U.S.A.,* ed. Robert A. Goldwin, Rand McNally and Company, 1961. Used by permission of the Public Affairs Conference Center, Kenyon College, Gambier, Ohio.

to changed circumstances. It resulted from a deliberate reform of the American political system which found expression primarily in the Pendleton Act of 1883. As is well known, this Act established a bipartisan Civil Service Commission charged, among other things, to provide open competitive examinations for entry into the "classified" federal service. . . .

The post-Civil War reform movement which led to this legislation was directed immediately at the civil service, but its more fundamental objective was the reform of political parties. While the reformers did not seek to eradicate parties, they were, like the American Founders, keenly aware that "party spirit, from the first, has been the terror of republics." It is, George Curtis said, "the one fire that needs no fanning. The first duty of patriotism is to keep that fire low." Specifically, the reformers were trying to rid the country of the spoils system, in which they saw three evils:

1. By distributing public office as the booty of party warfare, the spoils system introduced gross inefficiency and corruption into the public administration.

2. By basing political parties on a network of selfish private relationships, the spoils system distorted and frustrated the expression of the popular will.

3. By channelling men's minds along the lines of private and narrow group interest and away from a concern with the public interest, the spoils system corrupted American political life and character.

Unlike their successors, the early reformers—such men as George Curtis, Dorman Eaton, and Carl Schurz—thought that administrative inefficiency was the least of these evils. . . . In an important statement of the object of civil service reform in an editorial for *Harper's Weekly* Schurz conceded that one aim was "an improved conduct of the public business."

> But the ultimate end of civil service reform is something far more important than a mere improvement in the machinery of administration. It is to elevate the character of our political life by eliminating from it as much as possible the demoralizing elements of favoritism and of mercenary motives which under the spoils system have become the moving powers in our politics. It is to rescue our political parties, and in a great measure the management of our public affairs, from the control of men whose whole statesmanship consists in the low arts of office-mongering, and many of whom would never have risen to power had not the spoils system furnished them the means and opportunities for organizing gangs of political followers as mercenary as themselves. It is to restore ability, high character, and true public spirit once more to their legitimate spheres in our public life, and to make active politics once more attractive to men of self-respect and high patriotic aspirations.

Many of the reformers were Abolitionists in the controversy over slavery and regarded civil service reform as an extension of the same movement. Having freed the Negro slaves, they argued, it was time to free the civil service from its slavery to political parties. Like the system of chattel slavery, the spoils system corrupts slave, master, and the community that gives it countenance. . . .

[W]hile the problem was fundamentally a moral and political one, the solution was found in "something akin to a mechanical contrivance." Without attempting to plumb philosophical depths, the reformers reasoned that the immediate cause of political corruption was the spoils system; the spoils system, in turn, depended upon the discretion of appointing officers in choosing their subordinates. Abolish that discretion and you abolish the spoils system and the corruption flowing from it.

Although this chain of reasoning is not simply wrong, it is certainly insufficient. Civil service reform was not so efficacious as the reformers had expected in purifying politics and raising the moral tone of the community, and it brought new and unanticipated problems. Yet corruption *was* very considerably reduced, and politics *did* become less a matter of sheer self-seeking. . . .

It is undeniable, however, that the reformers grossly oversimplified the problem of popular government. They were inclined to think that, once the spoils system was out of the way, citizens would become pure, leaders noble, and politics patriotic. "[B]y making election, not a fight for plunder, but a contest of principle," civil service reform would make "the honest will of the people the actual government of the country." Although the reformers often described their movement as a return to the original principles of the American republic, they paid too little heed to the Founders' warning that a government fit for angels is not fit for men. Confronted with the need to rid American politics of selfishness run riot, they underestimated the enduring force of selfish interests, and consequently they failed to recognize sufficiently the permanent need to take account of such interests. . . .

With the passage of the Pendleton Act and the steady extension of the merit system in the federal service, the immediate objectives of the reformers were largely accomplished. Although the question of civil service reform erupted periodically, it ceased to be a major political issue. The reform movement did not die, but it moved from the political arena to the universities. The men associated with the second phase of reform were not primarily agitators, pamphleteers, and politicians, like Schurz and Curtis, but university professors, like Frank Goodnow, or professor-politicians, like Woodrow Wilson.

This second generation of reformer-political scientists sought to state systematically the theory of government implicit in the reform movement and to elaborate in more detail its practical consequences. In so doing they established the main lines from which most contemporary thinking about political parties and public administration derives. The key words are "responsible parties" and "efficient administration." As these men generally saw it, the ideal democracy consists, as it were, of two pyramids joined at the top. The will of the people flows up through the pyramid of politics where it is collected by political parties and formed into programs of legislation. The programs of the majority party then flow down through the administrative pyramid where they are implemented in the most efficient manner. According to this theory the prime requisites of a civil service are political neutrality and technical competence. The civil servant is not supposed to make policy. He decides, according to scientifically established technical criteria, the best, that is, most efficient, way to accomplish any given ends. Those ends are set by his political superiors who are responsible through the party to the people.

In spite of some fairly obvious difficulties, this theory proved to be extremely durable, because it seems to state simply and clearly the whole problem of democratic government: to ensure the free expression and the efficient implementation of the popular will. With customary diligence and thoroughness the academicians set about investigating and explaining how the pyramid of politics and the pyramid of administration ought to be governed, each according to its proper principle. . . . A new and vigorous discipline of administration has grown up within the universities, and it trains and the fosters a huge corps of professional administrators.

So successful is this movement that there has been a tendency to ignore the crucial question of the proper *connection* between administration and politics. The stock answer is that of course the political master gives the orders, but he should not meddle in the activities of his administrative servants; if he does he will only get in the way of the efficient implementation of his own orders. "Administrative questions are not political questions," Wilson said. "Although politics sets the tasks for administration, it should not be suffered to manipulate its offices." It is true that even the most ardent proponents of a neutral civil service rarely went so far as to assert that the intermediate and lower levels of public administration could be altogether free of direct political influence. There were even some doubts whether political control at the top could ever be sufficient to keep the administration politically responsible; but generally students and reformers of administration were too busy extending the merit system, neutralizing the civil service, and devising principles of administration to concern themselves much with the "external" problem of political control. In any case, the logic of the two pyramids, joined somehow at their respective peaks, seemed to settle the question in principle, whatever the practical difficulties. . . .

While many administrators and students of administration are still content to work quietly in the cloister of the neutral-civil service idea, others have discovered that the world is not so reasonable or so simple as they were taught in the "reform" school; and, like small boys in similar circumstances, they find a good deal of naughty pleasure in telling everyone about it. In spite of the extension of the merit system and the application of ever more sophisticated principles of administration, there seems to be as much "politics" in federal administration as there ever was. Administration is not, it appears, simply a matter of drawing logical deductions from a general statement of policy. No general statement can be so exhaustive as to permit the civil servant to act on the basis of a series of purely technical calculations, even if he were willing to do so. He is inevitably left with some discretion; he has to exercise his judgment; he has to participate in the making of policy. This is, of course, especially true at the higher levels, but the same principle applies, often in very significant ways, at lower levels as well.

If, then, we need a vast administration staffed largely by permanent officials and if they cannot be confined to merely technical decisions, the result of the attempt to neutralize the civil service is likely to be not a perfectly efficient and responsive executive machine, but a bureaucratic monster. A civil service free of detailed political control, trained in a purely instrumental science of administration, and insulated from the political life of the community will not be non-political; but it will be politically irresponsible. The spoils system, whatever its other effects, did at least ensure that the bureaucracy shared the political character of the community at large. There is not much serious consideration of going back to the spoils system, but it is argued very strongly that the civil service, being a political institution, must be *representative* of the political community that it serves if it is to be responsible. To the extent that the interests, opinions, and values of civil servants are intimately bound up with those of the community as a whole, any separate "bureaucratic" will or spirit will be out of the question.

Fortunately, in this view, the American civil service does represent the American society with a fair degree of faithfulness. Government offices are not reserved for any favored class or group, and educational prerequisites are usually modest. Appointment depends mainly on an individual's capacity to "do the job," thus permitting representation within the civil service of the diverse political, racial, ethnic, and religious groups which make up the American community. Moreover, entry is not restricted to the bottom rungs of the administrative ladder or to persons just out of school, so there is a constant and healthy infusion of new blood at all levels and a considerable movement between private life and the civil service. The proponents of a "representative bureaucracy" tend to be suspicious of "closed" career systems where there is little or no entry except at the bottom level and where the members ordinarily expect to spend their whole professional lives. The military services have, of course, long been open to suspicion on these grounds. Another favorite object of attack has been the foreign service, where long periods of residence outside the United States, the filling of higher positions exclusively from within the service, and a highly developed esprit de corps are seen to carry a threat of a rigid "inbred" bureaucracy, indifferent or hostile to American democratic values.

It seems, then, that the civil service reform movement has been turned on its head. The early reformers sought, as we have seen, to take the civil service out of politics and politics out of the civil service. A neutral civil service, properly organized and trained, was supposed to serve one party or to implement one policy just as willingly as any other. More than that, such a civil service could in principle be transplanted from one political environment to a totally different one, because there was thought to be, as Woodrow Wilson said, "but one rule of good administration for all governments alike." In recent years the idea of a neutral civil service has lost ground. It is now widely recognized that politics and administration are not capable of such a strict separation and that, in fact, all interesting administrative questions are political questions. It is seen to be futile and dangerous to attempt to deprive the civil service of a political function and a political character. The problem, rather, is to see that the civil service has a political character that will cause it to perform its political function well. That has been thought to require in the United States a thoroughly democratic or representative civil service. What began as a movement to neutralize the civil service has become a movement to democratize it.

Different as this view of a thoroughly democratized civil service is from the older one of a thoroughly neutralized civil service, they have one fundamental feature in common. Both assume that the civil service is an agency which ought to be responsive to the will or "values" of the people; both deny that the civil service should exercise a political will of its own. Only by questioning this common assumption is it possible to grasp the fundamental significance of the political role of the modern civil service. In the remainder of this paper we must consider the modern civil service not simply as an instrument of elected officials or as a reflector of widespread values, but as a political agency in its own right, endowed with certain qualities which give it a reasonable and legitimate claim to share in rule. . . .

[The] question of the kind of political neutrality that can be expected or desired of American civil servants is closely connected with a feature of the American Constitution that has long embarrassed party and civil service reformers, namely the system of checks and balances. The reformers, firmly persuaded by the logic of the two pyramids . . . , tended to regard the separation of powers as a "defect" in the American system, to be remedied either by drastic constitutional change or through the informal agency of reformed parties in control of a reformed administration. Even in their most generous and patriotic mood, they could scarcely see in this central feature of the American Constitution anything but a curiosity of the eighteenth-century mind—a once harmless nuisance grown under modern conditions into an intolerable obstacle to responsible and efficient government. The very fact that the civil service is constitutionally not simply subordinate to either the President or the Congress tends to obscure lines of command and, incidentally, to increase the political influence of the civil service. It is easy to see why the reformers, with their idea of a neutral civil service, thought that such a system could produce nothing but confusion and irresponsibility.

If, however, the civil service is regarded not as a neutral instrument but as a political institution, then the constitutional system of checks and balances appears in a different light. While the framers of the Constitution doubtless failed to anticipate the full significance of the administrative state, there is nevertheless a close harmony between the original intention of the system of checks and balances and the political role of the modern civil service. Without entering fully into this subject, we may say that the system of checks and balances was an attempt to institutionalize moderation; and one of the important ways it does this in modern American government is by adding to the political weight of the civil service which, more than any of the other active agencies of government, stands for moderation. Of course the Founders recognized that their "inventions of prudence" were not a sufficient condition of good government and might sometimes prove a positive handicap, and we must recognize the same about a politically influential civil service. But if the civil service is a political institution with a political function, it does not appear unreasonable that it should have some political power. In what follows we shall consider what the bureaucracy, in partnership with political parties, can and does contribute to American government.[1]

One manifestation of the basic problem of government by political parties is the fact that politicians who run for office in their capacity as leaders of organized parts, or parties, of the body politic are expected to assume a responsibility for the government of the whole. This formulation is obviously incomplete. American political parties themselves undertake to form particular individuals, groups, interests, and opinions into some kind of whole. This is not the place to discuss this broad responsibility or the various means by which American parties discharge it. It may be observed, however, that one means is the appointment of men who are not distinctively party men to fill even high political positions, to say nothing of the appointment of members of the opposite party. . . . Yet in spite of this and other qualifications, the fact remains that in a very important sense our system of government gives to a part the responsibility for governing the whole.

It is notorious that party politicians tend to learn moderation and responsibility when in office; but it is perhaps less generally recognized that one of their main teachers is the civil service. The common contrast between the politician, as the "practical man" experienced in "real life" and in touch with the wants and needs of the people, and the bureaucrat, as the remote, paper-shuffling office boy, is grossly overdrawn. In the first place, many civil servants have, in their particular fields, a kind of direct contact with the people and experience of the problems of government which even the politician whose ear

---

[1]Of what follows it may be said, with Blackstone, "This is the spirit of our constitution: not that I assert it is in fact quite so perfect as I have here endeavoured to describe it. . . ." I *Commentaries* 172.

never leaves the ground cannot possibly match. Moreover, modern government is to a large extent conducted by "shuffling papers," and it is of vital importance that they be shuffled well. Finally, a large part of the proposals for new policies and legislation come up through the civil service. Not only do civil servants exercise discretion in interpreting and applying the commands of their political superiors; they participate intimately in the formulation of those commands. They make proposals of their own and fight for them; they comment on the proposals of their political superiors—and may fight against them. They make a vital contribution to the process of deciding what is to be done. Government would come to a standstill if our "closet statesmen" in the civil service suddenly started doing only what they were told.

In the United States, of course, due partly to the constitutional system of checks and balances, the civil servant does not and perhaps cannot be expected to confine his statesmanship to the closet. Indeed, one of the peculiarities of American public administration is the fact that the civil servant may have more political knowledge and skill, even in the rather narrow sense, than his "political" superior. And he is almost certain to have, at least at first, more familiarity with the politics involved in actually running the government. A new Secretary or Assistant Secretary will normally find himself heavily dependent upon his experienced civil servants to facilitate not only the internal management of the agency but also its relations with Congress, interested organizations, other agencies of government, and even the White House itself. . . .

It is true that much of the contribution of the civil service to the art of government, even in the United States, is of a restraining and even negative kind. The civil servant, especially at the higher levels, has seen many programs tried, and many failures; even the successful innovations have usually fallen short of their makers' hopes. His experience has caused him to be sensitive to difficulties; he is an expert in seeking out unanticipated consequences. Even after a new policy has been decided upon, the civil servant is likely to explain, perhaps at exasperating length, why it cannot possibly be carried out the way his political chief wants. The civil servant is full of procedures, rules, and regulations, and he will (if he is performing properly) instruct his chief in the reasons for them. Orderly administration is not the most important quality of good government and it may sometimes have to be sacrificed to higher ends, but it is, generally speaking, indispensable. The cautious prudence and orderliness which tend to characterize the civil service are precisely that part of practical wisdom in which the party politician is likely to be deficient. . . .

The special kind of practical wisdom that characterizes the civil servant points to a more fundamental political function of the bureaucracy, namely to bring to bear on public policy its distinctive view of the common good or its way of looking at questions about the common good. The preoccupation of the civil service with rules and regulations, for example, is not aimed merely at orderly administration, important as that is. The rules and regulations, and the principle that there should *be* rules and regulations, represent a certain principle of justice, if only the principle of treating equals equally. Similar considerations apply to the civil servant's predilection for the way things have been done in the past. Generally speaking, to follow precedents is orderly, reasonable, and fair. One of the basic principles of American government is that governmental action should ordinarily be taken on the basis of established rules, however irritating that may sometimes be to a politician with a substantive program to put through. Like judges, civil servants have a special responsibility to preserve the rule of law.

Civil servants also bear a similarity to judges in their possession of what is, for most practical purposes, permanent tenure in office. Of course, like judges, they are influenced by the election returns—and it would be dangerous if they were not; but they have a degree of insulation from shifting political breezes. The rhythm of their official lives and thoughts is not governed so strictly as is that of the political executive by periodic elections. Their position enables them to mitigate the partisanship of party politics, and it gives them some protection from the powerful temptation, to which the party politician is always subject, to serve the people's inclinations rather than their interests.

Clement Attlee described the higher civil servant in Britain as having, in addition to long personal experience, "that mysterious tradition of the office wherein is somehow embalmed the wisdom of past generations." The civil service in the United States is of course far less time-encrusted, but here too the higher civil servant will ordinarily have long experience in government, nearly always longer than his political chiefs. Moreover the duties of the civil servant and the way he works—his concern for written records, for example—tend to make him conscious of the "long-termness" of political decisions to a degree that is unusual for transient party politicians. At its best, the civil service is a kind of democratic approximation to an hereditary aristocracy whose members are conscious of representing an institution of government which extends into the past and into the future beyond the life of any individual member. In our mobile democracy, the civil service is one of the few institutions we have for bringing the accumulated wisdom of the past to bear upon political decisions.

Perhaps the most important political contribution that a civil service can make is, of all those we have considered, the one the American civil service makes least. Neither the bureaucracy nor political parties merely "represents" or reflects the American polity; they also help to shape and guide that polity, and they perform this function by what they are as well as by what they do. The character of a country's public servants is one of the determinants of the character of its people. When George Washington sought honest, honorable, and loyal gentlemen to fill the public offices of the new country, he was concerned not only with getting the work of government done but also with distributing the patronage of government in such a way as to set the public stamp of approval on certain human qualities. When Andrew Jackson established the system of rotation in public office, he had the same broad objective in mind, but he sought to elevate the common man in the place of the gentleman. And what the civil service reformers feared most about the spoils system was the effect on the political character of the people of the example set by the kind of men which the spoils system tended to elevate. "Politics cannot be made a mere trade," George Curtis argued, "without dangerously relaxing the moral character of the country." . . .

Except for the removal of corruption, however, the reformers gave little thought to the kind of character and morality which their neutral, merely technical civil service would exemplify. One indication of the result is the fact that American civil servants themselves, though they may be thoroughly devoted to serving the common good, ordinarily prefer to identify themselves by their profession or occupation or "job" rather than by their public service. It is thought more respectable to be an agricultural economist or a personnel specialist than to be a civil servant. . . .

The civil service is, then, in possession of certain institutional qualities which give it a title to share with elected officials in rule. It has a distinctive competence in the art of government and a unique knowledge of the problems of government, without which stable and intelligent government under modern conditions would be literally impossible. It has, moreover, a distinctive view of the common good which can guide and supplement the view likely to be taken by elected party politicians. On the foundation of its procedures, its rules, its institutional memory and foresight, its traditions, its skepticism of political panaceas, and its protection from the whims of popularity, the civil service stands for the continuity and wholeness of American government.

It is not to be denied that bureaucracy suffers characteristic limitations and defects. Neither the party politician nor the bureaucrat has an unqualified claim to rule; neither is unqualifiedly competent or entitled to act on behalf of the whole people. Under ordinary circumstances the actual conduct of American government is in the charge of a partnership between them. We have emphasized the contributions of the bureaucratic part of this partnership, because they are less generally understood. But as the civil servant teaches, so also he is taught by the party politician. The civil servant is likely, for example, to overdo his concern with procedures and rules. He may be blind to the fact that procedural justice can do substantive injustice. It may be necessary for his political chief to show him that procedures have become so complex as to defeat their purpose or that the original reason for a rule has disappeared. While the civil servant may take a longer view of the common good, his view may also be distorted by a preoccupation with one program or a rather narrow range of programs. The broader range of responsibilities of the political chief may provide a corrective. Moreover, although the civil servant bears the immediate responsibility for government because he does (or is closer to) the actual governing, he does not bear the final responsibility. He may instruct his political chief, he may advise him, guide him, even manage him—but he does not have the last word. This means that he may be overruled, for good reasons or bad; but it also means that his way of thinking and acting is molded in part by the fact of his formal subordination. Even at his best he is not a political captain but a faithful, wise, and influential counsellor and servant.

This is connected with a final limitation of bureaucracy. Although a good civil service is one of the guardians of the traditional political wisdom of a regime, "sometimes it is necessary," as Attlee says, "to react violently against the tradition which was formed for a different state of society." While it is difficult to imagine Lord Attlee reacting violently against anything, it is clear that traditional bureaucratic wisdom may not suit changed circumstances. The very tradition which it is the responsibility of the bureaucrat to carry forward may require fundamental redefinition, and that is a task for which his duties, training, and experience disqualify him. During such times of crisis, "administration" does become radically subordinate to "politics"; the institution of the civil service does become to a much greater extent than usual an instrument of the man who is President. The peak of the spoils system is generally regarded as having come during Lincoln's first administration, and Lincoln removed the incumbents of almost all offices under his immediate control. He used the spoils of office to help bind together the Republican Party, the North, and thereby the Union. So much was this the paramount aim that, according to one historian, Lincoln "made no attempt to obtain the men best fitted to perform the functions of the various offices, except in case of the very highest; for minor places he did not even insist that a man be fit." The Civil War is an extreme example, but it is not the only one. The transformation which the civil service underwent at the hands of Franklin Roosevelt is well known. Roosevelt gave a new meaning to the civil service and to the Democratic Party in the course of giving a new meaning to American political life as a whole. During such critical times, the question of bureaucracy as such is almost entirely subordinated to the more fundamental question of political reconstruction. It is not unfair to say of the bureaucracy (and perhaps of political parties too) that it contributes least to government in the most important cases, provided it is remembered that a government requires a capacity for everyday competence, prudence, and public-spiritedness, as well as a capacity for greatness.

27

Constance Horner

The Civil Service: Competence, Character, and Constitutional Principles (1989, 1988)

As a Civil Service Commissioner in the early 1890s, Theodore Roosevelt was a firm believer in the use of written, objective examinations for making appointments to the federal service. He realized, however, that the "routine competitive examination was merely a means to an end," and that some positions could not be filled that way—the job of mounted cattle inspector, for instance. For that post—in best Rough Rider fashion—he recommended a test in "brand reading and shooting with rifle and revolver, in riding 'mean' horses and in roping and throwing steers." (Roosevelt 1925).

For over a decade, the issue of civil service hiring has been a "mean horse" for the United States—a source of bitter political contention, endless, complex lawsuits, and considerable confusion about first principles. Ever since the *Luevano* consent decree did away with the major testing device for government employment in 1982, an intense national debate has raged—in Congress, in the courts, in the press—between proponents of strict merit hiring, on the one hand, and of a racially representative workforce, on the other.

As a result, the United States has had no coherent, visible, effective civil service hiring system for almost a decade. What we have instead is a hiring *non*-system—one that is slow, legally trammelled, intellectually confused, and impossible to explain to potential candidates. It is almost certainly not fulfilling the spirit of our mandate to hire the most meritorious candidates.

Early in 1988 , the Office of Personnel Management (OPM)—the chief personnel agency for the Federal government, and successor to the US Civil Service Commission—decided that this state of affairs was no longer tolerable. We knew that we were facing serious labor shortages in the near future, and that the current non-system left us ill-equipped to compete with the private sector for the brightest young men and women. . . .

From Horner, "Securing Competence and Character," in *Governance: An International Journal of Policy and Administration,* Vol. 2, No. 2 (Spring, 1989). © copyright 1989 Research Committee on the Structure and Organization of Government of the International Political Science Association. Reprinted by permission.
The second selection is from "Remarks," at the Rotunda of the University of Virginia, October 14, 1988.

Something even more fundamental is at stake in the controversy over civil service hiring. For the way we bring people into the civil service has always been considerably more than a practical or technical matter—it is an important moral and political issue, as well.

Such was the design of those who established the civil service system in 1883. Practically speaking, their fledgling system was negligible, covering only about 10% of the workforce, mostly lower level clerks. But that modest step toward reform was, for them and for the nation, a profoundly important political symbol—it signified that the old, corrupt system of "spoils" was in retreat, and that a new system of political values reflecting non-partisanship and individual merit was in the ascendancy. . . .

Today as well, we expect our system of civil service hiring to reflect and reinforce our most important values and beliefs, and, by making them visible and compelling to our citizens, to elevate our political life. That we tolerate an incoherent, intellectually confused hiring non-system, then, is a significant moral failure on our part, because it sends garbled and ambiguous signals about those beliefs and values. . . .

In 1974, a comprehensive, general ability examination called the Professional and Administrative Career Exam (PACE) became the chief testing vehicle for the Federal government. It was used to fill GS-5 and 7, entry-level positions in 118 professional and administrative occupations, and it had some major virtues. It was a highly visible recruiting tool; it was economical; and it was considered to have a high level of validity—that is, it predicted well a person's subsequent performance on the job. And because it was a competitive exam open to all American citizens, it was thought to be a good way to open doors for minorities.

Nonetheless, because very small percentages of minority groups did well on the exam, it was soon charged with closing those doors. The court action that followed culminated in the *Luevano* consent decree, by the terms of which PACE was to be phased out over three years, and replaced by a series of job-specific exams that would, presumably, more accurately measure job abilities, *and* produce a representative work force.

Luevano unleashed a storm of controversy in this country. Supporters hailed it as a way to build a racially representative work force of high quality. Critics insisted that abandoning PACE meant abandoning the very principle of merit hiring, and embracing the repugnant notion of racial quotas. Two fundamental American values seemed to be irrevocably at odds: on the one hand, our deep belief in advancement on the basis of merit; on the other, our equally firm belief that advancement should be open to all. The lines were thus drawn in a contest that continues to this day.

Since the *Luevano* decree, PACE has in fact been dropped; job-specific exams have been developed for sixteen occupations formerly filled under that test; and agencies have been given more authority to hire job applicants without written examination. That approach itself now faces legal challenge, however, as the courts continue to try to solve through inflexible judicial edict a problem crying out for executive discretion.

In June, 1988, OPM exercised some of that discretion by proposing a new system of civil service hiring. That system puts the bitterness and philosophical confusion of the *Luevano* years behind us, and promises not only to meet the immediate, practical problems of hiring in times of labor shortage, but also to clarify the basic principles and commitments that we wish to see reflected in our civil service system.

It will meet the legitimate principled concerns of both sides in the *Luevano* controversy—rigorous competition for the best, and a racially and ethnically diverse workforce. But it will also incorporate a new concern or need, one that was missing from much of the contemporary hiring controversy. And that is the need to build a civil service possessing not only competence, but character as well.

To be sure, the notion of "character" has a rather quaint air about it today. It is one of those concepts that seems to have passed out of public discourse—or to have been driven out, by the sophisticated ridicule of our intellectual and cultural elites. Nonetheless, the mounting social and moral disasters all about us today—rampant drug abuse, rising crime rates, exploding illegitimate birth rates—all point to one conclusion: the rediscovery of character—the revival of the common sense view that personal, moral stature is an indispensable ingredient of a decent society and a sound political system—is one of the most desperate needs of our time.

More immediately, if we want our civil servants to exercise wisely the judgment and discretion that public service demands—if we want to *expand* those areas requiring judgment and discretion, as many of our management initiatives are designed to do—then we must seek more than technical expertise and intellect in our candidates. We must also look for certain essential human attributes and principles—among them perseverance, initiative, prudence, honesty, commitment to hard work, moral imagination, and human generosity. In short, we must seek character.

Frances Perkins, Franklin D. Roosevelt's Secretary of Labor, understood this need for both competence and character in a public servant. It was a misconception, she argued, to think that the most successful government executive is one who "reads, far into the night, volumes of information, studies profound reports, compares the views of experts, . . . and then by a process of pure logic arrives at a conclusion." Rather, she maintained, the best public servant operates as FDR himself did: "he had to have feeling as well as thought. His emotions, his intuitive understanding, his imagination, his moral and traditional bias, his sense of right and wrong—all entered into his thinking" (Perkins 1946). In short, competence *and* character are required.

Under our proposed hiring approach, federal agencies will be able to choose among a variety of staffing vehicles to fill entry-level jobs. We will retain and strengthen the smaller programs that have brought us so many fine candidates in the past, such as the Cooperative Education and Presidential Management Intern initiatives. But the two primary alternatives will be: First, direct recruiting and hiring on the basis of grade point average (GPA); and second, a battery of job specific cognitive exams, which are designed to include measures of experience and personal values.

Under the first, college recruiting approach, candidates will be eligible for consideration if they have compiled a certain GPA—probably a 3.0 or above on a 4.0 scale. GPA has long been recognized in the private sector as a useful measure of ability. Surveys indicate that between 25 and 30% of college graduates earn a 3.0 average, suggesting that GPA is in fact a reasonably rigorous indicator of a candidate's intellectual competence.

GPA measures more than technical ability, however—it also measures character. Individuals who have earned a 3.0 are more likely to be hardworking, motivated and ambitious. Even if students did not have the opportunity to attend a college of the first rank, the fact that they persevered in their studies—wherever they found themselves—is an important comment on their eligibility for employment.

Under the second, test-based approach to hiring, we intend to develop and make available to Federal agencies a series of occupationally based exams, covering some of the positions formerly filled by PACE. The exams will address the needs of those agencies that have to fill only a few jobs, by giving them quick and inexpensive access to a list of pre-screened applicants. Moreover, the exams will give candidates who have not graduated from college, or who have not earned a 3.0 there, the opportunity to demonstrate their employability.

Even these exams, however, will be designed to evaluate more than technical skills. We propose to include a measure, currently under study at OPM and broadly used in the private sector, called the Individual Achievement Record. This measure provides information on a candidate's self-discipline, school activities, leadership qualities, and problem-solving ability. Other parts of the exam will evaluate past employment and related aspects of an individual's experience. In short, we will be able to build measures of character directly into the written exams.

This new approach permits agencies to choose the hiring device most appropriate for them, given the conditions of the labor market. And as we have already seen, labor markets will be tight, and so competition will be intense for the shrinking pool of highly qualified candidates.

Our provision for direct hiring of quality college graduates gives us the means to compete in that tight market. We will no longer have to say to potential candidates, "yes, we'd love to have you with us, but first you have to take a test, and then be put on a list, and then sit around and wait." We will now be able to pursue quality candidates aggressively, and with something concrete to offer—a job, on the spot. At least one very important handicap will be removed from the federal recruiting process through this approach, which has the additional virtues of being easily understood, accessible, and highly visible.

To ensure that our new approach lives up to our expectations—and to correct it if it does not—we are at the same time launching a serious study of the quality of candidates it brings into public service. We will collect information on a number of indicators of quality—work experience, education, and class rank, for example—to see what sorts of people apply for our jobs, how well each branch of the new approach performs, and whether the best employees stay with us for the long term. For the first time, we will be able to evaluate and compare meaningfully different approaches to hiring.

Perhaps the most important aspect of the new proposal, however, is that it not only meets the practical recruiting needs of the government—it also moves the discussion of civil service hiring beyond the intellectual stalemate of the *Luevano* years, by addressing the legitimate concerns of both sides. It thereby clarifies the basic commitments we wish to incorporate in our civil service system, and the virtues we wish to cultivate in our public servants and citizens.

Critics of *Luevano,* for instance, were right to insist that merit is, and must continue to be, the core principle of civil service hiring. They went too far, however, when they identified merit in general with PACE in particular. Merit includes more than the technical skills measured by tests like PACE— it must be understood to include character, as well.

Although the estimate of character is described here as a new standard, it is in fact simply a return to an older and rich view of what the civil service merit system requires. As noted earlier, from its inception in the 19th century, civil service reform was always understood to have two purposes, one practical and one moral. Its practical purpose was to recruit public servants possessing the competence and technical proficiency to perform their jobs well. That practical end, however, was always considered secondary to a moral one: to secure public servants who were non-partisan, civic-minded, and the finest character.

Thus Carl Schurz could say in 1893 that one objective of civil service reform was "an improved conduct of the public business"—but the "ultimate end . . . is to restore ability, high character, and true public spirit once more to their legitimate spheres in our public life" (Schurz 1893). The early reformers, in turn, understood themselves to be operating in an even older and nobler tradition: that of George Washington, who insisted that "fitness of character" be the "primary object" in "every nomination to office" (White 1956). This rich and expansive view of the purposes behind civil service reform underlay Theodore Roosevelt's grasp of the limits of written, objective examinations.

Indeed, Roosevelt once had occasion to comment directly on the balance of competence and character sought in civil service hiring. In the late 1880s, an editorial in a Chicago newspaper came to his attention, suggesting that the fledgling civil service was not, in fact, based on genuine merit. Because it relied on written tests, the paper insisted, it was really only an "intelligence system," and did not measure the "first requisite of good service of any kind—character."

Roosevelt penned a strong rebuttal to this charge, pointing out that the civil service examination did, in fact, include various measures of a "candidate's good character," as well as written tests of intellectual capacity. "Our system certainly can be rightly called the intelligence system," he maintained, "for it does put a premium on such qualities as intelligence, efficiency, readiness and the like; but it is more just to call it the merit system, for we emphatically demand that all employees of the Government shall be honest, decent men of good moral standing" (U.S. Civil Service Commission 1958). In short, the original understanding of the merit system demanded both tests of competence, and measures of character.

Over time, however, and propelled by the "scientific management" enthusiasm of the early century, public sector administration came to be considered more a technical science than a high political art. As a result, the civil service's practical, proficiency-related purpose eclipsed its moral, character-related purpose. It became easy to fall into the trap of thinking that objective tests of technical skill measure the sum of "merit," as did the die-hard supporters of PACE.

Today, though, few believe that public administration can be reduced to a precise, technical science. We know that federal civil servants are constantly called upon to exercise judgment and discretion—to make decisions on the basis of prudence and broad political principle. Indeed, one of our goals at OPM is to enlarge the areas within which federal civil servants can exercise those qualities. But wise use of discretion requires more than technical expertise. As George Washington understood, it requires "fitness of character." It is time for us to acknowledge that ancient wisdom in modern civil service hiring.

While the pursuit of competence and character in the public service does not compromise the merit principle—indeed, it restores an older and fuller understanding of it—it should also produce a federal work force that reflects the diversity of the American public, thus meeting the legitimate expectations of the supporters of *Luevano*. To emphasize character in hiring is to emphasize an "equal opportunity" human trait. It is to judge people in part by how they play the hand life dealt them, because of the personal moral qualities they bring to bear on the way they live, the decisions they make, and the way they treat those with whom they live and work.

A candidate may not have had the opportunity to go to a first-rank college, but by virtue of hard work and ambition may have done very well. We want such a candidate, just as we want his or her peer from the best schools in the country—but only if that peer is also honest, hard-working, and civic-minded. Perhaps the new approach can best be summarized by saying: we are less interested in how many opportunities individuals have had, than in how fully they have exploited those they were given. We have good reason to believe that our new, flexible approach will produce healthy percentages of minority recruits, based on our experience with similar hiring devices over the past two decades. Under the decentralized, direct-hire system used since the demise of PACE, for instance, over 20% of our external hires have been black, and 6.7% have been Hispanic. Furthermore, the new job-specific exams developed by OPM are turning up results reflecting the population. . . .

For the past eight years, our primary challenge has been to bring federal power back into the channels laid for it by the U.S. Constitution. With that largely accomplished or well underway, we have now begun to consider once more the positive goals we might pursue through Federal power, in this renewed context of limited, yet energetic constitutional government. As we turn to those questions, we will find that we need, more than ever, a Federal workforce possessing competence and "fitness of character"; certain of its purpose and proud of its vocation; exercising judgment and discretion in service to the public. . . .

* * * * * * * * * *

[T]he study of management today is almost exclusively concerned with technique. It has very little to say about purpose. It can tell us how to coordinate and maneuver conflicting groups toward a common goal, but it cannot tell us what that goal should be. It can tell us how to "manage change," but it cannot tell us whether change is good or bad—whether we should be resisting it or speeding it along. In short, management knows a great deal about means, but very little about ends. Yet it is precisely an awareness of the distinctive ends or purposes to be served by an organization, that gives it a sense of unity and common calling.

What is the distinctive purpose of the Federal civil servant? Nothing could be clearer. We declare it openly and succinctly the first day on the job. In fact, we take an oath before God that we will carry out that purpose: to "support and defend the Constitution of the United States," and to "bear true faith and allegiance to the same." No other job in America exacts that pledge. It is the unique declaration of purpose of the public servant. It sets us apart from other professions, and forms the basis of a sense of singularity and unity.

Here, in our oath of office, is the source of the curriculum that all Federal civil servants must have in common. For surely we must come to know as much as we can about this document whose support and defense, we avow, is our unique purpose. We must read and know the Constitution's text. But we must also read and know the authoritative commentaries that explain it, as well as other major documents from our Founding. That includes the Declaration of Independence, *The Federalist Papers,* selections from the writings of the Anti-Federalists, Alexis de Tocqueville's superb commentary *Democracy in America,* selected addresses by our greatest presidents, and important decisions of the Supreme Court.

Madison and Jefferson composed a list very much like this one as they pondered together an appropriate curriculum for the future national leaders to be trained here at the University. These readings, Madison noted, would insure that the true doctrines of liberty, as exemplified in our political system, [are] inculcated in those who are to sustain and administer it.

Inculcating the "true doctrines of liberty" in our chief administrators is as essential today as when Jefferson and Madison first proposed it many years ago. But it requires far more than the customary "quickie" survey course that we have all taken and from which we have gotten not enough. It requires serious, sustained reflection on the important texts, and the principles and values they embody: liberty, equality, popular government, the rule of law, justice for all. To be effective, that reflection would have to permeate any course of study [of administrators].

The point is that a matter as concrete and practical as hiring for the civil service involves some of our nation's most fundamental political commitments. Without a clear, comprehensive understanding of those commitments—without a firm intellectual grounding in the texts that explain them—we simply would not be equipped to tackle this otherwise very practical issue. And that example could be repeated endlessly across the decisions that I—and all Federal civil servants—face daily in our jobs.

I am calling tonight for a commitment to what might be termed constitutional literacy. . . .

[O]ne antidote to growing specialization within the Federal executive service is to reinvigorate constitutional discourse, so we can meet once again on common ground. As Professor John Rohr puts it, we must "create within the bureaucracy a community of moral discourse centered on fundamental constitutional values."

Now, we may often disagree about what our shared commitment to constitutional values requires—what liberty or equality or justice demands in any given instance. But discourse about those principles should be the unique, common language of the Federal executive. Literacy in these concepts and ideas—constitutional literacy—can help unify and vivify the Federal executive corps. From many professions it can make one vocation.

Constitutional literacy would also help address another great problem in the civil service today—low morale—by nurturing a new sense of pride in the public servant. Serious attention to our oath of office and its meaning makes unmistakably clear that public service is so much more than "just a job." Our nation has in fact entrusted to our guardianship some of its most important values and principles. That is an awesome responsibility—but one that cannot fail to evoke a sense of dignity and high purpose in the civil servant.

If we are serious about reinvigorating a sense of self-respect in our civil service—if we truly wish to make our senior executives proud one again to be public servants, as well as lawyers and accountants and engineers— constitutional literacy will have to play a major role.

But along with pride, constitutional literacy inspires a kind of humility as well. As we examine the document and its purposes, we see that the executive branch is but one of three coordinate branches, and that the Federal government is but one level of governance in this nation. And we learn that all government ultimately must reflect the will of the people.

So we learn not only about the high purposes and ends we serve, but also about the constraints we must observe, as we go about our service. We see that ours is a limited, constitutionally circumscribed government, one that does not try to accomplish all desirable social ends through the agency of the public sector. That is a crucial lesson in modesty and self-restraint for the civil servant. . . .

overcome the deadlock caused by the separation of powers and the decentralized Congressional committee system.

Wilson had little success in establishing parliamentary government. Direct election of Senators and the rise of party primaries were the most Wilsonian reforms adopted in his day. But even recent reformers have been influenced by Wilson's ideas. Lloyd Cutler, for example, argues that the separation of powers makes it difficult for government to enact its programs and calls for changes that will bring American government closer to a parliamentary system.

The reforms of Congress in the mid-1970s may also be traced to a Wilsonian hostility to private interests and irresponsible power. To overcome these problems the reformers sought to make the internal organization of Congress more democratic. The result, however, has been to exacerbate the problem of decentralization with which Wilson was so concerned. As power has been dispersed to sub-committees and individual members, Congress appears to many to be less able than ever to produce coherent policy.

William F. Connelly, however, argues that Congress and Congressmen continue to operate as the Founders intended and that is for the good. Connelly shows that the Founders intended to create a tension between pluralist coalition building and coherent principled policy-making, between representation of individual constituencies and representation of the national interest, between the Congressman's self-interest and the interest of his or her constituency, and between principles and self-interest more broadly understood. Congressional critics and Congressional reformers have often failed to appreciate the complex character of Congress and have consequently misdiagnosed its problems and promoted inappropriate prescriptions for reform.

The Congressional Budget and Impoundment Control Act of 1974 also was based in part on a desire for reform of the internal operation of Congress, but its primary purpose was to transfer power over the budget process from the President to Congress. As David Nichols explains, the reform has largely been a failure. It has produced neither a more efficient budget process nor a transfer of power from the President to Congress. It has only produced more reform and more calls for reform. The problem according to Nichols is that once again reformers have failed to understand the fundamental character of the institutions they seek to reform and they have failed to develop reasonable goals for reform.

Similar problems arise in the debate over the power to make war. The authors of the War Powers Act said they only wanted to insure that the collective judgment of Congress and the President would apply to the use of the armed forces of the United States. But the War Powers Act was clearly based on the premise that even in foreign policy Congress should establish policy. The President is to carry out Congressional policy, not to act independently. Independent executive action was thought to be inconsistent with the rule of law and the primacy of Congress in the law-making process.

The Act has proved ineffective in restraining Presidential initiatives involving the armed forces, but the desire to limit Presidential power in foreign policy remains strong in Congress. The majority report of the Iran-Contra Committee presents the case for a greater Congressional role in foreign policy decision-making. The majority report concludes that many serious mistakes would have been avoided had the President not tried to circumvent the legitimate involvement of Congress. The minority report, however, presents a different view of the separation of powers. It concludes that many of the mistakes were just mistakes that could happen in any institutional setting. Moreover, the minority report traces many of the problems to previous attempts by Congress to micromanage foreign policy. According to the minority, reforms such as the Boland amendment have attempted to unconstitutionally restrict the independent foreign policy powers of the President. Congressional reformers have been reluctant to admit the legitimacy in principle of any independent Presidential discretion, but they have at the same time failed to develop any desirable or effective way to limit such discretion in practice.

Ultimately the resolution of this debate must turn on one's view of the Constitutional separation of powers. Does the Constitution create a government based on the notion of legislative supremacy or does it establish co-equal branches of government each with independent discretionary authority?

28

Alexander Hamilton and James Madison

On Congress (1788)

. . . A representative of the United States must be of the age of twenty-five years; must have been seven years a citizen of the United States; must, at the time of his election, be an inhabitant of the State he is to represent; and, during the time of his service, must be in no office under the United States. Under these reasonable limitations, the door of this part of the federal government is open to merit of every description, whether native or adoptive, whether young or old, and without regard to poverty or wealth, or to any particular profession or religious faith. . . .

As it is essential to liberty that the government in general should have a common interest with the people, so it is particularly essential that the branch of it under consideration should have an immediate dependence on, and an intimate sympathy with, the people. Frequent elections are unquestionably the only policy by which this dependence and sympathy can be effectually secured. . . .

[It has been objected that] the House of Representatives is not sufficiently numerous for the reception of all the different classes of citizens in order to combine the interests and feelings of every part of the community, and to produce a true sympathy between the representative body and its constituents. . . .

The idea of an actual representation of all classes of the people by persons of each class is altogether visionary. Unless it were expressly provided in the Constitution that each different occupation should send one or more members, the thing would never take place in practice. Mechanics and manufacturers will always be inclined, with few exceptions, to give their votes to merchants in preference to persons of their own professions or trades. Those discerning citizens are well aware that the mechanic and manufacturing arts furnish the materials of mercantile enterprise and industry. Many of them, indeed, are immediately connected with the operations of commerce. They know that the merchant is their natural patron and friend; and they are aware that however great the confidence they may justly feel in their own good sense, their interests can be more effectually

From Federalists 35, 52, 55, 57, 62, and 63, in *The Federalist*.

promoted by the merchant than by themselves. They are sensible that their habits in life have not been such as to give them those acquired endowments, without which in a deliberative assembly the greatest natural abilities are for the most part useless; and that the influence and weight and superior acquirements of the merchants render them more equal to a contest with any spirit which might happen to infuse itself into the public councils, unfriendly to the manufacturing and trading interests. These considerations and many others that might be mentioned prove, and experience confirms it, that artisans and manufacturers will commonly be disposed to bestow their votes upon merchants and those whom they recommend. We must therefore consider merchants as the natural representatives of all these classes of the community.

With regard to the learned professions, little need be observed; they truly form no distinct interest in society, and according to their situation and talents, will be indiscriminately the objects of the confidence and choice of each other and of other parts of the community.

Nothing remains but the landed interest; and this in a political view, and particularly in relation to taxes, I take to be perfectly united from the wealthiest landlord to the poorest tenant. No tax can be laid on land which will not affect the proprietor of millions of acres as well as the proprietor of a single acre. Every landholder will therefore have a common interest to keep the taxes on land as low as possible; and common interest may always be reckoned upon as the surest bond of sympathy. But if we even could suppose a distinction of interest between the opulent landholder and the middling farmer, what reason is there to conclude that the first would stand a better chance of being deputed to the national legislature than the last? . . .

It is said to be necessary that all classes of citizens should have some of their own number in the representative body in order that their feelings and interests may be the better understood and attended to. But we have seen that this will never happen under any arrangement that leaves the votes of the people free. Where this is the case, the representative body, with too few exceptions to have any influence on the spirit of the government, will be composed of landholders, merchants, and men of the learned professions. But where is the danger that the interests and feelings of the different classes of citizens will not be understood or attended to by these three descriptions of men? Will not the landholder know and feel whatever will promote or injure the interest of landed property? And will he not, from his own interest in that species of property, be sufficiently prone to resist every attempt to prejudice or encumber it? Will not the merchant understand and be disposed to cultivate, as far as may be proper, the interests of the mechanic and manufacturing arts to which his commerce is so nearly allied? Will not the man of the learned profession, who will feel a neutrality to the rivalships between the different branches of industry, be likely to prove an impartial arbiter between them, ready to promote either, so far as it shall appear to him conducive to the general interests of the society? . . .

[Furthermore,] a certain number [of members of the House] at least seems to be necessary to secure the benefits of free consultation and discussion, and to guard against too easy a combination for improper purposes; as, on the other hand, the number ought at most to be kept within a certain limit, in order to avoid the confusion and intemperance of a multitude. In all very numerous assemblies, of whatever character composed, passion never fails to wrest the sceptre from reason. . . .

The number of which this branch of the legislature is to consist, at the outset of the government, will be sixty-five. Within three years a census is to be taken, when the number may be augmented to one for every thirty thousand inhabitants; and within every successive period of ten years the census is to be renewed, and augmentations may continue to be made under the above limitation. It will not be thought an extravagant conjecture that the first census will, at the rate of one for every thirty thousand, raise the number of representatives to at least one hundred. . . . At the expiration of twenty-five years, according to the computed rate of increase, the number of representatives will amount to two hundred; and of fifty years, to four hundred. This is a number which, I presume, will put an end to all fears arising from the smallness of the body. . . .

[Moreover, the members of the House] will enter into the public service under circumstances which cannot fail to produce a temporary affection at least to their constituents. . . .

[T]hose ties which bind the representative to his constituents are strengthened by motives of a more selfish nature. His pride and vanity attach him to a form of government which favors his pretensions and gives him a share in its honors and distinctions. . . .

All these securities, however, would be found very insufficient without the restraint of frequent elections. Hence . . . the House of Representatives is so constituted as to support in the members an habitual recollection of their dependence on the people. Before the sentiments impressed on their minds by the mode of their elevation can be effaced by the exercise of power, they will be compelled to anticipate the moment when their power is to cease, when their exercise of it is to be reviewed, and when they must descend to the level from which they were raised; there forever to remain unless a faithful discharge of their trust shall have established their title to a renewal of it. . . .

Such will be the relation between the House of Representatives and their constituents. Duty, gratitude, interest, ambition itself, are the chords by which they will be bound to fidelity and sympathy with the great mass of the people. . . .

I must be permitted to add [one observation on the constitution of the House of Representatives.] It is, that in all legislative assemblies the greater the number composing them may be, the fewer will be the men who will in fact direct their proceedings. In the first place, the more numerous an assembly may be, of whatever characters composed, the greater is known to be the ascendancy of passion over reason. In the next place, the larger the number, the greater will be the proportion of members of limited information and of weak capacities. Now, it is precisely on characters of this description that the eloquence and address of the few are known to act with all their force. In the ancient republics, where the whole body of the people assembled in person, a single orator, or an artful statesman, was generally seen to rule with as complete a sway as if a sceptre had been placed in his single hand. On the same principle, the more multitudinous a representative assembly may be rendered, the more it will partake of the infirmities incident to collective meetings of the people. Ignorance will be the dupe of cunning, and passion the slave of sophistry and declamation. The people can never err more than in supposing that by multiplying their representatives beyond a certain limit, they strengthen the barrier against the government of a few. Experience will forever admonish them that, on the contrary, *after securing a sufficient number for the purposes of safety, of local information, and of diffusive sympathy with the whole society,* they will counteract their own views by every addition to their representatives. The countenance of the government may become more democratic, but the soul that animates it will be more oligarchic. The machine will be enlarged, but the fewer, and often the more secret, will be the springs by which its motions are directed. . . .

* * * * * * * * * *

I. The qualifications proposed for senators, as distinguished from those of representatives, consist in a more advanced age and a longer period of citizenship. A senator must be thirty years of age at least; as a representative must be twenty-five. And the former must have been a citizen nine years; as seven years are required for the latter. The propriety of these distinctions is explained by the nature of the senatorial trust, which, requiring greater extent of information and stability of character, requires at the same time that the senator should have reached a period of life most likely to supply these advantages; and which, participating immediately in transactions with foreign nations, ought to be exercised by none who are not thoroughly weaned from the prepossessions and habits incident to foreign birth and education. The term of nine years appears to be a prudent mediocrity between a total exclusion of adopted citizens, whose merits and talents may claim a share in the public confidence, and an indiscriminate and hasty admission of them, which might create a channel for foreign influence on the national councils.

II. It is equally unnecessary to dilate on the appointment of senators by the State legislatures. Among the various modes which might have been devised for constituting this branch of the government, that which has been proposed by the convention is probably the most congenial with the public opinion. It is recommended by the double advantage of favoring a select appointment, and of giving to the State governments such an agency in the formation of the federal government as must secure the authority of the former, and may form a convenient link between the two systems.

III. The equality of representation in the Senate is another point, which, being evidently the result of compromise between the opposite pretensions of the large and the small States, does not call for much discussion. If indeed it be right, that among a people thoroughly incorporated into one nation, every district ought to have a *proportional* share in the government, and that among independent and sovereign States, bound together by a simple league, the parties, however unequal in size, ought to have an *equal* share in the common councils, it does not appear to be without some reason that in a compound republic, partaking both of the national and federal character, the government ought to be founded on a mixture of the principles of proportional and equal representation. . . .

IV. The number of senators, and the duration of their appointment, come next to be considered. In order to form an accurate judgment on both these points, it will be proper to inquire into the purposes which are to be answered by a senate; and in order to ascertain these, it will be necessary to review the inconveniences which a republic must suffer from the want of such an institution.

First. It is a misfortune incident to republican government, though in a less degree than to other governments, that those who administer it may forget their obligations to their constituents, and prove unfaithful to their important trust. In this point of view, a senate, as a second branch of the legislative assembly, distinct from, and dividing the power with, a first, must be in all cases a salutary check on the government. It doubles the security to the people, by requiring the concurrence of two distinct bodies in schemes of usurpation or perfidy, where the ambition or corruption of one would otherwise be sufficient. . . . I will barely remark, that as the improbability of sinister combinations will be in proportion to the dissimilarity in the genius of the two bodies, it must be politic to distinguish them from each other by every circumstance which will consist with a due harmony in all proper measures, and with the genuine principles of republican government.

Secondly. The necessity of a senate is not less indicated by the propensity of all single and numerous assemblies to yield to the impulse of sudden and violent passions, and to be seduced by factious leaders into intemperate and pernicious resolutions. . . . All that need be remarked is, that a body which is to correct this infirmity ought itself to be free from it, and consequently ought to be less numerous. It ought, moreover, to possess great firmness, and consequently ought to hold its authority by a tenure of considerable duration.

Thirdly. Another defect to be supplied by a senate lies in a want of due acquaintance with the objects and principles of legislation. It is not possible that an assembly of men called for the most part from pursuits of a private nature, continued in appointment for a short time, and led by no permanent motive to devote the intervals of public occupation to a study of the laws, the affairs, and the comprehensive interests of their country, should, if left wholly to themselves, escape a variety of important errors in the exercise of their legislative trust. It may be affirmed, on the best grounds, that no small share of the present embarrassments of America is to be charged on the blunders of our governments; and that these have proceeded from the heads rather than the hearts of most of the authors of them. What indeed are all the repealing, explaining, and amending laws, which fill and disgrace our voluminous codes, but so many monuments of deficient wisdom; so many impeachments exhibited by each succeeding against each preceding session; so many admonitions to the people, of the value of those aids which may be expected from a well-constituted senate? . . .

Fourthly. The mutability in the public councils arising from a rapid succession of new members, however qualified they may be, points out, in the strongest manner, the necessity of some stable institution in the government. Every new election in the States is found to change one half of the representatives. From this change of men must proceed a change of opinions; and from a change of opinions, a change of measures. But a continual change even of good measures is inconsistent with every rule of prudence and every prospect of success. . . .

In the first place, it forfeits the respect and confidence of other nations, and all the advantages connected with national character. An individual who is observed to be inconstant to his plans, or perhaps to carry on his affairs without any plan at all, is marked at once, by all prudent people, as a speedy victim to his own unsteadiness and folly. His more friendly neighbors may pity him, but all will decline to connect their fortunes with his; and not a few will seize the opportunity of making their fortunes out of his. . . .

The internal effects of a mutable policy are still more calamitous. It poisons the blessing of liberty itself. It will be of little avail to the people, that the laws are made by men of their own choice, if the laws be so voluminous that they cannot be read, or so incoherent that they cannot be understood; if they be repealed or revised before they are promulgated, or undergo such incessant changes that no man, who knows what the law is to-day, can guess what it will be to-morrow. Law is defined to be a rule of action; but how can that be a rule, which is little known, and less fixed?

Another effect of public instability is the unreasonable advantage it gives to the sagacious, the enterprising, and the moneyed few over the industrious and uninformed mass of the people. Every new regulation concerning commerce or revenue, or in any manner affecting the value of the different species of property, presents a new harvest to those who watch the change, and can trace its consequences; a harvest, reared not by themselves, but by the toils and cares of the great body of their fellow-citizens. . . .

In another point of view, great injury results from an unstable government. The want of confidence in the public councils damps every useful undertaking, the success and profit of which may depend on a continuance of existing arrangements. What prudent merchant will hazard his fortunes in any new branch of commerce when he knows not but that his plans may be rendered unlawful before they can be executed? What farmer or manufacturer will lay himself out for the encouragement given to any particular cultivation or establishment, when he can have no assurance that his preparatory labors and advances will not render him a victim to an inconstant government? In a word, no great improvement or laudable enterprise can go forward which requires the auspices of a steady system of national policy.

But the most deplorable effect of all is that diminution of attachment and reverence which steals into the hearts of the people, towards a political system which betrays so many marks of infirmity, and disappoints so many of their flattering hopes. No government, any more than an individual, will long be respected without being truly respectable; nor be truly respectable, without possessing a certain portion of order and stability.

[A fifth] desideratum, illustrating the utility of a senate, is the want of a due sense of national character. Without a select and stable member of the government, the esteem of foreign powers will not only be forfeited by an unenlightened and variable policy, proceeding from the causes already mentioned, but the national councils will not possess that sensibility to the opinion of the world, which is perhaps not less necessary in order to merit, than it is to obtain, its respect and confidence.

An attention to the judgment of other nations is important to every government for two reasons: the one is, that, independently of the merits of any particular plan or measure, it is desirable, on various accounts, that it should appear to other nations as the offspring of a wise and honorable policy; the second is, that in doubtful cases, particularly where the national councils may be warped by some strong passion or momentary interest, the presumed or known opinion of the impartial world may be the best guide that can be followed. What has not America lost by her want of character with foreign nations; and how many errors and follies would she not have avoided, if the justice and propriety of her measures had, in every instance, been previously tried by the light in which they would probably appear to the unbiased part of mankind?

Yet however requisite a sense of national character may be, it is evident that it can never be sufficiently possessed by a numerous and changeable body. It can only be found in a number so small that a sensible degree of the praise and blame of public measures may be the portion of each individual; or in an assembly so durably invested with public trust, that the pride and consequence of its members may be sensibly incorporated with the reputation and prosperity of the community. . . .

I add, as a *sixth* defect, the want, in some important cases, of a due responsibility in the government to the people, arising from that frequency of elections which in other cases produces this responsibility. This remark will, perhaps, appear not only new, but paradoxical. . . .

Responsibility, in order to be reasonable, must be limited to objects within the power of the responsible party, and in order to be effectual, must relate to operations of that power, of which a ready and proper judgment can be formed by the constituents. The objects of government may be divided into two general classes: the one depending on measures which have singly an immediate and sensible operation; the other depending on a succession of well-chosen and well-connected measures, which have a gradual and perhaps unobserved operation.

The importance of the latter description to the collective and permanent welfare of every country, needs no explanation. And yet it is evident that an assembly elected for so short a term as to be unable to provide more than one or two links in a chain of measures, on which the general welfare may essentially depend, ought not to be answerable for the final result, any more than a steward or tenant, engaged for one year, could be justly made to answer for places or improvements which could not be accomplished in less than half a dozen years. Nor is it possible for the people to estimate the *share* of influence which their annual assemblies may respectively have on events resulting from the mixed transactions of several years. It is sufficiently difficult to preserve a personal responsibility in the members of a *numerous* body, for such acts of the body as have an immediate, detached, and palpable operation on its constituents.

The proper remedy for this defect must be an additional body in the legislative department, which, having sufficient permanency to provide for such objects as require a continued attention, and a train of measures, may be justly and effectually answerable for the attainment of those objects.

Thus far I have considered the circumstances which point out the necessity of a well-constructed Senate only as they relate to the representatives of the people. To a people as little blinded by prejudice or corrupted by flattery as those whom I address, I shall not scruple to add, that such an institution may be sometimes necessary as a defence to the people against their own temporary errors and delusions. As the cool and deliberate sense of the community ought, in all governments, and actually will in all free governments ultimately prevail over the views of its rulers; so there are particular moments in public affairs when the people, stimulated by some irregular passion, or some illicit advantage, or misled by the artful misrepresentations of interested men, may call for measures which they themselves will afterwards be the most ready to lament and condemn. In these critical moments, how salutary will be the interference of some temperate and respectable body of citizens, in order to check the misguided career, and to suspend the blow meditated by the people against themselves, until reason, justice, and truth can regain their authority over the public mind? . . .

29

Woodrow Wilson

The Need for Cabinet Government in the United States (1879, 1908, 1889)

. . . At its highest development, *representative* government is that form which best enables a free people to govern themselves. The main object of a representative assembly, therefore, should be the discussion of public business. They should legislate as if in the presence of the whole

From Wilson, "Cabinet Government in the United States," *International Review,* VII (August 1879); *Constitutional Government in the United States,* Columbia University Press, 1908; "An Address on the Nature of Democracy," in *The Papers of Woodrow Wilson,* ed. by Arthur S. Link, Vol. 6, Copyright © 1969 by Princeton University Press. Reprinted by permission of Princeton University Press.

country, because they come under the closest scrutiny and fullest criticism of all the representatives of the country speaking in open and free debate. . . .

Nothing can be more obvious than the fact that the very life of free, popular institutions is dependent upon their breathing the bracing air of thorough, exhaustive, and open discussions, or that select Congressional committees, whose proceedings must from their very nature be secret, are, as means of legislation, dangerous and unwholesome. . . .

Our Government is practically carried on by irresponsible committees. Too few Americans take the trouble to inform themselves as to the methods of Congressional management; and, as a consequence, not many have perceived that almost *absolute* power has fallen into the hands of men whose irresponsibility prevents the regulation of their conduct by the people from whom they derive their authority. . . .

Unless the rules of the House be suspended by a special two-thirds vote, every bill introduced must be referred, without debate, to the proper Standing Committee, with whom rests the privilege of embodying it, or any part of it, in their reports, or of rejecting it altogether. The House very seldom takes any direct action upon any measures introduced by individual members; its votes and discussions are almost entirely confined to committee reports and committee dictation. The whole attitude of business depends upon forty-seven Standing Committees. . . .

This is certainly a phase of representative government peculiar to ourselves. And yet its development was most natural and apparently necessary. It is hardly possible for a body of several hundred men, without official or authoritative leaders, to determine upon any line of action without interminable wrangling and delays injurious to the interests under their care. Left to their own resources, they would be as helpless as any other mass meeting. Without leaders having authority to guide their deliberations and give a definite direction to the movement of legislation; and, moreover, with none of that sense of responsibility which constantly rests upon those whose duty it is to work out to a successful issue the policies which they themselves originate, yet with full power to dictate policies which others must carry into execution,—a recognition of the need of some sort of leadership, and of a division of labor, led to the formation of these Standing Committees, to which are intrusted the shaping of the national policy in the several departments of administration, as well as the prerogatives of the initiative in legislation and leadership in debate. When theoretically viewed, this is an ingenious and apparently harmless device, but one which, in practice, subverts that most fundamental of all the principles of a free State,— the right of the people to a potential voice in their own government. Great measures of legislation are discussed and determined, not conspicuously in public session of the people's representatives, but in the unapproachable privacy of committee rooms.

But what less imperfect means of representative government can we find without stepping beyond the bounds of a true republicanism? . . .

What . . . is Cabinet government? What is the change proposed? Simply to give to the heads of the Executive departments—the members of the Cabinet—seats in Congress, with the privilege of the initiative in legislation and some part of the unbounded privileges now commanded by the Standing Committees. But the advocates of such a change—and they are now not a few—deceive themselves when they maintain that it would not necessarily involve the principle of ministerial responsibility,—that is, the resignation of the Cabinet upon the defeat of any important part of their plans. For, if Cabinet officers sit in Congress as official representatives of the Executive, this principle of responsibility must of necessity come sooner or later to be recognized. Experience would soon demonstrate the practical impossibility of their holding their seats, and continuing to represent the Administration, after they had found themselves unable to gain the consent of a majority to their policy. Their functions would be peculiar. They would constitute a link between the legislative and executive branches of the general Government, and, as representatives of the Executive, must hold the right of the initiative in legislation. Otherwise their position would be an anomalous one, indeed. There would be little danger and evident propriety in extending to them the first right of introducing measures relative to the administration of the several departments; and they could possess such a right without denying the fullest privileges to other members. But, whether granted this initiative or not, the head of each department would undoubtedly find it necessary to take a decided and open stand for or against every measure bearing upon the affairs of his department, by whomsoever introduced. No high-spirited man would long remain in an office in the business of which he was not permitted to pursue a policy which tallied with his own principles and convictions. If defeated by both Houses, he would naturally resign; and not many years would pass before resignation upon defeat would have become an established precedent,—and resignation upon defeat is the essence of responsible government. . . .

But, to give to the President the right to choose whomsoever he pleases as his constitutional advisers, after having constituted Cabinet officers *ex officio* members of Congress, would be to empower him to appoint a limited number of representatives, and would thus be plainly at variance with republican principles. The highest order of responsible government could, then, be established in the United States only by laying upon the President the necessity of selecting his Cabinet from among the number of representatives already chosen by the people. . . .

Under the conditions of Cabinet government . . . full and free debates are sure to take place. For what are these conditions? According as their policy stands or falls, the ministers themselves stand or fall; to the party which supports them each discussion involves a trial of strength with their opponents; upon it depends the amount of their success as a party; while to the opposition the triumph of ministerial plans means still further exclusion from office; their overthrow, accession to power. To each member of the assembly every debate offers an opportunity for placing himself, by able argument, in a position to command a place in any future Cabinet that may be formed from the ranks of his own party; each speech goes to the building up (or the tearing down) of his political fortunes. . . . Plainly, ministers must found their policies, an opposition must found its attacks, upon well-considered principles; for in this open sifting of debate, when every feature of every measure, even to the motives which prompted it, is the subject of out-spoken discussion and keen scrutiny, no chicanery, no party craft, no questionable principles can long hide themselves. . . .

In the severe, distinct, and sharp enunciation of underlying principles, the unsparing examination and telling criticism of opposite positions, the careful, painstaking unravelling of all the issues involved, which are incident to the free discussion of questions of public policy, we see the best, the only effective, means of educating public opinion. . . .

Only a single glance is necessary to discover how utterly Committee government must fail to give effect to public opinion. In the first place, the exclusion of debate prevents the intelligent formation of opinion on the part of the nation at large; in the second place, public opinion, when once formed, finds it impossible to exercise any immediate control over the action of its representatives. There is no one in Congress to speak for the nation. Congress is a conglomeration of inharmonious elements; a collection of men representing each his neighborhood, each his local interest; an alarmingly large proportion of its legislation is "special;" all of it is at best only a limping compromise between the conflicting interests of the innumerable localities represented. There is no guiding or harmonizing power. Are the people in favor of a particular policy,—what means have they of forcing it upon the sovereign legislature at Washington? None but the most imperfect. If they return representatives who favor it (and this is the most they can do), these representatives being under no directing power will find a mutual agreement impracticable among so many, and will finally settle upon some policy which satisfies nobody, removes no difficulty, and makes little definite or valuable provision for the future. They must, indeed, be content with whatever measure the appropriate committee chances to introduce. Responsible ministries, on the other hand, form the policy of their parties; the strength of their party is at their command; the course of legislation turns upon the acceptance or rejection by the Houses of definite and consistent plans upon which they determine. . . . The question would then no longer be, What representatives shall we choose to represent our chances in this haphazard game of legislation? but, What plans of national administration shall we sanction? Would not party programmes mean something then? . . .

But, above and beyond all this, a responsible Cabinet constitutes a link between the executive and legislative departments of the Government which experience declares in the clearest tones to be absolutely necessary in a well-regulated, well-proportioned body politic. None can so well judge of the perfections or imperfections of a law as those who have to administer it. . . .

When we come to speak of the probable influence of responsible Cabinet government upon the development of statesmanship and the renewal of the now perishing growth of statesmanlike qualities, we come upon a vital interest of the whole question. Will it bring with it worthy successors of Hamilton and Webster? Will it replace a leadership of trickery and cunning device by one of ability and moral strength? . . .

Crises give birth and a new growth to statesmanship because they are peculiarly periods of action, in which talents find the widest and the freest scope. They are periods not only of action, but also of unusual opportunity for gaining leadership and a controlling and guiding influence. It is opportunity for transcendent influence, therefore, which calls into active public life a nation's greater minds,—minds which might otherwise remain absorbed in the smaller affairs of private life. And we thus come upon the principle,—a principle which will appear the more incontrovertible the more it is looked into and tested,—that governmental forms will call to the work of administration able minds and strong hearts constantly or infrequently, according as they do or do not afford them at all times an opportunity of gaining and retaining a commanding authority and an undisputed leadership in the nation's councils. Now it certainly needs no argument to prove that government by supreme committees, whose members are appointed at the caprice of an irresponsible party chief, by seniority, because of reputation gained in entirely different fields, or because of partisan shrewdness, is not favorable to a full and strong development of statesmanship. . . . The cardinal feature of Cabinet government, on the other hand, is responsible leadership,—the leadership and authority of a small body of men who have won the foremost places in their party by a display of administrative talents, by evidence of high ability upon the floor of Congress in the stormy play of debate. . . .

It is said . . . that [Cabinet Government] would render the President a mere figure-head, with none of that stability of official tenure, or that traditional dignity, which are necessary to such figure-heads. Would the President's power be curtailed, then, if his Cabinet ministers simply took the place of the Standing Committees? Would it not rather be enlarged? He would then be in fact, and not merely in name, the head of the Government. . . .

The apparently necessary existence of a partisan Executive presents itself to many as a fatal objection to the establishment of the forms of responsible Cabinet government in this country. The President must continue to represent a political party, and must continue to be anxious to surround himself with Cabinet officers who shall always substantially agree with him on all political questions. . . . [However, i]t is not hard to believe that most presidents would find no greater inconvenience, experience no greater unpleasantness, in being at the head of a Cabinet composed of political opponents than in presiding, as they must now occasionally do, over a Cabinet of political friends who are compelled to act in all matters of importance according to the dictation of Standing Committees which are ruled by the opposite party. In the former case, the President may, by the exercise of whatever personal influence he possesses, affect the action of the Cabinet, and, through them, the action of the Houses; in the latter he is absolutely helpless. . . .

But against such a responsible system, the alarm-bell of *centralization* is again sounded, and all those who dread seeing too much authority, too complete control, placed within the reach of the central Government sternly set their faces against any such change. They deceive themselves. There could be no more despotic authority wielded under the forms of free government than our national Congress now exercises. It is a despotism which uses its power with all the caprice, all the scorn for settled policy, all the wild unrestraint which mark the methods of other tyrants as hateful to freedom.

Few of us are ready to suggest a remedy for the evils all deplore. We hope that our system is self-adjusting, and will not need our corrective interference. This is a vain hope! It is no small part of wisdom to know how long an evil ought to be tolerated, to see when the time has come for the people, from whom springs all authority, to speak its doom or prescribe its remedy. . . .

* * * * * * * * * *

. . . It was . . . [the] theory of checks and balances, which I have called the Newtonian theory of government, that prevailed in the convention which framed the Constitution of the United States,—which prevailed over the very different theory of Hamilton, that government was not a thing which you could afford to tie up in a nice poise, as if it were to be held at an inactive equilibrium, but a thing which must every day act with straightforward and unquestionable power, with definite purpose and consistent force, choosing its policies and making good its authority, like a single organism,—the theory which would have seemed to Darwin the theory of nature itself, the nature of men as well as the nature of animal organisms. Dominated by the immediate forces and aspirations of their own day, ruled in thought and action by the great contest in which they had found themselves engaged, to hold the royal power off from arbitrary interference with their interests and their liberties, they allowed themselves to become more interested in providing checks to government than in supplying it with energy and securing to it the necessary certainty and consistency of action. . . .

The most serious success of the convention in applying Whig theory to the government they were constructing was the complete separation of Congress and the executive which they effected. The English Whigs fought for long to oust the Crown from the power and intimate influence it had had in the House of Commons through its control of members' seats and its corrupting power of patronage: they succeeded only in placing the leaders of the Commons itself in executive authority in the stead of the Crown. The real executive authority of the English government is vested in the ministers of the day, who are in effect a committee of the House of Commons, and legislature and executive work together under a common party organization. The one is only an agency of the other: the ministers act for their party in the House. The separation of parliament and the Crown which the reformers of the early part of the last century finally succeeded in effecting was not, in fact, a separation of the legislature from the executive, but only a separation of the real from the nominal executive. . . . But our constitution-makers did their work during the earlier part of the struggle, when it seemed merely a contest to offset the authority of the king with effectual checks, and long before it had become evident that the outcome would be the substitution of an executive which represented the popular house for one which did not. . . .

[The results of] this absolute application of early Whig theory to the practice of our government . . . has been that, so far as the government itself is concerned, there is but one national voice in the country, and that is the voice of the President. His isolation has quite unexpectedly been his exaltation. The House represents localities, is made up of individuals whose interest is the interest of separate and scattered constituencies, who are drawn together, indeed, under a master, the Speaker, but who are controlled by no national force except that of their party, a force outside the government rather than within it. The Senate represents in its turn regions and interests distinguished by many conflicting and contrasted purposes, united only by exterior party organization and a party spirit not generated within the chamber itself. Only the President represents the country as a whole, and the President himself is cooperatively bound to the houses only by the machinery and discipline of party, not as a person and functionary, but as a member of an outside organization which exists quite independently of the executive and legislature.

It is extraordinary the influence the early Whig theory of political dynamics has had amongst us and the far-reaching consequences which have ensued from it. It is far from being a democratic theory. It is, on the contrary, a theory whose avowed object, at any rate as applied in America, was to keep government at a sort of mechanical equipoise by means of a standing amicable contest among its several organic parts, each of which it seeks to make representative of a special interest in the nation. It is particularly intended to prevent the will of the people as a whole from having at any moment an unobstructed sweep and ascendency. And yet in every step we have taken with the intention of making our governments more democratic, we have punctiliously kept to Whig mechanics. . . .

[Our government] can be solidified and drawn to system only by the external authority of party, an organization outside the government and independent of it. Not being drawn together by any system provided in our constitutions, being laid apart, on the contrary, in a sort of jealous dispersion and analysis by Whig theory enacted into law, it has been necessary to keep the several parts of the government in some kind of workable combination by outside pressure, by the closely knit imperative discipline of party, a body that has no constitutional cleavages and is free to tie itself into legislative and executive functions alike by its systematic control of the *personnel* of all branches of the government. . . .

But with us, who affect never to allow party majorities to get in complete control of governmental machinery if we can prevent it by constitutional obstacles, party programs are made up outside legislative chambers, by conventions constituted under the direction of independent politicians,—politicians, I mean, who are, at any rate in respect of that function, independent of the responsibilities of office and of public action; and these independent conventions, not charged with the responsibility of carrying out their programs, actually outline the policy of administrations and dictate the action of Congress, the irresponsible dictating to the responsible, and so, it may be, destroying the very responsibility itself. . . .

The satisfactions of power must be very great to attract so many men of unusual gifts to attempt the hazardous and little honored business of party management. We have made it necessary that we should have "bosses" and that they and their lieutenants should assign offices by appointment, but it is a very difficult and precarious business which they undertake. . . . [T]he people look askance at [this business] and often with a sudden disgust turn upon it. . . . [These occasional outbursts of discontent] come when the people happen to realize that under existing party machinery they have virtually no control at all over nominations for office, and that, having no real control over the choice of candidates, they are cut off from exercising real representative self-government,—that they have been solemnly taking part in a farce. . . .

[Y]et at the best the control which party exercises over government is uncertain. There can be, whether for the voter or for the managing politician himself, little more than a presumption that what party managers propose and promise will be done, for the separation of authority between the several organs of government itself still stands in the way. . . .

The principle of change, if change there is to be, should spring out of this question: Have we had enough of the literal translation of Whig theory into practice, into constitutions? Are we ready to make our legislatures and our executives our real bodies politic, instead of our parties? If we are, we must think less of checks and balances and more of coordinated power, less of separation of functions and more of the synthesis of action. If we are, we must decrease the number and complexity of the things the voter is called upon to do; concentrate his attention upon a few men whom he can make responsible, a few objects upon which he can easily center his purpose; make parties his instruments and not his masters by an utter simplification of the things he is expected to look to. . . .

* * * * * * * * * *

. . . [F]or us who stand in the dusty, matter-of-fact world of to-day there is even a touch of pathos in recollections of the ardour for democratic liberty that filled the air of Europe and America a century ago with such quickening influences. We may even catch ourselves regretting that the inoculations of experience have closed our systems against the infections of hopeful revolution. . . .

It is common to say, in explanation of our regret that that dawn and youth of democracy's day is past; that our principles are cooler now and more circumspect, with the coolness and circumspection of advanced years. It seems to some that as our sinews have hardened our enthusiasms have become tamer and more decorous: that as experience has grown idealism has declined.

But to speak thus is to speak with old self-deception as to the character of our politics. If we are suffering disappointment, it is the disappointment of an awakening: we were dreaming. For we never had any business harkening to Rousseau or consorting with Europe in revolutionary sentiment. Our Government, founded one hundred years ago, was no type of an experiment in advanced democracy, as we allowed Europe and even ourselves to suppose; it was simply an adaptation of English constitutional government. If we suffered Europe to study our institutions as instances in point touching experimentation in politics *she was the more deceived.* If we began the *first* century of our national existence under a similar impression ourselves, there is the greater reason why we should start out upon a *new* century of national life with accurate conceptions about our place in history. It is my modest purpose to-night to make such contribution as I may to this end. I shall, therefore, ask you to note:

(1) That there are certain influences astir in this century which make for democracy the world over, and that these influences owe their origin in part to the radical thought of the last century; but that it was not such forces that made us democratic, nor are we responsible for them.

(2) That, so far from owing our governments to these general influences, we began, not by carrying out any theory, but by simply carrying out a history, inventing nothing, only establishing a specialized species of English government. That we founded, not Democracy, but Constitutional government, in America.

(3) That the government which we set up thus in a quite normal manner has nevertheless *changed greatly* under our hands by reason both of growth and of the operation of the general democratic forces,—the European or rather world-wide democratic forces, of which I have spoken; and

(4) That the very *size* to which our governmental organism has attained, and more particularly this new connection of its character and destiny with the character and destiny of the common democratic forces of the age of steam and electricity have created new *problems of organization* which it behooves us to meet. . . .

First, then, for the forces which are bringing in democratic temper and method the world over. . . . They are freedom of thought and the diffusion of enlightenment among the people. Steam and electricity have cooperated with systematic popular education to accomplish this diffusion. The progress of popular education and the progress of democracy have been inseparable. The publication of their great *Encyclopedia* by Diderot and his associates in France in the last century was the sure sign of the change that was setting in. Learning was turning its face away from the studious few to the curious many. The intellectual movement of the modern time was emerging from the narrow courses of scholastic thought and beginning *to spread itself abroad* over the extended, if shallow, levels of the common mind. . . .

Organized popular education is, after all, however, only *one* of the quickening influences which have been producing the general enlightenment which is everywhere becoming the promise of general liberty: or, rather, it is only part of a great whole vastly larger than itself. Schools are but separated seedbeds in which only the staple thoughts of the steady and stay-at-home people are prepared and nursed. Not much of the world, after all, goes to school in the school-house. But through the mighty influences of commerce and the press *the world itself has become a school.* The air is alive with the multitudinous voices of information. . . .

Looked at in the large, the newspaper press is a type of democracy, bringing all men without distinction under comment made by any man without distinction; every topic reduced to a common standard of news; everything noted and argued about by everybody. . . .

In the newspapers, it is true, there is but little concerted between the writers; little but piece-meal opinion is created by their comment and argument; there is no common voice amidst their counsellings. But the *aggregate* voice thunders with tremendous volume; and that aggregate voice is 'public opinion.' Popular education and cheap printing and travel vastly thicken the ranks of thinkers everywhere that their influence is felt, and by rousing the multitude to take *knowledge* of the affairs of government directly prepare the time when the multitude will, so far as possible, take *charge* of the affairs of government,—the time when, to repeat Carlyle's phrase, democracy will become palpably extant.

But, mighty as such forces are,—democratic as they are,—no one can fail to see that they are inadequate to *produce of themselves* such a government as ours. There is little in them of *constructive* efficacy. They could not of themselves build any government at all. They are critical, analytical, questioning, quizzing forces;—but not architectural, not powers that devise and build. The influences of popular education, of the press, of travel, of commerce, of the innumerable agencies which nowadays send knowledge and thought in quick pulsations through every part and member of society, do not necessarily mold men for effective endeavour. They may only confuse and paralyze the mind with their myriad stinging lashes of excitement. They may only strengthen the impression that 'the world's a stage,' and that no one need do more than sit and look on through his ready glass, the newspaper. They overwhelm one with impressions, but do they give stalwartness to his manhood; do they make his hand any steadier on the plow, or his purpose any clearer with reference to the duties of the moment? They stream light about him, it may be, but do they clear his vision? Is he better able to see because they give him countless things to look at? Is he better able to judge because they fill him with a delusive sense of knowing everything? Activity of mind is not necessarily strength of mind. It may manifest itself in mere dumb show; it may run into jigs as well as into strenuous work at noble tasks. A man's farm does not yield its fruit the more abundantly in its season because he reads the world's news in the papers. A merchant's shipments do not multiply because he studies history. Banking is none the less hazardous to the banker's capital or taxing to his powers because the best writing of the best essayists is to be bought cheap.

Having thus expanded my first point by exhibiting the general forces of that democracy which we recognize as belonging to the age and to the world at large, rather than exclusively or even characteristically to ourselves, I now ask you to turn to view by contrast our origins in politics.

How different were the forces back of us! Nothing establishes the republican state save trained capacity for self-government, practical aptitude for public affairs, habitual soberness and temperateness of united action. When we look back to the moderate sagacity and steadfast, self- contained habit in self-government of the men to whom we owe the establishment of our institutions in the United States we are at once made aware that there is no communion between their democracy and the radical thought and restless spirit called by that name in Europe. . . . Democracy in America and in the English colonies, has had, almost from the first, a truly organic growth. There was nothing revolutionary in its movements: it had not to overthrow other polities; it had only to organize itself. . . .

Our democracy, plainly, was not a body of doctrine: it was a stage of development. Our democratic state was not a piece of developed theory, but a piece of developed habit. It was not created by mere aspirations or by new faith; it was built up by slow custom. . . .

Governments such as ours are founded upon discussion and government by discussion comes as late in political as scientific thought in intellectual development. It is a habit of state life created by long-established circumstance, and possible for a nation only in the adult age of its political life. The people which successfully maintains it must have gone through a period of political training which shall have prepared it by gradual steps of acquired privilege for assuming the entire control of its affairs. Long and slowly widening experience in local self-direction must have prepared them for national self-direction. . . .

So much for my second main point, as to the origins of our institutions in constitutional precedents rather than in democratic precepts. It is my object to consider, in the third place, the changes which have been or may be wrought in our institutions by means of the influences of the age, of our own growth as a political organism, and of our adulterated populations. . . .

[T]he forces peculiar to the new civilization of our day, and not only these but also the restless forces of European democratic thought and anarchic turbulence brought to us in such alarming masses by immigration, have deeply affected and may deeply modify the forms and habits of our politics.

All *vital* governments,—and by vital governments I mean those which have life *in their outlying members,* as well as life in their heads,—all systems in which self-government indeed *lives* and retains its self-possession must be governments *by neighbours,* by peoples homogeneous . . .

characterized within by the existence of easy neighborly knowledge of each other among their members. Not foreseeing steam and electricity or the diffusions of news and knowledge which we have witnessed, our fathers were right in thinking it impossible for the government which they had founded to spread without strain or break over the whole of the continent. Were not California now as near neighbor to the Atlantic states as Massachusetts once was to New York, national self-government on our present scale would assuredly hardly be possible or conceivable even. Modern science, scarcely less than our pliancy and steadiness in political habit, may be said to have created the United States of to-day. . . .

I wish to give full weight to these great advantages of our big and strenuous and yet familiar way of conducting affairs; but I wish at the same time to make very plain the influences which are pointing towards threatening changes in our politics—changes which threaten loss of organic wholeness and soundness in carrying on an efficient and honest government. The union of strength with bigness depends upon the maintenance of *character,* and it is just the character of the nation which is being most deeply affected and modified by the enormous immigration which year after year pours into the country from Europe: our own temperate blood, schooled to self-possession and to the measured conduct of self-government is receiving a constant infusion and yearly experiencing a partial corruption of foreign blood: our own equable habits have been crossed with the feverish habits of the restless old world. . . .

What was true of our early circumstances is not true of our present. We are not now simply carrying out under normal conditions the principles and habits of English constitutional history. Our tasks of construction are not done: we have, not simply to conduct but also to preserve and freshly adjust our government. Europe has sent her habits to us; and she has sent also her political philosophy,—that philosophy which has never been purged by the cold bath of practical politics. The communion which we did not have at first with her heated and mistaken ambitions, with her radical speculative habit in politics, with her readiness to experiment in forms of government, we may possibly have to suffer now that we are receiving her populations. Not only printing and steam and electricity have gotten hold of us to expand our English civilization, but also those general, and yet to us alien, forces of democracy of which I have spoken; and these are apt to tell disastrously upon our Saxon habits in government. . . .

I am now to speak of the *new problems* which have been prepared for our solution by reason of our growth and of the effects of immigration, and which may require as much political capacity for their proper solution as any that faced the architects of our government.

These problems are chiefly problems of organization and leadership. Were the nation homogeneous, were it composed simply of later generations of the same stock by which our institutions were planted, few adjustments of the old machinery of our politics would, perhaps, be necessary to meet the exigencies of growth. But every added element of variety, particularly every added element of foreign variety, complicates even the simpler questions of politics. The dangers attending that variety which is heterogeneity in so vast an organism as ours are of course the dangers of *disintegration,* nothing less: and it is unwise to think these dangers remote and merely contingent because they are not as yet pressing. We are conscious of oneness as a nation, of vitality, of strength, of progress; but are we often conscious of common thought in the concrete things of national policy? Does not our legislation, rather, wear the features of a vast conglomerate? Are we conscious of any national leadership: are we not, rather, dimly conscious of being pulled in a score of directions by a score of crossing influences and contending forces?

This vast and miscellaneous democracy of ours must be led: its giant faculties must be schooled and directed. Leadership cannot belong to the multitude: masses of men cannot be self-directed. Neither can groups of communities. We speak of the sovereignty of the people, but that sovereignty, we know very well, is of a peculiar sort, quite unlike the sovereignty of a king or of a small easily concerting group of confident men. It is judicial merely, not creative. It passes judgment or gives sanction, but it cannot direct or suggest. It furnishes standards, not policies. Questions of government are infinitely complex questions, and no multitude can of themselves form clear-cut, comprehensive, consistent conclusions touching them. And yet without such conclusions, without single and prompt purposes, government cannot be carried on. Neither legislation nor administration can be done at the ballot-box. The people can only accept the governing act of representatives. But the size of the modern democracy necessitates the exercise of persuasive power by dominant minds in the shaping of popular judgments in a very different way from that in which it was exercised in former times. . . . [All self-governing nations of to-day] are not a single audience within sound of an orator's voice; but a thousand audiences. Their actions do not spring from a single thrill of feeling, but from slow conclusions following upon much talk. The talk must slowly percolate through the whole mass. It cannot be sent through them straight like the pulse which is stirred by the call of a trumpet. A score of platforms in every neighborhood must ring with the insistent voice of controversy; and for a few hundreds who hear what is said by the public speakers, many thousands must read of the matter in the newspapers, discuss it interjectionally at the breakfast table, desultorily in the street-cars, laconically on the streets, dogmatically at dinner. And all this with a certain advantage, of course. Through so many stages of consideration passion cannot possibly hold out. *It gets chilled by over-exposure.* It finds the modern popular state organized for giving and hearing counsel in such a way that those who give it must be careful that it is such counsel as will *wear well,* and those who hear it handle and examine it enough to *test* its wearing qualities to the utmost.

All this, however, when looked at from another point of view, but illustrates an infinite difficulty of achieving *energy and organization.* There is a certain peril almost of disintegration attending such phenomena.

Everyone now knows familiarly enough how we accomplished the wide aggregations of self-government characteristic of the modern time, how we have articulated governments as vast and yet as whole as continents like our own. The instrumentality has been *representation,* of which the ancient world knew nothing, and lacking which it always lacked national integration. . . .

But not until recently have we been able to see the full effects of thus sending men to legislate for us at capitals distant the breadth of a continent. It makes the leaders of our politics many of them mere names to our consciousness instead of real persons, whom we have seen and heard, and whom we know. We have to accept rumors concerning them, we have to know them through the variously coloured accounts of others: we can seldom test our impressions of their sincerity by standing with them face to face. . . .

Our separation from our leaders is the greater peril because democratic government more than any other needs organization in order to escape disintegration, and it can have organization only by full knowledge of its leaders and full confidence in them. Just because it is a vast body to be persuaded it must know its persuaders: in order to be effective it must always have choice of men who are *impersonated policies.* Just because none but the finest mental batteries, with pure metals and unadulterated acids, can send a current through so huge and yet so rare a medium as democratic opinion, it is the more necessary to look to the excellence of these instrumentalities. There is no permanent place in democratic leadership except for him who 'hath clean hands and a pure heart'. If other men come temporarily into power among us, it is because we cut our leadership up into so many little parts and do not subject any one man to the purifying influences of centered responsibility. Never before was consistent leadership so necessary; never before was it necessary to concert measures over so vast areas, to adjust laws to so many interests, to make a compact and intelligible unit out of so many fractions, to maintain a central and dominant force where there are so many forces. . . .

Though we be the most law-abiding and law-directed nation in the world, law has not yet attained to such efficacy among us as to frame or adjust or administer *itself*. It may restrain but it cannot lead us: and I believe that unless we concentrate legislative leadership, leadership, i.e., in progressive policy, unless we give leave to our nationality and practice to it *by* such concentration, we shall sooner or later suffer something like national paralysis in the face of emergencies. We have no one in Congress who stands for the nation. Each man stands but for his part of the nation,—and so management and combination, which may be effected in the dark, are given the place that should be held by centered and responsible leadership, which would of necessity work in the focus of the national gaze. . . .

I believe that the only way in which we can preserve our nationality in its integrity and its old-time originative force in the face of growth and imported change is by *concentrating* it, by putting leaders forward vested with abundant authority in the conception and execution of policy. There is plenty of the old vitality in our national character to tell, if you will but give it leave. Give it leave and it will the more impress and mold those who come to us from abroad. I believe that we have not made enough of leadership.

> "A people is but the attempt of many
> To rise to the completer life of one;
> And those who live as models for the mass
> Are singly of more value than they all."

We shall not again have a true national life until we compact it by such legislative leadership as other nations have. But, once thus compacted and embodied, our nationality is safe. An accute English historical scholar has said that "the Americans of the United States are a nation because they once obeyed a king": we shall remain a nation only by obeying leaders. . . .

30

Lloyd N. Cutler

To Form a Government (1980)

Our society was one of the first to write a Constitution. This reflected the confident conviction of the Enlightenment that explicit written arrangements could be devised to structure a government that would be neither tyrannical nor impotent in its time, and to allow for future amendment as experience and change might require.

We are all children of this faith in a rational written arrangement for governing. Our faith should encourage us to consider changes in our Constitution—for which the framers explicitly allowed. . . .

A particular shortcoming in need of a remedy is the structural inability of our government to propose, legislate and administer a balanced program for governing. In parliamentary terms, one might say that under the U.S. Constitution it is not feasible to "form a Government." The separation of powers between the legislative and executive branches, whatever its merits in 1793, has become a structure that almost guarantees stalemate today. . . .

We elect one presidential candidate over another on the basis of our judgment of the overall program he presents, his ability to carry it out, and his capacity to adapt his program to new developments as they arise. We elected President Carter, whose program included, as one of its most important elements, the successful completion of the SALT II negotiations that his two predecessors had been conducting since 1972. . . .

But because we do not "form a Government," it [was] not . . . possible for President Carter to carry out this major part of his program. . . .

Treaties may indeed present special cases, and I do not argue here for any change in the historic two-thirds requirement. But our inability to "form a Government" able to ratify SALT II is replicated regularly over the whole range of legislation required to carry out any president's overall program, foreign and domestic. Although the enactment of legislation takes only a simple majority of both Houses, that majority is very difficult to achieve. Any part of the president's legislative program may be defeated, or amended into an entirely different measure, so that the legislative record of any presidency may bear little resemblance to the overall program the president wanted to carry out. Energy and the budget provide two . . . critical examples [from the Carter presidency]. Indeed, SALT II itself could have been presented for approval by a simple majority of each House under existing arms control legislation, but the administration deemed this task even more difficult than achieving a two-thirds vote in the Senate. And this difficulty is of course compounded when the president's party does not even hold the majority of the seats in both Houses, as was the case from 1946 to 1948, from 1954 to 1960 and from 1968 to 1976— or almost half the duration of the last seven administrations.

The Constitution does not require or even permit in such a case the holding of a new election, in which those who oppose the president can seek office to carry out their own overall program. Indeed, the opponents of each element of the president's overall program usually have a different makeup from one element to another. They would probably be unable to get together on any overall program of their own, or to obtain congressional votes to carry it out. As a result the stalemate continues, and because we do not form a Government, we have no overall program at all. We cannot fairly hold the president accountable for the success or failure of his overall program, because he lacks the constitutional power to put that program into effect.

Compare this with the structure of parliamentary governments. . . . The majority elects a Premier or Prime Minister from among its number, and he selects other leading members of the majority as the members of his Cabinet. The majority as a whole is responsible for forming and conducting the "government." If any key part of its overall program is rejected by the legislature, or if a vote of "no confidence" is carried, the "Government" must resign and either a new "Government" must be formed out of the existing legislature or a new legislative election must be held. If the program *is* legislated, the public can judge the results, and can decide at the next regular election whether to reelect the majority or turn it out. At all times the voting public knows who is in charge, and whom to hold accountable for success or failure.

In a parliamentary system, it is the duty of each majority member of the legislature to vote for each element of the Government's program, and the Government possesses the means to punish members if they do not. In a very real sense, each member's political and electoral future is tied to the fate of the Government his majority has formed. Politically speaking, he lives or dies by whether that Government lives or dies.

President Carter's party [had] a much larger majority percentage in both Houses of Congress than Chancellor Schmidt or Mrs. Thatcher. But [such] comfortable [majorities do] not even begin to assure that President Carter or any other president can rely on [those majorities] to vote for each element of his program. No member of [a] majority has the constitutional duty or the practical political need to vote for each element of the president's program.

Neither the president nor the leaders of the legislative majority have the means to punish him if he does not. In the famous phrase of Joe Jacobs, the fight manager, "it's every man for theirself."

Let me cite one example. In the British House of Commons, just as in our own House, some of the majority leaders are called the Whips. In the Commons, the Whips do just what their title implies. If the government cares about the pending vote, they "whip" the fellow members of the majority into compliance, under pain of party discipline if a member disobeys. On the most important votes, the leaders invoke what is called a three-line whip, which must be obeyed on pain of resignation or expulsion from the party.

In our House, the Majority Whip, who happens to be one of our very best Democratic legislators, can himself feel free to leave his Democratic president and the rest of the House Democratic leadership on a crucial vote, if he believes it important to his constituency and his conscience to vote the other way. When he does so, he is not expected or required to resign his leadership post; indeed he is back a few hours later "whipping" his fellow members of the majority to vote with the president and the leadership on some other issue. But all other members are equally free to vote against the president and the leadership when they feel it important to do so. The president and the leaders have a few sticks and carrots they can use to punish or reward, but nothing even approaching the power that Mrs. Thatcher's Government or Chancellor Schmidt's Government can wield against any errant member of the majority.

I am hardly the first to notice this fault. As Judge Carl McGowan has reminded us, that "young and rising academic star in the field of political science, Woodrow Wilson—happily unaware of what the future held for him in terms of successive domination of, and defeat by, the Congress—despaired in the late nineteenth century of the weakness of the Executive Branch vis-à-vis the Legislative, so much so that he concluded that a coalescence of the two in the style of English parliamentary government was the only hope."

As Wilson put it, "power and strict accountability for its use are the essential constituents of good Government." Our separation of executive and legislative power fractions power and prevents accountability.

In drawing this comparison, I am not blind to the proven weaknesses of parliamentary government, or to the virtues which our forefathers saw in separating the executive from the legislature. In particular, the parliamentary system lacks the ability of a separate and vigilant legislature to investigate and curb the abuse of power by an arbitrary or corrupt executive. Our own recent history has underscored this virtue of separating these two branches.

Moreover, our division of executive from legislative responsibility also means that a great many more voters are represented in positions of power, rather than as mere members of a "loyal opposition." . . .

But these virtues of separation are not without their costs. I believe these costs have been mounting in the last half-century, and that it is time to examine whether we can reduce the costs of separation without losing its virtues. . . . We are not about to revise our own Constitution so as to incorporate a true parliamentary system. But we do need to find a way of coming closer to the parliamentary concept of "forming a Government," under which the elected majority is able to carry out an overall program, and is held accountable for its success or failure.

There are several reasons why it is far more important in [the 1980s] than it was in 1940, 1900 or 1800 for our government to have the capability to formulate and carry out an overall program.

1) The first reason is that government is now constantly required to make a different kind of choice than usually in the past, a kind for which it is difficult to obtain a broad consensus. That kind of choice, which one may call "allocative," has become the fundamental challenge to government today. As a recent newspaper article put it:

> The domestic programs of the last two decades are no longer seen as broad campaigns to curb pollution or end poverty or improve health care. As these programs have filtered down through an expanding network of regulation, they single out winners and losers.

. . . During the second half of this century, our government has adopted a wide variety of national goals. Many of these goals—checking inflation, spurring economic growth, reducing unemployment, protecting our national security, assuring equal opportunity, increasing social security, cleaning up the environment, improving energy efficiency—conflict with one another, and all of them compete for the same resources. . . .

For balancing choices like these, a kind of political triage, it is almost impossible to achieve a broad consensus. Every group will be against some part of the balance. If the "losers" on each item are given a veto on that part of the balance, a sensible balance cannot be struck.

2) The second reason is that we live in an increasingly interdependent world. What happens in distant places is now just as consequential for our security and our economy as what happens in Seattle or Miami. . . . We have to respond as quickly and decisively to what happens abroad as to what happens within the portion of this world system that is governed under our Constitution.

New problems requiring new adjustments come up even more frequently over the foreign horizon than the domestic one. . . . The government has to be able to adapt its overall program to deal with each such event as it arises, and it has to be able to execute the adapted program with reasonable dispatch. Many of these adaptations—such as changes in the levels and direction of military and economic assistance—require joint action by the president and the Congress, something that is far from automatic under our system. And when Congress does act, it is prone to impose statutory conditions or prohibitions that fetter the president's policy discretion to negotiate an appropriate assistance package or to adapt it to fit even later developments. . . .

Indeed, the doubt that Congress will approve a presidential foreign policy initiative has seriously compromised our ability to make binding agreements with nations that "form a Government." Given the fate of SALT II and lesser treaties, and the frequent congressional vetoes of other foreign policy actions, other nations now realize that our executive branch commitments are not as binding as theirs, that Congress may block any agreement at all, and that at the very least they must hold something back for a subsequent round of bargaining with the Congress.

3) The third reason is the change in Congress and its relationship to the Executive. . . . There have been the well-intended democratic reforms of Congress, and the enormous growth of the professional legislative staff. The former ability of the president to sit down with ten or fifteen leaders in each House, and to agree on a program which those leaders could carry through Congress, has virtually disappeared. The committee chairmen and the leaders no longer have the instruments of power that once enabled them to lead. . . .

It is useful to compare this modern failure of our governmental structure with its earlier classic successes. There can be no structural fault, it might be said, so long as an FDR could put through an entire anti-depression program in 100 days, or an LBJ could enact a broad program for social justice three decades later. These infrequent exceptions, however, confirm the general rule of stalemate. . . .

If we decide we want the capability of forming a Government, the only way to do so is to amend the Constitution. Amending the Constitution, of course, is extremely difficult. Since 1793, when the Bill of Rights was added, we have amended the Constitution only 16 times. . . . But none has touched the basic separation of executive and legislative powers.

The most one can hope for is a set of modest changes that would make our structure work somewhat more in the manner of a parliamentary system, with somewhat less separation between the executive and the legislature than now exists.

There are several candidate proposals. Here are some of the more interesting ideas:

1) We now vote for a presidential candidate and a vice-presidential candidate as an inseparable team. We could provide that in presidential election years, voters in each congressional district would be required to vote for a trio of candidates, as a team, for president, vice-president and the House of Representatives. This would tie the political fortunes of the party's presidential

and congressional candidates to one another, and provide some incentive for sticking together after they are elected. Such a proposal could be combined with a four-year term for members of the House of Representatives. This would tie the presidential and congressional candidates even more closely, and has the added virtue of providing members with greater protection against the pressures of single-issue political groups. This combination is the brainchild of Congressman Jonathan Bingham of New York, and is now pending before the Congress.

In our bicameral legislature, the logic of the Bingham proposal would suggest that the inseparable trio of candidates for president, vice-president and member of Congress be expanded to a quintet including the two Senators, who would also have the same four-year term. But no one has challenged the gods of the Olympian Senate by advancing such a proposal.

2) Another idea is to permit or require the president to select 50 percent of his Cabinet from among the members of his party in the Senate and House, who would retain their seats while serving in the Cabinet. This would be only a minor infringement on the constitutional principle of separation of powers, but it would require a change in Article I, Section 6, which provides that "no person holding any office under the United States shall be a member of either house during his continuance in office." It would tend to increase the intimacy between the executive and the legislature, and add to their sense of collective responsibility. The 50-percent test would leave the president adequate room to bring other qualified persons into his Cabinet, even though they do not hold elective office.

3) A third intriguing suggestion is to provide the president with the power, to be exercised not more than once in his term, to dissolve Congress and call for new congressional elections. This is the power now vested in the president under the French Constitution. It would provide the opportunity that does not now exist to break an executive-legislative impasse, and to let the public decide whether it wishes to elect Senators and Congressmen who *will* legislate the president's overall program.

For obvious reasons, the president would invoke such a power only as a last resort, but his potential ability to do so could have a powerful influence on congressional responses to his initiatives. . . .

4) Another variant on the same idea is that in addition to empowering the president to call for new congressional elections, we might empower a majority or two-thirds of both Houses to call for new presidential elections. . . .

[My] point [here] is not to persuade the reader of the virtue of any particular amendment. I am far from persuaded myself. But I am convinced of these propositions:

We need to do better than we have in "forming a Government" for this country, and this need is becoming more acute.

The structure of our Constitution prevents us from doing significantly better.

It is time to start thinking and debating about whether and how to correct this structural fault.

31

Bruce F. Freed

House Reforms Enhance Subcommittees' Power (1976)

The Legislative Reorganization Act of 1946 reduced the number of standing House committees from 48 to 19. But as that reduction took place at the top, an explosion occurred at the bottom as the 19 standing committees spawned 106 subcommittees in the 80th Congress.

The creation of a larger network of subcommittees did not mean that power gravitated there. Until the early 1970s, most House committees were run by chairmen who were able to operate as autocrats, keeping most of the authority for themselves and a few senior members and giving very little to junior members or subcommittees. That was the case on the Education and Labor, Interior and Armed Services Committees.

Those chairmen could dominate committees because they had the backing of Speaker Sam Rayburn (D Texas 1913-61) and Speaker John W. McCormack (D Mass. 1928-71) and the support, or at least the acquiescence, of their panels' members. They could pack subcommittees with members who would do their bidding, decide how active subcommittees would be, when they would meet, what legislation they would consider and how much staff, if any, they could have.

The day of the committee autocrat began to wane with the revival of the House Democratic Caucus in 1969 and the retirement of McCormack as

From Freed, "House Reforms Enhance Subcommittees' Power," *Current American Government,* published by Congressional Quarterly, Spring, 1976. Reprinted by permission.

speaker in 1970. With McCormack's exit, these chairmen lost a powerful ally at the top of the House power structure.

The caucus revival meant that moderate and liberal Democrats elected to the House in the late 1950s and in the 1960s, who were frustrated by the old committee system that tended to freeze them out of power, at last had a vehicle to change the rules. They began to undercut the power of committee chairmen and strengthen that of the subcommittees where their potential power lay. . . .

The move to strengthen the autonomy of House subcommittees began in 1971 and culminated in decisions taken by the Democrats in the winter of 1974-75 forcing the Ways and Means Committee to establish subcommittees and authorizing subcommittee chairmen and ranking minority members to hire their own staff.

As a result, subcommittees have taken over from their parent committees much of the legislative workload. They are drafting major legislation in important areas such as energy and the environment, and their chairmen are managing bills on the House floor. On some committees, such as Interior, subcommittees are operating autonomously with large staffs of their own.

Because of these changes, some House members and congressional observers now talk about "subcommittee government" much as they had spoken of "committee government" in the 1960s. . . . [A] member of the House Rules Committee, which schedules most legislation for floor action, reports that subcommittees are reporting more legislation intact, without full committee consideration. . . .

Despite general support by Democrats for strengthening subcommittees, some members are beginning to question whether the shift has gone too far. . . . [M]any members are asking the following questions:

- Has the House become too fragmented?
- Are subcommittees operating too autonomously?
- Has the House leadership exerted strong enough leadership to effectively coordinate the efforts of the committees in drafting legislation and scheduling controversial measures for floor action?

"We're going the way of the Senate," warned an influential southern member. "We've spread the action by giving subcommittees more power and making it possible for members to play more active roles on them. But there's nothing at this point to coordinate what all these bodies are doing and to place some checks on their growing independence." . . .

The thrust of the changes was twofold: the authority of committee chairmen was curbed, and that of subcommittee leaders was strengthened. . . .

The great losers in the House power struggle of the late 1960s and early 1970s have been the committee chairmen. By the time the 94th Congress organized, they had given up much of their control to the heads of their panel's subcommittees and to junior committee members. . . .

Their powers have been pared in several ways through changes in House rules and positions adopted by the Democratic Caucus.

1. No House member can be chairman of more than one legislative subcommittee. That, in effect, made it possible to break the hold of senior conservative Democrats on key subcommittees and opened up opportunities for middle-level and junior Democrats on them. . . .

[2.] The new rules established a Democratic caucus on each committee and forced committee chairmen to start sharing authority with the panel's other Democratic members. It did that by giving the committee caucus the authority to select subcommittee chairmen, establish subcommittee jurisdictions, . . . and guarantee all members a major subcommittee assignment where vacancies make that possible.

Committee chairmen no longer could kill legislation quietly by pocketing it. Now they are required to refer bills to subcommittees within two weeks. . . .

3. All committees with more than 20 members must establish at least four subcommittees. This was directed at Ways and Means, which had operated without subcommittees during most of the 16-year chairmanship of Rep. Wilbur D. Mills (D Ark.). . . .

4. Another change was in subcommittee staffing. Subcommittee chairmen and ranking minority subcommittee members are now authorized to hire one staff person each to work directly for them on their subcommittees. A former representative's aide called this development "crucial." "Whether a subcommittee has its own staff is literally an index of how independent a subcommittee is," he said.

5. Committees are required to have written rules. This opened the way to checking the arbitrary power of committee chairmen and institutionalizing the subcommittees.

6. In an effort to spread participation even further, the Democratic Caucus in December, 1974, restricted senior Democrats to membership on only two of a committee's subcommittees. . . .

7. As of the beginning of the 94th Congress, chairmen of all the Appropriations subcommittees have to be approved by the House Democratic Caucus. . . .

The impact has been much greater on those committees that until recently had a tradition of strong central direction. In these cases—Ways and Means, Interstate and Foreign Commerce and Interior are prime examples—the committees have tended to become fragmented, with the chairman exercising much weaker control over the full committee and the subcommittees becoming much more aggressive. . . .

The strengthening of subcommittees has created more work for House members. Subcommittees are now holding more hearings and preparing more reports. . . .

With the broadening of committee opportunities, junior members have had to cope with a heavier workload as they participate more in subcommittee deliberations and floor debate. . . .

Subcommittee chairmen are gaining more influence on the House floor. On routine legislation, there is a growing tendency for them rather than the committee chairmen to give the cues to members on how to vote. . . .

On major legislation, subcommittee chairmen are dealing almost as equals with the chairmen of other committees. . . .

The increased independence and expertise of subcommittees have placed greater burdens on the House Democratic leadership. "In the past, the speaker only needed to think about a bill just as it approached the House floor," said Rep. Richard Bolling (D Mo.). "Now the speaker has to know what's happening at the subcommittee level where legislation is being generated. . . ."

According to [one political scientist], the speaker "under this new situation needs a big leadership staff to move around and find out what's going on." As he sees it, the problem is Speaker Carl Albert's (D Okla.) approach to leadership. "He is used to the situation where he deals with three or four leaders, where Ways and Means bills come to the House floor and are passed under a closed rule."

The strengthening of subcommittees, and the concurrent decentralization of the House, has its pluses and minuses, says Bolling. . . . For the most part, he considers "the pluses greater. You get greater specialization and oversight when you decentralize."

But the changes have had a much deeper impact and have transformed the character and operations of the House. They have made the legislative process much more untidy, freewheeling and unpredictable and have introduced more competing elements.

Among the benefits cited are the following:

More members have been brought into the legislative process, not only as subcommittee chairmen but as members of subcommittees that can play a more independent legislative role. . . .

With subcommittees playing a more active legislative and oversight role, citizens and interest groups have greater access to the legislative process in the House because of overlapping committee and subcommittee jurisdictions.

Independent subcommittees can delve into more legislative and oversight areas without interference from committee chairmen. . . .

Some House members and their staffs, however, feel decentralization of the House committee structure has gone too far, that subcommittees are becoming too autonomous. This trend, they say, makes it much more difficult to lead the House, delays the legislative process and exacerbates the problem of overlapping committee jurisdictions. . . . They could also lead to abuses by subcommittees, skeptics say.

The subcommittee reforms . . . have had contradictory effects. They have come at a time when House Democrats have been trying to pull themselves together by increasing the powers of the speaker, the Democratic Steering and Policy Committee and the House Democratic Caucus to better coordinate party policy on legislation and make the 290 Democrats a more coherent body. . . .

It has encouraged jurisdictional fights not only between committees but between subcommittees and committees. . . .

Committee jurisdictions, however, are only part of the problem. Another is the tendency for subcommittees to take on what some see as a life of their own. . . .

[Foley (D Wash.) said] "The rules today tend to be unbalanced because they pare the power of the committee chairmen, but place few restrictions on that of the subcommittee chairmen. I don't think this was really conscious, but it's there."

Foley cited as an example the rule requiring committee chairmen to refer bills to subcommittees within two weeks after they have been submitted to the panel. "That was due to old chairmen pigeonholing a bill," he said. "But there's no rule saying subcommittee chairmen can't pigeonhole a bill." . . .

32

William F. Connelly, Jr.

In Defense of Congress (1990)

In *Mr. Smith Goes to Washington* Jimmy Stewart pits his idealism against a Senate institution corrupted by party bosses, self-serving politicians and a cynical press. In this morality play, the pure-hearted, populist, good government reformer finally wins out over the Senate agents of selfish special interests, thus simultaneously reaffirming our faith in American political principles and our disdain for the institutions which embody those ideals. This classic competition is a mainstay of American political culture. This gap between our ideals and our institutions, according to Samuel Huntington, leads to a "disharmony" at the core of American politics. This dissonance is at once our defect and our virtue. Congress lives this conflict every day; Congress is this conflict.

Mr. Smith reflects the conventional wisdom on Congress. All too often, we begin with the facile assumption that members of Congress are venal, selfish, corrupt pawns of special interest groups, and that consequently, Congress, as an institution, is oriented to the status quo. Because special interests dominate Congress, the argument goes, the institution suffers from a bias against change. The political science literature, at times, seems to be a distillation of this conventional wisdom. For example, David Mayhew argues that members of Congress are single-minded seekers of re-election. Similarly, Morris Fiorina insists that Congress is the keystone to the rise of a Washington establishment in which "iron triangles" or "subgovernments" made up of interest groups, congressional committees and corresponding executive agencies, control policymaking. Members of Congress, Fiorina suggests, are more interested in constituent casework and porkbarrel activities than policy, and consequently "[p]ublic policy emerges from the system almost as an afterthought." The typical law is simply the sum total of enough bargains to build a majority coalition, according to this somewhat cynical view.

The self-interested model of political behavior may be a useful starting point in understanding Congress, but by itself, this perspective cannot explain the enormous complexity of the policy process. For starters, a desire for re-election forces congressmen to be attentive to the needs of others, namely, voters. Moreover, elections create incentives for members to reach out to as

By permission of the author.

many different individuals and groups as possible. Finally, while attentiveness to constituents' interests may be analytically distinct from a concern for good public policy, in practice the two are often linked.

Richard Fenno broadens Mayhew's analysis, pointing out that members of Congress may, in fact, have three goals: re-election, power within the institution, and good public policy. Fenno's analysis of individual motivation raises the possibility that members may be moved by institutional imperatives as well as personal ambition. At a minimum, members are constantly confronted with a conflict between their parochial re-election or constituency interests and Congress' collective responsibility to the nation. Combining these goals is often a challenge for Congress and its members. Indeed, every congressman is both a lawmaker for the nation and a representative for a part of that nation, consequently members are regularly torn between their "homestyle" and "hillstyle."

In order to understand Congress, however, we must look at the impact of the institution on the behavior of congressmen as well as the political environment in which Congress operates.

Institutional Analysis

Institutional analysis argues, according to Christopher J. Deering, that Congress is more than the sum of its parts, and that Congress, as an institution, has a life of its own. The Founders understood that institutions can affect the behavior of men, as they structured our institutions so as to curb the selfish tendencies of men and promote public interests. They tried to pit ambition against ambition and, perhaps more importantly, promote institutional loyalty and a sense of institutional responsibility.

Politicians elected to Congress, for example, naturally will be inclined to defend the institutional prerogatives of Congress against the President. Similarly, Senators will be quick to defend the Senate against encroachments by the House, and vice versa. As parties and committees came to play a role in Congress, members of political parties fought for their party's interest, and members of congressional committees tried to protect the institutional prerogatives of their committee. In each instance, members' "self-interests" are redefined, and they, in effect, adopt new constituencies apart from the original constituency that elected them to Congress. Members are constantly confronted with the dilemma of serving different, overlapping, and often conflicting constituencies, and are thus forced to choose between conflicting loyalties. Moreover, by virtue of their participation and involvement with these different institutions, members gain a stake in the success of each, learning what Tocqueville called "the art of associating." Members learn to identify with the institution, and a sense of "team play" or esprit de corp develops.

The Founders hoped for more from their constitutional institutions than ambition checking ambition, or a channeling of the competition among the "various and interfering interests." They wanted their institutional structures to promote deliberation, to enable the peoples' representatives to "refine and enlarge the public view." In Federalist #71 Hamilton suggests that the "republican principle requires that the deliberate sense of the community" should prevail.

> When occasions present themselves in which the *interests* of the people are at variance with their *inclinations,* it is the duty of the persons whom they have appointed to be the guardians of those interests to withstand the temporary delusion in order to give them time and opportunity for more cool and sedate reflection.

The Founders did not assume, as we so often do today, an easy identification between interests and inclinations, or needs and desires, whether of an individual, a group, or the nation. They recognized that reason must arbitrate between inclinations in order to arrive at interests. They did not expect that legislators exercising only an instrumental rationality would choose the best means to the ends demanded by factions or even simple majorities. Rather, they knew that legislating requires drawing conclusions, which is to say, choosing ends. They understood that persuasion is the crucial link between inclinations and decisions. They sought to promote deliberation through the structure of their institutions in spite of the din and clamor of vying factions. With Congress they succeeded tolerably well.

In Congress, whether on the Senate floor or in House committees, persuasion matters. In *The Senate Nobody Knows,* Bernard Asbell reports former Maine Senator Edmund Muskie's argument that in Congress knowledge is power: "People have all sorts of conspiratorial theories on what constitutes power in the Senate. . . . But real power up there comes from doing your work and knowing what you're talking about. Power is the ability to change someone's mind." Senator Richard Lugar or Congressman Lee Hamilton on foreign affairs, Sam Nunn or Les Aspin on national security, Bill Frenzel or Nancy Johnson on taxes, all are examples of members whose reputation and influence in Congress hinge on their competence and expertise. Such "workhorses" may not be as flashy as many congressional "showhorses," but their power is palpable and it is based on doing their homework and being persuasive; the institution rewards diligence and expertise. To be certain, neither chamber offers us what public interest groups like Common Cause demand, namely, pure deliberation on the merits of public policy in some sort of ideal olympian aloofness. Nevertheless, the structure of Congress promotes deliberation within the context of a political environment consisting of thousands of contending organized interests.

Key organizational characteristics of Congress—the role of bicameralism, House and Senate rules and procedures, and congressional parties and committees—all are in some fashion a function of constitutional structure and influence the activity of congressmen. We shall consider them in turn.

Bicameralism. One of the most important constitutional principles governing the behavior of Congress is bicameralism, which divides the legislature into the House and Senate. In order to counter the dominance of the legislature, the Founders, according to the *Federalist,* sought to "divide the legislature into different brances; and to render them, by different modes of election and different principles of action, as little connected with each other as the nature of their common functions and their common dependence on the society will admit."

The House and Senate are very different. The old joke about the Capitol Hill tourists who, after seeing the House and Senate, ask: "Okay, now where is Congress?" is very much on point. Upon closer inspection, new observers of congressional behavior are frequently amazed at how different the two chambers are in practice. Indeed, it is almost difficult to think of them as one institution after examining more carefully the operating principles of the House and Senate. Perhaps the most convincing evidence of the extraordinary difference between the two is the distrust and even hostility between the chambers, even when they are both controlled by the same party. Following unwritten norms, for example, members of each chamber refrain from even mentioning directly "the other chamber" in floor debate. This behavioral norm is a direct function of the constitutional principle of bicameralism.

Although the Founders saw bicameralism as a means of limiting legislative power relative to the executive branch, they also saw it as a way to strengthen the legislative function. In principle, a legislature should represent and deliberate. Two chambers chosen "by different modes of election" can better represent, albeit in different ways, the needs of their constituents. Furthermore, two chambers motivated by "different principles of action" will inevitably clash. House and Senate conflict and competition will just as inevitably augment the twin virtues or functions of any democratic legislature, namely public deliberation and consensus building.

The institutional conflict bicameralism invites has long been seen as a roadblock to policy change. Bicameralism contributes to the proliferation of what are frequently called "multiple veto points" in the legislative process, the implication being that this makes it easier to slow or halt the progress of legislation. Those same points in the legislative process, including committee and subcommittee consideration in each house, however, can also be seen as "multiple access points" inviting the added energy of policy entrepreneurs inside and outside of Congress. Bicameralism has the potential to make the legislative process more dynamic. During the '86 tax reform effort, for example, the competition between the Democratic controlled House Ways and

Means Committee and the Republican led Senate Finance Committee clearly helped advance the reformers' goal.

Moreover, while bicameralism divides the legislative power, it also focuses that power through a division of labor of sorts. The "advise and consent" clauses of the Constitution grant the Senate a special role in the area of foreign policy through its role in confirming executive nominations and ratifying treaties. Consequently, the Senate Foreign Relations Committee is generally recognized as being more prestigious than the House Foreign Affairs Committee. Similarly, the Constitution's "originating" clause, requiring all tax measures to originate in the House, historically has given the House Ways and Means Committee an advantage over the Senate Finance Committee in setting tax policy. The "specialization" these clauses engender are examples of the Constitution focusing power at the same time as it divides power. Again, bicameralism can strengthen as well as weaken Congress.

The specialization of the House and Senate in the legislative process can be seen in broader terms. The enormous difference between the operating principles (or what Madison called "different principles of action") of the two chambers flows from their constitutionally distinct "modes of election." Differences in the rules and procedures of the House and Senate derive, in the first instance, from the Constitution. For example, due to two year terms, smaller districts and a 435 person body, House members generally are closer to their constituents and less familiar with one another. The 100 persons in the Senate, drawn from fifty statewide districts for six year terms, are noted for a greater distance from constituents and greater familiarity with one another.

Rules and Procedures. The more partisan House thrives on conflict, whereas the Senate operates on the principles of comity and consensus. The House is governed by majority rule and the Senate by a time consuming concern for individual members' rights. Ironically, given its much larger size, the House is more efficient than the more deliberative Senate. The House is more efficient because of its detailed and elaborate rules; in the Senate, informal, yet painstaking, negotiations between the Majority and Minority Leaders determine floor scheduling of legislation. House members tend to be issue specialists and House Committees are reputed to be the "workshops" of Congress. Senators more often are generalists, more dependent on their larger staffs, and inclined to be less deferential to committee legislation on the floor. The Senate, as witness *Mr. Smith Goes to Washington,* is famous for its tradition of "unlimited debate," the filibuster, and the lack of a germaneness rule for floor amendments. Generally speaking, committees are more important in the House, and floor action more important in the Senate.

The differences between the House and Senate are exemplified by the way bills come to the floor. The powerful House Rules Committee, clearly an arm of the Speaker and majority party, acts as a gatekeeper in deciding which bills reach the floor with a "rule" or special order governing floor amendments and length of debate. Party leaders in the Senate, on the other hand, carefully hammer out "unanimous consent agreements" establishing ground rules for floor consideration of legislation in often lengthy negotiations. Because of its constant and literal attention to the principle of unanimous consent, it is surprising that the Senate is able to function at all, given that any member can object at virtually any time to a motion to proceed. In light of the range of ideologies and interests, and the panoply of issues debated on the floor, it is impressive that the Senate is able to act at all.

The different "principles of action" or functions of the House and Senate ultimately reflect differing expressions of democracy, referred to by political scientists as "adversary democracy" and "unitary democracy." While each chamber partakes of both forms of democracy, the characteristics of the former are more commonly found in the House and those of the latter in the Senate. According to Ross K. Baker, adversary democracy is "the faithful representation of the various interests of their states and districts by Senators and House members and the practice of bargaining among members for benefits and protections for those constituencies. Unitary democracy, in contrast, involves the establishment of a consensus among legislators on what is the common or national interest." Bicameralism enables Congress simultaneously to exhibit the character of both a pluralist democracy and a consensual democracy. Congress balances the desire to be responsive to its larger environment with need to act responsibly in the public interest.

Political Parties and Committees in Congress. Congress organizes itself for business by party and by committee. The two principles of organization conflict, thus augmenting "complex majority rule." Parties and committees are both more important in the House than in the Senate.

Party leadership in Congress is weak relative to parliamentary systems of government. Congressional leaders generally have less control over members' elections, and due to our separation of powers, constituents have relatively more control over members' elections, thus making congressmen more responsive to voters than to leaders. Moreover, Senate leadership is weaker than House leadership. The leader's "right to recognition" provides a case in point. The Speaker of the House, a constitutional officer, has the active right to recognize who on the House Floor gets to speak next. The Senate Majority leader, who at best is *primus inter pares* in the Senate, has a passive right to be recognized first whenever he stands up on the floor of the Senate.

Given the relative weakness of congressional party leadership, scholars have questioned whether there is real party leadership in our decentralized national legislature. Clearly Congress is not the President, and executive style leadership does not exist on the Hill. Nevertheless, leadership does exist depending on the timing and the issue. As a general rule, the more nationally salient an issue becomes, the more likely party leaders will get involved. On some issues, such as the 1990 budget summit with the President, party leaders play a more significant role. On most issues, however, partisan policy distinctions are less important than constituency service concerns. In such cases, committee or subcommittee leaders often may play a greater role. Especially in the Senate, there is even the possibility that individual "policy entrepreneurs" may come to the fore.

Party leaders in Congress regularly confront the dilemma of reconciling two diverse goals: party harmony and policy victory. This is a dilemma less likely to confront parliamentary leaders than congressional leaders in our separation of powers system because parliamentary leaders have more control over members' elections. Congressional leaders can "make their troops happy" by contributing what resources they have to aiding members' re-elections, or they can sharpen partisan conflict and force difficult policy choices on their followers. This basic division plagues leaders of both parties in both houses, but more so the House Democrats and House Republicans. Indeed, this division defines the two wings of the Democratic and Republican party caucuses in the House. The liberal wing of the House Democratic caucus, represented by the Democratic Study Group, is more inclined to urge a strategy of sharpening policy differences between the parties. Similarly, the House Republicans' conservative wing, embodied in Newt Gingrich's Conservative Opportunity Society, also frequently calls for heightening the obvious national policy divisions between the parties. Moderate elements in both parties are quick to argue that "all politics is local" and that "Congress is not Parliament," or in other words, the party should not jeopardize its members' reelection by artificially fueling principled national party differences. Who is right? Which strategy should party leaders follow: the pursuit of party harmony or policy victory? There may not be a right answer. Given the separation of powers and the nature of congressional elections, Congress is clearly not Parliament, but neither is it the local school board. Congress must address both local and national interests. Congress must be responsive and responsible.

At least since Woodrow Wilson, congressional reformers have criticized the strength of standing committees as well as the lack of strong party leadership. Wilson's lament that "congressional government is committee government" focuses on the seeming tendency of the committee system to augment the fragmentation and disintegration of the policy process. Reformers' incessant demands to style Congress after the British (but not the Italian!) Parliament, ignore the contributions the committee system makes to increasing policy-making coherence.

Committees sprang up naturally in the early decades of the Republic. They enabled Congress to cope with its own growth in numbers and workload, as well as, increasing demands on the federal government. The division of labor allows Congress to concentrate expertise, to address more systematically a constantly growing array of issues, and to exercise oversight of executive agencies more effectively. Following the committee reforms of the 1970's which "opened up" committees and weakened the role of committee chairmen, scholars are beginning to reassess the contribution of strong committees to policy coherence. Congressman David Price, while still a professor, recognized the potential for committees to act as a corrective to congressional fragmentation by structuring institutional incentives: "In other systems legislators are induced to do serious work by the prospect of promotion and preferment within the party or the government. In the American setting, where these structures have less to offer, the committee system represents an alternative incentive-producing mechanism indigenous to the legislature. Without committees, American legislators would have many fewer inducements to, and opportunities for, serious legislative and oversight activities."

Environmental Analysis

As should be evident by now, discussing the internal organization of Congress—committees, parties and bicameralism—makes little sense without taking into consideration the larger system or environment within which the institution operates. Elements in the environment of Congress include voters and constituents, public opinion, the media, interest groups, executive agencies, states, and the President. For our purposes here, we shall focus on interest groups and the President.

Interest Groups. If interest groups and lobbyists did not exist, Congress would have to invent them. The relationship is symbiotic, with lobbying groups of all stripes acting as virtual service bureaus in providing Congress with information. The caricature of lobbyists as wining, dining and bribing congressmen is misleading. As Bernard Asbell points out, "more than ninety-nine percent of lobbying effort is spent . . . [on] trying to persuade minds through facts and reason; some of it performed extremely well, some with comic incompetence." Moreover, there is a built in quality control in the lobbying process. All lobbyists speak from a known perspective, compete with many others arguing different positions, and need to maintain their reputation for telling the truth if they wish to be heard another day.

Who are these "special interests" Americans love to hate? They are us with our different interests, passions and opinions. Some critics argue that not all interests are able to organize; that there is a bias among organized interests favoring the status quo and those with the resources, education and skills to organize. Others respond that money does not automatically translate into power, or access into influence. During the 1970's, for example, AT & T, one of the most powerful corporations in America lost in its bid to halt the drive for deregulation of the telecommunications industry. During the 1986 tax reform effort enormous organized interests were unable to defeat the bill largely because they disagreed among themselves. The business of America may be business, but "Big Business" is hardly monolithic, and certainly not all powerful. More importantly, however, in a democracy "numbers" may be as significant as money, and in a media age, the ability to generate publicity can offset the talents of expensive lobbyists. Ralph Nader, and other "public interest advocates," have mastered tactics dating back at least to the Boston Tea Party.

Critics also argue that broad based interests, as opposed to narrow special interests or single issue groups, are inherently difficult to organize. While undoubtably true, the advent in the last three decades of electronic media based strategies and computerized direct mail or telemarketing techniques have helped to balance the ledger between so-called special and public interest groups, as witness the proliferation of reform organizations. Critics argue further that the broadest interest, the public interest, is impossible to organize and therefore chronically underrepresented.

Madison's response would likely be that the Constitution, and the institutions it created, *is* the organization of the public interest. For example, congressional elections offer an incentive to challengers to reach out to unorganized interests and disaffected individuals. And again, Congress as a deliberative institution can do more than merely register pressures from a myriad of interested factions. How else can one explain the elimination from the tax rolls in 1986 of six million of the working poor—what some have called the single largest act of legislative redistribution in recent decades? Once again, conventional critiques based on single-cause, self-interest models of political behavior are inadequate for explaining the complexities of Congress. Finally, it is worth noting that frequent attempts this century to regulate "special interest" lobbying have commonly run afoul of the First Amendment's protection of free speech, the right of association, and the right to petition government. Congress must remain open to its environment for this reason and because members owe their elections to their constituents, not to parties or Prime Ministers.

The President. Congress and the President need each other. They are like two halves of a whole; neither is a complete policy making process unto itself. Consequently policymaking is neither tidy nor especially efficient. Yet each brings its peculiar virtues to the relationship. The executive can act with energy, secrecy, dispatch and direction. Congress is deliberate. Congress is very good at talking, at second guessing the executive and equivocating. Congress is good at watching the executive, at providing oversight. It is a very open institution with few secrets. Congress is responsive to the multiplicity of interests and opinions in the nation; it is a good incubator for new ideas, including ones often borrowed by Presidents. In sum, Congress is creative chaos, but a chaos that on occasion can respond to the discipline of Presidents, public opinion or crises. The separation of powers makes Congress more open to its environment.

The Separation of Powers

The suggestion that the separation of powers prevents things from being done fails to recognize the differentiation of roles or functions at the heart of this central constitutional principle. Like bicameralism, the separation of powers does not merely limit the abuse of power, it also provides for the effective use of power. Congress is a powerful national legislature because of the institutional independence afforded by the separation of powers. Congress never fully surrenders to the executive its responsibility. The institutional independence or separation of Congress from the executive means that as a legislature it has more affirmative responsibility than its parliamentary counterpart. This institutional separation, in turn, allows Congress to more effectively exercise its legislative functions of deliberation and representation. Congress is more democratically responsive given its independence from the executive. Members are better able to represent the particular needs of their constituents, and the frequency of elections requires that they do so. Unlike a parliament, Congress cannot force consensus. If, for example, a general consensus on how to solve the budget deficit is lacking, Congress cannot create such a consensus. In this sense, Congress is more responsive to the whole as well as the parts. But at the same time Congress is designed to be more responsive, it also has more independent policy responsibility.

The functional separation of powers means that the two "political branches" can compete while they complement each other. Like the competition between the two houses of Congress, that between the president and Congress introduces more energy into the policy process. The competition also invites a more open and public deliberation between the branches, which in turn invites greater policy responsiveness.

A recent case study entitled *Taxing Choices: The Politics of Tax Reform* examines the passage of the 1986 Tax Reform Act in light of three different models of the policy process. The first is the traditional pluralist/incrementalist model which argues that policy results from bargaining and accommodation among disparate interests. The second is the presidential/majoritarian model which might be called the traditional model of reform politics in which presidents, acting on mandates, sweep in a new order of things. The third model, called the "new politics of reform," involves a combination of ideas, experts, the media, and political entrepreneurs. The authors of *Taxing Choices* argue that no one model adequately explains the passage of the 1986 Tax Reform Act. In effect, they argue that the policymaking process in America is all of the above, though they do not explain how that is possible.

James W. Ceaser, in an earlier discussion of the separation of powers, provides some insight into the flexibility of our constitutional order:

> The doctrine of separation of powers . . . does not define fully—nor was it ever intended to define fully—the exact character of the policy-making process. The Constitution is not completely silent or neutral about the character of the policy-making process, but in the final analysis there is not one single constitutional model for the policy-making function but only constitutional limits within which models must be constructed.

Ceaser argues that the flexibility of the separation of powers explains how the same constitutional order can provide for the era of congressional dominance in the 19th century *and* the rise of the imperial presidency in the period from the 1930's to the 1970's. However, the flexible and dynamic quality of the separation of powers might also explain the simultaneous existence of different "systems of power" as the authors of *Taxing Choices* call their three models. The constitutional separation of powers means that the American political system potentially and simultaneously is all three depending on timing, issues and participants.

The same congressional structure that requires members to be especially attentive to constituents, also allows some members to become, on occasion, policy entrepreneurs, and it invites a public deliberation about the merits of good public policy. The efforts of Ways and Means Chairman Dan Rostenkowski during passage of the '86 Tax Reform act in many ways typified pluralist politics. Senator Bill Bradley's and Congressman Jack Kemp's contributions to the '86 tax reform act are good examples of policy entrepreneurship. The competition between President Reagan and congressional Democrats provides an example of public deliberation.

Taken as a whole, the '86 tax reform effort depicts an institutionally bounded pluralist free market of policy entrepreneurship that combines the best elements of pluralism, party government and academic or bureaucratic expertise. Ambitious individuals operating within constitutional institutions that enhance competition and conflict and surrounded by a demanding environment make for a dynamic politics that is a far cry from the conventional image of Congress as suffering from a bias against change. Like the capitalist free markets described by economists, a pluralist free market regulated ("bounded") by institutional structures augments the energy and creativity that goes into policymaking. Politicians, beginning in a self-interested quest for re-election, search for compelling ideas and the support of diverse interests, and end by serving the public interest.

33

David K. Nichols

Reforming the Budget Reforms (1990)

Which came first: the deficit crisis or the reform of the budget process? As with all such profound questions there is no easy answer. The current cycle of budget process reform began in 1974, when the deficit was still at modest levels by today's standards. Surely the most important impetus for the 1974 Congressional Budget and Impoundment Control Act was Watergate and the extensive use of the impoundment power by Nixon. But even back in 1974 many members of Congress signed on to reform because they hoped that it would make Congress more fiscally responsible. As deficits have grown we have seen ever more reform and proposals for reform. Since 1974 Congress has adopted Gramm-Rudman-Hollins I and Gramm-Rudman-Hollins II, and Presidents Reagan and Bush have continually called for a balanced budget amendment and the line-item veto. Before this article is published Gramm-Rudman-Hollins III may well have been signed into law. Only the horror movie Friday the 13th has had more sequels than budget reform over the last sixteen years.

There is a tendency in American politics to assume that a bad policy is the result of a defective process. The policy in Viet Nam was a disaster, so we immediately jump to the conclusion that there is an imperial presidency that must be checked by the War powers act. Reagan sells arms to Iran and some members of the White House staff decide to expand private sector initiatives to foreign policy and we have another crisis in the foreign policy-making process. The budget deficit reaches unprecedented levels and we look for ways to change the process. We jump so quickly to look for an institutional solution to our policy problems that we sometimes neglect a more obvious cause—sometimes people make bad decisions. No process can protect the system from that very important fact.

The case of budget reform clearly demonstrates that when you attempt to cure policy problems with institutional reforms you will often fail. If you expect too much from institutional reform you are likely to receive very little. In fact, exaggerated expectations will probably lead you to adopt reforms that will make the situation worse in the long-run. This is especially true if you

By permission of the author.

add to a set of unrealistic goals a lack of appreciation of the institutional structures and incentives that shape the policy process. All too often reformers adopt or propose reforms that will not work because they are at odds with the institutional character of the Congress and the Presidency or because they fail to create any realistic incentives for responsible behavior on the part of either branch.

Is this an argument against institutional reform? In part, yes. As even our most revolutionary founder might say, institutions should not be changed for light or transient causes. Institutional reform may well have unintended consequences. Even if it does not, it may serve as an escape from the more immediate policy problem; it is easier to talk about budget reform than to discuss what programmatic cuts and what new taxes are necessary in order to cut the deficits. But sometimes reform is necessary. Sometimes it is clear that the current process isn't working and something needs to be done. The budget process looks like it is such a case. But before any more reform is undertaken, we need to think carefully about what the goals of procedural reform should be and what are realistic means to achieve those goals given the Constitutional structures within which policy is made.

Past Efforts at Reform

The correlation between budget deficits and budget reform is nothing new. For much of the 19th century there was little concern with the budget process and few formal procedures. The reason was that for much of the early 19th century there were budget surpluses. In 1834 Andrew Jackson even managed the remarkable feat of paying off the national debt. So for a very brief period not only was there no deficit, but there was no debt. The Civil War, however, brought large deficits and also the first major budget reform—the creation of separate appropriations committees to determine the level of funding for activities authorized by Congress. This was a lasting change, but it is worth noting that there was still no Presidential budget or Presidential budget office. The Secretary of the Treasury would assemble the requests from the various departments, but no one in the government, either in the legislative or the executive branch looked at the budget as a whole.

The increasing costs of veterans benefits, several economic downturns, and the Spanish American war gave rise to budget deficits around the turn of the century, and those deficits, in turn gave rise to calls for budget reform. Many people thought that someone should have responsibility for preparing a unified budget. But as the economy improved and the deficits dropped in the pre-World War I period, the movement for budget reform lost its momentum. It was only following the expansion of the national government and the national debt in World War I that Congress finally created the Bureau of the Budget in 1921. The BOB was originally a mere accounting agency. But during the crisis of the Depression, FDR tied the Bureau more directly to the President and made it an important part of the policy-making process. In 1971 Richard Nixon further enhanced its policy role and its Presidential ties when he initiated the transformation of the Bureau of the Budget into the Office of Management and the Budget. By the early Reagan years every one knew that the Director of OMB was David Stockman, and everyone knew that he was one of the most important policy-makers in Washington.

As is the case with the recent flurry of institutional reform, each of these earlier reforms was precipitated by economic problems. Unlike the recent reforms, however, the earlier changes in the budget process had more limited goals and for the most part reflected the institutional capacities of the president and Congress. The pre-1974 reforms did not promise balanced budgets or an end to economic problems. When these reformers saw that government budgeting was becoming increasingly complex, they turned first to the committee system of Congress to address the need for more specialized scrutiny. When fears arose regarding the lack of a unified budget the reformers looked not to Congress but to the most unified Constitutional office, the Presidency. Recent reformers have failed to appreciate the importance of both modest goals and institutional capacities.

Congressional Budget Reform

The 1974 Budget and Impoundment Control Act provides the first and in some respects best example. As we have noted, the primary impetus for the act came from the desire of Congress to restrict the powers of President Nixon, particularly his widespread use of the impoundment power. But the act did much more than restrict impoundment. It created a Congressional Budget Office to provide Congress with a source of information on the budget that would be independent of the executive branch. Moreover, it established a Senate and a House Budget Committee, that would for the first time prepare a unified Congressional budget resolution, a resolution that would look at both overall expenditures and overall revenues.

It was not just the impoundment portions of the act that were directed against Nixon and the "imperial presidency." The creation of the CBO and the establishment of a Congressional budget process culminating in a Congressional budget were also seen as ways to transfer authority over the budget process from the President to Congress. By providing Congress with independent information and allowing the Congress to develop its own unified budget, the reformers in Congress thought that they would be able to take much of the initiative on budgetary matters from the hands of the President.

Conservatives supported the new process because it promised to restrict the funding authority of the appropriations committees. The budget resolutions would establish a ceiling for appropriations in each area of government spending. Some conservatives believed that this would force members of Congress to take responsibility for the costs of the programs they proposed. According to this theory, it was easy for members of Congress to vote for a host of new and expensive programs when they were never forced to take responsibility for the size of the deficit or the size of the tax increase that would be necessary to pay for those programs. Under the new process, Congress would have to vote on a package that established programs, tax revenues and projected deficits. They could no longer compartmentalize the discussion of appropriations and revenues, and they could no longer ignore deficits.

Thus, the 1974 Act seemed to offer something for everyone. In practice, however, it not only failed to deliver on its promises, it actually backfired. During its first few years of operation the Congressional budget process had little if any effect on the respective power of the President and Congress or on the level of government spending approved by Congress. For the most part, the budget limits established in the budget resolution were based upon an estimate of what the Appropriations Committee would be likely to recommend. As budget analysts Allen Schick reports:

> In almost 100 interviews with Congressmen and staff, no one expressed the view that the budget allocations were knowingly set below legislative expectations. "We got all we needed," one committee staff director exulted. The chief clerk of an appropriation subcommittee complained that the budget target was too permissive: "We were faced with pressure to spend up to the full budget allocation. It's almost as if the budget committee bent over backwards to give Appropriations all that it wanted and then 'some.' "

It was of course necessary for the budget committees to take into account the expectations and recommendations of the appropriations committees, but the evidence is that they did little else. Members of Congress were so fearful that the process would be rejected, they hesitated to make any serious use of it. They believed that any serious attempt to use the new process to limit spending by the appropriations committees would result in a Congressional revolt against the process.

There was, however, one period when the Congressional budget resolution did serve to limit spending and redirect the priorities of the national government—the early Reagan years. When Reagan came to office calling for a tax cut, a decrease in domestic spending, and an increase in defense spending, the Budget resolution became the primary foucs of the budget policy process. Through an intense public and private lobbying effort Reagan was able to convince Congress to pass a budget resolution reflecting his priorities. Had Reagan had to lobby for each piece of his budget package in separate votes on appropriations and tax reduction it would have been difficult to sustain his momentum. With the reformed budget process Reagan was able to focus his lobbying activity on a few major votes on the budget resolution.

The irony is obvious. The process that was designed primarily to transfer power from the President to Congress "worked" only when a President wanted to institute a major change in budget priorities. Why did the process work for Reagan and not for Congress? It worked for Reagan because he was able to present a unified budget plan and to mobilize a national constituency in favor of it. It failed for Congress because Congress does not possess a unified perspective and its constituency is more local than national. Any student of the Constitutional separation of powers would be aware of these facts. Congress was designed to represent the parts of the nation, to be closest to the people, and to represent their immediate interests. Such representation is crucial to a democracy but it is not the kind of representation that is most likely to develop a unified national perspective. The President is one person representing the nation as a whole. He can present a vision of the whole and he can mobilize public opinion in support of that vision. The reformers of 1974 did not pay sufficient attention to these differences. Consequently, the Act that was to limit the President's power in the budget process helped Reagan to accomplish a massive change in budget priorities.

Gramm-Rudman-Hollins

Even Reagan's success under the process created in 1974 was short-lived. Congress began to have more and more difficulty passing budget resolutions and by the later Reagan years was frequently unable to reach agreement on appropriations bills. The federal government often operated on continuing resolutions or other stop-gap funding measures. But these problems have been eclipsed in the public debate by the growth of the budget deficit. In 1974, the deficit was $4.5 billion, by 1985 it was $220 billion, and after some decline the deficits have recently threatened to reach $300 billion. Not surprisingly the response to these budget deficits has been a call for reform of the process. The most popular means of salvation proposed by the Republicans has been the balanced budget amendment and the line-item veto. Neither of these suggestions has been adopted. What was adopted in 1985 was the Gramm-Rudman-Hollins Act.

GRH follows in the spirit of the balanced budget amendment, but is somewhat more modest in its promises. GRH assumed that the deficit problem was too big to be solved in one year, so it established a timetable for the gradual reduction of the budget deficit. It is unrealistic to go from $200 billion deficits to a balanced budget in one year, but a series of cuts over six years appears much more reasonable.

GRH appears reasonable in one other respect—it creates an institutional incentive for budget reduction. One important reason for the failure of the 1974 act to reduce spending was that no one in Congress had an incentive to provide meaningful limits in the budget resolution. Members had every reason to fear substantial limits. Such limits would threaten the process and, more to the point, they would threaten appropriations that were popular with their constituents. GRH offered a substantial incentive—sequestration. If Congress failed to make cuts or raise taxes in order to reduce the deficits to within the prescribed limits all programs of the federal government would be cut automatically by an equal percentage in order to bring the deficit to an acceptable level. No one ever wanted or expected sequestration to take place. Sequestration was a domestic form of mutual assured destruction. Congress and the President would be forced to reach agreement out of their mutual fear of the political holocaust resulting from sequestration.

If modest goals and institutional incentives are the key to successful reform, why hasn't GRH worked? Two problems with GRH soon became apparent. The first major problem arises from the fact that the budget is in important respects the product of guesswork. Sequestration was supposed to be automatic, but it wasn't possible to make it simply automatic. Before you can sequester, you must determine the amount of the deficit. But budget deficits are projections not hard and fast numbers. The unemployment rate, the interest rate, the growth in GNP and other factors affecting expenditures and revenues will vary after the budget is adopted. A budget is a projection for the next year based on certain economic assumptions. There are no "automatic" assumptions. Someone has to make a guess before a deficit is projected and before the need for and the amount of sequestration can be determined.

Under GRH the official responsible for that determination was the Comptroller-General. But in 1987 the Supreme Court ruled that the Comptroller-General was a legislative branch official and therefore ineligible to carry out the executive function of sequestration. In order to preserve sequestration, Congress was forced to revise GRH and transfer final authority over sequestration to the direction of OMB, an executive branch official.

Even had this problem not arisen there would have been a major problem under GRH, namely those reasonable increments of reduction were not all that reasonable. Congress had set a rather modest goal for the reduction of the budget in the first year of GRH. It was after all an election year. Not only was the first year goal modest, but changing economic forces pushed the deficit above the expected levels in the second year. Extraordinary cuts would have been necessary to meet the GRH targets for 1988. Faced with the prospect of drastic cuts or sequestration in an election year Congress punted, or perhaps more accurately they moved the first down marker. They took the opportunity presented to them by the need to rewrite the sequestration provisions to substantially reduce the deficit reduction targets for 1988 and 1989. Faced with a similar situation in the future, there is no reason to think that Congress will not follow a similar path. So much for mutual assured destruction.

Utopian Goals

The problem with GRH I or II is that in spite of more modest goals and some appreciation of the need for institutional incentives, it still falls short on both counts. The attempt to guarantee a balanced budget immediately or incrementally by means of an institutional reform is fundamentally misguided. Such reforms will almost always fail. Failure may even be a blessing. If you guarantee outcomes in advance, you will inevitably be forced to ignore changing circumstances and new information that should influence the outcome of the process.

Let us briefly consider the case of the balanced budget. Are deficits always bad? In 1980 Ronald Reagan called for a balanced budget amendment. Would either he or George Bush have approved of the results had such an amendment been in place since 1980? What would have happened to the Reagan tax cuts? What would have happened to defense spending? What would have been the political fallout from the drastic domestic cuts Reagan called for, if they would have actually been implemented? I think the answer is obvious. A balanced budget amendment would have eliminated any possibility of the Reagan revolution. Reagan wanted a balanced budget, but he wanted tax cuts and increased military spending more. Without a balanced budget amendment he was free to make those political choices. With such an amendment in place, he would have been robbed of that discretion.

Reagan often spoke as though deficits were the greatest evil, but he acted differently. Reagan is not alone in his rhetoric. How many politicians have asked the supposedly rhetorical question: Could you as an individual spend more money than you take in? Why should the federal government be any different? Won't it ultimately have to pay the price for fiscal irresponsibility? The problem with this line of reasoning is that it is based upon an utterly fallacious assumption. Most individuals do spend more than they take in, not because they are profligate but because that is the way the economy works. Capitalism is based on the idea of investment. For example, few individuals pay cash for a home. Most borrow. They mortgage their future. They go into debt in order to enjoy an asset they can't afford to pay for today. They are not irresponsible because that asset is worth something and it will be worth something in the future.

Government builds buildings, interstate highways, and missiles. It would have trouble converting some of these assets to cash, particularly in the case of the missiles. But these are assets with a value. They are presumably things that we as a nation need and would have to pay for if we didn't have them. It is no more unreasonable for government to borrow to invest in assets than it is for an individual or a business. Most state and local governments, in fact, do not keep books the way the federal government does. They distinguish between operating and capital expenditures, just as any individual or any business would do. Capital investments are not paid out of the operating budget in a lump sum, but are financed by bonds that are retired over a period of years. The adoption of such a procedure by the federal government might help to give us a more realistic picture of the "budget crisis."

Just as some individuals and businesses overdo deficit spending, so can the government. But simple-minded goals such as balanced budgets don't always help. We need to look at the circumstances to determine what level of debt is acceptable. We are outraged today by deficits approaching 5% of the GNP but we survived a deficit in 1943 that was 31% of the GNP. I don't think we want to reach those levels today, but I am even more convinced that we should not seek to guarantee a balanced budget in any and all circumstances. The goal of budget policy should be the formulation and implementation of a reasonable budget given the current political and economic realities. Fiscal responsibility should always be an important concern, but the simple-minded goal of a balanced budget is unrealistic and undesirable.

Institutional Disincentives

Perhaps we needn't worry too much about the utopian character of balanced budget requirements. There is no balanced budget amendment and Gramm-Rudman-Hollins has so far been unable to lead us to anything like a balanced budget. There is some truth to the assertion that GRH has at least forced politicians to keep the budget problem at the forefront of the political debate, but budget deficits between $150 and $200 Billion would be likely to have that effect with or without GRH. In general, GRH has created no effective institutional incentives for reducing the budget deficit over the long term. Its major contribution has been to create an institutional environment that encourages a preoccupation with quick fixes and discourages any significant change in long-term deficits.

The target figures for the next fiscal year become the touchstone for the budget debate. The political problem presented to the President and Congress is how to produce a budget that is consistent with the GRH target figures for next year. What is the problem with this approach? Why can't we solve the deficit crisis inch by inch? The reason is that long-term budget savings often entail short-term budget costs. It may be cheaper to buy some thing today than it will be tomorrow. Bringing the troops home from Europe will save money in the long-run, but it entails substantial costs this year. Cancelling certain programs may save money in the long run, but may require shut-down costs in the short-run. Some programs will cost money today, but will provide a stronger economy tomorrow. Between today and tomorrow political reality is often punctuated by elections. Politicians have very little incentive to incur immediate costs and defer benefits. GRH serves as a further disincentive to responsible behavior.

It is not surprising that faced with GRH targets politicians have proved to be remarkably adept pushing the deficit problem into the future. The transition rules for the Tax Reform Act of 1986 created a number of short-term revenue boosts. Asset sales have also served to decrease the deficits for a given year, but have little long-term effect. Other types of slight of hand are even more prevalent. By projecting unrealistically high growth in the GNP and unrealistically low unemployment and interest rates, virtually any deficit can be made to disappear. Congress often accuses the President of having unbridled faith in "rosy scenario", but when faced with program cuts or tax increases, members of Congress are quick to find their own pair of rose colored glasses.

Perhaps the greatest budget slight of hand has occurred with the savings and loan crisis. The S&L bailout has threatened to dramatically increase the deficits. What was the response? For purposes of GRH targets, the S&L bailout is not considered to be a part of the budget. How can that be? Simple, you pass a law. There is ample precedent for this approach. During Johnson's presidency the cost of guns and butter threatened to produce huge deficits. Johnson found an easy way to reduce the deficits. The social security trust fund had since its inception been excluded from the federal budget. The argument was that it was a self-financing program and all funds taken in by social security taxes should be used only for social security payments. But the social security trust fund was running a surplus and the rest of the government was running a deficit, so Johnson decided to bring social security under the umbrella of the federal budget. The immediate result was a reduction of the deficit. This change is now attacked by members of Johnson's own party. Some Democrats complain that the true size of the current deficit is masked by the surplus in the social security trust fund.

Should social security be on-budget or off-budget? There are reasonable arguments for both positions. What is not reasonable is that the decision is made on the basis of which option will better mask reality or which option will help to postpone accountability. The spirit of the current budget process is the spirit of Scarlet O'Hara—"I'll worry about that tomorrow."

A Modest Proposal for Reform

Any reform of the budget process should begin with a realistic set of goals. There should be no promises of balanced budgets or other guaranteed outcomes. A more modest set of goals would include: 1) some reasonable expectation that the process would be able to produce a budget in a timely fashion; 2) a process that holds elected officials responsible for the decisions they make or fail to make in the development of the budget; and 3) a reasonable expectation that the budget that is approved will be implemented.

Reformers must avoid the temptation to guarantee an outcome, such as a balanced budget. Members of Congress and the President should be given a free hand to decide what is reasonable in the circumstances. Moreover, because deficit projections are so elusive, it would be far better to have politicians focus on more substantial questions such as tax rates and expenditure levels.

There is still room for creative accounting in these areas, but flights of fancy are more restrained here than in the discussion of budget deficits.

The existing system has promised balanced budgets and often produced no budget at all. Congress has often failed to reach agreement on budget resolutions or appropriations bills or both. The system has discouraged decision-making and encouraged obfuscation. A reformed process should not try to make decisions about the budget in advance, but it should insure that decisions will be made. Any budget reform must set a firm deadline by which a budget will be in place and all decisions regarding appropriations and revenue rates will be made.

Reform should encourage political accountability not buck-passing and political irresponsibility. A new process should make clear who is responsible for making decisions at any given point in the process. Even more important, it should make clear who has refused to accept their responsibility for decision-making. In a government that spends over $1 Trillion someone somewhere must be making some decisions, and someone must be made to take responsibility.

Finally if we are to have a budget it should mean something. For years the President's budget was merely a recommendation. The real decisions were made in the appropriations and revenue committees. The new process promised to change, but it didn't deliver. The unified budget passed by Congress is a paper tiger. There are too many ways to get around budget limits. There is too much attention to uncontrollable deficits and too little to controllable tax rates and expenditures. A unified budget that determines revenues and expenditures is a good idea, but it must have some likelihood of meaningful implementation.

To that end I propose the adoption of the following budget process:

1. The President will submit a budget by 15th of January.
2. By May 1 Congress approves the President's budget or passes its own by concurrent resolution.
3. If Congress fails to act by this date, the President's budget takes effect.
4. Congress will pass appropriations bills, consistent with the budget by September 1.
5. If appropriations bills are passed in excess of the amounts provided for in the budget resolution, the President will be free to impound excess funds from the particular appropriations bill involved.
6. If a continuing resolution is passed in excess of the budget resolution, the President will be free to impound funds from any program within the continuing resolution to reach the levels required by the budget resolution.

The objections to such a proposal are easy to predict. The primary one is that it gives too much power to the President. Congress would never agree to allow the President to exercise so much of the power of the purse. The reply is that Congress can pass its own budget. Impoundment would then take place only when Congress ignored its own self-imposed limits. The President's budget would be implemented only when Congress was unable to do its job. Even when impoundment process is triggered, the President might be constrained by political pressures. He is not forced to impound. The virtue of the system is that it makes clear who is responsible for action or inaction at each stage.

The reform will insure responsibility and encourage action. The President will submit a budget. He will have every incentive to be realistic, because he may ultimately have to implement this budget. Congress will be encouraged to pass their own budget. They will know that the alternative is not inaction but the adoption of the President's budget.

Could each branch avoid action in this system? The answer is yes. Congress could avoid action and turn the problem over to the President. The President could ignore the budget resolution and fail to impound. But responsibility for inaction would be more clearly fixed. It is unlikely that both branches will pass up the opportunity to use the budget resolution as a means of establishing their priorities.

The proposed system takes advantage of the Constitutional separation of powers. It insures recognition of different perspectives and it relies on those different perspectives as an incentive for decision-making. It takes advantage of the tendency of the separation of powers when properly understood to encourage action and responsibility. Most commentators and practitioners would view this proposal as utopian, but it clearly offers more reasonable goals and more realistic incentives than the current system.

34

War Powers Resolution (1973)

Resolved by the Senate and House of Representatives of the United States of America in Congress assembled, That:

Section 1. This joint resolution may be cited as the "War Powers Resolution".

From War Powers Resolution, 87 Stat. 555 (1973)

Sec. 2. (a) It is the purpose of this joint resolution to fulfill the intent of the framers of the Constitution of the United States and insure that the collective judgment of both the Congress and the President will apply to the introduction of United States Armed Forces into hostilities, or into situations where imminent involvement in hostilities is clearly indicated by the circumstances, and to the continued use of such forces in hostilities or in such situations.

(b) Under article I, section 8, of the Constitution, it is specifically provided that the Congress shall have the power to make all laws necessary and proper for carrying into execution, not only its own powers but also all other powers vested by the Constitution in the Government of the United States, or in any department or officer thereof.

(c) The constitutional powers of the President as Commander-in-Chief to introduce United States Armed Forces into hostilities, or into situations where imminent involvement in hostilities is clearly indicated by the circumstances, are exercised only pursuant to (1) a declaration of war, (2) specific statutory authorization, or (3) a national emergency created by attack upon the United States, its territories or possessions, or its armed forces.

Sec. 3. The President in every possible instance shall consult with Congress before introducing United States Armed Forces into hostilities or into situations where imminent involvement in hostilities is clearly indicated by the circumstances, and after every such introduction shall consult regularly with the Congress until United States Armed Forces are no longer engaged in hostilities or have been removed from such situations.

Sec. 4. (a) In the absence of a declaration of war, in any case in which United States Armed Forces are introduced—

(1) into hostilities or into situations where imminent involvement in hostilities is clearly indicated by the circumstances;

(2) into the territory, airspace or waters of a foreign nation, while equipped for combat, except for deployments which relate solely to supply, replacement, repair, or training of such forces; or

(3) in numbers which substantially enlarge United States Armed Forces equipped for combat already located in a foreign nation;
the President shall submit within 48 hours to the Speaker of the House of Representatives and to the President pro tempore of the Senate a report, in writing, setting forth—

(A) the circumstances necessitating the introduction of United States Armed Forces;

(B) the constitutional and legislative authority under which such introduction took place; and

(C) the estimated scope and duration of the hostilities or involvement.

(b) The President shall provide such other information as the Congress may request in the fulfillment of its constitutional responsibilities with respect to committing the Nation to war and to the use of United States Armed Forces abroad. . . .

Sec. 5. (a) Each report submitted pursuant to section 4(a) (1) shall be . . . referred to the Committee on Foreign Affairs of the House of Representatives and to the Committee on Foreign Relations of the Senate for appropriate action. If, when the report is transmitted, the Congress has adjourned sine die or has adjourned for any period in excess of three calendar days, the Speaker of the House of Representatives and the President pro tempore of the Senate, if they deem it advisable (or if petitioned by at least 30 percent of the membership of their respective Houses) shall jointly request the President to convene Congress in order that it may consider the report and take appropriate action pursuant to this section.

(b) Within sixty calendar days after a report is submitted or is required to be submitted pursuant to section 4 (a) (1), whichever is earlier, the President shall terminate any use of United States Armed Forces with respect to which such report was submitted (or required to be submitted), unless the Congress (1) has declared war or has enacted a specific authorization for such use of United States Armed Forces, (2) has extended by law such sixty-day period, or (3) is physically unable to meet as a result of an armed attack upon the United States. Such sixty-day period shall be extended for not more than an additional thirty days if the President determines and certifies to the Congress in writing that unavoidable military necessity respecting the safety of United States Armed Forces requires the continued use of such armed forces in the course of bringing about a prompt removal of such forces.

(c) Notwithstanding subsection (b), at any time that United States Armed Forces are engaged in hostilities outside the territory of the United States, its possessions and territories without a declaration of war or specific statutory authorization, such forces shall be removed by the President if the Congress so directs by concurrent resolution. . . .

Sec. 8. . . . (d) Nothing in this joint resolution—

(1) is intended to alter the constitutional authority of the Congress or of the President, or the provisions of existing treaties; or

(2) shall be construed as granting any authority to the President with respect to the introduction of United States Armed Forces into hostilities or into situations wherein involvement in hostilities is clearly indicated by the circumstances which authority he would not have had in the absence of this joint resolution. . . .

[Passed over presidential veto Nov. 7, 1973.]

35

Report of the Congressional Committees Investigating the Iran-Contra Affair (1987)

Majority Report

. . . On November 3, 1986, Al-Shiraa, a Lebanese weekly, reported that the United States had secretly sold arms to Iran. Subsequent reports claimed that the purpose of the sales was to win the release of American hostages in Lebanon. These reports seemed unbelievable: Few principles of U.S. policy were stated more forcefully by the Reagan Administration than refusing to traffic with terrorists or sell arms to the Government of the Ayatollah Khomeini of Iran.

Although the Administration initially denied the reports, by mid-November it was clear that the accounts were true. The United States had sold arms to Iran and had hoped thereby to gain the release of American hostages in Lebanon. However, even though the Iranians received the arms, just as many Americans remained hostage as before. Three had been freed, but three more had been taken during the period of the sales.

There was still another revelation to come: on November 25 the Attorney General announced that proceeds from the Iran arms sales had been "diverted" to the Nicaraguan resistance at a time when U.S. military aid to the Contras was prohibited.

Iran and Nicaragua—twin thorns of U.S. foreign policy in the 1980s—were thus linked in a credibility crisis that raised serious questions about the adherence of the Administration to the Constitutional processes of Government. . . .

The common ingredients of the Iran and Contra policies were secrecy, deception, and disdain for the law. A small group of senior officials believed that they alone knew what was right. They viewed knowledge of their actions by others in the Government as a threat to their objectives. They told neither the Secretary of State, the Congress nor the American people of their actions. When exposure was threatened, they destroyed official documents and lied to Cabinet officials, to the public, and to elected representatives in Congress. They testified that they even withheld key facts from the President.

The United States Constitution specifies the process by which laws and policy are to be made and executed. Constitutional process is the essence of

From Senate Report No. 216, "Iran-Contra Investigation Report." Serial No. 13739 100th Congress First Session, Nov. 17, 1987.

our democracy and our democratic form of Government is the basis of our strength. Time and again we have learned that a flawed process leads to bad results, and that a lawless process leads to worse. . . .

The Administration's departure from democratic processes created the conditions for policy failure, and led to contradictions which undermined the credibility of the United States. . . .

It was stated on several occasions that the confusion, secrecy and deception surrounding the aid program for the Nicaraguan freedom fighters was produced in part by Congress' shifting positions on Contra aid.

But Congress' inconsistency mirrored the chameleon-like nature of the rationale offered for granting assistance in the first instance. Initially, Congress was told that our purpose was simply to interdict the flow of weapons from Nicaragua into El Salvador. Then Congress was told that our purpose was to harrass the Sandinistas to prevent them from consolidating their power and exporting their revolution. Eventually, Congress was told that our purpose was to eliminate all foreign forces from Nicaragua, to reduce the size of the Sandinista armed forces, and to restore the democratic reforms pledged by the Sandinistas during the overthrow of the Somoza regime.

Congress had cast a skeptical eye upon each rationale proffered by the Administration. It suspected that the Administration's true purpose was identical to that of the Contras—the overthrow of the Sandinista regime itself. Ultimately Congress yielded to domestic political pressure to discontinue assistance to the Contras, but Congress was unwilling to bear responsibility for the loss of Central America to communist military and political forces. So Congress compromised, providing in 1985 humanitarian aid to the Contras; and the NSC [National Security Council] staff provided what Congress prohibited: lethal support for the Contras.

Compromise is no excuse for violation of law and deceiving Congress. A law is no less a law because it is passed by a slender majority, or because Congress is open-minded about its reconsideration in the future. . . .

The NSC staff turned to private parties and third countries to do the Government's business. Funds denied by Congress were obtained by the Administration from third countries and private citizens. . . .

The solicitation of foreign funds by an Administration to pursue foreign policy goals rejected by Congress is dangerous and improper. . . .

Moreover, under the Constitution only Congress can provide funds for the Executive branch. The Framers intended Congress' "power of the purse" to be one of the principal checks on Executive action. It was designed, among other things, to prevent the Executive from involving this country unilaterally in a foreign conflict. The Constitutional plan does not prohibit a President from asking a foreign state, or anyone else, to contribute funds to a third party. But it does prohibit such solicitation where the United States exercises control over their receipt and expenditure. By circumventing Congress' power of the purse through third-country and private contributions to the Contras, the Administration undermined a cardinal principle of the Constitution. . . .

The Constitution of the United States gives important powers to both the President and the Congress in the making of foreign policy. The President is the principal architect of foreign policy in consultation with the Congress. The policies of the United States cannot succeed unless the President and the Congress work together.

Yet, in the Iran-Contra Affair, Administration officials holding no elected office repeatedly evidenced disrespect for Congress' efforts to perform its Constitutional oversight role in foreign policy:

• Poindexter testified, referring to his efforts to keep the covert action in support of the Contras from Congress: "I simply did not want any outside interference."

• North testified: "I didn't want to tell Congress anything" about this covert action.

• Abrams acknowledged in his testimony that, unless Members of Congressional Committees asked "exactly the right question, using exactly the right words, they weren't going to get the right answers," regarding solicitation of third-countries for Contra support.

• And numerous other officials made false statements to, and misled, the Congress.

Several witnesses at the hearings stated or implied that foreign policy should be left solely to the President to do as he chooses, arguing that shared powers have no place in a dangerous world. But the theory of our Constitution is the opposite: policies formed through consultation and the democratic process are better and wiser than those formed without it. Circumvention of Congress is self-defeating, for no foreign policy can succeed without the bipartisan support of Congress.

In a system of shared powers, decision-making requires mutual respect between the branches of government.

The Committees were reminded by Secretary Shultz during the hearings that "trust is the coin of the realm." Democratic government is not possible without trust between the branches of government and between the government and the people. Sometimes that trust is misplaced and the system falters. But for officials to work outside the system because it does not produce the results they seek is a prescription for failure. . . .

Under our Constitution, both the Congress and the Executive are given specific foreign policy powers. The Constitution does not name one or the other branch as the exclusive actor in foreign policy. Each plays a role in our system of checks and balances to ensure that our foreign policy is effective, sustainable and in accord with our national interests.

Key participants in the Iran-Contra Affair had serious misconceptions about the roles of Congress and the President in the making of foreign policy. . . .

The argument that Congress has but a minor role in foreign policy-making is contradicted by the language of the Constitution, and by over 200 years of history. It is also shortsighted and ultimately self-defeating. American foreign policy and our system of government cannot succeed unless the President and Congress work together. . . . During the public hearings, both Poindexter and North characterized Congress as meddlers in the President's arena. . . .

North also repeatedly stated his view that "it was within the purview of the President of the United States to conduct secret activities . . . to further the policy goals of the United States." North claimed that the President had the power under the Constitution to conduct "secret diplomacy" because "the President can do what he wants with his own staff." He stated that the President had a "very wide mandate to carry out activities, secretly or publicly, as he chooses.". . . The Constitution itself gives no support to the argument that the President has a mandate so broad. The words "foreign policy" do not appear in the Constitution, and the Constitution does not designate the President as the sole or dominant actor in foreign policy.

The only foreign policy powers expressly granted to the Executive in the Constitution are the powers to nominate Ambassadors, to negotiate treaties, and to direct the Armed Forces as Commander-in-Chief. Two of these powers are specifically conditioned on Senate approval: the Senate, through its power of advise and consent, can confirm or reject Ambassadors and ratify or reject treaties.

On the other hand, the Constitution expressly grants Congress the power to regulate foreign commerce, to raise and support armies, to provide and maintain a navy, and to declare war. Congress is given the exclusive power of the purse. The Executive may not spend funds on foreign policy projects except pursuant to an appropriation by Congress. . . . In testifying before these Committees, North and Poindexter indicated their view that whatever power Congress may have in foreign policy derived solely from its power of the purse. They reasoned that so long as public money was not expended, Congress had no role and the President was free to pursue his foreign policy goals using private and third-country funds. . . .

These claims by North and Poindexter strike at the very heart of the system of checks and balances. To permit the President and his aides to carry out covert actions by using funds obtained from outside Congress undermines the Framers' belief that "the purse and the sword must never be in the same hands." . . . By seeking private and third-country aid for the Contras without Congressional notification—much less approval—the Administration did more than engage in an unfortunate fundraising effort that opened the door to expectations of secret return favors. This clandestine financing operation undermined the powers of Congress as a co-equal branch and subverted the Constitution. . . . The sharing of power over foreign policy requires consultation, trust, and coordination. As President Reagon told a joint session of

Congress on April 27, 1983: "The Congress shares both the power and the responsibility for our foreign policy." . . . The questions before these Committees concerning the foreign policy roles of Congress and the President are not abstract issues for legal scholars. They are practical considerations essential to the making of good foreign policy and the effective functioning of government. The theory of the Constitution is that policies formed through consultation and the democratic process are better, and wiser, than those formed without it.

The Constitution divided foreign policy powers between the legislative and executive branches of government. That division of power is fundamental to this system, and acts as a check on the actions of each branch of government. Those who would take shortcuts in the constitutional process—mislead the Congress or withhold information—show their contempt for what the Framers created. Shortcuts that bypass the checks and balances of the system, and excessive secrecy by those who serve the President, do not strengthen the President. They weaken the President and the constitutional system of government.

Minority Report

We emphatically reject the idea that through these mistakes, the executive branch subverted the law, undermined the Constitution, or threatened democracy. The President is every bit as much of an elected representative of the people as is a Member of Congress. In fact, he and the Vice President are the only officials elected by the whole Nation. Nevertheless, we do believe the mistakes relate in a different way to the issue of democratic accountability. They provide a good starting point for seeing what both sides of the great legislative-executive branch divide must do to improve the way the Government makes foreign policy. . . . Congress has a hard time even conceiving of itself as contributing to the problem of democratic accountability. But the record of ever-changing policies toward Central America that contributed to the NSC staff's behavior is symptomatic of a frequently recurring problem. When Congress is narrowly divided over highly emotional issues, it frequently ends up passing intentionally ambiguous laws or amendments that postpone the day of decision. In foreign policy, those decisions often take the form of restrictive amendments on money bills that are open to being amended again *every year,* with new, and equally ambiguous, language replacing the old. . . . The Constitution created the Presidency to be a separate branch of government whose occupant would have substantial discretionary power to act. He was not given the power of an 18th century monarch, but neither was he meant to be a creature of Congress. The country needs a President who can exercise the powers the Framers intended. As long as any President has those powers, there will be mistakes. It would be disastrous to respond to the possibility of error by further restraining and limiting the powers of the office. Then, instead of seeing occasional actions turn out to be wrong, we would be increasing the probability that future Presidents would be unable to act decisively, thus guaranteeing ourselves a perpetually paralyzed, reactive, and unclear foreign policy in which mistake by inaction would be the order of the day. . . . Judgments about the Iran-Contra Affair ultimately must rest upon one's views about the proper roles of Congress and the President in foreign policy. There were many statements during the public hearings, for example, about the rule of law. But the fundamental law of the land is the Constitution. Unconstitutional statutes violate the rule of law every bit as much as do willful violations of constitutional statutes. It is essential, therefore, to frame any discussion of what happened with a proper analysis of the Constitutional allocation of legislative and executive power in foreign affairs.

One point stands out from the historical record: the Constitution's Framers expected the President to be much more than a minister or clerk. The President was supposed to execute the laws, but that was only the beginning. He also was given important powers, independent of the legislature's, and these substantively were focused on foreign policy. . . .

The need for an effective foreign policy, it turned out, was one of the main reasons the country needs an "energetic government," according the Alexander Hamilton in *Federalist* Nos. 22 and 23. Madison made the same point in No. 37: "Energy in Government is essential to that security against external and internal danger, and to that prompt and salutary execution of the laws, which enter into the very definition of good Government." The relevance of these observations about the *government's* power is that the Framers saw energy as being primarily an executive branch characteristic.

Energy is the main theme of *Federalist* No. 70 ("energy in the executive is a leading character in the definition of good government.") It is said to be important primarily when "decision, activity, secrecy, and dispatch" were needed. . . . Presidents asserted their constitutional independence from Congress early. They engaged in secret diplomacy and intelligence activities, and refused to share the results with Congress if they saw fit. They unilaterally established U.S. military and diplomatic policy with respect to foreign belligerent states, in quarrels involving the United States, and in quarrels involving only third parties. They enforced this policy abroad, using force if necessary. They engaged U.S. troops abroad to serve American interests without congressional approval, and in a number of cases apparently against explicit directions from Congress. They also had agents engage in what would commonly be referred to as covert actions, again without Congressional approval. In short, Presidents exercised a broad range of foreign policy powers for which they neither sought nor received Congressional sanction through statute.

This history speaks volumes about the Constitution's allocation of powers between the branches. It leaves little, if any, doubt that the President was expected to have the primary role of conducting the foreign policy of the United

States. Congressional actions to limit the President in this area therefore should be reviewed with a considerable degree of skepticism. If they interfere with core presidential foreign policy functions, they should be struck down. Moreover, the lesson of our constitutional history is that doubtful cases should be decided in favor of the President. . . . The Constitution gives important foreign policy powers both to Congress and to the President. Neither can accomplish very much over the long term by trying to go it alone. The President cannot use the country's resources to carry out policy without congressional appropriations. At the same time, Congress can prohibit some actions, and it can influence others, but it cannot act by itself, and it is not institutionally designed to accept political responsibility for specific actions. Action or implementation is a peculiarly executive branch function.

The Constitution's requirement for cooperation does not negate the separaton of powers. Neither branch can be permitted to usurp functions that belong to the other. As we have argued throughout, and as the Supreme Court reaffirmed in 1983, "the powers delegated to the three branches are functionally identifiable." The executive branch's functions are the ones most closely related to the need for secrecy, efficiency, dispatch, and the acceptance by one person, the President, of political responsibility for the result. This basic framework must be preserved if the country is to have an effective foreign policy in the future.

Chapter IV

The Presidency

Alexander Hamilton says that "Energy in the executive is a leading character in the definition of good government." Hamilton understands the potential conflict between an energetic government and republican principles, but he claims that an energetic executive is essential to the defense of the nation against foreign attacks and the steady administration of the laws. The ingredients that will produce an energetic executive are a unified presidential office, a term of sufficient duration, adequate financial support, and competent powers. These ingredients would insulate the President from an undue dependence on Congress and public opinion. He would have the independent resources necessary to the energetic execution of his office.

Ceaser argues that Presidents increasingly look not to their Constitutional office but to public opinion as a source of executive energy. Ceaser traces this development to the Progressives who saw public opinion as a more democratic and more powerful source of authority. But Ceaser thinks this is a dangerous trend. He contends that the reliance on popular opinion will undermine the exercise of Constitutionally created power, and will lead to an excessive reliance on popular rhetoric. The more rhetoric is seen as a source of authority, the more politicians will be tempted to make exaggerated claims in search of increased power. It is this overemphasis on Presidential rhetoric, Jeffrey Tulis claims, that was responsible for many of the major shortcomings of the Reagan administration. Ceaser and Tulis believe that a return to a more Hamiltonian conception of the office of the Presidency would lead to more realistic expectations and more competent government.

In a 1960 campaign speech John F. Kennedy argues that his understanding of the Presidential office was far more important than his position on any particular policy issue. Kennedy accepts Hamilton's call for an energetic executive and criticizes those who wish to substitute rhetoric for more substantive political results. But Kennedy is also willing to look to popular opinion and popular rhetoric as a source of presidential authority. He accepts Theodore Roosevelt's idea of the Presidency as a "bully pulpit." Kennedy wants the president "to summon his national constituency" and "alert the people to our dangers and our opportunities."

Can the Presidency become a bully pulpit without undermining the President's institutional sources of authority? Lincoln saw the potential for ambitious men to subvert the Constitution in search of extraordinary powers and honors. Lincoln's solution, however, relied to a great extent on rhetoric. Lincoln did not wish to encourage the passionate rhetoric that would fan the flames of a mob, he looked instead to a cooler more reasonable rhetoric that would support the Constitution and the laws. Only through the persuasive powers of rhetoric could the President maintain the institutions of government created by the Constitution.

The rule of law must not only be supplemented by a judicious rhetoric, it must sometimes give way to action without specific legal authorization. When President Truman seized the steel mills during the Korean War, he claimed that such discretionary authority was implied in the executive power vested in him by the Constitution and by his constitutional duty "to take care that the laws be faithfully executed." But the Supreme Court found his action to be beyond the Constitutional authority of the President.

In other cases the Court has given the President a broad claim to discretionary authority. In *Curtiss-Wright Export Corporation v. United States* the Court distinguished the authority of the national government over domestic affairs, which is derived from the Constitution, and its authority over foreign affairs, which inheres in the concept of nationhood. The latter would exist whether or not the Constitution provided for it. Since the President represents the nation in foreign affairs, the Court's reasoning suggests that the President may exercise this virtually unlimited reservoir of extra-Constitutional authority.

The Court glossed over the fact that it is the Constitution that makes the President the representative of the nation in foreign affairs. Nonetheless, the idea of discretionary powers beyond the reach of Constitutional limitations has remained an important strain of judicial interpretation. The immediate problem in the case of *Korematsu v. U.S.* is whether distinctions based on race can ever be legitimate. But Justices Jackson and Frankfurter take the opportunity of the case to elaborate their different views of the discretionary authority of the executive. Both admit that military necessity may occasionally take precedence over the protection of individual rights. But Justice Jackson says that even if such action is absolutely necessary, we should never call it Constitutional. To do so would be to establish a dangerous precedent that would undermine the protection of rights. Frankfurter disagrees. He finds it more dangerous to place the actions of the executive outside of the Constitution in any circumstance. Whether or not there is an emergency, Frankfurter wants to retain the possibility of Constitutional restraint. He concludes that the Constitution can and should be understood to include the possibility of effective action in an emergency.

Frankfurter's argument brings to mind Lincoln's defense of his suspension of the writ of habeas corpus. Lincoln claims that in times of emergency the government must deprive citizens of liberty without due process of law; indeed, in granting power to suspend the writ of habeas corpus, the Constitution itself recognizes the necessity for doing so. According to Lincoln the Presidential office established by the Constitution permits and even demands the exercise of discretion in extraordinary situations. Statesmanship is necessary for the preservation of the Constitution and the rule of law.

Frederick Douglass's speech on the statesmanship of Lincoln provides a fitting conclusion to the discussion of the presidency. Douglass captures the essence of Lincoln's statesmanship: Lincoln's recognition of the need for compromise, his appreciation of the virtues and limits of law, and his sense of when to follow, when to lead, and when to ignore popular opinion. Douglass also recognizes that although Lincoln had different personal interests from his own, and represented different social interests, their common belief in certain fundamental principles provided a basis for mutual respect and political action.

36

Alexander Hamilton

On the Presidency (1788)

There is an idea, which is not without its advocates, that a vigorous Executive is inconsistent with the genius of republican government. The enlightened well-wishers to this species of government must at least hope that the supposition is destitute of foundation; since they can never admit its truth, without at the same time admitting the condemnation of their own principles. Energy in the Executive is a leading character in the definition of good government. It is essential to the protection of the community against foreign attacks; it is not less essential to the steady administration of the laws; to the protection of property against those irregular and high-handed combinations which sometimes interrupt the ordinary course of justice; to the security of liberty against the enterprises and assaults of ambition, of faction, and of anarchy. . . .

A feeble execution is but another phrase for a bad execution; and a government ill executed, whatever it may be in theory, must be, in practice, a bad government.

Taking it for granted, therefore, that all men of sense will agree in the necessity of an energetic Executive, it will only remain to inquire, what are the ingredients which constitute this energy? How far can they be combined with those other ingredients which constitute safety in the republican sense? And how far does this combination characterize the plan which has been reported by the convention?

The ingredients which constitute energy in the Executive are, first, unity; secondly, duration; thirdly, an adequate provision for its support; fourthly, competent powers.

The ingredients which constitute safety in the republican sense are, first, a due dependence on the people; secondly, a due responsibility. . . .

That unity is conducive to energy will not be disputed. Decision, activity, secrecy, and despatch will generally characterize the proceedings of one man in a much more eminent degree than the proceedings of any greater number; and in proportion as the number is increased, these qualities will be diminished.

This unity may be destroyed in two ways: either by vesting the power in

From Federalists 70–73, in *The Federalist*.

two or more magistrates of equal dignity and authority; or by vesting it ostensibly in one man, subject, in whole or in part, to the control and cooperation of others, in the capacity of counsellors to him. . . .

Wherever two or more persons are engaged in any common enterprise or pursuit, there is always danger of difference of opinion. If it be a public trust or office, in which they are clothed with equal dignity and authority, there is peculiar danger of personal emulation and even animosity. From either, and especially from all these causes, the most bitter dissensions are apt to spring. Whenever these happen, they lessen the respectability, weaken the authority, and distract the plans and operations of those whom they divide. If they should unfortunately assail the supreme executive magistracy of a country, consisting of a plurality of persons, they might impede or frustrate the most important measures of the government, in the most critical emergencies of the state. And what is still worse, they might split the community into the most violent and irreconcilable factions, adhering differently to the different individuals who composed the magistracy. . . .

Upon the principles of a free government, inconveniences from the source just mentioned must necessarily be submitted to in the formation of the legislature; but it is unnecessary, and therefore unwise, to introduce them into the constitution of the Executive. It is here too they may be most pernicious. In the legislature, promptitude of decision is oftener an evil than a benefit. The differences of opinion, and the jarrings of parties in that department of the government, though they may sometimes obstruct salutary plans, yet often promote deliberation and circumspection, and serve to check excesses in the majority. When a resolution too is once taken, the opposition must be at an end. That resolution is a law, and resistance to it punishable. But no favorable circumstances palliate or atone for the disadvantages of dissension in the executive department. Here, they are pure and unmixed. There is no point at which they cease to operate. They serve to embarrass and weaken the execution of the plan or measure to which they relate, from the first step to the final conclusion of it. They constantly counteract those qualities in the Executive which are the most necessary ingredients in its composition,—vigor and expedition, and this without any counterbalancing good. In the conduct of war, in which the energy of the Executive is the bulwark of the national security, every thing would be to be apprehended from its plurality. . . .

But one of the weightiest objections to a plurality in the Executive, and which lies as much against the last as the first plan, is, that it tends to conceal faults and destroy responsibility. Responsibility is of two kinds—to censure and to punishment. The first is the more important of the two, especially in an elective office. Man, in public trust, will much oftener act in such a manner as to render him unworthy of being any longer trusted, than in such a manner as to make him obnoxious to legal punishment. But the multiplication of the Executive adds to the difficulty of detection in either case. It often becomes impossible, amidst mutual accusations, to determine on whom the blame or the punishment of a pernicious measure, or series of pernicious measures, ought really to fall. . . .

Duration in office has been mentioned as the second requisite to the energy of the Executive authority. This has relation to two objects: to the personal firmness of the executive magistrate, in the employment of his constitutional powers; and to the stability of the system of administration which may have been adopted under his auspices. With regard to the first, it must be evident, that the longer the duration in office, the greater will be the probability of obtaining so important an advantage. It is a general principle of human nature, that a man will be interested in whatever he possesses, in proportion to the firmness or precariousness of the tenure by which he holds it; will be less attached to what he holds by a momentary or uncertain title, than to what he enjoys by a durable or certain title; and, of course, will be willing to risk more for the sake of the one, than for the sake of the other. This remark is not less applicable to a political privilege, or honor, or trust, than to any article of ordinary property. The inference from it is, that a man acting in the capacity of chief magistrate, under a consciousness that in a very short time he *must* lay down his office, will be apt to feel himself too little interested in it to hazard any material censure or perplexity, from the independent exertion of his powers, or from encountering the ill-humors, however transient, which may happen to prevail, either in a considerable part of the society itself, or even in a predominant faction in the legislative body. . . .

There are some who would be inclined to regard the servile pliancy of the Executive to a prevailing current, either in the community or in the legislature, as its best recommendation. But such men entertain very crude notions, as well of the purposes for which government was instituted, as of the true means by which the public happiness may be promoted. The republican principle demands that the deliberate sense of the community should govern the conduct of those to whom they intrust the management of their affairs; but it does not require an unqualified complaisance to every sudden breeze of passion, or to every transient impulse which the people may receive from the arts of men, who flatter their prejudices to betray their interest. It is a just observation, that the people commonly *intend* the PUBLIC GOOD. This often applies to their very errors. But their good sense would despise the adulator who should pretend that they always *reason right* about the *means* of promoting it. They know from experience that they sometimes err; and the wonder is that they so seldom err as they do, beset, as they continually are, by the wiles of parasites and sycophants, by the snares of the ambitious, the avaricious, the desperate, by the artifices of men who possess their confidence more than they deserve it, and of those who seek to possess rather than to deserve it. When occasions present themselves, in which the interests of the people are at variance with their inclinations, it is the duty of the persons whom they have appointed to be the guardians of those interests, to withstand the temporary delusion, in order to give them time and opportunity for more cool and sedate reflection. Instances might be cited in which a conduct of this kind has saved the people from very fatal consequences of their own mistakes, and has procured lasting monuments of their gratitude to the men who had courage and magnanimity enough to serve them at the peril of their displeasure.

But however inclined we might be to insist upon an unbounded complaisance in the Executive to the inclinations of the people, we can with no propriety contend for a like complaisance to the humors of the legislature. The latter may sometimes stand in opposition to the former, and at other times the people may be entirely neutral. In either supposition, it is certainly desirable that the Executive should be in a situation to dare to act his own opinion with vigor and decision. . . .

It cannot be affirmed, that a duration of four years, or any other limited duration, would completely answer the end proposed; but it would contribute towards it in a degree which would have a material influence upon the spirit and character of the government. Between the commencement and termination of such a period, there would always be a considerable interval, in which the prospect of annihilation would be sufficiently remote, not to have an improper effect upon the conduct of a man imbued with a tolerable portion of fortitude; and in which he might reasonably promise himself, that there would be time enough before it arrived, to make the community sensible of the propriety of the measures he might incline to pursue. Though it be probable that, as he approached the moment when the public were, by a new election, to signify their sense of his conduct, his confidence, and with it his firmness, would decline; yet both the one and the other would derive support from the opportunities which his previous continuance in the station had afforded him, of establishing himself in the esteem and goodwill of his constituents. . . .

With a positive duration of considerable extent, I connect the circumstance of reeligibility. The first is necessary to give to the officer himself the inclination and the resolution to act his part well, and to the community time and leisure to observe the tendency of his measures, and thence to form an experimental estimate of their merits. The last is necessary to enable the people, when they see reason to approve of his conduct, to continue him in his station, in order to prolong the utility of his talents and virtues, and to secure to the government the advantage of permanency in a wise system of administration.

Nothing appears more plausible at first sight, nor more ill-founded upon close inspection than scheme which in relation to the present point has had some respectable advocates,—I mean that of continuing the chief magistrate in office for a certain time, and then excluding him from it, either for a limited period or forever after. This exclusion, whether temporary or perpetual, would have nearly the same effects, and these effects would be for the most part rather pernicious than salutary.

One ill effect of the exclusion would be a diminution of the inducements to good behavior. There are few men who would not feel much less zeal in the discharge of a duty, when they were conscious that the advantages of the station with which it was connected must be relinquished at a determinate period, than when they were permitted to entertain a hope of *obtaining,* by *meriting,* a continuance of them. This position will not be disputed so long as it is admitted that the desire of reward is one of the strongest incentives of human conduct; or that the best security for the fidelity of mankind is to make their interest coincide with their duty. Even the love of fame, the ruling passion of the noblest minds, which would prompt a man to plan and undertake extensive and arduous enterprises for the public benefit, requiring considerable time to mature and perfect them, if he could flatter himself with the prospect of being allowed to finish what he had begun, would, on the contrary, deter him from the undertaking, when he foresaw that he must quit the scene before he could accomplish the work, and must commit that, together with his own reputation, to hands which might be unequal or unfriendly to the task. The most to be expected from the generality of men, in such a situation, is the negative merit of not doing harm, instead of the positive merit of doing good.

Another ill effect of the exclusion would be the temptation to sordid views, to peculation, and, in some instances, to usurpation. An avaricious man, who might happen to fill the office, looking forward to a time when he must at all events yield up the emoluments he enjoyed, would feel a propensity, not easy to be resisted by such a man, to make the best use of the opportunity he enjoyed while it lasted, and might not scruple to have recourse to the most corrupt expedients to make the harvest as abundant as it was transitory; though the same man, probably, with a different prospect before him, might content himself with the regular perquisites of his situation, and might even be unwilling to risk the consequences of an abuse of his opportunities. His avarice might be a guard upon his avarice. Add to this that the same man might be vain or ambitious, as well as avaricious. And if he could expect to prolong his honors by his good conduct, he might hesitate to sacrifice his appetite for them to his appetite for gain. But with the prospect before him of approaching an inevitable annihilation, his avarice would be likely to get the victory over his caution, his vanity, or his ambition.

37

James W. Ceaser, Glen E. Thurow,
Jeffrey K. Tulis, Joseph Bessette

The Rise of the Rhetorical Presidency (1981)

Popular or mass rhetoric, which presidents once employed only rarely, now serves as one of their principal tools in attempting to govern the nation. Whatever doubts Americans may now entertain about the limitations of presidential leadership, they do not consider it unfitting or inappropriate for presidents to attempt to "move" the public by programmatic speeches that exhort and set forth grand and ennobling views.

It was not always so. Prior to this century, popular leadership through rhetoric was suspect. Presidents rarely spoke directly to the people, preferring communications between the branches of the government. Washington seldom delivered more than one major speech per year of his administration, and that one—the Annual Address—was almost mandated by the Constitution and was addressed to Congress. Jefferson even ceased delivering the address in person, a precedent that continued until Woodrow Wilson's appearance before Congress in 1913. The spirit of these early presidents' examples was followed throughout the nineteenth century. The relatively few popular speeches that were made differed in character from today's addresses. Most were patriotic orations, some raised constitutional issues, and several spoke to the conduct of war. Very few were domestic "policy speeches" of the sort so common today, and attempts to move the nation by means of an exalted picture of a perfect ideal were almost unknown. . . .

Today, a president has an assembly line of speechwriters efficiently producing words that enable him to say something on every conceivable occasion. Unless a president is deliberately "hiding" in the White House, a week scarcely goes by without at least one major news story devoted to coverage of a radio or TV speech, an address to Congress, a speech to a convention, a press conference, a news release, or some other presidential utterance. But more important even than the quantity of popular rhetoric is the fact that presidential speech and action increasingly reflect the opinion that speaking *is* governing. Speeches are written to become the events to which people react no less than "real" events themselves. . . .

From Ceaser, Thurow, Tulis, and Bessette, "The Rise of the Rhetorical Presidency," in *Presidential Studies Quarterly* (Spring, 1981). Reprinted by permission of *Presidential Studies Quarterly*.

The excess of speech has perhaps fed a cynicism about it that is the opposite of [a] boundless faith in rhetoric. . . . Yet, despite this cynicism, it seems increasingly the case that for many who comment on and form opinions about the presidency, word rivals deed as the measure of presidential performance. The standard set for presidents has in large degree become an artifact of their own inflated rhetoric and one to which they frequently fall victim. While part of this difficulty can be blamed on the ineptness of certain presidents' rhetorical strategies, it is also the case that presidents operate in a context that gives them much less discretion over their rhetoric than one might think. The problem is thus not one simply of individual rhetorics, but is rather an institutional dilemma for the modern presidency. Beginning with the campaign, the candidates are obliged to demonstrate their leadership capacity through an ever growing number of rhetorical performances, with the potential impact of their words on future problems of governing often being the least of their concerns. The pressure to "say something" continues after the president has begun to govern. Presidents not only face the demand to explain what they have done and intend to do, but they also have come under increasing pressure to speak out on perceived crises and to minister to the moods and emotions of the populace. In the end, it may be the office of the presidency that is weakened by this form of leadership, puffed up by false expectations that bear little relationship to the practical tasks of governing and undermined by the resulting cynicism.

How did the rhetorical presidency come into existence? What are its strengths and weaknesses? Can presidents escape its burdens, and to what extent should they try to do so? These are some of the important questions that need addressing.

The rise of the rhetorical presidency has been primarily the result of three factors: (1) a modern doctrine of presidential leadership, (2) the modern mass media, and (3) the modern presidential campaign. Of these three, doctrine is probably the most important.

As strange as it may seem to us today, the framers of our Constitution looked with great suspicion on popular rhetoric. Their fear was that mass oratory, whether crudely demogogic or highly inspirational, would undermine the rational and enlightened self-interest of the citizenry which their system was designed to foster and on which it was thought to depend for its stability. The framers' well-known mistrust of "pure" democracy by an assembly—and by extension, of the kind of representative government that looked only to public opinion as its guide—was not based, as is generally supposed, on a simple doubt about the people's capacity go govern, but on a more complex case concerning the evils that would result from the interplay between the public and popular orators.

In democracies, they reasoned, political success and fame are won by those orators who most skillfully give expression to transient, often inchoate, public opinion. Governing by this means, if indeed it can be called governing, leads to constant instability as leaders compete with each other to tap the latest mood passing through the public. The paradox of government by mood is that it fosters neither democratic accountability nor statesmanly efficiency. Freed from the necessity to consult public opinion, understood as "the cool and deliberate sense of the community," popular orators would be so chained to public opinion, understood as "mood," that discretion and flexibility essential to statesmanship would be undermined.

The framers were not so impractical as to think that popular rhetoric could be entirely avoided in a republican system. But the government they designed was intended to minimize reliance on popular oratory and to establish institutions which could operate effectively without the immediate support of transient opinion. All of the powers of governing were to be given, not directly to the people, but to their representatives. These representatives would find themselves in a tripartite government in which the various tasks of governing would be clearly discernible and assigned, and in which they would be forced to deal with knowledgeable and determined men not easily impressed by facile oratory. As part of their solution, the framers were counting on the large size of the nation, which at the time erected a communication barrier that would mute the impact of national popular rhetoric, whether written or oral. Beyond this, the framers instituted a presidential selection system that was designed to preclude active campaigning by the candidates. As for the presidency itself, the framers discouraged any idea that the president should serve as a leader of the people who would stir mass opinion by rhetoric; their conception was rather that of a constitutional officer who would rely for his authority on the formal powers granted by the Constitution and on the informal authority that would flow from the office's strategic position.

These limitations on popular rhetoric did not mean, however, that presidents were expected to govern in silence. Ceremonial occasions presented a proper forum for reminding the public of the nation's basic principles; and communications to Congress, explicitly provided for by the Constitution, offered a mechanism by which the people also could be informed on matters of policy. Yet this intrabranch rhetoric, though public, was not meant to be popular. Addressed in the first instance to a body of informed representatives, it would possess a reasoned and deliberative character; and insofar as some in the public would read these speeches and state papers, they would implicitly be called on to raise their understanding to the level of characteristic deliberative speech.

Nineteenth century politics in America did not, of course, follow exactly the framer's model of an essentially nonrhetorical regime. . . . Yet the amount of nineteenth century presidential rhetoric that even loosely could be called popular is very little indeed, and the presidency remained, with some slight alterations, a constitutional office rather than the seat of popular leadership.

The Inaugural and the Annual Address (now called the State of the Union) were the principal speeches of a president given wide dissemination. The character of the Inaugural Address illustrates the general character of presidential popular speech during the period. Given on a formal occasion, it tended to follow a pattern which was set by Jefferson's First Inaugural Address in which he delivered an exposition of the principles of the Union and its republican character. . . .

Against this tradition Woodrow Wilson gave the Inaugural Address (and presidential speech generally) a new theme. Instead of showing how the policies of the incoming administration reflected the principles of our form of government, Wilson sought to articulate the unspoken desires of the people by holding out a vision of their fulfillment. Presidential speech, in Wilson's view, should articulate what is "in our hearts" and not necessarily what is in our Constitution. . . . Wilson articulated the doctrinal foundation of the rhetorical presidency and thereby provided an alternative theoretical model to that of the framers. . . .

The Wilsonian concept of the rhetorical presidency consists of two interfused elements. First, the president should employ oratory to create an active public opinion that, if necessary, will pressure Congress into accepting his program: "He [the president] has no means of compelling Congress except through public opinion." In advancing policy, deliberative, intrabranch rhetoric thus becomes secondary to popular rhetoric, and the president "speaks" to Congress not directly but through his popular addresses. Second, in order to reach and move the public, the character of the rhetoric must tap the public's feelings and articulate its wishes. Rhetoric does not instill old and established principles as much as it seeks to infuse a sense of vision into the president's particular legislative program.

> A nation is led by a man who . . . speaks, not the rumors of the street, but a new principle for a new age; a man in whose ears the voices of the nation do not sound like the accidental and discordant notes that come from the voice of a mob, but concurrent and concordant like the united voices of a chorus, whose many meanings, spoken by melodious tongues, unite in his understanding in a single meaning and reveal to him a single vision, so that he can speak what no man else knows, the common meaning of the common voice.

If the doctrine of the rhetorical presidency leaves us today with the occasional feeling that it is hollow or outworn, it is not because of a decline in its influence but because of the inevitable consequences of its ascendancy. . . .

The second factor that accounts for the rise of the rhetorical presidency is the modern mass media. The media did not create the rhetorical presidency—doctrine did—but it facilitated its development and has given to it some of its special characteristics. The mass media, meaning here primarily radio and television, must be understood first from the perspective of its technical capacities. It has given the president the means by which to communicate directly and instantaneously with a large national audience, thus tearing down the communications barrier on which the framers had relied to insulate representative institutions from direct contact with the populace. Besides increasing the size of the president's audience, the mass media have changed the mode by which he communicates with the public, replacing the written with the spoken word delivered in a dramatic visible performance. The written word formerly provided a partial screen or check against the most simplistic argumentations, as it allowed more control of the text by the reader and limited the audience to those with the most interest in politics. . . .

The influence of the mass media on presidential rhetoric is not limited to its technical capacities. The mass media have also created a new power center in American politics in the form of television news. If the technical aspect of the media has given the president an advantage or an opportunity, the existence of television news often serves as a rival or an impediment. Journalists are filters in the communication process, deciding what portions of the president's non-televised speeches they will show and how their arguments will be interpreted. When presidents speak in public today, their most important audience is not the one they are personally addressing, but rather the public as it is reached through the brief cuts aired on the news. Speeches accordingly tend to be written so that any segment can be taken to stand by itself—as a self-contained lead. Argument gives way to aphorism.

The direct impact of the news media's interpretation of the president's words is perhaps less important for presidential rhetoric than the indirect influence that derives from the character of news itself. Television news not only carries the messages of governing officials to the people; it also selects the issues that are presented to the government for "action" of some sort. "Real" expressions of mass opinion, which in the past were sporadic, are replaced by the news media's continuous "sophisticated" analyses that serve as a surrogate audience, speaking to the government and supposedly representing to it what the people are saying and thinking. Driven by its own inner dynamic to find and sustain exciting issues and to present them in dramatic terms, the news media create—or give the impression of creating—national moods and currents of opinion which appear to call for some form of action by the government and especially by the president.

The media and the modern presidency feed on each other. The media have found in the presidency a focal point on which to concentrate their peculiarly simplistic and dramatic interpretation of events; and the presidency has found a vehicle in the media that allows it to win public attention and with that attention the reality, but more often the pretense, of enhanced power. . . .

The modern presidential campaign is the third factor that accounts for the rise of the rhetorical presidency. The roots of the modern campaign go back to Wilson and the Progressives and to many of the same ideas that helped to create the rhetorical presidency. Prior to 1912, the parties were largely responsible for conducting the campaigns, and the candidates, with few exceptions, restricted their communications to letters of acceptance of the nomination. Wilson was the first victorious presidential candidate to have engaged in a full-scale speaking tour during the campaign. In his view, it was essential that the candidates replace the parties as the main rhetorical instruments of the campaign. This change would serve not only to downgrade the influence of traditional parties but also to prepare the people for the new kind of presidency that he hoped to establish. Indeed, with Wilson the distinction between campaigning and governing is blurred, as both involve the same essential function of persuading through popular oratory.

Although Wilson himself did not campaign extensively in the preconvention period, he supported the idea of a preconvention campaign and pushed for nomination by national primaries. His ideal of a truly open presidential nomination campaign in which all candidates must take the "outside" route was not fully realized, however, until after the reforms that followed the 1968 election. Over the past three campaigns (1972, 1976 and 1980) we have seen the development of one of the most peculiarly irresponsible rhetorical processes ever devised. For a period of what is now well over a year, the various contenders have little else to offer except their rhetoric. Undisciplined by the responsibility of matching word to deed, they seek to create events out of their speeches, all the while operating under the constant media-created pressure to say something new. As their goal is to win power, and as that goal, especially in the preconvention period, is remote, candidates can easily afford to disregard the impact of their speech on the demands of governing and instead craft their rhetoric with a view merely to persuading. . . .

The presidential campaign is important for the kinds of inflated expectations it raises, but it is even more important for the effects it has on the process of governing. So formative has the campaign become of our tastes for oratory and of our conception of leadership that presidential speech and governing have come more and more to imitate the model of the campaign. . . .

The inflated expectations engendered by the rhetorical presidency have by now become a matter of serious concern among those who study the presidency. In response to this problem, a growing number of scholars have begun to argue that presidents should remove themselves from much day-to-day management of government and reserve themselves for crisis management. If this argument means only that presidents should not immerse themselves in details or spread themselves too thin, no one could quarrel with it. But if it means that the president should abandon the articulation of a broad legislative program or avoid general management of the bureaucracy at a time when the bureaucracy is becoming more and more unmanageable, then the argument is misguided. If the president does not give coherence to policy or enforce discipline on the Executive branch, who will? Certainly not Congress. The president remains our only national officer who, as Jefferson once said, "commands a view of the whole ground." A retrenched presidency that cedes much of its authority to others and merely reacts to crisis is hardly the answer to our difficulties. . . .

The roots of the rhetorical presidency extend so deeply into our political structure and national consciousness that talk of change may seem futile; and yet the evident failures of the current doctrine, together with the growing scholarly debate about the crisis of the presidency, suggest that the moment has arrived for a discussion of alternatives. It should not be forgotten that the foundations of the rhetorical presidency were deliberately laid by Woodrow Wilson and that other presidents might establish new doctrines. If a sensible reform of the institution is ever possible, the key will be found in reversing the order of President Carter's July 1979 formulation—that is, in restoring the president to his natural place as the head of government, and subordinating his awkward role of an itinerant leader of the people. But how could such change take place, and what would the contours of the office look like?

First, since the modern campaign is the source of so many of the problems of the presidency, it is evident that no reform of the office can hope to succeed without change in the selection process. The operative theoretical principle that must govern this change is that the selection process should be thought of not as an end in itself, but as a means of promoting, or at least not undermining, the character of the presidential office. Construed in practical terms, this principle translates into a call for electoral reform that would reduce the duration of the campaign, especially in the preconvention period. The elimination or dramatic reduction in the number of presidential primaries and the return of the power of selection to the parties would be helpful. This change would not eliminate the campaign, but it would reduce its public phase to a shorter period and thus focus public attention on the speechmaking that takes place after the nomination. . . .

Second, presidents should reduce the number of their speeches. As they speak less, there is at least the chance that their words will carry more weight; and if their words carry more weight, then perhaps more thought will be given to speech that can sensibly direct action. What applies to speeches applies equally to press conferences. Press conferences without cameras would probably allow for a more detailed exchange of information between the president and the press corps and avoid the pressures on the president (and the journalists) to make each news conference dramatic and newsworthy. Written messages might replace many presently oral performances, and personal television appearances would be reserved for truly important issues of public concern.

Third, it is obvious that a reduction in the quantity of rhetoric itself is not enough; its character must also change. To avoid inspirational rhetoric does not mean that the president must abandon firm principles, practical ideals or even a political poetry that connects this generation with the moorings of our political system. Indeed, such a rhetoric is perfectly consistent with the dignity of a head of state and the character of our political order. In respect to policy, however, presidents must recapture the capacity to address the nation's enlightened self-interest no less than its sense of idealism and the related capacity to approach Congress directly rather than through the people.

The gravest problem of the rhetorical presidency, however, goes deeper than any issue confined to presidential practice. It extends to the basic questions of how our nation can be governed. No one would deny that presidents need to hold up America's basic principles and on occasion mobilize the public to meet genuine challenges. Indeed, in a liberal system of government that frees men's acquisitive instincts and allows them to devote their energies to individual material improvement, there is room on occasion for presidents to lift up the public's vision to something beyond the clash of interests. But under the influence of the rhetorical presidency, we have seen an ever-increasing reliance on inspirational rhetoric to deal with the normal problems of politics. If there is a place for such rhetoric, it is necessary also to be aware of its danger and of the corresponding need to keep it within limits.

By itself, rhetoric does not possess the power to make citizens devote themselves selflessly to the common weal, particularly where the basic principles of society protect and encourage men's independent and private activities. The founders of our country created a complex representative government designed to foster a knowledgeable concern for the common good in the concrete circumstances of political life that would be difficult, if not impossible, to elicit directly from a people led by orators. What the continued use of inspirational rhetoric fosters is not a simple credibility problem, but a deep tension between the publicly articulated understanding of the nature of our politics and the actual springs that move the system. No wonder, then, that some politicians, deceived by their own rhetoric, find it difficult to come to terms with the job of governing a nation of complex multiple interests. Far from reinforcing our country's principles and protecting its institutions, the rhetorical presidency leads us to neglect our principles for our hopes and to ignore the benefits and needs of our institutions for a fleeting sense of oneness with our leaders.

38

Jeffrey K. Tulis

Ronald Reagan, The Great Communicator (1987)

In Ronald Reagan, America found the rhetorical president. In the conduct of his administration, we can find the dilemmas of governance in modern America.

Among the consequences of Reagan's election to the presidency was the the rewriting of textbooks on American government. It was no longer possible to maintain that interest groups, subgovernments, the checks and balances system, iron triangles, and a demoralized public would frustrate the efforts of any president to accomplish substantial policy objectives, to maintain popularity, and to avoid blame for activities beyond his control.

At the time of the midterm elections in 1986, Reagan could boast of major legislative victories (budget cuts, tax reform, militarization), foreign policy victories (Grenada, the Philippines), substantial changes in the management of the bureaucracy (more centralized control, regulatory reform), a reinspiriting of the population, and a landslide reelection. Most importantly, Reagan's victories on domestic policy were substantial enough to signal a political realignment, although not a shift in party identification as that notion is usually understood. The Reagan realignment is rather a deeper shift in what the parties stand for, in the conspectus of legitimate public policy, and in some institutional arrangements designed to perpetuate these policy shifts (for example, the destruction of the Office of Economic Opportunity on one hand, and massive numbers of judicial appointments on the other). Democrats now talk like Republicans.

If these dramatic results reminded us of the powerful potential of the rhetorical presidency, the political scandal that followed the discovery of weapons payments from Iran to Nicaragua forced political observers to reconsider their enthusiasm for it. How could the president not know what was going on in his National Security Council? Journalists dusted off, rewrote, rethought, and republished old stories of how the president of the United States spends his day. A story usually suitable for the Sunday supplement during a slow week suddenly was of acute political interest.

The credibility of Reagan's policies was shaken by the credibility of his insistence not to know what they were. *Time* interviewed White House staffers and the president himself. They discovered a president who often spent more of his day in photo opportunities and greeting dignitaries than in policy discussion, a president who rarely called staffers to probe or elaborate upon their very brief memos to him, a president who allegedly prepared for the Iceland summit by reading a novel.

> Only when it comes to his speeches is Reagan truly a hands-on-President. His writers supply the substance; he adds the homespun parables. His attention to speeches reflects his own perception of the job: on many issues he sees himself less as an originator of policy than as the chief marketer of it. [*Time* (Dec., 8, 1986)].

The continual attempts to mobilize the public through the use of personal or charismatic power delegitimizes constitutional or normal authority. Garry Will noted this phenomenon in the administration of John Kennedy, a president committed to the welfare state. Attempting to pit public opinion against his own government, Kennedy developed a "counter-insurgency" style of domestic leadership that paralleled his adventures abroad. Under charismatic rule, order inheres in the leader, not in the routines of governance. Kennedy aide Theodore Sorenson described some of the institutional consequences of his president's personal presidency:

> [Kennedy] ignored Eisenhower's farewell recommendation to create a First Secretary of the Government to oversee all foreign affairs agencies. He abandoned the practice of the Cabinet's and the National Security Council's making group decisions like corporate boards of directors. He abolished the practice of White House staff meetings and weekly Cabinet meetings. He abolished the pyramid structure of the White House staff. . . .

Successors to a charismatic leader inherit "a delegitimated set of procedures" and are themselves compelled "to go outside of procedures—further delegitimating the very office they [hold]." The routinization of crisis, endemic to the rhetorical presidency, is accompanied by attempted repetitions of charisma. In Reagan's case this cycle was further reinforced by an ideology and a rhetoric opposed to the Washington establishment, to bureaucrats and bureaucracies. "In the present crisis," Reagan said at his Inauguration, "government is not the solution to our problem; government *is* the problem."

One must note that Reagan and his advisers have been sensitive to some of the pitfalls of the rhetorical presidency that I have mentioned. This administration has given considerable attention to the structure of speeches, crafting them not just for the immediate presentation but as written documents as well. While systematic research has not yet been done on the (currently incomplete) Reagan corpus of speeches, preliminary study indicates that a substantial number of those speeches contain an ordered argument and relatively few, compared to the most recent presidents, are mere laundry lists of points. The number of references to the Constitution is also substantial (although many of them also illustrate the warning I made that one not assume intelligent constitutional positions by virtue of the mere invocation of the word). Press conferences have become more formalized, with the president regaining substantial control over them. Taken together, these sorts of reforms were intended to recover some of the authority inherent in the office, to contribute to the deliberative process, and to raise important constitutional concerns.

If these developments signal an attempt to attenuate some of the dilemmas of rhetorical leadership, Reagan's love of the movie line and the offhand remark have exacerbated other problems. Under the auspices of the Wilsonian constitution, the "new way," everything a president says is "official." No president has made as much policy as Reagan has on the run, about to board a helicopter, plane, or limousine. . . .

The Great Communicator embodies the ambivalence of the rhetorical presidency. A brief review of three major policy campaigns that Reagan considers successes—tax reform, the budget victory of 1981, and the Strategic Defense Initiative—will illustrate this ambivalence more clearly. . . .

Tax Reform

. . . [T]he issue [of tax reform] did occupy a central position in Reagan's political agenda. It was the first issue mentioned in his 1985 Inaugural Address, and in his State of the Union Address a month later. He introduced his tax plan in May in a prime-time television address, and he then engaged in several trips around the country to campaign for the legislation. At crucial junctures, but only at the behest of supporters from both parties, the president . . . entered the deliberative process. . . . Reagan timed his support of various versions of the legislation to "keep the process moving." On a dramatic personal trip to Capitol Hill, Reagan convinced fellow Republicans in the House to support a bill that they did not favor in order to get one that they approved out of the Senate by promising them that he would veto any final bill that did not overcome their most substantial objections.

Reagan's campaign, directed by Secretary of the Treasury James Baker, carefully coordinated the development of draft legislation by the Treasury with simultaneous deliberations on the Hill. From the beginning there was bipartisan interest in the bill. The skepticism that any such a bill could pass was due to the very factor that made possible a good bill. Tax reform had been a continuing subject of discussion on the Hill for decades, and the intense preoccupation of several legislators, such as Senator Bill Bradley, for several years. On the House side, Congressman Dan Rostenkowski combined substantive expertise with an exceptional ability to bargain in a way that did not compromise principle. Indeed, sometimes bargains improved the substantive merits of the bill, as for example the deal to retain IRA deductions for the middle class, but eliminate them for the rich. These extensive hearings were even more thorough than they appeared, since they built upon years of deliberation on the subject.

Political observers were skeptical that tax reform could pass because it seemed to exemplify the very properties that make "collective goods" difficult to realize in our individualistic, interest-based political system. The thousands of provisions of the tax code that would be altered represented the fruits of lobbying of thousands of interest groups who would campaign to preserve their benefits. At the same time, the concrete economic benefit to individuals was projected to be relatively small. Certainly it was perceived to be small, as numerous public opinion polls revealed that most citizens thought that the tax bill would not help them personally, and a majority even believed that the economy as a whole would not be much improved by it. What was in it for the masses?

Reagan's statesmanship was based on the insight that tax reform, despite the economic arguments that informed its legislation, was not fundamentally an economic reform. Rather, it was a political reform that concretely and dramatically raised the issue of the meaning and status of *fairness* and *law-abidingness* in American politics.

The day after passage of the tax reform bill, one of the leading sponsors, Senator Bob Packwood, told the press, "This bill is not about economics, it's about fairness." This echoed the theme that the Republican president had articulated two years previously in his 1984 State of the Union Address, where he had directed his then-Treasury Secretary Donald Regan to develop a plan "to simplify the entire tax code so all taxpayers, big and small, are treated fairly." Fairness was connected to law-abidingness because the unfairness of the code stemmed, in large measure, from complications and loopholes that made evasion both easy and common. The tax code served as a nice metaphor for the integrity of the legal system as a whole, as well as an objective indicator of the law-abidingness of the American people. . . .

It is in regime-level dispute that the rhetorical presidency is most needed, and happily, it is there that it is most likely to be successful. Success is not guaranteed, of course. Oratorical skill, well-timed and principled (and not-so-principled) bargains, coordination with congressional leaders, media attention, and other contingencies (such as the other current problems facing the nation) all affect the likelihood that one will succeed. It also remains possible for a president to exploit conditions like these to secure a policy to his liking but to the detriment of the regime. Nevertheless, it is in cases like this one that the promise and the noble possibility of the rhetorical presidency display themselves.

The Budget Victory of 1981

As with Lyndon Johnson and his War on Poverty, Reagan's first substantial political victory as president came quickly, drawing upon the "capital" of popularity following his election. Reagan's campaign, like Johnson's, combined exaggerated rhetorical claims and skillful preemption of the deliberative process by avoidance or reconstruction of the rules of legislative debate, with an unstated appeal to public sympathy.

Johnson's victory benefited from the fellow-feeling generated by the national mourning for an assassinated president. Reagan benefited from the sympathy generated by his own near-assassination. He recovered from the poorest approve-to-disapprove ratio recorded by the Gallup poll for any president's second month in office, which had followed his initial televised announcement of plans for many billions of dollars of tax cuts and governmental spending cuts.

Instead of a War on Poverty, Reagan provided a characterization of the economy as "the worst economic mess since the great depression," along with a fantastic diagnosis and prescription of the problem drawn from a school of economics known as "supply side." I call the theory fantastic because Reagan refused to alter it in the face of repeated claims by almost all economists, including many members of his administration, that there was little evidence to support his theory or the particular projections that he made on the basis of it.

Reagan's theory did not so much structure congressional debate as supplant it. Reagan's Office of Management and Budget Director David Stockman figured out a way to subvert a parliamentary measure, known as the reconciliation procedure, that Congress had devised to give itself a greater role in the construction of the federal budget. Reagan skillfully made that procedure an instrument of presidential policy. After a dramatic speech to a joint session of Congress, Reagan won a substantial victory on a general budget resolution. When Rules Committee Democrats tried to force votes on specific appropriations contained in the authorizing resolution, Reagan lobbied on television and on the phone to secure a single up or down vote; and he succeeded, winning in the House 232 to 193. Kernell reports the reaction of Majority Leader James Wright, who "complained bitterly that the administration was trying to 'dictate every last scintilla, every last phrase' of legislation."

Reagan not only tried to dictate the details of legislation, he succeeded. The legislation effectively gutted all the Great Society programs inherited from Johnson's rhetorical presidency fifteen years earlier. Like Johnson's, this massive public policy was prepared hastily in the executive branch, and like the War on Poverty, the nation's legislature played no substantive role in planning the program. In short, there was no public deliberation. Finally, like Johnson's rhetorical campaign, this one created the terms by which the policy would later be held to account and the terms on which subsequent debate would proceed. Later in the term, Reagan achieved substantial tax cuts, but he also became saddled, contrary to the projections of his theory, with the largest national debt in American history.

Star Wars

. . . On March 23, 1983, Reagan addressed the nation on television.

The subject I want to discuss with you, peace and national security, is both timely and important. Timely, because I've reached a decision which offers hope for our children in the 21st century, a decision I'll tell you about in a few moments. And important because there's a very big decision that you must make for yourselves. . . .

I've become more and more deeply convinced that the human spirit must be capable of rising above dealing with other nations and human beings by threatening their existence. . . .

What if a free people could live secure in the knowledge that their security did not rest upon the threat of instant U.S. retaliation to deter a Soviet attack, that we could intercept and destroy strategic ballistic missiles before they reached our own soil or that of our allies? . . .

I clearly recognize that defensive systems have their limitations and raise certain problems and ambiguities. If paired with offensive systems, they can be viewed as fostering an aggressive policy; and no one wants that. But with these considerations in mind, I call upon the scientific community in our country, those who gave us nuclear weapons, to turn their great talents now to the cause of mankind and world peace, to give us the means of rendering these nuclear weapons impotent and obsolete. . . .

My fellow Americans, tonight we're launching an effort which holds the promise of changing the course of human history.

This is the program that has come to be known as "Star Wars." The media gave the program the appellation, and it has stuck because it seems to capture the idea of Reagan's speech better than "SDI" does. "Star Wars" seems suitable for a policy that sounds more like science fiction than shrewd defense. And indeed, the policy might have first occurred to Reagan in the late 1940s, when he played the character Brass Bancroft in a movie about a U.S. intelligence agent (Brass) whose mission is to recover a secret weapon that America has developed that renders enemy guns impotent.

In Reagan's vision, defensive systems are not a supplement or adjunct to offensive weapons but an intended replacement of them. This is why his speech fostered the view that to be effective they would have to work perfectly, one hundred percent. In subsequent speeches, the president spoke of the possibility of trading technology with the Soviets in his new defensible world. . . .

The president's own strategic advisers did not so much criticize the policy as reinterpret it in a more defensible, and much more technical, manner. In dozens of speeches, Paul Nitze, Kenneth Adelman, Secretaries George Shultz and Caspar Weinberger, and others articulated a very different policy than the president's, albeit one that they publicly claimed to be the same as his.

In the view of the president's advisers, defensive systems were a means of improving deterrence, not an alternative to it. They were a means made increasingly necessary by the Soviets' own developments in this area, a factor not mentioned by the president. In this view, defensive systems could be effective whether or not they were ultimately capable of providing a fully protective shield for the nation. . . .

[The case of] Star Wars raises the possibility that rhetoric designed to make a complex or technical issue intelligible and appealing to those who are not in a position to understand the "real" policy will come to constitute the policy it was supposed to explain. . . .

Possessed of [great] rhetorical skill, Reagan was able to establish his program. Senator Sam Nunn, a proponent of a strong defense and of SDI has perceived the potential for long-term failure engendered by this kind of leadership. The president's rhetoric ". . . causes the scientific community to be shooting in a very broad fashion and is very injurious to a sound program. . . . [It is] probably a political plus in the short term. But in the long term, it's a real trap, not for this president, but for the one who has to go before the American people and say, 'Oops. I realize Reagan said we're going to protect Peoria, but now let me tell you why we've got to protect missile Fields in Montana.' "

Finally, the case of Star Wars raises an issue of still greater gravity. Reagan apparently thinks that the program is designed to protect Peoria. He serves as a better illustration than any previous president of the possibility and danger that presidents might come themselves to think in the terms initially designed to persuade those not capable of fully understanding the policy itself. . . .

39

John F. Kennedy

Campaign Speech on the Presidency (1960)

The modern presidential campaign covers every issue in and out of the platform from cranberries to creation. But the public is rarely alerted to a candidate's views about the central issue on which all the rest turn. That central issue—and the point of my comments this noon—is not the farm problem or defense or India. It is the Presidency itself. Of course a candidate's views on specific policies are important—but Theodore Roosevelt and William Howard Taft shared policy views with entirely different results in the White House. Of course it is important to elect a good man with good intentions—but Woodrow Wilson and Warren G. Harding were both good men of good intentions—so were Lincoln and Buchanan—but there is a Lincoln Room in the White House, and no Buchanan Room.

The history of this nation—its brightest and its bleakest pages—has been written largely in terms of the different views our Presidents have had of the Presidency itself. This history ought to tell us that the American people in 1960 have an imperative right to know what any man bidding for the Presidency thinks about the place he is bidding for—whether he is aware of and willing to use the powerful resources of that office—whether his model will be Taft or Roosevelt—Wilson or Harding.

Not since the days of Woodrow Wilson has any candidate spoken on the Presidency itself before the votes have been irrevocably cast. Let us hope that the 1960 campaign, in addition to discussing the familiar issues where our positions too often blur, will also talk about the Presidency itself—as an instrument for dealing with those issues—as an office with varying roles, powers, and limitations.

During the past eight years, we have seen one concept of the Presidency at work. Our needs and hopes have been eloquently stated—but the initiative and follow-through have too often been left to others. And too often his own objectives have been lost by the President's failure to override objections from within his own party, in the Congress or even in his Cabinet.

Speech delivered to the National Press Club by John F. Kennedy on January 14, 1960. © 1960 by The New York Times Company. Reprinted by permission.

The American people in 1952 and 1956 may well have preferred this detached, limited concept of the Presidency after twenty years of fast-moving, creative presidential rule. Perhaps historians will regard this as necessarily one of those frequent periods of consolidation, a time to draw breath, to recoup our national energy. To quote the State of the Union Message: "No Congress . . . on surveying the state of the nation, has met with a more pleasing prospect than that which appears at the present time." Unfortunately this is not Mr. Eisenhower's last message to the Congress, but Calvin Coolidge's. He followed to the White House Mr. Harding, whose "sponsor" declared very frankly that the times did not demand a first-rate President. If true, the times and the man met.

But the question is what do the times—and the people—demand for the next four years in the White House?

They demand a vigorous proponent of the national interest—not a passive broker for conflicting private interests. They demand a man capable of acting as the commander in chief of the grand alliance, not merely a bookkeeper who feels that his work is done when the numbers on the balance sheet come out even. They demand that he be the head of a responsible party, not rise so far above politics as to be invisible—a man who will formulate and fight for legislative policies, not be a casual bystander to the legislative process.

Today a restricted concept of the Presidency is not enough. For beneath today's surface gloss of peace and prosperity are increasingly dangerous, unsolved, long-postponed problems—problems that will inevitably explode to the surface during the next four years of the next Administration—the growing missile gap, the rise of Communist China, the despair of the underdeveloped nations, the explosive situations in Berlin and in the Formosa Straits, the deterioration of NATO, the lack of an arms control agreement, and all the domestic problems of our farms, cities, and schools.

This Administration has not faced up to these and other problems. Much has been said—but I am reminded of the old Chinese proverb: "There is a great deal of noise on the stairs but nobody comes into the room." The President's State of the Union Message reminded me of the exhortation from "King Lear" that goes: "I will do such things—what they are I know not . . . but they shall be the wonders of the earth."

In the decade that lies ahead—in the challenging, revolutionary Sixties—the American Presidency will demand more than ringing manifestoes issued from the rear of the battle. It will demand that the President place himself in the very thick of the fight, that he care passionately about the fate of the people he leads, that he be willing to serve them at the risk of incurring their momentary displeasure.

Whatever the political affiliation of our next President, whatever his views may be on all the issues and problems that rush in upon us, he must above all be the Chief Executive in every sense of the word. He must be prepared to exercise the fullest powers of his office—all that are specified and some that are not. He must master complex problems as well as receive one-page memoranda. He must originate action as well as study groups. He must reopen the channels of communication between the world of thought and the seat of power.

Ulysses Grant considered the President "a purely administrative officer." If he administered the government departments efficiently, delegated his functions smoothly, and performed his ceremonies of state with decorum and grace, no more was to be expected of him. But that is not the place the Presidency was meant to have in American life. The President is alone, at the top—the loneliest job there is, as Harry Truman has said. If there is destructive dissension among the services, he alone can step in and straighten it out—instead of waiting for unanimity. If administrative agencies are not carrying out their mandate—if a brushfire threatens some part of the globe—he alone can act, without waiting for the Congress. If his farm program fails, he alone deserves the blame, not his Secretary of Agriculture.

"The President is at liberty, both in law and conscience, to be as big a man as he can." So wrote Professor Woodrow Wilson. But President Woodrow Wilson discovered that to be a big man in the White House inevitably brings cries of dictatorship. So did Lincoln and Jackson and the two Roosevelts. And so may the next occupant of that office, if he is the man the times demand. But how much better it would be, in the turbulent Sixties, to have a Roosevelt or a Wilson than to have another James Buchanan, cringing in the White House, afraid to move.

Nor can we afford a Chief Executive who is praised primarily for what he did not do, the disasters he prevented, the bills he vetoed—a President wishing his subordinates would produce more missiles or build more schools. We will need instead what the Constitution envisioned: a Chief Executive who is the vital center of action in our whole scheme of government.

This includes the legislative process as well. The President cannot afford—for the sake of the office as well as the nation—to be another Warren G. Harding, described by one backer as a man who "would, when elected, sign whatever bill the Senate sent him—and not send bills for the Senate to pass." Rather he must know when to lead the Congress, when to consult it and when he should act alone. Having served fourteen years in the Legislative Branch, I would not look with favor upon its domination by the Executive. Under our government of "power as the rival of power," to use Hamilton's phrase, Congress must not surrender its responsibilities. But neither should it dominate. However large its share in the formulation of domestic programs, it is the President alone who must make the major decisions of our foreign policy.

That is what the Constitution wisely commands. And even domestically, the President must initiate policies and devise laws to meet the needs of the nation. And he must be prepared to use all the resources of his office to insure the enactment of that legislation—even when conflict is the result. By the end of his term Theodore Roosevelt was not popular in the Congress—particularly when he criticized an amendment to the Treasury appropriation which forbade the use of Secret Service men to investigate congressmen! And the feeling was mutual, Roosevelt saying: "I do not much admire the Senate, because it is such a helpless body when efficient work is to be done." And Woodrow Wilson was even more bitter after his frustrating quarrels—asked if he might run for the Senate in 1920, he replied: "Outside of the United States, the Senate does not amount to a damn. And inside the United States, the Senate is mostly despised. They haven't had a thought down there in fifty years."

But, however bitter their farewells, the facts of the matter are that Roosevelt and Wilson did get things done—not only through their Executive powers but through the Congress as well. Calvin Coolidge, on the other hand, departed from Washington with cheers of Congress still ringing in his ears. But when his World Court bill was under fire on Capitol Hill he sent no messages, gave no encouragement to the bill's leaders and paid little or no attention to the whole proceeding—and the cause of world justice was set back. To be sure, Coolidge had held the usual White House breakfasts with congressional leaders—but they were aimed, as he himself said, at "good fellowship," not a discussion of "public business." And at his press conferences, according to press historians, where he preferred to talk about the local flower show and its exhibits, reporters who finally extracted from him a single sentence— "I am against that bill"—would rush to file tongue-in-cheek dispatches, proclaiming that: "President Coolidge, in a fighting mood, today served notice on Congress that he intended to combat, with all the resources at his command, the pending bill. . . ."

But in the coming years, we will need a real fighting mood in the White House—a man who will not retreat in the face of pressure from his congressional leaders—who will not let down those supporting his views on the floor. Divided government over the past six years has only been further confused by this lack of legislative leadership. To restore it next year will help restore purpose to both the Presidency and the Congress.

The facts of the matter are that legislative leadership is not possible without party leadership, in the most political sense—and Mr. Eisenhower prefers to stay above politics (although a weekly news magazine last fall reported the startling news that "President Eisenhower is emerging as a major political figure"). When asked, early in his first term, how he liked the "game of politics," he replied with a frown that his questioner was using a derogatory phrase. "Being President," he said, "is a very great experience . . . but the word 'politics' . . . I have no great liking for that." But no President, it seems to me, can escape politics. He has not only been chosen by the nation—he has been chosen by his party. And if he insists that he is "President of all the people" and should, therefore, offend none of them—if he blurs the issues and differences between the parties—if he neglects the party machinery and avoids his party's leadership—then he has not only weakened the political party as an instrument of the democratic process—he has dealt a blow to the democratic process itself. I prefer the example of Abe Lincoln, who loved politics with the passion of a born practitioner. For example, he waited up all night in 1863 to get the crucial returns on the Ohio governorship. When the Unionist candidate was elected, Lincoln wired: "Glory to God in the highest! Ohio has save the nation!"

But the White House is not only the center of political leadership. It must be the center of moral leadership—a "bully pulpit," as Theodore Roosevelt described it. For only the President represents the national interest. And upon him alone converge all the needs and aspirations of all parts of the country, all departments of the government, all nations of the world. It is not enough merely to represent prevailing sentiment—to follow McKinley's practice, as described by Joe Cannon, of "keeping his ear so close to the ground he got it full of grasshoppers." We will need in the Sixties a President who is willing and able to summon his national constituency to its finest hour—to alert the people to our dangers and our opportunities—to demand of them the sacrifices that will be necessary. Despite the increasing evidence of a lost national purpose and a soft national will, F.D.R.'s words in his first inaugural still ring true: "In every dark hour of our national life, a leadership of frankness and vigor has met with that understanding and support of the people themselves which is essential to victory."

Roosevelt fulfilled the role of moral leadership. So did Wilson and Lincoln, Truman and Jackson and Teddy Roosevelt. They led the people as well as the government—they fought for great ideals as well as bills. And the time has come to demand that kind of leadership again. And so, as this vital campaign begins, let us discuss the issues the next President will face—but let us also discuss the powers and tools with which he must face them. For he must endow that office with extraordinary strength and vision. He must act in the image of Abraham Lincoln summoning his wartime Cabinet to a meeting on the Emancipation Proclamation. That Cabinet had been carefully chosen to please and reflect many elements in the country. But "I have gathered you together," Lincoln said, "to hear what I have written down. I do not wish your advice about the main matter—that I have determined for myself." And later when he went to sign it after several hours of exhausting handshaking that had left his arm weak, he said to those present: "If my name goes down in history, it will be for this act. My whole soul is in it. If my hand trembles when I sign this proclamation, all who examine the document hereafter will say: 'He hesitated.' " But Lincoln's hand did not tremble. He did not hesitate. He did not equivocate. For he was the President of the United States. It is in this spirit that we must go forth in the coming months and years.

40

Abraham Lincoln

The Perpetuation of Our Political Institutions (1838)

As a subject for the remarks of the evening, *the perpetuation of our political institutions,* is selected.

In the great journal of things happening under the sun, we, the American People, find our account running, under date of the nineteenth century of the Christian era. We find ourselves in the peaceful possession, of the fairest portion of the earth, as regards extent of territory, fertility of soil, and salubrity of climate. We find ourselves under the government of a system of political institutions, conducing more essentially to the ends of civil and religious liberty, than any of which the history of former times tells us. We, when mounting the stage of existence, found ourselves the legal inheritors of these fundamental blessings. We toiled not in the acquirement or establishment of them—they are a legacy bequeathed us, by a *once* hardy, brave, and patriotic, but *now* lamented and departed race of ancestors. Their's was the task (and nobly they performed it) to possess themselves, and through themselves, us, of this goodly land; and to uprear upon its hills and its valleys, a political edifice of liberty and equal rights; 'tis ours only, to transmit these, the former, unprofaned by the foot of an invader; the latter, undecayed by the lapse of time, and untorn by usurpation—to the latest generation that fate shall permit the world to know. This task of gratitude to our fathers, justice to ourselves, duty to posterity, and love for our species in general, all imperatively require us faithfully to perform.

How, then, shall we perform it? At what point shall we expect the approach of danger? By what means shall we fortify against it? Shall we expect some transatlantic military giant, to step the Ocean, and crush us at a blow? Never! All the armies of Europe, Asia and Africa combined, with all the treasure of the earth (our own excepted) in their military chest; with a Buonaparte for a commander, could not by force, take a drink from the Ohio, or make a track on the Blue Ridge, in a trial of a thousand years.

From *The Collected Works of Abraham Lincoln,* Vol. I, Rutgers University Press, 1953.

At what point then is the approach of danger to be expected? I answer, if it ever reach us, it must spring up amongst us. It cannot come from abroad. If destruction be our lot, we must ourselves be its author and finisher. As a nation of freemen, we must live through all time, or die by suicide.

I hope I am over wary; but if I am not, there is, even now, something of ill-omen amongst us. I mean the increasing disregard for law which pervades the country; the growing disposition to substitute the wild and furious passions, in lieu of the sober judgment of Courts; and the worse than savage mobs, for the executive ministers of justice. This disposition is awfully fearful in any community; and that it now exists in ours, though grating to our feelings to admit, it would be a violation of truth, and an insult to our intelligence, to deny. Accounts of outrages committed by mobs, form the every-day news of the times. They have pervaded the country, from New England to Louisiana;—they are neither peculiar to the eternal snows of the former, nor the burning suns of the latter;—they are not the creature of climate—neither are they confined to the slaveholding, or the nonslaveholding States. Alike, they spring up among the pleasure hunting masters of Southern slaves, and the order loving citizens of the land of steady habits. Whatever, then, their cause may be, it is common to the whole country.

It would be tedious, as well as useless, to recount the horrors of all of them. Those happening in the State of Mississippi, and at St. Louis, are, perhaps, the most dangerous in example, and revolting to humanity. In the Mississippi case, they first commenced by hanging the regular gamblers: a set of men, certainly not following for a livelihood, a very useful, or very honest occupation, but one which, so far from being forbidden by the laws, was actually licensed by an act of the Legislature, passed but a single year before. Next, negroes, suspected of conspiring to raise an insurrection, were caught up and hanged in all parts of the State: then, white men, supposed to be leagued with the negroes; and finally, strangers, from neighboring States, going thither on business, were, in many instances, subjected to the same fate. Thus went on this process of hanging, from gamblers to negroes, from negroes to white citizens, and from these to strangers; till, dead men were seen literally dangling from the boughs of trees upon every road side; and in numbers almost sufficient, to rival the native Spanish moss of the country, as a drapery of the forest.

Turn, then, to that horror-striking scene at St. Louis. A single victim was only sacrificed there. His story is very short; and is, perhaps, the most highly tragic, of any thing of its length, that has ever been witnessed in real life. A mulatto man, by the name of McIntosh, was seized in the street, dragged to the suburbs of the city, chained to a tree, and actually burned to death; and all within a single hour from the time he had been a freeman, at-tending to his own business, and at peace with the world.

Such are the effects of mob law; and such are the scenes, becoming more and more frequent in this land so lately famed for love of law and order; and the stories of which, have even now grown too familiar, to at-tract anything more, than an idle remark.

But you are, perhaps, ready to ask, "What has this to do with the perpetuation of our political institutions?" I answer, it has much to do with it. Its direct consequences are, comparatively speaking, but a small evil; and much of its danger consists, in the proneness of our minds, to regard its direct, as its only consequences. Abstractly considered, the hanging of the gamblers at Vicksburg, was of but little consequence. They constitute a portion of population, that is worse than useless in any community; and their death, if no pernicious example be set by it, is never matter of reasonable regret with any one. If they were annually swept, from the stage of existence, by the plague or small pox, honest men would, perhaps, be much profited, by the operation. Similar too, is the correct reasoning, in regard to the burning of the negro at St. Louis. He had forfeited his life, by the perpetration of an outrageous murder, upon one of the most worthy and respectable citizens of the city; and had he not died as he did, he must have died by the sentence of the law, in a very short time afterwards. As to him alone, it was as well the way it was, as it could otherwise have been. But the example in either case, was fearful. When men take it in their heads today, to hang gamblers, or burn murderers, they should recollect, that, in the confusion usually attending such transactions, they will be as likely to hang or burn some one, who is neither a gambler nor a murderer as one who is; and that, acting upon the example they set, the mob of tomorrow, may, and probably will, hang or burn some of them, by the very same mistake. And not only so; the innocent, those who have ever set their faces against violations of law in every shape, alike with the guilty, fall victims to the ravages of mob law; and thus it goes on, step by step; till all the walls erected for the defence of the persons and property of individuals, are trodden down, and disregarded. But all this even, is not the full extent of the evil. By such examples, by instances of the perpetrators of such acts going unpunished, the lawless in spirit, are encouraged to become lawless in practice; and having been used to no restraint, but dread of punishment, they thus become, absolutely unrestrained. Having ever regarded Govern-ment as their deadliest bane, they make a jubilee of the suspension of its operations; and pray for nothing so much, as its total annihilation. While, on the other hand, good men, men who love tranquility, who desire to abide by the laws, and enjoy their benefits, who would gladly spill their blood in the defence of their country; seeing their property destroyed; their families insulted, and their lives endangered; their persons injured; and seeing nothing in prospect that forebodes a change for the better; become tired of, and disgusted with, a Government that offers them no protection; and are not much averse to a change in which they imagine they have nothing to lose. Thus, then, by the operation of this mobocratic spirit, which all must admit, is now abroad in the land, the strongest bulwark of any Government, and particularly of those constituted like ours, may effectually be broken down and destroyed—I mean the *attachment* of the People. Whenever this effect shall be produced among us; whenever the vicious portion of population shall be permitted to gather in bands of hundreds and thousands, and burn churches, ravage and rob provision stores, throw printing presses into rivers, shoot editors,* and hang and burn obnoxious persons at pleasure, and with impunity; depend on it, this Government cannot last. By such things, the feelings of the best citizens will become more or less alienated from it; and thus it will be left without friends, or with too few, and those few too weak, to make their friendship effectual. At such a time and under such circumstances, men of sufficient talent and ambition will not be wanting to seize the opportunity, strike the blow, and overturn that fair fabric, which for the last half century, had been the fondest hope, of the lovers of freedom, throughout the world.

I know the American People are *much* attached to their Government;—I know they would suffer *much* for its sake;—I know they would endure evils long and patiently, before they would ever think of exchanging it for another. Yet, notwithstanding all this, if the laws be continually despised and disregarded, if their rights to be secure in their persons and property, are held by no better tenure than the caprice of a mob, the alienation of their affections from the Government is the natural consequence; and to that, sooner or later, it must come.

Here then, is one point at which danger may be expected.

The question recurs "how shall we fortify against it?" The answer is simple. Let every American, every lover of liberty, every well wisher to his posterity, swear by the blood of the Revolution, never to violate in the least particular, the laws of the country; and never to tolerate their violation by others. As the patriots of seventy-six did to the support of the Declaration of Independence, so to the support of the Constitution and Laws, let every American pledge his life, his property, and his sacred honor;—let every man remember that to violate the law, is to trample on the blood of his father, and to tear the character [charter?] of his own, and his children's liberty. Let reverence for the laws, be breathed by every American mother, to the

---

*On November 7, 1787, the Abolitionist newspaper editor, Elijah Parish Lovejoy, was lynched at Alton, Illinois.

lisping babe, that prattles on her lap—let it be taught in schools, in seminaries, and in colleges;—let it be written in Primmers, spelling books, and in Almanacs;—let it be preached from the pulpit, proclaimed in legislative halls, and enforced in courts of justice. And, in short, let it become the *political religion* of the nation; and let the old and the young, the rich and the poor, the grave and the gay, of all sexes and tongues, and colors and conditions, sacrifice unceasingly upon its altars.

While ever a state of feeling, such as this, shall universally, or even, very generally prevail throughout the nation, vain will be every effort, and fruitless every attempt, to subvert our national freedom.

When I so pressingly urge a strict observance of all the laws, let me not be understood as saying there are no bad laws, nor that grievances may not arise, for the redress of which, no legal provisions have been made. I mean to say no such thing. But I do mean to say, that, although bad laws, if they exist, should be repealed as soon as possible, still while they continue in force, for the sake of example, they should be religiously observed. So also in unprovided cases. If such arise, let proper legal provisions be made for them with the least possible delay; but, till then, let them if not too intolerable, be borne with.

There is no grievance that is a fit object of redress by mob law. In any case that arises, as for instance, the promulgation of abolitionism, one of two positions is necessarily true; that is, the thing is right within itself, and therefore deserves the protection of all law and all good citizens; or, it is wrong, and therefore proper to be prohibited by legal enactments; and in neither case, is the interposition of mob law, either necessary, justifiable, or excusable.

But, it may be asked, why suppose danger to our political institutions? Have we not preserved them for more than fifty years? And why may we not for fifty times as long?

We hope there is no *sufficient* reason. We hope all dangers may be overcome; but to conclude that no danger may ever arise, would itself be extremely dangerous. There are now, and will hereafter be, many causes, dangerous in their tendency, which have not existed heretofore; and which are not too insignificant to merit attention. That our government should have been maintained in its original form from its establishment until now, is not much to be wondered at. It had many props to support it through that period, which now are decayed, and crumbled away. Through that period, it was felt by all, to be an undecided experiment; now, it is understood to be a successful one. Then, all that sought celebrity and fame, and distinction, expected to find them in the success of that experiment. Their *all* was staked upon it:—their destiny was *inseparably* linked with it. Their ambition aspired to display before an admiring world, a practical demonstration of the truth of a proposition, which had hitherto been considered, at best no better, than problematical; namely, *the capability of a people to govern themselves.* If they succeeded, they were to be immortalized; their names were to be transferred to counties and cities, and rivers and mountains; and to be revered and sung, and toasted through all time. If they failed, they were to be called knaves and fools, and fanatics for a fleeting hour; then to sink and be forgotten. They succeeded. The experiment is successful; and thousands have won their deathless names in making it so. But the game is caught; and I believe it is true, that with the catching, end the pleasures of the chase. This field of glory is harvested, and the crop is already appropriated. But new reapers will arise, and *they,* too, will seek a field. It is to deny, what the history of the world tells us is true, to suppose that men of ambition and talents will not continue to spring up amongst us. And, when they do, they will as naturally seek the gratification of their ruling passion, as others have *so* done before them. The question then, is, can that gratification be found in supporting and maintaining an edifice that has been erected by others? Most certainly it cannot. Many great and good men sufficiently qualified for any task they should undertake, may ever be found, whose ambition would aspire to nothing beyond a seat in Congress, a gubernatorial or a presidential chair; *but such belong not to the family of the lion, or the tribe of the eagle.* What! think you these places would satisfy an Alexander, a Caesar, or a Napoleon? Never! Towering genius disdains a beaten path. It seeks regions hitherto unexplored. It sees *no distinction* in adding story to story, upon the monuments of fame, erected to the memory of others. It *denies* that it is glory enough to serve under any chief. It *scorns* to tread in the footsteps of *any* predecessor, however illustrious. It thirsts and burns for distinction; and, if possible, it will have it, whether at the expense of emancipating slaves, or enslaving freemen. Is it unreasonable then to expect, that some man possessed of the loftiest genius, coupled with ambition sufficient to push it to its utmost stretch, will at some time, spring up among us? And when such a one does, it will require the people to be united with each other, attached to the government and laws, and generally intelligent, to successfully frustrate his designs.

Distinction will be his paramount object; and although he would as willingly, perhaps more so, acquire it by doing good as harm; yet, that opportunity being past, and nothing left to be done in the way of building up, he would set boldly to the task of pulling down.

Here then, is a probable case, highly dangerous, and such a one as could not have well existed heretofore.

Another reason which *once was;* but which, to the same extent, is *now no more,* has done much in maintaining our institutions thus far. I mean the powerful influence which the interesting scenes of the revolution had upon the *passions* of the people as distinguished from their judgment. By this influence, the jealousy, envy, and avarice, incident to our nature, and so common to a state of peace, prosperity, and conscious strength, were, for the time, in a great measure smothered and rendered inactive; while the deep rooted principles of *hate,* and the powerful motive of *revenge,* instead of being turned against each other, were directed exclusively against the British nation. And thus, from the force of circumstances, the basest principles of our nature, were either made to lie dormant, or to become the active agents in the advancement of the noblest of causes—that of establishing and maintaining civil and religious liberty.

But this state of feeling *must fade, is fading, has faded,* with the circumstances that produced it.

I do not mean to say, that the scenes of the revolution *are now* or *ever will be* entirely forgotten; but that like every thing else, they must fade upon the memory of the world, and grow more and more dim by the lapse of time. In history, we hope, they will be read of, and recounted, so long as the bible shall be read;—but even granting that they will, their influence *cannot be* what it heretofore has been. Even then, they *cannot be* so universally known, nor so vividly felt, as they were by the generation just gone to rest. At the close of that struggle, nearly every adult male had been a participator in some of its scenes. The consequence was, that of those scenes, in the form of a husband, a father, a son or a brother, a *living history was* to be found in every family—a history bearing the indubitable testimonies of its own authenticity, in the limbs mangled, in the scars of wounds received, in the midst of the very scenes related—a history, too, that could be read and understood alike by all, the wise and the ignorant, the learned and the unlearned. But *those* histories are gone. They *can* be read no more forever. They *were* a fortress of strength; but, what invading foemen could *never do,* the silent artillery of time *has done;* the levelling of its walls. They are gone. They *were* a forest of giant oaks; but the all-resistless hurricane has swept over them, and left only, here and there, a lonely trunk, despoiled of its verdure, shorn of its foliage; unshading and unshaded, to murmur in a few more gentle breezes, and to combat with its mutilated limbs, a few more ruder storms, then to sink, and be no more.

They *were* pillars of the temple of liberty; and now, that they have crumbled away, that temple must fall, unless we, their descendants, supply their places with other pillars, hewn from the solid quarry of sober reason. Passion has helped us; but can do so no more. It will in future be our enemy. Reason, cold, calculating, unimpassioned reason, must furnish all the materials for our future support and defence. Let those materials be molded into *general intelligence, sound morality* and, in particular, *a reverence for the constitution and laws;* and, that we improved to the last; that we remained free to the last; that we revered his name to the last; that, during his long sleep, we permitted no hostile foot to pass over or desecrate his resting place; shall be that which to learn and last trump shall awaken our WASHINGTON.

Upon these let the proud fabric of freedom rest, as the rock of its basis; and as truly as has been said of the only greater institution, " *the gates of hell shall not prevail against it.* "

41

Youngstown Sheet and Tube Co.
v. Sawyer (1952)

Mr. Justice Black *delivered the opinion of the Court:*

We are asked to decide whether the President was acting within his constitutional power when he issued an order directing the Secretary of Commerce to take possession of and operate most of the Nation's steel mills. . . .

The President's power, if any, to issue the order must stem from an act

From *Youngstown Sheet & Tube Co. v. Sawyer,* 343 U.S. 579 (1952).

of Congress or from the Constitution itself. There is no statute that expressly authorizes the President to take possession of property as he did here. Nor is there any act of Congress to which our attention has been directed from which such a power can fairly be implied. . . .

Moreover, the use of the seizure technique to solve labor disputes in order to prevent work stoppages was not only unauthorized by any congressional enactment; prior to this controversy, Congress has refused to adopt that method of settling labor disputes. When the Taft-Hartley Act was under consideration in 1947, Congress rejected an amendment which would have authorized such governmental seizures in cases of emergency. . . .

It is clear that if the President had authority to issue the order he did, it must be found in some provisions of the Constitituion. And it is not claimed that express constitutional language grants this power to the President. The contention is that presidential power should be implied from the aggregate of his powers under the Constitution. Particular reliance is placed on provisions in Article II which say that "the executive Power shall be vested in a President . . ."; that "he shall take Care that the Laws be faithfully executed"; and that he "shall be Commander in Chief of the Army and Navy of the United States."

The order cannot properly be sustained as an exercise of the President's military power as Commander in Chief of the Armed Forces. The Government attempts to do so by citing a number of cases unholding broad powers in military commanders engaged in day-to-day fighting in a theater of war. Such cases need not concern us here. Even though "theater of war" be an expanding concept, we cannot with faithfulness to our constitutional system hold that the Commander in Chief of the Armed Forces has the ultimate power as such to take possession of private property in order to keep labor disputes from stopping production. This is a job for the Nation's lawmakers, not for its military authorities.

Nor can the seizure order be sustained because of the several constitutional provisions that grant executive power to the President. In the framework of our Constitution, the President's power to see that the laws are faithfully executed refutes the idea that he is to be a lawmaker. The Constitution limits his functions in the law-making process to the recommending of laws he thinks wise and the vetoing of laws he thinks bad. And the Constitution is neither silent nor equivocal about who shall make laws which the President is to execute. . . .

The President's order does not direct that a congressional policy be executed in a manner prescribed by Congress—it directs that a presidential policy be executed in a manner prescribed by the President. The preamble of the order itself, like that of many statutes, sets out reasons why the President believes certain policies should be adopted, proclaims these policies as rules of conduct to be followed, and again, like a statute, authorizes a government official to promulgate additional rules and regulations consistent with the policy proclaimed and needed to carry that policy into execution. The power of Congress to adopt such public policies as those proclaimed by the order is beyond question. It can authorize the taking of private property for public use. It can make laws regulating the relationships between employers and employees, prescribing rules designed to settle labor disputes, and fixing wages and working conditions in certain fields of our economy. . . .

The Founders of this Nation entrusted the lawmaking power to the Congress alone in both good and bad times. It would do no good to recall the historical events, the fears of power and the hopes for freedom that lay behind their choice. Such a view would but confirm our holding that this seizure order cannot stand. . . .

Mr. Chief Justice Vinson, *dissenting:*

. . . Those who suggest that this is a case involving extraordinary powers should be mindful that these are extraordinary times. A world not yet recovered from the devastation of World War II has been forced to face the threat of another and more terrifying global conflict. . . .

The steel mills were seized for a public use. The power of eminent domain, invoked in this case, is an essential attribute of sovereignty and has long been recognized as a power of the Federal Government. . . .

Admitting that the Government could seize the mills, plaintiffs claim that the implied power of eminent domain can be exercised only under an Act of Congress; under no circumstances, they say, can that power be exercised by the President unless he can point to an express provision in enabling legislation. . . .

Under this view, the President is left powerless at the very moment when the need for action may be most pressing and when no one, other than he, is immediately capable of action. Under this view, he is left powerless because a power not expressly given to Congress is nevertheless found to rest exclusively with Congress. . . .

A review of executive action demonstrates that our Presidents have on many occasions exhibited the leadership contemplated by the Framers when they made the President Commander in Chief, and imposed upon him the trust to "take Care that the Laws be faithfully executed." With or without explicit statutory authorization, Presidents have at such times dealt with national emergencies by acting promptly and resolutely to enforce legislative programs, at least to save those programs until Congress could act. Congress and the courts have responded to such executive initiative with consistent approval. . . .

Jefferson's initiative in the Louisiana Purchase, the Monroe Doctrine, and Jackson's removal of Government deposits from the Bank of the United States further serve to demonstrate by deed what the Framers described by words when they vested the whole of the executive power in the President.

Without declaration of war, President Lincoln took energetic action with the outbreak of the Civil War. He summoned troops and paid them out of the Treasury without appropriation therefor. He proclaimed a naval blockade of the Confederacy and seized ships violating that blockade. Congress, far from denying the validity of these acts, gave them express approval. The most striking action of President Lincoln was the Emancipation Proclamation, issued in aid of the successful prosecution of the Civil War, but wholly without statutory authority.

In an action furnishing a most apt precedent for this case, President Lincoln directed the seizure of rail and telegraph lines leading to Washington without statutory authority. Many months later, Congress recognized and confirmed the power of the President to seize railroads and telegraph lines and provided criminal penalties for interference with Government operation. This Act did not confer on the President any additional powers of seizure. Congress plainly rejected the view that the President's acts had been without legal sanction until ratified by the legislature. Sponsors of the bill declared that its purpose was only to confirm the power which the President already possessed. Opponents insisted a statute authorizing seizure was unnecessary and might even be construed as limiting existing Presidential powers. . . .

[The Chief Justice then cites other examples of the exercise of emergency powers by American Presidents.]

Focusing now on the situation confronting the President on the night of April 8, 1952, we cannot but conclude that the President was performing his duty under the Constitution "to take care that the laws be faithfully executed"—a duty described by President Benjamin Harrison as "the central idea of the office."

The President reported to Congress the morning after the seizure that he acted because a work stoppage in steel production would immediately imperil the safety of the Nation by preventing execution of the legislative programs for procurement of military equipment. And, while a shutdown could be averted by granting the price concessions requested by plaintiffs, granting such concessions would disrupt the price stabilization program also enacted by Congress. Rather than fail to execute either legislative program, the President acted to execute both.

Much of the argument in this case has been directed at straw men. We do not now have before us the case of a President acting solely on the basis of his own notions of the public welfare. Nor is there any question of unlimited executive power in this case. The President himself closed the door to any such claim when he sent his Message to Congress stating his purpose to abide by any action of Congress, whether approving or disapproving his seizure action. Here, the President immediately made sure that Congress was fully informed of the temporary action he had taken only to preserve the legislative programs from destruction until Congress could act.

The absence of a specific statute authorizing seizure of the steel mills as a mode of executing the laws—both the military procurement program and the anti-inflation program—has not until today been thought to prevent the President from executing the laws. Unlike an administrative commission confined to the enforcement of the statute under which it was created, or the head of a department when administering a particular statute, the President is a constitutional officer charged with taking care that a "mass of legislation" be executed. Flexibility as to mode of execution to meet critical situations is a matter of practical necessity. . . .

42

United States v. Curtiss-Wright
Export Corporation (1936)

Mr. Justice Sutherland *delivered the opinion of the Court:*

On January 27, 1936, an indictment was returned in the court below, the first count of which charges that appellees, beginning with the 29th day of May, 1934, conspired to sell in the United States certain arms of war, namely, fifteen machine guns, to Bolivia, a country then engaged in armed conflict in the Chaco, in violation of the Joint Resolution of Congress approved May 28, 1934, and the provisions of a proclamation issued on the same day by the President of the United States pursuant to authority conferred by section 1 of the resolution. In pursuance of the conspiracy, the

From *United States v. Curtiss-Wright Export Corporation,* 299 U.S. 304 (1936).

commission of certain overt acts was alleged, details of which need not be stated. The Joint Resolution follows:

> *Resolved by the Senate and House of Representatives of the United States of America in Congress assembled,* That if the President finds that the prohibition of the sale of arms and munitions of war in the United States to those countries now engaged in armed conflict in the Chaco may contribute to the reestablishment of peace between those countries, and if after consultation with the governments of other American Republics and with their cooperation, as well as that of such other governments as he may deem necessary, he makes proclamation to that effect, it shall be unlawful to sell, except under such limitations and exceptions as the President prescribes, any arms or munitions of war in any place in the United States to the countries now engaged in that armed conflict, or to any person, company, or association acting in the interest of either country, until otherwise ordered by the President or by Congress.
>
> Sec. 2. Whoever sells any arms or munitions of war in violation of section 1 shall, on conviction, be punished by a fine not exceeding $10,000 or by imprisonment not exceeding two years, or both.

The President's proclamation, after reciting the terms of the joint Resolution, declares:

> Now, therefore, I, Franklin D. Roosevelt, President of the United States of America, acting under and by virtue of the authority conferred in me by the said joint resolution of Congress, do hereby declare and proclaim that I have found that the prohibition of the sale of arms and munitions of war in the United States to those countries now engaged in armed conflict in the Chaco may contribute to the reestablishment of peace between these countries, and that I have consulted with the governments of other American Republics and have been assured of the cooperation of such governments as I have deemed necessary as contemplated by the said joint resolution; and I do hereby admonish all citizens of the United States and every person to abstain from every violation of the provisions of the joint resolution above set forth, hereby made applicable to Bolivia and Paraguay, and I do hereby warn them that all violations of such provisions will be rigorously prosecuted. . . .

On November 14, 1935, this proclamation was revoked, in the following terms:

> Now, therefore, I, Franklin D. Roosevelt, President of the United States of America, do hereby declare and proclaim that I have found that the prohibition of the sale of arms and munitions of war in the United States to Bolivia or Paraguay will no longer be necessary as a contribution to the reestablishment of peace between those countries. . . .

Appellees severally demurred . . . [urging] that the Joint Resolution effects an invalid delegation of legislative power to the executive. . . .

It is contended that by the Joint Resolution the going into effect and continued operation of the resolution was conditioned (a) upon the President's judgment as to its beneficial effect upon the reestablishment of peace between the countries engaged in armed conflict in the Chaco; (b) upon the making of a proclamation, which was left to his unfettered discretion, thus constituting an attempted substitution of the President's will for that of Congress; (c) upon the making of a proclamation putting an end to the operation of the resolution, which again was left to the President's unfettered discretion; and (d) further, that the extent of its operation in particular cases was subject to limitation and exception by the President, controlled by no standard. In each of these particulars, appellees urge that Congress abdicated its essential functions and delegated them to the Executive.

Whether, if the Joint Resolution had related solely to internal affairs, it would be open to the challenge that it constituted an unlawful delegation of legislative power to the Executive, we find it unnecessary to determine. The whole aim of the resolution is to affect a situation entirely external to the United States, and falling within the category of foreign affairs. The determination which we are called to make, therefore, is whether the Joint Resolution, as applied to that situation, is vulnerable to attack under the rule that forbids a delegation of the lawmaking power. In other words, assuming (but not deciding) that the challenged delegation, if it were confined to internal affairs, would be invalid, may it nevertheless be sustained on the ground that its exclusive aim is to afford a remedy for a hurtful condition within foreign territory?

It will contribute to the elucidation of the question if we first consider the differences between the powers of the federal government in respect of foreign or external affairs and those in respect of domestic or internal affairs. That there are differences between them, and that these differences are fundamental, may not be doubted.

The two classes of powers are different, both in respect of their origin and their nature. The broad statement that the federal government can exercise no powers except those specifically enumerated in the Constitution, and such implied powers as are necessary and proper to carry into effect the enumerated powers, is categorically true only in respect of our internal affairs. In that field, the primary purpose of the Constitution was to carve from the general mass of legislative powers *then possessed by the states* such portions as it was thought desirable to vest in the federal government, leaving those not included in the enumeration still in the states. That this doctrine applies only to powers which the states had is self-evident. And since the states severally never possessed international powers, such powers could not have been carved from the mass of state powers but obviously were transmitted to the United States from some other source. During the Colonial period, those powers were possessed exclusively by and were entirely under the control of the Crown. By the Declaration of Independence, "the

Representatives of the United States of America" declared the United (not the several) Colonies to be free and "independent states," and as such to have "full Power to levy War, conclude Peace, contract Alliances, establish Commerce and to do all other Acts and Things which Independent States may of right do."

As a result of the separation from Great Britain by the colonies, acting as a unit, the powers of external sovereignty passed from the Crown not to the colonies severally, but to the colonies in their collective and corporate capacity as the United States of America. Even before the Declaration, the colonies were a unit in foreign affairs, acting through a common agency— namely, the Continental Congress, composed of delegates from the thirteen colonies. That agency exercised powers of war and peace, raised an army, created a navy, and finally adopted the Declaration of Independence. Rulers come and go; governments end and forms of government change; but sovereignty survives. A political society cannot endure without a supreme will somewhere. Sovereignty is never held in suspense. When, therefore, the external sovereignty of Great Britain in respect of the colonies ceased, it immediately passed to the Union. That fact was given practical application almost at once. The treaty of peace, made on September 3, 1783, was concluded between his Brittanic Majesty and the "United States of America."

The Union existed before the Constitution, which was ordained and established among other things to form "a more perfect Union." Prior to that event, it is clear that the Union, declared by the Articles of Confederation to be "perpetual," was the sole possessor of external sovereignty, and in the Union it remained without change save in so far as the Constitution in express terms qualified its exercise. The Framers' Convention was called and exerted its powers upon the irrefutable postulate that though the states were several their people in respect of foreign affairs were one. In that convention, the entire absence of state power to deal with those affairs was thus forcefully stated by Rufus King:

> The states were not "sovereigns" in the sense contended for by some. They did not possess the peculiar features of sovereignty,—they could not make war, nor peace, nor alliances, nor treaties. Considering them as political beings, they were dumb, for they could not speak to any foreign sovereign whatever. They were deaf, for they could not hear any propositions from such sovereign. They had not even the organs or faculties of defence or offence, for they could not of themselves raise troops, or equip vessels, for war.

It results that the investment of the federal government with the powers of external sovereignty did not depend upon the affirmative grants of the Constitution. The powers to declare and wage war, to conclude peace, to make treaties, to maintain diplomatic relations with other sovereignties, if they had never been mentioned in the Constitution, would have vested in the federal government as necessary concomitants of nationality. Neither the Constitution nor the laws passed in pursuance of it have any force in foreign territory unless in respect of our own citizens; and operations of the nation in such territory must be governed by treaties, international understandings and compacts, and the principles of international law. As a member of the family of nations, the right and power of the United States in that field are equal to the right and power of the other members of the international family. Otherwise, the United States is not completely sovereign. The power to acquire territory by discovery and occupation, the power to make such international agreements as do not constitute treaties in the constitutional sense [citations omitted], none of which is expressly affirmed by the Constitution, nevertheless exist as inherently inseparable from the conception of nationality. This the court recognized, and in each of the cases cited found the warrant for its conclusions not in the provisions of the Constitution, but in the law of nations. . . .

Not only, as we have shown, is the federal power over external affairs in origin and essential character different from that over internal affairs, but participation in the exercise of the power is significantly limited. In this vast external realm, with its important, complicated, delicate and manifold problems, the President alone has the power to speak or listen as a representative of the nation. He *makes* treaties with the advice and consent of the Senate; but he alone negotiates. Into the field of negotiation the Senate cannot intrude; and Congress itself is powerless to invade it. As Marshall said in his great argument of March 7, 1800, in the House of Representatives, "The President is the sole organ of the nation in its external relations, and its sole representative with foreign nations." The Senate Committee on Foreign Relations at a very early day in our history (February 15, 1816), reported to the Senate, among other things, as follows:

> The President is the constitutional representative of the United States with regard to foreign nations. He manages our concerns with foreign nations and must necessarily be most competent to determine when, how, and upon what subjects negotiation may be urged with the greatest prospect of success. For his conduct he is responsible to the Constitution. The committee considers this responsibility the surest pledge for the faithful discharge of his duty. They think the interference of the Senate in the direction of foreign negotiations calculated to diminish that responsibility and thereby to impair the best security for the national safety. The nature of transactions with foreign nations, moveover, requires caution and unity of design, and their success frequently depends on secrecy and dispatch.

It is important to bear in mind that we are here dealing not alone with an authority vested in the President by an exertion of legislative power, but with such an authority plus the very delicate, plenary and exclusive power of the President as the sole organ of the federal government in the field of international relations—a power which does not require as a basis for its exercise an act of Congress, but which, of course, like every other governmental power, must be exercised in subordination to the applicable provisions of the Constitution. It is quite apparent that if, in the maintenance of our international relations, embarrassment—perhaps serious embarrassment—is to be avoided and success for our aims achieved, congressional legislation which is to be made effective through negotiation and inquiry within the international field must often accord to the President a degree of discretion and freedom from statutory restriction which would not be admissible were domestic affairs alone involved. Moreover, he, not Congress, has the better opportunity of knowing the conditions which prevail in foreign countries, and especially is this true in time of war. He has his confidential sources of information. He has his agents in the form of diplomatic, consular and other officials. Secrecy in respect of information gathered by them may be highly necessary, and the premature disclosure of it productive of harmful results. Indeed, so clearly is this true that the first President refused to accede to a request to lay before the House of Representatives the instructions, correspondence and documents relating to the negotiation of the Jay Treaty—a refusal the wisdom of which was recognized by the House itself and has never since been doubted. In his reply to the request, President Washington said:

> The nature of foreign negotiations requires caution, and their success must often depend on secrecy; and even when brought to a conclusion a full disclosure of all the measures, demands, or eventual concessions which may have been proposed or contemplated would be extremely impolitic; for this might have a pernicious influence on future negotiations, or produce immediate inconveniences, perhaps danger and mischief, in relation to other powers. The necessity of such caution and secrecy was one cogent reason for vesting the power of making treaties in the President, with the advice and consent of the Senate, the principle on which that body was formed confining it to a small number of members. To admit, then, a right in the House of Representatives to demand and to have as a matter of course all the papers respecting a negotiation with a foreign power would be to establish a dangerous precedent.

The marked difference between foreign affairs and domestic affairs in this respect is recognized by both houses of Congress in the very form of their requisitions for information from the executive departments. In the case of every department except the Department of State, the resolution *directs* the official to furnish the information. In the case of the State Department, dealing with foreign affairs, the President is *requested* to furnish the information "if not incompatible with the public interest." A statement that to furnish the information is not compatible with the public interest rarely, if ever, is questioned.

When the President is to be authorized by legislation to act in respect of a matter intended to affect a situation in foreign territory, the legislator properly bears in mind the important consideration that the form of the President's action—or, indeed, whether he shall act at all—may well depend, among other things, upon the nature of the confidential information which he has or may thereafter receive, or upon the effect which his action may have upon our foreign relations. This consideration, in connection with what we have already said on the subject, discloses the unwisdom of requiring Congress in this field of governmental power to lay down narrowly definite standards by which the President is to be governed. As this court said in Mackenzie v. Hare, "As a government, the United States is invested with all the attributes of sovereignty. As it has the character of nationality it has the powers of nationality, especially those which concern its relations and intercourse with other countries. *We should hesitate long before limiting or embarrassing such powers.*" (Italics supplied.)

In the light of the foregoing observations, it is evident that this court should not be in haste to apply a general rule which will have the effect of condemning legislation like that under review as constituting an unlawful delegation of legislative power. The principles which justify such legislation find overwhelming suport in the unbroken legislative practice which has prevailed almost from the inception of the national government to the present day.

Let us examine, in chronological order, the acts of legislation which warrant this conclusion:

The Act of June 4, 1794, authorized the President to lay, regulate and revoke embargoes. He was "authorized" whenever, in his opinion, the public safety shall so require, "to lay the embargo upon all ships and vessels in the ports of the United States, including those of foreign nations, "under such regulations as the circumstances of the case may require, and to continue or revoke the same, whenever he shall think proper." A prior joint resolution of May 7, 1794, had conferred *unqualified* power on the President to grant clearances, notwithstanding an existing embargo, to ships or vessels belonging to citizens of the United States bound to any port beyond the Cape of Good Hope. . . .

[The other examples are omitted.]

Practically every volume of the United States Statutes contains one or more acts or joint resolutions of Congress authorizing action by the President in respect of subjects affecting foreign relations, which either leave the exercise of the power to his unrestricted judgment, or provide a standard far more general than that which has always been considered requisite with regard to domestic affairs. . . .

The result of holding that the joint resolution here under attack is void and unenforceable as constituting an unlawful delegation of legislative power would be to stamp this multitude of comparable acts and resolutions as likewise invalid. And while this court may not, and should not, hesitate to declare acts of Congress, however many times repeated, to be unconstitutional if beyond all rational doubt it finds them to be so, an impressive array of legislation such as we have just set forth, enacted by nearly every Congress from the beginning of our national existence to the present day, must be given unusual weight in the process of reaching a correct determination of the problem. A legislative practice such as we have here, evidenced not by only occasional instances, but marked by the movement of a steady stream for a century and a half of time, goes a long way in the direction of proving the presence of unassailable ground for the constitutionality of the practice, to be found in the origin and history of the power involved, or in its nature, or in both combined. . . .

The uniform, long-continued and undisputed legislative practice just disclosed rests upon an admissible view of the Constitution which, even if the practice found far less support in principle than we think it does, we should not feel at liberty at this late day to disturb.

We deem it unnecessary to consider, *seriatim,* the several clauses which are said to evidence the unconstitutionality of the Joint Resolution as involving an unlawful delegation of legislative power. It is enough to summarize by saying that, both upon principle and in accordance with precedent, we conclude there is sufficient warrant for the broad discretion vested in the President to determine whether the enforcement of the statute will have a beneficial effect upon the reestablishment of peace in the affected countries; whether he shall make proclamation to being the resolution into operation; whether and when the resolution shall cease to operate and to make proclamation accordingly; and to prescribe limitations and exceptions to which the enforcement of the resolution shall be subject. . . .

The judgment of the court below must be reversed. . . .

43

Korematsu v. United States (1944)

Mr. Justice Black delivered the opinion of the Court.

The petitioner, an American citizen of Japanese descent, was convicted in the federal district court for remaining in San Leandro, California, a "Military Area," contrary to Civilian Exclusion Order No. 34 of the Commanding General of the Western Command, U.S. Army, which directed that after May 9, 1942, all persons of Japanese ancestry should be excluded from that area. No question was raised as to petitioner's loyalty to the United States. The Circuit Court of Appeals affirmed, and the importance of the constitutional question involved caused us to grant certiorari.

It should be noted, to begin with, that all legal restrictions which curtail the civil rights of a single racial group are immediately suspect. That is not to say that all such restrictions are unconstitutional. It is to say that courts must subject them to the most rigid scrutiny. Pressing public necessity may sometimes justify the existence of such restrictions; racial antagonism never can.

In the instant case prosecution of the petitioner was begun by information charging violation of an Act of Congress, of March 21, 1942, which provides that "whoever shall enter, remain in, leave, or commit any act in any military area or military zone prescribed, under the authority of an Executive order of the President, by Secretary of War, or by any military commander designated by the Secretary of War, contrary to the restrictions applicable to any such area or zone or contrary to the order of the Secretary of War or any such military commander, shall, if it appears that he knew or should have known of the existence and extent of the restrictions or order and that his act was in violation thereof, be guilty of a misdemeanor and upon conviction shall be liable to a fine of not to exceed $5,000 or to imprisonment for not more than one year, or both, for each offense."

Exclusion Order No. 34, which the petitioner knowingly and admittedly violated was one of a number of military orders and proclamations, all of which were substantially based upon Executive Order No. 9066, 7 Fed. Reg. 1407. That order, issued after we were at war with Japan, declared that "the successful prosecution of the war requires every possible protection

From *Korematsu v. United States,* 323 U.S. 214 (1944).

against espionage and against sabotage to national-defense material, national-defense premises, and national-defense utilities. . . .

One of the series of orders and proclamations, a curfew order, which like the exclusion order here was promulgated pursuant to Executive Order 9066, subjected all persons of Japanese ancestry in prescribed West Coast military areas to remain in their residences from 8 P.M. to 6 A.M.. As is the case with the exclusion order here, that prior curfew order was designed as a "protection against espionage and against sabotage." In Kiyoshi Hirabayashi v. United States, we sustained a conviction obtained for violation of the curfew order. The Hirabayashi conviction and this one thus rest on the same 1942 Congressional Act and the same basic executive and military orders, all of which orders were aimed at the twin dangers of espionage and sabotage. . . .

In the light of the principles we announced in the Hirabayashi case, we are unable to conclude that it was beyond the war power of Congress and the Executive to exclude those of Japanese ancestry from the West Coast war area at the time they did. True, exclusion from the area in which one's home is located is a far greater deprivation than constant confinement to the home from 8 P.M. to 6 A.M.. Nothing short of apprehension by the proper military authorities of the gravest imminent danger to the public safety can constitutionally justify either. But exclusion from a threatened area, no less than curfew, has a definite and close relationship to the prevention of espionage and sabotage. The military authorities, charged with the primary responsibility of defending our shores, concluded that curfew provided inadequate protection and ordered exclusion. They did so, as pointed out in our Hirabayashi opinion, in accordance with Congressional authority to the military to say who should, and who should not, remain in the threatened areas.

In this case the petitioner challenges the assumptions upon which we rested our conclusions in the Hirabayashi case. He also urges that by May 1942, when Order No. 34 was promulgated, all danger of Japanese invasion of the West Coast had disappeared. After careful consideration of these contentions we are compelled to reject them.

Here, as in the Hirabayashi case, "we cannot reject as unfounded the judgment of the military authorities and of Congress that there were disloyal members of that population, whose number and strength could not be precisely and quickly ascertained. We cannot say that the war-making branches of the Government did not have ground for believing that in a critical hour such persons could not readily be isolated and separately dealt with, and constituted a menace to the national defense and safety, which demanded that prompt and adequate measures be taken to guard against it."

Like curfew, exclusion of those of Japanese origin was deemed necessary because of the presence of an unascertained number of disloyal members of the group, most of whom we have no doubt were loyal to this country. It was because we could not reject the finding of the military authorities that it was impossible to bring about an immediate segregation of the disloyal from the loyal that we sustained the validity of the curfew order as applying to the whole group. In the instant case, temporary exclusion of the entire group was rested by the military on the same ground. The judgment that exclusion of the whole group was for the same reason a military imperative answers the contention that the exclusion was in the nature of group punishment based on antagonism to those of Japanese origin. That there were members of the group who retained loyalties to Japan has been confirmed by investigations made subsequent to the exclusion. Approximately five thousand American citizens of Japanese ancestry refused to swear unqualified allegiance to the United States and to renounce allegiance to the Japanese Emperor, and several thousand evacuees requested repatriation to Japan.

We uphold the exclusion order as of the time it was made and when the petitioner violated it. In doing so, we are not unmindful of the hardships imposed by it upon a large group of American citizens. But hardships are part of war, and war is an aggregation of hardships. All citizens alike, both in and out of uniform, feel the impact of war in greater or lesser measure. Citizenship has its responsibilities as well as its privileges, and in time of war the burden is always heavier. Compulsory exclusion of large groups of citizens from their homes, except under circumstances of direct emergency and peril, is inconsistent with our basic governmental institutions. But when under conditions of modern warfare our shores are threatened by hostile forces, the power to protect must be commensurate with the threatened danger.

It is argued that on May 30, 1942, the date the petitioner was charged with remaining in the prohibited area, there were conflicting orders outstanding, forbidding him both to leave the area and to remain there. Of course, a person cannot be convicted for doing the very thing which it is a crime to fail to do. But the outstanding orders here contained no such contradictory commands. . . .

It does appear, however, that on May 9, the effective date of the exclusion order, the military authorities had already determined that the evacuation should be effected by assembling together and placing under guard all those of Japanese ancestry, at central points, designated as "assembly centers," in order "to insure the orderly evacuation and resettlement of Japanese voluntarily migrating from military area No. 1 to restrict and regulate such migration." Public Proclamation No. 4, 7 Fed. Reg. 2601.

And on May 19, 1942, eleven days before the time petitioner was charged with unlawfully remaining in the area, Civilian Restrictive Order No. 1, 8 Fed. Reg. 982, provided for detention of those of Japanese ancestry in assembly or relocation centers. It is now argued that the validity of the exclusion order cannot be considered apart from the orders requiring him, after departure from the area, to report and to remain in an assembly or relocation center. The contention is that we must treat these separate orders as one and inseparable; that, for this reason, if detention in the assembly or relocation center would have illegally deprived the petitioner of his liberty, the exclusion order and his conviction under it cannot stand. . . .

Since the petitioner has not been convicted of failing to report or to remain in an assembly or relocation center, we cannot in this case determine the validity of those separate provisions of the order. It is sufficient here for us to pass upon the order which petitioner violated. To do more would be to go beyond the issues raised, and to decide momentous questions not contained within the framework of the pleadings or the evidence in this case. It will be time enough to decide the serious constitutional issues which petitioner seeks to raise when an assembly or relocation order is applied or is certain to be applied to him, and we have its terms before us.

Some of the members of the Court are of the view that evacuation and detention in an Assembly Center were inseparable. After May 3, 1942, the date of Exclusion Order No. 34, Korematsu was under compulsion to leave the area not as he would choose but via an Assembly Center. The Assembly Center was conceived as a part of the machinery for group evacuation. The power to exclude includes the power to do it by force if necessary. And any forcible measure must necessarily entail some degree of detention or restraint whatever method of removal is selected. But whichever view is taken, it results in holding that the order under which petitioner was convicted was valid.

It is said that we are dealing here with the case of imprisonment of a citizen in a concentration camp solely because of his ancestry, without evidence or inquiry concerning his loyalty and good disposition towards the United States. Our task would be simple, our duty clear, were this a case involving the imprisonment of a loyal citizen in a concentration camp because of racial prejudice. Regardless of the true nature of the assembly and relocation centers—and we deem it unjustifiable to call them concentration camps with all the ugly connotations that term implies—we are dealing specifically with nothing but an exclusion order. To cast this case into outlines of racial prejudice, without reference to the real military dangers which were presented, merely confuses the issue. Korematsu was not excluded from the Military Area because of hostility to him or his race. He was excluded because we are at war with the Japanese Empire, because the properly constituted military authorities feared an invasion of our West Coast and felt constrained to take proper security measures, because they decided that the military urgency of the situation demanded that all citizens of Japanese ancestry be segregated from the West Coast temporarily, and finally, because Congress, reposing its confidence in this time of war in our military leaders—as inevitably it must—determined that they should have the power to do just this. There was evidence of disloyalty on the part of some, the military authorities considered that the need for action was great, and time was short. We cannot—by availing ourselves of the calm perspective of hindsight—now say at that time these actions were unjustified.

Affirmed.

Mr. Justice Frankfurter, concurring. . . . I join in the opinion of the Court, but should like to add a few words of my own.

The provisions of the Constitution which confer on the Congress and the President powers to enable this country to wage war are as much part of the Constitution as provisions looking to a nation at peace. And we have had recent occasion to quote approvingly the statement of former Chief Justice Hughes that the war power of the Government is "the power to wage war sucessfully." Therefore, the validity of action under the war power must be judged wholly in the context of war. That action is not to be stigmatized as lawless because like action in times of peace would be lawless. To talk about a military order that expresses an allowable judgment of war needs by those entrusted with the duty of conducting war as "an unconstitutional order" is to suffuse a part of the Constitution with an atmosphere of unconstitutionality. The respective spheres of action of military authorities and of judges are of course very different. But within their sphere, military authorities are no more outside the bounds of obedience to the Constitution than are judges within theirs. "The war power of the United States, like its other powers . . . is subject to applicable constitutional limitations," Hamilton v. Kentucky Distilleries Company. To recognize that military orders are "reasonably expedient military precautions" in time of war and yet to deny them constitutional legitimacy makes of the Constitution an instrument for dialectic subtleties not reasonably to be attributed to the hardheaded Framers, of whom a majority had had actual participation in war. If a military order such as that under review does not transcend the means appropriate for conducting war, such action by the military is as constitutional as would be any authorized action by the Interstate Commerce Commission within the limits of the constitutional power to regulate commerce. And being an exercise of the war power explicitly granted by the Constitution for safeguarding the national life by prosecuting war effectively, I find nothing in the

Constitution which denies to Congress the power to enforce such a valid military order by making its violation an offense triable in the civil courts. To find that the Constitution does not forbid the military measures now complained of does not carry with it approval of that which Congress and the Executive did. That is their business, not ours.

Mr. Justice Murphy, dissenting.

This exclusion of "all persons of Japanese ancestry, both alien and nonalien," from the Pacific Coast area on a plea of military necessity in the absence of martial law ought not to be approved. Such exclusion goes over "the very brink of constitutional power" and falls into the ugly abyss of racism.

In dealing with matters relating to the prosecution and progress of a war, we must accord great respect and consideration to the judgments of the military authorities who are on the scene and who have full knowledge of the military facts. The scope of their discretion must, as a matter of necessity and common sense, be wide. And their judgments ought not to be overruled lightly by those whose training and duties ill-equip them to deal intelligently with matters, so vital to the physical security of the nation.

At the same time, however, it is essential that there be definite limits to military discretion, especially where martial law has not been declared. Individuals must not be left impoverished of their constitutional rights on a plea of military necessity that has neither substance nor support. Thus, like other claims conflicting with the asserted constitutional rights of the individual, the military claim must subject itself to the judicial process of having its reasonableness determined and its conflicts with other interests reconciled. "What are the allowable limits of military discretion, and whether or not they have been over-stepped in a particular case, are judicial questions."

The judicial test of whether the Government, on a plea of military necessity, can validly deprive an individual of any of his constitutional rights is whether the deprivation is reasonably related to a public danger that is so "immediate, imminent, and impending" as not to admit of delay and not to permit the intervention of ordinary constitutional processes to alleviate the danger. Civilian Exclusion Order No. 34, banishing from a prescribed area of the Pacific Coast "all persons of Japanese ancestry, both alien and nonalien," clearly does not meet that test. Being an obvious racial discrimination, the order deprives all those within its scope of the equal protection of the laws as guaranteed by the Fifth Amendment. It further deprives these individuals of their constitutional rights to live and work where they will, to establish a home where they choose and to move about freely. In excommunicating them without benefit of hearings, this order also deprives them of all their constitutional rights to procedural due process. Yet no reasonable relation to an "immediate, imminent, and impending" public danger is evident to support this racial restriction which is one of the most sweeping and complete deprivations of constitutional rights in the history of this nation in the absence of martial law.

It must be conceded that the military and naval situation in the spring of 1942 was such as to generate a very real fear of invasion of the Pacific Coast, accompanied by fears of sabotage and espionage in that area. The military command was therefore justified in adopting all reasonable means necessary to combat these dangers. In adjudging the military action taken in light of the then apparent dangers, we must not erect too high or too meticulous standards; it is necessary only that the action have some reasonable relation to the removal of the dangers of invasion, sabotage and espionage. But the exclusion, either temporarily or permanently, of all persons with Japanese blood in their veins has no such reasonable relation. And that relation is lacking because the exclusion order necessarily must rely for its reasonableness upon the assumption that *all* persons of Japanese ancestry may have a dangerous tendency to commit sabotage and espionage and to aid our Japanese enemy in other ways. It is difficult to believe that reason, logic or experience could be marshalled in support of such an assumption.

That this forced exclusion was the result in good measure of this erroneous assumption of racial guilt rather than bona fide military necessity is evidenced by the Commanding General's Final Report on the evacuation from the Pacific Coast area. In it he refers to all individuals of Japanese descent as "subversive," as belonging to "an enemy race" whose "racial strains are undiluted," and as constituting "over 112,000 potential enemies . . . at large today" along the Pacific Coast. In support of this blanket condemnation of all persons of Japanese descent, however, no reliable evidence is cited to show that such individuals were generally disloyal, or had generally so conducted themselves in this area as to constitute a special menace to defense installations or war industries, or had otherwise by their behavior furnished reasonable ground for their exclusion as a group.

Justification for the exclusion is sought, instead, mainly upon questionable racial and sociological grounds not within the realm of expert military judgment, supplemented by certain semi-military conclusions drawn from an unwarranted use of circumstantial evidence. Individuals of Japanese ancestry are condemned because they are said to be "a large, unassimilated, tightly knit racial group, bound to an enemy nation by strong ties of race, culture, custom and religion." They are claimed to be given to "emperor worshipping ceremonies" and to "dual citizenship." Japanese language schools and allegedly pro-Japanese organizations are cited as evidence of possible group disloyalty, together with facts as to certain persons being educated and residing at length in Japan. It is intimated that many of these individuals deliberately resided "adjacent to strategic points," thus enabling them "to carry into execution a tremendous program of sabotage on a mass scale should any considerable number of them have been inclined to do so." The need for protective custody is also asserted. The report refers without identity to "numerous incidents of violence" as well as to other admittedly unverified or cumulative incidents. From this, plus certain other events not shown to have been connected with the Japanese Americans, it is concluded that the "situation was fraught with danger to the Japanese population itself" and that the general public "was ready to take matters into its own hands." Finally, it is intimated, though not directly charged or proved, that persons of Japanese ancestry were responsible for three minor isolated shellings and bombings of the Pacific Coast area, as well as for unidentified radio transmissions and night signalling.

The main reasons relied upon by those responsible for the forced evacuation, therefore, do not prove a reasonable relation between the group characteristics of Japanese Americans and the dangers of invasion, sabotage and espionage. The reasons appear, instead, to be largely an accumulation of much of the misinformation, half-truths and insinuations that for years have been directed against Japanese Americans by people with racial and economic prejudices—the same people who have been among the foremost advocates of the evacuation. A military judgment based upon such racial and sociological considerations is not entitled to the great weight ordinarily given the judgments based upon strictly military considerations. Especially is this so when every charge relative to race, religion, culture, geographical location, and legal and economic status has been substantially discredited by independent studies made by experts in these matters.

The military necessity which is essential to the validity of the evacuation order thus resolves itself into a few intimations that certain individuals actively aided the enemy, from which it is inferred that the entire group of Japanese Americans could not be trusted to be or remain loyal to the United States. No one denies, of course, that there were some disloyal persons of Japanese descent on the Pacific Coast who did all in their power to aid their ancestral land. Similar disloyal activities have been engaged in by many persons of German, Italian and even more pioneer stock in our country. But to infer that examples of individual disloyalty prove group disloyalty and justify discriminatory action against the entire group is to deny that under our system of law individual guilt is the sole basis for deprivation of rights. Moreover, this inference, which is at the very heart of the evacuation orders, has been used in support of the abhorrent and despicable treatment of minority groups by the dictatorial tyrannies which this nation is now pledged to destroy. To give constitutional sanction to that inference is this case, however well-intentioned may have been the military command on the Pacific Coast, is to adopt one of the cruelest of the rationales used by our enemies to destroy the dignity of the individual and to encourage and open the door to discriminatory actions against other minority groups in the passions of tomorrow.

No adequate reason is given for the failure to treat these Japanese Americans on an individual basis by holding investigations and hearings to separate the loyal from the disloyal, as was done in the case of persons of German and Italian ancestry. See House Report No 2124 (77th Cong., 2d Sess.) 247-52. It is asserted merely that the loyalties of this group "were unknown and time was of the essence." Yet nearly four months elapsed after Pearl Harbor before the first exclusion order was issued; nearly eight months went by until the last order was issued; and the last of these "subversive" persons was not actually removed until almost eleven months had elapsed. Leisure and deliberation seem to have been more of the essence than speed. And the fact that conditions were not such as to warrant a declaration of martial law adds strength to the belief that the factors of time and military necessity were not as urgent as they have been represented to be.

Moreover, there was no adequate proof that the Federal Bureau of Investigation and the military and naval intelligence services did not have the espionage and sabotage situation well in hand during this long period. Nor is there any denial of the fact that not one person of Japanese ancestry was accused or convicted of espionage or sabotage after Pearl Harbor while they were still free, a fact which is some evidence of the loyalty of the vast majority of these individuals and of the effectiveness of the established methods of combatting these evils. It seems incredible that under these circumstances it would have been impossible to hold loyalty hearings for the mere 112,000 persons involved—or at least for the 70,000 American citizens—especially when a large part of this number represented children and elderly men and women. Any inconvenience that may have accompanied an attempt to conform to precedural due process cannot be said to justify violations of constitutional rights of individuals.

I dissent, therefore, from this legalization of racism. Racial discrimination in any form and in any degree has no justifiable part whatever in our democratic way of life. It is unattractive in any setting but it is utterly revolting among a free people who have embraced the principles set forth in the Constitution of the United States. All residents of this nation are kin in some way by blood or culture to a foreign land. Yet they are primarily and necessarily a part of the new and distinct civilization of the United States. They must accordingly be treated at all times as the heirs of the American experiment and as entitled to all the rights and freedoms guaranteed by the Constitution.

Mr. Justice Jackson, dissenting.

. . . [T]he "law" which this prisoner is convicted of disregarding is not found in an act of Congress, but in a military order. . . . And it is said that if the military commander had reasonable military grounds for promulgating the orders, they are constitutional and become law, and the Court is required to enforce them. There are several reasons why I cannot subscribe to this doctrine.

It would be impracticable and dangerous idealism to expect or insist that each specific military command in an area of probable operations will conform to conventional tests of constitutionality. When an area is so beset that it must be put under military control at all, the paramount consideration is that its measures be successful, rather than legal. The armed services must protect a society, not merely its Constitution. The very essence of the military job is to marshal physical force, to remove every obstacle to its effectiveness, to give it every strategic advantage. Defense measures will not, and often should not, be held within the limits that bind civil authority in peace. No court can require such a commander in such circumstances to act as a reasonable man; he may be unreasonably cautious and exacting. Perhaps he should be. But a commander in temporarily focusing the life of a community on defense is carrying out a military program; he is not making law in the sense the courts know the term. He issues orders, and they may have a certain authority as military commands, although they may be very bad as constitutional law.

But if we cannot confine military expedients by the Constitution, neither would I distort the Constitution to approve all that the military may deem expedient. That is what the Court appears to be doing, whether consciously or not. I cannot say, from any evidence before me, that the orders of General DeWitt were not reasonably expedient military precautions, nor could I say that they were. But even if they were permissible military procedures, I deny that it follows that they are constitutional. If, as the Court holds, it does follow, then we may as well say that any military order will be constitutional and have done with it.

The limitation under which courts always will labor in examining the necessity for a military order are illustrated by this case. How does the Court know that these orders have a reasonable basis in necessity? No evidence whatever on that subject has been taken by this or any other court. There is sharp controversy as to the credibility of the DeWitt report. So the Court, having no real evidence before it, has no choice but to accept General DeWitt's own unsworn, self-serving statement, untested by any cross-examination, that what he did was reasonable. And thus it will always be when courts try to look into the reasonableness of a military order.

In the very nature of things military decisions are not susceptible of intelligent judicial appraisal. They do not pretend to rest on evidence, but are made on information that often would not be admissible and on assumptions that could not be proved. Information in support of an order could not be disclosed to courts without danger that it would reach the enemy. Neither can courts act on communications made in confidence. Hence courts can never have any real alternative to accepting the mere declaration of the authority that issued the order that it was reasonably necessary from a military viewpoint.

Much is said of the danger to liberty from the Army program for deporting and detaining these citizens of Japanese extraction. But a judicial construction of the due process clause that will sustain this order is a far more subtle blow to liberty than the promulgation of the order itself. A military order, however unconstitutional, is not apt to last longer than the military emergency. Even during that period a succeeding commander may revoke it all. But once a judicial opinion rationalizes such an order to show that it conforms to the Constitution, or rather rationalizes the Constitution to show that the Constitution sanctions such an order, the Court for all time has validated the principle of racial discrimination in criminal procedure and of transplanting American citizens. The principle then lies about like a loaded weapon ready for the hand of any authority that can bring forward a plausible claim of an urgent need. Every repetition imbeds that principle more deeply in our law and thinking and expands it to new purposes. All who observe the work of courts are familiar with what Judge Cardozo described as "the tendency of a principle to expand itself to the limit of its logic." A military commander may overstep the bounds of constitutionality, and it is an incident. But if we review and approve, that passing incident becomes the doctrine of the Constitution. There it has a generative power of its own, and all that it creates will be in its own image. . . .

I should hold that a civil court cannot be made to enforce an order which violates constitutional limitations even if it is a reasonable exercise of military authority. The courts can exercise only the judicial power, can apply only law, and must abide by the Constitution, or they cease to be civil courts and become instruments of military policy.

Of course the existence of a military power resting on force, so vagrant, so centralized, so necessarily heedless of the individual, is an inherent threat to liberty. But I would not lead people to rely on this Court for a review that seems to me wholly delusive. The military reasonableness of these orders can only be determined by military superiors. If the people ever let command of the war power fall into irresponsible and unscrupulous hands, the courts wield no power equal to its restraint. The chief restraint upon those who command the physical forces of the country, in the future as in the past, must be their responsibility to the political judgments of their contemporaries and to the moral judgments of history.

My duties as justice as I see them do not require me to make a military judgment as to whether General DeWitt's evacuation and detention program was a reasonable military necessity. I do not suggest that the courts should have attempted to interfere with the Army in carrying out its task. But I do not think they may be asked to execute a military expedient that has no place in law under the Constitution. I would reverse the judgment and discharge the prisoner.

44

Abraham Lincoln

On the Suspension of the Writ of Habeas Corpus (1863)

Hon Erastus Corning and others*

Gentlemen Your letter of May 19th. inclosing the resolutions of a public meeting held at Albany, New York on the 16th of the same month, was received several days ago.

The resolutions, as I understand them, are resolvable into two propositions—first, the expression of a purpose to sustain the cause of the Union, to secure peace through victory, and to support the administration in every constitutional, and lawful measure to suppress the rebellion; and

---

*On June 30, Corning and others replied: ". . . We have carefully considered the grounds on which your pretensions to more than regal authority are claimed to rest; and if we do not misinterpret the misty and clouded forms of expression in which those pretensions are set forth, your meaning is that while the rights of the citizen are protected by the Constitution in time of peace, they are suspended or lost in time of war, or when invasion or rebellion exist. You do not, like many others in whose minds, reason and love of regulated liberty seem to be overthrown by the excitements of the hour, attempt to base this conclusion upon a supposed military necessity existing outside of and transcending the Constitution, a military necessity behind which the Constitution itself disappears in a total eclipse. We do not find this gigantic and monstrous heresy put forth in your plea for absolute power, but we do find another equally subversive of liberty and law, and quite as certainly tending to the establishment of despotism. Your claim to have found not outside, but within the Constitution, a principle or germ of arbitrary power, which in time of war expands at once into an absolute sovereignty, wielded by one man; so that liberty perished, or is dependent on his will, his discretion or his caprice. This extraordinary doctrine, you claim to derive wholly from that clause of the Constitution, which, in case of invasion or rebellion, permits the writ of habeas corpus to be suspended. Upon this ground your whole argument is based.

"You must permit us, to say to you with all due respect, but with the earnestness demanded by the occasion, that the American people will never acquiese in this doctrine. . . ." The Robert Todd Lincoln Collection of the Papers of Abraham Lincoln, Library of Congress.

From *The Collected Works of Abraham Lincoln,* Vol. VI, Rutgers University Press, 1953.

secondly, a declaration of censure upon the administration for supposed unconstitutional action such as the making of military arrests.

And, from the two propositions a third is deduced, which is, that the gentlemen composing the meeting are resolved on doing their part to maintain our common government and country, despite the folly or wickedness, as they may conceive, of any administration. This position is eminently patriotic, and as such, I thank the meeting, and congratulate the nation for it. My own purpose is the same; so that the meeting and myself have a common object, and can have no difference, except in the choice of means or measures, for effecting that object.

And here I ought to close this paper, and would close it, if there were no apprehension that more injurious consequences, than any merely personal to myself, might follow the censures systematically cast upon me for doing what, in my view of duty, I could not forbear. The resolutions promise to support me in every constitutional and lawful measure to suppress the rebellion; and I have not knowingly employed, nor shall knowingly employ, any other. But the meeting, by their resolutions, assert and argue, that certain military arrests and proceedings following them for which I am ultimately responsible, are unconstitutional. I think they are not. The resolutions quote from the constitution, the definition of treason; and also the limiting safe-guards and guarantees therein provided for the citizen, on trials for treason, and on his being held to answer for capital or otherwise infamous crimes, and, in criminal prosecutions, his right to a speedy and public trial by an impartial jury. They proceed to resolve "That these safe-guards of the rights of the citizen against the pretentions of arbitrary power, were intended more *especially* for his protection in times of civil commotion." And, apparently, to demonstrate the proposition, the resolutions proceed "They were secured substantially to the English people, *after* years of protracted civil war, and were adopted into our constitution at the *close* of the revolution." Would not the demonstration have been better, if it could have been truly said that these safe-guards had been adopted, and applied *during* the civil wars and *during* our revolution, instead of *after* the one, and at the *close* of the other. I too am devotedly for them *after* civil war, and *before* civil war, and at all times "except when, in cases of Rebellion or Invasion, the public Safety may require" their suspension. The resolutions proceed to tell us that these safe-guards "have stood the test of seventy-six years of trial, under our republican system, under circumstances which show that while they constitute the foundation of all free government, they are the elements of the enduring stability of the Republic." No one denies that they have so stood the test up to the beginning of the present rebellion if we except a certain matter at New Orleans hereafter to be mentioned; nor does anyone question that they will stand the same test much longer after the rebellion closes. But these provisions of the constitution have no application to the case we have in hand, because the arrests complained of were not made for treason—that is, not for *the* treason defined in the constitution, and upon the conviction of which, the punishment is death—; nor yet were they made to hold persons to answer for any capital, or otherwise infamous crimes; nor were the proceedings following, in any constitutional or legal sense, "criminal prosecutions." The arrests were made on totally different grounds, and the proceedings following, accorded with the grounds of the arrests. Let us consider the real case with which we are dealing, and apply to it the parts of the constitution plainly made for such cases.

Prior to my installation here it had been inculcated that any State had a lawful right to secede from the national Union; and that it would be expedient to exercise the right, whenever the devotees of the doctrine should fail to elect a President to their own liking. I was elected contrary to their liking; and accordingly, so far as it was legally possible, they had taken seven states out of the Union, had seized many of the United States Forts, and had fired upon the United States' Flag, all before I was inaugurated; and, of course, before I had done any offical act whatever. The rebellion, thus began soon ran into the present civil war; and, in certain respects, it began on very unequal terms between the parties. The insurgents had been preparing for it more than thirty years, while the government had taken no steps to resist them. The former had carefully considered all the means which could be truned to their account. It undoubtedly was a well pondered reliance with them that in their own unrestricted effort to destroy Union, constitution, and law, all together, the government would, in great degree, be restrained by the same constitution and law, from arresting their progress. Their sympathizers pervaded all departments of the government, and nearly all communities of the people. From this material, under cover of "Liberty of speech" "Liberty of the press" and *"Habeas corpus"* they hoped to keep on foot amongst us a most efficient corps of spies, informers, suppliers, and aiders and abettors of their cause in a thousand ways. They knew that in times such as they were inaugurating, by the constitution itself, the "Habeas corpus" might be suspended; but they also knew they had friends who would make a question as to *who* was to suspend it; meanwhile their spies and others might remain at large to help on their cause. Or if, as has happened, the executive should suspend the writ, without ruinous waste of time, instances of arresting innocent persons might occur, as are always likely to occur in such cases; and then a clamor could be raised in regard to this, which might be, at least, of some service to the insurgent cause. It needed no very keen perception to discover this part of the enemies' programme, so soon as by open hostilities their machinery was fairly put in motion. Yet, thoroughly imbued with a reverence for the guarranteed rights of individuals, I was slow to adopt the strong measures, which by degrees I have been forced to regard as being within the exceptions of the constitution, and as indispensable to the public Safety. Nothing is better known to history than that courts of justice are utterly incompetent to such cases. Civil courts are organized chiefly for trials of individuals, or, at most, a few individuals acting in concert; and this in quiet times, and on charges of crimes well defined in the law. Even in times of peace, bands of horse-thieves and robbers frequently grow too numerous and powerful for the ordinary courts of justice. But what comparison, in numbers, have such bands ever borne to the insurgent sympathizers even in many of the loyal states? Again, a jury too frequently have at least one member, more ready to hand the panel than to hang the traitor. And yet again, he who dissuades one man from volunteering, or induces one soldier to desert, weakens the Union cause as much as he who kills a union soldier in battle. Yet this dissuasion, or inducement, may be so conducted as to be no defined crime of which any civil court would take cognizance.

Ours is a case of Rebellion—so called by the resolutions before me—in fact, a clear, flagrant, and gigantic case of Rebellion; and the provision of the constitution that "The privilege of the writ of Habeas Corpus shall not be suspended, unless when in cases of Rebellion or Invasion, the public Safety may require it" is *the* provision which specially applies to our present case. This provision plainly attests the understanding of those who made the constitution that ordinary courts of justice are inadequate to "cases of Rebellion"—attests their purpose that in such cases, men may be held in custody whom the courts acting on ordinary rules, would discharge. Habeas Corpus, does not discharge men who are proved to be guilty of defined crime; and its suspension is allowed by the constitution on purpose that, men may be arrested and held, who cannot be proved to be guilty of defined crime, "when, in cases of Rebellion or Invasion the public Safety may require it." This is precisely our present case—a case of Rebellion, wherein the public Safety does require the suspension. Indeed, arrests by process of courts, and arrests in cases of rebellion, do not proceed altogether upon the same basis. The former is directed at the small percentage of ordinary and continuous perpetration of crime; while the latter is directed at sudden and extensive uprisings against the government, which, at most, will succeed or fail, in no great length of time. In the latter case, arrests are made, not so much for what has been done, as for what probably would be done. The latter is more for the preventive, and less for the vindictive, than the former. In such cases the purposes of men are much more easily understood, than in cases of ordinary crime. The man who stands by and says nothing, when the peril of his government is discussed, cannot be misunderstood. If not hindered, he is sure to help the enemy. Much more, if he talks ambiguously—talks for his country with "buts" and "ifs" and "ands." Of how little value the constitutional provision I have quoted will be rendered, if arrests shall never be made until defined crimes shall have been committed, may be illustrated by a few notable examples. Gen. John C. Breckienridge, Gen. Robert E. Lee, Gen. Joseph E. Johnston, Gen. John B. Magruder, Gen. William B. Preston, Gen. Simon B. Buckner, and Comodore [Franklin] Buchanan, now occupying the very highest places in the rebel war service, were all within the power of the government since the rebellion began, and were nearly as well known to be traitors then as now. Unquestionably if we had seized and held them, the insurgent cause would be much weaker. But no one of them had then committed any crime defined in the law. Every one of them if arrested would have been discharged on Habeas Corpus, were the writ allowed to operate. In view of these and similar cases, I think the time not unlikely to come when I shall be blamed for having made too few arrests rather than too many.

By the third resolution the meeting indicate their opinion that military arrests may be constitutional in localities where rebellion actually exists; but that such arrests are unconstitutional in localities where rebellion, or insurrection, does not actually exist. They insist that such arrests shall not be made "outside of the lines of necessary military occupation, and the scenes of insurrection." Inasmuch, however, as the constitution itself makes no such distinction, I am unable to believe that there is any such constitutional distinction. I concede that the class of arrests complained of, can be constitutional only when, in cases of Rebellion or Invasion, the public Safety may require them; and I insist that in such cases, they are constitutional *wherever* the public safety does require them—as well in places to which they may prevent the rebellion extending, as in those where it may be already prevailing—as well where they may restrain mischievous interference with the raising and supplying of armies, to suppress the rebellion, as where the rebellion may actually be—as well where they may restrain the enticing men out of the army, as where they would prevent mutiny in the army—equally constitutional at all places where they will conduce to the public Safety, as against the dangers of Rebellion or Invasion.

Take the particular case mentioned by the meeting. They assert in substance that Mr. Vallandigham was by a military commander, seized and tried "for no other reason than words addressed to a public meeting, in criticism of the course of the administration, and in condemnation of the military orders of that general." Now, if there be no mistake about this—if this assertion is the truth and the whole truth—if there was no other reason for the arrest, then I concede that the arrest was wrong. But the arrest, as I understand, was made for a very different reason. Mr. Vallandigham avows his hostility to the war on the part of the Union; and his arrest was made because he was laboring, with some effect, to prevent the raising of troops, to encourage desertions from the army, and to leave the rebellion without an adequate military force to suppress it. He was not arrested because he was damaging the political prospects of the administration, or the personal interests of the commanding general; but because he was damaging the army, upon the existence, and vigor of which, the life of the nation depends. He was warring upon the military; and this gave the military constitutional jurisdiction to lay hands upon him. If Mr. Vallandigham was not damaging the military power of the country, then his arrest was made on mistake of fact, which I would be glad to correct, on reasonably satisfactory evidence.

I understand the meeting, whose resolutions I am considering, to be in favor of suppressing the rebellion by military force—by armies. Long experience has shown that armies cannot be maintained unless desertion shall be punished by the severe penalty of death. The case requires, and the law and the constitution, sanction this punishment. Must I shoot a simple-minded soldier boy who deserts, while I must not touch a hair of a wiley agitator who induces him to desert? This is none the less injurious when effected by getting a father, or brother, or friend, into a public meeting, and there working upon his feelings, till he is persuaded to write the soldier boy, that he is fighting in a bad cause, for a wicked administration of a contemptible government, too weak to arrest and punish him if he shall desert. I think that in such a case, to silence the agitator, and save the boy, is not only constitutional, but, withal, a great mercy.

If I be wrong on this question of constitutional power, my error lies in believing that certain proceedings are constitutional when, in cases of rebellion or Invasion, the public Safety requires them, which would not be constitutional when, in absence of rebellion or invasion, the public Safety does not require them—in other words, that the constitution is not in it's application in all respects the same, in cases of Rebellion or invasion, involving the public Safety, as it is in times of profound peace and public security. The constitution itself makes the distinction; and I can no more be persuaded that the government can constitutionally take no strong measure in time of rebellion, because it can be shown that the same could not be lawfully taken in time of peace, than I can be persuaded that a particular drug is not good medicine for a sick man, because it can be shown to not be good food for a well one. Nor am I able to appreciate the danger, apprehended by the meeting, that the American people will, by means of military arrests during the rebellion, lose the right of public discussion, the liberty of speech and the press, the law of evidence, trial by jury, and Habeas corpus, throughout the indefinite peaceful future which I trust lies before them, any more than I am able to believe that a man could contract so strong an appetite for emetics during temporary illness, as to persist in feeding upon them through the remainder of his healthful life.

In giving the resolutions that earnest consideration which you request of me, I cannot overlook the fact that the meeting speak as "Democrats." Nor can I, with full respect for their known intelligence, and the fairly presumed deliberation with which they prepared their resolutions, be permitted to suppose that this occurred by accident, or in any way other than that they preferred to designate themselves "democrats" rather than "American citizens." In this time of national peril I would have preferred to meet you upon a level one step higher than any party platform; because I am sure that from such more elevated position, we could do better battle for the country we all love, than we possibly can from those lower ones, where from the force of habit, the prejudices of the past, and selfish hopes of the future, we are sure to expend much of our ingenuity and strength, in finding fault with, and aiming blows at each other. But since you have denied me this, I will yet be thankful, for the country's sake, that not all democrats have done so. He on whose discretionary judgment Mr. Vallandigham was arrested and tried, is a democrat, having no old party affinity with me; and the judge who rejected the constitutional view expressed in these resolutions, by refusing to discharge Mr. V. on Habeas Corpus, is a democrat of better days than these, having received his judicial mantle at the hands of President Jackson. And still more, of all those democrats who are nobly exposing their lives and shedding their blood on the battle-field, I have learned that many approve the course taken with Mr. V. while I have not heard of a single one condemning it. I can not assert that there are none such. . . .

45

Frederick Douglass

Oration in Memory of Abraham Lincoln (1876)

. . . We stand today at the national center to perform something like a national act—an act which is to go into history; and we are here where every pulsation of the national heart can be heard, felt, and reciprocated. A thousand wires, fed with thought and winged with lightning, put us in instantaneous communication with the loyal and true men all over this country.

Few facts could better illustrate the vast and wonderful change which has taken place in our condition as a people than the fact of our assembling here for the purpose we have today. Harmless, beautiful, proper, and praiseworthy as this demonstration is, I cannot forget that no such demonstration would have been tolerated here twenty years ago. The spirit of slavery and barbarism, which still lingers to blight and destroy in some dark and distant parts of our country, would have made our assembling here the signal and excuse for opening upon us all the flood-gates of wrath and violence. That we are here in peace today is a compliment and a credit to American civilization, and a prophecy of still greater national enlightenment and progress in the future. I refer to the past not in malice, for this is no day for malice; but simply to place more distinctly in front the gratifying and glorious change which has come both to our white fellow-citizens and ourselves, and to congratulate all upon the contrast between now and then; the new dispensation of freedom with its thousand blessings to both races, and the old dispensation of slavery with its ten thousand evils to both races—white and black. . . .

[W]e are here to express, as best we may, by appropriate forms and ceremonies, our grateful sense of the vast, high, and preëminent services rendered to ourselves, to our race, to our country, and to the whole world by Abraham Lincoln.

The sentiment that brings us here to-day is one of the noblest that can stir and thrill the human heart. It has crowned and made glorious the high places of all civilized nations with the grandest and most enduring works of art, designed to illustrate the characters and perpetuate the memories of great public men. It is the sentiment which from year to year adorns with fragrant

From "Oration in Memory of Abraham Lincoln," delivered at the Unveiling of the Freedmen's Monument in Memory of Abraham Lincoln, in Lincoln Park, Washington, D.C., April 14, 1876.

and beautiful flowers the graves of our loyal, brave, and patriotic soldiers who fell in defence of the Union and liberty. It is the sentiment of gratitude and appreciation. . . .

For the first time in the history of our people, and in the history of the whole American people, we join in this high worship, and march conspicuously in the line of this time-honored custom. First things are always interesting, and this is one of our first things. It is the first time that, in this form and manner, we have sought to do honor to an American great man, however deserving and illustrious. I commend the fact to notice; let it be told in every part of the Republic; let men of all parties and opinions hear it; let those who despise us, not less than those who respect us, know that now and here, in the spirit of liberty, loyalty, and gratitude, let it be known everywhere, and by everybody who takes an interest in human progress and in the amelioration of the condition of mankind, that . . . we, the colored people, newly emancipated and rejoicing in our blood-bought freedom, near the close of the first century in the life of this Republic, have now and here unveiled, set apart, and dedicated a monument of enduring granite and bronze, in every line, feature, and figure of which the men of this generation may read, and those of after-coming generations may read, something of the exalted character and great works of Abraham Lincoln, the first martyr President of the United States.

Fellow-citizens, in what we have said and done today, and in what we may say and do hereafter, we disclaim everything like arrogance and assumption. We claim for ourselves no superior devotion to the character, history, and memory of the illustrious name whose monument we have here dedicated today. We fully comprehend the relation of Abraham Lincoln both to ourselves and to the white people of the United States. Truth is proper and beautiful at all times and in all places, and it is never more proper and beautiful in any case than when speaking of a great public man whose example is likely to be commended for honor and imitation long after his departure to the solemn shades, the silent continents of eternity. It must be admitted, truth compels me to admit, even here in the presence of the monument we have erected to his memory, Abraham Lincoln was not, in the fullest sense of the word, either our man or our model. In his interests, in his associations, in his habits of thought, and in his prejudices, he was a white man.

He was preëminently the white man's President, entirely devoted to the welfare of white men. He was ready and willing at any time during the first years of his administration to deny, postpone, and sacrifice the rights of humanity in the colored people to promote the welfare of the white people of this country. In all his education and feeling he was an American of the Americans. He came into the Presidential chair upon one principle alone, namely, opposition to the extension of slavery. His arguments in furtherance of this policy had their motive and mainspring in his patriotic devotion to the interests of his own race. To protect, defend, and perpetuate slavery in the states where it existed Abraham Lincoln was not less ready than any other President to draw the sword of the nation. He was ready to execute all the supposed guarantees of the United States Constitution in favor of the slave system anywhere inside the slave states. He was willing to pursue, recapture, and send back the fugitive slave to his master, and to suppress a slave rising for liberty, though his guilty master were already in arms against the Government. The race to which we belong were not the special objects of his consideration. Knowing this, I concede to you, my white fellow-citizens, a preëminence in this worship at once full and supreme. First, midst, and last, you and yours were the objects of his deepest affection and his most earnest solicitude. You are the children of Abraham Lincoln. We are at best only his step-children; children by adoption, children by forces of circumstances and necessity. . . .

Fellow-citizens, ours is no new-born zeal and devotion—merely a thing of this moment. The name of Abraham Lincoln was near and dear to our hearts in the darkest and most perilous hours of the Republic. We were no more ashamed of him when shrouded in clouds of darkness, of doubt, and defeat than when we saw him crowned with victory, honor, and glory. Our faith in him was often taxed and strained to the uttermost, but it never failed. When he tarried long in the mountain; when he strangely told us that we were the cause of the war; when he still more strangely told us that we were to leave the land in which we were born; when he refused to employ our arms in defence of the Union; when, after accepting our services as colored soldiers, he refused to retaliate our murder and torture as colored prisoners; when he told us he would save the Union if he could with slavery; when he revoked the Proclamation of Emancipation of General Fremont; when he refused to remove the popular commander of the Army of the Potomac, in the days of its inaction and defeat, who was more zealous in his efforts to protect slavery than to suppress rebellion; when we saw all this, and more, we were at times grieved, stunned, and greatly bewildered; but our hearts believed while they ached and bled. Nor was this, even at that time, a blind and unreasoning superstition. Despite the mist and haze that surrounded him; despite the tumult, the hurry, and confusion of the hour, we were able to take a comprehensive view of Abraham Lincoln, and to make reasonable allowance for the circumstances of his position. We saw him, measured him, and estimated him; not by stray utterances to injudicious and tedious delegations, who often tried his patience; not by isolated facts torn from their connection; not by any partial and imperfect glimpses, caught at inopportune moments; but by a broad survey, in the light of the stern logic of great events, and in view of that divinity which shapes our ends, rough hew them how we will, we came to the conclusion that the hour and the man of our redemption had somehow met in the person of Abraham Lincoln. It mattered little to us what language he might employ on special occasions; it mattered little to us, when we fully knew him, whether he was swift or slow in his movements; it was enough for us that Abraham

Lincoln was at the head of a great movement, and was in living and earnest sympathy with that movement, which, in the nature of things, must go on until slavery should be utterly and forever abolished in the United States.

When, therefore, it shall be asked what we have to do with the memory of Abraham Lincoln, or what Abraham Lincoln had to do with us, the answer is ready, full, and complete. Though he loved Caesar less than Rome, though the Union was more to him than our freedom or our future, under his wise and beneficent rule we saw ourselves gradually lifted from the depths of slavery to the heights of liberty and manhood; under his wise and beneficent rule, and by measures approved and vigorously pressed by him, we saw that the handwriting of ages, in the form of prejudice and proscription, was rapidly fading away from the face of our whole country; under his rule, and in due time, about as soon after all as the country could tolerate the strange spectacle, we saw our brave sons and brothers laying off the rags of bondage, and being clothed all over in the blue uniforms of the soldiers of the United States; under his rule we saw two hundred thousand of our dark and dusky people responding to the call of Abraham Lincoln, and with muskets on their shoulders, and eagles on their buttons, timing their high footsteps to liberty and union under the national flag; under his rule we saw the independence of the black republic of Haiti, the special object of slaveholding aversion and horror, fully recognized, and her minister, a colored gentleman, duly received here in the city of Washington; under his rule we saw the internal slave-trade, which so long disgraced the nation, abolished, and slavery abolished in the District of Columbia; under his rule we saw for the first time the law enforced against the foreign slave trade, and the first slave-trader hanged like any other pirate or murderer; under his rule, assisted by the greatest captain of our age, and his inspiration, we saw the Confederate States, based upon the idea that our race must be slaves, and slaves forever, battered to pieces and scattered to the four winds; under his rule, and in the fullness of time, we saw Abraham Lincoln, after giving the slaveholders three months' grace in which to save their hateful slave system, penning the immortal paper, which, though special in its language, was general in its principles and effect, making slavery forever impossible in the United States. Though we waited long, we saw all this and more. . . .

I have said that President Lincoln was a white man, and shared the prejudices common to his countrymen towards the colored race. Looking back to his times and to the condition of his country, we are compelled to admit that this unfriendly feeling on his part may be safely set down as one element of his wonderful success in organizing the loyal American people for the tremendous conflict before them, and bringing them safely through that conflict. His great mission was to accomplish two things: first, to save his country from dismemberment and ruin; and, second, to free his country from the great crime of slavery. To do one or the other, or both, he must have the earnest sympathy and the powerful coöperation of his loyal fellow-countrymen. Without this primary and essential condition to success his efforts must have been vain and utterly fruitless. Had he put the abolition of slavery before the salvation of the Union, he would have inevitably driven from him a powerful class of the American people and rendered resistance to rebellion impossible. Viewed from the genuine abolition ground, Mr. Lincoln seemed tardy, cold, dull, and indifferent; but measuring him by the sentiment of his country, a sentiment he was bound as a statesman to consult, he was swift, zealous, radical, and determined.

Though Mr. Lincoln shared the prejudices of his white fellow-countrymen against the Negro, it is hardly necessary to say that in his heart of hearts he loathed and hated slavery. . . . The man who could say, "Fondly do we hope, fervently do we pray, that this mighty scourge of war shall soon pass away, yet if God wills it continue till all the wealth piled by two hundred years of bondage shall have been wasted, and each drop of blood drawn by the last shall have been paid for by one drawn by the sword, the judgments of the Lord are true and righteous altogether," gives all needed proof of his feeling on the subject of slavery. He was willing, while the South was loyal, that it should have its pound of flesh, because he thought that it was so nominated in the bond; but farther than this no earthly power could make him go.

Fellow-citizens, whatever else in this world may be partial, unjust, and uncertain, time, time! is impartial, just, and certain in its action. In the realm of mind, as well as in the realm of matter, it is a great worker, and often works wonders. The honest and comprehensive statesman, clearly discerning the needs of his country, and earnestly endeavoring to do his whole duty, though covered and blistered with reproaches, may safely leave his course to the silent judgment of time. Few great public men have ever been the victims of fiercer denunciation than Abraham Lincoln was during his administration. He was often wounded in the house of his friends. Reproaches came thick and fast upon him from within and from without, and from opposite quarters. He was assailed by Abolitionists; he was assailed by slaveholders; he was assailed by the men who were for peace at any price; he was assailed by those who were for a more vigorous prosecution of the war; he was assailed for not making the war an abolition war; and he was bitterly assailed for making the war an abolition war.

But now behold the change: the judgment of the present hour is, that taking him for all in all, measuring the tremendous magnitude of the work before him, considering the necessary means to ends, and surveying the end from the beginning, infinite wisdom has seldom sent any man into the world better fitted for his mission than Abraham Lincoln. His birth, his training, and his natural endowments, both mental and physical, were strongly in his favor. Born and reared among the lowly, a stranger to wealth and luxury, compelled to grapple single-handed with the flintiest hardships of life, from tender youth to sturdy manhood, he grew strong in the manly and heroic qualities demanded by the great mission to which he was called by the votes of his countrymen. The hard condition of his early life, which would have depressed and broken down weaker men, only gave greater life, vigor, and buoyancy to the heroic spirit of Abraham Lincoln. He was ready for any kind and any quality of work. . . .

All day long he could split heavy rails in the woods, and half the night long he could study his English Grammar by the uncertain flare and glare of the light made by a pine-knot. He was at home on the land with his axe, with his maul, with gluts, and his wedges; and he was equally at home on water, with his oars, with his poles, with his planks, and with his boat-hooks. And whether in his flat-boat on the Mississippi River, or at the fireside of his frontier cabin, he was a man of work. A son of toil himself, he was linked in brotherly sympathy with the sons of toil in every loyal part of the Republic. This very fact gave him tremendous power with the American people, and materially contributed not only to selecting him to the Presidency, but in sustaining his administration of the Government.

Upon his inauguration as President of the United States, an office, even when assumed under the most favorable conditions, fitted to tax and strain the largest abilities, Abraham Lincoln was met by a tremendous crisis. He was called upon not merely to administer the Government, but to decide, in the face of terrible odds, the fate of the Republic.

A formidable rebellion rose in his path before him; the Union was already practically dissolved; his country was torn and rent asunder at the center. Hostile armies were already organized against the Republic, armed with the munitions of war which the Republic had provided for its own defence. The tremendous question for him to decide was whether his country should survive the crisis and flourish, or be dismembered and perish. His predecessor in office had already decided the question in favor of national dismemberment, by denying to it the right of self-defence and self-preservation—a right which belongs to the meanest insect.

Happily for the country, happily for you and for me, the judgment of James Buchanan, the patrician, was not the judgment of Abraham Lincoln, the plebeian. He brought his strong common sense, sharpened in the school of adversity, to bear upon the question. He did not hesitate, he did not doubt, he did not falter; but at once resolved that at whatever peril, at whatever cost, the union of the States should be preserved. . . . The trust that Abraham Lincoln had in himself and in the people was surprising and grand, but it was also enlightened and well founded. He knew the American people better than they knew themselves, and his truth was based upon this knowledge.

Fellow-citizens, the fourteenth day of April, 1865, of which this is the eleventh anniversary, is now and will ever remain a memorable day in the annals of this Republic. It was on the evening of this day, while a fierce and sangui-nary rebellion was in the last stages of its desolating power; while its armies were broken and scattered before the invincible armies of Grant and Sherman; while a great nation, torn and rent by war, was already beginning to raise to the skies loud anthems of joy at the dawn of peace, it was startled, amazed, and overwhelmed by the crowning crime of slavery—the assassination of Abraham Lincoln. It was a new crime, a pure act of malice. No purpose of the rebellion was to be served by it. It was the simple gratification of a hell-black spirit of revenge. But it has done good after all. It has filled the country with a deeper abhorrence of slavery and a deeper love for the great liberator.

Had Abraham Lincoln died from any of the numerous ills to which flesh is heir; had he reached that good old age of which his vigorous constitution and his temperate habits gave promise; had he been permitted to see the end of his great work; had the solemn curtain of death come down but gradually— we should still have been smitten with a heavy grief, and treasured his name lovingly. But dying as he did die, by the red hand of violence, killed, assassi-nated, taken off without warning, not because of personal hate—for no man who knew Abraham Lincoln could hate him—but because of his fidelity to union and liberty, he is doubly dear to us, and his memory will be precious forever.

Fellow-citizens, I end, as I began, with congratulations. We have done a good work for our race today. In doing honor to the memory of our friend and liberator, we have been doing highest honors to ourselves and those who come after us; we have been fastening ourselves to a name and fame imperishable and immortal; we have also been defending ourselves from a blighting scandal. When now it shall be said that the colored man is soulless, that he has no appreciation of benefits or benefactors; when the foul reproach of ingratitude is hurled at us, and it is attempted to scourge us beyond the range of human brotherhood, we may calmly point to the monument we have this day erected to the memory of Abraham Lincoln.

Chapter V

The Judiciary

In *The Federalist* Hamilton argues that the Supreme Court's power of judicial review follows from the concept of a limited constitution. Because there are limits to governmental activity, acts that exceed those limits are void, and therefore cannot be applied in particular cases by the Court. Judicial review signifies not judicial supremacy, but constitutional supremacy. The particular function of the court is thus to protect the rule of law.

Although the Constitution establishes the rule of law, there must be discretion for those who enact and administer the laws, or for the strictly political or elected branches of government. It is often difficult to draw the line between the discretion necessary for governing and the arbitrary exercise of power. In its job of defending the Constitution, the Court must often draw that line, deciding what matters are justiciable and what matters are political. In making that decision the Court itself exercises discretion. The possibility of arbitrary rule by the Judiciary parallels that of arbitrary rule by administrators, since neither the Court nor the administrator can avoid exercising discretion in particular cases before them. But although administrators are accountable to a political superior, the members of the Judiciary are relatively independent, holding office during good behavior. Hamilton argues that it is safe to give the Judiciary such independence, since it is the weakest of the three branches. Judges are able to declare laws unconstitutional only when a case is brought before them, and they depend on the Executive to enforce their decisions.

The anti-Federalist writer Brutus is not persuaded by Hamilton's argument. He believes that the Court has the potential to become the most dangerous branch of government. If as in Britain the Court had no power to override the Acts of the legislature, there would be less danger from life tenure for judges. But life tenure combined with the power of judicial review holds the potential for the exercise of unrestrained arbitrary power.

Both Jefferson and Lincoln later expressed distrust of an arbitrary and powerful Court. Jefferson went so far as to deny that the Court possessed the power of judicial review. Each branch of government, Jefferson believed, must interpret the Constitution insofar as it applies to itself. He admits that "contradictory decisions" could arise undeı his scheme, but he relies on "the prudence of public functionaries, and the authority of public opinion" to "produce accommodation." In the absence of enlightened public opinion and statesmanship, Jefferson's version of separation of powers would lead to conflict between the branches and great confusion about the meaning of the law. Lincoln, like Jefferson, recognizes the danger of judicial review, but his position is more prudent. He emphasizes that while American citizens must abide by the *Dred Scott* decision, it applies only to the case at hand and cannot act as a precedent.

In *Marbury v. Madison* the Court declares a law of Congress unconstitutional. Marshall, speaking for the Court, explains why the Constitution implies that the Court has this power. Paradoxically, Congress went beyond its powers in enlarging those of the Court. In asserting the power of judicial review, Marshall also declared that the Court's own powers were limited by the Constitution. It was those limits that Congress had attempted to exceed in the Judiciary Act of 1789.

Marshall both affirms and limits judicial authority in another way as well. He distinguishes between acts of Executive officers that are and are not reviewable by the Court. An administrative officer is legally accountable for those acts that a law directs him to do, but not for those acts that the President directs him to do when exercising the discretionary political powers given him by the Constitution. *United States v. Nixon* goes beyond *Marbury* in restricting Executive discretion. There the issue is the discretion of the President himself rather than that of an administrative officer. Although the Court holds that "executive privilege" is implied in the office of the Presidency, it asserts that the Court itself is the judge of its applicability. The implications of the Court's opinion in *U.S. v. Nixon* entail a danger of judicial supremacy, not to Congress, but to the Presidency.

The question of the relation between the Court and the political branches is also raised by the reapportionment cases. Dissenting in those cases, Harlan claims that the Court has usurped power that rightly belongs to political branches, in particular, to the state legislatures. He looks back to the intention of the Framers of the Equal Protection Clause of the Fourteenth Amendment in order to show that it cannot be read to guarantee an apportionment of state legislatures on a one-man, one-vote basis. The Court, according to Harlan, has in effect amended the Constitution by placing an unjustifiable interpretation on the Fourteenth Amendment.

Stewart differs from Harlan in maintaining that apportionment does fall under the Equal Protection Clause and is therefore reviewable by the Court, but he differs from Warren and the Court's majority in denying the constitutional necessity of the one-man, one-vote principle. By forcing all state legislatures to apply that principle, Stewart argues, the Court stifles the local diversity and initiative that are essential to federalism. Furthermore, the Court misunderstands the principle of majority by coalition, so essential to the American tradition: the principle of one-man, one-vote allows a majority to run roughshod over minorities. On the other hand, apportionment schemes giving some voice to sparsely-populated areas is more likely to produce a majority composed of "a medley of component voices." Although the Equal Protection Clause does not require one-man, one-vote, Stewart argues, it does limit state legislatures in two ways. It demands that the criteria on the basis of which legislatures are apportioned be reasonably related to a legitimate end and that the apportionment not prevent majority rule. This allows for an appropriate diversity in apportionment in different states. For example, states might preserve local communities, formed either by natural boundaries or historical circumstances, by assuring them a voice in the legislature.

In spite of their different understandings of the relation between apportionment and the Equal Protection Clause, Harlan and Stewart agree that the Court's imposition of one-man, one-vote on state legislatures undermines federalism. Harlan further suggests that political reform by the Judiciary undermines democratic government. He warns that if people depend on the Court to solve political problems rather than on their own efforts in the political arena, a complacent body politic might result.

Justice William J. Brennan, Jr. provides a contemporary defense not only of judicial review but also of judicial activism. Brennan claims that the Court must look beyond the text of the Constitution and the intention of its framers in order to deal with problems that arise in a modern world. He believes that the Constitution establishes a Court in order to protect the rights of minorities and the rights of individuals. The Court need not rely on any specific statutory or Constitutional language, but should instead look to these broader Constitutional goals.

Judge Robert Bork, however, argues that the doctrine of judicial activism is merely a convenient rationalization that allows judges to impose their own personal policy preferences on the Constitution and the nation. Bork believes that if the Constitution is to protect the rights of the people in the long-run, the text of the document and the intention of its framers must provide the boundaries within which judicial interpretation takes place. If the Constitution fails to settle an issue it is up to the more political branches of government to fill in the gaps through legislation or Constitutional amendment.

Like Brennan, Jefferson fears that the framers of a Constitution may not be able to anticipate the changing needs of the nation. But unlike Brennan Jefferson knows that his position ultimately calls into question an enduring Constitutional system. Jefferson does not think a Court can breathe life into an old Constitution. Men have no right to bind a future generation. Each generation must create its own Constitution. In response, Madison argued that generations are linked by the fact that later ones are beneficiaries of earlier ones, and to that extent obliged to follow their prescriptions. Since Madison was replying to Jefferson's objection to a "perpetual constitution," he must have had in mind his own generation's work of founding and the endurance of his own handiwork as the link among the individuals who were to live under the Constitution. Furthermore, a new government every generation, Madison argued, would not maintain the prejudice of the people in favor of the government "which is a salutary aid to the most rational government." Or, as he put it in Federalist 49, frequent appeals to the people about the fundamental principles of government would "deprive the government of that veneration that time bestows on everything."

In *California v. Bakke,* the judges reveal their different views of judicial review. As L. Peter Schultz points out, most of the Justices advocate that notion of a "living Constitution," which changes according to the problems and needs of the age. But although the majority of judges emphasize the necessity of a Constitution adaptable to the times, they differ in their understanding of how constitutional change should occur. Those judges who believe in an active Court hold that the Judiciary branch should reinterpret or adapt the Constitution from time to time. In *Bakke,* they uphold an expansion of the Equal Protection Clause of the Fourteenth Amendment so as to justify affirmative action programs. Their jurisprudence resembles that of the Court in the reapportionment cases, where the Court's interpretation of Equal Protection overturned state apportionment schemes. The activists' position in *Bakke,* however, was not endorsed by a majority of the Court. Another group of Justices, proponents of judicial self-restraint, refused to reach the Constitutional question of Equal Protection. They too advocate the "living Constitution," but they believe that it is the more political branches of government which should apply the changing standards of the age. These judges invalidated the affirmative action plan of the University of California on the ground that it violated the Civil Rights Act, which forbad state-funded institutions from making racial classifications. Whether the advocates of the "living Constitution" actively attempt to adapt the Constitution to their perception of the changing times, or restrain themselves in favor of the adaptations coming from the people and the more political branches, their understanding of the Constitution owes much to Jefferson's idea that one generation should not bind future generations and his hope for frequent constitutional conventions. The elaboration and protection of the permanent principles in the Constitution, which Hamilton and Marshall thought was one of the Court's highest roles, is found in the *Bakke* case, according to Schultz, only in the position of Justice Powell. Powell does join the "restraintists" to overturn affirmative action. But, unlike the restraintists, he is active in that he reaches the constitutional issue. Nonetheless, he is "restrained" in deciding the case on the basis of enduring constitutional principles, refusing to expand those principles to suit the passing exigencies or even the latest prejudices of the times. It is only by such a combination of activism and restraint, Schultz argues, that judicial statesmanship can emerge.

46

Alexander Hamilton

The Role of the Supreme Court (1788)

. . . As to the tenure by which the judges are to hold their places: this chiefly concerns their duration in office; the provisions for their support; the precautions for their responsibility.

According to the plan of the convention, all judges who may be appointed by the United States are to hold their offices *during good behavior*. . . . The standard of good behavior for the continuance in office of the judicial magistracy, is certainly one of the most valuable of the modern improvements in the practice of government. In a monarchy it is an excellent barrier to the despotism of the prince; in a republic it is a no less excellent barrier to the encroachments and oppressions of the representative body. And it is the best expedient which can be devised in any government, to secure a steady, upright, and impartial administration of the laws.

Whoever attentively considers the different departments of power must perceive, that, in a government in which they are separated from each other, the judiciary, from the nature of its functions, will always be the least dangerous to the political rights of the Constitution; because it will be least in a capacity to annoy or injure them. The Executive not only dispenses the honors, but holds the sword of the community. The legislature not only commands the purse, but prescribes the rules by which the duties and rights of every citizen are to be regulated. The judiciary, on the contrary, has no influence over either the sword or the purse; no direction either of the strength or of the wealth of the society; and can take no active resolution whatever. It may truly be said to have neither FORCE nor WILL, but merely judgment; and must ultimately depend upon the aid of the executive arm even for the efficacy of its judgments.

This simple view of the matter suggests several important consequences. It proves incontestably, that the judiciary is beyond comparison the weakest of the three departments of power; that it can never attack with success either of the other two; and that all possible care is requisite to enable it to defend itself against their attacks. It equally proves, that though individual oppression may now and then proceed from the courts of justice,

From Federalist 78, in *The Federalist.*

the general liberty of the people can never be endangered from that quarter; I mean so long as the judiciary remains truly distinct from both the legislature and the Executive. For I agree, that "there is no liberty, if the power of judging be not separated from the legislative and executive powers." And it proves, in the last place, that as liberty can have nothing to fear from the judiciary alone, but would have every thing to fear from its union with either of the other departments; that as all the effects of such a union must ensue from a dependence of the former on the latter, notwithstanding a nominal and apparent separation; that as, from the natural feebleness of the judiciary, it is in continual jeopardy of being overpowered, awed, or influenced by its coordinate branches; and that as nothing can contribute so much to its firmness and independence as permanency in office, this quality may therefore be justly regarded as an indispensable ingredient in its constitution, and, in a great measure, as the citadel of the public justice and the public security.

The complete independence of the courts of justice is peculiarly essential in a limited Constitution. By a limited Constitution, I understand one which contains certain specified exceptions to the legislative authority; such, for instance, as that it shall pass no bills of attainder, no *ex-post-facto* laws, and the like. Limitations of this kind can be preserved in practice no other way than through the medium of courts of justice, whose duty it must be to declare all acts contrary to the manifest tenor of the Constitution void. Without this, all the reservations of particular rights or privileges would amount to nothing.

Some perplexity respecting the rights of the courts to pronounce legislative acts void, because contrary to the constitution, has arisen from an imagination that the doctrine would imply a superiority of the judiciary to the legislative power. It is urged that the authority which can declare the acts of another void, must necessarily be superior to the one whose acts may be declared void. As this doctrine is of great importance in all the American constitutions, a brief discussion of the ground on which it rests cannot be unacceptable.

There is no position which depends on clearer principles, than that every act of a delegated authority, contrary to the tenor of the commission under which it is exercised, is void. No legislative act, therefore, contrary to the Constitution, can be valid. To deny this, would be to affirm, that the deputy is greater than his principal; that the servant is above his master; that the representatives of the people are superior to the people themselves; that men acting by virtue of powers, may do not only what their powers do not authorize, but what they forbid.

If it be said that the legislative body are themselves the constitutional judges of their own powers, and that the construction they put upon them is conclusive upon the other departments, it may be answered, that this cannot be the natural presumption, where it is not to be collected from any particular provisions in the Constitution. It is not otherwise to be supposed, that the Constitution could intend to enable the representatives of the people to substitute their *will* to that of their constituents. It is far more rational to suppose, that the courts were designed to be an intermediate body between the people and the legislature, in order, among other things, to keep the latter within the limits assigned to their authority. The interpretation of the laws is the proper and peculiar province of the courts. A constitution is, in fact, and must be regarded by the judges, as a fundamental law. It therefore belongs to them to ascertain its meaning, as well as the meaning of any particular act proceeding from the legislative body. If there should happen to be an irreconcilable variance between the two, that which has the superior obligation and validity ought, of course, to be preferred; or, in other words, the Constitution ought to be preferred to the statute, the intention of the people to the intention of their agents.

Nor does this conclusion by any means suppose a superiority of the judicial to the legislative power. It only supposes that the power of the people is superior to both; and that where the will of the legislature, declared in its statutes, stands in opposition to that of the people, declared in the Constitution, the judges ought to be governed by the latter rather than the former. They ought to regulate their decisions by the fundamental laws, rather than by those which are not fundamental.

This exercise of judicial discretion, in determining between two contradictory laws, is exemplified in a familiar instance. It not uncommonly happens, that there are two statutes existing at one time, clashing in whole or in part with each other, and neither of them containing any repealing clause or expression. In such a case, it is the province of the courts to liquidate and fix their meaning and operation. So far as they can, by any fair construction, be reconciled to each other, reason and law conspire to dictate that this should be done; where this is impracticable, it becomes a matter of necessity to give effect to one, in exclusion of the other. The rule which has obtained in the courts for determining their relative validity is, that the last in order of time shall be preferred to the first. . . . [The Courts] thought it reasonable, that between the interfering acts of an *equal* authority, that which was the last indication of its will should have the preference.

But in regard to the interfering acts of a superior and subordinate authority, of an original and derivative power, the nature and reason of the thing indicate the converse of that rule as proper to be followed. They teach us that the prior act of a superior ought to be preferred to the subsequent act of an inferior and subordinate authority; and that accordingly, whenever a particular statute contravenes the Constitution, it will be the duty of the judicial tribunals to adhere to the latter and disregard the former.

It can be of no weight to say that the courts, on the pretence of a repugnancy, may substitute their own pleasure to the constitutional intentions of the legislature. This might as well happen in the case of two contradictory statutes; or it might as well happen in every adjudication upon any single statute. The courts must declare the sense of the law; and if they should be disposed to exercise WILL instead of JUDGMENT, the consequence would equally be the substitution of their pleasure to that of the legislative body. The observation, if it prove any thing, would prove that there ought to be no judges distinct from that body.

If, then, the courts of justice are to be considered as the bulwarks of a limited Constitution against legislative encroachments, this consideration will afford a strong argument for the permanent tenure of judicial offices since nothing will contribute so much as this to that independent spirit in the judges which must be essential to the faithful performance of so arduous a duty.

This independence of the judges is equally requisite to guard the Constitution and the rights of individuals from the effects of those ill humors, which the arts of designing men, or the influence of particular conjunctures, sometimes disseminate among the people themselves, and which, though they speedily give place to better information, and more deliberate reflection, have a tendency, in the meantime, to occasion dangerous innovations in the government, and serious oppressions of the minor party in the community. Though I trust the friends of the proposed Constitution will never concur with its enemies, in questioning that fundamental principle of republican government, which admits the right of the people to alter or abolish the established Constitution, whenever they find it inconsistent with their happiness, yet it is not to be inferred from this principle, that the representatives of the people, whenever a momentary inclination happens to lay hold of a majority of their constituents, incompatible with the provisions in the existing Constitution, would, on that account, be justifiable in a violation of those provisions; or that the courts would be under a greater obligation to connive at infractions in this shape, than when they had proceeded wholly from the cabals of the representative body. Until the people have, by some solemn and authoritative act, annulled or changed the established form, it is binding upon themselves collectively, as well as individually; and no presumption, or even knowledge, of their sentiments, can warrant their representatives in a departure from it, prior to such an act. But it is easy to see, that it would require an uncommon portion of fortitude in the judges to do their duty as faithful guardians of the Constitution, where legislative invasions of it had been instigated by the major voice of the community.

But it is not with a view to infractions of the Constitution only, that the independence of the judges may be an essential safeguard against the effects of occasional ill humors in the society. These sometimes extend no farther than to the injury of the private rights of particular classes of citizens, by unjust and partial laws. Here also the firmness of the judicial magistracy is of vast importance in mitigating the severity and confining the operation of such laws. It not only serves to moderate the immediate mischiefs of those which may have been passed but it operates as a check upon the legislative body in passing them; who, perceiving that obstacles to the success of iniquitous intention are to be expected from the scruples of the courts, are in a manner compelled, by the very motives of the injustice they meditate, to qualify their attempts. . . .

Periodical appointments, however regulated, or by whomsoever made, would, in some way or other, be fatal to [the judges'] necessary independence. . . .

There is yet a further and a weightier reason for the permanency of the judicial offices, which is deducible from the nature of the qualifications they require. It has been frequently remarked, with great propriety, that a voluminous code of laws is one of the inconveniences necessarily connected with the advantages of a free government. To avoid an arbitrary discretion in the courts, it is indispensable that they should be bound down by strict rules and precedents, which serve to define and point out their duty in every particular case that comes before them; and it will readily be conceived from the variety of controversies which grow out of the folly and wickedness of mankind, that the records of those precedents must unavoidably swell to a very considerable bulk, and must demand long and laborious study to acquire a competent knowledge of them. Hence it is, that there can be but few men in the society who will have sufficient skill in the laws to qualify them for the stations of judges. And making the proper deductions for the ordinary depravity of human nature, the number must be still smaller of those who unite the requisite integrity with the requisite knowledge. These considerations apprise us, that the government can have no great option between fit character; and that a temporary duration in office, which would naturally discourage such characters from quitting a lucrative line of practice to accept a seat on the bench, would have a tendency to throw the administration of justice into hands less able, and less well qualified, to conduct it with utility and dignity. . . .

47

Brutus

The Problem of Judicial Review (1787)

. . . [T]he supreme court under this constitution [will] be exalted above all other power in the government, and subject to no controul. . . . I question whether the world ever saw, in any period of it, a court of justice invested with such immense powers, and yet placed in a situation so little responsible. Certain it is, that in England, and in the several states, where we have been taught to believe, the courts of law are put upon the most prudent establishment, they are on a very different footing.

The judges in England, it is true, hold their offices during their good behaviour, but then their determinations are subject to correction by the house of lords; and their power is by no means so extensive as that of the proposed supreme court of the union.—I believe they in no instance assume the authority to set aside an act of parliament under the idea that it is inconsistent with their constitution. They consider themselves bound to decide according to the existing laws of the land, and never undertake to controul them by adjudging that they are inconsistent with the constitution—much less are they vested with the power of giving an *equitable* construction to the constitution.

The judges in England are under the controul of the legislature, for they are bound to determine according to the laws passed by them. But the judges under this constitution will controul the legislature, for the supreme court are authorised in the last resort, to determine what is the extent of the powers of the Congress; they are to give the constitution an explanation, and there is no power above them to set aside their judgment. The framers of this constitution appear to have followed that of the British, in rendering the judges independent, by granting them their offices during good behaviour, without following the constitution of England, in instituting a tribunal in which their errors may be corrected; and without adverting to this, that the judicial under this system have a power which is above the legislative, and which indeed transcends any power before given to a judicial by any free government under heaven.

I do not object to the judges holding their commissions during good behaviour. I suppose it a proper provision provided they were made properly responsible. But I say, this system has followed the English government in this, while it has departed from almost every other principle of their jurisprudence,

From Brutus XV, *New York Journal,* March 20, 1787.

under the idea, of rendering the judges independent; which, in the British constitution, means no more than that they hold their places during good behaviour, and have fixed salaries, they have made the judges *independent,* in the fullest sense of the word. There is no power above them, to controul any of their decisions. There is no authority that can remove them, and they cannot be controuled by the laws of the legislature. In short, they are independent of the people, of the legislature, and of every power under heaven. Men placed in this situation will generally soon feel themselves independent of heaven itself. Before I proceed to illustrate the truth of these assertions, I beg liberty to make one remark—Though in my opinion the judges ought to hold their offices during good behaviour, yet I think it is clear, that the reasons in favour of this establishment of the judges in England, do by no means apply to this country.

The great reason assigned, why the judges in Britain ought to be commissioned during good behaviour, is this, that they may be placed in a situation, not to be influenced by the crown, to give such decisions, as would tend to increase its powers and prerogatives. While the judges held their places at the will and pleasure of the king, on whom they depended not only for their offices, but also for their salaries, they were subject to every undue influence. If the crown wished to carry a favorite point, to accomplish which the aid of the courts of law was necessary, the pleasure of the king would be signified to the judges. And it required the spirit of a martyr, for the judges to determine contrary to the king's will.—They were absolutely dependent upon him both for their offices and livings. The king, holding his office during life, and transmitting it to his posterity as an inheritance, has much stronger inducements to increase the prerogatives of his office than those who hold their offices for stated periods, or even for life. Hence the English nation gained a great point, in favour of liberty. When they obtained the appointment of the judges, during good behaviour, they got from the crown a concession, which deprived it of one of the most powerful engines with which it might enlarge the boundaries of the royal prerogative and encroach on the liberties of the people. But these reasons do not apply to this country, we have no hereditary monarch; those who appoint the judges do not hold their offices for life, nor do they descend to their children. The same arguments, therefore, which will conclude in favor of the tenor of the judge's offices for good behaviour, lose a considerable part of their weight when applied to the state and condition of America. But much less can it be shewn, that the nature of our government requires that the courts should be placed beyond all account more independent, so much so as to be above controul.

I have said that the judges under this system will be *independent* in the strict sense of the word: To prove this I will shew—That there is no power above them that can controul their decisions, or correct their errors. There is no authority that can remove them from office for any errors or want of capacity, or lower their salaries, and in many cases their power is superior to that of the legislature.

1st. There is no power above them that can correct their errors or controul their decisions—The adjudications of this court are final and irreversible, for there is no court above them to which appeals can lie, either in error or on the merits.—In this respect it differs from the courts in England, for there the house of lords is the highest court, to whom appeals, in error, are carried from the highest of the courts of law.

2d. They cannot be removed from office or suffer a dimunition of their salaries, for any error in judgement or want of capacity.

It is expressly declared by the constitution,—"That they shall at stated times receive a compensation for their services which shall not be diminished during their continuance in office."

The only clause in the constitution which provides for the removal of the judges from office, is that which declares, that "the president, vice-president, and all civil officers of the United States, shall be removed from office, on impeachment for, and conviction of treason, bribery, or other high crimes and misdemeanors." By this paragraph, civil officers, in which the judges are included, are removable only for crimes. Treason and bribery are named, and the rest are included under the general terms of high crimes and misdemeanors.—Errors in judgement, or want of capacity to discharge the duties of the office, can never be supposed to be included in these words, *high crimes and misdemeanors.* A man may mistake a case in giving judgment, or manifest that he is incompetent to the discharge of the duties of a judge, and yet give no evidence of corruption or want of integrity. To support the charge, it will be necessary to give in evidence some facts that will shew, that the judges commited the error from wicked and corrupt motives.

3d. The power of this court is in many cases superior to that of the legislature. I have shewed, in a former paper, that this court will be authorised to decide upon the meaning of the constitution, and that, not only according to the natural and ob[vious] meaning of the words, but also according to the spirit and intention of it. In the exercise of this power they will not be subordinate to, but above the legislature. For all the departments of this government will receive their powers, so far as they are expressed in the constitution, from the people immediately, who are the source of power. The legislature can only exercise such powers as are given them by the constitution, they cannot assume any of the rights annexed to the judicial, for this plain reason, that the same authority which vested the legislature with their powers, vested the judicial with theirs—both are derived from the same source, both therefore are equally valid, and the judicial hold their powers independently of the legislature, as the legislature do of the judicial.—The supreme court then have a right, independent of the legislature, to give a construction to the constitution and every part of it, and there is no power provided in this system to correct their construction or do it away. If, therefore, the legislature pass any laws, inconsistent with the sense the judges put upon the constitution, they will declare it void; and therefore in this respect their power is superior to that of the legislature. . . .

48

Thomas Jefferson

Against Judicial Review (1815)

The . . . question, whether the judges are invested with exclusive authority to decide on the constitutionality of a law, has been heretofore a subject of consideration with me in the exercise of official duties. Certainly there is not a word in the constitution which has given that power to them more than to the executive or legislative branches. Questions of property, of character and of crime being ascribed to the judges, through a definite course of legal proceeding, laws involving such questions belong, of course, to them; and as they decide on them ultimately and without appeal, they of course decide *for themselves.* The constitutional validity of the law or laws again prescribing executive action, and to be administered by that branch ultimately and without appeal, the executive must decide for *themselves* also, whether, under the constitution, they are valid or not. So also as to laws governing the proceedings of the legislature, that body must judge *for itself* the constitutionality of the law, and equally without appeal or control from its co-ordinate branches. And, in general, that branch which is to act ultimately, and without appeal, on any law, is the rightful expositor of the validity of the law, uncontrolled by the opinions of the other co-ordinate authorities. It may be said that contradictory decisions may arise in such case, and produce inconvenience. This is possible, and is a necessary failing in all human proceedings. Yet the prudence of the public functionaries, and authority of public opinion, will generally produce accommodation. Such an instance of difference occurred between the judges of England (in the time of Lord Holt) and the House of Commons, but the prudence of those bodies prevented inconvenience from it. So in the cases of Duane and of William Smith of South Carolina, whose characters of citizenship stood precisely on the same ground, the judges in a question of meum and tuum which came before them, decided that Duane was not a citizen; and in a question of membership, the House of Representatives, under the same words of the same provision, adjudged William Smith to be a citizen. Yet no inconvenience has ensued from these contradictory decisions. This is

From *The Writings of Thomas Jefferson,* Vol. IX, G.P. Putnam's Sons, 1898.

what I believe myself to be sound. But there is another opinion entertained by some men of such judgment and information as to lessen my confidence in my own. That is, that the legislature alone is the exclusive expounder of the sense of the constitution, in every part of it whatever. And they allege in its support, that this branch has authority to impeach and punish a member of either of the others acting contrary to its declaration of the sense of the constitution. It may indeed be answered, that an act may still be valid although the party is punished for it, right or wrong. However, this opinion which ascribes exclusive exposition to the legislature, merits respect for its safety, there being in the body of the nation a control over them, which, if expressed by rejection on the subsequent exercise of their elective franchise, enlists public opinion against their exposition, and encourages a judge or executive on a future occasion to adhere to their former opinion. Between these two doctrines, every one has a right to choose, and I know of no third meriting any respect. . . .

49

Abraham Lincoln

The Authority of the Supreme Court (1857)

. . . And now as to the Dred Scott decision. That decision declares two propositions—first, that a negro cannot sue in the U.S. Courts; and secondly, that Congress cannot prohibit slavery in the Territories. It was made by a divided court—dividing differently on the different points. Judge Douglas does not discuss the merits of the decision; and, in that respect, I shall follow his example, believing I could no more improve on McLean and Curtis, than he could on Taney.

From Speech at Springfield, Illinois, June 26, 1857, in *The Collected Works of Abraham Lincoln,* Vol. II, Rutgers University Press, 1953.

He denounces all who question the correctness of that decision, as offering violent resistance to it. But who resists it? Who has, in spite of the decision, declared Dred Scott free, and resisted the authority of his master over him?

Judicial decisions have two uses—first, to absolutely determine the case decided, and secondly, to indicate to the public how other similar cases will be decided when they arise. For the latter use, they are called "precedents" and "authorities."

We believe, as much as Judge Douglas, (perhaps more) in obedience to, and respect for the judicial department of government. We think its decisions on Constitutional questions, when fully settled, should control, not only the particular cases decided, but the general policy of the country, subject to be disturbed only by amendments of the Constitution as provided in that instrument itself. More than this would be revolution. But we think the Dred Scott decision is erroneous. We know the court that made it, has often over-ruled its own decisions, and we shall do what we can to have it to over-rule this. We offer no *resistance* to it.

Judicial decisions are of greater or less authority as precedents, according to circumstances. That this should be so, accords both with common sense, and the customary understanding of the legal profession.

If this important decision had been made by the unanimous concurrence of the judges, and without any apparent partisan bias, and in accordance with legal public expectation, and with the steady practice of the departments throughout our history, and had been in no part, based on assumed historical facts which are not really true; or, if wanting in some of these, it had been before the court more than once, and had there been affirmed and re-affirmed through a course of years, it then might be, perhaps would be, factious, nay, even revolutionary, to not acquiesce in it as a precedent.

But when, as it is true we find it wanting in all these claims to the public confidence, it is not resistance, it is not factious, it is not even disrespectful, to treat it as not having yet quite established a settled doctrine for the country—But Judge Douglas considers this view awful. Hear him:

"The courts are the tribunals prescribed by the Constitution and created by the authority of the people to determine, expound and enforce the law. Hence, whoever resists the final decision of the highest judicial tribunal, aims a deadly blow to our whole Republican system of government—a blow, which if successful would place all our rights and liberties at the mercy of passion, anarchy and violence. I repeat, therefore, that if resistance to the decisions of the Supreme Court of the United States, in a matter like the points decided in the Dred Scott case, clearly within their jurisdiction as defined by the Constitution, shall be forced upon the country as a political issue, it will become a distinct and naked issue between the friends and the enemies of the Constitution—the friends and the enemies of the supremacy of the laws.''

Why this same Supreme court once decided a national bank to be constitutional; but Gen. Jackson, as President of the United States, disregarded the decision, and vetoed a bill for a re-charter, partly on constitutional ground, declaring that each public functionary must support the Constitution, *"as he understands it."* But hear the General's own words. Here they are, taken from his veto message:

"It is maintained by the advocates of the bank, that its constitutionality, in all its features, ought to be considered as settled by precedent, and by the decision of the Supreme Court. To this conclusion I cannot assent. Mere precedent is a dangerous source of authority, and should not be regarded as deciding questions of constitutional power, except where the acquiescence of the people and the States can be considered as well settled. So far from this being the case on this subject, an argument against the bank might be based on precedent. One Congress in 1791, decided in favor of a bank; another in 1811, decided against it. One Congress in 1815 decided against a bank; another in 1816 decided in its favor. Prior to the present Congress, therefore, the precedents drawn from that source were equal. If we resort to the States, the expressions of legislative, judicial and executive opinions against the bank have been probably to those in its favor as four to one. There is nothing in precedent, therefore, which if its authority were admitted, ought to weigh in favor of the act before me.''

I drop the quotations merely to remark that all there ever was, in the way of precedent up to the Dred Scott decision, on the points therein decided, had been against that decision. But hear Gen. Jackson further—

"If the opinion of the Supreme court covered the whole ground of this act, it ought not to control the co-ordinate authorities of this Government. The Congress, the executive and the court, must each for itself be guided by its own opinion of the Constitution. Each public officer, who takes an oath to support the Constitution, swears that he will support it as he understands it, and not as it is understood by others.'' . . .

50

Marbury v. Madison (1803)

Chief Justice Marshall *delivered the opinion of the Court:*

At the last term on the affidavits then read and filed with the clerk, a rule was granted in this case, requiring the secretary of state to show cause why a mandamus should not issue, directing him to deliver to William Marbury his commission as a justice of the peace for the county of Washington in the District of Columbia.

No cause has been shown, and the present motion is for a mandamus. The peculiar delicacy of this case, the novelty of some of its circumstances, and the real difficulty attending the points which occur in it, require a complete exposition of the principles on which the opinion to be given by the court is founded.

In the order in which the court has viewed this subject the following questions have been considered and decided.

1st. Has the applicant a right to the commission he demands?

2d. If he has a right, and that right has been violated, do the laws of his country afford him a remedy?

3d. If they do afford him a remedy, is it a mandamus issuing from this court?

The first object of inquiry is,

1st. Has the applicant a right to the commission he demands?

[The Court's discussion showing Marbury's right to the commission is omitted.]

Mr. Marbury, then, since his commission was signed by the President, and sealed by the Secretary of State, was appointed; and as the law creating the office, gave the officer a right to hold for five years, independent of the executive, the appointment was not revocable, but vested in the officer legal rights, which are protected by the laws of his country.

To withhold his commission, therefore, is an act deemed by the court not warranted by law, but violative of a vested legal right.

This brings us to the second inquiry; which is,

2d. If he has a right, and that right has been violated, do the laws of his country afford him a remedy?

From *Marbury v. Madison,* 1 Cranch 137 (1803).

The very essence of civil liberty certainly consists in the right of every individual to claim the protection of the laws, whenever he receives an injury. One of the first duties of government is to afford that protection. In Great Britain the king himself is sued in the respectful form of a petition, and he never fails to comply with the judgment of his court. . . .

The government of the United States has been emphatically termed a government of laws, and not of men. It will certainly cease to deserve this high appellation, if the laws furnish no remedy for the violation of a vested legal right. . . .

[T]he question, whether the legality of an act of the head of a department be examinable in a court of justice or not, must always depend on the nature of that act.

If some acts be examinable, and others not, there must be some rule of law to guide the court in the exercise of its jurisdiction.

In some instances there may be difficulty in applying the rule to particular cases; but there cannot, it is believed, be much difficulty in laying down the rule.

By the constitution of the United States, the President is invested with certain important political powers, in the exercise of which he is to use his own discretion, and is accountable only to his country in his political character and to his own conscience. To aid him in the performance of these duties, he is authorized to appoint certain officers, who act by his authority, and in conformity with his orders.

In such cases, their acts are his acts; and whatever opinion may be entertained of the manner in which executive discretion may be used, still there exists, and can exist, no power to control that discretion. The subjects are political. They respect the nation, not individual rights, and being intrusted to the executive, the decision of the executive is conclusive. The application of this remark will be perceived by adverting to the act of congress for establishing the department of foreign affairs. This officer, as his duties were prescribed by that act, is to conform precisely to the will of the President. He is the mere organ by whom that will is communicated. The acts of such an officer, as an officer, can never be examinable by the courts.

But when the legislature proceeds to impose on that officer other duties; when he is directed peremptorily to perform certain acts; when the rights of individuals are dependent on the performance of those acts; he is so far the officer of the law; is amenable to the laws for his conduct; and cannot at his discretion sport away the vested rights of others.

The conclusion from this reasoning is, that where the heads of departments are the political or confidential agents of the executive, merely to execute the will of the President, or rather to act in cases in which the executive possesses a constitutional or legal discretion, nothing can be more perfectly clear than that their acts are only politically examinable. But where a specific duty is assigned by law, and individual rights depend upon the performance of that duty, it seems equally clear that the individual who considers himself injured, has a right to resort to the laws of his country for a remedy. . . .

It is, then, the opinion of the Court,

1st. That by signing the commission of Mr. Marbury, the President of the United States appointed him a justice of peace for the county of Washington, in the District of Columbia; and that the seal of the United States, affixed thereto by the Secretary of State, is conclusive testimony of the verity of the signature, and of the completion of the appointment; and that the appointment conferred on him a legal right to the office for the space of five years.

2d. That, having this legal title to the office, he has a consequent right to the commission; a refusal to deliver which is a plain violation of that right, for which the laws of his country afford him a remedy.

It remains to be inquired whether,

3d. He is entitled to the remedy for which he applies. This depends on,

1st. The nature of the writ applied for; and,

2d. The power of this court.

1st. The nature of the writ. . . .

This writ, if awarded, would be directed to an officer of government, and its mandate to him would be, to use the words of Blackstone, "to do a particular thing therein specified, which appertains to his office and duty, and which the court has previously determined, or at least supposes, to be consonant to right and justice." Or, in the words of Lord Mansfield, the applicant, in this case, has a right to execute an office of public concern, and is kept out of possession of that right.

These circumstances certainly concur in this case.

Still, to render the mandamus a proper remedy, the officer to whom it is to be directed, must be one to whom, on legal principles, such writ may be directed; and the person applying for it must be without any other specific and legal remedy.

1st. With respect to the officer to whom it would be directed. The intimate political relation subsisting between the President of the United States and the heads of departments, necessarily renders any legal investigation of the acts of one of those high officers peculiarly irksome, as well as delicate; and excites some hesitation with respect to the propriety of entering into such investigation. Impressions are often received without much reflection or examination, and it is not wonderful that in such a case as this the assertion, by an individual, of his legal claims in a court of justice, to which claims it is the duty of that court to attend, should at first view be considered by some, as an attempt to intrude into the cabinet, and to inter-meddle with the prerogatives of the executive.

It is scarcely necessary for the court to disclaim all pretensions to such jurisdiction. An extravagance, so absurd and excessive, could not have been entertained for a moment. The province of the court is, solely, to decide on the rights of individuals, not to inquire how the executive, or executive offi-cers, perform duties in which they have a discretion. Questions in their nature political, or which are, by the constitution and laws, submitted to the executive, can never be made in this court.

But, if this be not such a question; if, so far from being an intrusion into the secrets of the cabinet, it respects a paper which, according to law, is upon record, and to a copy of which the law gives a right, on the payment of ten cents; if it be no intermeddling with a subject over which the executive can be considered as having exercised any control; what is there in the ex-alted station of the officer, which shall bar a citizen from asserting, in a court of justice, his legal rights, or shall forbid a court to listen to the claim, or to issue a mandamus directing the performance of a duty, not depending on executive discretion, but on particular acts of congress, and the general principles of law?

If one of the heads of departments commits any illegal act, under col-our of his office, by which an individual sustains an injury, it cannot be pretended that his office alone exempts him from being sued in the ordinary mode of proceeding, and being compelled to obey the judgment of the law. How, then, can his office exempt him from this particular mode of deciding on the legality of his conduct if the case be such a case as would, were any other individual the party complained of, authorize the process? . . .

. . . [W]here he is directed by law to do a certain act affecting the ab-solute rights of individuals, in the performance of which he is not placed under the particular direction of the President, and the performance of which the President cannot lawfully forbid, and therefore is never presumed to have forbidden; as for example to record a commission, or a patent for land, which has received all the legal solemnities; or to give a copy of such record; in such cases, it is not perceived on what ground the courts of the country are further excused from the duty of giving judgment that right be done to an injured individual, than if the same services were to be per-formed by a person not the head of a department. . . .

This, then, is a plain case for a mandamus, either to deliver the com-mission, or a copy of it from the record; and it only remains to be inquired,

Whether it can issue from this court.

The act to establish the judicial courts of the United States authorizes the Supreme Court "to issue writs of mandamus in cases warranted by the principles and usages of law, to any courts appointed, or persons holding office, under the authority of the United States."

The Secretary of State, being a person holding an office under the authority of the United States, is precisely within the letter of the description, and if this court is not authorized to issue a writ of mandamus to such an officer, it must be because the law is unconstitutional, and therefore absolutely incapable of conferring the authority, and assigning the duties which its words purport to confer and assign.

The constitution vests the whole judicial power of the United States in one Supreme Court, and such inferior courts as congress shall, from time to time, ordain and establish. This power is expressly extended to all cases arising under the laws of the United States; and, consequently, in some form, may be exercised over the present case; because the right claimed is given by a law of the United States.

In the distribution of this power it is declared that "the Supreme Court shall have original jurisdiction in all cases affecting ambassadors, other public ministers and consuls, and those in which a state shall be a party. In all other cases, the Supreme Court shall have appellate jurisdiction."

It has been insisted, at the bar, that as the original grant of jurisdiction, to the Supreme and inferior courts, is general, and the clause, assigning original jurisdiction to the Supreme Court, contains no negative or restrictive words, the power remains to the legislature, to assign original jurisdiction to that court in other cases than those specified in the article which has been recited; provided those cases belong to the judicial power of the United States.

If it had been intended to leave it in the discretion of the legislature to apportion the judicial power between the supreme and inferior courts according to the will of that body, it would certainly have been useless to have proceeded further than to have defined the judicial power, and the tribunals in which it should be vested. The subsequent part of the section is mere surplusage, is entirely without meaning, if such is to be the construction. If congress remains at liberty to give this court appellate jurisdiction, where the constitution has declared their jurisdiction shall be original; and original jurisdiction where the constitution has declared it shall be appellate; the distribution of jurisdiction, made in the constitution, is form without substance. . . .

It is the essential criterion of appellate jurisdiction, that it revises and corrects the proceedings in a cause already instituted, and does not create that cause. Although, therefore, a mandamus may be directed to courts, yet to issue such a writ to an officer for the delivery of a paper, is in effect the same as to sustain an original action for that paper, and, therefore, seems not to belong to appellate but to original jurisdiction. Neither is it necessary in such a case as this, to enable the court to exercise its appellate jurisdiction.

The authority, therefore, given to the Supreme Court, by the act establishing the judicial courts of the United States, to issue writs of mandamus to public officers, appears not to be warranted by the constitution; and it becomes necessary to inquire whether a jurisdiction so conferred can be exercised.

The question, whether an act, repugnant to the constitution, can become the law of the land, is a question deeply interesting to the United States; but, happily, not of an intricacy proportioned to its interest. It seems only necessary to recognize certain principles, supposed to have been long and well established, to decide it.

That the people have an original right to establish, for their future government, such principles, as, in their opinion, shall most conduce to their own happiness is the basis on which the whole American fabric has been erected. The exercise of this original right is a very great exertion; nor can it, nor ought it, to be frequently repeated. The principles, therefore, so established, are deemed fundamental. And as the authority from which they proceed is supreme, and can seldom act, they are designed to be permanent.

This original and supreme will organizes the government, and assigns to different departments their respective powers. It may either stop here, or establish certain limits not to be transcended by those departments.

The government of the United States is of the latter description. The powers of the legislature are defined and limited; and that those limits may not be mistaken, or forgotten, the constitution is written. To what purpose are powers limited, and to what purpose is that limitation committed to writing, if these limits may, at any time, be passed by those intended to be restrained? The distinction between a government with limited and unlimited powers is abolished, if those limits do not confine the persons on whom they are imposed, and if acts prohibited and acts allowed, are of equal obligation. It is a proposition too plain to be contested, that the constitution controls any legislative act repugnant to it; or, that the legislature may alter the constitution by an ordinary act.

Between these alternatives there is no middle ground. The constitution is either a superior paramount law, unchangeable by ordinary means, or it is on a level with ordinary legislative acts, and, like other acts, is alterable when the legislature shall please to alter it.

If the former part of the alternative be true, then a legislative act contrary to the constitution is not law: if the latter part be true, then written constitutions are absurd attempts, on the part of the people, to limit a power in its own nature illimitable.

Certainly all those who have framed written constitutions contemplate them as forming the fundamental and paramount law of the nation, and, consequently, the theory of every such government must be, that an act of the legislature, repugnant to the constitution, is void.

This theory is essentially attached to a written constitution, and is, consequently, to be considered, by this court, as one of the fundamental principles of our society. It is not therefore to be lost sight of in the further consideration of this subject.

If an act of the legislature, repugnant to the constitution, is void, does it, notwithstanding its invalidity, bind the courts, and oblige them to give it effect? Or, in other words, though it be not law, does it constitute a rule as operative as if it was a law? This would be to overthrow in fact what was established in theory; and would seem, at first view, an absurdity too gross to be insisted on. It shall, however, receive a more attentive consideration.

It is emphatically the province and duty of the judicial department to say what the law is. Those who apply the rule to particular cases, must of necessity expound and interpret that rule. If two laws conflict with each other, the courts must decide on the operation of each.

So if a law be in opposition to the constitution; if both the law and the constitution apply to a particular case, so that the court must either decide that case conformably to the law, disregarding the constitution; or conformably to the constitution, disregarding the law; the court must determine which of these conflicting rules governs the case. This is of the very essence of judicial duty.

If, then, the courts are to regard the constitution, and the constitution is superior to any ordinary act of the legislature, the constitution, and not such ordinary act, must govern the case to which they both apply.

Those, then, who controvert the principle that the constitution is to be considered, in court, as a paramount law, are reduced to the necessity of maintaining that courts must close their eyes on the constitution, and see only the law.

This doctrine would subvert the very foundation of all written constitutions. It would declare that an act which, according to the principles and theory of our government, is entirely void, is yet, in practice, completely obligatory. It would declare that if the legislature shall do what is expressly forbidden, such act, notwithstanding the express prohibition, is in reality effectual. It would be giving to the legislature a practical and real omnipotence, with the same breath which professes to restrict their powers within narrow limits. It is prescribing limits, and declaring that those limits may be passed at pleasure.

That it thus reduces to nothing what we have deemed the greatest improvement on political institutions, a written constitution, would of itself be sufficient, in America, where written constitutions have been viewed with so much reverence, for rejecting the construction. But the peculiar expressions of the constitution of the United States furnish additional arguments in favour of its rejection.

The judicial power of the United States is extended to all cases arising under the constitution.

Could it be the intention of those who gave this power, to say that in using it the constitution should not be looked into? That a case arising under the constitution should be decided without examining the instrument under which it arises?

This is too extravagant to be maintained.

In some cases, then, the constitution must be looked into by the judges. And if they can open it at all, what part of it are they forbidden to read or to obey?

There are many other parts of the constitution which serve to illustrate this subject.

It is declared that "no tax or duty shall be laid on articles exported from any state." Suppose a duty on the export of cotton, of tobacco, or of flour; and a suit instituted to recover it. Ought judgment to be rendered in such a case? Ought the judges to close their eyes on the constitution, and only see the law?

The constitution declares "that no bill of attainder or ex post facto law shall be passed."

If, however, such a bill should be passed, and a person should be prosecuted under it; must the court condemn to death those victims whom the constitution endeavors to preserve?

"No person," says the constitution, "shall be convicted of treason unless on the testimony of two witnesses to the same overt act, or on confession in open court."

Here the language of the constitution is addressed especially to the courts. It prescribes, directly for them, a rule of evidence not to be departed from. If the legislature should change that rule, and declare one witness, or a confession out of court, sufficient for conviction, must the constitutional principle yield to the legislative act?

From these, and many other selections which might be made, it is apparent, that the framers of the constitution contemplated that instrument as a rule for the government of courts, as well as of the legislature.

Why otherwise does it direct the judges to take an oath to support it? This oath certainly applies in an especial manner, to their conduct in their official character. How immoral to impose it on them, if they were to be used as the instruments, and the knowing instruments, for violating what they swear to support! . . .

It is also not entirely unworthy of observation, that in declaring what shall be the supreme law of the land, the constitution itself is first mentioned; and not the laws of the United States generally, but those only which shall be made in pursuance of the constitution, have that rank.

Thus, the particular phraseology of the constitution of the United States confirms and strengthens the principle, supposed to be essential to all written constitutions, that a law repugnant to the constitution is void; and that courts, as well as other departments, are bound by that instrument. . . .

51

United States v. Nixon (1974)

Mr. Chief Justice Burger *delivered the opinion of the Court:*

On March 1, 1974, a grand jury of the United States District Court for the District of Columbia returned an indictment charging seven named individuals with various offenses, including conspiracy to defraud the United States and to obstruct justice. Although he was not designated as such in the indictment, the grand jury named the President, among others, as an unindicted coconspirator. On April 18, 1974, upon motion of the Special Prosecutor, see n. 8, *infra,* a subpoena *duces tecum* was issued pursuant to Rule 17(c) to the President by the United States District Court and made returnable on May 2, 1974. This subpoena required the production, in advance of the September 9 trial date, of certain tapes, memoranda, papers, transcripts or other writings relating to certain precisely identified meetings between the President and others. The Special Prosecutor was able to fix the time, place and persons present at these discussions because the White House daily logs and appointment records had been delivered to him. On April 30, the President publicly released edited transcripts of 43 conversations; portions of 20 conversations subject to subpoena in the present case were included. On May 1, 1974, the President's counsel, filed a "special appearance" and a motion to quash the subpoena, under Rule 17(c). This motion was accompanied by a formal claim of privilege. . . .

In the District Court, the President's counsel argued that the court lacked jurisdiction to issue the subpoena because the matter was an intra-

From *United States v. Nixon,* 418 U.S. 683 (1974).

branch dispute between a subordinate and superior officer of the Executive Branch and hence not subject to judicial resolution. That argument has been renewed in this Court with emphasis on the contention that the dispute does not present a "case" or "controversy" which can be adjudicated in the federal courts. The President's counsel argues that the federal courts should not intrude into areas committed to the other branches of Government. He views the present dispute as essentially a "jurisdictional" dispute within the Executive Branch which he analogizes to a dispute between two congressional committees. Since the Executive Branch has exclusive authority and absolute discretion to decide whether to prosecute a case, it is contended that a President's decision is final in determining what evidence is to be used in a given criminal case. . . .

The mere assertion of a claim of an "intra-branch dispute," without more, has never operated to defeat federal jurisdiction; justiciability does not depend on such a surface inquiry. In United States v. ICC, the Court observed, "courts must look behind names that symbolize the parties to determine whether a justiciable case or controversy is presented."

Our starting point is the nature of the proceeding for which the evidence is sought—here a pending criminal prosecution. It is a judicial proceeding in a federal court alleging violation of federal laws and is brought in the name of the United States as sovereign. Under the authority of Article II, § 2, Congress has vested in the Attorney General the power to conduct the criminal litigation of the United States Government. It has also vested in him the power to appoint subordinate officers to assist him in the discharge of his duties. Acting pursuant to those statutes, the Attorney General has delegated the authority to represent the United States in these particular matters to a Special Prosecutor with unique authority and tenure. The regulation gives the Special Prosecutor explicit power to contest the invocation of executive privilege in the process of seeking evidence deemed relevant to the performance of these specially delegated duties. . . .

So long as this regulation remains in force the Executive Branch is bound by it, and indeed the United States as the sovereign composed of the three branches is bound to respect and to enforce it. Moreover, the delegation of authority to the Special Prosecutor in this case is not an ordinary delegation by the Attorney General to a subordinate officer: with the authorization of the President, the Acting Attorney General provided in the regulation that the Special Prosecutor was not to be removed without the "consensus" of eight designated leaders of Congress. . . .

Here at issue is the production or nonproduction of specified evidence deemed by the Special Prosecutor to be relevant and admissible in a pending criminal case. It is sought by one official of the Government within the scope of his express authority; it is resisted by the Chief Executive on the ground of his duty to preserve the confidentiality of the communications of the President. Whatever the correct answer on the merits, these issues are "of a type which are traditionally justiciable." . . .

[W]e turn to the claim that the subpoena should be quashed because it demands "confidential conversations between a President and his close advisors that it would be inconsistent with the public interest to produce." The first contention is a broad claim that the separation of powers doctrine precludes judicial review of a President's claim of privilege. The second contention is that if he does not prevail on the claim of absolute privilege, the court should hold as a matter of constitutional law that the privilege prevails over the subpoena *duces tecum*.

In the performance of assigned constitutional duties each branch of the Government must initially interpret the Constitution, and the interpretation of its powers by any branch is due great respect from the others. The President's counsel, as we have noted, reads the Constitution as providing an absolute privilege of confidentiality for all presidential communications. Many decisions of this Court, however, have unequivocally reaffirmed the holding of Marbury v. Madison, that "it is emphatically the province and duty of the judicial department to say what the law is."

No holding of the Court has defined the scope of judicial power specifically relating to the enforcement of a subpoena for confidential presidential communications for use in a criminal prosecution, but other exercises of powers by the Executive Branch and the Legislative Branch have been found invalid as in conflict with the Constitution. Powell v. McCormack, *supra; Youngstown, supra.* In a series of cases, the Court interpreted the explicit immunity conferred by express provisions of the Constitution on Members of the House and Senate by the Speech or Debate Clause, U.S. Const. Art. I, § 6. Since this Court has consistently exercised the power to construe and delineate claims arising under express powers, it must follow that the Court has authority to interpret claims with respect to powers alleged to derive from enumerated powers.

Our system of government "requires that federal courts on occasion interpret the Constitution in a manner at variance with the construction given the document by another branch." Powell v. McCormack. And in Baker v. Carr, the Court stated:

> "[D]eciding whether a matter has in any measure been committed by the Constitution to another branch of government, or whether the action of that branch exceeds whatever authority has been committed, is itself a delicate exercise in constitutional interpretation, and is a responsibility of this Court as ultimate interpreter of the Constitution."

Notwithstanding the deference each branch must accord the others, the "judicial power of the United States" vested in the federal courts by

Art. III, § 1 of the Constitution can no more be shared with the Executive Branch than the Chief Executive, for example, can share with the Judiciary the veto power, or the Congress share with the Judiciary the power to override a presidential veto. Any other conclusion would be contrary to the basic concept of separation of powers and the checks and balances that flow from the scheme of a tripartite government. The Federalist, No. 47, p. 313. We therefore reaffirm that it is "emphatically the province and the duty" this Court "to say what the law is" with respect to the claim of privilege presented in this case.

In support of his claim of absolute privilege, the President's counsel urges two grounds one of which is common to all governments and one of which is peculiar to our system of separation of powers. The first ground is the valid need for protection of communications between high government officials and those who advise and assist them in the performance of their manifold duties; the importance of this confidentiality is too plain to require further discussion. Human experience teaches that those who expect public dissemination of their remarks may well temper candor with a concern for appearances and for their own interests to the detriment of the decision-making process. Whatever the nature of the privilege of confidentiality of presidential communications in the exercise of Art. II powers the privilege can be said to derive from the supremacy of each branch within its own assigned area of constitutional duties. Certain powers and privileges flow from the nature of enumerated powers; the protection of the confidentiality of presidential communications has similar constitutional underpinnings.

The second ground asserted by the President's counsel in support of the claim of absolute privilege rests on the doctrine of separation of powers. Here it is argued that the independence of the Executive Branch within its own sphere, Humphrey's Executor v. United States, insulates a president from a judicial subpoena in an ongoing criminal prosecution, and thereby protects confidential presidential communications.

However, neither the doctrine of separation of powers, nor the need for confidentiality of high level communications, without more, can sustain an absolute, unqualified presidential privilege of immunity from judicial process under all circumstances. The President's need for complete candor and objectivity from advisers calls for great deference from the courts. However, when the privilege depends solely on the broad, undifferentiated claim of public interest in the confidentiality of such conversations, a confrontation with other values arises. Absent a claim of need to protect military, diplomatic or sensitive national security secrets, we find it difficult to accept the argument that even the very important interest in confidentiality of presidential communications is significantly diminished by production of such material for *in camera* inspection with all the protection that a district court will be obliged to provide.

The impediment that an absolute, unqualified privilege would place in the way of the primary constitutional duty of the Judicial Branch to do justice in criminal prosecutions would plainly conflict with the function of the courts under Art. III. In designing the structure of our Government and dividing and allocating the sovereign power among three coequal branches, the Framers of the Constitution sought to provide a comprehensive system, but the separate powers were not intended to operate with absolute independence. . . . To read the Art. II powers of the President as providing an absolute privilege as against a subpoena essential to enforcement of criminal statutes on no more than a generalized claim of the public interest in confidentiality of nonmilitary and nondiplomatic discussions would upset the constitutional balance of "a workable government" and gravely impair the role of the courts under Art. III.

Since we conclude that the legitimate needs of the judicial process may outweigh presidential privilege, it is necessary to resolve those competing interests in a manner that preserves the essential functions of each branch. The right and indeed the duty to resolve that question does not free the judiciary from according high respect to the representations made on behalf of the President.

The expectation of a President to the confidentiality of his conversations and correspondence, like the claim of confidentiality of judicial deliberations, for example, has all the values to which we accord deference for the privacy of all citizens and added to those values the necessity for protection of the public interest in candid, objective, and even blunt or harsh opinions in presidential decisionmaking. A President and those who assist him must be free to explore alternatives in the process of shaping policies and making decisions and to do so in a way many would be unwilling to express except privately. These are the considerations justifying a presumptive privilege for presidential communications. The privilege is fundamental to the operation of government and inextricably rooted in the separation of powers under the Constitution. In Nixon v. Sirica, the Court of Appeals held that such presidential communications are "presumptively privileged," and this position is accepted by both parties in the present litigation. We agree with Mr. Chief Justice Marshall's observation, therefore, that "in no case of this kind would a court be required to proceed against the President as against an ordinary individual." United States v. Burr.

But this presumptive privilege must be considered in light of our historic commitment to the rule of law. This is nowhere more profoundly manifest than in our view that "the twofold aim [of criminal justice] is that guilt shall not escape or innocence suffer." Berger v. Unitzd States. We have elected to employ an adversary system of criminal justice in which the parties contest all issues before a court of law. The need to develop all relevant facts in the adversary system is both fundamental and comprehensive. The ends of criminal justice would be defeated if judgments were to be founded on a partial or speculative presentation of the facts. The very integrity of the judicial system and public confidence in the system depend on full disclosure of all the facts, within the framework of the rules of evidence. To ensure that justice is done, it is imperative to the function of courts that compulsory process be available for the production of evidence needed either by the prosecution or by the defense.

Only recently the Court restated the ancient proposition of law, albeit in the context of a grand jury inquiry rather than a trial, " 'that the public . . . has a right to every man's evidence' except for those persons protected by a constitutional, common law, or statutory privilege." The privileges referred to by the Court are designed to protect weighty and legitimate competing interests. Thus, the Fifth Amendment to the Constitution provides that no man "shall be compelled in any criminal case to be a witness against himself." And, generally, an attorney or a priest may not be required to disclose what has been revealed in professional confidence. These and other interests are recognized in law by privileges against forced disclosure, established in the Constitution, by statute, or at common law. Whatever their origins, these exceptions to the demand for every man's evidence are not lightly created nor expansively construed, for they are in derogation of the search for truth.

In this case the President challenges a subpoena served on him as a third party requiring the production of materials for use in a criminal prosecution on the claim that he has a privilege against disclosure of confidential communications. He does not place his claim of privilege on the ground they are military or diplomatic secrets. As to these areas of Art. II duties the courts have traditionally shown the utmost deference to presidential responsibilities. . . . In United States v. Reynolds, dealing with a claimant's demand for evidence in a damage case against the Government the Court said:

> "It may be possible to satisfy the court, from all the circumstances of the case, that there is a reasonable danger that compulsion of the evidence will expose military matters which, in the interest of national security, should not be divulged. When this is the case, the occasion for the privilege is appropriate, and the court should not jeopardize the security which the privilege is meant to protect by insisting upon an examination of the evidence, even by the judge alone, in chambers."

No case of the Court, however, has extended this high degree of deference to a President's generalized interest in confidentiality. Nowhere in the Constitution, as we have noted earlier, is there any explicit reference to a privilege of confidentiality, yet to the extent this interest relates to the effective discharge of a President's powers, it is constitutionally based.

The right to the production of all evidence at a criminal trial similarly has constitutional dimensions. The Sixth Amendment explicitly confers upon every defendant in a criminal trial the right "to be confronted with the witnesses against him" and "to have compulsory process for obtaining witnesses in his favor. Moreover, the Fifth Amendment also guarantees that no person shall be deprived of liberty without due process of law. It is the manifest duty of the courts to vindicate those guarantees and to accomplish that it is essential that all relevant and admissible evidence be produced.

In this case we must weigh the importance of the general privilege of confidentiality of presidential communications in performance of his responsibilities against the inroads of such a privilege on the fair administration of criminal justice.* The interest in preserving confidentiality is weighty indeed and entitled to great respect. However we cannot conclude that advisers will be moved to temper the candor of their remarks by the infrequent occasions of disclosure because of the possibility that such conversations will be called for in the context of a criminal prosecution.

On the other hand, the allowance of the privilege to withhold evidence that is demonstrably relevant in a criminal trial would cut deeply into the guarantee of due process of law and gravely impair the basic function of the courts. A President's acknowledged need for confidentiality in the communications of his office is general in nature, whereas the constitutional need for production of relevant evidence in a criminal proceeding is specific and central to the fair adjudication of a particular criminal case in the administration of justice. Without access to specific facts a criminal prosecution may be totally frustrated. The President's broad interest in confidentiality of communications will not be vitiated by disclosure of a limited number of conversations preliminarily shown to have some bearing on the pending criminal cases.

We conclude that when the ground for asserting privilege as to subpoenaed materials sought for use in a criminal trial is based only on the generalized interest in confidentiality, it cannot prevail over the fundamental demands of due process of law in the fair administration of criminal justice. The generalized assertion of privilege must yield to the demonstrated, specific need for evidence in a pending criminal trial. . . .

---

*We are not here concerned with the balance between the President's generalized interest in confidentiality and the need for relevant evidence in civil litigation, nor with that between the confidentiality interest and congressional demands for information, nor with the President's interest in preserving state secrets. We address only the conflict between the President's assertion of a generalized privilege of confidentiality against the constitutional need for relevant evidence in criminal trials.

52

Reapportionment Cases (1964)

Mr. Chief Justice Warren delivered the opinion of the Court [in
Reynolds v. Sims].

. . . Plaintiffs below alleged that the last apportionment of the
Alabama Legislature was based on the 1900 federal census, despite the requirement of the State Constitution that the legislature be reapportioned
decennially. They asserted that, since the population growth in the State
from 1900 to 1960 had been uneven, Jefferson and other counties were now
victims of serious discrimination with respect to the allocation of legislative
representation. . . .

[The district court found that neither the apportionment at the time nor
any of the new plans submitted by the Alabama Legislature was wholly acceptable under the Equal Protection Clause.]

A predominant consideration in determining whether a State's legislative apportionment scheme constitutes an invidious discrimination violative of rights asserted under the Equal Protection Clause is that the rights
allegedly impaired are individual and personal in nature. . . .

[T]he judicial focus must be concentrated upon ascertaining whether
there has been any discrimination against certain of the State's citizens
which constitutes an impermissible impairment of their constitutionally
protected right to vote. . . . Undoubtedly, the right of suffrage is a fundamental matter in a free and democratic society. Especially since the right
to exercise the franchise in a free and unimpaired manner is preservative of
other basic civil and political rights, any alleged infringement of the right of
citizens to vote must be carefully and meticulously scrutinized. . . .

Legislators represent people, not trees or acres. Legislators are elected
by voters, not farms or cities or economic interests. As long as ours is a
representative form of government, and our legislatures are those instruments of government elected directly by and directly representative of the
people, the right to elect legislators in a free and unimpaired fashion is a
bedrock of our political system. It could hardly be gainsaid that a constitutional claim had been asserted by an allegation that certain otherwise quali-

From *Reynolds v. Sims,* 377 U.S. 533 (1964) and *Lucas v. Forty-fourth General
Assembly of Colorado,* 377 U.S. 713 (1964).

fied voters had been entirely prohibited from voting for members of their state legislature. And, if a State should provide that the votes of citizens in one part of the State should be given two times, or five times, or 10 times the weight of votes of citizens in another part of the State, it could hardly be contended that the right to vote of those residing in the disfavored areas had not been effectively diluted. . . . Of course, the effect of state legislative districting schemes which give the same number of representatives to unequal numbers of constituents is identical. Overweighting and overvaluation of the votes of those living here has the certain effect of dilution and undervaluation of the votes of those living there. The resulting discrimination against those individual voters living in disfavored areas is easily demonstrable mathematically. . . . Weighting the votes of citizens differently, by any method or means, merely because of where they happen to reside, hardly seems justifiable. . . .

[R]epresentative government is in essence self-government through the medium of elected representatives of the people, and each and every citizen has an inalienable right to full and effective participation in the political processes of his State's legislative bodies. Most citizens can achieve this participation only as qualified voters through the election of legislators to represent them. Full and effective participation by all citizens in state government requires, therefore, that each citizen has an equally effective voice in the election of members of his state legislature. . . .

We are told that the matter of apportioning representation in a state legislature is a complex and many-faceted one. We are advised that States can rationally consider factors other than population in apportioning legislative representation. We are admonished not to restrict the power of the States to impose differing views as to political philosophy on their citizens. We are cautioned about the dangers of entering into political thickets and mathematical quagmires. Our answer is this: a denial of constitutionally protected rights demands judicial protection; our oath and our office require no less of us. . . .

[O]ne of the proposed plans, that contained in the so-called 67-Senator Amendment, at least superficially resembles the scheme of legislative representation followed in the Federal Congress. Under this plan, each of Alabama's 67 counties is allotted one senator, and no counties are given more than one Senate seat. Arguably, this is analogous to the allocation of two Senate seats, in the Federal Congress, to each of the 50 States, regardless of population. Seats in the Alabama House, under the proposed constitutional amendment, are distributed by giving each of the 67 counties at least one, with the remaining 39 seats being allotted among the more populous counties on a population basis. This scheme, at least at first glance, appears to resemble that prescribed for the Federal House of Representatives, where the 435 seats are distributed among the States on a population basis, although each State, regardless of its population, is given at least one Congressman. . . .

The system of representation in the two Houses of the Federal Congress is one ingrained in our Constitution, as part of the law of the land. It is one conceived out of compromise and concession indispensable to the establishment of our federal republic. . . .

Political subdivisions of States—counties, cities, or whatever—never were and never have been considered as sovereign entities. Rather, they have been traditionally regarded as subordinate governmental instrumentalities created by the State to assist in the carrying out of state governmental functions. As stated by the Court in *Hunter v. City of Pittsburgh,* these governmental units are "created as convenient agencies for exercising such of the governmental powers of the State as may be entrusted to them," and the "number, nature and duration of the powers conferred upon [them] . . . and the territory over which they shall be exercised rests in the absolute discretion of the State." The relationship of the States to the Federal Government could hardly be less analogous. . . .

Since we find the so-called federal analogy inapposite to a consideration of the constitutional validity of state legislative apportionment schemes, we necessarily hold that the Equal Protection Clause requires both houses of a state legislature to be apportioned on a population basis. . . .

We do not believe that the concept of bicameralism is rendered anachronistic and meaningless when the predominant basis of representation in the two state legislative bodies is required to be the same—population. A prime reason for bicameralism, modernly considered, is to insure mature and deliberate consideration of, and to prevent precipitate action on, proposed legislative measures. Simply because the controlling criterion for apportioning representation is required to be the same in both houses does not mean that there will be no differences in the composition and complexion of the two bodies. Different constituencies can be represented in the two houses. One body could be composed of single-member districts while the other could have at least some multimember districts. The length of terms of the legislators in the separate bodies could differ. The numerical size of the two bodies could be made to differ, even significantly, and the geographical size of districts from which legislators are elected could also be made to differ. And apportionment in one house could be arranged so as to balance off minor inequities in the representation of certain areas in the other house. In summary, these and other factors could be, and are presently in many States, utilized to engender differing complexions and collective attitudes in the two bodies of a state legislature, although both are apportioned substantially on a population basis. . . .

A State may legitimately desire to maintain the integrity of various political subdivisions, insofar as possible, and provide for compact districts of contiguous territory in designing a legislative apportionment scheme. Valid considerations may underlie such aims. Indiscriminate districting, without any regard for political subdivision or natural or historical boundary lines, may be little more than an open invitation to partisan gerrymandering. . . .

But neither history alone, nor economic or other sorts of group interests, are permissible factors in attempting to justify disparities from population-based representation. Citizens, not history or economic interests, cast votes. . . . Modern developments and improvements in transportation and communications make rather hollow, in the mid-1960's, most claims that deviations from population-based representation can validly be based solely on geographical considerations. . . .

A consideration that appears to be of more substance in justifying some deviations from population-based representation in state legislatures is that of insuring some voice to political subdivisions, as political subdivisions. Several factors make more than insubstantial claims that a State can rationally consider according political subdivisions some independent representation in at least one body of the state legislature, as long as the basic standard of equality of population among districts is maintained. Local governmental entities are frequently charged with various responsibilities incident to the operation of state government. In many States much of the legislature's activity involves the enactment of so-called local legislation, directed only to the concerns of particular political subdivisions. And a State may legitimately desire to construct districts along political subdivision lines to deter the possibilities of gerrymandering. However, permitting deviations from population-based representation does not mean that each local governmental unit or political subdivision can be given separate representation, regardless of population. Carried too far, a scheme of giving at least one seat in one house to each political subdivision (for example, to each county) could easily result, in many States, in a total subversion of the equal-population principle in that legislative body. . . .

Mr. Chief Justice Warren delivered the opinion of the Court [in *Lucas v. Colorado General Assembly*].

. . . At the November 1962 general election, the Colorado electorate adopted proposed Amendment No. 7 by a vote of 305,700 to 172,725, and defeated proposed Amendment No. 8 by a vote of 311,749 to 149,822. Amendment No. 8, rejected by a majority of the voters, prescribed an apportionment plan pursuant to which seats in both houses of the Colorado Legislature would purportedly be apportioned on a population basis.

Amendment No. 7, on the other hand, provided for the apportionment of the House of Representatives on the basis of population, but essentially maintained the existing apportionment in the Senate, which was based on a combination of population and various other factors. . . .

Plaintiffs below requested a declaration that Amendment No. 7 was unconstitutional under the Fourteenth Amendment since resulting in substantial disparities from population-based representation in the Senate, and asked for a decree reapportioning both houses of the Colorado Legislature on a population basis. . . . Finding that the disparities from a population basis in the apportionment of Senate seats were based upon rational considerations, the court below stated that the senatorial apportionment under Amendment No. 7 "recognizes population as a prime, but not controlling, factor and gives effect to such important considerations as geography, compactness and contiguity of territory, accessibility, observance of natural boundaries, [and] conformity to historical divisions such as county lines and prior representation districts. . . ." Stressing also that the apportionment plan had been recently adopted by popular vote in a statewide referendum, the Court states:

> "[Plaintiffs'] argument that the apportionment of the Senate by Amendment No. 7 is arbitrary, invidiously discriminatory, and without any rationality . . . [has been answered by] the voters of Colorado. . . .*

*Continuing, the court below stated:
"The initiative gives the people of a state no power to adopt a constitutional amendment which violates the Federal Constitution. Amendment No. 7 is not valid just because the people voted for it. . . . [But] the traditional and recognized criteria of equal protection . . . are arbitrariness, discrimination, and lack of rationality. The actions of the electorate are material to the application of the criteria. The contention that the voters have discriminated against themselves appalls rather than convinces. . . .

"The electorate of every county from which the plaintiffs come preferred Amendment No. 7. In the circumstances it is difficult to comprehend how the plaintiffs can sue to vindicate a public right. . . ."

And, earlier in its opinion on the merits, the District Court stated: "With full operation of the one-man, one-vote principle, the Colorado electorate by an overwhelming majority approved a constitutional amendment creating a Senate, the membership of which is not apportioned on a strict population basis. By majority process the voters have said that minority process in the Senate is what they want. A rejection of their choice is a denial of the will of the majority. If the majority becomes dissatisfied with that which it has created, it can make a change at an election in which each vote counts the same as every other vote."

. . . [T]he maximum population-variance ratio, under the revised senatorial apportionment, [of Amendment 7] is about 3.6-to-1. Denver and the three adjacent suburban counties contain about one-half of the State's total 1960 population of 1,753,947, but are given only 14 out of 39 senators. The Denver, Pueblo, and Colorado Springs metropolitan areas, containing 1,191,832 persons, about 68%, or over two-thirds of Colorado's population, elect only 20 of the State's 39 senators, barely a majority. The average population of Denver's eight senatorial districts, under Amendment No. 7, is 61,736, while the five least populous districts contain less than 22,000 persons each. Divergences from population-based representation in the Senate are growing continually wider, since the underrepresented districts in the Denver, Pueblo, and Colorado Springs metropolitan areas are rapidly gaining in population, while many of the overrepresented rural districts have tended to decline in population continuously in recent years.

Several aspects of this case serve to distinguish it from the other cases involving state legislative apportionment also decided this date. Initially, one house of the Colorado Legislature is at least arguably apportioned substantially on a population basis under Amendment No. 7 and the implementing statutory provisions. . . . Additionally, the Colorado scheme of legislative apportionment here attacked is one adopted by a majority vote of the Colorado electorate almost contemporaneously with the District Court's decision on the merits in this litigation. Thus, the plan at issue did not result from prolonged legislative inaction. . . .

Finally, this case differs from the others decided this date in that the initiative device provides a practicable political remedy to obtain relief against alleged legislative malapportionment in Colorado. . . .

Except as an interim remedial procedure justifying a court in staying its hand temporarily, we find no significance in the fact that a nonjudicial, political remedy may be available for the effectuation of asserted rights to equal representation in a state legislature. . . . An individual's constitutionally protected right to cast an equally weighted vote cannot be denied even by a vote of a majority of a State's electorate, if the apportionment scheme adopted by the voters fails to measure up to the requirements of the Equal Protection Clause. . . .

[A]ppellees' argument, accepted by the court below, that the apportionment of the Colorado Senate, under Amendment No. 7, is rational because it takes into account a variety of geographical, historical, topographic and economic considerations fails to provide an adequate justification for the substantial disparities from population-based representation in the allocation of Senate seats to the disfavored populous areas. . . .

Mr. Justice Stewart, whom Mr. Justice Clark joins, dissenting [in *Lucas v. Colorado*].*

It is important to make clear at the outset what these cases are not about. They have nothing to do with the denial or impairment of any person's right to vote. Nobody's right to vote has been denied. Nobody's right to vote has been restricted. Nobody has been deprived of the right to have his vote counted. . . .

Simply stated, the question is to what degree, if at all, the Equal Protection Clause of the Fourteenth Amendment limits each sovereign State's freedom to establish appropriate electoral constituencies from which representatives to the State's bicameral legislative assembly are to be chosen. The Court's answer is a blunt one, and, I think, woefully wrong. The Equal Protection Clause, says the Court, "requires that the seats in both houses of a bicameral state legislature must be apportioned on a population basis."

After searching carefully through the Court's opinions in these and their companion cases, I have been able to find but two reasons offered in support of this rule. First, says the Court, it is "established that the fundamental principle of representative government in this country is one of equal representation for equal numbers of people. . . ." With all respect, I think that this is not correct, simply as a matter of fact. It has been unanswerably demonstrated before now that this "was not the colonial system, it was not the system chosen for the national government by the Constitution, it was not the system exclusively or even predominantly practiced by the States at the time of adoption of the Fourteenth Amendment, it is not predominantly practiced by the States today." Secondly, says the Court, unless legislative districts are equal in population, voters in the more populous districts will suffer a "debasement" amounting to a constitutional injury. As the Court explains it, "To the extent that a citizen's right to vote is debased, he is that much less a citizen." We are not told how or why the vote of a person in a more populated legislative district is "debased," or how or why he is less a citizen, nor is the proposition self-evident. I find it impossible to understand how or why a voter in California, for instance, either feels or is less a citizen than a voter in Nevada, simply because, despite their population disparities, each of those States is represented by two United States Senators. . . .

The rule announced today is at odds with long-established principles of constitutional adjudication under the Equal Protection Clause, and it stifles values of local individuality and initiative vital to the character of the Federal Union which it was the genius of our Constitution to create.

What the Court has done is to convert a particular political philosophy into a constitutional rule, binding upon each of the 50 States, from Maine

*Mr. Justice Stewart concurred in *Reynolds v. Sims*.

to Hawaii, from Alaska to Texas, without regard and without respect for the many individualized and differentiated characteristics of each State, characteristics stemming from each State's distinct history, distinct geography, distinct distribution of population, and distinct political heritage. . . .

I could not join in the fabrication of a constitutional mandate which imports and forever freezes one theory of political thought into our Constitution, and forever denies to every State any opportunity for enlightened and progressive innovation in the design of its democratic institutions, so as to accommodate within a system of representative government the interests and aspirations of diverse groups of people, without subjecting any group or class to absolute domination by a geographically concentrated or highly organized majority.

Representative government is a process of accommodating group interests through democratic institutional arrangements. Its function is to channel the numerous opinions, interests, and abilities of the people of a State into the making of the State's public policy. Appropriate legislative apportionment, therefore, should ideally be designed to insure effective representation in the State's legislature, in cooperation with other organs of political power, of the various groups and interests making up the electorate. In practice, of course, this ideal is approximated in the particular apportionment system of any State by a realistic accommodation of the diverse and often conflicting political forces operating within the State. . . .

[A] system of legislative apportionment which might be best for South Dakota, might be unwise for Hawaii with its many islands, or Michigan with its Northern Peninsula. I do know enough to realize that Montana with its vast distances is not Rhode Island with its heavy concentrations of people. I do know enough to be aware of the great variations among the several States in their historic manner of distributing legislative power—of the Governors' Councils in New England, of the broad powers of initiative and referendum retained in some States by the people, of the legislative power which some States give to their Governors, by the right of veto or otherwise, of the widely autonomous home rule which many States give to their cities. The Court today declines to give any recognition to these considerations and countless others, tangible and intangible, in holding unconstitutional the particular systems of legislative apportionment which these States have chosen. Instead, the Court says that the requirements of the Equal Protection Clause can be met in any State only by the uncritical, simplistic, and heavy-handed application of sixth-grade arithmetic.

But legislators do not represent faceless numbers. They represent people, or, more accurately, a majority of the voters in their districts—people with identifiable needs and interests which require legislative representation, and which can often be related to the geographical areas in which these people live. The very fact of geographic districting, the constitutional validity of which the Court does not question, carries with it an acceptance of the idea of legislative representation of regional needs and interests. Yet if geographical residence is irrelevant, as the Court suggests, and the goal is solely that of equally "weighted" votes, I do not understand why the Court's constitutional rule does not require the abolition of districts and the holding of all elections at large.

The fact is, of course, that population factors must often to some degree be subordinated in devising a legislative apportionment plan which is to achieve the important goal of ensuring a fair, effective, and balanced representation of the regional, social, and economic interests within a State. And the further fact is that throughout our history the apportionments of State Legislatures have reflected the strongly felt American tradition that the public interest is composed of many diverse interests, and that in the long run it can better be expressed by a medley of component voices than by the majority's monolithic command. What constitutes a rational plan reasonably designed to achieve this objective will vary from State to State, since each State is unique, in terms of topography, geography, demography, history, heterogeneity and concentration of population, variety of social and economic interests, and in the operation and interrelation of its political institutions. But so long as a State's apportionment plan reasonably achieves, in the light of the State's own characteristics, effective and balanced representation of all substantial interests, without sacrificing the principle of effective majority rule, that plan cannot be considered irrational.

This brings me to what I consider to be the proper constitutional standards to be applied in these cases. . . . A recent expression by the Court of these principles will serve as a generalized compendium:

> "[T]he Fourteenth Amendment permits the States a wide scope of discretion in enacting laws which affect some groups of citizens differently than others. The constitutional safeguard is offended only if the classification rests on grounds wholly irrelevant to the achievement of the State's objective. . . . ."

These principles reflect an understanding respect for the unique values inherent in the Federal Union of States established by our Constitution. They reflect, too, a wise perception of this Court's role in that constitutional system. The point was never better made than by Mr. Justice Brandeis, dissenting in *New State Ice Co. v. Liebmann.* The final paragraph of that classic dissent is worth repeating here:

> "To stay experimentation in things social and economic is a grave responsibility. Denial of the right to experiment may be fraught with serious consequences to the Nation. It is one of the happy incidents of the federal system

that a single courageous State may, if its citizens choose, serve as a laboratory; and try novel social and economic experiments without risk to the rest of the country. This Court has the power to prevent an experiment. We may strike down the statute which embodies it on the ground that, in our opinion, the measure is arbitrary, capricious or unreasonable. . . . But in the exercise of this high power, we must be ever on our guard, lest we erect our prejudices into legal principles. If we would guide by the light of reason, we must let our minds be bold.''

. . . Moving from the general to the specific, I think that the Equal Protection Clause demands but two basic attributes of any plan of state legislative apportionment. First, it demands that, in the light of the State's own characteristics and needs, the plan must be a rational one. Secondly, it demands that the plan must be such as not to permit the systematic frustration of the will of a majority of the electorate of the State. I think it is apparent that any plan of legislative apportionment which could be shown to reflect no policy, but simply arbitrary and capricious action or inaction, and that any plan which could be shown systematically to prevent ultimate effective majority rule, would be invalid under accepted Equal Protection Clause standards. But, beyond this, I think there is nothing in the Federal Constitution to prevent a State from choosing any electoral legislative structure it thinks best suited to the interests, temper, and customs of its people. . . .

In the Colorado House, the majority unquestionably rules supreme, with the population factor untempered by other considerations. In the Senate rural minorities do not have effective control, and therefore do not have even a veto power over the will of the urban majorities. It is true that, as a matter of theoretical arithmetic, a minority of 36% of the voters could elect a majority of the Senate, but this percentage has no real meaning in terms of the legislative process. Under the Colorado plan, no possible combination of Colorado senators from rural districts, even assuming *arguendo* that they would vote as a bloc, could control the Senate. To arrive at the 36% figure, one must include with the rural districts a substantial number of urban districts, districts with substantially dissimilar interests. There is absolutely no reason to assume that this theoretical majority would ever vote together on any issue so as to thwart the wishes of the majority of the voters of Colorado. Indeed, when we eschew the world of numbers, and look to the real world of effective representation, the simple fact of the matter is that Colorado's three metropolitan areas, Denver, Pueblo, and Colorado Springs, elect a majority of the Senate.

The State of Colorado is not an economically or geographically homogeneous unit. The Continental Divide crosses the State in a meandering line from north to south, and Colorado's 104,247 square miles of area are almost equally divided between high plains in the east and rugged mountains in the west. The State's population is highly concentrated in the urbanized eastern edge of the foothills, while farther to the east lies that agricultural area of Colorado which is a part of the Great Plains. The area lying to the west of the Continental Divide is largely mountainous, with two-thirds of the population living in communities of less than 2,500 inhabitants or on farms. Livestock raising, mining and tourism are the dominant occupations. This area is further subdivided by a series of mountain ranges containing some of the highest peaks in the United States, isolating communities and making transportation from point to point difficult, and in some places during the winter months almost impossible. The fourth distinct region of the State is the South Central region, in which is located the most economically depressed area in the State. A scarcity of water makes a state-wide water policy a necessity, with each region affected differently by the problem.

The District Court found that the people living in each of these four regions have interests unifying themselves and differentiating them from those in other regions. Given these underlying facts, certainly it was not irrational to conclude that effective representation of the interests of the residents of each of these regions was unlikely to be achieved if the rule of equal population districts were mechanically imposed; that planned departures from a strict per capita standard of representation were a desirable way of assuring some representation of distinct localities whose needs and problems might have passed unnoticed if districts had been drawn solely on a per capita basis; a desirable way of assuring that districts should be small enough in area, in a mountainous State like Colorado, where accessibility is affected by configuration as well as compactness of districts, to enable each senator to have firsthand knowledge of his entire district and to maintain close contact with his constituents; and a desirable way of avoiding the drawing of district lines which would submerge the needs and wishes of a portion of the electorate by grouping them in districts with larger numbers of voters with wholly different interests.

It is clear from the record that if per capita representation were the rule in both houses of the Colorado Legislature, counties having small populations would have to be merged with larger counties having totally dissimilar interests. Their representatives would not only be unfamiliar with the problems of the smaller county, but the interests of the smaller counties might well be totally submerged to the interests of the larger counties with which they are joined. Since representatives representing conflicting interests might well pay greater attention to the views of the majority, the minority interest could be denied any effective representation at all. Its votes would not be merely "diluted," an injury which the Court considers of constitutional dimensions, but rendered totally nugatory. . . .

[T]he majority has consciously chosen to protect the minority's interests, and under the liberal initiative provisions of the Colorado Constitution, it retains the power to reverse its decision to do so. Therefore, there can be no question of frustration of the basic principle of majority rule. . . .

Mr. Justice Harlan dissenting [in *Reynolds v. Sims, Lucas v. Colorado, et. al.*].

In these cases the Court holds that seats in the legislatures of six States [Ala., Col., Del., Md., N.Y., and Va.] are apportioned in ways that violate the Federal Constitution. . . . These decisions . . . have the effect of placing basic aspects of state political systems under the pervasive overlordship of the federal judiciary. . . . I must register my protest.

Today's holding is that the Equal Protection Clause of the Fourteenth Amendment requires every State to structure its legislature so that all the members of each house represent substantially the same number of people; other factors may be given play only to the extent that they do not significantly encroach on this basic "population" principle. Whatever may be thought of this holding as a piece of political ideology—and even on that score the political history and practices of this country from its earliest beginnings leave wide room for debate . . .—I think it demonstrable that the Fourteenth Amendment does not impose this political tenet on the States or authorize this Court to do so. . . .

Stripped of aphorisms, the Court's argument boils down to the assertion that petitioners' right to vote has been invidiously "debased" or "diluted" by systems of apportionment which entitle them to vote for fewer legislators than other voters, an assertion which is tied to the Equal Protection Clause only by the constitutionally frail tautology that "equal" means "equal."

Had the Court paused to probe more deeply into the matter, it would have found that the Equal Protection Clause was never intended to inhibit the States in choosing any democratic method they pleased for the apportionment of their legislatures. This is shown by the language of the Fourteenth Amendment taken as a whole, by the understanding of those who proposed and ratified it, and by the political practices of the States at the time the Amendment was adopted. It is confirmed by numerous state and congressional actions since the adoption of the Fourteenth Amendment. . . .

Since it can, I think, be shown beyond doubt that state legislative apportionments, as such, are wholly free of constitutional limitations, save such as may be imposed by the Republican Form of Government Clause (Const., Art. IV, § 4), the Court's action now bringing them within the purview of the Fourteenth Amendment amounts to nothing less than an exercise of the amending power by this Court. . . .

The Court relies exclusively on that portion of § 1 of the Fourteenth Amendment which provides that no State shall "deny to any person within its jurisdiction the equal protection of the laws." . . .

I am unable to understand the Court's utter disregard of the second section which expressly recognizes the States' power to deny "or in any way" abridge the right of their inhabitants to vote for "the members of the [State] Legislature," and its express provision of a remedy for such denial or abridgment. The comprehensive scope of the second section and its particular reference to the state legislatures precludes the suggestion that the first section was intended to have the result reached by the Court today. . . .

The history of the adoption of the Fourteenth Amendment provides conclusive evidence that neither those who proposed nor those who ratified the Amendment believed that the Equal Protection Clause limited the power of the States to apportion their legislatures as they saw fit. Moreover, the history demonstrates that the intention to leave this power undisturbed was deliberate and was widely believed to be essential to the adoption of the Amendment. . . .

[Representative Thaddeus Stevens explained:]

"This amendment . . . allows Congress to correct the unjust legislation of the States, so far that the law which operates upon one man shall operate *equally* upon all. Whatever law punishes a white man for a crime shall punish the black man precisely in the same way and to the same degree. Whatever law protects the white man shall afford 'equal' protection to the black man. . . ."

. . . In unmistakable terms, he recognized the power of a State to withhold the right to vote:

"If any State shall exclude any of her adult male citizens from the elective franchise, or abridge that right, she shall forfeit her right to representation in the same proportion. . . ."

. . . Much of the debate concerned the change in the basis of representation effected by the second section, and the speakers stated repeatedly, in express terms or by unmistakable implication, that the States retained the power to regulate suffrage within their borders. . . .

Speaking for the Senate Chairman of the Reconstruction Committee, who was ill, Senator Howard, also a member of the Committee, explained . . .

    . . . *"But, sir, the first section of the proposed amendment does not give to either of these classes the right of voting.* The right of suffrage is not, in law, one of the privileges or immunities thus secured by the Constitution. It is merely the creature of law. It has always been regarded in this country as the result of positive local law, not regarded as one of those fundamental rights lying at the basis of all society and without which a people cannot exist except as slaves, subject to a depotism [*sic*]." [Emphasis supplied by Justice Harlan.]

Discussing the second section, he expressed his regret that it did "not recognize the authority of the United States over the question of suffrage in the several States at all. . . ." He justified the limited purpose of the Amendment in this regard as follows:

    . . . "The committee were of opinion that the States are not yet prepared to sanction so fundamental a change as would be the concession of the right of suffrage to the colored race. We may as well state it plainly and fairly, so that there shall be no misunderstanding on the subject. It was our opinion that three fourths of the States of this Union could not be induced to vote to grant the right of suffrage, even in any degree or under any restriction, to the colored race. . . .
    "The second section leaves the right to regulate the elective franchise still with the States, and does not meddle with that right." [Emphasis supplied by Justice Harlan.]

. . .Debates over readmission were extensive. In at least one instance, the problem of state legislative apportionment was expressly called to the attention of Congress. Objecting to the inclusion of Florida in the Act of June 25, 1868, Mr. Farnsworth stated on the floor of the House:

"I might refer to the apportionment of representatives. By this constitution representatives in the Legislature of Florida are apportioned in such a manner as to give to the sparsely-populated portions of the State the control of the Legislature. The sparsely-populated parts of the State are those where there are very few negroes, the parts inhabited by the white rebels. . . ."

The response of Mr. Butler is particularly illuminating:

"All these arguments, all these statements, all the provisions of this constitution have been submitted to the Judiciary Committee of the Senate, and they have found the constitution republican and proper. This constitution has been submitted to the Senate, and they have found it republican and proper. It has been submitted to your own Committee on Reconstruction, and they have found it republican and proper, and have reported it to this House."

. . . Even if one were to accept the majority's belief that it is proper entirely to disregard the unmistakable implications of the second section of the Amendment in construing the first section, one is confounded by its disregard of all this history. There is here none of the difficulty which may attend the application of basic principles to situations not contemplated or understood when the principles were framed. . . .

In this summary of what the majority ignores, note should be taken of the Fifteenth and Nineteenth Amendments. . . .

If constitutional amendment was the only means by which all men and, later, women, could be guaranteed the right to vote at all, even for *federal* officers, how can it be that the far less obvious right to a particular kind of apportionment of *state* legislatures—a right to which is opposed a far more plausible conflicting interest of the State than the interest which opposes the general right to vote—can be conferred by judicial construction of the Fourteenth Amendment? Yet, unless one takes the highly implausible view that the Fourteenth Amendment controls methods of apportionment but leaves the right to vote itself unprotected, the conclusion is inescapable that the Court has, for purposes of these cases, relegated the Fifteenth and Nineteenth Amendments to the same limbo of constitutional anachronisms to which the second section of the Fourteenth Amendment has been assigned. . . .

Generalities cannot obscure the cold truth that cases of this type are not amenable to the development of judicial standards. No set of standards can guide a court which has to decide how many legislative districts a State shall have, or what the shape of the districts shall be, or where to draw a particular district line. No judicially manageable standard can determine whether a State should have single-member districts or multimember districts or some combination of both. No such standard can control the balance between keeping up with population shifts and having stable districts. In all these respects, the courts will be called upon to make particular decisions with respect to which a principle of equally populated districts will be of no assistance whatsoever. Quite obviously, there are limitless possibilities for districting consistent with such a principle. Nor can these problems be avoided by judicial reliance on legislative judgments so far as possible. Reshaping or combining one or two districts, or modifying just a few district lines, is no less a matter of choosing among many possible solutions, with varying political consequences, than reapportionment broadside. . . .

It is well to remember that the product of today's decisions will not be readjustment of a few districts in a few States which most glaringly depart from the principle of equally populated districts. It will be a redetermination, extensive in many cases, of legislative districts in all but a few States.

Although the Court—necessarily, as I believe—provides only generalities in elaboration of its main thesis, its opinion nevertheless fully demonstrates how far removed these problems are from fields of judicial competence. Recognizing that "indiscriminate districting" is an invitation to "partisan gerrymandering," *ante,* pp. 43-44, the Court nevertheless excludes virtually every basis for the formation of electoral districts other than "indiscriminate districting." . . .

I believe that the vitality of our political system, on which in the last analysis all else depends, is weakened by reliance on the judiciary for political reform; in time a complacent body politic may result.

These decisions also cut deeply into the fabric of our federalism. What must follow from them may eventually appear to be the product of State Legislatures. Nevertheless, no thinking person can fail to recognize that the aftermath of these cases, however desirable it may be thought in itself, will have been achieved at the cost of a radical alteration in the relationship between the States and the Federal Government, more particularly the Federal Judiciary. Only one who has an overbearing impatience with the federal system and its political processes will believe that that cost was not too high or was inevitable.

Finally, these decisions give support to a current mistaken view of the Constitution and the constitutional function of this Court. This view, in a nutshell, is that every major social ill in this country can find its cure in some constitutional "principle," and that this Court should "take the lead" in promoting reform when other branches of government fail to act. The Constitution is not a panacea for every blot upon the public welfare, nor should this Court, ordained as a judicial body, be thought of as a general haven for reform movements. The Constitution is an instrument of government, fundamental to which is the premise that in a diffusion of governmental authority lies the greatest promise that this Nation will realize liberty for all its citizens. This Court, limited in function in accordance with that premise, does not serve its high purpose when it exceeds its authority, even to satisfy justified impatience with the slow workings of the political process. For when, in the name of constitutional interpretation, the Court *adds* something to the Constitution that was deliberately excluded from it, the Court in reality substitutes its view of what should be so for the amending process. . . .

53

William J. Brennan, Jr.

Constitutional Interpretation (1985)

. . . [T]he text I have chosen for exploration is the amended Constitution of the United States, which, of course, entrenches the Bill of Rights and the Civil War amendments, and draws sustenance from the bedrock principles of another great text, the Magna Carta. So fashioned, the Constitution embodies the aspiration to social justice, brotherhood, and human dignity that brought this nation into being. The Declaration of Independence, the Constitution and the Bill of Rights solemnly committed the United States to be a country where the dignity and rights of all persons were equal before all authority. In all candor we must concede that part of this egalitarianism in America has been more pretension than realized fact. But we are an aspiring people, a people with faith in progress. Our amended Constitution is the lodestar for our aspirations. Like every text worth reading, it is not crystalline. The phrasing is broad and the limitations of its provisions are not clearly marked. Its majestic generalities and ennobling pronouncements are both luminous and obscure. This ambiguity of course calls forth interpretation, the interaction of reader and text. The encounter with the constitutional text has been, in many senses, my life's work.

My approach to this text may differ from the approach of other participants in this symposium to their texts. Yet such differences may themselves stimulate reflection about what it is we do when we "interpret" a text. Thus I will attempt to elucidate my approach to the text as well as my substantive interpretation.

Perhaps the foremost difference is the fact that my encounters with the constitutional text are not purely or even primarily introspective; the Constitution cannot be for me simply a contemplative haven for private moral reflection. My relation to this great text is inescapably public. That is not to say that my reading of the text is not a personal reading, only that the personal reading perforce occurs in a public context, and is open to critical scrutiny from all quarters.

The Constitution is fundamentally a public text—the monumental charter of a government and a people—and a Justice of the Supreme Court must apply

From "Address to the Text and Teaching Symposium," Georgetown University, October 12, 1985, Washington, D.C.

it to resolve public controversies. For, from our beginning, a most important consequence of the constitutionally created separation of powers has been the American habit, extraordinary to other democracies, of casting social, economic, philosophical and political questions in the form of lawsuits, in an attempt to secure ultimate resolution by the Supreme Court. In this way, important aspects of the most fundamental issues confronting our democracy may finally arrive in the Supreme Court for judicial determination. Not infrequently, these are the issues upon which contemporary society is most deeply divided. They arouse our deepest emotions. The main burden of my twenty-nine terms on the Supreme Court has thus been to wrestle with the Constitution in this heightened public context, to draw meaning from the text in order to resolve public controversies.

Two other aspects of my relation to this text warrant mention. First, constitutional interpretation for a federal judge is, for the most part, obligatory. When litigants approach the bar of court to adjudicate a constitutional dispute, they may justifiably demand an answer. Judges cannot avoid a definitive interpretation because they feel unable to, or would prefer not to, penetrate to the full meaning of the Constitution's provisions. Unlike literary critics, judges cannot merely savor the tensions or revel in the ambiguities inhering in the text—judges must resolve them.

Second, consequences flow from a Justice's interpretation in a direct and immediate way. A judicial decision respecting the incompatibility of Jim Crow with a constitutional guarantee of equality is not simply a contemplative exercise in defining the shape of a just society. It is an order—supported by the full coercive power of the State—that the present society change in a fundamental aspect. Under such circumstances the process of deciding can be a lonely, troubling experience for fallible human beings conscious that their best may not be adequate to the challenge. We Justices are certainly aware that we are not final because we are infallible; we know that we are infallible only because we are final. One does not forget how much may depend on the decision. More than the litigants may be affected. The course of vital social, economic and political currents may be directed.

These three defining characteristics of my relation to the constitutional text—its public nature, obligatory character, and consequentialist aspect—cannot help but influence the way I read that text. When Justices interpret the Constitution they speak for their community, not for themselves alone. The act of interpretation must be undertaken with full consciousness that it is, in a very real sense, the community's interpretation that is sought. Justices are not platonic guardians appointed to wield authority to their personal moral predilections. Precisely because coercive force must attend any judicial decision to countermand the will of a contemporary majority, the Justices must render constitutional interpretations that are received as legitimate. The source of legitimacy is, of course, a wellspring of controversy in legal and political circles. At the core of the debate is what the late Yale Law School Professor Alexander Bickel labeled "the counter-majoritarian difficulty." Our commitment to self-governance in a representative democracy must be reconciled with vesting in electorally unaccountable Justices the power to invalidate the expressed desires of representative bodies on the ground of inconsistency with higher law. Because judicial power resides in the authority to give meaning to the Constitution, the debate is really a debate about how to read the text, about constraints on what is legitimate interpretation.

There are those who find legitimacy in fidelity to what they call "the intentions of the Framers." In its most doctrinaire incarnation, this view demands that Justices discern exactly what the Framers thought about the question under consideration and simply follow that intention in resolving the case before them. It is a view that feigns self-effacing deference to the specific judgments of those who forged our original social compact. But in truth it is little more than arrogance cloaked as humility. It is arrogant to pretend that from our vantage we can gauge accurately the intent of the Framers on application of principle to specific, contemporary questions. All too often, sources of potential enlightenment such as records of the ratification debates provide sparse or ambiguous evidence of the original intention. Typically, all that can be gleaned is that the Framers themselves did not agree about the application or meaning of particular constitutional provisions, and hid their differences in cloaks of generality. Indeed, it is far from clear whose intention is relevant— that of the drafters, the congressional disputants, or the ratifiers in the states— or even whether the idea of an original intention is a coherent way of thinking about a jointly drafted document drawing its authority from a general assent of the states. And apart from the problematic nature of the sources, our distance of two centuries cannot but work as a prism refracting all we perceive. One cannot help but speculate that the chorus of lamentations calling for interpretation faithful to "original intention"—and proposing nullification of interpretations that fail this quick litmus test—must inevitably come from persons who have no familiarity with the historical record.

Perhaps most importantly, while proponents of this facile historicism justify it as a depoliticization of the judiciary, the political underpinnings of such a choice should not escape notice. A position that upholds constitutional claims only if they were within the specific contemplation of the Framers in effect establishes a presumption of resolving textual ambiguities against the claim of constitutional right. It is far from clear what justifies such a presumption against claims of right. Nothing intrinsic in the nature of interpretation—if there is such a thing as the "nature" of interpretation—commands such a passive approach to ambiguity. This is a choice no less political than any other; it expresses antipathy to claims of the minority rights against the majority. Those who would restrict claims of right to the values of 1789 specifically articulated in the Constitution turn a blind eye to social progress and eschew adaptation of overarching principles to changes of social circumstance.

Another, perhaps more sophisticated, response to the potential power of judicial interpretation stresses democratic theory: because ours is a government of the people's elected representatives, substantive value choices should by and large be left to them. This view emphasizes not the transcendant historical authority of the Framers but the predominant contemporary authority of the elected branches of government. Yet it has similar consequences for the nature of proper judicial interpretation. Faith in the majoritarian process counsels restraint. Even under more expansive formulations of this approach, judicial review is appropriate only to the extent of ensuring that our democratic process functions smoothly. Thus, for example, we would protect freedom of speech merely to ensure that the people are heard by their representatives, rather than as a separate, substantive value. When, by contrast, society tosses up to the Supreme Court a dispute that would require invalidation of a legislature's substantive policy choice, the Court generally would stay its hand because the Constitution was meant as a plan of government and not as an embodiment of fundamental substantive values.

The view that all matters of substantive policy should be resolved through the majoritarian process has appeal under some circumstances, but I think it ultimately will not do. Unabashed enshrinement of majority will would permit the imposition of a social caste system or wholesale confiscation of property so long as a majority of the authorized legislative body, fairly elected, approved. Our Constitution could not abide such a situation. It is the very purpose of a Constitution—and particularly of the Bill of Rights—to declare certain values transcendent, beyond the reach of temporary political majorities. The majoritarian process cannot be expected to rectify claims of minority right that arise as a response to the outcomes of that very majoritarian process. . . .

Faith in democracy is one thing, blind faith quite another. Those who drafted our Constitution understood the difference. One cannot read the text without admitting that it embodies substantive value choices; it places certain values beyond the power of any legislature. Obvious are the separation of powers; the privilege of the Writ of Habeas Corpus; prohibition of Bills of Attainder and *ex post facto* laws; prohibition of cruel and unusual punishments; the requirement of just compensation for official taking of property; the prohibition of laws tending to establish religion or enjoining the free exercise of religion; and, since the Civil War, the banishment of slavery and official race discrimination. With respect to at least such principles, we simply have not constituted ourselves as strict utilitarians. While the Constitution may be amended, such amendments require an immense effort by the People as a whole.

To remain faithful to the content of the Constitution, therefore, an approach to interpreting the text must account for the existence of these substantive value choices, and must accept the ambiguity inherent in the effort to apply them to modern circumstances. The Framers discerned fundamental principles through struggles against particular malefactions of the Crown; the struggle shapes the particular contours of the articulated principles. But our acceptance of the fundamental principles has not and should not bind us to those precise, at times anachronistic, contours. Successive generations of Americans have continued to respect these fundamental choices and adopt them as their own guide to evaluating quite different historical practices. Each generation has the choice to overrule or add to the fundamental principles enunciated by the Framers; the Constitution can be amended or it can be ignored. Yet with respect to its fundamental principles, the text has suffered neither fate. Thus, if I may borrow the words of an esteemed predecessor, Justice Robert Jackson, the burden of judicial interpretation is to translate "the majestic generalities of the Bill of Rights, conceived as part of the pattern of liberal government in the eighteenth century, into concrete restraints on officials dealing with the problems of the twentieth century." *Board of Education v. Barnette,* [319 U.S. 624, 639 (1943),].

We current justices read the Constitution in the only way that we can: as Twentieth Century Americans. We look to the history of the time of framing and to the intervening history of interpretation. But the ultimate question must be, what do the words of the text mean in our time? For the genius of the Constitution rests not in any static meaning it might have had in a world that is dead and gone, but in the adaptability of its great principles to cope with current problems and current needs. What the constitutional fundamentals meant to the wisdom of other times cannot be their measure to the vision of our time. Similarly, what those fundamentals mean for us, our descendants will learn, cannot be the measure to the vision of their time. This realization is not, I assure you, a novel one of my own creation. Permit me to quote from one of the opinions of our Court, *Weems v. United States,* [217 U.S. 349,] written nearly a century ago:

> Time works changes, brings into existence new conditions and purposes. Therefore, a principle to be vital must be capable of wider application than the mischief which gave it birth. This is peculiarly true of constitutions. They are not ephemeral enactments, designed to meet passing occasions. They are, to use the words of Chief Justice John Marshall, 'designed to approach immortality as nearly as human institutions can approach it.' The future is their care and provision for events of good and bad tendencies of which no prophesy can be made. In the application of a constitution, therefore, our contemplation cannot be only of what has been, but of what may be.

Interpretation must account for the transformative purpose of the text. Our Constitution was not intended to preserve a preexisting society but to make a new one, to put in place new principles that the prior political community had not sufficiently recognized. Thus, for example, when we interpret the Civil War Amendments to the charter—abolishing slavery, guaranteeing blacks equality under law, and guaranteeing blacks the right to vote—we must remember that those who put them in place had no desire to enshrine the status quo. Their goal was to make over their world, to eliminate all vestige of slave caste.

Having discussed at some length how I, as a Supreme Court Justice, interact with this text, I think it time to turn to the fruits of this discourse. For the Constitution is a sublime oration on the dignity of man, a bold commitment by a people to the ideal of libertarian dignity protected through law. Some reflection is perhaps required before this can be seen.

The Constitution on its face is, in large measure, a structuring text, a blueprint for government. And when the text is not prescribing the form of government it is limiting the powers of that government. The original document, before addition of any of the amendments, does not speak primarily of the rights of man, but of the abilities and disabilities of government. When one reflects upon the text's preoccupation with the scope of government as well as its shape, however, one comes to understand that what this text is about is the relationship of the individual and the state. The text marks the metes and bounds of official authority and individual autonomy. When one studies the boundary that the text marks out, one gets a sense of the vision of the individual embodied in the Constitution.

As augmented by the Bill of Rights and the Civil War amendments, this text is a sparkling vision of the supremacy of the human dignity of every individual. This vision is reflected in the very choice of democratic self-governance: the supreme value of a democracy is the presumed worth of each individual. And this vision manifests itself most dramatically in the specific prohibitions of the Bill of Rights, a term which I henceforth will apply to describe not only the original first eight amendments, but the Civil War amendments as well. It is a vision that has guided us as a people throughout our history, although the precise rules by which we have protected fundamental human dignity have been transformed over time in response to both transformations of social condition and evolution of our concepts of human dignity.

Until the end of the nineteenth century, freedom and dignity in our country found meaningful protection in the institution of real property. In a society still largely agricultural, a piece of land provided men not just with sustenance but with the means of economic independence, a necessary precondition of political independence and expression. Not surprisingly, property relationships formed the heart of litigation and of legal practice, and lawyers and judges tended to think stable property relationships the highest aim of the law.

But the days when common law property relationships dominated litigation and legal practice are past. To a growing extent economic existence now depends on less certain relationships with government—licenses, employment, contracts, subsidies, unemployment benefits, tax exemptions, welfare and the like. Government participation in the economic existence of individuals is pervasive and deep. Administrative matters and other dealings with government are at the epicenter of the exploding law. We turn to government and to the law for controls which would never have been expected or tolerated before this century, when a man's answer to economic oppression or difficulty was to move two hundred miles west. Now hundreds of thousands of Americans live entire lives without any real prospect of the dignity and autonomy that ownership of real property could confer. Protection of the human dignity of such citizens requires a much modified view of the proper relationship of individual and state.

In general, problems of the relationship of the citizen with government have multiplied and thus have engendered some of the most important constitutional issues of the day. As government acts ever more deeply upon those areas of our lives once marked "private," there is an even greater need to see that individual rights are not curtailed or cheapened in the interest of what may temporarily appear to be the "public good." And as government continues in its role of provider for so many of our disadvantaged citizens, there is an even greater need to ensure that government act with integrity and consistency in its dealings with these citizens. To put this another way, the possibilities for collision between government activity and individual rights will increase as the power and authority of government itself expands, and this growth, in turn, heightens the need for constant vigilance at the collision points. If our free society is to endure, those who govern must recognize human dignity and accept the enforcement of constitutional limitations on their power conceived by the Framers to be necessary to preserve that dignity and the air of freedom which is our proudest heritage. Such recognition will not come from a technical understanding of the organs of government, or the new forms of wealth they administer. It requires something different, something deeper—a personal confrontation with the wellsprings of our society. . . .

I do not mean to suggest that we have in the last quarter century achieved a comprehensive definition of the constitutional ideal of human dignity. We are still striving toward that goal, and doubtless it will be an eternal quest. For if the interaction of this Justice and the constitutional text over the years confirms any single proposition, it is that the demands of human dignity will never cease to evolve. . . .

54

Robert H. Bork

Testimony Before the Senate Judiciary Committee (1987)

Judge Bork: I want to begin by thanking the President for placing my name in nomination for this most important position. . . .

As you have said, quite correctly, Mr. Chairman, and as others have said here today, this is in large measure a discussion of judicial philosophy, and I want to make a few remarks at the outset on that subject of central interest.

That is, my understanding of how a judge should go about his or her work. That may also be described as my philosophy of the role of a judge in a constitutional democracy.

The judge's authority derives entirely from the fact that he is applying the law and not his personal values. That is why the American public accepts the decisions of its courts, accepts even decisions that nullify the laws a majority of the electorate or of their representatives voted for.

The judge, to deserve that trust and that authority, must be every bit as governed by law as is the Congress, the President, the State Governors and legislatures, and the American people. No one, including a judge, can be above the law. Only in that way will justice be done and the freedom of Americans assured.

How should a judge go about finding the law? The only legitimate way, in my opinion, is by attempting to discern what those who made the law intended. The intentions of the lawmakers govern whether the lawmakers are the Congress of the United States enacting a statute or whether they are those who ratified our Constitution and its various Amendments.

Where the words are precise and the facts simple, that is a relatively easy task. Where the words are general, as is the case with some of the most profound protections of our liberties—in the Bill of Rights and in the Civil War Amendments—the task is far more complex. It is to find the principle or value that was intended to be protected and to see that it is protected.

As I wrote in an opinion for our court, the judge's responsibility "is to discern how the framers' values, defined in the context of the world they knew, apply in the world we know."

From Hearings Before the Committee on the Judiciary, United States Senate, 100th Congress First Session, Sept. 15, 1987, Senate No. J–100–64.

If a judge abandons intention as his guide, there is no law available to him and he begins to legislate a social agenda for the American people. That goes well beyond his legitimate power.

He or she then diminishes liberty instead of enhancing it. That is why I agree with Judge Learned Hand, one of the great jurists in our history, when he wrote that the judge's "authority and his immunity depend upon the assumption that he speaks with the mouths of others: the momentum of his utterances must be greater than any which his personal reputation and character can command if it is to do the work assigned to it—if it is to stand against the passionate resentments arising out of the interests he must frustrate." To state that another way, the judge must speak with the authority of the past and yet accommodate that past to the present.

The past, however, includes not only the intentions of those who first made the law, it also includes those past judges who interpreted it and applied it in prior cases. That is why a judge must have great respect for precedent. It is one thing as a legal theorist to criticize the reasoning of a prior decision, even to criticize it severely, as I have done. It is another and more serious thing altogether for a judge to ignore or overturn a prior decision. That requires much careful thought.

Times come, of course, when even a venerable precedent can and should be overruled. The primary example of a proper overruling is *Brown* v. *Board of Education*, the case which outlawed racial segregation accomplished by government action. *Brown* overturned the rule of separate but equal laid down 58 years before in *Plessy* v. *Ferguson*. Yet *Brown*, delivered with the authority of a unanimous Court, was clearly correct and represents perhaps the greatest moral achievement of our constitutional law.

Nevertheless, overruling should be done sparingly and cautiously. Respect for precedent is a part of the great tradition of our law, just as is fidelity to the intent of those who ratified the Constitution and enacted our statutes. That does not mean that constitutional law is static. It will evolve as judges modify doctrine to meet new circumstances and new technologies. Thus, today we apply the first amendment's guarantee of the freedom of the press to radio and television, and we apply to electronic surveillance the fourth amendment's guarantee of privacy for the individual against unreasonable searches of his or her home.

I can put the matter no better than I did in an opinion on my present court. Speaking of the judge's duty, I wrote: "The important thing, the ultimate consideration, is the constitutional freedom that is given into our keeping. A judge who refuses to see new threats to an established constitutional value and hence provides a crabbed interpretation that robs a provision of its full, fair and reasonable meaning, fails in his judicial duty. That duty, I repeat, is to ensure that the powers and freedoms the framers specified are made effective in today's circumstances."

But I should add to that passage that when a judge goes beyond this and reads entirely new values into the Constitution, values the framers and the ratifiers did not put there, he deprives the people of their liberty. That liberty, which the Constitution clearly envisions, is the liberty of the people to set their own social agenda through the processes of democracy.

Conservative judges frustrated that process in the mid-1930's by using the concept they had invented, the 14th amendment's supposed guarantee of a liberty of contract, to strike down laws designed to protect workers and labor unions. That was wrong then and it would be wrong now.

My philosophy of judging, Mr. Chairman, as you pointed out, is neither liberal nor conservative. It is simply a philosophy of judging which gives the Constitution a full and fair interpretation but, where the Constitution is silent, leaves the policy struggles to the Congress, the President, the legislatures and executives of the 50 States, and to the American people.

I welcome this opportunity to come before the committee and answer whatever questions the members may have. I am quite willing to discuss with you my judicial philosophy and the approach I take to deciding cases. I cannot, of course, commit myself as to how I might vote on any particular case and I know you would not wish me to do that. . . .

55

Thomas Jefferson and James Madison

Exchange on the Binding of Generations (1789-1790)

Thomas Jefferson to James Madison

Paris September 6, 1789.

Dear Sir

I sit down to write to you without knowing by what occasion I shall send my letter. I do it because a subject comes into my head which I would wish to develop a little more than is practicable in the hurry of the moment of making up general dispatches.

The question whether one generation of men has a right to bind another, seems never to have been stated either on this or our side of the water. Yet it is a question of such consequences as not only to merit decision, but place also, among the fundamental principles of every government. The course of reflection in which we are immersed here on the elementary principles of society has presented this question to my mind; and that no such obligation can be so transmitted I think very capable of proof.—I set out on this ground, which I suppose to be self evident, *'that the earth belongs in usufruct to the living':* that the dead have neither powers nor rights over it. The portion occupied by any individual ceases to be his when himself ceases to be, and reverts to the society. If the society has formed no rules for the appropriation of its lands in severality, it will be taken by the first occupants. These will generally be the wife and children of the decedent. If they have formed rules of appropriation, those rules may give it to the wife and children, or to some one of them, or to the legatee of the deceased. So they may give it to his creditor. But the child, the legatee, or creditor takes it, not by any natural right, but by a law of the society of which they are members, and to which they are subject. Then no man can, by *natural right,* oblige the lands he occupied, or the persons who succeed him in that occupation, to the payment of debts contracted by him. For if he could, he might, during his own life, eat up the usufruct of the lands for

From *The Papers of Thomas Jefferson,* Vol. 15, Princeton University Press, 1969.

several generations to come, and then the lands would belong to the dead, and not to the living, which would be the reverse of our principle.

What is true of every member of the society individually, is true of them all collectively, since the rights of the whole can be no more than the sum of the rights of the individuals.—To keep our ideas clear when applying them to a multitude, let us suppose a whole generation of men to be born on the same day, to attain mature age on the same day, and to die on the same day, leaving a succeeding generation in the moment of attaining their mature age all together. Let the ripe age be supposed of 21 years, and their period of life 34 years more, that being the average term given by the bills of mortality to persons who have already attained 21 years of age. Each successive generation would, in this way, come on, and go off the stage at a fixed moment, as individuals do now. Then I say the earth belongs to each of these generations, during its course, fully, and in their own right. The 2d. generation receives it clear of the debts and incumberances of the 1st. the 3d of the 2d. and so on. For if the 1st. could charge it with a debt, then the earth would belong to the dead and not the living generation. Then no generation can contract debts greater than may be paid during the course of its own existence. . . .—But a material difference must be noted between the succession of an individual, and that of a whole generation. Individuals are parts only of a society, subject to the laws of the whole. These laws may appropriate the portion of land occupied by a decendent to his creditor rather than to any other, or to his child on condition he satisfies the creditor. But when a whole generation, that is, the whole society dies, as in the case we have supposed, and another generation or society succeeds, this forms a whole, and there is no superior who can give their territory to a third society, who may have lent money to their predecessors beyond their faculties of paying.

What is true of a generation all arriving to self-government on the same day, and dying all on the same day, is true of those in a constant course of decay and renewal, with this only difference. A generation coming in and going out entire, as in the first case, would have a right in the 1st. year of their self-dominion to contract a debt for 33. years, in the 10th. for 24. in the 20th. for 14. in the 30th. for 4. whereas generations, changing daily by daily deaths and births, have one constant term, beginning at the date of their contract, and ending when a majority of those of full age at that date shall be dead. The length of that term may be estimated from the tables of mortality, corrected by the circumstances of climate, occupation &c. peculiar to the country of the contractors. Take, for instance, the table of M. de Buffon wherein he states 23,994 deaths, and the ages at which they happened. Suppose a society in which 23,994 persons are born every year, and live to the ages stated in this table. The conditions of that society will be as follows. 1st. It will consist constantly of 617,703. persons of all ages. 2ly. Of those living at any one instant of time, one half will be dead in 24 years 8 months. 3dly. 10,675 will arrive every year at the age of 21 years complete. 4ly. It will constantly have 348,417 persons of all ages above 21 years. 5ly. And the half of those of 21 years and upwards living at any one instant of time will be dead in 18 years 8 months, or say 19 years as the nearest integral number. Then 19 years is the term beyond which neither the representatives of a nation, nor even the whole nation itself assembled, can validly extend a debt. . . .

I suppose that the received opinion, that the public debts of one generation devolve on the next, has been suggested by our seeing habitually in private life that he who succeeds to lands is required to pay the debts of his ancestor or testator: without considering that this requisition is municipal only, not moral; flowing from the will of the society, which has found it convenient to appropriate lands, become vacant by the death of their occupant, on the condition of a payment of his debts: but that between society and society, or generation and generation, there is no municipal obligation, no umpire but the law of nature. We seem not to have perceived that, by the law of nature, one generation is to another as one independent nation to another.

The interest of the national debt of France being in fact but a two thousandth part of its rent roll, the payment of it is practicable enough: and so becomes a question merely of honor, or of expediency. But with respect to future debts, would it not be wise and just for that nation to declare, in the constitution they are forming, that neither the legislature, nor the nation itself, can validly contract more debt than they may pay within their own age, or within the term of 19 years? And that all future contracts will be deemed void as to what shall remain unpaid at the end of 19 years from their date? This would put the lenders, and the borrowers also, on their guard. By reducing too the faculty of borrowing within its natural limits, it would bridle the spirit of war, to which too free a course has been procured by the inattention of money-lenders to this law of nature, that succeeding generations are not responsible for the preceding.

On similar ground it may be proved that no society can make a perpetual constitution, or even a perpetual law. The earth belongs always to the living generation. They may manage it then, and what proceeds from it, as they please, during their usufruct. They are masters too of their own persons, and consequently may govern them as they please. But persons and property make the sum of the objects of government. The constitution and the laws of their predecessors extinguished then in their natural course with those who gave them being. This could preserve that being till it ceased to be itself, and no longer. Every constitution then, and every law, naturally expires at the end of 19 years. If it be enforced longer, it is an act of force, and not of right.—It may be said that the succeeding generation exercising in fact the power of repeal, this leaves them as free as if the constitution or law had been expressly limited to 19 years only. In the first place, this objection admits the right, in proposing an equivalent. But the power of repeal is not an equivalent. It might be indeed if every form of government were so perfectly contrived that the will of the majority could always be obtained fairly and without impediment. But this is true of no form. The people cannot assemble themselves. Their representation is unequal and vicious. Various checks are opposed to every legislative proposition. Factions get possession of the public councils. Bribery corrupts them. Personal interests lead them astray from the general interests of their constituents: and other impediments arise so as to prove to every practical man that a law of limited duration is much more manageable than one which needs a repeal. . . .

Turn this subject in your mind, my dear Sir, and particularly as to the power of contracting debts; and develop it with that perspicuity and cogent logic so peculiarly yours. Your station in the councils of our country gives you an opportunity of producing it to public consideration, of forcing it into discussion. At first blush it may be rallied, as a theoretical speculation: but examination will prove it to be solid and salutary. It would furnish matter for a fine preamble to our first law for appropriating the public revenue; and it will exclude at the threshold of our new government the contagious and ruinous errors of this quarter of the globe, which have armed despots with means, not sanctioned by nature, for binding in chains their fellow men. We have already given in example one effectual check to the Dog of war by transferring the power of letting him loose from the Executive to the Legislative body, from those who are to spend to those who are to pay. I should be pleased to see this second obstacle held out by us also in the first instance. No nation can make a declaration against the validity of long-contracted debts so disinterestedly as we, since we do not owe a shilling which may not be paid with ease, principal and interest, within the time of our own lives.—Establish the principle also in the new law to be passed for protecting copyrights and new inventions, by securing the exclusive right for 19 instead of 14 years. Besides familiarizing us to this term, it will be an instance the more of our taking reason for our guide, instead of English precedent, the habit of which fetters us with all the political heresies of a nation equally remarkable for its early excitement from some errors, and long slumbering under others. . . .

James Madison to Thomas Jefferson

New York Feb. 4, 1790

Dear Sir

Your favor of Jan. 9 enclosing one of Sept. last did not get to hand till a few days ago. The idea which the latter evolves is a great one; and suggests many interesting reflections to legislators; particularly when contracting and providing for public debts. Whether it can be received in the extent to which your reasonings carry it, is a question which I ought to turn more in my thoughts than I have yet been able to do, before I should be justified in making up a full opinion on it. My first thoughts lead me to view the doctrine as not *in all respects,* compatible with the course of human affairs. I will endeavor to sketch the grounds of my skepticism.

> "As the Earth belongs to the living, not to the dead, a living generation can bind itself only: in every Society the will of the majority binds the whole: according to the laws of mortality, a majority of those ripe for the exercise of their will do not live beyond the term of 19 years: to this term then is limited the validity of every act of the Society; nor can any act be continued beyond this term without an *express* declaration of the public will." This I understand to be the outline of the argument.

The acts of a political society may be divided into three classes.

1. The fundamental constitution of the government
2. Laws involving some stipulation, which renders them irrevocable at the will of the legislature.
3. Laws involving no such irrevocable quality.

1. However applicable in theory the doctrine may be to a Constitution, it seems liable in practice to some weighty objections.

Would not a government ceasing of necessity at the end of a given term, unless prolonged by some constitutional act, previous to its expiration, be too subject to the casualty and consequences of an interregnum?

Would not a government so often revised become too mutable and novel to retain that share of prejudice in its favor which is a salutary aid to the most rational government?

Would not such a periodical revision engender pernicious factions that might not otherwise come into existence; and agitate the public mind more frequently and more violently than might be expedient?

2. In the second class of acts involving stipulations, must not exceptions at least to the doctrine, be admitted?

If the earth be the gift of *nature* to the living, their title can extend to the earth in its *natural* state only. The *improvements* made by the dead form a debt against the living who take the benefit of them. This debt cannot be otherwise discharged than by a proportionate obedience to the will of the authors of the improvements.

But a case less liable to be controverted may perhaps be stated. Debts may be incurred with a direct view to the interest of the unborn as well as of the living: Such are debts for repelling a conquest, the evils of which descend through many generations. Debts may even be incurred principally for the benefit of posterity: Such perhaps is the debt incurred by the U. States. In these instances the debts might not be dischargeable within the term of 19 years.

There seems then to be some foundation in the nature of things; in the relation which one generation bears to another, for the *descent* of obligations from one to another. Equity may require it. Mutual good may be promoted by it. And all that seems indispensable in stating the account between the dead and the living, is to see that the debits against the latter do not exceed the advances made by the former. Few of the incumbrances entailed on nations by their predecessors would bear a liquidation even on this principle.

3. Objections to the doctrine, as applied to the third class of acts must be merely practical. But in that view alone they appear to be material.

Unless such temporary laws should be kept in force by acts regularly anticipating their expiration, all the rights depending on positive laws, that is most of the rights of property would become absolutely defunct, and the most violent struggles ensue between the parties interested in reviving and those interested in reforming the antecedent state of property. Nor does it seem improbable that such an event might be suffered to take place. The checks and difficulties opposed to the passage of laws which render the power of repeal inferior to an opportunity to reject as a security against oppression, would here render the latter an insecure provision against anarchy. Add to this that the very possibility of an event so hazardous to the rights of property could not but depreciate its value; that the approach of the crisis would increase the effect; that the frequent return of periods superceding all the obligations depending on antecedent laws and usages, must by weakening the sense of them, co-operate with motives to licenciousness already too powerful; and that the general uncertainty and vicisitudes of such a state of things would, on one side, discourage every useful effort of steady industry pursued under the sanction of existing laws, and on the other, give an immediate advantage to the more sagacious over the less sagacious part of the society.

I can find no relief from such embarrassments, but in the received doctrine that a *tacit* assent may be given to established governments and laws, and that this assent is to be inferred from the omission of an express revocation. It seems more practicable to remedy by well constituted governments, the pestilent operation of this doctrine, in the unlimited sense in which it is at present received than it is to find a remedy for the evils necessarily springing from an unlimited admission of the contrary doctrine.

Is it not doubtful whether it be possible to exclude wholly the idea of an implied or tacit assent, without subverting the very foundation of civil society?

On what principle is it that the voice of the majority binds the minority? It does not result I conceive from a law of nature but from compact founded on utility. A greater proportion might be required by the fundamental constitution of society, if under any particular circumstances it were judged eligible. Prior therefore to the establishment of this principle, *unanimity* was necessary; and rigid theory, accordingly presupposes the assent of every individual to the rule, which subjects the minority to the will of the majority. If this assent cannot be given tacitly, or be not implied where no positive evidence forbids, no person born in society, could on attaining ripe age, be bound by any acts, of the majority, and either a unanimous renewal of every law would be necessary, as often as a new member should be added to the society, or the express consent of every new member be obtained to the rule by which the majority decides for the whole.

If these observations be not misapplied, it follows that a limitation of the validity of all acts to the computed life of the generation establishing them, is in some cases not required by theory, and in others not consistent with practice. They are not meant however to impeach either the utility of the principle as applied to the cases you have particularly in view, or the general importance of it in the eye of the philosophical legislator. On the contrary it would give me singular pleasure to see it first announced to the world in a law of the U. States, and always kept in view as a salutary restraint on living generations from unjust and unnecessary burdens on their successors. This is a pleasure however which I have no hope of enjoying. The spirit of philosophical legislation has not prevailed at all in some parts of America, and is by no means the fashion of this part, or of the present representative body. The evils suffered or feared from weakness in government and licenciousness in the people, have turned the attention more towards the means of strengthening the powers of the former, than of narrowing their extent in the minds of the latter. Besides this it is so much easier to descry the little difficulties immediately incident to every great plan, than to comprehend its general and remote benefits, that further light must be added to the councils of our country before many truths which are seen through the medium of philosophy, become visible to the naked eye of the ordinary politician.

56

James Madison

Federalist 49 (1788)

The author of the *Notes on the State of Virginia,* quoted in the last paper, has subjoined to that valuable work the draught of a constitution, which had been prepared in order to be laid before a convention expected to be called in 1783, by the legislature, for the establishment of a constitution for that commonwealth. . . . One of the precautions which he proposes, and on which he appears ultimately to rely as a palladium to the weaker departments of power against the invasions of the stronger, is perhaps altogether his own. . . .

His proposition is "that whenever any two of the three branches of government shall concur in opinion, each by the voices of two thirds of their whole number, that a convention is necessary for altering the Constitution, or *correcting breaches of it,* a convention shall be called for the purpose."

As the people are the only legitimate fountain of power, and it is from them that the constitutional charter, under which the several branches of government hold their power, is derived, it seems strictly consonant to the republican theory to recur to the same original authority, not only whenever it may be necessary to enlarge, diminish, or new-model the powers of government, but also whenever any one of the departments may commit encroachments on the chartered authorities of the others. The several departments being perfectly co-ordinate by the terms of their common commission, neither of them, it is evident, can pretend to an exclusive or superior right of settling the boundaries between their respective powers; and how are the encroachments of the stronger to be prevented, or the wrongs of the weaker to be redressed, without an appeal to the people themselves, who, as the grantors of the commission, can alone declare its true meaning, and enforce its observance? . . .

In the next place, it may be considered as an objection inherent in the principle that as every appeal to the people would carry an implication of some defect in the government, frequent appeals would, in great measure, deprive the government of that veneration which time bestows on everything, and without which perhaps the wisest and freest governments would

From *The Federalist.*

not possess the requisite stability. If it be true that all governments rest on opinion, it is no less true that the strength of opinion in each individual, and its practical influence on his conduct, depend much on the number which he supposes to have entertained the same opinion. The reason of man, like man himself, is timid and cautious when left alone, and acquires firmness and confidence in proportion to the number with which it is associated. When the examples which fortify opinion are *ancient* as well as *numerous,* they are known to have a double effect. In a nation of philosophers, this consideration ought to be disregarded. A reverence for the laws would be sufficiently inculcated by the voice of an enlightened reason. But a nation of philosophers is as little to be expected as the philosophical race of kings wished for by Plato. And in every other nation, the most rational government will not find it a superfluous advantage to have the prejudices of the community on its side.

The danger of disturbing the public tranquillity by interesting too strongly the public passions is a still more serious objection against a frequent reference of constitutional questions to the decision of the whole society. Notwithstanding the success which has attended the revisions of our established forms of government and which does so much honor to the virtue and intelligence of the people of America, it must be confessed that the experiments are of too ticklish a nature to be unnecessarily multiplied. We are to recollect that all the existing constitutions were formed in the midst of a danger which repressed the passions most unfriendly to order and concord; of an enthusiastic confidence of the people in their patriotic leaders, which stifled the ordinary diversity of opinions on great national questions; of a universal ardor for new and opposite forms, produced by a universal resentment and indignation against the ancient government; and whilst no spirit of party connected with the changes to be made, or the abuses to be reformed, could mingle its leaven in the operation. The future situations in which we must expect to be usually placed do not present any equivalent security against the danger which is apprehended.

But the greatest objection of all is that the decisions which would probably result from such appeals would not answer the purpose of maintaining the constitutional equilibrium of the government. We have seen that the tendency of republican governments is to an aggrandizement of the legislative at the expense of the other departments. The appeals to the people, therefore, would usually be made by the executive and judiciary departments. But whether made by one side or the other, would each side enjoy equal advantages on the trial? Let us view their different situations. The members of the executive and judiciary departments are few in number, and can be personally known to a small part only of the people. The latter, by the mode of their appointment, as well as by the nature and permanency of it, are too far removed from the people to share much in their preposses-sions. The former are generally the objects of jealousy and their administra-tion is always liable to be discolored and rendered unpopular. The members of the legislative department, on the other hand, are numerous. They are distributed and dwell among the people at large. Their connections of blood, of friendship, and of acquaintance embrace a great proportion of the most influential part of the society. The nature of their public trust im-plies a personal influence among the people, and that they are more imme-diately the confidential guardians of the rights and liberties of the people. With these advantages it can hardly be supposed that the adverse party would have an equal chance for a favorable issue.

But the legislative party would not only be able to plead their cause most successfully with the people. They would probably be constituted themselves the judges. The same influence which had gained them an elec-tion into the legislature would gain them a seat in the convention. . . .

57

California v. Bakke (1978)

Mr. Justice POWELL announced the judgment of the Court.

This case presents a challenge to the special admissions program of the petitioner, the Medical School of the University of California at Davis, which is designed to assure the admission of a specified number of students from certain minority groups. The Superior Court of California sustained respon-dent's challenge, holding that petitioner's program violated the California Constitution, Title VI of the Civil Rights Act of 1964, and the Equal Protec-tion Clause of the Fourteenth Amendment. The court enjoined petitioner from considering respondent's race or the race of any other applicant in making admissions decisions. It refused, however, to order respondent's admission to the Medical School, holding that he had not carried his burden of proving

From *Regents of the University of California v. Allan Bakke,* 438 U.S. 277 (1978).

that he would have been admitted but for the constitutional and statutory violations. The Supreme Court of California affirmed those portions of the trial court's judgment declaring the special admissions program unlawful and enjoining petitioner from considering the race of any applicant. It modified that portion of the judgment denying respondent's requested injunction and directed the trial court to order his admission.

For the reasons stated in the following opinion, I believe that so much of the judgment of the California court as holds petitioner's special admissions program unlawful and directs that respondent be admitted to the Medical School must be affirmed. . . .

I also conclude for the reasons stated in the following opinion that the portion of the court's judgment enjoining petitioner from according any consideration to race in its admissions process must be reversed. . . .

In this Court the parties neither briefed nor argued the applicability of Title VI of the Civil Rights Act of 1964. Rather, as had the California court, they focused exclusively upon the validity of the special admissions program under the Equal Protection Clause. Because it was possible, however, that a decision on Title VI might obviate resort to constitutional interpretation, we requested supplementary briefing on the statutory issue. . . .

The language of § 601, 78 Stat. 252, like that of the Equal Protection Clause, is majestic in its sweep:

> "No person in the United States shall, on the ground of race, color, or national origin, be excluded from participation in, be denied the benefits of, or be subjected to discrimination under any program or activity receiving Federal financial assistance."

The concept of "discrimination," like the phrase "equal protection of the laws," is susceptible of varying interpretations, for as Mr. Justice Holmes declared, "[a] word is not a crystal, transparent and unchanged, it is the skin of a living thought and may vary greatly in color and content according to the circumstances and the time in which it is used." We must, therefore, seek whatever aid is available in determining the precise meaning of the statute before us. . . .

The problem confronting Congress was discrimination against Negro citizens at the hands of recipients of federal moneys. . . . Over and over again, proponents of the bill detailed the plight of Negroes seeking equal treatment in such programs. There simply was no reason for Congress to consider the validity of hypothetical preferences that might be accorded minority citizens . . . .

In addressing that problem, supporters of Title VI repeatedly declared that the bill enacted constitutional principles. . . . In the Senate, Senator Humphrey declared that the purpose of Title VI was "to insure that Federal funds are spent in accordance with the Constitution and the moral sense of the Nation." Senator Ribicoff agreed that Title VI embraced the constitutional standard: "Basically, there is a constitutional restriction against discrimination in the use of federal funds; and Title VI simply spells out the procedure to be used in enforcing that restriction." Other Senators expressed similar views. . . .

In view of the clear legislative intent, Title VI must be held to proscribe only those racial classifications that would violate the Equal Protection Clause or the Fifth Amendment. . . .

The parties do disagree as to the level of judicial scrutiny to be applied to the special admissions program. Petitioner argues that the court below erred in applying strict scrutiny . . . . That level of review, petitioner asserts, should be reserved for classifications that disadvantage "discrete and insular minorities." Respondent, on the other hand, contends that the California court correctly rejected the notion that the degree of judicial scrutiny accorded a particular racial or ethnic classification hinges upon membership in a discrete and insular minority and duly recognized that the "rights established [by the Fourteenth Amendment] are personal rights." . . .

The special admissions program is undeniably a classification based on race and ethnic background. To the extent that there existed a pool of at least minimally qualified minority applicants to fill the 16 special admissions seats, white applicants could compete only for 84 seats in the entering class, rather than the 100 open to minority applicants. . . .

The guarantees of the Fourteenth Amendment extend to all persons. . . . The guarantee of equal protection cannot mean one thing when applied to one individual and something else when applied to a person of another color. If both are not accorded the same protection, then it is not equal. . . . Racial and ethnic distinctions of any sort are inherently suspect and thus call for the most exacting judicial examination. . . .

Although many of the Framers of the Fourteenth Amendment conceived of its primary function as bridging the vast distance between members of the Negro race and the white "majority," the Amendment itself was framed in universal terms, without reference to color, ethnic origin, or condition of prior servitude. As this Court recently remarked in interpreting the 1866 Civil Rights Act to extend to claims of racial discrimination against white persons, "the 39th Congress was intent upon establishing in the federal law a broader principle than would have been necessary simply to meet the particular and immediate plight of the newly freed Negro slaves." . . .

Over the past 30 years, this Court has embarked upon the crucial mission of interpreting the Equal Protection Clause with the view of assuring to all persons "the protection of equal laws." . . .

Petitioner urges us to adopt for the first time a more restrictive view of the Equal Protection Clause and hold that discrimination against members of the white "majority" cannot be suspect if its purpose can be characterized as "benign." . . . It is far too late to argue that the guarantee of equal protection to *all* persons permits the recognition of special wards entitled to a degree of protection greater than that accorded others. . . .

[T]he difficulties entailed in varying the level of judicial review according to a perceived "preferred" status of a particular racial or ethnic minority are intractable. The concepts of "majority" and "minority" necessarily reflect temporary arrangements and political judgments. As observed above, the white "majority" itself is composed of various minority groups, most of which can lay claim to a history of prior discrimination at the hands of the State and private individuals. Not all of these groups can receive preferential treatment and corresponding judicial tolerance of distinctions drawn in terms of race and nationality, for then the only "majority" left would be a new minority of white Anglo-Saxon Protestants. There is no principled basis for deciding which groups would merit "heightened judicial solicitude" and which would not. Courts would be asked to evaluate the extent of the prejudice and consequent harm suffered by various minority groups. Those whose societal injury is thought to exceed some arbitrary level of tolerability then would be entitled to preferential classifications at the expense of individuals belonging to other groups. Those classifications would be free from exacting judicial scrutiny. As these preferences began to have their desired effect, and the consequences of past discrimination were undone, new judicial rankings would be necessary. The kind of variable sociological and political analysis necessary to produce such rankings simply does not lie within the judicial competence—even if they otherwise were politically feasible and socially desirable.

Moreover, there are serious problems of justice connected with the idea of preference itself. First, it may not always be clear that a so-called preference is in fact benign. . . . [P]referential programs may only reinforce common stereotypes holding that certain groups are unable to achieve success without special protection based on a factor having no relationship to individual worth. [Moreover,] there is a measure of inequity in forcing innocent persons in respondent's position to bear the burdens of redressing grievances not of their making.

By hitching the meaning of the Equal Protection Clause to these transitory considerations, we would be holding, as a constitutional principle, that judicial scrutiny of classifications touching on racial and ethnic background may vary with the ebb and flow of political forces. Disparate constitutional tolerance of such classifications well may serve to exacerbate racial and ethnic antagonisms rather than alleviate them. Also, the mutability of a constitutional principle, based upon shifting political and social judgments, undermines the chances for consistent application of the Constitution from one generation to the next, a critical feature of its coherent interpretation. In expounding the Constitution, the Court's role is to discern "principles sufficiently absolute to give them roots throughout the community and continuity over significant periods of time, and to lift them above the level of the pragmatic political judgments of a particular time and place." . . .

We have held that in "order to justify the use of a suspect classification, a State must show that its purpose or interest is both constitutionally permissible and substantial, and that its use of the classification is 'necessary . . . to the accomplishment' of its purpose or the safeguarding of its interest." The special admissions program purports to serve the purposes of: (i) "reducing the historic deficit of traditionally disfavored minorities in medical schools and in the medical profession," (ii) countering the effects of societal discrimination; (iii) increasing the number of physicians who will practice in communities currently underserved; and (iv) obtaining the educational benefits that flow from an ethnically diverse student body. It is necessary to decide which, if any, of these purposes is substantial enough to support the use of a suspect classification.

If petitioner's purpose is to assure within its student body some specified percentage of a particular group merely because of its race or ethnic origin, such a preferential purpose must be rejected not as insubstantial but as facially invalid. Preferring members of any one group for no reason other than race or ethnic origin is discrimination for its own sake. This the Constitution forbids. . . .

We have never approved a classification that aids persons perceived as members of relatively victimized groups at the expense of other innocent individuals in the absence of judicial, legislative, or administrative findings of constitutional or statutory violations. After such findings have been made, the governmental interest in preferring members of the injured groups at the expense of others is substantial, since the legal rights of the victims must be vindicated. In such a case, the extent of the injury and the consequent remedy will have been judicially, legislatively, or administratively defined. Also, the remedial action usually remains subject to continuing oversight to assure that it will work the least harm possible to other innocent persons competing for the benefit. Without such findings of constitutional or statutory violations, it cannot be said that the government has any greater interest in helping one individual than in refraining from harming another. Thus, the government has no compelling justification for inflicting such harm.

Petitioner does not purport to have made, and is in no position to make, such findings. Its broad mission is education, not the formulation of any legislative policy or the adjudication of particular claims of illegality. . . .

Petitioner identifies, as another purpose of its program, improving the delivery of health-care services to communities currently underserved. It may be assumed that in some situations a State's interest in facilitating the health care of its citizens is sufficiently compelling to support the use of a suspect classification. But there is virtually no evidence in the record indicating that petitioner's special admissions program is either needed or geared to promote that goal. . . . [T]here are more precise and reliable ways to identify applicants who are genuinely interested in the medical problems of minorities than by race. An applicant of whatever race who has demonstrated his concern for disadvantaged minorities in the past and who declares that practice in such a community is his primary professional goal would be more likely to contribute to alleviation of the medical shortage than one who is chosen entirely on the basis of race and disadvantage. . . .

The fourth goal asserted by petitioner is the attainment of a diverse student body. This clearly is a constitutionally permissible goal for an institution of higher education. Physicians serve a heterogeneous population. An otherwise qualified medical student with a particular background—whether it be ethnic, geographic, culturally advantaged or disadvantaged—may bring to a professional school of medicine experiences, outlooks, and ideas that enrich the training of its student body and better equip its graduates to render with understanding their vital service to humanity. . . .

It may be assumed that the reservation of a specified number of seats in each class for individuals from the preferred ethnic groups would contribute to the attainment of considerable ethnic diversity in the student body. But petitioner's argument that this is the only effective means of serving the interest of diversity is seriously flawed. . . . The diversity that furthers a compelling state interest encompasses a far broader array of qualifications and characteristics of which racial or ethnic origin is but a single though important element. . . .

The experience of other university admissions programs, which take race into account in achieving the educational diversity valued by the First Amendment, demonstrates that the assignment of a fixed number of places to a minority group is not a necessary means toward that end. An illuminating example is found in the Harvard College program . . . .

In such an admissions program, race or ethnic background may be deemed a "plus" in a particular applicant's file, yet it does not insulate the individual from comparison with all other candidates for the available seats. . . . This kind of program treats each applicant as an individual in the admissions process. The applicant who loses out on the last available seat to another candidate receiving a "plus" on the basis of ethnic background will not have been foreclosed from all consideration for that seat simply because he was not the right color or had the wrong surname. It would mean only that his combined qualifications, which may have included similar nonobjective factors, did not outweigh those of the other applicant. His qualifications would have been weighed fairly and competitively, and he would have no basis to complain of unequal treatment under the Fourteenth Amendment. . . .

In summary, it is evident that the Davis special admissions program involves the use of an explicit racial classification never before countenanced by this Court. It tells applicants who are not Negro, Asian, or Chicano that they are totally excluded from a specific percentage of the seats in an entering class. No matter how strong their qualifications, quantitative and extracurricular, including their own potential for contribution to educational diversity, they are never afforded the chance to compete with applicants from the preferred groups for the special admissions seats. At the same time, the preferred applicants have the opportunity to compete for every seat in the class.

The fatal flaw in petitioner's preferential program is its disregard of individual rights as guaranteed by the Fourteenth Amendment. Such rights are not absolute. But when a State's distribution of benefits or imposition of burdens hinges on ancestry or the color of a person's skin, that individual is entitled to a demonstration that the challenged classification is necessary to promote a substantial state interest. Petitioner has failed to carry this burden. For this reason, that portion of the California court's judgment holding petitioner's special admissions program invalid under the Fourteenth Amendment must be affirmed.

In enjoining petitioner from ever considering the race of any applicant, however, the courts below failed to recognize that the State has a substantial interest that legitimately may be served by a properly devised admissions program involving the competitive consideration of race and ethnic origin. For this reason, so much of the California court's judgment as enjoins petitioner from any consideration of the race of any applicant must be reversed. . . .

Opinion of Mr. Justice BRENNAN, Mr. Justice WHITE, Mr. Justice MARSHALL, and Mr. Justice BLACKMUN, concurring in the judgment in part and dissenting in part.

The threshold question we must decide is whether Title VI of the Civil Rights Act of 1964 bars recipients of federal funds from giving preferential consideration to disadvantaged members of racial minorities as part of a program designed to enable such individuals to surmount the obstacles imposed by racial discrimination. . . .

In our view, Title VI prohibits only those uses of racial criteria that would violate the Fourteenth Amendment if employed by a State or its agencies; it does not bar the preferential treatment of racial minorities as a means of remedying past societal discrimination to the extent that such action is consistent with the Fourteenth Amendment. . . .

The history of Title VI . . . reveals one fixed purpose: to give the Executive Branch of Government clear authority to terminate federal funding of private programs that use race as a means of disadvantaging minorities in a manner that would be prohibited by the Constitution if engaged in by government. . . . Congress' equating of Title VI's prohibition with the commands of the Fifth and Fourteenth Amendments, its refusal precisely to define that racial discrimination which it intended to prohibit, and its expectation that the statute would be administered in a flexible manner, compel the conclusion that Congress intended the meaning of the statute's prohibition to evolve with the interpretation of the commands of the Constitution. Thus, any claim that the use of racial criteria is barred by the plain language of the statute must fail in light of the remedial purpose of Title VI and its legislative history. . . .

Section 602 of Title VI instructs federal agencies to promulgate regulations interpreting Title VI. These regulations, which, under the terms of the statute, require Presidential approval, are entitled to considerable deference in construing Title VI. Consequently, it is most significant that the Department of Health, Education, and Welfare (HEW), which provides much of the federal assistance to institutions of higher education, has adopted regulations *requiring* affirmative measures designed to enable racial minorities which have been previously discriminated against by a federally funded institution or program to overcome the effects of such actions and *authorizing* the voluntary undertaking of affirmative-action programs by federally funded institutions that have not been guilty of prior discrimination in order to overcome the effects of conditions which have adversely affected the degree of participation by persons of a particular race. . . . These regulations clearly establish that where there is a need to overcome the effects of past racially discriminatory or exclusionary practices engaged in by a federally funded institution, race-conscious action is not only permitted but required to accomplish the remedial objectives of Title VI. . . .

Finally, congressional action subsequent to the passage of Title VI eliminates any possible doubt about Congress' views concerning the permissibility of racial preferences for the purpose of assisting disadvantaged racial minorities. It confirms that Congress did not intend to prohibit and does not now believe that Title VI prohibits the consideration of race as part of a remedy for societal discrimination even where there is no showing that the institution extending the preference has been guilty of past discrimination nor any judicial finding that the particular beneficiaries of the racial preference have been adversely affected by societal discrimination. . . .

Our cases have always implied that an "overriding statutory purpose" could be found that would justify racial classifications. . . . And in *North Carolina Board of Education v. Swann* we held, again unanimously, that a statute mandating color-blind school-assignment plans could not stand "against the background of segregation," since such a limit on remedies would "render illusory the promise of *Brown [I]*."

We conclude, therefore, that racial classifications are not *per se* invalid under the Fourteenth Amendment. Accordingly, we turn to the problem of articulating what our role should be in reviewing state action that expressly classifies by race. . . .

Unquestionably we have held that a government practice or statute which restricts "fundamental rights" or which contains "suspect classifications" is to be subjected to "strict scrutiny" and can be justified only if it furthers a compelling government purpose and, even then, only if no less restrictive alternative is available. But no fundamental right is involved here. Nor do whites as a class have any of the "traditional indicia of suspectness: the class is not saddled with such disabilities, or subjected to such a history of purposeful unequal treatment, or relegated to such a position of political powerlessness as to command extraordinary protection from the majoritarian political process." . . .

[B]ecause of the significant risk that racial classifications established for ostensibly benign purposes can be misused, causing effects not unlike those created by invidious classifications, it is inappropriate to inquire only whether there is any conceivable basis that might sustain such a classification. Instead, to justify such a classification an important and articulated purpose for its use must be shown. In addition, any statute must be stricken that stigmatizes any group or that singles out those least well represented in the political process to bear the brunt of a benign program. . . .

Davis' articulated purpose of remedying the effects of past societal discrimination is, under our cases, sufficiently important to justify the use of race-conscious admissions programs where there is a sound basis for concluding that minority underrepresentation is substantial and chronic, and that the handicap of past discrimination is impeding access of minorities to the Medical School. . . .

Properly construed . . . our prior cases unequivocally show that a state government may adopt race-conscious programs if the purpose of such programs is to remove the disparate racial impact its actions might otherwise have and if there is reason to believe that the disparate impact is itself the product of past discrimination, whether its own or that of society at large. There is no question that Davis' program is valid under this test.

Certainly, on the basis of the undisputed factual submissions before this Court, Davis had a sound basis for believing that the problem of underrepresentation of minorities was substantial and chronic and that the problem was attributable to handicaps imposed on minority applicants by past and present racial discrimination. Until at least 1973, the practice of medicine in this country was, in fact, if not in law, largely the prerogative of whites. . . .

Davis clearly could conclude that the serious and persistent underrepresentation of minorities in medicine depicted by these statistics is the result of handicaps under which minority applicants labor as a consequence of a background of deliberate, purposeful discrimination against minorities in education and in society generally, as well as in the medical profession. From the inception of our national life, Negroes have been subjected to unique legal disabilities impairing access to equal educational opportunity. . . . The generation of minority students applying to Davis Medical School since it opened in 1968—most of whom were born before or about the time *Brown I* was decided—clearly have been victims of this discrimination. Judicial decrees recognizing discrimination in public education in California testify to the fact of widespread discrimination suffered by California-born minority applicants; many minority group members living in California, moreover, were born and reared in school districts in Southern States segregated by law. Since separation of school-children by race "generates a feeling of inferiority as to their status in the community that may affect their hearts and minds in a way unlikely ever to be undone," *Brown I,* the conclusion is inescapable that applicants to medical school must be few indeed who endured the effects of *de jure* segregation, the resistance to *Brown I,* or the equally debilitating pervasive private discrimination fostered by our long history of official discrimination, and yet come to the starting line with an education equal to whites. . . .

The second prong of our test—whether the Davis program stigmatizes any discrete group or individual and whether race is reasonably used in light of the program's objectives—is clearly satisfied by the Davis program.

It is not even claimed that Davis' program in any way operates to stigmatize or single out any discrete and insular, or even any identifiable, non-minority group. Nor will harm comparable to that imposed upon racial minorities by exclusion or separation on grounds of race be the likely result of the program. It does not, for example, establish an exclusive preserve for minority students apart from and exclusive of whites. Rather, its purpose is to overcome the effects of segregation by bringing the races together. True, whites are excluded from participation in the special admissions program, but this fact only operates to reduce the number of whites to be admitted in the regular admissions program in order to permit admission of a reasonable percentage—less than their proportion of the California population—of otherwise underrepresented qualified minority applicants.

Nor was Bakke in any sense stamped as inferior by the Medical School's rejection of him. Indeed, it is conceded by all that he satisfied those criteria regarded by the school as generally relevant to academic performance better than most of the minority members who were admitted. Moreover, there is absolutely no basis for concluding that Bakke's rejection as a result of Davis' use of racial preference will affect him throughout his life in the same way as the segregation of the Negro schoolchildren in *Brown I* would have affected them. Unlike discrimination against racial minorities, the use of racial preferences for remedial purposes does not inflict a pervasive injury upon individual whites in the sense that wherever they go or whatever they do there is a significant likelihood that they will be treated as second-class citizens because of their color. . . .

Accordingly, we would reverse the judgment of the Supreme Court of California holding the Medical School's special admissions program unconstitutional and directing respondent's admission, as well as that portion of the judgment enjoining the Medical School from according any consideration to race in the admissions process.

Mr. Justice BLACKMUN.

I participate fully, of course, in the opinion that bears the names of my Brothers BRENNAN, WHITE, MARSHALL, and myself. I add only some general observations that hold particular significance for me, and then a few comments on equal protection.

It is gratifying to know that the Court at least finds it constitutional for an academic institution to take race and ethnic background into consideration as one factor, among many, in the administration of its admissions program. I presume that that factor always has been there, though perhaps not conceded or even admitted. It is a fact of life, however, and a part of the real world of which we are all a part. The sooner we get down the road toward accepting and being a part of the real world, and not shutting it out and away from us, the sooner will these difficulties vanish from the scene.

I suspect that it would be impossible to arrange an affirmative-action program in a racially neutral way and have it successful. To ask that this be so is to demand the impossible. In order to get beyond racism, we must first take account of race. There is no other way. And in order to treat some persons equally, we must treat them differently. We cannot—we dare not—let the Equal Protection Clause perpetuate racial supremacy.

So the ultimate question, as it was at the beginning of this litigation, is: Among the qualified, how does one choose?

A long time ago, as time is measured for this Nation, a Chief Justice, both wise and farsighted, said:

"In considering this question, then, we must never forget, that it is *a constitution* we are expounding." *McCulloch v. Maryland.*

In the same opinion, the Great Chief Justice further observed:

"Let the end be legitimate, let it be within the scope of the constitution, and all means which are appropriate, which are plainly adapted to that end, which are not prohibited, but consist with the letter and spirit of the constitution, are constitutional."

More recently, one destined to become a Justice of this Court observed:

"The great generalities of the constitution have a content and a significance that vary from age to age." B. Cardozo.

And an educator who became a President of the United States said:

> "But the Constitution of the United States is not a mere lawyer's document: it is a vehicle of life, and its spirit is always the spirit of the age." W. Wilson, Constitutional Government in the United States.

These precepts of breadth and flexibility and ever-present modernity are basic to our constitutional law. Today, again, we are expounding a *Constitution*. The same principles that governed *McCulloch's* case in 1819 govern *Bakke's* case in 1978. There can be no other answer.

Mr. Justice STEVENS, with whom THE CHIEF JUSTICE, Mr. Justice STEWART, and Mr. Justice REHNQUIST join, concurring in the judgment in part and dissenting in part.

. . . Both petitioner and respondent have asked us to determine the legality of the University's special admissions program by reference to the Constitution. Our settled practice, however, is to avoid the decision of a constitutional issue if a case can be fairly decided on a statutory ground. "If there is one doctrine more deeply rooted than any other in the process of constitutional adjudication, it is that we ought not to pass on questions of constitutionality . . . unless such adjudication is unavoidable." The more important the issue, the more force there is to this doctrine. In this case, we are presented with a constitutional question of undoubted and unusual importance. Since, however, a dispositive statutory claim was raised at the very inception of this case, and squarely decided in the portion of the trial court judgment affirmed by the California Supreme Court, it is our plain duty to confront it. Only if petitioner should prevail on the statutory issue would it be necessary to decide whether the University's admissions program violated the Equal Protection Clause of the Fourteenth Amendment.

Section 601 of the Civil Rights Act of 1964 provides:

> "No person in the United States shall, on the ground of race, color, or national origin, be excluded from participation in, be denied the benefits of, or be subjected to discrimination under any program or activity receiving Federal financial assistance."

The University, through its special admissions policy, excluded Bakke from participation in its program of medical education because of his race. The University also acknowledges that it was, and still is, receiving federal financial assistance. The plain language of the statute therefore requires affirmance of the judgment below. . . .

Title VI is an integral part of the far-reaching Civil Rights Act of 1964. No doubt, when this legislation was being debated, Congress was not directly concerned with the legality of "reverse discrimination" or "affirmative action" programs. Its attention was focused on the problem at hand, the "glaring . . . discrimination against Negroes which exists throughout our Nation," and, with respect to Title VI, the federal funding of segregated facilities. The genesis of the legislation, however, did not limit the breadth of the solution adopted. Just as Congress responded to the problem of employment discrimination by enacting a provision that protects all races, so, too, its answer to the problem of federal funding of segregated facilities stands as a broad prohibition against the exclusion of *any* individual from a federally funded program "on the ground of race." . . .

Petitioner contends, however, that exclusion of applicants on the basis of race does not violate Title VI if the exclusion carries with it no racial stigma. No such qualification or limitation of § 601's categorical prohibition of "exclusion" is justified by the statute or its history. . . . The legislative history reinforces this reading. The only suggestion that § 601 would allow exclusion of nonminority applicants came from opponents of the legislation . . . . In response, the proponents of the legislation gave repeated assurances that the Act would be "colorblind" in its application. . . .

As with other provisions of the Civil Rights Act, Congress' expression of its policy to end racial discrimination may independently proscribe conduct that the Constitution does not. However, we need not decide the congruence— or lack of congruence—of the controlling statute and the Constitution since the meaning of the Title VI ban on exclusion is crystal clear: Race cannot be the basis of excluding anyone from participation in a federally funded program. . . .

The University's special admissions program violated Title VI of the Civil Rights Act of 1964 by excluding Bakke from the medical school because of his race. It is therefore our duty to affirm the judgment ordering Bakke admitted to the University.

58

L. Peter Schultz

The Supreme Court, Affirmative Action, and the Judicial Function (1990)

The Bakke case presents a most interesting "alignment of forces" on the court. On the one hand, four Justices, viz., Berger, Rehnquist, Stevens and Stewart, voted to invalidate the Davis affirmative action program under the Civil Rights Act of 1964. For reasons to be discussed shortly, these four Justices may be labeled "restraintists." On the other hand, four Justices, viz., Blackmun, Brennan, Marshall and White voted to uphold the Davis program under the 1964 Civil Rights Act and under the Constitution. These Justices may be called "activists." Finally, there is Justice Powell who unlike the restraintists reached the constitutional issue, but unlike the activists found the Davis program unconstitutional. The question arises then: What is Justice Powell, an activist, a restraintist, or something else altogether? This comment explores this question with an eye to illuminating the function of the Supreme Court.

We begin with the "restraintists" and their spokesman, Justice Stevens. At first, it may seem odd to label these Justices "restraintists" insofar as the doctrine of judicial restraint was born out of a concern with judicial activity that invalidated legislative or executive action, especially legislation deemed to be "progressive." However, applying this label to Justice Stevens, et. al., in *Bakke* is accurate for two reasons. First, Stevens stakes a claim to this label in his opinion:

> Our settled practice is to avoid the decision of a constitutional issue if a case can be fairly decided on a statutory ground. "If there is one doctrine more deeply rooted than any other in the process of constitutional adjudication, it is that we ought not pass on questions of constitutionality" unless such adjudication is unavoidable. The more important the issue, the more force there is to this doctrine.

And Justice Stevens argues that the doctrines should be applied even in cases such as *Bakke* which present "a constitutional question of undoubted and unusual importance."

By permission of the author.

There is little doubt then that Stevens wants to appear as a restraintist following a deeply rooted principle which commends judicial modesty vis-à-vis constitutional issues. Moreover, this stance is consistent with the doctrine of judicial restraint because, whatever the practical concerns that motivated the formulation of this doctrine, its assumptions point to the conclusion that the Court should not, except when absolutely necessary, decide constitutional questions. The doctrine's two basic assumptions are (1) the Court is not democratic and (2) the Constitution is or should be "alive." These assumptions are related in that "the living Constitution" puts a premium on adaptation in accordance with the wishes of the people. Restraintists do not dispute "the notion of a living Constitution," but they do dispute the legitimacy or ability of the Court to breathe life into that document. Primarily, bestowing life on the Constitution is the function of the more representative or political departments of the government, Congress and the executive or the same departments of state governments. This implies, however, that for the most part the court's judicial function does not comprehend deciding constitutional questions. As Stevens' opinion in *Bakke* illustrates, the Court should limit its concern to statutory interpretation whenever possible. Avoiding the constitutional aspect of "questions of undoubted and unusual importance" comports fully with the doctrine of judicial restraint, even if such avoidance results in invalidating "progressive" legislation.

While seemingly commendable for its modesty, such a stance is potentially injurious to the Constitution. Is the Constitution a clean slate upon which Congress and the states may write largely as they please? So the doctrine of judicial restraint implies, especially as this doctrine is expressed by Justice Stevens: "The more important the issue, the more force there is to this doctrine [of avoidance]." That is, for the most important issues, judicial silence is most appropriate. Now a few cases come to mind—e.g. *Dred Scott*—when avoidance of constitutional issues may have been commendable. But were judicial avoidance to become the rule in cases of such great import, the silence might be deafening and perhaps fatal to constitutional government.

Interestingly the Constitution fares little better with the activists, who agree with the restraintists that the Constitution is "alive". However, lacking the modesty of the restraintists, the activists are willing to supply this "defect" by helping to assure the "viability" of the Constitution through adaptation. Justice Blackmun, after quoting Chief Justice Marshall in *McCulloch* that "it is a constitution we are expounding", (2808) quotes first Cardozo and then Woodrow Wilson as follows:

> The great generalities of the Constitution have a content and significance that vary from age to age.
>
> . . . the Constitution of the United States is not a mere lawyer's document, it is a vehicle of life, and its spirit is always the spirit of the ages.

Blackmun concludes by asserting that "These precepts of breadth and flexibility and *ever-present modernity* are basic to our constitutional law. Today, again, we are expounding a *Constitution*." (2808)

Now to say that the spirit of the Constitution "is *always* the spirit of the age" is to say that the Constitution has no abiding spirit of its own. Whatever else might be said of this assertion, it is not one that finds support in Marshall's opinion in *McCulloch*. There Marshall said: "Let the end be legitimate, let it be within the scope of the constitution, and all means which are appropriate, which are fairly adapted to that end, which are not prohibited, but consist with the letter and *spirit of the constitution,* are constitutional." For Marshall, the means employed toward legitimate ends should be judged by the Constitution, by *its* spirit. Also, the ends as well as the means should be judged by the Constitution. For Marshall, "the great generalities of the Constitution" are not distinguished by their "flexibility" or "ever-present modernity" but by their comprehensiveness. When Marshall admonishes us to remember that the Court is expounding a constitution, he admonishes us to remember not that the Constitution is infinitely "progressive" or adaptable to an ever-emerging "reality", but that its principles comprehend "the various crises of human affairs." Thus for Marshall, constitutional *interpretation,* saying what the law is, is the foremost function of the Court, whereas for the activists in *Bakke* the Court's foremost function is constitutional *adaptation.*

The activists are not aware, however, of the degree to which they "tinker" with the Constitution. For them, "the spirit of the age" is determined by history and necessity, past deeds and current needs. Past discrimination justifies race conscious policies today because, in the words of Justice Blackmun, "We cannot—we dare not—let the Equal Protection Clause perpetuate racial supremacy." (2807) These policies are temporary, their necessity ending where the results of past injustices are eradicated. The problem here is that "ideals" rather than needs determine the spirit of any age and the policies which arise therein. Affirmative action policies are no exception, resting on an ideal—simple egalitarianism—which is at odds with equal opportunity or the notion of life as a race among competing but unequally endowed individuals. Affirmative action programs cannot be temporary because that which they are said to modify, equal opportunity, does not and was not intended to result in the degree of equality sought by radical egalitarians. The activists in *Bakke* are not then the servants of "reality" or "progress" they pretend to be; rather, they are the vanguard of an egalitarian ideal in conflict with equal opportunity. As Woodrow Wilson knew, keeping the Constitution in touch with "the spirit of the age" sometimes requires radical reform or change.

Apparently aware of this, Justice Powell cautions against allowing the questions raised in *Bakke* to be settled either without reference to or by adaptation of constitutional principle. He rejects the restraintists' attempt to avoid the constitutional issue, arguing that given the purpose of the 1964 Civil Rights Act affirmative action programs need to be considered under the Fourteenth Amendment. Speaking to the activists, Powell argues that the Constitution's principles protect all individuals, thereby prohibiting almost all racial classifications or race conscious policies:

> The guarantee of the Fourteenth Amendment extends to all persons. Its language is explicit. . . . It is settled beyond question that the "rights created by . . . the Fourteenth Amendment are . . . guaranteed to the individual. The rights established are personal rights." The guarantee of equal protection cannot mean one thing when applied to one individual and something else when applied to a person of another color. (2747-8)

Moreover, Powell rejects the activists' position that the Fourteenth Amendment permits "benign" discrimination—drawing distinctions that favor rather than stigmatize a particular group. Such discrimination is not permissible, Powell maintains, because there is "no *principled* basis for deciding which groups would merit 'heightened judicial solicitude' and which would not. . . . By hitching the meaning of the Equal Protection clause to . . . transitory considerations, we would be holding, *as a constitutional principle,* that judicial scrutiny of classifications touching on racial and ethnic background may vary with the ebb and flow of political forces." (2751-2) Again, the activists have no principled way to determine which state-imposed racial classifications "stigmatize." All such classifications cause "resentment" and justifiably so: "One should not lightly dismiss *the inherent unfairness* of . . . a system of allocating benefits and privileges on the basis of color and ethnic origin." (2750, note 34). The activists "offer no principle for deciding whether preferential classifications reflect a benign remedial purpose or a malevolent stigmatic classification, since they . . . accept mere *post hoc* declarations by an isolated state entity . . . unadorned by particularized findings of past discrimination." *(ibid.)*

If the Constitution is color-blind, why then does Justice Powell not strike down all race-conscious policies? Powell's refusal to do this has left him open to the charge that his "judicial statesmanship" is merely a thinly-veiled policy of expediency. Not so much constitutional principle as compromise explains Powell's opinion in *Bakke*.

Powell's argument is that the color-blind principle or rule has never been absolute: "All legal restrictions which curtail the civil rights of a single racial group are immediately suspect . . . not to say . . . unconstitutional . . . [But] courts must subject them to the most rigid scrutiny." (2748) Subjecting the Davis program to such scrutiny, it is unconstitutional because it excludes some applicants from competing for some seats *solely* on grounds of race: "The fatal flaw in the petitioner's preferential program is its disregard of individual rights as guaranteed by the Fourteenth Amendment." (2763) Powell does find a constitutional justification for considering race as one factor in admissions, viz., the first amendment and academic freedom asserted for the sake of diversity: "it is not too much to say that the 'nation's future depends upon leaders trained through wide exposure' to the ideas and mores of students as diverse as this Nation of many peoples." (2761) Viewed in this way, the Constitution does not require educational institutions to ignore race any more than it requires them to ignore religion, sex or place of residence. However, the Constitution does forbid such institutions excluding anyone *solely* on grounds of race.

Does Powell's opinion meet the standard of judicial statesmanship? If judicial statesmanship refers to enunciating absolute rules, then it cannot be said Powell rises to the challenge. But if judicial statesmanship refers to enunciating deeply-rooted or constitutionally nurtured principles, then Powell has risen to the occasion. Of course, Powell's interpretation of the strict scrutiny test will not satisfy all, but it does appear consistent with the Fourteenth Amendment in that race cannot be the determinative factor in allocating privileges. Race may be considered but it may not be considered *decisive*.

Although in *Bakke* Powell exercised judicial statesmanship in applying constitutional principle, the post-*Bakke* Court has not always followed this standard in dealing with affirmative action. In some instances, those in which the burdens implied by affirmative action are diffused, the Court has upheld state action that gives preferential treatment to minorities. This is the case in *Fulilove v. Klutznick* (1980), where the Court held a federal law constitutional although it required that ten per cent of all federal funds for local public works projects be allocated to minority-owned businesses. While such state action is inconsistent with *Bakke's* holding that race cannot be the determinative or decisive factor in allocating privileges, the burden on non-minority businesses was diffused and indirect. In other cases, where the burden imposed by preferential policies is direct and burdensome, as when someone loses a job, the Court has not allowed race-conscious policies. In two 1980 cases (*Firefighters Local Union 1784 v. Stotts* and *Wygant v. Jackson Board of Education*), for example, where the Court upheld the claims of whites who had been laid off before blacks with less seniority, the burden was direct and heavy. In allowing diffused burdens, and in forbidding direct ones, the Court appears to be reacting against the infliction of pain rather than upholding constitutional principle. Without the kind of appeal to constitutional principle that we find in Powell's opinion in *Bakke,* the Court follows a policy of accommodation toward whatever wind seems strongest—or whatever pain seems greatest—in particular cases.

But why should we be concerned with whether the Court rose to the level of judicial statesmanship, i.e., of thinking through and applying fundamental constitutional principles? After all, the Court is a political institution, as are

Congress and the presidency. Why should the Court be expected to recur to constitutional principle rather than solving political problems in the most timely way?

The answer, it must be admitted, is not perfectly clear. Timeliness is often of the essence in politics. As Publius knew, energy is one, and may even be the essential, ingredient of good government. But energy, according to Publius, belonged primarily to the Executive. Other institutions of government were intended to embody and foster other characteristics of good government. Publius also wrote that "veneration" of and "reverence" for the law are indispensable to stable and decent government. If time is to generate the requisite veneration for law, as Publius hoped, the fundamental law or the Constitution cannot be seen to change with the temporary needs of the age, as proponents of the "living Constitution" proclaim. Moreover, Publius may be incorrect in assuming that time always produces veneration, for in a democracy "old" is often treated as a suspect category. Judicial statesmanship—recurrence to the permanent principles of the Constitution—not only counteracts the notion of change implied in the doctrine of a "living Constitution," but in the best cases explains to citizens why the old is good. It is asking much of any institution, and especially a political institution, to reach so high, but such is the function constitutional government forces the Supreme Court to perform.

Chapter VI

Politics and Economics

How much government regulation of the economy is desirable? What is the proper relationship between politics and economics? Conservatives typically support some version of laissez-faire capitalism, while liberals advocate some version of the welfare state. Milton Friedman argues for minimal interference in the economy, on the ground that economic freedom is both itself an important component of freedom and the condition for political freedom. For Friedman, economic power should be independent of political power in order to check political power; socialism, by destroying economic liberty, destroys a protector of political freedom. Furthermore, a market economy can coordinate the activities of large numbers of individuals without resorting to coercion: each person pursues his own interest by voluntarily entering into relations with others. Government therefore should be primarily an umpire of economic activity.

Friedman's views stand in sharp contrast to the welfare state that Franklin D. Roosevelt established and defended. According to FDR, the rights of the Declaration of Independence must be redefined as social conditions change. By adding to the freedoms of religion and speech the new freedoms, the freedom from fear and the freedom from want, FDR gives to politics a new aim—making men happy by contenting them with their lot. Since a commercial society depends on the dynamism of individual acquisitiveness in a competitive market, FDR's new freedoms promote a distrust of such a society. Cooperation will replace competition in a future where the individual advances along a road on which thousands of others also advance, practicing "reciprocal self-denial" for the sake of the common advantage.

FDR says that the task has become one of distributing and administering rather than producing wealth. However, it is not entirely clear in his thought whether it is the success or the failure of the commercial republic that dictates the redefinition of political goals. He argues that we must end competition because the frontiers have closed and opportunity for advancement no longer exists. Yet he also speaks of the enjoyment of the fruits of scientific progress with an ever rising standard of living as one of the basic things we can expect government to provide in the welfare state.

Both the viability and the desirability of the welfare state are, however, open to question. Irving Kristol argues that the welfare state is premised on the belief that the government can "manage and manipulate" aggregate demand so as to maintain a healthy economy. But Kristol contends that such comprehensive centralized planning is impossible. Furthermore, he suggests that the attempt to "manage" the economy destroys the individual incentives that cause a productive economy. Kristol claims that supply-side economics seeks to correct the utopianism of centralized planning and to restore the incentives necessary for a sound economy.

In the early 19th century Alexis de Tocqueville expressed the fear that in democracies the people would gradually give up their independence in exchange for the security offered by a powerful national government. Such a state would be a "soft despotism" in which men become passive, their basic needs taken care of by a benevolent government on whom they would eventually become completely dependent. Equal prosperity might be attained at the price of dignity and freedom.

A consideration of earlier views on the relationship between government and economics helps to place the current debate in a broader perspective. As we see from his *Report on Manufacturers,* Hamilton favors government regulation of the economy. Congress is empowered to do so, he argues, by the general welfare clause of the Constitution. The constitutionality of much New Deal legislation is also derived from this clause. Although Hamilton thus shares with FDR a concept of active government, Hamilton is one of the greatest proponents of a commercial republic. He wants government to promote manufactures in order to increase productivity and therewith the wealth of the community. A prosperous nation, he argues, is a strong nation, subservient to no other country. FDR's emphasis on "the sufficiency of life" rather than Hamilton's "plethora of riches" seems to make him more like Jefferson than Hamilton, who thought that the United States should aspire "to a state of opulence." We cannot, however, conclude that FDR advocated Hamilton's means to Jefferson's ends. While both FDR and Jefferson decry the desire for excess, Jefferson speaks of the self-sufficiency of the farmer rather than the simple sufficiency of life. He opposes the promotion of manufactures because of the effect such work has on men—subservience, venality, and the stifling of virtue. Artisans are not fit citizens of a republic but the tools of a despot. In both Jefferson and Hamilton, we can see an emphasis on independence and pride that is missing in FDR's thought. For Jefferson, farming promotes the self-dependence of the individual; for Hamilton, manufactures promotes the self-dependence of the nation.

While Jefferson and Hamilton disagree about the character of the republic that economic policy should promote, they both consider the long-term political effects of economic policy on the kind of country the United States should be. Such considerations are absent in both FDR and Friedman. While

Friedman does make freedom his end, he does not adequately consider the political conditions and ends of economic freedom. For both FDR and Friedman, politics is in the service of economics: for Friedman government regulates the acquisition of material benefits, and for FDR government itself is the dispenser of these benefits. The subordination of the public to the private stems from a denial that there are standards of right and wrong that a people can hold in common. Friedman, for example, argues that we should not coerce someone we see making a mistake, for, after all, he may be right and we wrong. Similarly, FDR cannot maintain that men have any rights in common, such as the natural rights referred to in the Declaration: since statesmen must redefine human rights as the social conditions change, there are at best only different rights for different social conditions.

Zuckert thinks that economic policy should be made to serve political ends. What economic policies, she asks, best enable a regime to guarantee to all the right to pursue happiness? She examines the rule of the middle-class majority to see whether it can be justified by its effects on the two economic extremes, the rich and the poor. The majority's claim that it secures the right of all to pursue happiness is supported because the majority both protects the wealth of the rich *and* gives welfare to the poor. Policies that include economic incentives are appropriate to such a regime because they foster habits in the citizens, such as individual effort, forethought, and self-control, that are necessary to maintain a free regime. Zuckert turns to Tocqueville as a model. Because private economic associations foster the habits conducive to political freedom, Tocqueville taught democratic statesmen that they should encourage the formation of such associations. Tocqueville thus offers some hope that we may avoid the soft despotism of the welfare state by means of carefully-framed policies. Zuckert both reminds us of this possibility and also shows us that welfare can be consistent with the premises of our regime and does not necessarily require a reformulation of them on egalitarian grounds.

59

Milton Friedman

Capitalism and Freedom (1962)

In a much quoted passage in his inaugural address, President Kennedy said, "Ask not what your country can do for you—ask what you can do for your country." It is a striking sign of the temper of our times that the controversy about this passage centered on its origin and not on its content. Neither half of the statement expresses a relation between the citizen and his government that is worthy of the ideals of free men in a free society. The paternalistic "what your country can do for you" implies that government is the patron, the citizen the ward, a view that is at odds with the free man's belief in his own responsibility for his own destiny. The organismic, "what you can do for your country" implies that government is the master or the deity, the citizen, the servant or the votary. To the free man, the country is the collection of individuals who compose it, not something over and above them. . . . He recognizes no national purpose except as it is the consensus of the purposes for which the citizens severally strive.

The free man will ask neither what his country can do for him nor what he can do for his country. He will ask rather "What can I and my compatriots do through government" to help us discharge our individual responsibilities, to achieve our several goals and purposes, and above all, to protect our freedom? . . . Government is necessary to preserve our freedom, it is an instrument through which we can exercise our freedom; yet by concentrating power in political hands, it is also a threat to freedom. . . .

How can we benefit from the promise of government while avoiding the threat to freedom? . . .

First, the scope of government must be limited. Its major function must be to protect our freedom both from the enemies outside our gates and from our fellow-citizens: to preserve law and order, to enforce private contracts, to foster competitive markets. Beyond this major function, government may enable us at times to accomplish jointly what we would find it more difficult or expensive to accomplish severally. However, any such use of government is fraught with danger. We should not and cannot avoid using government in this way. But there should be a clear and large balance of advantages before we do. By relying primarily on voluntary co-operation and private enterprise, in both economic and other activities, we can insure that the private sector is a check on the powers of the governmental sector and an effective protection of freedom of speech, of religion, and of thought.

The second broad principle is that government power must be dispersed. If government is to exercise power, better in the county than in the state, better in the state than in Washington. If I do not like what my local community does, be it in sewage disposal, or zoning, or schools, I can move to another local community, and though few may take this step, the mere possibility acts as a check. If I do not like what my state does, I can move to another. If I do not like what Washington imposes, I have few alternatives in this world of jealous nations. . . .

The preservation of freedom is the protective reason for limiting and decentralizing governmental power. But there is also a constructive reason. The great advances of civilization, whether in architecture or painting, in science or literature, in industry or agriculture, have never come from centralized government. . . .

Government can never duplicate the variety and diversity of individual action. At any moment in time, by imposing uniform standards in housing, or nutrition, or clothing, government could undoubtedly improve the level of living of many individuals; by imposing uniform standards in schooling, road construction, or sanitation, central government could undoubtedly improve the level of performance in many local areas and perhaps even on the average of all communities. But in the process, government would replace progress by stagnation, it would substitute uniform mediocrity for the variety essential for that experimentation which can bring tomorrow's laggards above today's mean. . . .

As it developed in the late eighteenth and early nineteenth centuries, the intellectual movement that went under the name of liberalism emphasized freedom as the ultimate goal and the individual as the ultimate entity in the society. It supported laissez faire at home as a means of reducing the role of the state in economic affairs and thereby enlarging the role of the individual. . . .

Beginning in the late nineteenth century, and especially after 1930 in the United States, the term liberalism came to be associated with a very different emphasis, particularly in economic policy. It came to be associated with a readiness to rely primarily on the state rather than on private voluntary arrangements to achieve objectives regarded as desirable. The catchwords became welfare and equality rather than freedom. The nineteenth-century liberal regarded an extension of freedom as the most effective way to promote welfare and equality; the twentieth-century liberal regards welfare and equality as either prerequisites of or alternatives to freedom. In the name of welfare and equality, the twentieth-century liberal has come to favor a revival of the very policies of state intervention and paternalism against which classical liberalism fought. . . .

* * * * * * * * * *

It is widely believed that politics and economics are separate and largely unconnected; that individual freedom is a political problem and material welfare an economic problem; and that any kind of political arrangements can be combined with any kind of economic arrangements. The chief contemporary manifestation of this idea is the advocacy of "democratic socialism" by many who condemn out of hand the restrictions on individual freedom imposed by "totalitarian socialism" in Russia, and who are persuaded that it is possible for a country to adopt the essential features of Russian economic arrangements and yet to ensure individual freedom through political arrangements. The thesis of this chapter is that such a view is a delusion. . . .

Economic arrangements play a dual role in the promotion of a free society. On the one hand, freedom in economic arrangements is itself a component of freedom broadly understood, so economic freedom is an end in itself. In the second place, economic freedom is also an indispensable means toward the achievement of political freedom.

The first of these roles of economic freedom needs special emphasis because intellectuals in particular have a strong bias against regarding this aspect of freedom as important. They tend to express contempt for what they regard as material aspects of life. . . .

A citizen of the United States who under the laws of various states is not free to follow the occupation of his own choosing unless he can get a license for it, is likewise being deprived of an essential part of his freedom. So is the man who would like to exchange some of his goods with, say, a Swiss for a watch but is prevented from doing so by a quota. So also is the Californian who was thrown into jail for selling Alka Seltzer at a price below that set by the manufacturer under so-called "fair trade" laws. So also is the farmer who cannot grow the amount of wheat he wants. And so on. Clearly, economic freedom, in and of itself, is an extremely important part of total freedom.

Viewed as a means to the end of political freedom, economic arrangements are important because of their effect on the concentration or dispersion of power. The kind of economic organization that provides economic freedom directly, namely, competitive capitalism, also promotes political freedom because it separates economic power from political power and in this way enables the one to offset the other. . . .

What are the logical links between economic and political freedom? In discussing these questions we shall consider first the market as a direct component of freedom, and then the indirect relation between market arrangements and political freedom. A by-product will be an outline of the ideal economic arrangements for a free society.

As liberals, we take freedom of the individual, or perhaps the family, as our ultimate goal in judging social arrangements. Freedom as a value in this sense has to do with the interrelations among people. . . . [I]n a society freedom has nothing to say about what an individual does with his freedom; it is not an all-embracing ethic. Indeed, a major aim of the liberal is to leave the ethical problem for the individual to wrestle with. The "really" important ethical problems are those that face an individual in a free society—what he should do with his freedom. . . .

The basic problem of social organization is how to co-ordinate the economic activities of large numbers of people. . . .

Literally millions of people are involved in providing one another with their daily bread, let alone with their yearly automobiles. The challenge to the believer in liberty is to reconcile this widespread interdependence with individual freedom.

Fundamentally, there are only two ways of co-ordinating the economic activities of millions. One is central direction involving the use of coercion—the technique of the army and of the modern totalitarian state. The other is voluntary co-operation of individuals—the technique of the market place.

The possibility of co-ordination through voluntary co-operation rests on the elementary—yet frequently denied—proposition that both parties to an economic transaction benefit from it, *provided the transaction is bilaterally voluntary and informed.*

Exchange can therefore bring about co-ordination without coercion. A working model of a society organized through voluntary exchange is a *free private enterprise exchange economy*—what we have been calling competitive capitalism. . . .

[I]n the complex enterprise and money-exchange economy, co-operation is strictly individual and voluntary *provided: (a)* that enterprises are private, so that the ultimate contracting parties are individuals and *(b)* that individuals are effectively free to enter or not to enter into any particular exchange, so that every transaction is strictly voluntary. . . .

So long as effective freedom of exchange is maintained, the central feature of the market organization of economic activity is that it prevents one person from interfering with another in respect of most of his activities. The consumer is protected from coercion by the seller because of the presence of other sellers with whom he can deal. The seller is protected from coercion by the consumer because of other consumers to whom he can sell. The employee is protected from coercion by the employer because of other employers for whom he can work, and so on. And the market does this impersonally and without centralized authority. . . .

The existence of a free market does not of course eliminate the need for government. On the contrary, government is essential both as a forum for determining the "rules of the game" and as an umpire to interpret and enforce the rules decided on. What the market does is to reduce greatly the range of issues that must be decided through political means, and thereby to minimize the extent to which government need participate directly in the game. The characteristic feature of action through political channels is that it tends to require or enforce substantial conformity. The great advantage of the market, on the other hand, is that it permits wide diversity. It is, in political terms, a system of proportional representation. Each man can vote, as it were, for the color of tie he wants and get it; he does not have to see what color the majority wants and then, if he is in the minority, submit.

It is this feature of the market that we refer to when we say that the market provides economic freedom. But this characteristic also has implications that go far beyond the narrowly economic. Political freedom means the absence of coercion of a man by his fellow men. . . . By removing the organization of economic activity from the control of political authority, the market eliminates this source of coercive power. It enables economic strength to be a check to political power rather than a reinforcement. . . .

One feature of a free society is surely the freedom of individuals to advocate and propagandize openly for a radical change in the structure of the society—so long as the advocacy is restricted to persuasion and does not include force or other forms of coercion. It is a mark of the political freedom of a capitalist society that men can openly advocate and work for socialism. Equally, political freedom in a socialist society would require that men be free to advocate the introduction of capitalism. How could the freedom to advocate capitalism be preserved and protected in a socialist society?

In order for men to advocate anything, they must in the first place be able to earn a living. This already raises a problem in a socialist society, since all jobs are under the direct control of political authorities. . . .

For advocacy of capitalism to mean anything, the proponents must be able to finance their cause—to hold public meetings, publish pamphlets, buy radio time, issue newspapers and magazines, and so on. How could they raise the funds? There might and probably would be men in the socialist society with large incomes, perhaps even large capital sums in the form of government bonds and the like, but these would of necessity be high public officials. . . .

The only recourse for funds would be to raise small amounts from a large number of minor officials. But this is no real answer. To tap these sources, many people would already have to be persuaded, and our whole problem is how to initiate and finance a campaign to do so. Radical movements in capitalist societies have never been financed this way. They have typically been supported by a few wealthy individuals who have become persuaded. . . . This is a role of inequality of wealth in preserving political freedom that is seldom noted—the role of the patron. . . .

[I]ndeed, it is not even necessary to persuade people or financial institutions with available funds of the soundness of the ideas to be propagated. It is only necessary to persuade them that the propagation can be financially successful; that the newspaper or magazine or book or other venture will be profitable. . . .

But we are not yet through. In a free market society, it is enough to have the funds. The suppliers of paper are as willing to sell it to the *Daily Worker* as to the *Wall Street Journal.* In a socialist society, it would not be enough to have the funds. The hypothetical supporter of capitalism would have to persuade a government factory making paper to sell to him, the government printing press to print his pamphlets, a government post office to distribute them among the people, a government agency to rent him a hall in which to talk, and so on. . . .

By contrast, it is clear how a free market capitalist society fosters freedom.

A striking practical example of these abstract principles is the experience of Winston Churchill. From 1933 to the outbreak of World War II, Churchill was not permitted to talk over the British radio, which was, of course, a government monopoly administered by the British Broadcasting Corporation. Here was a leading citizen of his country, a Member of Parliament, a former cabinet minister, a man who was desperately trying by every device possible to persuade his countrymen to take steps to ward off the menace of Hitler's Germany. He was not permitted to talk over the radio to the British people because the BBC was a government monopoly and his position was too "controversial." . . .

Another example of the role of the market in preserving political freedom, was revealed in our experience with McCarthyism. Entirely aside from the substantive issues involved, and the merits of the charges made, what protection did individuals, and in particular government employees, have against irresponsible accusations and probings into matters that it went against their conscience to reveal? Their appeal to the Fifth Amendment would have been a hollow mockery without an alternative to government employment.

Their fundamental protection was the existence of a private-market economy in which they could earn a living. . . .

* * * * * * * * * *

The "social security" program is one of those things on which the tyranny of the status quo is beginning to work its magic. Despite the controversy that surrounded its inception, it has come to be so much taken for granted that its desirability is hardly questioned any longer. Yet it involves a large-scale invasion into the personal lives of a large fraction of the nation without, so far as I can see, any justification that is at all persuasive, not only on liberal principles, but on almost any other. I propose to examine the biggest phase of it, that which involves payments to the aged.

As an operational matter, the program known as old age and survivor's insurance (OASI) consists of a special tax imposed on payrolls, plus payments to persons who have reached a specified age, of amounts determined by the age at which payments begin, family status, and prior earning record.

As an analytical matter, OASI consists of three separable elements:

1. The requirement that a wide class of persons must purchase specified annuities, i.e., compulsory provision for old age.

2. The requirement that the annuity must be purchased from the government; i.e., nationalization of the provision of these annuities.

3. A scheme for redistributing income, insofar as the value of the annuities to which people are entitled when they enter the system is not equal to the taxes they will pay.

Clearly, there is no necessity for these elements to be combined. . . .

Let us therefore consider each of these elements in turn to see how far, if at all, each can be justified. It will facilitate our analysis, I believe, if we consider them in reverse order.

1. Income redistribution. The present OASI program involves two major kinds of redistribution; from some OASI beneficiaries to others; from the general taxpayer to OASI beneficiaries.

The first kind of redistribution is primarily from those who entered the system relatively young, to those who entered it at an advanced age. The latter are receiving, and will for some time be receiving, a greater amount as benefits than the taxes they paid could have purchased. Under present tax and benefit schedules, on the other hand, those who entered the system at a young age will receive decidedly less.

I do not see any grounds—liberal or other—on which this particular redistribution can be defended. . . .

The second kind of redistribution arises because the system is not likely to be fully self-financing. During the period when many were covered and paying taxes, and few had qualified for benefits, the system appeared to be self-financing and indeed to be having a surplus. But this appearance depends on neglecting the obligation being accumulated with respect to the persons paying the tax. It is doubtful that the taxes paid have sufficed to finance the accumulated obligation. . . .

[Could] a subsidy from the general taxpayer . . . be justified if it is required[?] I see no grounds on which such a subsidy can be justified. We may wish to help poor people. Is there any justification for helping people whether they are poor or not because they happen to be a certain age? Is this not an entirely arbitrary redistribution?

The only argument I have ever come across to justify the redistribution involved in OASI is one that I regard as thoroughly immoral despite its wide use. This argument is that OASI redistribution on the average helps low-income people more than high-income people despite a large arbitrary element; that it would be better to do this redistribution more efficiently; but that the community will not vote for the redistribution directly though it will vote for it as part of a social security package. In essence, what this argument says is that the community can be fooled into voting for a measure that it opposes by presenting the measure in a false guise. . . .

2. *Nationalization of the provision of required annuities.* Suppose we avoid redistribution by requiring each person to pay for the annuity he gets, in the sense of course, that the premium suffices to cover the present value of the annuity, account being taken both of mortality and interest returns. What justification is there then for requiring him to purchase it from a governmental concern? If redistribution is to be accomplished, clearly the taxing power of the government must be used. But if redistribution is to be no part of the program . . . why not permit individuals who wish to do so to purchase their annuities from private concerns? . . .

Possible economies of scale are no argument for nationalizing the provision of annuities. If they are present, and the government sets up a concern to sell annuity contracts, it may be able to undersell competitors by virtue of its size. In that case, it will get the business without compulsion. If it cannot undersell them, then presumably economies of scale are not present or are not sufficient to overcome other diseconomies of governmental operation. . . .

3. *Compulsory Purchase of Annuities.* . . . One possible justification for such compulsion is strictly paternalistic. People could if they wished decide to do individually what the law requires them to do as a group. But they are separately short-sighted and improvident. "We" know better than "they" that it is in their own good to provide for their old age to a greater extent than they would voluntarily; we cannot persuade them individually; but we can persuade 51 per cent or more to compel all to do what is in their own good. This paternalism is for responsible people, hence does not even have the excuse of concern for children or madmen.

This position is internally consistent and logical. A thorough-going paternalist who holds it cannot be dissuaded by being shown that he is making a mistake in logic. He is our opponent on grounds of principle, not simply a well-meaning but misguided friend. Basically, he believes in dictatorship, benevolent and maybe majoritarian, but dictatorship none the less.

Those of us who believe in freedom must believe also in the freedom of individuals to make their own mistakes. If a man knowingly prefers to live for today, to use his resources for current enjoyment, deliberately choosing a penurious old age, by what right do we prevent him from doing so? We may argue with him, seek to persuade him that he is wrong, but are we entitled to use coercion to prevent him from doing what he chooses to do? Is there not always the possibility that he is right and that we are wrong? Humility is the distinguishing virtue of the believer in freedom; arrogance, of the paternalist. . . .

A possible justification on liberal principles for compulsory purchase of annuities is that the improvident will not suffer the consequence of their own action but will impose costs on others. We shall not, it is said, be willing to see the indigent aged suffer in dire poverty. We shall assist them by private and public charity. Hence the man who does not provide for his old age will become a public charge. Compelling him to buy an annuity is justified not for his own good but for the good of the rest of us. . . .

The belief that a large fraction of the community would become public charges if not compelled to purchase annuities owed its plausibility, at the time OASI was enacted, to the Great Depression. . . . This experience was unprecedented and has not been repeated since. It did not arise because people were improvident and failed to provide for their old age. . . .

Private arrangements for the care of the aged have altered greatly over time. Children were at one time the major means whereby people provided for their own old age. As the community became more affluent, the mores changed. The responsibilities imposed on children to care for their parents declined and more and more people came to make provision for old age in the form of accumulating property or acquiring private pension rights. More recently, the development of pension plans over and above OASI has accelerated. Indeed, some students believe that a continuation of present trends points to a society in which a large fraction of the public scrimps in their productive years to provide themselves with a higher standard of life in old age than they ever enjoyed in the prime of life. Some of us may think such a trend perverse, but if it reflects the tastes of the community, so be it.

Compulsory purchase of annuities has therefore imposed large costs for little gain. It has deprived all of us of control over a sizable fraction of our income, requiring us to devote it to a particular purpose, purchase of a retirement annuity, in a particular way, by buying it from a government concern. It has inhibited competition in the sale of annuities and the devel-

opment of retirement arrangements. It has given birth to a large bureaucracy that shows tendencies of growing by what it feeds on, of extending its
scope from one area of our life to another. And all this, to avoid the danger
that a few people might become charges on the public. . . .

60

Franklin Delano Roosevelt

The New Goals of Politics (1932, 1935, 1941)

. . . The issue of Government has always been whether individual
men and women will have to serve some system of Government or economics, or whether a system of Government and economics exists to serve individual men and women. . . .

A glance at the situation today only too clearly indicates that equality
of opportunity as we have known it no longer exists. Our industrial plant is
built; the problem just now is whether under existing conditions it is not
overbuilt. Our last frontier has long since been reached, and there is practically no more free land. . . .

Just as freedom to farm has ceased, so also the opportunity in business
has narrowed. It still is true that men can start small enterprises, trusting to
native shrewdness and ability to keep abreast of competitors; but area after
area has been preempted altogether by the great corporations, and even in
the fields which still have no great concerns, the small man starts under a
handicap. . . . If the process of concentration goes on at the same rate, at
the end of another century we shall have all American industry controlled

From Roosevelt, "The Commonwealth Club Address" (Sept., 1932), in *The Public
Papers and Addresses of Franklin D. Roosevelt,* Vol. I, Random House, 1938;
"Address to the Young Democratic Clubs of America" (Aug., 1935), in *The Public
Papers and Addresses of Franklin D. Roosevelt,* Vol. IV, 1938; "The Four
Freedoms Speech" (1941), in *Development of United States Foreign Policy: Ad-
dresses and Messages of Franklin D. Roosevelt* (77th Cong., 2d sess.; Senate Doc.
No. 188, Serial No. 10676 [Washington, 1942]).

by a dozen corporations, and run by perhaps a hundred men. But plainly, we are steering a steady course toward economic oligarchy, if we are not there already.

Clearly, all this calls for a reappraisal of values. A mere builder of more industrial plants, a creator of more railroad systems, an organizer of more corporations, is as likely to be a danger as a help. The day of the great promoter or the financial Titan, to whom we granted anything if only he would build, or develop, is over. Our task now is not discovery or exploitation of natural resources, or necessarily producing more goods. It is the soberer, less dramatic business of administering resources and plants already in hand, of seeking to reestablish foreign markets for our surplus production, of meeting the problem of underconsumption, of adjusting production to consumption, of distributing wealth and products more equitably, of adapting existing economic organizations to the service of the people. The day of enlightened administration has come. . . .

As I see it, the task of Government in its relation to business is to assist the development of an economic declaration of rights, an economic constitutional order. This is the common task of statesman and business man. It is the minimum requirement of a more permanently safe order of things.

Happily, the times indicate that to create such an order not only is the proper policy of Government, but it is the only line of safety for our economic structures as well. We know, now, that these economic units cannot exist unless prosperity is uniform, that is, unless purchasing power is well distributed throughout every group in the nation. That is why even the most selfish of corporations for its own interest would be glad to see wages restored and unemployment ended and to bring the Western farmer back to his accustomed level of prosperity and to assure a permanent safety to both groups. That is why some enlightened industries themselves endeavor to limit the freedom of action of each man and business group within the industry in the common interest of all; why business men everywhere are asking a form of organization which will bring the scheme of things into balance, even though it may in some measure qualify the freedom of action of individual units within the business. . . .

We have now to apply the earlier concepts of American Government to the conditions of today.

The Declaration of Independence discusses the problem of Government in terms of a contract. Government is a relation of give and take, a contract, perforce, if we would follow the thinking out of which it grew. Under such a contract rulers were accorded power, and the people consented to that power on consideration that they be accorded certain rights. The task of statesmanship has always been the redefinition of these rights in terms of a changing and growing social order. New conditions impose new requirements upon Government and those who conduct Government.

I held, for example, in proceedings before me as Governor, the purpose of which was the removal of the Sheriff of New York, that under modern conditions it was not enough for a public official merely to evade the legal terms of official wrongdoing. He owed a positive duty as well. I said in substance that if he had acquired large sums of money, he was when accused required to explain the sources of such wealth. To that extent this wealth was colored with a public interest. I said that in financial matters, public servants should, even beyond private citizens, be held to a stern and uncompromising rectitude.

I feel that we are coming to a view through the drift of our legislation and our public thinking in the past quarter century that private economic power is, to enlarge an old phrase, a public trust as well. I hold that continued enjoyment of that power by any individual or group must depend upon the fulfillment of that trust. The men who have reached the summit of American business life know this best; happily, many of these urge the binding quality of this greater social contract.

The terms of that contract are as old as the Republic, and as new as the new economic order.

Every man has a right to life; and this means that he has also the right to make a comfortable living. He may by sloth or crime decline to exercise that right; but it may not be denied him. We have no actual famine or dearth; our industrial and agricultural mechanism can produce enough and to spare. Our Government formal and informal, political and economic, owes to everyone an avenue to possess himself of a portion of that plenty sufficient for his needs, through his own work.

Every man has a right to his own property; which means a right to be assured, to the fullest extent attainable, in the safety of his savings. By no other means can men carry the burdens of those parts of life which, in the nature of things, afford no chance of labor; childhood, sickness, old age. In all thought of property, this right is paramount; all other property rights must yield to it. If, in accord with this principle, we must restrict the operations of the speculator, the manipulator, even the financier, I believe we must accept the restriction as needful, not to hamper individualism but to protect it.

These two requirements must be satisfied, in the main, by individuals who claim and hold control of the great industrial and financial combinations which dominate so large a part of our industrial life. They have undertaken to be, not business men, but princes of property. I am not prepared to say that the system which produces them is wrong. I am very clear that they must fearlessly and competently assume the responsibility which goes with the power. . . .

[T]he responsible heads of finance and industry instead of acting each for himself, must work together to achieve the common end. They must, where necessary, sacrifice this or that private advantage; and in reciprocal self-denial must seek a general advantage. It is here that formal Government—political Government, if you choose—comes in. Whenever in the pursuit of this objective the lone wolf, the unethical competitor, the reckless promoter, the Ishmael or Insull whose hand is against every man's, declines to join in achieving an end recognized as being for the public welfare, and threatens to drag the industry back to a state of anarchy, the Government may properly be asked to apply restraint. . . .

* * * * * * * * * *

. . . I say from my heart that no man of my generation has any business to address youth unless he comes to that task not in a spirt of exultation, but in a spirit of humilty. I cannot expect you of a newer generation to believe me, of an older generation, if I do not frankly acknowledge that had the generation that brought you into the world been wiser and more provident and more unselfish, you would have been saved from needless difficult problems and needless pain and suffering. We may not have failed you in good intentions but we have certainly not been adequate in results. Your task, therefore, is not only to maintain the best in your heritage, but to labor to lift from the shoulders of the American people some of the burdens that the mistakes of a past generation have placed there. . . .

The severity of the recent depression, toward which we had been heading for a whole generation, has taught us that no economic or social class in the community is so richly endowed and so independent of the general community that it can safeguard its own security, let alone assure security for the general community.

The very objectives of young people have changed. In the older days a great financial fortune was too often the goal. To rule through wealth, or through the power of wealth, fired our imagination. This was the dream of the golden ladder—each individual for himself.

It is my firm belief that the newer generation of America has a different dream. You place emphasis on sufficiency of life, rather than on a plethora of riches. You think of the security for yourself and your family that will give you good health, good food, good education, good working conditions, and the opportunity for normal recreation and occasional travel. Your advancement, you hope, is along a broad highway on which thousands of your fellow men and women are advancing with you.

You and I know that this modern economic world of ours is governed by rules and regulations vastly more complex than those laid down in the days of Adam Smith or John Stuart Mill. They faced simpler mechanical processes and social needs. It is worth remembering, for example, that the business corporation, as we know it, did not exist in the days of Washington and Hamilton and Jefferson. Private businesses then were conducted solely by individuals or by partnerships in which every member was immediately and wholly responsible for success or failure. Facts are relentless. We must adjust our ideas to the facts of today. . . .

In 1911, twenty-four years ago, when I was first a member of the New York State Legislature, a number of the younger members of the Legislature worked against these old conditions and called for laws governing factory inspection, for workmen's compensation and for the limitation of work for women and children to fifty-four hours, with one day's rest in seven. Those of us who joined in this movement in the Legislature were called reformers, socialists, and wild men. We were opposed by many of the same organizations and the same individuals who are now crying aloud about the socialism involved in social security legislation, in bank deposit insurance, in farm credit, in the saving of homes, in the protection of investors and the regulation of public utilities. The reforms, however, for which we were condemned twenty-four years ago are taken today as a matter of course. And so, I believe, will be regarded the reforms that now cause such concern to the reactionaries of 1935. We come to an understanding of these new ways of protecting people because our knowledge enlarges and our capacity for organized action increases. People have learned that they can carry their burdens effectively only by cooperation. We have found out how to conquer the ravages of diseases that years ago were regarded as unavoidable and inevitable. We must learn that many other social ills can be cured.

Let me emphasize that serious as have been the errors of unrestrained individualism, I do not believe in abandoning the system of individual enterprise. The freedom and opportunity that have characterized American development in the past can be maintained if we recognize the fact that the individual system of our day calls for the collaboration of all of us to provide, at the least, security for all of us. Those words "freedom" and "opportunity" do not mean a license to climb upwards by pushing other people down.

Any paternalistic system which tries to provide for security for everyone from above only calls for an impossible task and a regimentation utterly uncongenial to the spirit of our people. But Government cooperation to help make the system of free enterprise work, to provide that minimum security without which the competitive system cannot function, to restrain the kind of individual action which in the past has been harmful to the community—that kind of governmental cooperation is entirely consistent with the best tradition of America. . . .

More than ever, we cherish the elective form of democratic government, but progress under it can easily be retarded by disagreements that relate to method and to detail rather than to the broad objectives upon which we are agreed. It is as if all of us were united in the pursuit of a common goal, but that each and every one of us were marching along a separate road of our own. If we insist on choosing different roads, most of us will not reach our common destination. . . .

Therefore, to the American youth of all parties I submit a message of confidence—Unite and Challenge! Rules are not necessarily sacred; principles are. The methods of the old order are not, as some would have you believe, above the challenge of youth. . . .

* * * * * * * * * *

. . . [T]here is nothing mysterious about the foundations of a healthy and strong democracy. The basic things expected by our people of their political and economic systems are simple. They are:

Equality of opportunity for youth and for others.

Jobs for those who can work.

Security for those who need it.

The ending of special privilege for the few.

The preservation of civil liberties for all.

The enjoyment of the fruits of scientific progress in a wider and constantly rising standard of living.

These are the simple, basic things that must never be lost sight of in the turmoil and unbelievable complexity of our modern world. The inner and abiding strength of our economic and political systems is dependent upon the degree to which they fulfill these expectations.

Many subjects connected with our social economy call for immediate improvement.

As examples:

We should bring more citizens under the coverage of old-age pensions and unemployment insurance.

We should widen the opportunities for adequate medical care.

We should plan a better system by which persons deserving or needing gainful employment may obtain it.

I have called for personal sacrifice. I am assured of the willingness of almost all Americans to respond to that call.

A part of the sacrifice means the payment of more money in taxes. . . .

In the future days, which we seek to make secure, we look forward to a world founded upon four essential human freedoms.

The first is freedom of speech and expression—everywhere in the world.

The second is freedom of every person to worship God in his own way—everywhere in the world.

The third is freedom from want—which, translated into world terms, means economic understandings which will secure to every nation a healthy peacetime life for its inhabitants—everywhere in the world.

The fourth is freedom from fear—which, translated into world terms, means a world-wide reduction of armaments to such a point and in such a thorough fashion that no nation will be in a position to commit an act of physical aggression against any neighbor—anywhere in the world.

That is no vision of a distant millennium. It is a definite basis for a kind of world attainable in our own time and generation. That kind of world is the very antithesis of the so-called new order of tyranny which the dictators seek to create with the crash of a bomb.

To that new order we oppose the greater conception—the moral order. A good society is able to face schemes of world domination and foreign revolutions alike without fear.

Since the beginning of our American history, we have been engaged in change—in a perpetual peaceful revolution—a revolution which goes on steadily, quietly adjusting itself to changing conditions—without the concentration camp or the quick-lime in the ditch. The world order which we seek is the cooperation of free countries, working together in a friendly, civilized society.

This nation has placed its destiny in the hands and heads and hearts of its millions of free men and women; and its faith in freedom under the guidance of God. Freedom means the supremacy of human rights everywhere. Our support goes to those who struggle to gain those rights or keep them. Our strength is our unity of purpose.

To that high concept there can be no end save victory.

61

Irving Kristol

Ideology and Supply-Side Economics (1981)

The terms being applied—by the media, by politicians, by economists—
to President Reagan's economic program, and most particularly to the tax-
cutting aspect of this program, are "bold," "revolutionary," "a risky experiment," and so on. Clearly, a great many people are nervous about "supply-
side" economics, and seem to have difficulty understanding its rationale. This
is quite odd. For there is nothing really bold, or revolutionary, or experimental
about this program. Nor is it at all difficult to understand. . . .

It must be said that the term itself, "supply-side economics," may be a
source of initial confusion. It originates in deliberate contrast to the prevailing
Keynesian approach, which emphasizes the need for government to manage
and manipulate—through fiscal and monetary policies—aggregate demand so
as to maintain full employment. Supply-side economists say government cannot really do this, no matter how many clever economists it hires, but that if
business enterprise is permitted to function with a minimum of interference,
it will invest and innovate, so as to *create* the requisite demand for the goods
it produces.

There is certainly a difference in perspective here. Supply-side economists look at the economy from ground level, as it were—i.e., from the point
of view of the entrepreneurs and investors who are identified as the prime
movers. Keynesian economists look at the economy from above—from the
standpoint of a government that is a *deus ex machina,* and which, in its om-
niscience, intervenes discreetly to preserve a harmonious economic universe.
But it is wrong to infer that we live in a Manichean world in which Supply
and Demand are continually at odds, so that we always are having to declare
allegiance to one as against the other. They are, rather, opposite sides of the
same coin, coexisting of necessity, and there can be no question of *choosing*
between them.

More precisely, it is absurd *economically* to think in terms of such a
choice. Beyond a certain point, a tax on production becomes a tax on consumption—the goods become too expensive and demand falls. Similarly, beyond a certain point a tax on consumption becomes a tax on production—the

Reprinted from *Commentary,* Spring, 1981, by permission of the author.

decrease in demand inhibits supply. Shifting taxes from the one to the other may provide marginal benefits on occasion. But a tax on commercial transactions and economic activity is always a tax on *both* production and consumption.

When, however, one moves from a purely analytical-economic mode of thought to a political-ideological one—when, in short, one moves from economic analysis to economic policy—then the difference in perspective has significant implications. Supply-side economics naturally gives rise to an emphasis on growth, not redistribution. It aims at improving everyone's economic circumstances over time, but not necessarily in the same degree or in the same period of time. The aggregate demand created by economic activity, as seen from the supply-side, is indifferent to the issue of equality. Its bias is consequently in favor of a free market for economic activity, because this provides the most powerful economic incentives for investment, innovation, and growth. Those, on the other hand, for whom economic equality is at least as important as economic growth will always want to see government "restructure" this aggregate demand and will be indifferent to the issue of economic incentives.

However, there is another—incidental but important—source of controversy which has already been referred to, and that is the threat that supply-side economics represents to the economics profession as at present constituted. There can be little doubt that the nature of the controversy would be a lot clearer, and we would all be less befuddled, if it were not for the fact that so many distinguished economists are publicly accusing supply-side economics of being inconsistent with the principles of economic science as these are taught in graduate school and incarnated in, say, articles in the *American Economic Review.* To make matters worse, the accusation has a lot of truth in it, which is why so much of the writing in favor of supply-side economics originates outside the academic universe.

Thus one cannot understand the controversy over supply-side economics without paying some attention to the condition of the economics profession and to its vested interests, both intelllectual and material. This condition is, at the moment, painfully ambiguous.

For more than three decades, we have all been looking to our best economists for guidance on economic policy. To that end we even established, after World War II, an extraordinary institution called the Council of Economic Advisers: three economists, with staff, who are supposed to provide the President and Congress with *authoritative* guidance on our economic problems, prospects, and policies. . . .

From what do their authority and expertise derive? They derive from the ambitious reconstruction of economic science after World War II in which the scheme of Keynesian macroeconomics was wedded to new, rigorous, analytical, largely mathematical techniques so as to provide, not a general, abstract model of the economic "system"—the 19th century gave us that—but a specific model of *our* economy at *this* particular time. Such a model consists of hundreds of complex correlations, spawned by econometric research, which relate one aspect of our national economic activity to another (or to many others), all fed into a computer which, having been properly programmed, can inform us as to where our economy has been coming from (to adopt a useful term from another part of the culture), where it is now, and whither it is drifting. . . . [T]his enterprise, . . . has come to be called "the neoclassical synthesis," or "neo-Keynesian" economics. . . .

It all went reasonably well for a couple of decades, though just *what* went reasonably well is itself one source of controversy. The neo-Keynesians will say that their sound analysis and good advice were at least partly responsible for our healthy economy from 1945 to 1970. Critics will argue that it was the existence of a healthy economy, created by businessmen and statesmen blissfully ignorant of sophisticated economic theories, that permitted economists to bask in a kind of reflected glory. (These critics point to the remarkable economic recoveries of Germany and Japan in a period when those nations had yet to learn of the neoclassical synthesis.)

But there can be no dispute over the fact that, beginning around 1970, it ceased going well and began to go badly. Not only were those annual forecasts too often very wide of the mark (especially with regard to inflation), but our economics establishment—for that is what it is, by now—could not explain the phenomenon of "stagflation," a combination of inflation and lagging economic growth that neo-Keynesian theory regards as an impossibility. . . .

Simultaneously, and inevitably, a great many people began to take a hard and critical look at the presuppositions of neo-Keynesian economics—and, above all, at the model of the economy upon which it relies. . . .

The new critique of the neo-Keynesian model . . . asserted that *this kind* of model, for all its complexity and sophistication—or one can even say because of its complexity and sophistication—reveals profound misconceptions about the nature of economic behavior, and especially about the kind of economic behavior that leads to economic growth.

It is important to realize that the conventional models are utterly blind to entrepreneurship and innovation (technological or otherwise). They can deal with quantifiable aggregates (like "investment") but what cannot be quantified they ignore. Basically, theirs is a kind of Newtonian model of an economic system, with all the "forces" balancing each other out—except sometimes, when (for reasons still unclear) there is a mismatch between overall supply and overall demand, on which occasions the government, like some benign deity, pumps in the missing quantity of demand and restores the system to equilibrium. All specifically human motivations, intentions, aspirations are ignored. It is the results of past human *behavior* that the model blandly reflects, and always after the fact. In a sense, the revolt against neo-Keynesian economics is part of a larger revulsion, visible in other social sciences as well, against behaviorism as an adequate guide to human reality.

Economists attuned to the theories incarnated in such models cannot explain the "whys" of economic phenomena. They cannot, for instance, explain why economies grow, and why some economies grow faster than others. . . .

Is that surprising? Only if we forget that economics is still a "social" science—the most methodologically rigorous of them all, to be sure, but still a social science—and not a "natural" science like physics or chemistry. We are hardly astonished, after all, if our political scientists fail to come up with a rigorous theory of political change, or if our sociologists fail to come up with a rigorous theory of social change, one which informs us precisely and authoritatively as to where our polity and society have been, where they are, where they are going. That is because we understand intuitively that any such theory, dealing with human beings, would require a degree of self-knowledge—of our present characters and personalities, from which we could make strong inferences as to our future motivations and actions—which is, by the nature of things, unavailable. (If we had any such complete self-knowledge we would be God—the Being in Whom thought and existence are one.) But economics, in striving to become an objective and positive science like physics, has promised us exactly this kind of self-knowledge, at least insofar as we are economic men and women. . . .

Supply-side economics may be viewed as a kind of "humanistic" rebellion against the mathematical-mechanical type of economic analysis in which economic aggregates, themselves dubious in nature, are related to one another so as to achieve a supposedly accurate series of snapshots of the economic universe we inhabit—something comparable to the universe we perceive when we go to a planetarium. Supply-side economics is uninterested in such a beautifully architected equilibrium because it believes this is the wrong paradigm for understanding an economy that consists of the *purposive* yet *inconstant* behavior of millions of individuals. Purposive, because economic behavior generally has as its goal the improvement of one's economic conditions. Inconstant, because only the individual himself can define "improvement" for us, and his behavior will be profoundly influenced by all sorts of contingent factors—religious heritage, family relations, and, not least, the actions of government. . . .

Nothing conveys more clearly the radically different perspectives on economic activity of supply-side and neo-Keynesian theory than the issue of incentives. . . .

Supply-side economics takes incentives—the innate human impulse to better one's condition, as Adam Smith would put it—as the *fons et origo* of economic activity and, most important, of economic growth. We do indeed know of primitive cultures where that impulse is either weak or missing—and where economic growth is, as a consequence, also weak or missing. We know, too, of historical societies where the impulse has been frustrated by religious or political authorities—and where economic growth has been sporadic and cyclical. It is only with the emergence of a modern, commercial civilization, in which self-interested transactions in the marketplace are morally vindicated and politically tolerated, that the impulse to better one's condition becomes translated into steady, progressive economic growth over decades and centuries.

Now, one way of frustrating that impulse, and economic growth as well, is to tax it. This accords with both common sense and common observation. As a matter of fact, it is a proposition that any economist, even the most devoted neo-Keynesian, will casually agree to. But when you suggest that one way of encouraging economic growth is to *decrease* the taxes on economic activity, many of these same economists will suddenly and inexplicably balk.

This balkiness is unquestionably ideological. These are people who are persuaded that the "collective goods" our taxes pay for—not only public works but also a more equal distribution of income—give us fair value, if not in purely economic terms. This is a perfectly sensible argument in defense of a tax system, but it is rarely made in the United States in 1981, presumably because it is not so evident that our taxes are actually getting us our "money's worth" in those collective goods. Instead, these economists engage in the most curious kind of research to refute the notion that anyone's incentive will be affected by a cut in taxes.

This research involves polling people, asking them whether they will work harder if their taxes are cut by 10 percent or 20 percent—or will they, perhaps, just consume more, by way of goods or leisure? Such studies often find that it makes little or no difference. . . .

Who on earth ever said that, in a commercial society such as ours, we achieve economic growth by having to work harder? On the contrary: the whole point of economic growth is that people should work *less hard*—but more productively. The human impulse to work less hard is just as strong as the human impulse to better one's condition—always has been, one suspects always will be. It is the genius of market capitalism to satisfy both of these impulses at once by encouraging entrepreneurship, the incentive to innovate, among that minority of human beings who are, unlike most of us, peculiarly "economic activists." The existence of such human beings—of entrepreneurs who, by innovating, make us all more productive without necessarily being less lazy—is simply ignored in the atomistic poll data or the aggregate statistics that economists so solemnly analyze.

It does not matter in the least whether you or I will respond to a tax cut by sharpening our economic incentives. Some of us will, some of us will not. What does matter is that there is out there, in the real business world as distinct from the academic world of the economists, a minority who will respond in this way—not necessarily the nicest people, not necessarily the smartest people, but the ones who, for whatever reason, relish economic success. For such people, the incentives to save and invest (and invest again) are extraordinarily powerful, and it is the incentives of these "economic activists" that are blunted and thwarted by a heavy tax burden. . . .

Still, taxes do have to be paid to acquire the necessary and desirable level of public services, and the question is immediately posed: how do we know, in fact, that taxes are *too* high? . . . This brings us to the so-called "Laffer curve". . . .

All that the Laffer curve says is that, *after a certain point,* a tax—or the tax level as a whole—can become counterproductive. It is the point at which people experience taxes as an excessive and unfair burden—they are not getting their "money's worth" for the tax they pay—with the result that their incentives to economic activity are adversely affected. The tax, in effect, *represses* economic activity to such an extent that, if it were substantially reduced, the government would end up collecting more in tax revenues, since there would be a lot more economic activity contributing to these tax revenues. . . .

The question that academic critics of the Laffer curve raise is whether the American tax system has gone beyond the point of diminishing returns. "How do we know this?" they ask querulously. "Prove it," they demand. To judge by last November's election results, a clear majority of Americans are already convinced. But academic economists want *academic* proof—not, one suspects, because of their devotion to pure science, but because they would really prefer that government collect money and redistribute it more equally than see everyone improve his condition unequally through untrameled economic growth.

The academic question as to whether we are beyond the point of diminishing returns in our tax system is unanswerable in strictly academic terms. It is a matter for *political* judgment, since it all depends on how people *feel* about the level of taxation. In wartime they feel one way; in peacetime, another. Yes, people always do grumble about taxes, at just about any level, but they don't always do something about it. They don't always make strenuous efforts to avoid or evade; they don't always regard overtime (at time-and-a-half pay) with indifference or hostility. . . .

Though one cannot provide the kind of elegant, mathematical proof economists wish, there are in fact some persuasive signs that the American economy has gone too far up on the Laffer curve. One is our flourishing (because untaxed) underground economy—just how large it is, no one knows. . . .

Another such sign is the tens of billions of dollars that seek and find legal tax shelters, investments that would not exist except for their relative tax advantage and which are therefore, by definition as it were, uneconomic. . . .

The real opposition to the Laffer curve has less to do with economics than with liberal egalitarianism. . . . Does anyone really think that, even if we could prove beyond the shadow of a doubt that reducing the tax rates on more affluent Americans would result in their actually paying more in taxes than they now do, the reductions would become less controversial? There are many people, including quite a few economists, for whom it is more important to have a symbolic tax rate of 70 percent on very high incomes even if very few of the rich actually pay it, than to have an effective tax rate of, say, 40 percent which many of the rich would pay instead of fooling around with (often problematic) tax shelters.

But there are some thoughtful people who, having little quarrel with the general tenor of supply-side economics, nevertheless wonder whether it is appropriate in today's inflationary economy. . . .

That classical tradition has its own policy for coping with inflation. And, in truth, it is a policy that has always worked. It involves slowing down the rate of growth of the money supply to bring it in line with the growth in productivity. It also involves reducing governmental expenditures and bringing the budget into balance. . . . Both of these measures, taken jointly, induce a recession, during which all of the distortions caused by inflation are "purged" from (or "wrung out of") the economic system. After the recession has achieved this effect, a normal economic recovery may be expected to set in, and non-inflationary growth is once again possible. . . .

I have noted that these policies have in fact worked in the past. But would they work under the present, truly novel, circumstances? . . . One of the novel things about our present economic condition is not merely the endemic high inflation but the existence of a welfare state. This means that as the economy slows down, government expenditures actually increase, as the number of people who are now "in need" increases, and all sorts of welfare programs are triggered. The deficit, instead of going down, tends to go up—especially since tax revenues are also decreasing. As a result, whereas a relatively shallow and short-lived recession could do the trick in a pre-welfare state economy, what is now required is a deep and prolonged recession. (This is what Margaret Thatcher has discovered, to her dismay.) The economic costs of such a recession are so enormous as to make it a most questionable instrument of policy.

And the political costs are, to put it bluntly, intolerable. . . .

That is why the Reagan administration has added a cut in tax rates, for business firms and individuals, to the traditional dual strategy of fighting inflation by slowing down the growth of the money supply and of government spending. It is the only possible answer to our predicament—encouraging economic growth so as to annul or at least ameliorate the recessionary effects of other anti-inflationary policies. . . .

Will it work? There are plenty of good reasons for thinking it will. True, it might temporarily increase the deficit and the national debt—but if the predicted growth eventually occurs, both deficit and debt will be imposed on a larger and stronger economy which can easily support them.

Moreover, we do have some solid historical evidence that the "feedback" effects of cuts in tax rates, in terms of increased tax revenues, are always larger than our economists and Treasury officials—whose econometric models cannot cope with such "feedback" effects—expect to be the case. This is what happened with the Kennedy-Johnson tax cuts which were as large, in terms of the 1964 economy, as the Reagan tax cuts are in the 1981 economy. There is no reason why it should not happen again.

One final point, often overlooked. Because of the increase in social-security taxes that has taken effect this year, and because of automatic "bracket creep" in the income tax resulting from inflation, we shall in effect be experiencing something like a $40-billion tax *increase* in 1981. No economist of any persuasion, no politician of any persuasion, no commentator (liberal or conservative) has been heard to say that such a tax increase would be good for the economy in its present condition. Yet many of these same people are volubly disturbed by a tax cut that will, in 1981, at best keep our tax burden in a steady state, and in 1982 only alleviate it modestly.

Somehow, the current condition of economic theory, combined with existing ideological trends, has given us a level of public discourse on economic policy that is disgracefully inadequate to our economic and political realities. No one, critical though he may be, seems even to feel the need to offer a practicable alternative to Reagan's economic policy. One even suspects that many critics of supply-side economics want above all to see it fail, since its success would threaten their ideological investments.

62

Alexis de Tocqueville

Soft Despotism (1840)

The principle of equality, which makes men independent of each other, gives them a habit and a taste for following in their private actions no other guide than their own will. This complete independence, which they constantly enjoy in regard to their equals and in the intercourse of private life, tends to make them look upon all authority with a jealous eye and speedily suggests to them the notion and the love of political freedom. Men living at such times have a natural bias towards free institutions. Take any one of them at a venture and search if you can his most deep-seated instincts, and you will find that, of all governments, he will soonest conceive and most highly value that government whose head he has himself elected and whose administration he may control.

Of all the political effects produced by the equality of conditions, this love of independence is the first to strike the observing and to alarm the timid; nor can it be said that their alarm is wholly misplaced, for anarchy has a more formidable aspect in democratic countries than elsewhere. . . .

⌐I am convinced, however, that anarchy is not the principal evil that democratic ages have to fear, but the least. For the principle of equality begets two tendencies: the one leads men straight to independence and may suddenly drive them into anarchy; the other conducts them by a longer, more secret, but more certain road to servitude. Nations readily discern the former tendency and are prepared to resist it; they are led away by the latter, without perceiving its drift; hence it is peculiarly important to point it out.⌐

Personally, far from finding fault with equality because it inspires a spirit of independence, I praise it primarily for that very reason. I admire it because it lodges in the very depths of each man's mind and heart that indefinable feeling, the instinctive inclination for political independence, and thus prepares the remedy for the ill which it engenders. It is precisely for this reason that I cling to it.

The notion of secondary powers placed between the sovereign and his subjects occurred naturally to the imagination of aristocratic nations, because those communities contained individuals or families raised above the common level and apparently destined to command by their birth, their education, and their wealth. This same notion is naturally wanting in the minds of men in democratic ages, for converse reasons; it can only be introduced artificially, it can only be kept there with difficulty. . . . Moreover, in politics as well as in philosophy and in religion the intellect of democratic nations is peculiarly open to simple and general notions. Complicated systems are repugnant to it, and its favorite conception is that of a great nation composed of citizens all formed upon one pattern and all governed by a single power.

The very next notion to that of a single and central power which presents itself to the minds of men in the ages of equality is the notion of uniformity of legislation. As every man sees that he differs but little from those about him, he cannot understand why a rule that is applicable to one man should not be equally applicable to all others. Hence the slightest privileges are repugnant to his reason; the faintest dissimilarities in the political institutions of the same people offend him, and uniformity of legislation appears to him to be the first condition of good government. . . .

As the conditions of men become equal among a people, individuals seem of less and society of greater importance; or rather every citizen, being assimilated to all the rest, is lost in the crowd, and nothing stands conspicuous but the great and imposing image of the people at large. . . .

As the men who inhabit democratic countries have no superiors, no inferiors, and no habitual or necessary partners in their undertakings, they readily fall back upon themselves and consider themselves as beings apart. I had occasion to point this out at considerable length in treating of individualism. Hence such men can never, without an effort, tear themselves from their private affairs to engage in public business. . . .

I have also had occasion to show how the increasing love of well-being and the fluctuating character of property cause democratic nations to dread all violent disturbances. The love of public tranquillity is frequently the only passion which these nations retain. . . .

As in periods of equality no man is compelled to lend his assistance to his fellow men, and none has any right to expect much support from them, everyone is at once independent and powerless. These two conditions, which must never be either separately considered or confounded together, inspire the citizen of a democratic country with very contrary propensities. His independence fills him with self-reliance and pride among his equals; his debility makes him feel from time to time the want of some outward assistance, which he cannot expect from any of them, because they are all impotent and unsympathizing. In this predicament he naturally turns his eyes to that imposing power which alone rises above the level of universal depression. . . .

⌐My object is to remark that all these various rights which have been successively wrested, in our time, from classes, guilds, and individuals have not served to raise new secondary powers on a more democratic basis, but have uniformly been concentrated in the hands of the sovereign. Everywhere the state acquires more and more direct control over the humblest members of the community and a more exclusive power of governing each of them in his smallest concerns.⌐

Almost all the charitable establishments of Europe were formerly in the hands of private persons or of guilds; they are now almost all dependent on the supreme government, and in many countries are actually administered by that power. The state almost exclusively undertakes to supply bread to the hungry, assistance and shelter to the sick, work to the idle, and to act as the sole reliever of all kinds of misery.

Education, as well as charity, has become in most countries at the present day a national concern. The state receives, and often takes, the child from the arms of the mother to hand it over to official agents; the state undertakes to train the heart and to instruct the mind of each generation. Uniformity prevails in the courses of public instruction as in everything else; diversity as well as freedom is disappearing day by day. . . .

There exists among the modern nations of Europe one great cause, independent of all those which have already been pointed out, which perpetually contributes to extend the agency or to strengthen the prerogative of the supreme power, though it has not been sufficiently attended to: I mean the growth of manufactures, which is fostered by the progress of social equality. Manufacturers generally collect a multitude of men on the same spot, among whom new and complex relations spring up. These men are exposed by their calling to great and sudden alternations of plenty and want, during which public tranquillity is endangered. It may also happen that these employments sacrifice the health and even the life of those who gain by them or of those who live by them. Thus the manufacturing classes require more regulation, superintendence, and restraint than the other classes of society, and it is natural that the powers of government should increase in the same proportion as those classes. . . .

⌐As a nation becomes more engaged in manufactures, the lack of roads, canals, harbors, and other works of a semi-public nature, which facilitate the acquisition of wealth, is more strongly felt; and as a nation becomes more democratic, private individuals are less able, and the state more able, to execute works of such magnitude.⌐ I do not hesitate to assert that the manifest tendency of all governments at the present time is to take upon themselves alone the execution of these undertakings, by which means they daily hold in closer dependence the population which they govern.

⌐On the other hand, in proportion as the power of a state increases and its necessities are augmented, the state consumption of manufactured produce is always growing larger; and these commodities are generally made in the arsenals or establishments of the government. Thus in every kingdom the ruler becomes the principal manufacturer: he collects and retains in his service a vast number of engineers, architects, mechanics, and handicraftsmen.⌐

Not only is he the principal manufacturer, but he tends more and more to become the chief, or rather the master, of all other manufacturers. As private persons become powerless by becoming more equal, they can effect nothing in manufactures without combination; but the government naturally seeks to place these combinations under its own control.

It must be admitted that these collective beings, which are called companies, are stronger and more formidable than a private individual can ever be, and that they have less of the responsibility for their own actions; whence it seems reasonable that they should not be allowed to retain so great an independence of the supreme government as might be conceded to a private individual. . . .

⌐[T]he incessant increase of the prerogative of the supreme government, [becomes] more centralized, more adventurous, more absolute, more extensive, the people perpetually falling under the control of the public administration, led insensibly to surrender to it some further portion of their individual independence, till the very men who from time to time upset a throne and trample on a race of kings bend more and more obsequiously to the slightest dictate of a clerk.⌐ . . .

⌐I seek to trace the novel features under which despotism may appear in the world. The first thing that strikes the observation is an innumerable multitude of men, all equal and alike, incessantly endeavoring to procure the petty and paltry pleasures with which they glut their lives. Each of them, living apart, is as a stranger to the fate of all the rest; his children and his private friends constitute to him the whole of mankind. As for the rest of his fellow citizens, he is close to them, but he does not see them; he touches them, but he does not feel them; he exists only in himself and for himself alone; and if his kindred still remain to him, he may be said at any rate to have lost his country.⌐

Above this race of men stands an immense and tutelary power, which takes upon itself alone to secure their gratifications and to watch over their fate. That power is absolute, minute, regular, provident, and mild. It would be like the authority of a parent if, like that authority, its object was to prepare men for manhood; but it seeks, on the contrary, to keep them in perpetual childhood: it is well content that the people should rejoice, provided they think of nothing but rejoicing. For their happiness such a government willingly labors, but it chooses to be the sole agent and the only arbiter of that happiness; it provides for their security, foresees and supplies their necessities, facilitates their pleasures, manages their principal concerns, directs their industry, regulates the descent of property, and subdivides their inheritances: what remains, but to spare them all the care of thinking and all the trouble of living?

Thus it every day renders the exercise of the free agency of man less useful and less frequent; it circumscribes the will within a narrower range and gradually robs a man of all the uses of himself. The principle of equality has prepared men for these things; it has predisposed men to endure them and often to look on them as benefits.

After having thus successively taken each member of the community in its powerful grasp and fashioned him at will, the supreme power then extends its arm over the whole community. It covers the surface of society with a network of small complicated rules, minute and uniform, through which the most original minds and the most energetic characters cannot penetrate, to rise above the crowd. The will of man is not shattered, but softened, bent, and guided; men are seldom forced by it to act, but they are constantly restrained from acting. Such a power does not destroy, but it prevents existence; it does not tyrannize, but it compresses, enervates, extinguishes, and stupefies a people, till each nation is reduced to nothing better than a flock of timid and industrious animals, of which the government is the shepherd.

I have always thought that servitude of the regular, quiet, and gentle kind which I have just described might be combined more easily than is commonly believed with some of the outward forms of freedom, and that it might even establish itself under the wing of the sovereignty of the people.

Our contemporaries are constantly excited by two conflicting passions: they want to be led, and they wish to remain free. As they cannot destroy either the one or the other of these contrary propensities, they strive to satisfy them both at once. They devise a sole, tutelary, and all-powerful form of government, but elected by the people. They combine the principle of centralization and that of popular sovereignty; this gives them a respite: they console themselves for being in tutelage by the reflection that they have chosen their own guardians. Every man allows himself to be put in leading-strings, because he sees that it is not a person or a class of persons, but the people at large who hold the end of his chain.

By this system the people shake off their state of dependence just long enough to select their master and then relapse into it again. A great many persons at the present day are quite contented with this sort of compromise between administrative despotism and the sovereignty of the people; and they think they have done enough for the protection of individual freedom when they have surrendered it to the power of the nation at large. This does not satisfy me: the nature of him I am to obey signifies less to me than the fact of extorted obedience. . . .

It is in vain to summon a people who have been rendered so dependent on the central power to choose from time to time the representatives of that power; this rare and brief exercise of their free choice, however important it may be, will not prevent them from gradually losing the faculties of think-ing, feeling, and acting for themselves, and thus gradually falling below the level of humanity. . . .

63

Thomas Jefferson

Against Manufacturing (1787)

. . . The political economists of Europe have established it as a princi-ple, that every State should endeavor to manufacture for itself; and this principle, like many others, we transfer to America, without calculating the difference of circumstance which should often produce a difference of result. In Europe the lands are either cultivated, or locked up against the cultivator. Manufacture must therefore be resorted to of necessity not of choice, to support the surplus of their people. But we have an immensity of land courting the industry of the husbandman. Is it best then that all our citizens should be employed in its improvement, or that one half should be called off from that to exercise manufactures and handicraft arts for the other? Those who labor in the earth are the chosen people of God, if ever He had a chosen people, whose breasts He has made His peculiar deposit for substantial and genuine virtue. It is the focus in which he keeps alive that sacred fire, which otherwise might escape from the face of the earth. Corruption of morals in the mass of cultivators is a phenomenon of which no age nor nation has furnished an example. It is the mark set on those, who, not looking up to heaven, to their own soil and industry, as does the

From Jefferson, "Query XIX," in *Notes on the State of Virginia,* London, 1787.

husbandman, for their subsistence, depend for it on casualties and caprice of customers. Dependence begets subservience and venality, suffocates the germ of virtue, and prepares fit tools for the designs of ambition. This, the natural progress and consequence of the arts, has sometimes perhaps been retarded by accidental circumstances; but, generally speaking, the proportion which the aggregate of the other classes of citizens bears in any State to that of its husbandmen, is the proportion of its unsound to its healthy parts, and is a good enough barometer whereby to measure its degree of corruption. While we have land to labor then, let us never wish to see our citizens occupied at a workbench, or twirling a distaff. Carpenters, masons, smiths, are wanting in husbandry; but, for the general operations of manufacture, let our workshops remain in Europe. It is better to carry provisions and materials to workmen there, than bring them to the provisions and materials, and with them their manners and principles. The loss by the transportation of commodities across the Atlantic will be made up in happiness and permanence of government. The mobs of great cities add just so much to the support of pure government, as sores do to the strength of the human body. It is the manners and spirit of a people which preserve a republic in vigor. A degeneracy in these is a canker which soon eats to the heart of its laws and constitution.

64

Alexander Hamilton

Report on Manufactures (1791)

The Secretary of the Treasury, in obedience to the order of the House of Representatives, of the 15th day of January, 1790, has applied his attention, at as early a period as his other duties would permit, to the subject of manufactures; and particularly to the means of promoting such as will tend to render the United States, independent on foreign nations for military and

From Hamilton, *Report on Manufactures,* in *Reports of the Secretary of the Treasury of the United States,* Vol. I (Washington, 1837).

other essential supplies. And he thereupon respectfully submits the following Report. . . .

There still are respectable patrons of opinions, unfriendly to the encouragement of manufactures. The following are, substantially, the arguments by which these opinions are defended.

"In every country (say those who entertain them) agriculture is the most beneficial and *productive* object of human industry. This position, generally, if not universally true, applies with peculiar emphasis to the United States, on account of their immense tracts of fertile territory, uninhabited and unimproved. Nothing can afford so advantageous an employment for capital and labour, as the conversion of this extensive wilderness into cultivated farms. Nothing equally with this, can contribute to the population, strength and real riches of the country.

"To endeavor, by the extraordinary patronage of government, to accelerate the growth of manufactures, is, in fact, to endeavor, by force and art, to transfer the natural current of industry from a more, to a less beneficial channel. Whatever has such a tendency must necessarily be unwise. Indeed it can hardly ever be wise in a government, to attempt to give a direction to the industry of its citizens. This under the quicksighted guidance of private interest, will, if left to itself, infallibly find its own way to the most profitable employment: and 'tis by such employment, that the public prosperity will be most effectually promoted. . . .

"If contrary to the natural course of things, an unseasonable and premature spring can be given to certain fabrics, by heavy duties, prohibitions, bounties, or by other forced expedients; this will only be to sacrifice the interests of the community to those of particular classes. . . ."

. . .[I]t is necessary to advert carefully to the considerations, which plead in favour of manufactures, and which appear to recommend the special and positive encouragement of them; in certain cases, and under certain reasonable limitations.

It ought readily to be conceded that the cultivation of the earth—as the primary and most certain source of national supply—as the immediate and chief source of subsistence to man—as the principal source of those materials which constitute the nutriment of other kinds of labor—as including a state most favourable to the freedom and independence of the human mind—one, perhaps, most conducive to the multiplication of the human species—has *intrinsically a strong claim to pre-eminence over every other kind of industry.*

But, that it has a title to anything like an exclusive predilection, in any country, ought to be admitted with great caution. . . .

It has been maintained that agriculture is, not only, the most productive, but the only productive, species of industry. . . .

To this it has been answered. . . .

"That the annual produce of the land and labour of a country can only be increased in two ways—by some improvement in the *productive powers* of the useful labour, which actually exists within it, or by some increase in the quantity of such labour: That with regard to the first, the labor of artificers being capable of greater subdivision and simplicity of operation than that of cultivators, it is susceptible, in a proportionably greater degree, of improvement in its *productive powers,* whether to be derived from an accession of skill, or from the application of ingenious machinery; in which particular, therefore, the labor employed in the culture of land can pretend to no advantage over that engaged in manufactures. . . ."

. . . But while the *exclusive* productiveness of agricultural labour has been thus denied and refuted, the superiority of its productiveness has been conceded without hesitation. . . .

One of the arguments made use of in support of the idea may be pronounced both quaint and superficial—It amounts to this—That in the productions of the soil, nature co-operates with man; and that the effect of their joint labour must be greater than that of the labour of man alone.

This however, is far from being a necessary inference. It is very conceivable, that the labor of man alone, laid out upon a work requiring great skill and art to bring it to perfection, may be more productive, *in value,* than the labour of nature and man combined, when directed towards more simple operations and objects: And when it is recollected to what an extent the agency of nature, in the application of the mechanical powers, is made auxiliary to the prosecution of manufactures, the suggestion, which has been noticed, loses even the appearance of plausibility.

It might also be observed, with a contrary view, that the labor employed in agriculture is in a great measure periodical and occasional, depending on seasons, liable to various and long intermissions; while that occupied in many manufactures is constant and regular, extending through the year, embracing in some instances night as well as day. It is also probable, that there are among the cultivators of land, more examples of remissness, than among artificers. The farmer, from the peculiar fertility of his land, or some other favorable circumstance, may frequently obtain a livelihood, even with a considerable degree of carelessness in the mode of cultivation; but the artisan can with difficulty effect the same object, without exerting himself pretty equally with all those who are engaged in the same pursuit. And if it may likewise be assumed as a fact, that manufactures open a wider field to exertions of ingenuity than agriculture, it would not be a strained conjecture, that the labour employed in the former, being at once more *constant,* more uniform and more ingenious, than that which is employed in the latter, will be found, at the same time more productive. . . .

It is now proper to proceed a step further, and to enumerate the principal circumstances, from which it may be inferred—that manufacturing establishments not only occasion a positive augmentation of the produce and revenue of the society, but that they contribute essentially to rendering them greater than they could possibly be, without such establishments. These circumstances are—

1. The division of labour.
2. An extension of the use of machinery.
3. Additional employment to classes of the community not ordinarily engaged in the business.
4. The promoting of emigration from foreign countries.
5. The furnishing greater scope for the diversity of talents and dispositions which discriminate men from each other.
6. The affording a more ample and various field for enterprize.
7. The creating in some instances a new, and securing in all, a more certain and steady demand for the surplus produce of the soil.

Each of these circumstances has a considerable influence upon the total mass of industrious effort in a community: Together, they add to it a degree of energy and effect, which are not easily conceived. . . .

It has justly been observed, that there is a scarcely any thing of greater moment in the economy of a nation than the proper division of labour. The separation of occupations causes each to be carried to a much greater perfection, than it could possibly acquire, if they were blended. This arises principally from three circumstances—

1st. The greater skill and dexterity naturally resulting from a constant and undivided application to a single object. It is evident, that these properties must increase, in proportion to the separation and simplification of objects and the steadiness of the attention devoted to each; and must be less in proportion to the complication of objects, and the number among which the attention is distracted.

2nd. The economy of time, by avoiding the loss of it, incident to a frequent transition from one operation to another of a different nature. This depends on various circumstanes—the transition itself—the orderly disposition of the implements, machines and materials employed in the operation to be relinquished—the preparatory steps to the commencement of a new one—the interruption of the impulse, which the mind of the workman acquires, from being engaged in a particular operation—the distractions, hesitations and reluctances, which attend the passage from one kind of business to another.

3rd. An extension of the use of machinery. A man occupied on a single object will have it more in his power, and will be more naturally led to exert his imagination in devising methods to facilitate and abrige labour, than if he were perplexed by a variety of independent and dissimilar operations. . . .

The employment of Machinery forms an item of great importance in the general mass of national industry. 'Tis an artificial force brought in aid of the natural force of man; and, to all the purposes of labour, is an increase of hands; an accession of strength, *unencumbered too by the expense of maintaining the laborer.* May it not therefore be fairly inferred, that those occupations, which give greatest scope to the use of this auxiliary, contribute most to the general Stock of industrious effort, and, in consequence, to the general product of industry? . . .

In places where [manufacturing] institutions prevail, besides the persons regularly engaged in them, they afford occasional and extra employment to industrious individuals and families, who are willing to devote the leisure resulting from the intermissions of their ordinary pursuits to collateral labours, as a resource for multiplying their acquisitions or their enjoyments. The husbandman himself experiences a new source of profit and support from the increased industry of his wife and daughters; invited and stimulated by the demands of the neighboring manufactories.

Besides this advantage of occasional employment to classes having different occupations, there is another, of a nature allied to it, and of a similar tendency. This is—the employment of persons who would otherwise be idle (and in many cases a burden on the community) either from the bias of temper, habit, infirmity of body, or some other cause, indisposing or disqualifying them for the toils of the country. It is worthy of particular remark, that, in general, women and children are rendered more useful, and the latter more early useful by manufacturing establishments, than they would otherwise be. Of the number of persons employed in the cotton manufactories of Great Britain, it is computed that four sevenths nearly are women and children; of whom the greatest proportion are children, and many of them of a very tender age. . . .

It is a just observation, that minds of the strongest and most active powers for their proper objects fall below mediocrity and labour without effect, if confined to uncongenial pursuits. And it is thence to be inferred, that the results of human exertion may be immensely increased by diversifying its objects. When all the different kinds of industry obtain in a community, each individual can find his proper element, and can call into activity the whole vigour of his nature. And the community is benefitted by the services of its respective members, in the manner, in which each can serve it with most effect. . . .

To cherish and stimulate the activity of the human mind, by multiplying the objects of enterprise, is not among the least considerable of the expedients, by which the wealth of a nation may be promoted. Even things in themselves not positively advantageous, sometimes become so, by their tendency to provoke exertion. Every new scene which is opened to the busy nature of man to rouse and exert itself, is the addition of a new energy to the general stock of effort.

The spirit of enterprise, useful and prolific as it is, must necessarily be contracted or expanded in proportion to the simplicity or variety of the occupations and productions, which are to be found in a society. . . .

[Creating a new demand and securing a more certain and steady demand for surplus produce of the soil] is a principal mean, by which the establishment of manufactures contributes to an augmentation of the produce or revenue of a country, and has an immediate and direct relation to the prosperity of agriculture.

It is evident, that the exertions of the husbandman will be steady or fluctuating, vigorous or feeble, in proportion to the steadiness or fluctuation, adequateness or inadequateness, of the markets on which he must depend, for the vent of the surplus, which may be produced by his labor; and that such surplus in the ordinary course of things will be greater or less in the same proportion.

For the purpose of this vent, a domestic market is greatly to be preferred to a foreign one; because it is the nature of things, far more to be relied upon. . . .

[T]he multiplication of manufactories not only furnishes a market for those articles which have been accustomed to be produced in abundance in a country, but it likewise creates a demand for such as were either unknown or produced in inconsiderable quantities. The bowels as well as the surface of the earth are ransacked for articles which were before neglected. Animals, plants and minerals acquire a utility and a value which were before unexplored. . . .

If the system of perfect liberty to industry and commerce were the prevailing system of nations, the arguments which dissuade a country, in the predicament of the United States, from the zealous pursuit of manufactures, would doubtless have great force. . . . In such a state of things, each country would have the full benefit of its peculiar advantages to compensate for its deficiencies or disadvantages. . . .

But the system which has been mentioned, is far from characterising the general policy of nations. The prevalent one has been regulated by an opposite spirit. The consequence of it is, that the United States are to a certain extent in the situation of a country precluded from foreign commerce. They can indeed, without difficulty obtain from abroad the manufactured supplies, of which they are in want; but they experience numerous and very injurious impediments to the emission and vent of their own commodities. . . .

In such a position of things, the United States cannot exchange with

Europe on equal terms; and the want of reciprocity would render them the victim of a system which should induce them to confine their views to agriculture, and refrain from manufactures. A constant and increasing necessity, on their part, for the commodities of Europe, and only a partial and occasional demand for their own, in return, could not but expose them to a state of impoverishment, compared with the opulence to which their political and natural advantages authorise them to aspire. . . .

The conversion of their waste into cultivated lands is certainly a point of great moment in the political calculations of the United States. . . .

But it does, by no means, follow, that the progress of new settlements would be retarded by the extension of manufactures. The desire of being an independent proprietor of land is founded on such strong principles in the human breast, that where the opportunity of becoming so is as great as it is in the United States, the proportion will be small of those, whose situations would otherwise lead to it, who would be diverted from it towards manufactures. . . .

The remaining objections to a particular encouragement of manufacturers in the United States now require to be examined.

One of these turns on the proposition, that industry, if left to itself, will naturally find its way to the most useful and profitable employment: whence it is inferred that manufactures without the aid of government will grow up as soon and as fast, as the natural state of things and the interest of the community may require.

Against the solidity of this hypothesis, in the full latitude of the terms, very cogent reasons may be offered. These have relation to—the strong influence of habit and the spirit of imitation—the fear of want of success in untried enterprises—the intrinsic difficulties incident to first essays towards a competition with those who have previously attained to perfection in the business to be attempted—the bounties premiums and other artificial encouragements, with which foreign nations second the exertions of their own citizens in the branches, in which they are to be rivalled.

Experience teaches, that men are often so much governed by what they are accustomed to see and practise, that the simplest and most obvious improvements, in the most ordinary occupations, are adopted with hesitation, reluctance, and by slow gradations. The spontaneous transition to new pursuits, in a community long habituated to different ones, may be expected to be attended with proportionably greater difficulty. When former occupations ceased to yield a profit adequate to the subsistence of their followers, or when there was an absolute deficiency of employment in them, owing to the superabundance of hands, changes would ensue; but these changes would be likely to be more tardy than might consist with the interest either of individuals or of the society. In many cases they would not happen, while a bare support could be insured by an adherence to ancient courses; though a resort to a more profitable employment might be practicable. To produce the desirable changes as early as may be expedient, may therefore require the incitement and patronage of government.

The apprehension of failing in new attempts is perhaps a more serious impediment. There are dispositions apt to be attracted by the mere novelty of an undertaking—but these are not always the best calculated to give it success. To this, it is of importance that the confidence of cautious sagacious capitalists, both citizens and foreigners, should be excited. And to inspire this description of persons with confidence, it is essential, that they should be made to see in any project, which is new, and for that reason alone, if, for no other, precarious, the prospect of such a degree of countenance and support from government, as may be capable of overcoming the obstacles, inseparable from first experiments.

The superiority antecedently enjoyed by nations, who have preoccupied and perfected a branch of industry, constitutes a more formidable obstacle, than either of those, which have been mentioned, to the introduction of the same branch into a country in which it did not before exist. To maintain between the recent establishments of one country and the long matured establishments of another country, a competition upon equal terms, both as to quality and price, is in most cases impracticable. The disparity, in the one or in the other, or in both, must necessarily be so considerable as to forbid a successful rivalship, without the extraordinary aid and protection of government.

But the greatest obstacle of all to the successful prosecution of a new branch of industry in a country, in which it was before unknown, consists, as far as the instances apply, in the bounties premiums and other aids which are granted, in a variety of cases, by the nations, in which the establishments to be imitated are previously introduced. . . .

Not only the wealth, but the independence and security of a country, appear to be materially connected with the prosperity of manufactures. Every nation, with a view to those great objects, ought to endeavour to possess within itself all the essentials of national supply. These comprise the means of *subsistence, habitation, clothing,* and *defence.*

The possession of these is necessary to the perfection of the body politic; to the safety as well as to the welfare of the society; the want of either is the want of an important organ of political life and motion; and in the various crises which await a state, it must severely feel the effects of any such deficiency. The extreme embarrassments of the United States during the late war, from an incapacity of supplying themselves, are still matter of keen recollection: A future war might be expected again to exemplify the mischiefs and dangers of a situation to which that incapacity is still in too great a degree applicable, unless changed by timely and vigorous exertion. To effect this change, as fast as shall be prudent, merits all the attention and all the Zeal of our Public Councils; 'tis the next great work to be accomplished. . . .

[Among the political means for promoting manufactures that Hamilton discusses are duties on foreign articles competing with domestic ones, prohibitions of competing articles, pecuniary bounties for new enterprises, premiums, exempting materials of manufacture from duties, encouraging new inventions and discoveries, and facilitating transportation of commodities. In discussing objections to bounties, Hamilton wrote:]

It is a species of encouragement more positive and direct than any other, and for that very reason, has a more immediate tendency to stimulate and uphold new enterprises, increasing the chances of profit, and diminishing the risks of loss, in the first attempts. . . .

A question has been made concerning the constitutional right of the government of the United States to apply this species of encouragement, but there is certainly no good foundation for such a question. The National Legislature has express authority "To lay and collect taxes, duties, imposts, and excises, to pay the debts, and provide for the *common defence* and *general welfare*" with no other qualfications than that "all duties, imposts, and excises shall be *uniform* throughout the United States and that no capitation or other direct tax shall be laid unless in proportion to numbers ascertained by a census or enumeration taken on the principles prescribed in the Constitution," and that "no tax or duty shall be laid on articles exported from any State."

These three qualifications excepted the power to *raise money* is *plenary* and *indefinite,* and the objects to which it may be *appropriated* are no less comprehensive than the payment of the public debts, and the providing for the common defence and *general welfare.* The terms *"general welfare"* were doubtless intended to signify more than was expressed or imported in those which preceded; otherwise, numerous exigencies incident to the affairs of a nation would have been left without a provision. The phrase is as comprehensive as any that could have been used; because it was not fit that the constitutional authority of the Union to appropriate its revenues should have been restricted within narrower limits than the "General Welfare" and because this necessarily embraces a vast variety of particulars, which are susceptible neither of specification or of definition.

It is therefore of necessity left to the discretion of the National Legislature, to pronounce upon the objects, which concern the general welfare, and for which under that description, an appropriation of money is requisite and proper. And there seems to be no room for a doubt that whatever concerns the general interest of *learning,* of *agriculture,* of *manufactures,* and of *commerce,* are within the sphere of the national councils, *as far as regards an application of money.* . . .

65

Catherine Zuckert

The Political Lessons of
Economic Life (1977)

. . . The argument of this paper is that strictly economic analysis [of public policy] both abstracts from important politically determined conditions and distorts the alternatives by stating them in quantitative and commensurable terms. If the political conditions are clearly stated, however, economic incentives and interests do provide a particularly appropriate and effective means of achieving the ends of public policy. They are appropriate because the basic political institutions of the United States constitute just such an attempt to establish the conditions in which individuals seeking their own self-interest, largely economic, will in the process serve public interests as well. The principles of the institutions can, therefore, provide a model for the design of more specific public policies, if those principles are understood as setting the conditions in which private interests work rather than mere processes of accommodation. . . .

I. The Attractions and Limitations of Economic Analysis

If policy issues and questions of priority could be established merely by listing our collective and some special group desires-demands, determining what it would cost to satisfy each separately and in various combinations, and comparing them, then economic analysis would supply an adequate foundation for policy determination, though merely listing and calculating all the alternatives would itself constitute a tremendous task. . . .

As the report on energy issued by the Congressional Budget Office in February, 1977, shows, however, the most a list of alternative goals and policies can do is to show the mutually incompatible requirements of simultaneously desired ends—in this particular case, to minimize pollution, and cost to consumers, to achieve conservation and efficient allocation of resources, and to maintain the requirements of national defense. The economic analysis in itself cannot establish the priorities and thus it does

By permission of the author.

not provide standards by which to choose among competing goals and methods of achieving them.

Economists themselves are the first to emphasize that the accuracy and predictability of economic analysis depends upon stringently defined assumptions about the desires and behavior of individuals or firms, the goods to be exchanged and the conditions of exchange. "All other things being equal," individuals (or firms) will "rationally" seek to maximize their gain and minimize their cost. . . . The explicit admission that individuals do not, in fact, always act "rationally" to maximize their gains and that all goods, especially political "goods" are not actually commensurable, makes the direct application of an economic framework of analysis to questions of public policy extremely problematic. . . .

Economic rationality does not and will not suffice to maintain a nation. It is never, for example, in the interest of an "economic man" to risk his life for his country. . . .

The conflict between the requirement that governmental programs constitute the most efficient use of economic resources and the need for consent, hence for some participation of the individuals or groups to be regulated, has long been noted. American laws often represent a compromise among several competing goals, so that a calculation of the suitability or efficiency of the means of administering the program becomes almost impossible. . . .

The desirability for voluntary compliance becomes [a] source of the attraction of economic frameworks of analysis, however, when those analyses proceed in terms of "incentives." Policies incorporating "incentives" have the advantage of making the outcome a product of individual choice and hence "free." They are thus both ideologically and politically attractive. And they are more likely to be effective. Such policies are designed to make it in the economic self-interest of individuals to serve the public end, so that there is eager cooperation rather than resistance, active or passive, to government regulations and their enforcement. Economic "incentives" do, therefore, constitute important means or "tools" of democratic government. The difficulty is that the tool does not prescribe the limitations or the goals of its use.

Economic methods of decision and allocations of resources look particularly attractive at a time when direct public regulation, in energy, schools, or welfare, for example, does not seem to work, at least not very well. And as skepticism about present governmental programs grows, so does interest in the suggestions Milton Friedman has made about ways to replace public with private decisions by utilizing the market. . . .

In the name of freedom, Friedman would like to minimize governmental regulation and to maximize individual choice. He seeks, therefore, to minimize politics and extend the sphere of economic decision. By sharpening the the public's understanding of the issues and requiring that one decision be made for everyone, Friedman argues, political debate serves to coalesce opposing sides and to intensify conflict. The resulting decision forces the minority to obey the majority. Since political action rests so much on the threat of force, it should be kept to a minimum. The market, on the other hand, operates as a voluntary system of proportional representation. The majority can buy most of the goods it prefers at the cheapest price through the economies of scale, yet the minority may still purchase the more expensive version. Neither is coerced. So long as there is a market, the goods will be produced. Indeed, since producers seek new markets, the choice and variety is apt to expand. Thus, in all possible cases, the economic process should replace the political process as a means of reaching agreement. . . .

Friedman's proposals [,however,] systematically substitute short-run preferences for long-run conditions or goals, because his goal is stated negatively, as minimizing government, and so the only positive measure becomes the expression of divergent individual preferences. He does not ask whether these choices undermine the conditions of choice in the long-run. . . .

Friedman admits that there are some "indivisible" goods such as national defense which can be provided only on an "either/or" basis and so require governmental support. But, he argues, the public should pay what the service is worth rather than coercing young men to provide it by conscripting them. Thus he suggested the institution of a "volunteer army." Salaries in the armed forces should be competitive with those in private industry. The result may be that Americans pay what they think that defense is worth; Congress spends more every year. Manpower, procurement, and research and development have all dropped, however, because so much of the total defense budget must now go to salaries and pensions, though, to put it kindly, the capabilities of the people employed has not much improved. So we pay more and get less; what an uneconomic result! Of course, the volunteer army was not in fact instituted for economic reasons; rather it served the political goal of substantially reducing the major source of opposition to the war in Vietnam. . . . The result is that we seem to have gained domestic peace in the short run at the cost of national defense over the long haul. . . .

Friedman's proposals are as attractive as they are, because they seem to maximize individual choice and efficiency at the same time. They fail because he does not take sufficient account of either the conditions necessary to present individuals with real choices or the long-run effects of the choices they make. Individuals do not have "real" choices unless (a) they know what the alternatives are and (b) they can choose without risking probable death or permanent damage. The man who "chooses" between starvation and "starvation wages" does not have much choice at all. Both education and income distribution are to a large extent subject to governmental action, however. . . . If we could specify the political conditions and institutions which set the context for the operation of economic incentives, we might then be able to be more specific about the desired and predictable political results. (We would then have defined the limitations of the operation of economic incentives as well.) But here we reach the central problem. Many agree that the economic approach is limited and that there is a broader political dimension. But no one seems able to say exactly what that political dimension is. The common sensical answer of "government" seems too restrictive; it puts too much emphasis on the external institutional framework and so detracts attention from the forces that actually make the institutions work. Yet the more inclusive definitions of politics as "power" or "authoritative allocation of values" are too broad to distinguish political from other activities and too abstract to provide much guidance for policymakers. . . .

II. The Close Relation of Politics and Economics in the Modern Liberal Regime

America remains basically a liberal regime. The national "creed" declares:

> We hold these truths to be self-evident; that all men are created equal, that they are endowed by their Creator with certain inalienable rights, and that among these are life, liberty, and the pursuit of happiness;—that to secure these rights, governments are instituted among men. . . .

American governmental institutions secure the rights to life and liberty by establishing a legal system that not only forbids "impairing the obligation of contract" but also requires "due process" and "equal protection of the laws." Thus they also establish the necessary conditions for the growth of an advanced economy, because a high degree of order (predictability and peace) is required to make economic investment rational and so to increase productivity. Governments provide the conditions for economic growth not for their own sake, however, but only in order to secure a more fundamental political end, to secure the "right" to the "pursuit of happiness." Both modern politics and modern economics ultimately serve the same political goal in attempting to establish the conditions under which each person can pursue his own vision of the good life. As a result, economic and political ends and means are easily fused and confused. It proves imperative to remember the priority of the political ends, however, if our policies are to be effective in the long run.

As Tocqueville also observed, instituting government on the basis of equal rights does not necessarily result in rule of or for all individuals. The need to secure equal conditions for all may justify the rule of a few with much force. Even with free institutions, securing the equal rights of all means, in practice, the rule of the majority for the interests of the majority.

> No one has yet found a political structure that equally favors the growth and prosperity of all the classes composing society. When the rich alone rule, the interests of the poor are always in danger; and when the poor make the law, the interests of the rich run great risks. . . . The real advantage of democracy is not, as some have said, to favor the prosperity of all, but only to serve the well-being of the greatest number.

The modern regime is still a regime, therefore; it is a democracy. The difference is that the majority now come from the middle class and use their power not to seize the goods of others (at home or abroad) but only to establish the conditions in which all individuals can pursue their own (largely economic) self-interest.

Though limited, even self-restrained in its ends, if not its power, and justified to itself only insofar as it secures the rights or opportunities of all, the modern regime constitutes a variety of majority rule. And that fact has several consequences. Recognition of the effective control of the majority creates fear at both the economic extremes. Second, although the modern majority does not explicitly require and directly reward living in a typically middle-class fashion or penalize those who do not, the laws which merely allow all individuals to follow their self-interest in effect require them to do so as well. They do not forbid aristocratic leisure or non-conformist rebellion; they merely make them economically impractical if not altogether unfeasible. If a person is actually forced to work to support himself he will have to do something for which there is a market; and it is a "mass market." The conformism and "middle-class morality" of America have been much criticized. I will, on the contrary, argue that these oft-derided characteristics are useful, perhaps even essential to maintaining decent free, political institutions.

First, we must look at the fate and prospects of the two threatened minorities, because in the fate of these minorities we will find the contradiction or affirmation of the majority's claim to rule for the benefit of everyone. Much early American political thought was concerned with the preservation of rights, especially the property rights of the minority (rich) from expropriation by the majority (previously poor). The chief protection consisted in the widespread participation in these rights; men with their own special interests and properties would not seek to have special interests prosecuted and property rights violated. . . . People have an interest in placing ceilings on wealth only if they are sure they themselves will never succeed in exceeding them. So long as they think they or their children may join the rich, they will protect the rights of wealth as they protect their own opportunities, especially if they see that the accumulation of wealth serves through investment to increase their opportunities to become rich as well. The preservation of the rights of the rich then depends upon maintaining conditions in which middle class people may hope to grow rich and seeing the rich contribute to the increase of these opportunities through demonstrating superior enterprise and inventive investment in the place of conspicuous consumption.

From this point of view, American income tax legislation makes much more sense than the surface contradictions indicate. As a result, perhaps, of the "closing of the frontier" and more surely expressing a sense of a growing and more rigid gap between the rich of Scott Fitzgerald and the ordinary man, the progressive income tax is enacted on the thought that those who benefit most from the system should pay more to support it, not just absolutely but relatively as well. Yet as soon as the progressive tax is enacted, the exceptions begin and grow precisely because the majority are willing, even anxious to have the wealth generated used to further general social and economic ends, especially those which create more opportunity for more people to join in the economic benefit. In effect, American tax laws allow the rich to retain some of their earnings to give others incentive to earn more; through deductions they allow the rich to keep control of even more of their income and property so long as they devote it to publicly desired uses and goals. The tax laws, thus, in effect, produce social responsibility in the rich, if not a social conscience.

The advantages of tax incentives have already been emphasized. What has not been sufficiently publicized, largely as a result of the incremental process whereby the tax law is drafted and amended over many years, is that the "exemptions," "loopholes," and deductions that have been exposed with so much ire of late, all serve as indirect means of executing public policy, and that they often work much better to achieve the desired ends than direct public regulations. . . .

If the concern of older defenders of the liberal regime was to make its claim to secure rights of all good against the ancient democratic proclivity to expropriate the rich, modern defenders have been more concerned to show not only that it allows each man to keep what he has gained but also that it enables all its citizens to gain. Even if the middle class extends the protection of life, liberty, and property it establishes in its own self-interest to the rich, its rule remains selfish and thus fundamentally unjust unless its rule also protects and benefits the poor minority. The modern middle-class majority does not, after all, justify its rule on the basis of its excellence of character, so much as on its ability to secure the rights of all. Securing the right to pursue happiness does not mean guaranteeing prosperity, much less happiness. That would be incompatible with individual freedom. It does mean in practice securing the option to participate in the economic system that provides the means for that broader pursuit. And securing that option becomes exceedingly complicated in a highly differentiated economy.

Some taxation is always justified, because the individual always owes part of his gain to the existence of an ordered society. His wealth is not simply, although it is surely in part, a product of his individual effort, ingenuity and foresight. For the same reason, an individual may come to grief through no personal fault of his own. He becomes a victim of the "system" from which he previously benefited. He may be highly trained in aerodynamics, for example, and still find himself unemployed. In order for the market to work, there must be shifts in labor as well as capital; yet the shifts in labor may result in grievous and undeserved suffering for significant numbers. Without assistance, displaced workers may fall into destitution and so create an enduring economic problem rather than a cyclical adjustment by moving into another area and/or trade. There are greater obstacles to the flow of resources than theory allows; so governmental action for relief (unemployment) and support for retraining becomes necessary not only on charitable but also on economic grounds. As any member of the middle-class can see, he, too, can become a victim. It is thus not surprising that the majority has passed legislation to help the victims of technological advance and shifts in supply and demand.

Much of the welfare system in the U.S. dispenses such temporary relief. The aged and handicapped constitute the second major category of recipients who are unable to participate in the economic system through no personal fault of their own. Though the legally instituted system could provide more incentive for family care of the aged and hiring the handicapped in order to reduce further weakening of family ties and personal (in contrast with "official") concern for human dignity, these programs are not very controversial. The controversy and the failure of the welfare system to help the poor occurs when the system does not serve merely to relieve suffering caused by economic dislocation but rather to perpetuate and even extend the need for support. This failure becomes even more problematic when a large number of the individuals involved visibly belong to a group that has previously suffered both legal and informal discrimination and oppression. *Prima facie* the regime does not secure the rights of all its citizens; and its legitimacy is thus brought into question. . . .

If the dominant groups in society were merely interested in maintaining their economy, they would use force to suppress any disruptive or potentially disruptive group. So long as the propertyless, so long as those who see no ground to hope that effort on their part will result in an improvement of their situation remain a minority—and they must begin as such—, force is a more economic and more efficient means of dealing with the problem than a complicated system of welfare payments. The reason why liberal societies attempt to institute the welfare state is not to maintain their wealth, but to maintain the grounds upon which they believe their wealth, both individual and social, is justified. And that justification for both the wealth and its necessarily unequal distribution is only that it is the way and, indeed, the only way of producing means sufficient to allow individuals to pursue their different visions of happiness. . . .

In the attempt to raise benefits to a decent level, we have, [however], created a situation in which it pays the head of a family to quit his 40-hour-a-week job at the minimum wage to go on welfare, or, in the absence of AFDC-U, to desert his family so they will become eligible for assistance and thereby maximize their total disposable income. Surely the incentives should be revised. This would be the major advantage of the institution of a negative income tax.

A negative income tax would create an incentive to work, even part-time or at low wages that does not presently exist. But it would not do much to encourage the development of the habits and skills necessary to enter the economy on a truly self-sufficient level. Could incentives not be used more positively? . . .

III. Economic Incentives as Means of Public Education

The reason economic incentives tend to be more legitimate and effective [than direct governmental regulation] is that they are peculiarly consonant with the principles of this regime. They work on the basis of choice and are, to that extent, free. Economic considerations can, to be sure, have coercive power. In incentives, that power operates indirectly and is designed to operate to the advantage of both individual and public. The choice offered is not between two indifferent alternatives; an incentive means that one alternative will be clearly economically advantageous. But the difference between such a choice and direct command or conditioning to the point that the individual no longer sees that there is an alternative remains considerable. Incentives work, moreover, because they do not serve merely as means to unrelated ends. Rather, by using incentives, one encourages the development and so one teaches the economic rationality necessary to make both the liberal economy and the liberal polity go. Economic rationality involves not only the weighing of alternatives in terms of their respective costs and benefits. It also entails the ability to identify long-run interests and to calculate the means necessary to secure those interests (forethought) as well as the discipline to carry out the plan. Economic analysis assumes, of course, economic rationality; and the analysis describes reality only insofar as that rationality exists. Public policies incorporating the use of economic incentives thus support general economic interests, not only by augmenting investment and labor resources but, more importantly, by establishing the conditions in which economic operations work. The habits of thought we call economic rationality are desirable not only for their strictly economic results but even more for their political effects.

American public policy should be designed to encourage individual effort, forethought and self-control, rather than supporting individuals only after they fail, as at present, because it is only through the development of such skills and habits that an individual can participate in the political community in a meaningful way or take real control of his own life. These skills and habits are the absolutely necessary conditions for the maintenance of a free regime. People are not born with these abilities; they learn them, and government can have a role in this broad form of education. Self-control is a very old-fashioned virtue that has been brought into question repeatedly in recent years by being re-named repression. Yet it is quite clear upon reflection that choice has no practical meaning whatsoever if one is not able to pause long enough to identify the alternatives or lacks the ability to identify the means necessary to achieve his desired end and the discipline to execute them. Quite simply, if one does not control oneself, one will be controlled by external forces or by others. The benefits of incentive structures in policy do not thus inhere solely or even primarily in their economic results. They lie rather in the kind of training they provide.

The present controversy concerning abortion legislation may provide a non-economic example of the connection between forethought and freedom. . . . We do, as a result of the Supreme Court decision, have a limited right to abortions. But, as Georgie Ann Geyer has argued, this right has effects opposed to those desired by most of its advocates. Instead of giving women the power to control their own lives, she observes, the availability of abortion has enabled women to deny the character and responsibility for their own and their partners' sexual acts at the time they occur. The result resembles the traditional situation the reformers wished to overturn: the women alone suffer the consequences and take responsibility, after the fact. Women will be free, Ms. Geyer argues, only if they are willing to take charge of their own lives, and this requires both thinking ahead and self-discipline. . . .

The self-discipline that well-designed economic policies can produce, becomes more apparent perhaps in present policy debates about energy and health. Virtually all economists now agree that the government should let the market determine the price of energy (though some would then subsidize the necessities of the poorer segment of the populations), because they think both private and public users will consume most efficiently when inefficiency becomes expensive. They thus express a long-standing American belief that economic self-interest can lead people to sacrifice some present comfort more effectively than moralistic appeals to public spirit.

Likewise, the major pending proposals for increased federal involvement in health care take the form of insurance rather than a national service on the model of Great Britain, even though the U.S. has a nascent public health service which could grow incrementally. One reason is that the major commitment and justification for the program is, like welfare policy in general, to prevent the individual from falling into irreversible destitution. There is the further general belief that, all other things being equal, it is better for the individual to look out for himself than for the government to take care of him; and insurance appears more compatible with this belief than government service. . . . The hope is to design a policy which will protect individuals from unsupportable financial burdens and yet allocate resources more efficiently by making the individual bear some portion of the cost. If it costs the individual more to use more expensive services, he will be more apt to use the least expensive suitable treatment, and there will be some restrictions on demand. Cost again "disciplines" the individual. . . .

Understanding economic activity as a means of encouraging the self-restraint fundamental to liberal politics has implications for strictly economic policy as well, of course. It would not, for example, support the "macroeconomic" policies based on the now-familiar Keynesian notion that government can expand production by increasing consumption, either directly through increased governmental spending or indirectly by stimulating private demand by lowering taxes, that the United States government has undertaken following Kennedy's 1962 speech. The idea is that firms will respond to increased demand by increasing investment and production, so increasing the demand for labor, salaries, and ultimately consumption and demand again . . . and so on—the famous "multiplier effect." Such policies encourage credit-buying, both public and private; and are inflationary if supply proves, as it has, not to be simply expandable. But the inflationary effects are by no means the most important or fundamental. Quite simply, credit-buying produces bad habits. It not only encourages people to seek immediate fulfillment of their present desires without considering whether they actually have or will have the means and so diminishes both self-restraint and calculation. It also supports and encourages unrealistic expectations of ever increasing prosperity and productivity and dangerous suspicions of public wrongdoing when these fail to materialize. One can continue to hope that the energy crisis with its obvious message of the value of conservation and forethought will reverse the trend. . . .

Liberal democracies can and have traditionally used economic incentives (or self-interest) in order to encourage the self-control that constitutes the practical meaning of freedom. The problem is that in using economic incentives, the political value, the training, can be lost in the rhetoric of productivity and the apparent worship of wealth for its own sake. Analyzing public policies solely or primarily in terms of their economic costs and benefits, especially only over the short-run, presses further in this direction. Since both economic and political institutions in a liberal regime are explicitly only a means to a further end, individual freedom, the distinction and ordering of the two interdependent means can easily become confused, if not obliterated. The most pressing danger to the institutions of this nation from both left and right—partly because it is not seen—is that they would both reverse the economic and political priorities and thus return us to the ancient source of political corruption, the subordination of political to economic ends of either productivity in itself or equality of economic resources.

Public support for following one's own economic interest inevitably breeds distrust. If one "knows" that all others are merely out for their self-interest and only their self-interest, one is not apt to trust them too far. Yet no individual by himself can provide himself with even the economic means requisite to offer him a choice of ways of life. The economy is a social product involving interdependence and cooperation, and there is no cooperation without trust. The pursuit of economic self-interest purely does not suffice even to achieve its own narrow aims. But it can serve as an education in the broadest sense; it can become the basis of habits of self-control which would enable one person to believe another capable of carrying out his promises and thus productive of trust if the political ends, the community interest and benefits are made clear.

IV. The Place of Economic Incentives and Interests in the American Political System

American political institutions are often thought to be founded on distrust. Madison's words in *Federalist* 51 to this effect are among his most famous.

> Ambition must be made to counteract ambition. The interest of the man must be connected with the constitutional rights of the place.

. . . Yet it is only partly true that the foundation is distrust. In *Federalist* 10 [Madison] explicitly recognizes that a direct conflict of interest, especially economic interest, produces tyranny—in direct democracies, tyranny of the majority. The point of encouraging and celebrating the multiplicity of interests in the extended sphere is not that the conflict of contending groups in itself necessarily produces the best outcome. Rather, the advantage of developing a multiplicity of interests is that, given representative institutions, the only way to form a majority and so to act at all is then through compromise and cooperation. Both require not only the qualification of particular interests, but the assertion of some common interest as well. If no group itself constitutes a majority and cannot get its narrow interest directly through political action, the political interest it will hold in common with other groups will always include the preservation of the rights of minorities. The majorities form, moreover, not to act directly but only to elect representatives. These representatives are directly responsible to the people through elections, but there is a "cushion" inserted by means of these elections, held in large districts incorporating many interests, between the actual process by which policy is decided in the legislature and direct economic pressures.

The system is intended to keep elected representatives "in line," however, and there is more attention paid to problems of corruption in the form of bribery in the *Federalist Papers* than in most recent treatises in political science, with the possible exception of those directed explicitly at "Watergate." Neither the "checks" nor elections would in themselves suffice. Rather, one had to tie the interest of the man to the office, so that it would be more in his interest to remain in office than to gouge the public treasury. Hamilton makes an explicit argument to this effect in support of an open-ended series of four year Presidential terms in #72. The institutions of the federal government are intentionally designed to produce public trust by "engineering" private interest. . . .

This paper concludes with a consideration of Tocqueville, because the French observer is the only writer thus far to have applied the concept of regime directly to American politics. And he shows the importance of economic behavior, not primarily for productivity, but as a kind of civil training which maintains the opinions and habits necessary for the operation of a liberal polity. . . .

[Tocqueville] does [not] believe . . . groups arise "spontaneously." On the contrary, he states

> The common interests of civil life seldom naturally induce great numbers to act together. A great deal of artifice is required to produce such a result.

If a citizen merely defines his interest solely in economic terms, he is not apt to join associations. "One cannot take part in most civil associations without risking some of one's property." By concentrating on short-run, monetary gain, citizens will lose the political abilities and so destroy the conditions under which they will be able to live free or satisfying lives, to enjoy even their economic gains in the long run.

> Intent only on getting rich, they do not notice the close connection between private fortunes and general prosperity. They find it a tiresome inconvenience to exercise political rights which distract them from industry. When required

to elect representatives, to support authority by personal service, or to discuss public business together, they find they have no time. They cannot waste their precious time in unrewarding work. . . . Such folk think they are following the doctrine of self-interest, but they have a very crude idea thereof, and the better to guard their interests, they neglect the chief of them, that is, to remain their own masters.

Tocqueville's interest in the formation of private associations is that individuals attain the organizational skills and the experience of having some effect on what happens. He praises the decentralized and thus more participatory political institutions of the United States chiefly because political life accustoms people to the idea and formation of associations that break down the isolation and feeling of powerlessness of isolated individuals. . . . Tocqueville admits that federal institutions are complicated and may result in some inefficiency in administration. But the political advantages far outweigh the costs. By involving people in making the decisions that determine the conditions in which they live, decentralized political institutions (local governments) make the connection between the individual's fate and the community very clear. They give individuals confidence that they can have an effect, so these institutions encourage all sorts of new enterprises, private even more than public. . . .

This effect of the structure of the political institutions becomes more important as American life becomes urban rather than agrarian and the employees of large organizations far outnumber independent farmers and entrepreneurs. The informal tendency of these organizations to foster conformity, buttressed by the leadership's legal and economic power over the members has been well-documented. Tocqueville foresaw such a development.

> It is easy to see the time coming in which men will be less and less able to produce, by each alone, the commonest bare necessities of life. The tasks of government must perpetually increase, and its efforts to cope with them must spread its net ever wider. The more government takes the place of associations, the more will individuals lose the idea of forming associations and need the government to come to their help. This is a vicious circle of cause and effect.

The complexities of modern economics make individuals factually and fundamentally interdependent. The political doctrine that no man has a right to rule another also means that no man has an obligation to support another. Thus, Tocqueville observes, when an individual feels his vulnerability to economic pressures he tends to look to the government rather than to his fellows. Although the government can help the man's economic situation, its direct assistance compounds his feeling of dependency. And that feeling makes the individual more conformist and timid, less independent in spirit and mind. Governmental assistance does not reduce the individual to such a feeling of helplessness, however, if he has a part in determining governmental policy and its effect in his particular case. Thus Tocqueville argues, governments and governmental programs can be designed to induce rather than depress individual enterprise. Designing programs with this end becomes most important because the dominant forces in modern civil societies push in the other direction. Governments cannot make their citizens independent or enterprising—directly. They can create conditions which encourage the development of the attitudes, habits and abilities which enable individuals to act on their own behalf. . . .

Chapter VII

Foreign Policy and
the American Regime

Should morality enter into our deliberation about foreign policy? If it should, what does morality demand? Cropsey presents the arguments for two predominant foreign policy perspectives: one states that we have a duty to other nations, while the other advocates a crude and calculating self-interest. Finding that both the morality of selfless duty and a self-interest that abstracts from virtue are inadequate guides to action, Cropsey offers a synthesis of these two positions that meets the demands of both morality and survival. This synthesis is a self-regarding morality based on nobility and honor rather than on altruism. Unfortunately, the American regime, Cropsey argues, vacillates between the two extremes that he criticizes, and is therefore not likely to adopt a self-regarding morality of honor.

Morgenthau's account of the history of American foreign policy sub-stantiates Cropsey's claim that the American regime alternates between the extremes of self-interest and selfless duty. For Morgenthau there are three periods in American history: that of the Founding generation, which advocated a policy of national interest in abstraction from moral considerations; a period where national interests were pursued but couched in moralistic terms; and the period since Woodrow Wilson, in which, contemptuous of calculating self-interest, the United States pursues moral goals in its dealings with other nations. Morgenthau calls for a return to the interest-oriented politics of Hamilton and Washington. Neglect of national interest, he argues, will lead to the death of the nation, and there is no morality except in the context of national communities. Morgenthau's argument for national survival, however, does not answer the question of why our nation is worth preserving. His argument for national self-preservation addresses all nations, whereas Cropsey argues that it is the character of the nation that makes the nation worth preserving.

Furthermore, we may question whether Hamilton and Washington did in fact ignore moral considerations in their foreign policy. Although Washington and Hamilton advocate national self-preservation, they conceive of the nation as having a certain character or excellence, and think that the preservation of that character is necessary to the nation's preservation. In Hamilton's Pacificus papers as well as in Washington's Farewell Address, foreign policy deliberations involve both national interest and morality, if morality is conceived of as self-dependence or self-respect rather than altruism. Although Hamilton argues that, given the circumstances, we should not go to war in aid of France, he tells us that we must be ready to defend our rights and to vindicate our honor. He does condemn "self-denying gratitude" toward other nations and "moral" considerations that harm the nation. But when Hamilton asks whether, by aiding France, our usefulness to the cause of liberty would outweigh the harm to ourselves, he assumes that there *are* circumstances in which we should assist others in a fight for liberty. Indeed, for Hamilton the cause of liberty, pursued with justice and good faith, appears to be the nation's highest purpose.

Although Morgenthau justifies self-interest, and Cropsey teaches us what kind of self-interest is justifiable, Woodrow Wilson proposes that the self-interest of states be replaced by the common will of mankind. Morality must replace expediency, just as national competition must give way to international cooperation. Wilson applauds the end of interest-based balance of power politics, for the same reason that he opposed the interest-based character of domestic affairs, including the separation of powers and checks and balances. The pursuit of particular or distinct interests, on both the domestic and international levels, leads to divisiveness that must be overcome; the unification of citizens in the United States under the direction of the Wilsonian statesman parallels the unification or the brotherhood of all men, as promoted and interpreted by such a statesman.

It is unclear that either self-interest or morality will provide an adequate guide for U.S. foreign policy in the 1990s. As James Pontuso explains, the Cold War presented a situation in which the United States could pursue a foreign policy that was both self-interested and moral. Communism was a threat both to our interests and anathema to our principles. But the end of the Cold War appears to eliminate the major threat to our national survival and the major opponent to our democratic principles. Some commentators have even gone so far as to say that it signals the end of history. Democracy has triumphed and foreign policy, understood as the clash of great powers or great principles, is no longer necessary.

Pontuso claims, however, that even if the optimism regarding Communism's demise proves to be well founded, the fundamental causes of international conflict have not been banished. In fact, the ideological conflict between democracy and communism may have served to restrain the more traditional sources of international conflict such as nationalism. According to Pontuso there is something in human nature, a love of one's own, or a desire for honor, that leads individuals and nations to distinguish themselves from others. It is this desire for distinction that has historically been at the root of international conflict. The challenge of U.S. foreign policy in the 1990s may be to recover an appreciation of those sources of conflict that are sown in the nature of man.

66

Joseph Cropsey

The Moral Basis of
International Action (1961)

The power of nations to inflict pain, destruction, and death in warfare has been brought to such a peak that men feel themselves compelled as never before to find means for preventing that power from being used. The instruments of mutilation and devastation are tremendous and their action comprehensive to such a degree that their employment would produce effects that shock the mind, for they reach perhaps to the impairment of the human race as a whole. It is by no means easy to obtain agreement as to the essence of moral offense in general; but it is transcendently easy to obtain agreement that it would be monstrous, and if monstrous then immoral, for men to burn up the moiety of mankind and to denature the loins of those who survive. . . .

It therefore appears that each nation is by duty bound to practice a voluntary restraint, to limit its own action and power of action in the interest of some good which is not its obvious, immediate self-benefit. For the sake of fulfilling a duty to the rest of mankind, each nation should to some extent deprive itself of the means to supremacy or even of defense. As we reflect on this duty, we notice how well it corresponds with what appears as the notion of morality at large. Morality is a standard of conduct which guides men to recognize and show concern for others, and to act out of some larger motive than the convenience, safety and well-being of themselves.

The demand of morality may be said to be in the direction of deliberate self-incapacitation. So far as this is true, morality is in apparent conflict with policy, or in other words with calculation in the interest of the actor. This is admitted both by the friends of morality, who see it as moderating the brutal egotism of life, and by the cynics, who see it as the delusion by

From Cropsey, "The Moral Basis of International Action," in *America Armed,* ed. Robert A. Goldwin, Rand McNally College Publishing Company, 1961. Reprinted by permission of the Public Affairs Conference Center, Kenyon College, Gambier, Ohio.

which the strong are seduced to abstain from benefiting from their strength. . . .

The common violation of morality suggests that something fundamental in human nature is outraged by the demand that the interest of another be made the measure of a man's or nation's action. The demand of morality appears to conflict with natural self-love and with the power of calculation that supports it. Nevertheless, to think only of oneself is perhaps more an offense against rationality than against decency. Other men and other nations have a concrete, objective existence which cannot sensibly be ignored, not merely because they will protest and retaliate, but because, from an impartial point of view, their being and their interest are equal in importance to the actor's. If one avoids the plain folly of picking himself out of the whole human race and making a special case of himself, he will easily be led to grant that he has no right to live by one set of rules and to expect everyone else to live by another. He must keep the others in mind when he seeks to form the rules of his own behavior. He will see that the fundamental likeness of all human beings in their humanity leads to the fundamental equality of all human beings in their rights. . . .

Thus it would appear that morality as self-limitation is the dictate of reason, based upon a rational being's power of seeing his relation to others with an impartial, objective eye. . . .

[M]en have a unique power to control or govern themselves. A beast can be trained, indeed, and it will show signs of apprehension when it breaks a rule, but there is no reason to suppose that it experiences anything but a fear of consequences when it does so. When it behaves well, it does so out of mere obedience. Men, however, do not merely obey; they are capable of themselves positively willing to do what is also required of them externally. They are thus unique in the whole world as willing, self-controlling, rational beings. This is a most important fact, for as a result of it, men have an overriding absolute worth or, as is often said, a dignity. The dignity of man is absolute; men therefore have an absolute moral obligation to one another, and incidentally, corresponding absolute moral claims on one another. . . .

The worth of man is so great that our duty to each other cannot be based upon any calculation of interest. To base our actions toward each other upon some calculation of interest leads to the contamination of every seemingly good deed: we would be truthful only to preserve our credit, kind only to preserve ourselves from retaliation, grateful only to encourage benefactions, and so on. Actions so performed would not express any recognition of man's dignity; all of them on the contrary would imply the treatment of other men as things to be manipulated, by cunning appearances, for the benefit of the actor—who would deserve to be so called for more than one reason.

It is clear that this conception of moral duty, resting upon the premise of man's capacity for willing, really rests upon the premise of man's capacity for willing freely—or, in brief, upon man's radical freedom. . . .

I shall try to show that such a notion of an absolute moral obligation rests upon error and cannot be the guide to action; it does not oblige because it cannot and ought not to oblige in practice.

1. The rule of absolute moral obligation is derived from a generalization about all mankind, and it pretends to oblige every man toward all of mankind. It claims a status similar to that of a law of nature. But it is a fact, as objective as any moral metaphysic, that men live not under the moral laws of nature but as members of nations under positive laws. The existence of bodies politic with different legal systems is the sovereign practical fact. The inference from this fact is that homogeneous mankind is superseded in practice by politically differentiated mankind; that laws obliging all mankind must be mediated by the legislation of the nations. The fundamental condition for the translation of absolute moral duty into political practice therefore does not exist in the world. . . . From the variety of moral foundations beneath the several political societies, two things follow: the duty of each society toward every other is affected by the character of the one toward which action is to be directed, just as our moral duty to act toward parsons and pickpockets, bearing in mind their common humanity, does not eventuate in the same conduct toward both. And second, since not all societies (and perhaps no societies) subscribe in their constituting principles to the view that there is an absolute moral duty of man to man, any nation that derived its practice from such a view would involve itself in the difficulties described next.

2. If absolute moral duty as described is to be the guide of any nation's practice, it would have to be recognized by mankind generally, that is, by all the nations or by the important nations as the guide to their actions. If it were not, then obedience to the moral law would inevitably entail suicide, or if not suicide, then disgrace. Coincidentally, obedience to the moral law would guarantee the triumph of the immoral, of those who feel little need to obey the moral law. A moral law that brings the obedient to death and shame and guarantees the success of its violators is not fit to be discussed at length by men with practical responsibilities. . . .

Our first general conclusion is that moral laws are not "absolute" in their force but must be obeyed in such a way that the result of obeying them is consistent with morality or simple decency. Morality uninformed by sound judgment is theoretically, let alone practically, null. This means that we must and do believe that deceitfulness is immoral, yet espionage is not to be eschewed; homicide is baneful, yet we must be ready to destroy the enemy; intervention in foreign sovereignties is reprehensible, yet we may not hang back from it.

Historically, the belief in a rational and objective ground of morality has led to views of mutual obligation quite different from the principle of absolute duty just examined. If rational and objective mean founded on common observations that anyone can make and verify at any time, then there is no more rational and objective foundation for morality than this: that all men, like all living things, have an overpowering preference for themselves, each one devoted to his own interest more than to anything in the world, with "interest" subject to some latitude of definition but not very much. But in that case it is both impractical and theoretically unsound to argue that man's duty to man must be understood as abstracted from every consideration of interest and consequences. Human nature would rule that out. . . .

It was noticed long ago that the ends of self-interest are best promoted by strictly enforceable agreements to live and let live, agreements by which each binds himself to abstain from the goods and persons of the others in order himself to be immune from destruction. It goes without saying that such agreements would be not useless but dangerous to those who entered into them if there were not effective arbitrators to enforce them, and to punish violations; otherwise, faithless contractors would exploit the simple who honor their engagements.

On this view of the human situation, morality may be said to grow out of, or to be replaced by, or to be identical with rational selfishness. Selfishness dictates that each individual respect the absolute right of others, and that he and the others ratify the tenders of their mutual consideration by submitting to be ruled by laws with penalties attached. Let us call this the condition of institutionalized mutual regard.

What does this notion have to contribute to our understanding of the moral ground underlying international action, military or other? What is the character of the moral obligation that nations have toward one another? . . .

If morality means to follow the dictate of survival under legal restraints in the interest of everybody's equal right to follow the same dictate, but among the nations there are no legal restraints of any significance, then plainly the nations' moral obligation dissolves into the right of naked power wielded by each country in its own behalf. . . .

It is disturbing to reflect that if one begins with the rational and objective natural rights of men to life and security, one ends with the reduction of international morality to violence or threats of violence, and nothing more. This conclusion is unacceptable for, if admitted, it would render us incapable of judging the moral quality of Hitler's acts to strengthen the Third Reich and Churchill's acts to strengthen Great Britain. But the need and the possibility of making that discrimination are facts as rational and objective as the common impulse toward self-preservation. . . .

In presenting the two moral extremes, the one of absolute duty to all men as men and the other of simple calculation in the interest of the agent, we have run into these difficulties: either the moral action of the one party exposes him to ruin at the hands of an immoral antagonist (with the consequence that morality leads invariably to the triumph of evil); or the possibility of moral discrimination disappears entirely, leaving as the only criterion of action the submoral criterion of success in survival. In either case, what begins as morality ends as immorality.

With this behind us, we can set down the requirements of a moral ground for international action, military and other. And if it turns out that no moral system can without self-contradiction meet these requirements, then we may conclude that morality is irrelevant to the conduct of nations, and all is just in hate and lust. The requirements for such a moral order are these: (1) That a nation be able to abide by the rules of right conduct without harm to itself even if every other nation in the world ignore or violate them. (2) That notwithstanding the full compatibility of the moral order with survival and victory, the rule of morality not simply dissolve into the right of the stronger, that is, the criterion of success.

Beginning again, we recur to the simplest and most generally admitted notion as to the meaning of morality: morality is self-restraint. Hitherto, we have taken self-restraint to mean a voluntary holding back either from violating an abstract precept of duty or from injuring others. The implicit supposition has been that the overriding problem to which morality addresses itself is how to define the duties or rights of men, the extreme solutions to the problem being either duty apart from calculation or calculation apart from duty. But there is no need for morality to mean either the one or the other so exclusively. This becomes clear to us when we consult the normal human understanding of what conduct deserves blame and what deserves praise. We blame people who deceive, defraud, plunder, attack, and murder; but curiously we also blame those who are vacillating, miserly, gluttonous, lewd, or craven, although it is not possible to say, for example, "gluttonous toward others." These latter defects are not primarily the sources of injury to other men. They are rather flaws of weakness, for example, the weakness of being unrestrainedly fond of some external good, or of being incapable of exercising that amount of self-control that enables a man to come to a conclusion or to suppress cruel, effete, or otherwise disgusting passions. We might note at the same time that a man overcome with the sense of duty, who plunged incontinently, that is, unrestrainedly into every situation where good needed to be done, would come under deserved censure as a dangerous meddler, especially if the only good accomplished was the salving of his conscience. There is a path between morality in the service of preservation and morality in the service of duty, abstractly considered; and that path is the one indicated by the general understanding of mankind. It follows the rule that self-restraint is not confined to the agent's acts against others but touches his character more comprehensively. . . .

Morality . . . is not intelligible as an abstract or formal principle but only as the sum of concrete characteristics, the possession of which enables the agent to deserve praise and respect. Morality without virtues is vanity.

What are those praiseworthy characteristics, and what does any of this have to do with the international action of the United States? The answer to the first will be tantamount to the answer to the second. Neither a nation nor a man can avoid shame if it is craven, heedless, self-indulgent, wanton in ease, irresolute in deliberation, wastrel in pleasure, squeamish in contest, faint in adversity. Virtue is etymologically related to manliness; but the relation is evidently more than etymological. . . .

I believe that if we test this rule of morality, which rises more or less directly out of common human experience, we will find that it meets the two conditions laid down earlier as being indispensable if the moral criterion is to be applicable to the nation's action. We are at no disadvantage if all the world but us behave brutally, foolishly, aggressively, deceitfully, and in every other way immorally. Prudence and decency demand of us that we make every effort to withstand every attempt that can be made against us; to do less would be contemptible and thus immoral. To do as much would be to work toward safety through morality. It goes without saying that morality so conceived utterly excludes those avoidable deeds of massive violence that can be defended only on the premise that success justifies everything. Certainly success is not the touchstone of morality as naturally understood, and it is not sensible to infer righteousness from survival, nor vice from failure. It is indeed possible to be respectable in defeat and contemptible in victory; but it is not possible to be respectable in defeat if defeat is the result of sloth, decadence, or a failure of nerve.

By this view, war and therefore the preparation for war are, in themselves, neither morally good nor morally bad, any more than homicide is morally good or bad. The homicide of a police officer upon a fleeing criminal is morally good, the homicide of a fleeing criminal upon a police officer morally bad. War is dreadful, and the preparation for it painful; but a theory that defines the painful as the immoral is nothing but hedonism or an encouragement to hedonism, no matter what appeals it may make to sentiment, conscience, or a show of rights. War is bad but it is not bad in the way that a supine indifference to disgrace and slavery are bad, for the latter comes from moral corruption and the former only from a fearful necessity that some men cannot, because of the vice of others, avoid.

War is bad because pain and death are bad, and death worse than pain. But we must reflect on the order of things, and recognize the difference between the death of men and the death of nations. Individuals die, but those remaining make up the loss. Cities are reduced to material chaos, but in an amazingly short time the destruction is repaired. The resurrection of a regime, however, is a thing rarely seen. The Constitution subverted, liberty disappears, and the human flotsam remaining suffer the ultimate demoralization, which is not death but subjection to the unlimited will of a master. Those who would investigate war and peace as part of the moral problem may never stray out of sight of the fact that the necessary condition for all morality is freedom, and the condition for freedom is the absolute integrity of the body politic—guaranteed by the power and willingness to make war.

It is evident that morality can retain its connection with self-restraint without collapsing into self-incapacitation. On the contrary, the demands of morality, seen in their relation to freedom and honor, are more energizing than they are paralyzing. Then the question arises whether there is anything at all that could contribute to the greatness and safety of the nation for which a justification could not be found by appealing to honor. The answer to this is surely No if the appeal to honor is a specious pretext, and as surely Yes if the appeal to honor is itself honorable. But assuming for the moment that the appeal to honor is not hypocritical, what sort of act would a nation be compelled to deny itself for purely moral reasons, contrary to its urgent interest? Is there something dishonorable, for example, in espionage? In deceitful counterintelligence? In the apprehension of a rebel by means of a ruse? In the subversion of a foreign government with which we are not at war? Not one of these questions can be answered except with knowledge of concrete circumstances. The most relevant circumstance is the character of the nation doing the deed in question, and the character of the men or nation to which it is done. . . .

Those who raise the question, Who shall judge? do so, very often, in the belief that it is self-evidently absurd for us to be judge of our own morality. In truth it is no less, and perhaps far more absurd to hope that a reliable judgment on our morality will be brought by a poll of the nations, many of which are moved by animosity and envy, and more by ignorance. . . . The teaching of morality may be reduced to this: we must do everything that needs to be done to insure the survival of ourselves, our friends, and our free principles, indulging neither ourselves nor others, avoiding sentimentality no less than brutality, and mindful that if we weakly hang back, we will ignominiously hang alone. Those who desire to see this wisdom reduced to a punched-tape program must await their translation to another, better universe; likewise those who wish to see it purged of all severity.

It will surely be objected that to imperil the human race on the point of honor is to inflate Quixotism from an eccentricity to a calamity. We must therefore try to keep separate in our minds these two principles of action: the one, that it is wrong and dishonorable weakly to submit to domination; and the second, quite different, that what deserves to be defended should be defended, and what deserves to be resisted should be resisted, but that it is not sober to make a virtue out of defense and resistance regardless of the worth of things to be defended and resisted. In other words, the appeal to honor alone is defective, and must be perfected by a showing that honor is aroused in a good cause; otherwise it is suspected of being a euphemism for truculence or ferocious obstinacy. Do we have any reason for believing that the sovietization of the world is an evil commensurate with the peril created by opposing it? that it is the menace to dignity and freedom it was earlier said to be? To answer this question fully would require a full statement of the character of communism; here we can provide only the barest intimation.

Marxism begins with materialism and ends with the homogeneity of mankind. Marxist materialism differs from traditional materialism in attaching fundamental importance to the process of production, that is, to self-preservation by means of "technology," primitive or complex. The problem of preservation is primarily a technological, not a political problem for Marx. Indeed the complete solution of the problem of preservation is radically nonpolitical: when the means of production are commonly owned and production is made a wholly social process, politics, or ruling and being ruled, will cease among men. The aspiration of communism is a total solution of the economic problem by means that would reduce all mankind to a single classless, that is, homogeneous mass: a huge herd of sheep safely grazing. Human distinction is the source of the human problem, and therefore distinction must be terminated. The "heroes" will be "heroes of the shovel" and "heros of the loom": heroes of social production. This could be called the ultimate vulgarization of humanity, or the final indignity. We see it foreshadowed in the substitution of the shoe for the gavel in council, and the hairy chest for the clean collar in diplomacy. Because dignity is inseparable from distinction, the resistance to sovietization was said to be in the interest of human dignity.

What of freedom? Communism aims at life without the state, or without formal government. . . . The formlessness of the herd without distinction exposes it perpetually to the highest concentration of irresponsible authority—wielded for the noble end of administration, all other problems having vanished. More simply, a flock demands a shepherd.

The bias of Marxism toward matter and in opposition to form bears fruit in an unprecedented threat to human dignity and freedom. Honorable resistance to sovietization is thus more than merely honorable.

Readers may be pardoned for failing to see in the Soviet Union now a population of grazing sheep. Far from a fat and torpid flock, they are an active, patriotic, spirited community, exhilarated by their hard-won achievements, conscious of greatness and lusting for its gratifications. That they are all these things is a vindication, not a contradiction of what was said above: finding their revolution confronted by hindrances, they compel themselves to rise to formidable heights of exertion. They are in the irrational condition of heroically laboring to destroy the possibility of any future heroic labor, while congratulating themselves on their own heroism. It is not the self-contradiction but the menace in their doings that is our present concern, and how we must respond to it.

We are in the position of respecting and praising the sense of honor, and of discerning it well-developed in our enemy. We will prove his right to rule us if we do not prevent him from exercising it; and we can maintain our right to be free only by being in a position to exercise it. In plain language, to his irresistible force we must oppose an immovable obstacle. . . .

There is not one iota of preponderance on the side of the view that the activator of the great force will choose to dash it against an absolute resistance. But if he entertains any reasonable doubt that our response will be absolute and remorseless, he will have less reason to keep the peace. This means that at a certain moment we must harden ourselves to look at the beauties of peace and prepare to see in their stead a contaminated chaos peopled with human carrion. If we cannot stand this thought, we are not ready to fight and will therefore be compelled to do so—or to truckle and prostrate ourselves.

On one condition would the sacrifice of ruin not be excessive: if we triumphed and the enemy were in the end destroyed. It is absurd to say that there are no victors in war. The one who survives in freedom is the victor; the one who must humble himself and surrender his ways and institutions at the dictate of his enemy is vanquished. . . .

Perhaps it will be said that there can be no victory where there are no survivors. . . . Then there must not be a next war. To argue so is plausible, but . . . inconclusive, for the argument tells us nothing about the form in which the cost of avoiding war must be paid. It might be that we pay for peace by abject surrender. That is unthinkable. It is unthinkable because the argument in favor of doing so is based upon the premise that, morally and politically, nothing matters—nothing, that is, except survival. The proper name for this position is not philanthropic morality but nihilism without intestines. The fortified species of nihilism also argues that nothing matters—except success. We have lost contact with the human spirit if we can no longer sense the repulsiveness of nihilism and the depravity of it in its emasculated form. If nothing matters, then human life does not matter. (Who would mourn it?) If anything matters, it is the decency of life and the possible self-respect of men. Still, where there is life there is hope for some amendment of any evil. We agree, and recommend the thought to our enemy; it deserves his consideration no less than ours. In brief, there is one cost of avoiding war which is more than we can afford: subhuman self-abasement.

Then we must pay for peace by making such a preparation for war that apprehensions for the safety of mankind will for once begin to influence the calculations of the enemy. If he is beyond or beneath a care for man's preservation, he is the manifest enemy of the race, fit to be hedged in or destroyed, certainly requiring to be diligently guarded against. If he is capable of such a care, then we need not, as truly we ought not assume the whole burden of providence. . . .

We seem to have concluded that the dictate of morality coincides with the interest of men and nations whose purposes are compatible with freedom and high-mindedness. This conclusion was the one intended.

In the course of our attempt to clarify the moral basis of international action, we have been led to take up two extreme but not unrepresentative examples of moral doctrine and a third which avoids the extremes. To simplify, the three could be said to turn, respectively, on Duty, Rights, and Honor. The conclusion has been that the first two are, for the purposes of guiding international action, imperfect, and the third is to be preferred. Supposing this for the moment to be true, of what practical value is the conclusion? Is it possible for a nation simply to adopt the moral principle of its choice for application to its international business? There is reason to doubt that this can be done with complete ease or freedom. The reason is that each nation is given its character by the elaborate set of moral judgments already embodied in its system of laws and practices. Implicit in the laws and customs is a notion of what action is just, what is proper and decent, what is worthy of esteem—in brief, of morality. . . . If all our notions of tolerable conduct are fashioned by one system of judgments, can we act externally on another? . . .

The problem is made especially severe by the kinship that exists between our general moral outlook as a community and the two moral dispensations described above as the "extremes." When we go back to the Declaration of Independence, for example, we read of man's inalienable rights—which are the same natural rights that we noticed earlier in the discussion—all derivative from the natural right of all men to self-preservation. The Declaration enumerates the inalienable rights to life, liberty, and the pursuit of happiness; the Constitution speaks of life, liberty, and property. The replacement made by the Constitution is not of the nature of a revision but a clarification: the rights to life, liberty, and property are inseparably connected with happiness, in our moral and political understanding as a nation. It is only when each man is guaranteed in his person that his property is secure, and only when he is safeguarded in his property that his person is inviolate. Our political system makes provision for translating those natural rights into a meaningful ground of civil life by wedding the institutions of capitalism to those of constitutional government. Political freedom is possible on various bases; in the Western world it exists on the foundation of certain economic institutions, and the concurrence of capitalism and modern democracy is by no means a coincidence. Liberty and prosperity, the aims of our order, are provided for at one and the same time by a principle that authorizes the individuals to act in their own behalf under the protection of a government to whose rule they give their consent so long as it defends them in their freedom to act in their own behalf. The essence of acting in one's own behalf is calculation. This is the basis for the remark made at the head of this paragraph, to the effect that deep in our own moral and political foundations there is a kinship with the extreme moral principle named after "Rights," leading to undiluted calculation.

But the assertion was also made that as a nation we have an affinity for the opposite moral extreme as well, the one called by the name of "absolute Duty." Long ago, the reduction of morality to the rules of calculation was seen to be open to various objections. One line of objection was to the effect that when morality collapses into mere calculation, patriotism or love of the common good tends to languish or to disappear. This view when broadened or exaggerated becomes the criticism that, under the reign of private calculation or institutionalized egotism, care for the absolute worth or dignity of man as man vanishes, and life deteriorates accordingly in the moral respect. Those who hold this view feel a need to oppose "human rights" to "property rights." The objection on behalf of patriotism or civic virtue found a certain expression in the yearning for republican, agrarian simplicity often voiced in our earlier history. The criticism on behalf of man as man is more characteristic of the reforming or Liberal tendency as it now is among us. What began as solicitude for a sort of virtue that can become patriotism has been replaced by a solicitude for humanity or Society, a care that need not eventuate in patriotism.

Thus our moral life as a nation vibrates between the poles of calculation and a radicalized alternative to it, the former polarizing on Property, the latter on hostility to it and on radical, undiscriminating Equality. The former is at the heart of our national conservatism, the latter epitomizes contemporary Liberalism. Neither . . . pays heed above all to honor, the sober mean somewhere between calculation and duty.

There is indeed a lack of perfect congruity between our ruling moral predilections and the preferred moral basis of international action. But if we must act on the strength of what we are rather than what we might wish to be, there is little doubt as to the course we ought to follow. One of the two poles of our moral world stands as an encouragement to men to love their theory of homogeneous mankind more than they love their country and their countrymen, where the demands of the two come in competition. The other pole, grounded on the perhaps low but surely solid principle of calculation, is not out of contact with the intermediate moral ground of decent self-regard or honor. Husbanding our strength, gathering our allies, and preparing to avoid the supreme disaster of servility and disgrace, we at least avoid the imprudence of opposing armed brutality with impotent dogma. Our enemy is abundantly furnished with dogma, but his action is notably unobstructed by it. His moral ground contains two elements, as does our own. One of them, if made the spring of his action, would bring down his regime and his empire in instant ruin. It is no less than the replacement of political life as known on earth by an absolute morality, to be inculcated among men by the economic institutions of communism. The other is Revolution—its necessity, its goodness, its inevitability. They are respectively his end and his means. The first is never allowed to get in the way of the second, which is the ruling element of his moral nature. It behooves us to remain in touch with our adversary on this simple level in order to oppose him—undistracted by sentimental dogma which he mocks, game theory which he ignores, and all other sophistications that are wasted upon a political intelligence which rightly or wrongly regards coercion as the ultimate rationality. Under the circumstances, we may allow ourselves to be led by calculation where perhaps we cannot be taught to soar by honor.

We began by thinking of man's duty to mankind. Reflecting on morality in its connection with the deeds of nations, we could not avoid the themes of honor and nobility, or more largely of human excellence. Human excellence, as it finds its expression among the masses of men ranked in their nations, is called civilization. Whatever reminds us of civilization reminds us at the same time of our duty to civilization, which means in practice to civilized men. What begins as a reflection on duty to man ends, under the influence of a glimpse at human superiority, as a reflection on duty to civilized man and to civilized nations. The way to discharge our duty to civilization is to sustain it where it exists before trying to inspire it where it never has been. Upon this point, remote from doctrinairism, the morality of calculation and the morality of honor come within sight of one another. The resulting gain in strategic competence brings them within earshot of one another. We must not despair if they never join hands.

67

Hans J. Morgenthau

The Mainsprings of
American Foreign Policy (1950)

. . . [T]his generation of Americans must shed the illusions of their fathers and grandfathers and relearn the great principles of statecraft which guided the path of the republic in its first decade and—in moralistic disguise—in the first century of its existence. . . .

This classic age of American statecraft comes to an end with the physical disappearance of that generation of American statesmen. . . . Until very recently the American people seemed to be content to live in a political desert. . . . What in that period, stretching over more than a century, went under the name of foreign policy was either improvisation in the face of an urgent problem which had to be dealt with somehow, or—and especially in our century—the invocation of some abstract moral principle in the image of which the world was to be made over. Improvisation as a substitute for foreign policy was largely successful, for in the past the margin of American and allied power to spare generally exceeded the degree to which American improvidence fell short of the demands of the hour. The invocation of abstract moral principles was in part hardly more than an innocuous pastime; for embracing everything it came to grips with nothing. In part, however, it was a magnificent instrument for marshalling public opinion in support of war and warlike policies—and for losing the peace to follow. The intoxication with moral abstractions which as a mass phenomenon started with the Spanish-American War, and which in our time has become the prevailing substitute for political thought, is indeed one of the great sources of weakness and failure in American foreign policy. . . .

In the Western Hemisphere we have always endeavored to preserve the unique position of the United States as a predominant power without rival. We have not been slow in recognizing that this predominance was not likely to be effectively threatened by any one American nation or combination of them, acting without support from outside the Western Hemisphere. It was,

From Morgenthau, "The Mainsprings of American Foreign Policy," *American Political Science Review,* December 1950. Reprinted by permission of the American Political Science Association.

then, imperative for the United States to isolate the Western Hemisphere from the political and military policies of non-American nations. . . .

Since a threat to the national interest of the United States in the Western Hemisphere can come only from outside it, that is, historically from Europe, the United States has always striven to prevent the development of conditions in Europe which would be conducive to a European nation's interference in the affairs of the Western Hemisphere or to a direct attack upon the United States. Such conditions would be most likely to arise if a European nation had gained such predominance that it could afford to look across the sea for conquest without fear of being menaced at the center of its power, that is, in Europe itself. It is for this reason that the United States has consistently—the War of 1812 is the sole major exception—pursued policies aiming at the maintenance of the balance of power in Europe. . . . It is by virtue of this concern that the United States has intervened in both World Wars on the side of the initially weaker coalition and that its European policies have so largely paralleled those of Great Britain; for from Henry VIII to this day Great Britain has invariably pursued one single objective in Europe: the maintenance of the balance of power.

With Asia the United States has been vitally concerned only since the turn of the century, and the relation of Asia to the national interest of the United States has never been obvious or clearly defined. . . . Yet beneath the confusions, reversals of policy, and moralistic generalities, which have made up the surface of our Asiatic policy since McKinley, one can detect an underlying consistency which, however vaguely, reflects the permanent interest of the United States in Asia. . . .

However unsure of itself the Asiatic policy of the United States has been, it has always assumed that the domination of China by another nation would create so great an accumulation of power as to threaten the security of the United States.

Not only with regard to Asia, however, but wherever American foreign policy has operated, political thought has been divorced from political action. . . . We have acted on the international scene, as all nations must, in power-political terms; we have tended to conceive of our actions in non-political, moralistic terms. This aversion to seeing problems of international politics as they are and the inclination to viewing them instead in non-political, moralistic terms can be attributed both to certain misunderstood peculiarities of the American experience in foreign affairs and to the general climate of opinion prevailing in the Western world during the better part of the nineteenth and the first decade of the twentieth centuries. . . .

The expansion of the United States up to the Spanish-American War seemed to provide conclusive proof both for the distinctiveness and moral superiority of American foreign policy. The settlement of the better part of a continent by the thirteen original states seemed to be an act of civilization rather than of conquest and as such essentially different from, and morally superior to, the imperialistic ventures, wars of conquest, and colonial acquisitions with which the history of other nations is replete. Yet it was not so much political virtue as the contiguity of the sparsely settled object of conquest with the original territory of departure, which put the mark of uniqueness upon American expansion. . . . Furthermore, the utter political, military, and numerical inferiority of the Indian opponent tended to obscure the element of power, which was less obtrusive in, but no more absent from, the continental expansion of the United States than the expansionist movements of other nations. . . .

American isolation was an established political fact until the end of the nineteenth century. . . .

From the shores of the North American continent, the citizens of the new world watched the strange spectacle of the struggle for power unfolding on the distant scenes of Europe, Africa, and Asia. Since for the better part of the nineteenth century their foreign policy enabled them to retain the role of spectators, what was actually the result of a passing historic constellation appeared to Americans as a permanent condition, self-chosen as well as naturally ordained. At worst they would continue to watch the game of power politics played by others. At best the time was close at hand when, with democracy established everywhere, the final curtain would fall and the game of power politics would no longer be played.

To aid in the achievement of this goal was conceived to be part of America's mission. . . .

To understand the American mission in such selfless, humanitarian terms was the easier as the United States—in contrast to the other great powers—was generally not interested, at least outside the Western Hemisphere, in a particular advantage to be defined in terms of power or of territorial gain. Its national interest was exhausted by the preservation of its predominance in the Western Hemisphere and of the balance of power in Europe and Asia. . . .

In one sense, this ideal of a free, peaceful, and prosperous world, from which popular government had banished power politics forever, was a natural outgrowth of the American experience. In another sense, this ideal expressed in a particularly eloquent and consistent fashion the general philosophy which during the better part of the nineteenth century dominated the Western world. This philosophy contains two basic propositions: that the struggle for power on the international scene is a mere accident of history, naturally associated with non-democratic government and, hence, destined to disappear with the triumph of democracy throughout the world; and that, in consequence, conflicts between democratic and non-democratic nations must be conceived not as struggles for mutual advantage in terms of power but primarily as a contest between good and evil, which can only end with the complete triumph of good and with evil being wiped off the face of the earth. . . .

The illusion that a nation can escape, if it only wants to, from power politics into a realm where action is guided by moral principles rather than by considerations of power, not only is deeply rooted in the American mind; it also took more than a century for this illusion to crowd out the older notion that international politics is an unending struggle for power in which the interests of individual nations must necessarily be defined in terms of power. Out of the struggle between these two opposing conceptions three types of American statesmen emerge: the realist, thinking in terms of power and represented by Alexander Hamilton; the ideological, acting in terms of power, thinking in terms of moral principles, and represented by Thomas Jefferson and John Quincy Adams; the moralist, thinking and acting in terms of moral principles and represented by Woodrow Wilson. To these three types, three periods of American foreign policy roughly correspond: the first covering the first decade of the history of the United States as an independent nation, the second covering the nineteenth century to the Spanish-American War, the third covering the half century after that war. . . .

On April 22, 1793, Washington issued a proclamation of neutrality, and it was in defense of that proclamation that Hamilton wrote the "Pacificus" and "Americanus" articles. Among the arguments directed against the proclamation were three derived from moral principles. Faithfulness to treaty obligations, gratitude toward a country which had lent its assistance to the colonies in their struggle for independence, and the affinity of republican institutions were cited to prove that the United States must side with France. Against these moral principles, Hamilton invoked the national interest of the United States. . . .

Must a nation subordinate its security, its happiness, nay, its very existence to the respect for treaty obligations, to the sentiment of gratitude, to sympathy with a kindred political system? This was the question which Hamilton proposed to answer, and his answer was an unequivocal "no." Hamilton unswervingly applied one standard to the issues raised by the opposition to Washington's proclamation of neutrality: the national interest of the United States. He put the legalistic and moralistic arguments of the oppostion . . . into the context of the concrete power situation in which the United States found itself on the international scene. . . .

Considerations such as these, recognized for what they are, have guided American foreign policy but for a short period, that is, as long as the Federalists were in power. *The Federalist* and Washington's Farewell Address are their classic expression. . . . During the century following their brief flowering, they have by and large continued to influence policies as well, under the cover, as it were, of those moral principles with which from Jefferson onward American statesmen have liked to justify their moves on the international scene. . . . [W]hat the moral law demanded was by a felicitous coincidence always identical with what the national interest seemed to require. Political thought and political action moved on different planes, which, however, were so inclined as to merge in the end. . . .

The Monroe Doctrine's moral postulates of anti-imperialism and mutual non-intervention were the negative conditions for the safety and enduring greatness of the United States. . . .

This period initiated by McKinley, in which moral principles no longer justify the enduring national interest as in the second, but replace it as a guide for action, finds its fulfillment in the political thought of Woodrow Wilson. Wilson's thought not only disregards the national interest, but is explicitly opposed to it on moral grounds. "It is a very perilous thing," he said in his address at Mobile on October 27, 1913,

> to determine the foreign policy of a nation in the terms of material interest. It not only is unfair to those with whom you are dealing, but it is degrading as regards your own actions. . . . We dare not turn from the principle that morality and not expediency is the thing that must guide us, and that we will never condone iniquity because it is most convenient to do so.

. . . Not only did the crusading fervor of moral reformation obliterate the awareness of the United States' traditional interest in the maintenance of the European balance of power, to be accomplished through the defeat of Germany. Wilson's moral fervor also had politically disastrous effects, for which there is no precedent in the history of the United States. Wilson's moral objective required the destruction of the Kaiser's autocracy, and this happened also to be required by the political interests of the United States. The political interests of the United States required, beyond this immediate objective of total victory, the restoration of the European balance of power, traditional guarantor of American security. Yet it was in indignation at the moral deficiencies of that very balance of power, "forever discredited," as he thought, that Wilson had asked the American people to take up arms against the Central Powers! Once military victory had put an end to the immediate threat to American security, the very logic of his moral position—let us remember that consistency is the moralist's supreme virtue—drove him toward substituting for the concrete national interest of the United States the general postulate of a brave new world where the national interest of the United States, as that of all nations, would disappear in a community of interests comprising mankind.

Consequently, Wilson considered it to be the purpose of victory not to restore a new, viable balance of power, but to make an end to it once and forever. . . .

Faced with the national interests of the great allied powers, Wilson had nothing to oppose or support them with but his moral principles, with the result that the neglect of the American national interest was not compensated for by the triumph of political morality. In the end Wilson had to consent to a series of uneasy compromises which were a betrayal of his moral principles—for principles can, by their very nature, not be made the object of compromise—and which satisfied nobody's national aspirations. . . .

Yet Wilson returned to the United States, unaware of his failure. He offered the American people what he had offered the allied nations at Paris: moral principles divorced from political reality. "The day we have left behind us," he proclaimed at Los Angeles on September 20, 1919,

> was a day of balances of power. It was a day of "every nation take care of itself or make a partnership with some other nation or group of nations to hold the peace of the world steady or to dominate the weaker portions of the world." Those were the days of alliances. This project of the League of Nations is a great process of disentanglement. . . .

[W]hat is significant for the course which American foreign policy was to take in the interwar years is not so much that the American people rejected Wilsonianism, but that they rejected it by ratifying the denial of the American tradition of foreign policy which was implicit in the political thought of Wilson. . . . The isolationism of the interwar period could delude itself into believing that it was but the restorer of the early realist tradition of American foreign policy. . . . The isolationists of the twenties and thirties did not see what was the very essence of the policies of the Founding Fathers—that both the isolated and the preponderant position of the United States in the Western Hemisphere was not a fact of nature, and that the freedom from entanglements in European conflicts was not the result of mere abstention on the part of the United States. Both benefits were the result of political conditions outside the Western Hemisphere and of policies carefully contrived and purposefully executed in their support. For the realists of the first period, isolation was an objective of policy, which had to be striven for to be attained. For the isolationists of the interwar period, isolation was, as it were, a natural state, which only needed to be left undisturbed in order to continue forever. Conceived in such terms, it was the very negation of foreign policy. . . .

In a profound sense [isolationism and Wilsonianism] are brothers under the skin. Both are one in maintaining that the United States has no interest in any particular political and military constellation outside the Western Hemisphere. While isolationism stops here, Wilsonianism asserts that the American national interest is nowhere in particular but everywhere, being identical with the interests of mankind itself. The political awareness of both refuses to concern itself with the concrete issues with regard to which the national interest must be asserted. . . .

When internationalism triumphed in the late thirties, it did so in the moral terms of Wilsonianism. . . .

The practical results of this philosophy of international affairs, as applied to the political war and post-war problems, were, then, bound to be quite similar to those which had made the allied victory in the First World War politically meaningless. . . .

The thought that the war might be waged in view of a new balance of power to be established after the war, occurred in the West only to Winston Churchill—and, of course, to Joseph Stalin. . . .

The equation of political moralism with morality and of political realism with immorality is itself untenable. . . . The basic fact of international politics is the absence of a society able to protect the existence, and to promote the interests, of the individual nations. For the individual nations to take care of their own national interests is, then, a political necessity. There can be no moral duty to neglect them; for as the international society is at present constituted, the consistent neglect of the national interest can only lead to national suicide. Yet it can be shown that there exists even a positive moral duty for the individual nation to take care of its national interests.

Self-preservation for the individual as well as for societies is not only a biological and psychological necessity, but in the absence of an overriding moral obligation a moral duty as well. In the absence of an integrated international society, in particular, the attainment of a modicum of order and the realization of a minimum of moral values are predicated upon the existence of national communities capable of preserving order and realizing moral values within the limits of their power. It is obvious that such a state of affairs falls far short of that order and realized morality to which we are accustomed in national societies. The only relevant question is, however, what the practical alternative is to these imperfections of an international society based upon the national interests of its component parts. The attainable alternative is not a higher morality realized through the application of universal moral principles, but moral deterioration through either political failure or the fanaticism of political crusades. . . .

68

Alexander Hamilton

On Neutrality Toward France (1793-1794)

. . . The . . . objection to the Proclamation [of Neutrality] namely that it is inconsistent with the Treaties between the United States and France will now be examined. . . .

The Alliance between the United States and France is a *Defensive Alliance.* In the Caption of it it is denominated a "Treaty of Alliance eventual and *defensive.*" . . .

[I]n determining the *legal* and *positive* obligations of the UStates the only point of inquiry is—whether the War was *in fact* begun by France or by her enemies. . . . [I]n a *defensive* alliance, when *war is made upon* one of the allies, the other is bound to fulfil the conditions stipulated on its part, without inquiry whether the war is rightfully begun or not—as on the other hand when war is begun by one of the allies the other is exempted from the obligation of assisting; however just the commencement of it may have been. . . .

[T]hough the manifest injustice of the war has been affirmed by some, to be a good cause for not executing the formal obligations of a treaty, I have no where found it maintained, that the justice of a war is a consideration, which can *oblige* a nation to do what its formal obligations do not require; as in the case of a *defensive* alliance, to furnish the succours stipulated, though the formal obligation did not exist, by reason of the ally having begun the war, instead of being the party attacked.

But if this were not the true doctrine, an impartial examination would prove, that with respect to some of the powers, France is not blameless in the circumstances, which preceded and led to the war with those powers; that if she received, she also gave cause of offense, and that the justice of the War on her side is, in those cases, not a little problematical. . . .

[France] gave a general and just cause of alarm to Nations, by that Decree of the 19th. of November 1792 whereby the Convention, in the name of the French Nation, declare that they will grant *fraternity* and *assistance* to every People who *wish* to recover their liberty and charge the Executive

From Hamilton, "Pacificus II-IV" and "Americanus I-II," *The Papers of Alexander Hamilton,* Vol. XV and XVI, Columbia University Press, 1969.

Power to send the necessary orders to *the Generals* to give assistance to such people, and to *defend those citizens who may have been or who may be vexed for the cause of liberty;* which decree was ordered to be printed *in all languages.*

When a Nation has actually come to a resolution to throw off a yoke, under which it may have groaned, and to assert its liberties—it is justifiable and meritorious in another nation to afford assistance to the one which has been oppressed & is *in the act* of liberating itself; but it is not warrantable for any Nation *beforehand* to hold out a general invitation to insurrection and revolution, by promising to assist *every people* who may *wish* to recover their liberty and to defend *those citizens,* of every country, *who may have been or who may be vexed for the cause of liberty;* still less to commit to the *Generals* of its armies the discretionary power of judging when the Citizens of a foreign Country have been vexed for the cause of Liberty by their own government. . . .

Such a conduct as that indicated by this Decree has a natural tendency to disturb the tranquillity of nations, to excite fermentation and revolt every where; and therefore justified neutral powers, who were in a situation to be affected by it in taking measures to repress the spirit by which it had been dictated.

But the principle of this Decree received a more particular application to Great Britain by some subsequent circumstances.

Among the proofs of this are two answers, which were given by the President of the National Convention at a public sitting on the 28th. of November. . . .

"Nature and *principles* draw *towards us* England Scotland and Ireland. Let the cries of friendship resound through the two *REPUBLICS.*"
"Principles are waging war against Tyranny, which will fall under the blows of philosophy. *Royalty in Europe is either destroyed or on the point of perishing,* on the ruins of feudality; and the *Declaration of Rights placed by the side of thrones is a devouring fire which will consume them. WORTHY Republicans.*"

Declarations of this sort cannot but be considered as a direct application of the principle of the Decree to Great Britain; as an open patronage of a Revolution in that Country; a conduct which proceeding from the head of the body that governed France in the presence and on behalf of that body was unquestionably an offense and injury to the Nation to which it related.

The decree of the 15 of November is another cause of offence to all the Governments of Europe. By That Decree *"The French Nation declares, that it will treat as enemies the people,* who *refusing* or *renouncing* liberty and equality *are desirous* of preserving their *Prince* and *privileged casts*—or of *entering into an accomodation* with them &c."* This decree was little short of a declaration of War against all Nations, having *princes* and *privileged classes*. . . .

Whatever partiality may be entertained for the general object of the French Revolution, it is impossible for any well informed or soberminded man not to condemn the proceedings which have been stated; as repugnant to the general rights of Nations, to the true principles of liberty, to the freedom of opinion of mankind; & not to acknowledge as a consequence of this, that the justice of the war on the part of France, with regard to some of the powers with which she is engaged, is from those causes questionable enough to free the UStates from all embarrassment on that score; if it be at all incumbent upon them to go into the inquiry.

The policy of a defensive alliance is so essentially distinct from that of an offensive one, that it is every way important not to confound their effects. The first kind has in view the prudent object of mutual defence, when either of the allies is involuntarily forced into a war by the attack by some third power. The latter kind subjects the peace of each ally to the will of the other, and obliges each to partake in the wars of policy & interest, as well as in those of safety and defence, of the other. To preserve their boundaries distinct it is necessary that each kind should be governed by plain and obvious rules. This would not be the case, if instead of taking the simple fact of who begun the war as a guide, it was necessary to travel into metaphysical niceties about the justice or injustice of the cause which led to it. . . .

France at the time of issuing the proclamation was engaged & likely to be engaged in war, with all or almost all Europe; without a single ally in that quarter of the Globe.

In such a state of things, it is evident, that however she may be able to defend herself at home (a thing probably still practicable if her factions can be appeased, and system and order introduced) she cannot make any *external* efforts, in any degree proportioned to those which can be made against her.

By this situation of things alone, the United States would be dispensed from an obligation to embark in her quarrel.

It is known that we are wholly destitute of naval force. France, with all the great maritime Powers united against her, is unable to supply this deficiency. She can not afford us that species of cooperation, which is necessary to render our efforts useful to her and to prevent our experiencing the entire destruction of our Trade and the most calamitous inconveniences in other respects.

Our guarantee does not respect France herself. It does not relate to her own immediate defence or preservation. It relates merely to the defence & preservation of her American colonies; objects of which (though of considerable importance) she might be deprived and yet remain a great and powerful and a happy Nation. . . .

There would be no proportion between the mischiefs and perils, to which the UStates would expose themselves by embarking in the War, and the benefit *which the nature of their stipulation aims at securing* to France, or that, which it would be in their power actually to render her, by becoming a party.

This disproportion would be a valid reason for not executing the Guarantee. All contracts are to receive a reasonable construction. Self preservation is the first duty of a Nation; and though in the performance of stipulations relating to war, good faith requires that the *ordinary hazards* of war should be fairly encountered, because they are directly contemplated by such stipulations, yet it does not require that *extraordinary* and *extreme* hazards should be run; especially where the object, for which they are to be run, is only a *partial* and *particular* interest of the ally, for whom they are to to be run.

As in the present instance good faith does not require, that the UStates should put in jeopardy their essential interests, perhaps their very existence, in one of the most unequal contests, in which a nation could be engaged—to secure to France what?—her West India Islands and other less important possessions in America. . . .

[Another] objection to the Proclamation is, that it is inconsistent with the gratitude due to France, for the services rendered us in our own Revolution. . . .

[I]t may not be without use to indulge some reflections on this very favourite topic of gratitude to France; since it is at this shrine we are continually invited to sacrifice the true interests of the Country; as if *"All for love and the world well lost"* were a fundamental maxim in politics.

Faith and Justice between nations are virtues of a nature sacred and unequivocal. They cannot be too strongly inculcated nor too highly respected. Their obligations are definite and positive their utility unquestionable. . . .

But the same cannot be said of gratitude. . . .

The basis of gratitude, is a benefit received or intended, which there was no right to claim, originating in a regard to the interest or advantage of the party, on whom the benefit is or is meant to be conferred. If a service is rendered from views *chiefly* relative to the immediate interest of the party, who renders it, and is productive of reciprocal advantages, there seems scarcely in such a case to be an adequate basis for a sentiment like that of gratitude. . . .

Between individuals, occasion is not unfrequently given to the exercise of gratitude. Instances of conferring benefits, from kind and benevolent dispositions or feelings towards the person benefitted, without any other interest on the part of the person, who confers the benefit, than the pleasure of doing a good action, occur every day among individuals. But among nations they perhaps never occur. It may be affirmed as a general principle, that the predominant motive of good offices from one nation to another is the interest or advantage of the Nations, which performs them.

Indeed the rule of morality is in this respect not exactly the same between Nations as between individuals. The duty of making its own welfare the guide of its actions is much stronger upon the former than upon the latter; in proportion to the greater magnitude and importance of national compared with individual happiness, to the greater permanency of the effects of national than of individual conduct. Existing Millions and for the most part future generations are concerned in the present measures of a government: While the consequences of the private actions of an individual, for the most part, terminate with himself or are circumscribed within a narrow compass.

Whence it follows, that an individual may on numerous occasions meritoriously indulge the emotions of generosity and benevolence; not only without an eye to, but even at the expence of his own interest. But a Nation can rarely be justified in pursuing a similar course; and when it does so ought to confine itself within much stricter bounds. Good offices, which are indifferent to the Interest of a Nation performing them, or which are compensated by the existence or expectation of some reasonable equivalent or which produce an essential good to the nation, to which they are rendered, without real detriment to the affairs of the nation rendering them, prescribe the limits of national generosity or benevolence.

It is not meant here to advocate a policy absolutely selfish or interested in nations; but to show that a policy regulated by their own interest, as far as justice and good faith permit, is, and ought to be their prevailing policy: and that either to ascribe to them a different principle of action, or to deduce from the supposition of it arguments for a self-denying and self-sacrificing gratitude on the part of a Nation, which may have received from another good offices, is to misconceive or mistake what usually are and ought to be the springs of National Conduct. . . .

An examination into the question how far *regard to the cause of Liberty* ought to induce the United States to take part with France in the present war, is rendered necessary by the efforts which [some] are making to establish an opinion that it ought to have that effect. In order to make a right judgment on the point, it is requisite to consider the question under two aspects.

I. Whether the cause of France be truly the cause of Liberty, pursued with justice and humanity, and in a manner likely to crown it with honorable success.

II. Whether the degree of service we could render, by participating in the conflict, was likely to compensate, by its utility to the cause, the evils which would probably flow from it to ourselves.

If either of these questions can be answered in the negative, it will result, that the consideration which has been stated ought not to embark us in the war. . . .

All who are not wilfully blind must see and acknowlege that this Country at present enjoys an unexampled state of prosperity. That war would interrupt it need not be affirmed. We should then by war lose the advantage of that astonishing progress in strength wealth and improvement, which we are now making, and which if continued for a few years will place our national rights and interests upon immoveable foundations. This loss alone would be of infinite moment: it is such a one as no prudent or good man would encounter but for some clear necessity or some positive duty.

If while Europe is exhausting herself in a destructive war, this country can maintain its peace, the issue will open to us a wide field of advantages, which even imagination can with difficulty compass.

But a check to the *progress* of our prosperity is not the greatest evil to be anticipated. Considering the naval superiority of the enemies of France we cannot doubt that our commerce would be in a great degree annihilated by a war. Our Agriculture would of course with our commerce receive a deep wound. The exportations which now contribute to animate it could not fail to be essentially diminished. Our mechanics would experience their full share of the common calamity. That lively and profitable industry which now spreads a smile over all our cities and Towns would feel an instantaneous and rapid decay. . . .

The certain evils of our joining France in the war are sufficient dissuasives from so intemperate a measure. . . .

To defend its own rights, to vindicate its own honor, there are occasions when a Nation ought to hazard even its existence. Should such an occasion occur, I trust those who are now most averse to commit the peace of the country will not be the last to face the danger, nor the first to turn their backs upon it.

But let us at least have the consolation of not having rashly courted misfortune. Let us have to act under the animating reflection of being engaged in repelling wrongs which we neither sought nor merited, in vindicating our rights, invaded without provocation, in defending our honor violated without cause. Let us not have to reproach ourselves with having voluntarily bartered blessings for calamities.

But we are told that our own Liberty is at stake upon the event of the war against France—that if she falls we shall be the next victim. The combined powers, it is said, will never forgive in us the origination of those principles which were the germs of the French Revolution. They will endeavour to eradicate them from the world.

If this suggestion were ever so well founded, it would perhaps be a sufficient answer to it to say, that our interference is not likely to alter the case—that it could only serve prematurely to exhaust our strength.

But other answers more conclusive present themselves.

The war against France requires on the part of her enemies efforts unusually violent. They are obliged to strain every nerve, to exert every resource. However it may terminate, they must find themselves spent in an extreme degree; a situation not very favourable to the undertaking a new, and even to Europe combined, an immense enterprize.

To subvert by force republican Liberty in this Country, nothing short of entire conquest would suffice. This conquest, with our present increased population; greatly distant as we are from Europe, would either be impracticable or would demand such exertions, as following immediately upon those which will have been requisite to the subversion of the French Revolution, would be absolutely ruinous to the undertakers. . . .

There are too great errors in our reasoning upon this subject. One is that the combined Powers will certainly attribute to us the same principles which they deem so exceptionable in France; the other, that our principles are in fact the same.

If left to themselves, they will all except one naturally see in us a people who originally resorted to a Revolution in Government as a refuge from encroachment on rights and privileges *antecedently* enjoyed—not as a people who from choice have sought a radical and entire change in the established Government, in pursuit of new privileges and rights carried to an extreme, not reconciliable perhaps with any form of regular Government. They will see in us a people who have a due respect for property and personal security—who in the midst of our revolution abstained with exemplary moderation from everything violent or sanguinary instituting governments adequate to the protection of persons and property; who since the completion of our revolution have in a very short period, from mere reasoning and reflection, without tumult or bloodshed adopted a form of general Government calculated as well as the nature of things would permit—to remedy antecedent defects—to give strength and security to the Nation—to rest the foundations of Liberty on the basis of Justice Order and Law—who at all times have been content to govern ourselves; unmeddling in the Governments or Affairs of other Nations: in fine, they will see in us sincere Republicans but decided enemies to licentiousness and anarchy—sincere republicans but decided friends to the freedom of opinion, to the order and tranquility of all Mankind. They will not see in us a people whose best passions have been misled and whose best qualities have been perverted from their true aim by headlong fanatical or designing leaders to the perpetration of acts from which humanity shrinks—to the commission of outrages, over which the eye of reason weeps—to the profession and practice of principles which tend to shake the foundations of morality—to dissolve the social bands—to disturb the peace of mankind—to substitute confusion [for] order, anarchy [for] Government.

Such at least is the light in which the Reason or the passions of the Powers confederated against France lead them to view her principles and conduct. And it is to be lamented that so much cause has been given for their opinions. If on our part, we give no incitement to their passions, facts too prominent and too decisive to be combated will forbid their reason to bestow the same character upon us.

It is therefore matter of real regret that there should be an effort on our part to level the distinctions, which discriminate our case from that of France—to confound the two cases in the view of foreign powers—and to hazard our own principles, by persuading ourselves of a similitude which does not exist. . . .

But let us not corrupt ourselves by false comparisons or glosses—nor shut our eyes to the true nature of transactions which ought to grieve and warn us—not rashly mingle our destiny in the consequences of the errors and extravagances of another nation.

69

James Madison

First Inaugural Address (1809)

. . . Indulging no passions which trespass on the rights or the repose of other nations, it has been the true glory of the United States to cultivate peace by observing justice, and to entitle themselves to the respect of the nations at war by fulfilling their neutral obligations with the most scrupulous impartiality. . . .

This unexceptionable course could not avail against the injustice and violence of the belligerent powers. In their rage against each other, or impelled by more direct motives, principles of retaliation have been introduced

From *Inaugural Addresses of the Presidents of the United States,* United States Government Printing Office, 1969.

equally contrary to universal reason and acknowledged law. How long their arbitrary edicts will be continued in spite of the demonstrations that not even a pretext for them has been given by the United States, and of the fair and liberal attempt to induce a revocation of them, can not be anticipated. Assuring myself that under every vicissitude the determined spirit and united councils of the nation will be safeguards to its honor and its essential interests, I repair to the post assigned me with no other discouragement than what springs from my own inadequacy to its high duties. If I do not sink under the weight of this deep conviction it is because I find some support in a consciousness of the purposes and a confidence in the principles which I bring with me into this arduous service.

To cherish peace and friendly intercourse with all nations having correspondent dispositions; to maintain sincere neutrality toward belligerent nations; to prefer in all cases amicable discussion and reasonable accommodation of differences to a decision of them by an appeal to arms; to exclude foreign intrigues and foreign partialities, so degrading to all countries and so baneful to free ones; to foster a spirit of independence too just to invade the rights of others, too proud to surrender our own, too liberal to indulge unworthy prejudices ourselves and too elevated not to look down upon them in others; to hold the union of the States as the basis of their peace and happiness; to support the Constitution, which is the cement of the Union, as well in its limitations as in its authorities; to respect the rights and authorities reserved to the States and to the people as equally incorporated with and essential to the success of the general system; . . . to promote by authorized means improvements friendly to agriculture, to manufactures, and to external as well as internal commerce; to favor in like manner the advancement of science and the diffusion of information as the best aliment to true liberty; to carry on the benevolent plans which have been so meritoriously applied to the conversion of our aboriginal neighbors from the degradation and wretchedness of savage life to a participation [in] the improvements of which the human mind and manners are susceptible in a civilized state—as far as sentiments and intentions such as these can aid the fulfillment of my duty, they will be a resource which can not fail me. . . .

70

Woodrow Wilson

Fourth Liberty Loan Speech (1918)

. . . I have come . . . to seek an opportunity to present to you some thoughts which I trust will serve to give you, in perhaps fuller measure than before, a vivid sense of the great issues involved, in order that you may appreciate and accept with added enthusiasm the grave significance of the duty of supporting the Government by your men and your means to the utmost point of sacrifice and self-denial. No man or woman who has really taken in what this war means can hesitate to give to the very limit of what he or she has; and it is my mission here to-night to try to make it clear once more what the war really means. You will need no other stimulation or reminder of your duty. . . .

No statesman or assembly created [the purposes of the war]; no statesman or assembly can alter them. They have arisen out of the very nature and circumstances of the war. The most that statesmen or assemblies can do is to carry them out or be false to them. They were perhaps not clear at the outset; but they are clear now. The war has lasted more than four years and the whole world has been drawn into it. The common will of mankind has been substituted for the particular purposes of individual states. Individual statesmen may have started the conflict, but neither they nor their opponents can stop it as they please. It has become a peoples' war, and peoples of all sorts and races, of every degree of power and variety of fortune, are involved in its sweeping processes of change and settlement. We came into it when its character had become fully defined and it was plain that no nation could stand apart or be indifferent to its outcome. Its challenge drove to the heart of everything we cared for and lived for. The voice of the war had become clear and gripped our hearts. Our brothers from many lands, as well as our own murdered dead under the sea, were calling to us, and we responded, fiercely and of course. . . .

From Wilson, "Address to Public Meeting in New York, Opening the Fourth Liberty Loan," in *Selected Addresses and Public Papers of Woodrow Wilson,* The Modern Library.

The issues of the war are these:

Shall the military power of any nation or group of nations be suffered to determine the fortunes of peoples over whom they have no right to rule except the right of force?

Shall strong nations be free to wrong weak nations and make them subject to their purpose and interest?

Shall peoples be ruled and dominated, even in their own internal affairs, by arbitrary and irresponsible force or by their own will and choice?

Shall there be a common standard of right and privilege for all peoples and nations or shall the strong do as they will and the weak suffer without redress?

Shall the assertion of right be haphazard and by casual alliance or shall there be a common concert to oblige the observance of common rights?

No man, no group of men, chose these to be the issues of the struggle. They *are* the issues of it; and they must be settled,—by no arrangement or compromise or adjustment of interests, but definitely and once for all and with a full and unequivocal acceptance of the principle that the interest of the weakest is as sacred as the interest of the strongest. . . .

We are all agreed that there can be no peace obtained by any kind of bargain or compromise with the governments of the Central Empires, because we have dealt with them already and have seen them deal with other governments that were parties to this struggle, at Brest-Litovsk and Bucharest. They have convinced us that they are without honor and do not intend justice. They observe no covenants, accept no principle but force and their own interest. We cannot "come to terms" with them. They have made it impossible. The German people must by this time be fully aware that we cannot accept the word of those who forced this war upon us. We do not think the same thoughts or speak the same language of agreement.

It is of capital importance that we should also be explicitly agreed that no peace shall be obtained by any kind of compromise or abatement of the principles we have avowed as the principles for which we are fighting. . . .

If it be in deed and in truth the common object of the Governments associated against Germany and of the nations whom they govern, as I believe it to be, to achieve by the coming settlements a secure and lasting peace, it will be necessary that all who sit down at the peace table shall come ready and willing to pay the price, the only price, that will procure it; and ready and willing, also, to create in some virile fashion the only instrumentality by which it can be made certain that the agreements of the peace will be honored and fulfilled.

That price is impartial justice in every item of the settlement, no matter whose interest is crossed; and not only impartial justice, but also the satisfaction of the several peoples whose fortunes are dealt with. That indispensable instrumentality is a League of Nations formed under covenants that will be efficacious. Without such an instrumentality, by which the peace of the world can be guaranteed, peace will rest in part upon the word of outlaws and only upon that word. For Germany will have to redeem her character, not by what happens at the peace table, but by what follows.

And, as I see it, the constitution of that League of Nations and the clear definition of its objects must be a part, is in a sense the most essential part, of the peace settlement itself. It cannot be formed now. If formed now, it would be merely a new alliance confined to the nations associated against a common enemy. It is not likely that it could be formed after the settlement. It is necessary to guarantee the peace; and the peace cannot be guaranteed as an afterthought. The reason, to speak in plain terms again, why it must be guaranteed is that there will be parties to the peace whose promises have proved untrustworthy, and means must be found in connection with the peace settlement itself to remove that source of insecurity. It would be folly to leave the guarantee to the subsequent voluntary action of the Governments we have seen destroy Russia and deceive Rumania.

But these general terms do not disclose the whole matter. Some details are needed to make them sound less like a thesis and more like a practical program. These, then, are some of the particulars, and I state them with the greater confidence because I can state them authoritatively as representing this Government's interpretation of its own duty with regard to peace:

First, the impartial justice meted out must involve no discrimination between those to whom we wish to be just and those to whom we do not wish to be just. It must be a justice that plays no favorites and knows no standard but the equal rights of the several peoples concerned;

Second, no special or separate interest of any single nation or any group of nations can be made the basis of any part of the settlement which is not consistent with the common interest of all;

Third, there can be no leagues or alliances or special covenants and understandings within the general and common family of the League of Nations.

Fourth, and more specifically, there can be no special, selfish economic combinations within the League and no employment of any form of economic boycott or exclusion except as the power of economic penalty by exclusion from the markets of the world may be vested in the League of Nations itself as a means of discipline and control.

Fifth, all international agreements and treaties of every kind must be made known in their entirety to the rest of the world. . . .

We still read Washington's immortal warning against "entangling alliances" with full comprehension and an answering purpose. But only special and limited alliances entangle; and we recognize and accept the duty of a new day in which we are permitted to hope for a general alliance which will avoid entanglements and clear the air of the world for common understandings and the maintenance of common rights. . . .

As I have said, neither I nor any other man in governmental authority created or gave form to the issues of this war. I have simply responded to them with such vision as I could command. But I have responded gladly and with a resolution that has grown warmer and more confident as the issues have grown clearer and clearer. . . .

Our enthusiasm for them grows more and more irresistible as they stand out in more and more vivid and unmistakable outline. . . . It is the peculiarity of this great war that while statesmen have seemed to cast about for definitions of their purpose and have sometimes seemed to shift their ground and their point of view, the thought of the mass of men, whom statesmen are supposed to instruct and lead, has grown more and more unclouded; more and more certain of what it is that they are fighting for. National purposes have fallen more and more into the background and the common purpose of enlightened mankind has taken their place. The counsels of plain men have become on all hands more simple and straightforward and more unified than the counsels of sophisticated men of affairs, who still retain the impression that they are playing a game of power and playing for high stakes. That is why I have said that this is a peoples' war, not a statesmen's. Statesmen must follow the clarified common thought or be broken.

I take that to be the significance of the fact that assemblies and associations of many kinds made up of plain workaday people have demanded, almost every time they came together, and are still demanding, that the leaders of their Governments declare to them plainly what it is, exactly what it is, that they were seeking in this war, and what they think the items of the final settlement should be. They are not yet satisfied with what they have been told. They still seem to fear that they are getting what they ask for only in statesmen's terms,—only in the terms of territorial arrangements and divisions of power, and not in terms of broadvisioned justice and mercy and peace and the satisfaction of those deep-seated longings of oppressed and distracted men and women and enslaved peoples that seem to them the only things worth fighting a war for that engulfs the world. Perhaps statesmen have not always recognized this changed aspect of the whole world of policy and action. . . .

But I, for one, am glad to attempt the answer again and again, in the hope that I may make it clearer and clearer that my one thought is to satisfy those who struggle in the ranks and are, perhaps above all others, entitled to a reply whose meaning no one can have any excuse for misunderstanding. . . . "Peace drives" can be effectively neutralized and silenced only by showing that every victory of the nations associated against Germany brings the nations nearer the sort of peace which will bring security and reassurance to all peoples and make the recurrence of another such struggle of pitiless force and bloodshed forever impossible, and that nothing else can. Germany is constantly intimating the "terms" she will accept; and always finds that the world does not want terms. It wishes the final triumph of justice and fair dealing.

71

James F. Pontuso

Is There Anything Bad About the End of the Cold War? (1990)

Sitting on my desk is a piece of the Berlin Wall. One of my students gave it to me. It is not really much to look at, just a three inch fragment of roughly made concrete with some indecipherable scribbling on one side in blue iridescent paint. Yet this little hunk of rubble represents one of the momentous events of the twentieth century, and perhaps a turning point in human history. For most of our lives the Cold War dominated the relations among countries. Whether they wanted to or not, all nations, even those not directly involved, had to make foreign policy in light of the conflict between the Communist powers of the East and the liberal democracies of the West. The Berlin Wall was a symbol of that struggle. Ostensibly it was built to keep Western troublemakers out of East Germany, but it actually was constructed to prohibit East Berliners from fleeing their tyrannical system of government. When the Wall was torn down, it seemed to mark the end of the contest between East and West. Not only was East Berlin liberated, but all of Eastern Europe broke free from the Soviet orbit. We all are aware that wars, even cold ones, are distasteful things. So, what could be bad about the end of the Cold War?

This question raises an important preliminary issue that must be considered. Is the Cold War really over?

Certainly the disagreement that initiated the Cold War has ended. The Cold War began at the conclusion of World War II when the Soviet Union used its military might to plant Communist governments in the nations of Eastern Europe. During World War II the United States, Great Britain, and the Soviet Union had fought as allies against the Nazis. As the war neared its end, the leaders of those nations Franklin Roosevelt, Winston Churchill, and Joseph Stalin met to map out an arrangement that would bring stability to Europe and peace to the rest of the world. It was decided that each of the Great Powers would have a sphere of influence. Since the Soviet army occupied Eastern Europe there was little doubt that it would be within the Soviet realm. Furthermore, the Soviets desired to have a buffer between themselves and Western powers, especially Germany, as a means of avoiding the catastrophic losses (estimated at 20 million people) they had suffered during the war. The difficulty was that the agreement between the Great Powers was faulty. It promised that the governments of Eastern Europe would be freely elected *and* that they would be congenial toward the Soviet Union. However, if the people of Eastern Europe were actually given a choice, they would never have elected leaders sympathetic to the Soviet Union. There were long-standing hostilities toward Russia, some going back centuries, that were only made worse by the fear of Communist domination.

Governments congenial to the Soviet Union were established, but only after Stalin brutally crushed all political movements in Eastern Europe and installed Communist leaders who mimicked the Soviet line. Harry Truman, who had become President after Roosevelt's death, pressed Stalin to comply with the other half of the agreement—democratic elections—but to no avail. Truman also worried that the Soviets were supporting Communist insurgences in Turkey, Greece and Iran. He feared that Stalin might use the same fierce tactics to establish Communist governments in those nations. To counter Soviet moves, the United States began to rearm and redeploy its military forces, so recently withdrawn from Europe at the conclusion of the war. The idea was to encircle the Soviet Union with a group of alliances and to prohibit it from further expansion. That principle became the cornerstone of Western policy toward the Soviets, and remained so for more than forty years. Although there were a number of wars during that era, such as Korea, Vietnam, and Afghanistan, direct confrontation between the superpowers was avoided because of the fear of mutual nuclear annihilation.

Such were the origins of the Cold War. But it is important to remember that there were deeper reasons for the discord. The most fundamental was ideology. Karl Marx, on whose ideas the Soviets claimed to base their system, argued that the bourgeois way of life, that is the political and social system of a liberal democracy such as the United States, was the source of great suffering and injustice. He claimed that the natural rights Americans so cherish were in actuality nothing more than a mechanism of class oppression. In order to perform tasks more efficiently, Marx reasoned, every society employs a division of labor. Over time, these divisions evolve into social classes. Some people benefit more from this economic arrangement than do others. In bourgeois societies the class difference becomes particularly acute, since the owners of businesses, or capitalists, use their wealth and position to amass great fortunes. The political rights guaranteed in capitalist states (for example, in the United States, by such documents as the Declaration of Independence and the Bill of Rights) insure that no one will interfere with the owners' liberty to acquire more, always more.

On the other hand, Marx held that although the workers are "free" to vote and to sell their labor to the highest bidder, they are reduced to subsistence wages. This "iron law," as he called it, is true because of the intense competition inherent in capitalism. In order to keep up with their rivals, corporations are compelled to produce goods rapidly and efficiently, and at the same time to lower the cost of production. To attain these goals the owners must introduce ever more complex machines and simultaneously reduce wages. Thus, the laborers, the most numerous class, become alienated from their toil and, indeed, their very existence. They are made to work at tedious jobs, the result of assembly–line techniques and advanced machinery, for meager wages, the absolute minimum expenditure needed to maintain them as functioning units of production. All fulfillment is lost in such labor, since the workers have control over neither the finished product nor the means by which those products are created. For the workers, political freedom results in slavery and degradation.

Marx theorized that after a time the flaws of capitalism would become apparent. Capitalism's very efficiency would cause its downfall. It would produce such a glut of goods that consumption would fall behind production, resulting in massive layoffs and eventually economic collapse. The inequity of a system in which the owners enjoy all the luxuries of life but do not labor and the workers labor but live in poverty would become so apparent that the workers would finally seize the means of production and transform the social arrangement so that all would share equally in its bounty. The inexorable movement of history made it inevitable that a new era would be born in which there was real equality, full liberty, and universal brotherhood.

Some people in the West came to agree with Marx's goals of equality, liberation and community, but most viewed his ideals with suspicion. The latter group believed that no matter how humane the aim, Marx's principles were impractical. Human beings are not equal in ability or determination. The attempt to make all people equal necessitates denying liberty to some, normally the talented. In other words, Marx's promise to make people equal, in fact, results in denying equality of opportunity to most. The critics of Marx also maintained that total liberation was not feasible. Human beings need some form of government to restrain their baser instincts. By its very nature, government implies that there will be restrictions on people's liberty. Even universal community is unrealistic; for in all of recorded history people have found it normal to live in distinct political communities.

Even more worrisome than the principles of Communist countries were their practices. Marx's philosophy led people to believe that society could be thoroughly reformed. Thus, Communist rulers worked tirelessly to usher in the intended changes. But most people could not measure up to this perfect image; they were often more concerned with their own interests than with the triumph of Communism. In an effort to make reality conform to theory, Communist rulers employed the most severe forms of discipline. When still the people failed to meet expectations, Communists became vicious. Despite the tightly controlled media in Communist countries, stories of ruthlessness and savagery filtered into the West from émigrés and others who had escaped. The tales were almost too fantastic to believe. Millions of people were executed for political offenses. Even more were sent to forced labor camp where the majority died from overwork. The crimes of these people consisted of being born into the wrong social class (bourgeois), or of opposing the government in any way. Under Stalin a person could be jailed for, among other things, "anti-Soviet thought" or for being a "wife or child of a enemy of the people." For many years Communist rulers denied these allegations, and the people of the West, although wary, thought them exaggerated. But revelations since the rise of Mikhail Gorbachev show that many of the most far-fetched stories were true.

Not only did Marxism make Communists cruel to their own citizens, it made them hostile to the West. A variety of methods were employed with the purpose of overthrowing Western democracies. For instance, disclosures from once secret files of the former Communist governments in Eastern Europe indicate that for many years sanctuary and aid were given to a number of terrorists groups intent on undermining the fabric of Western society.

It is not exactly clear what motivated Gorbachev to move the Soviet Union down the road of reform. It might have been that he decided on a policy of accommodation because the Soviets could not compete in the massive military build-up of the 1980s under Ronald Reagan. Perhaps he was driven to make changes because of the terrible state of the Soviet economy. Or maybe he is just a reformer. For whatever reason, Gorbachev has brought about important reverses in Soviet behavior. There is greater freedom of speech and press. To a degree Soviet citizens can participate in government. Marxist economics has been discarded and attempts to introduce free-market exchanges are underway. The Soviet Union did not interfere when the nations of Eastern Europe liberated themselves from Communism. It has agreed to scale back its military budget and has limited the aid it gives to opponents of the West.

These are certainly encouraging signs, but no one can know if they will last. Predictions are always difficult because part of political life is unpredictable; it rests on chance. After all, the Chinese Communists were further down the road of reform than the Soviets, but in June 1989 they ruthlessly crushed a pro-democracy movement. And Gorbachev has a great many problems that could lead to a turnabout of Soviet progress. The Soviet economy is a wreck and is not showing signs of great improvement. The many nationalities that make up the Soviet Union distrust one another and despise the Russians. If Gorbachev abandons Marxism completely, the Communist party will lose its legitimacy and thereby its mandate to rule. But many Communists have benefited from their high positions. Will they relinquish their wealth and prestige without a fight?

In spite of these reservations, however, let us assume that the Cold War is over. Is this a good thing? Yes, for the most part, it is. The threat of war and global destruction is diminished. The tyrannical system of politics and economics that opposed our way of life is no longer so threatening. And from a humanitarian point of view, we should be pleased that the peoples of Eastern Europe, and to a lesser extent the Soviet Union, are free.

So, what can be bad about the end of the Cold War? One thesis, put forward by Francis Fukuyama, an official of the State Department, contends that the termination of the Cold War indicates that history has come to an end. Fukuyama, whose theory was quickly coined "endism," does not maintain that time is about to stop. Rather, he argues that the West won the Cold War and that its political principles predominate over the entire world. Turning Marx's historical analysis around, Fukuyama argues that over the past two hundred years, liberal democracy has triumphed over all its enemies: monarchy, autocracy, Fascism and now Communism. The ideas of liberal democracy are now almost universally accepted as the proper way to organize political communities. Those nations that have not yet adopted the institutions of liberal democracy will eventually do so because behavior follows theory, practices follow ideas. What Fukuyama means by the end of history, then, is that there will no longer be revolutionary movements based on new philosophic doctrines to challenge the status quo. No seminal events or epoch-changing upheavals, as occurred during the American, French and Russian revolutions, will mark the future.

For Fukuyama the victory of liberal democracy is a good thing, except that life will be boring. After all, those people whose careers were spent defending the West will no longer have anything to do with themselves. For instance, in a 1990 commencement address, former secretary of defense James Schlesinger reminisced wistfully about his experiences as a cold warrior. Although he was delighted that his efforts had brought about success, he wondered what could replace the "excitement, challenge, and fun" of protecting the United States from totalitarianism. There are many such people who must now discover other outlets for their energies.

Fukuyama also states that the truimph of the West is likely to bring about a stable and peaceful world. This is surely a fine thing, but he wonders what people will do with themselves during an era of universal peace and prosperity. Perhaps, shopping malls will suddenly be filled with browsers, video rentals will skyrocket, and the demand for professional wrestling, already America's most lucrative "sport," will reach an all-time high. People will pursue only material, i.e., bodily pleasures, or expend themselves in mindless distractions. There will be nothing to inspire people; no excitement, no desire for distinction, no need for noble sacrifice, no cause to spur courageous acts, and not even an impulse toward beauty. The serious question that Fukuyama raises is whether life will be satisfying if those magnificent endeavors people have so honored in the past are no longer required. Examples from our popular culture, such as the enormous popularity of the *Star Wars* movie trilogy, suggest that there is something in the human soul that is stirred at the sight of stalwart people in a desperate situation acting gallantly for the sake of a righteous cause.

Although Fukuyama makes some interesting claims, there is a serious problem with his analysis of the international situation. It is unlikely that life will be tranquil as the result of the end of the Cold War. The new source of discord in the world, as Fukuyama mentions in passing, will be nationalism. We can already see evidence of national rivalries disrupting the peace. The Soviet Union has been plagued by violent quarrels in Azerbaijan, Armenia, and Georgia. Several of the newly liberated Eastern European nations have experienced ethnic antagonisms. Even in the West national disharmony is evident. Quebec and the English-speaking provinces of Canada are having difficulty reconciling their cultural differences. In the United States tension between ethnic groups has risen, as has been so aptly captured in Tom Wolfe's novel *Bonfire of the Vanities.*

Why is nationalism likely to become a disruptive force in international relations? Two of America's statesmen can help us understand the phenomena. "There are certain social principles in human nature," Alexander Hamilton stated at the New York convention to ratify the Constitution, "from which we may draw the most solid conclusions with respect to the conduct of individuals, and of communities. We love our families, more than we love our neighbors: We love our neighbors, more than our countrymen in general. The human affections, like solar heat, lose their intensity, as they depart the center." This "love of one's own," as it might be called, is more than mere selfishness. In fact, it overcomes our individualism and draws us together into political communities. As such, it can be the source of civic mindedness and dedication to one's friends and fellow countrymen. By caring for one's own, however, one must exclude outsiders, since the range which human affections can be stretched does not seem to be indefinite. (This inclination explains why sporting events are more fun to watch when one has a home team to root for.) Other people, too, form themselves into communities and, because the interests of these communities are sometimes at odds, there are bound to be clashes.

It is exactly because of these conflicts that some citizens are able to show their commitment to the community. They are willing to risk their own safety in order to protect their family, country, or way of life, and, of course, to achieve acclaim for themselves in the process. Indeed, there seems to be an element of the human soul that longs to transcend the physical part of our being. It is this urge that makes us discipline and suppress our bodily desires in hopes of achieving something extraordinary. This impulse motivates people to expose themselves to hazards in order to attain honor. There is also a darker side to this passion. Those under its influence are sometimes not constrained by laws or morality. They strike out at others either from the pleasure of defeating a rival or from the sheer exhilaration of breaking the norms of society in order to exhibit their prominence. Neglecting these aspects of human nature, Fukuyama is too optimistic about the universal success of liberal democracy, which requires that human beings rationally and harmoniously pursue their goals.

During the years of the Cold War ethnic and national rivalries were kept at bay by the intense ideological struggle that gripped the world and by the discipline that the superpowers imposed on their allies. People on both sides of the Iron Curtain put aside their parochial distrust of each other in order to combat a more threatening enemy. Abraham Lincoln, the second of our statesmen who can help us understand this problem, argued that a common opponent can be a powerful source of unity. During the first fifty years of our nationhood, he explained, "the jealousy, envy, and avarice, incident to our nature, and so common to a state of peace, prosperity and conscious strength, were, for the time, in a great measure smothered and rendered inactive; while the deep rooted principle of *hate,* and the powerful motive of *revenge,* instead of being turned against each other, were directed exclusively against the British nation." Now that the Cold War is over and the fear of the common enemy is gone, the spirit of "hatred" and "revenge" within the former political blocs is likely to predominate. Fukuyama is correct to assert that the foreseeable future will lack the titanic struggles for the hearts and minds of the human race that have occurred in the last two centuries. Yet, petty wars between nationalities and factional strife among ethnic groups within nations are likely to become the occasion for international disharmony.

It is good that the Cold War is over. But observers of politics ought to recall Hamilton's statement that, "Tis the portion of man assigned to him by the eternal allotment of Providence that every good he enjoys, shall be alloyed with ills."

Chapter VIII

Liberty and Equality

The two dominant principles of the American Regime are liberty and equality. But what do they mean? Are they unqualified goods or do they require limitation? Are they mutually reinforcing, or are they at odds with one another? When the Supreme Court interprets and applies the Bill of Rights and the Fourteenth Amendment, it explores the meaning of these two principles.

Communities, in order to govern themselves, require citizens who are capable of governing themselves and sufficiently informed to make sound judgements about community affairs. Freedom of speech is necessary for self-government. Anastaplo argues that the First Amendment absolutely prohibits Congress from abridging political speech, that is, speech about the duties and concerns of self-governing citizens. Any governmental censorship of the press, he argues, will undermine our regime as a self-governing community. Ironically, Anastaplo argues that one of our culture's most pervasive forms of speech, television, is in need of restraint. Television, he claims, is making Americans less able to govern themselves. As a nationalizing force, television breaks down smaller communities and neighborhoods—isolating individuals and producing a conformity of tastes and desires reduced to the lowest common denominator. Anastaplo therefore proposes that we abolish television. Such a move is not forbidden, he says, because the First Amendment extends absolute protection only to political speech; indeed, we must abolish television in order to protect the self-governing community the First Amendment was meant to serve.

Although few Supreme Court justices would be willing to permit a limitation of speech as radical as that proposed by Anastaplo, most judges agree that the First Amendment does not protect all kinds of expression. In *Miller v. California,* the Court affirmed its earlier holdings that obscenity is not protected by the First Amendment. Moreover, under the Court's ruling, obscenity should be judged by the local standards of the various states rather than by a uniform national standard. This decision supports federalism by permitting each state to perpetuate its own standards of decency. The Court's opinion assumes that it is appropriate for states to do this. Perhaps a self-governing community is possible only when citizens have a certain moral character and share standards of decency.

Douglas dissents in *Miller* on the ground that the First Amendment forbids the government to ban publications merely because some people are offended by them. What shocks one man "may be sustenance for [his] neighbor." Government should not favor any standard of decency, according to Douglas, because such standards are merely matters of taste. Freedom is made necessary by the equality of all opinions and desires. Douglas' taking freedom as an absolute ironically undermines community, which is supported by common standards, and promotes national uniformity.

Perhaps the most controversial issue concerning the definition and limits of liberty in recent years has been the issue of abortion. Both the "pro life" and the "pro choice" camps consider themselves to be the defenders of individual rights. Pro lifers appeal to the rights of the unborn child while pro choice advocates appeal to the right of a woman to control her own body. By making either the rights of the fetus or the rights of the mother paramount, each side seeks to decide the conflict by recourse to an unqualified definition of rights or liberty. It is precisely these absolutist perspectives that make resolution of the issue next to impossible.

The Court, however, has not spoken in absolutist terms. In *Roe v. Wade* even Justice Blackmun speaks of the need to take into account not only the rights of the mother but also the state's interest in protecting potential life and in establishing standards of medical safety. But Justice Blackmun's majority opinion also divides pregnancy into three parts: the first trimester in which neither the concerns of medical safety nor the state's interest in potential life justify interference with a woman's "right to privacy;" the second trimester in which concerns of medical safety may allow for state regulation; and the third in which both the concern for safety and the state interest in potential life allow for regulation. This division is based upon Blackmun's understanding of the point in pregnancy when an abortion becomes more dangerous than child birth and the point in pregnancy when the fetus may be viable outside of the mother's body. But, as Justice O'Connor points out in her dissent in *Akron,* development in medical technology will lead to constant changes in the point of viability and in the relative safety of abortion.

The opinion of the Court in *Roe* has led to confusion and controversy over the extent of state regulation of abortion that is permissable. The case of *Minnesota v. Hodgson* provides a good example of the various interpretations that are possible. The liberal wing of the Court, including Blackmun, see *Roe* as establishing an absolute right to an abortion in the first trimester of pregnancy and an almost absolute right in the second trimester. On the other side, White, Rhenquist and Kennedy are willing to allow an almost unlimited range of restrictions on abortion rights. Although they have hesitated to overturn *Roe,* they are willing to defer to almost any legislative decision to restrict abortion. Justice Scalia, having indicated in an earlier case that he would overturn *Roe,* complains here that the attempt of the Court to draw lines defining precisely what types of restrictions are legitimate is not the function of the Court and leads only to further confusion.

Justices O'Connor and Stevens appear most willing to accept the framework set forth in *Roe*, but unlike the more liberal wing, they take seriously the need for balancing the rights of the mother and with other legitimate state interests. They are not willing to judge particular cases on the basis of an unqualified right of the mother or unquestioned deference to legislative concerns. They see a need for the Court to define the extent and limits of rights. For them, the doctrine of individual rights does not require or even allow an absolutist interpretation.

The meaning of equality under the Fourteenth Amendment has also been the subject of a range of interpretations by the Supreme Court. In *Plessy v. Ferguson* the Court ruled that equality had a very limited meaning. The Constitutional standard of "the equal protection of the laws" in no way prevented state legislatures from instituting legal segregation. The only requirement was that separate accommodations be equal. In practice, even this limited nod toward equality was largely ignored for many years. It was not until 1954 and the decision of *Brown v. Board of Education* that the separate but equal doctrine was overturned. But the *Brown* decision raised new questions about the meaning of equality. Not only did the Court say that the state could not impose distinctions based on race, the Court also called into question the legitimacy of any policy that resulted in inequalities between the races. Segregation was wrong, according to the Court, because it produced feelings of inferiority and did irremedial damage to the hearts and minds of black children. But can the elimination of feelings of inferiority be the goal of the Court, or should the Court limit itself to preventing legally sanctioned inequalities. Or, in more familiar terms, is the goal of the Constitution equal opportunity or equal outcome?

In his dissent in *Plessy v. Ferguson* Justice Harlan argues that equal opportunity should be the standard. According to Harlan, the Constitution and the laws should be color blind. He would permit neither a color consciousness that justifies legal segregation or a color consciousness that guarantees equality of result by instituting "benign discrimination."

Eugene McCarthy argues that the goal of many current reforms is not equality of opportunity but equality itself. The limitations on campaign contributions, for example, are "attempts to equalize the non-voting influence on candidates." Further results of the emphasis on equality, he argues, include such guarantees as a college diploma to all. He finds this "security of equalization" degrading to the human personality. Kurt Vonnegut depicts the horrors of an egalitarian society where outstanding individuals are handicapped in order that they be made equal to everybody else. The radical egalitarianism McCarthy and Vonnegut criticize has its counterpart in the belief in absolute freedom—both stem from a leveling of distinctions between higher and lower.

Jefferson, on the other hand, defends equality as the condition for the emergence of a natural aristocracy. In free elections citizens will elevate men of uncommon virtue and ability to public office. But a system of public education is necessary to prepare people to select the natural aristocracy and to prepare the natural aristocracy for its tasks. From the free schools in each community, the best students would be selected for further education at district schools, and the best selected from these to attend a university. Public education, like free election, would separate the wheat from the chaff.

Tocqueville suggests reasons why Jefferson's scheme for education is not likely to be actualized in America. Equality, he says, produces men who envy excellence rather than men wishing to elevate it. Moreover, in equal social conditions, there is a universal competition for the goods of life; consequently, there is much ambition to rise without any hope of rising very far. But is the emergence of a natural aristocracy likely in such a situation? The greatest danger for America, Tocqueville believes, is the mediocrity rather than the boldness of desires. Therefore it would be beneficial, he concludes, if the community were from time to time exposed to matters of difficulty and danger "in order to raise ambition and give it a field of action."

72

George Anastaplo

Self-Government and the Mass Media:
A Practical Man's Guide (1974)

Delenda est Carthago.
—Cato the Elder

It should be instructive, in considering the significance among us of the mass media, to consider how we deal today with the press and the television industry. . . .

There is considerable effort made by some theorists to have us treat these two means of communication the same way. To treat them the same way not only would overlook vital differences between them, but would also threaten the integrity of our regime even more than it may already be. We must, above all, be practical about these matters.

We should take care, whatever we may say or do, not to undermine the privileges and hence the usefulness of a press that has traditionally had a vital part to play in our constitutional system. . . .

Although the prohibition in the First Amendment is absolute (we see here a restraint upon Congress which is unqualified, among other Bill of Rights restraints which *are* qualified) the absolute prohibition does not relate to all forms of expression, but only to that which the term "freedom of speech, or of the press" was then taken to encompass: political speech, that is, speech having to do with the duties and concerns of self-governing citizens. Thus, for example, this constitutional provision is not primarily or directly concerned with what we now call artistic expression or with the problem of obscenity. Rather, the First Amendment acknowledges that the sovereign citizen body

From Anastaplo, "Self-Government and the Mass Media: A Practical Man's Guide," in *The Mass Media and Modern Democracy,* ed. Harry M. Clor, Rand McNally College Publishing Company, 1974. Reprinted by permission of the Public Affairs Conference Center, Kenyon College, Gambier, Ohio. Corrections were made by the author. This article will be republished in Anastaplo, *The American Moralist: On Law Ethics and Government* (Athens, Ohio: Ohio University Press/Swallow Press, 1991).

The author has developed further his discussion of these matters in Anastaplo, *Human Being and Citizen: Essays on Virtue, Freedom, and the Common Good,* (Chicago: Swallow Press, 1975). He is also the author of *The Constitution of 1787: A Commentary* (Baltimore: Johns Hopkins University Press, 1989).

has the right freely to discuss public business, a privilege theretofore claimed only for members of legislative bodies. . . .

I am prepared to defend the propositions that, for the sake of our way of life, there cannot be in ordinary constitutional circumstances *any* previous restraints of publications and that there should be even more "previous restraint" than we now have of the television industry. . . .

The right of the people to know, of which we hear much today, includes the duty to think. This has, as a precondition, the opportunity to learn as well as the ability to discern what it is necessary to learn. Information and opinions about vital matters of public concern are needed among us on a day-to-day basis.

Even more important than day-to-day concerns, however, and indeed central to this paper, are several perennial questions: what kind of people is presupposed by institutions that include the absolute prohibition, at least in practice, of previous restraints on the press? What produces and preserves such a people? Is not a people of a certain character, rather than merely a with certain information, political opinions and morale, presupposed by our institutions? . . .

Vital to a people's self-governance are its experience and ability in forming and choosing its leaders and policies. This means that the character of our people cannot be left only to chance, to private influences, or to the vagaries of a "free trade in ideas." We should be concerned to preserve in our people a character that permits it to use responsibly the extensive freedom of speech and of the press traditionally and constitutionally available to it. . . .

The modern mass media tend more toward centralization of power, while the old-fashioned press tended to be more localizing in it efforts and effects. The local is apt to be both more provincial and healthier; certainly, it is to be encouraged in this day and age. When we go "national" today, whether in the media or in politics, everything tends to become somewhat more gross and less discriminating. A facile simplification is rewarded and hence promoted. Is there then a tendency toward homogeneity of tastes and opinions as well as a general lowering of effective moral, political, and intellectual standards?

Industrialization with its marvels-laden technology can be said to be responsible for such developments. With such developments comes also the sense of helplessness and of rootlessness to which modern man is peculiarly subject. In modern circumstances one has less the impression of being "one's own man," of being able to do things for oneself. One is forced into a passive role, not the role of the alert observer but that of the pampered slave. . . .

The press continues to provide us with the serious searching out and recording of the news of the day, whereas television is in this respect for the most part parasitic. I believe it significant that the newscaster on television is rarely the man who has investigated the story being broadcast. Rather, he is usually part of a "show" that draws primarily on what newspapermen have gathered and put on the wire. Thus there is no necessary connection between the influence or "image" of television "personalities" and their competence. These television personalities wield tremendous influence, but such influence is both ephemeral and beyond their comprehension and hence their control. . . .

To speak as I have of "public opinion" is to recognize in *public* a body that acts and is somehow keyed to political concerns; it is also to recognize in *opinion* something that does depend ultimately upon notions of right and wrong and hence upon reason. This is quite different from the passive audiences upon which television depends and which it creates.

The television industry, in its distinctive modernity, is representative of the mass media and their infatuation with appearances. The term *mass media* aptly records what happens when modern electronic technology is applied to communications. The decisive factor becomes the necessarily "mass" character of passive and pacified audiences made up of countless private or isolated parties. The emphasis in the term *media* is upon the industry as little more than a conduit. Does not a people lose its moral and hence political sense when it becomes the "masses"? One may even be obliged to consider whether some previous restraint of the press might not become necessary if the people should, because of the debilitating effects of the mass media, become so childish as to be unable to govern itself. . . .

The effects of television are pervasive and are felt both directly and indirectly: directly through what almost six hours a day of *exposure* (not necessarily of viewing) do to the souls of our people; indirectly through the adjustments the press and others consider themselves obliged to make to compete with the television industry in capturing people's attention and thus being able to stay in business.

It should be noticed that much of the time devoted to television must be taken from other activities, such as reading, writing, conversation or courting or playing. What had been the effect on us heretofore of such activities? What is the effect of their radical curtailment? It is unrealistic to assume that such revolutionary changes as we have undergone have no significant effect on the souls of people.

Commercial considerations are obviously much more important for television than for the press, whatever may be said about the influence of advertisers upon publishers. Television was invented during a more commercial age than was printing; the press developed more naturally as an extension of thinking and writing rather than as an agency for advertising and selling. The commercial aspects of the press simply cannot assert themselves as much as the commercial aspects of television do. For example, one can easily ignore the advertisements in a newspaper. No one doubts the considerable effect that sponsors have in the United States upon the content of television programs and upon audiences. The commercial aspects of television, however important they may be in so many critiques of the industry, are not our primary concern. Nor does the specific content of television broadcasting concern us here, insofar as this can be corrected by a people determined to do so, but rather the very form of it and the consequent effects of the displacement by television of the other means by which souls have been engaged heretofore. . . .

[A]re not the good things on television always an incidental part of the whole? Are not even the good uses to which television has been put due in large part to chance? The issues that capture public attention and get considerable "play" are all too often contrived or accidental. However adept television may be at exposing some public figures, the professional television personalities are themselves litte more than animated masks so far as the viewing audience is concerned. Why this should be so depends on the very nature of the medium.

Distortion and superficiality are among the inevitable effects of television, including effects of the technology itself that are accentuated by the expense of television and its consequent need for large audiences. Television cannot help but cater to the worst in us, even when it is trying to do its best. Certain things are made to appear easier than they really are. Shallow illusions are promoted, including the illusion that the viewer can learn enough from capsule presentations (a kind of discourse by headline) to get a serious notion of what is going on in the world and to be able to make sensible judgments and responsible choices. Television seems to liberate even while it really cripples, and it does this in so enticing a manner as to drive its competitors either out of the "market" or into suicidal imitation.

Thus, television helps create the illusion that it has informed us and that we have "participated" in something we have witnessed "close up." It emphasizes that one must "get it" at once; one can't tarry to look at what has been broadcast, to take one's time studying what one may not understand. One must get it all *now*, for something else is coming soon. One is discouraged from looking back: everything is before us; recollection and reflection are discouraged or at least made difficult. Is not all this more appropriate for entertainment than for serious discourse? . . .

The electronic media are very voracious and insatiable. Consequently, they promote novelty which seems to fit in better with youthfulness, with those who are by nature always changing and experimenting. A "culture" keyed to or shaped by the mass media is bound to be youth-oriented, an unnatural state of affairs for a community. There is constant change, with a consequent profound dissatisfaction and rootlessness. Fashions become more important and character less. Since the visual is necessarily emphasized, the length of discourse that can be presented on television is much shorter than serious issues require, much less than what would be possible in a meeting hall. Yet most viewers *are* given the impression that television presents enough. . . .

It is sometimes said that the young, and some of the old, know today much more about the world—how big and diverse it is, for example—than people did a generation ago. The mass media no doubt contribute to this sense of liberation: they do "open up" the world. But because of the inefficiency of television (consider the amount of material that can be spoken as against what can be read in a given time) one simple cannot get much detail beyond the immediately visible. Even the "educated" young probably know less than any generation heretofore about what has gone before or about the serious questions to which men have always addressed themselves. The young spread themselves over much more than did their predecessors, but much more thinly. Hence they cannot begin to know themselves. Yet they readily believe themselves to be more enlightened than their predecessors. . . .

Children, as well as adults, are discouraged by television from becoming practiced in reading. Once television becomes available, reading appears to most people laborious and even less attractive; the attention span is likely to be shortened for activities requiring deliberate effort; discipline is not encouraged for serious work, and this suggests that everyday passions are even more likely to make themselves felt than they have always been. The general deterioration of serious reading ability will eventually lead to deterioration of the ability to write. Does not this entail for us the impairment of the ability to think seriously?

Despite what is said about television's ability to "take the clothes off a man," his television "image" is likely to be quite different from what he is truly like. In fact, it may be virtually impossible for anyone to be more than an image before the camera. But one's written statements may be very much what one is. In fact, they may be essentially what one is, insofar as one is a thinking being. . . .

Serious association with one another, whether for purposes of entertainment, education, worship, politics, or sports, is undermined by television, especially since viewers and performers (or, as they once were, people and leaders) can make no serious contact with one another. For example, politicians tailor what they say and eventually believe to what can be "put across" on the television screen. The screen depends upon and encourages the wrong kind of simplification. No matter how complicated the subject presented may be, it is all too often pretended if not sincerely believed that it can be adequately dealt with, as if magically, in a few minutes. . . .

Yet it is also felt that something like television is needed for an aggregate as large as the United States has become. It is, some might even say, a necessary evil to cure an even worse one, the divisiveness of bigness.

Television does bring us all together, in a way, but too many at a time and at too low a level. In the process it breaks down smaller communities that until its coming had still been viable despite the onslaughts of the automobile and of the Second World War. The isolation of people, whether the elderly or the infirm or the housewife, that is intensified if not induced by the disruption of our towns and urban neighborhoods, seems to lead to a "need" for television. . . .

The easy intrusion of television into our lives undermines what friendship and influence should mean. Appearance becomes even more important than it had been. It is my impression that television fits better with an emphasis upon presidential rather than congressional or state politics. Rule by television plebiscite seems to be developing among us, a kind of rule that is peculiarly responsive to the volatile mass taste that television promotes and serves. The constitutional tendency of television—of the way of life that permits and is in turn shaped by television—is to unleash desires and arouse expectations that undermine among us the moderation of tradition, the restraints both of diversity and of a genuine respect of quality, and the requirements and advantages of federalism.

This social indictment of television can be summed up thus: Each of us is constantly addressed by television apart from the others, and yet none of us is ever really spoken to. The ability to read, and hence to think and to join in serious common discourse, suffers. Every kind of association is filtered through the camera and stripped of its humanity. The community is depreciated while a hollow privacy is emphasized; communal tastes are reduced to the lowest common denominator and then shamelessly catered to. Spectacle replaces theater; feeling replaces thought; image replaces character. The world shaped by television is an empty one, starved and frenetic, dreamlike and debilitating. It can be expected to culminate eventually in a crippling mediocrity and perhaps even in tyranny. . . .

It has long seemed obvious to me that the television industry should be abolished completely in this country and that nothing short of this can purge its crippling influence from American life. If this is indeed a society open to experimentation, then let us deliberately experiment for at least a decade with the remedy of complete suppression of television.

If television should be abolished, we should be obliged to go out again into our streets, if only to attend more movies. Local entertainment, local gatherings (religious as well as secular), and even genuine popular culture might become important again. Even more importantly, the intrinsically harmful influences of television would no longer have to be contended with.

Is it not revealing that something so harmful as television should have become so entrenched so soon? It is like noxious weeds that happen to be blown in by the wind. Its abolition today is, of course, virtually unthinkable; yet we did not have it a generation ago, however natural it may now seem to most of us.

If we move against television, we reassert ourselves as a community even as we act together on behalf of communal interests. We would show we care about what affects us, thereby again becoming a community. We would show as well that we recognize that mere desires should not govern our lives, that temperance is vital to enduring happiness. . . .

I see in the abolition of television no serious First Amendment problem. Rather than abridge the "freedom of speech" guaranteed by the First Amendment, the abolition of television, and hence a radical reform of the mass media, would enlarge freedom of speech among us. Television interferes, I have argued, with serious general education in a country such as ours: it affects the ability to read and hence the ability to think and the very status of thought among us, playing up to the passions as it does. The abolition of television would probably contribute *among us* to the preservation of self-government and hence genuine freedom. . . .

We are, of course, [not] likely to abolish television. . . .

What *can* be done about television, short of the total abolition I have advocated? Various reforms, which reflect some of the criticisms I have made in this paper, can be attempted. I collect here, as illustrative of how one may begin to think about reforms, a half-dozen suggestions:

1. There should be a curtailment in the amount of television available daily. It would be good *not* to have continuous television, but only a couple of hours of transmission at a time, followed by extended intermissions during which there is no local transmission at all. It would also be good to have certain evenings of the week, and perhaps most, if not all, of Sunday, completely free from television as well as from most other commerical activity. . . .

2. The commercial influence upon television in this country should be reduced. It would be good to experiment with the means by which British commercial television has ensured that there be no identification of advertisers with particular programs.

3. What is the relation between television's pervasive commercialism and its national programming? Whatever it may be, there is much to be said for encouraging local programming, thereby emphasizing the importance of the local community. We should expect with more local programming a decline in the professional quality of programs, at least until local talent begins to assert itself.

4. The immediate effect of television on our political life should be eliminated if we are to be left free and equipped to assess such things as television upon that way of life. Should not television be explicitly reserved for entertainment, leaving the discussion of politics to more appropriate forums? . . .

5. If there is to be politics on television, the emphasis should be on lengthy talks and extended civic proceedings. It would probably be prudent to reconsider the "fairness doctrine," for that may provide an overly zealous administration in Washington too great an opportunity to control the political discourse of the country. Insofar as television is permitted to provide a forum for political discourse, it is good for us that it should be able to rely on First Amendment privileges.

6. The nonpolitical content of television, with a view to the effects on viewers of such things as portrayals of violence and legitimation of greed, should be periodically assessed by civic-minded people who recognize that the virtues, vices, and accomplishments of human beings are not without causes. . . .

7. It should go without saying that any family or neighborhood which "deprives" itself of television is likely to be better off than those families or neighborhoods addicted to it. It may become generally apparent someday, perhaps even in time to make a difference, that the many who are saddled with television are being exploited by the few who profit from it, and that the exploited are so deluded as to "choose" this form of self-enslavement. This is like the relationship between cigarette manufacturers and their victims. It may then become generally apparent that any community respectful of its integrity or concerned about the under-privileged should abolish television root and branch. . . .

It *is* instructive that we do not (perhaps, by now, cannot) see the risks we are running, and that we will not do anything serious, partly because of immediate pleasures and profits, partly because of profound confusion about causes and effects, and about the nature itself of cause and effect, in moral and political matters. An attempt to return ourselves to a more austere and healthier way of life, a life more conducive to a republican form of government and to the full development of the human soul is virtually unthinkable. It would also be instructive if the reader, in attempting to assess the argument I have presented here, should be induced to investigate and to make explicit what we take for granted as to *how* a particular way of life is established and perpetuated. . . .

73

Miller v. California (1973)

Mr. Chief Justice Burger *delivered the opinion of the Court.*

This is one of a group of "obscenity-pornography" cases being reviewed by the Court in a re-examination of standards enunciated in earlier cases involving what Mr. Justice Harlan called "the intractable obscenity problem."

Appellant conducted a mass mailing campaign to advertise the sale of illustrated books, euphemistically called "adult" material. After a jury trial, he was convicted of violating California Penal Code § 311.2(a), a misdemeanor, by knowingly distributing obscene matter, and the Appellate Department, Superior Court of California, County of Orange, summarily affirmed the judgment without opinion. Appellant's conviction was specifically based on his conduct in causing five unsolicited advertising brochures to be sent through the mail in an envelope addressed to a restaurant in Newport Beach, California. The envelope was opened by the manager of the restaurant and his mother. They had not requested the brochures; they complained to the police. . . .

This case involves the application of a State's criminal obscenity statute to a situation in which sexually explicit materials have been thrust by aggressive sales action upon unwilling recipients who had in no way indicated any desire to receive such materials. . . .

[S]ince the Court now undertakes to formulate standards more concrete than those in the past, it is useful for us to focus on two of the landmark cases in the somewhat tortured history of the Court's obscenity decisions. In Roth v. United States, the Court sustained a conviction under a federal statute punishing the mailing of "obscene, lewd, lascivious or filthy . . ." materials. The key to that holding was the Court's rejection of the claim that obscene materials were protected by the First Amendment. Five Justices joined in the opinion stating:

> "All ideas having even the slightest redeeming social importance— unorthodox ideas, controversial ideas, even ideas hateful to the prevailing climate of opinion—have the full protection of the [First Amendment] guaranties, unless excludable because they encroach upon the limited area of more important interest. But implicit in the history of the First Amendment is the rejection

From *Miller v. California,* 413 U.S. 15 (1973).

of obscenity as utterly without redeeming social importance. . . . This is the same judgment expressed by this Court in Chaplinsky v. New Hampshire:

" '. . . There are certain well-defined and narrowly limited classes of speech, the prevention and punishment of which have never been thought to raise any Constitutional problem. *These include the lewd and obscene. . . . It has been well observed that such utterances are no essential part of any exposition of ideas, and are of such slight social value as a step to truth that any benefit that may be derived from them is clearly outweighed by the social interest in order and morality. . . .*' [Emphasis by Court in *Roth* opinion.]

"We hold that obscenity is not within the area of constitutionally protected speech or press."

Nine years later, in Memoirs v. Massachusetts, the Court veered sharply away from the *Roth* concept and, with only three Justices in the plurality opinion, articulated a new test of obscenity. The plurality held that under the *Roth* definition

"as elaborated in subsequent cases, three elements must coalesce: it must be established that (a) the dominant theme of the material taken as a whole appeals to a prurient interest in sex; (b) the material is patently offensive because it affronts contemporary community standards relating to the description or representation of sexual matters; and (c) the material is utterly without redeeming social value."

. . . While *Roth* presumed "obscenity" to be "utterly without redeeming social importance," *Memoirs* required that to prove obscenity it must be affirmatively established that the material is "*utterly* without redeeming social value." Thus, even as they repeated the words of *Roth,* the *Memoirs* plurality produced a drastically altered test that called on the prosecution to prove a negative, *i.e.,* that the material was "*utterly* without redeeming social value"—a burden virtually impossible to discharge under our criminal standards of proof. . . .

This much has been categorically settled by the Court, that obscene material is unprotected by the First Amendment. . . . We acknowledge, however, the inherent dangers of undertaking to regulate any form of expression. State statutes designed to regulate obscene materials must be carefully limited. See Interstate Circuit, Inc. v. Dallas. As a result, we now confine the permissible scope of such regulation to works which depict or describe sexual conduct. That conduct must be specifically defined by the applicable state law, as written or authoritatively construed. A state offense must also be limited to works which, taken as a whole, appeal to the prurient interest in sex, which portray sexual conduct in a patently offensive way, and which, taken as a whole, do not have serious literary, artistic, political, or scientific value.

The basic guidelines for the trier of fact must be: (a) whether "the average person, applying contemporary community standards" would find that the work, taken as a whole, appeals to the prurient interest, (b) whether the work depicts or describes, in a patently offensive way, sexual conduct specifically defined by the applicable state law; and (c) whether the work, taken as a whole, lacks serious literary, artistic, political, or scientific value. We do not adopt as a constitutional standard the "*utterly* without redeeming social value" test of Memoirs v. Massachusetts; that concept has never commanded the adherence of more than three Justices at one time.[1] . . .

At a minimum, prurient, patently offensive depiction or description of sexual conduct must have serious literary, artistic, political, or scientific value to merit First Amendment protection. For example, medical books for the education of physicians and related personnel necessarily use graphic illustrations and descriptions of human anatomy. In resolving the inevitably sensitive questions of fact and law, we must continue to rely on the jury system, accompanied by the safeguards that judges, rules of evidence, presumption of innocence, and other protective features provide, as we do with rape, murder, and a host of other offenses against society and its individual members.[2] . . .

Under a National Constitution, fundamental First Amendment limitations on the powers of the States do not vary from community to community, but this does not mean that there are, or should or can be, fixed, uniform national standards of precisely what appeals to the "prurient interest" or is "patently offensive." These are essentially questions of fact, and our Nation is simply too big and too diverse for this Court to reasonably expect that such standards could be articulated for all 50 States in a single formulation, even assuming the prerequisite consensus exists. When triers of fact are asked to decide whether "the average person, applying contemporary community standards" would consider certain materials "prurient," it would be unrealistic to require that the answer be based on some abstract formulation. The adversary system, with lay jurors as the usual ultimate fact-finders in criminal prosecutions, has historically permitted triers of fact to draw on the standards of their community, guided always by limiting instructions on the law. To require a State to structure obscenity proceedings around evidence of a *national* "community standard" would be an exercise in futility. . . .

During the trial, both the prosecution and the defense assumed that the relevant "community standards" in making the factual determination of obscenity were those of the State of California, not some hypothetical standard of the entire United States of America. Defense counsel at trial never objected to the testimony of the State's expert on community standards or to the instructions of the trial judge on "statewide" standards. . . .

We conclude that neither the State's alleged failure to offer evidence of "national standards," nor the trial court's charge that the jury consider state community standards, were constitutional errors. Nothing in the First Amendment requires that a jury must consider hypothetical and unascertainable "national standards" when attempting to determine whether certain materials are obscene as a matter of fact. . . .

It is neither realistic nor constitutionally sound to read the First Amendment as requiring that the people of Maine or Mississippi accept public depiction of conduct found tolerable in Las Vegas, or New York City.[3] . . .

People in different States vary in their tastes and attitudes, and this diversity is not to be strangled by the absolutism of imposed uniformity. As the Court made clear in Mishkin v. New York, the primary concern with requiring a jury to apply the standard of "the average person, applying contemporary community standards" is to be certain that, so far as material is not aimed at a deviant group, it will be judged by its impact on an average person, rather than a particularly susceptible or sensitive person—or indeed a totally insensitive one. . . .

The dissenting Justices sound the alarm of repression. But, in our view, to equate the free and robust exchange of ideas and political debate with commercial exploitation of obscene material demeans the grand conception of the First Amendment and its high purposes in the historic struggle for freedom. It is a "misuse of the great guarantees of free speech and free press. . . ." The First Amendment protects works which, taken as a whole, have serious literary, artistic, political, or scientific value, regardless of whether the government or a majority of the people approve of the ideas these works represent. "The protection given speech and press was fashioned to assure unfettered interchange of *ideas* for the bringing about of political and social changes desired by the people," Roth v. United States. But the public portrayal of hard-core sexual conduct for its own sake, and for the ensuing commercial gain, is a different matter. . . .

Mr. Justice Douglas, dissenting.

. . . The difficulty is that we do not deal with constitutional terms, since "obscenity" is not mentioned in the Constitution or Bill of Rights. And the First Amendment makes no such exception from "the press" which it undertakes to protect. . . . So there are no constitutional guidelines for deciding what is and what is not "obscene." The Court is at large because we deal with tastes and standards of literature. What shocks me may be sustenance for my neighbor. What causes one person to boil up in rage over one pamphlet or movie may reflect only his neurosis, not shared by others. . . .

The idea that the First Amendment permits government to ban publications that are "offensive" to some people puts an ominous gloss on freedom of the press. That test would make it possible to ban any paper or any journal or magazine in some benighted place. The First Amendment was designed "to invite dispute," to induce "a condition of unrest," to "create dissatisfaction with conditions as they are," and even to stir "people to anger." Terminiello v. Chicago. The idea that the First Amendment permits punishment for ideas that are "offensive" to the particular judge or jury sitting in judgment is astounding. No greater leveler of speech or literature has ever been designed. To give the power to the censor, as we do today, is to make a sharp and radical break with the traditions of a free society. The First Amendment was not fashioned as a vehicle for dispensing tranquilizers to the people. Its prime function was to keep debate open to "offensive" as well as to "staid" people. The tendency throughout history has been to subdue the individual and to exalt the power of government. The use of the standard "offensive" gives authority to government that cuts the very vitals out of the First Amendment. As is intimated by the Court's opinion, the materials before us may be garbage. But so is much of what is said in political campaigns, in the daily press, on TV, or over the radio. By reason of the First Amendment—and solely because of it—speakers and publishers have not been threatened or subdued because their thoughts and ideas may be "offensive" to some. . . .

We deal with highly emotional, not rational, questions. To many the Song of Solomon is obscene. I do not think we, the judges, were ever given the constitutional power to make definitions of obscenity. If it is to be defined, let the people debate and decide by a constitutional amendment what they want to ban as obscene and what standards they want the legislatures and the courts to apply. Perhaps the people will decide that the path towards a mature, integrated society requires that all ideas competing for acceptance must have no censor. Perhaps they will decide otherwise. Whatever the choice, the courts will have some guidelines. Now we have none except our own predilections.

NOTES

1. "A quotation from Voltaire in the flyleaf of a book will not constitutionally redeem an otherwise obscene publication. . . ." We also reject, as a constitutional standard, the ambiguous concept of "social importance."
2. The mere fact juries may reach different conclusions as to the same material does not mean that constitutional rights are abridged. As this Court observed in Roth v. United States, "it is common experience that different juries may reach different results under any criminal statute. That is one of the consequences we accept under our jury system. . . ."

3. In Jacobellis v. Ohio, two Justices argued that application of "local" community standards would run the risk of preventing dissemination of materials in some places because sellers would be unwilling to risk criminal conviction by testing variations in standards from place to place. The use of "national" standards, however, necessarily implies that materials found tolerable in some places, but not under the "national" criteria, will nevertheless be unavailable where they are acceptable. Thus, in terms of danger to free expression, the potential for suppression seems at least as great in the application of a single nationwide standard as in allowing distribution in accordance with local tastes, a point which Mr. Justice Harlan often emphasized.

Appellant also argues that adherence to a "national standard" is necessary "in order to avoid unconscionable burdens on the free flow of interstate commerce." . . . . Obscene material may be validly regulated by a State in the exercise of its traditional local power to protect the general welfare of its population despite some possible incidental effect on the flow of such materials across state lines.

74

Roe v. Wade (1973)

Mr. Justice Blackmun delivered the opinion of the Court:
. . . Three reasons have been advanced to explain historically the enactment of criminal abortion laws in the 19th century and to justify their continued existence.

It has been argued occasionally that these laws were the product of a Victorian social concern to discourage illicit sexual conduct. Texas, however, does not advance this justification in the present case, and it appears that no court or commentator has taken the argument seriously. The appellants and amici contend, moreover, that this is not a proper state purpose at all and suggest that, if it were, the Texas statutes are overbroad in protecting it since the law fails to distinguish between married and unwed mothers.

A second reason is concerned with abortion as a medical procedure. When most criminal abortion laws were first enacted, the procedure was a hazardous one for the woman. . . .

From *Roe v. Wade,* 410 U.S. 113 (1973).

Modern medical techniques have altered this situation. Appellants and various amici refer to medical data indicating that abortion in early pregnancy, this is, prior to the end of the first trimester, although not without its risk, is now relatively safe. Mortality rates for women undergoing early abortions, where the procedure is legal, appear to be as low as or lower than the rates for normal childbirth. Consequently, any interest of the State in protecting the woman from an inherently hazardous procedure, except when it would be equally dangerous for her to forgo it, has largely disappeared. Of course, important state interests in the area of health and medical standards do remain.

The State has a legitimate interest in seeing to it that abortion, like any other medical procedure, is performed under circumstances that insure maximum safety for the patient. This interest obviously extends at least to the performing physician and his staff, to the facilities involved, to the availability of aftercare, and to adequate provision for any complication or emergency that might arise. The prevalence of high mortality rates at illegal "abortion mills" strengthens, rather than weakens, the State's interest in regulating the conditions under which abortions are performed. Moreover, the risk to the woman increases as her pregnancy continues. Thus, the State retains a definite interest in protecting the woman's own health and safety when an abortion is proposed at a late stage of pregnancy.

The third reason is the State's interest—some phrase it in terms of duty—in protecting prenatal life. Some of the argument for this justification rests on the theory that a new human life is present from the moment of conception. The State's interest and general obligation to protect life then extends, it is argued, to prenatal life. Only when the life of the pregnant mother herself is at stake, balanced against the life she carries within her, should the interest of the embryo or fetus not prevail. Logically, of course, a legitimate state interest in this area need not stand or fall on acceptance of the belief that life begins at conception or at some other point prior to live birth. In assessing the State's interest, recognition may be given to the less rigid claim that as long as at least *potential* life is involved, the State may assert interests beyond the protection of the pregnant woman alone. . . .

The Constitution does not explicitly mention any right of privacy. In a line of decisions, however, going back perhaps as far as *Union Pacific R. Co. v. Botsford* (1891) . . . , the Court has recognized that a right of personal privacy, or a guarantee of certain areas or zones of privacy, does exist under the Constitution. In varying contexts, the Court or individual Justices have, indeed, found at least the roots of that right in the First Amendment, *Stanley v. Georgia* (1969) . . . ; in the Fourth and Fifth Amendments, *Terry* v. *Ohio* (1968) . . . , *Katz* v. *United States* (1967) . . . ; in the penumbras of the Bill of Rights, *Griswold* v. *Connecticut* (1965) . . . ; in the Ninth Amendment, id., at 486, . . . (Goldberg, J., concurring); or in the concept of liberty guaranteed by the first section of the Fourteenth Amendment, see *Meyer* v. *Nebraska* (1923). . . . These decisions make it clear that only personal rights that can be deemed "fundamental" or "implicit in the concept of ordered liberty," *Palko* v. *Connecticut* (1937) . . . , are included in this guarantee of personal privacy. They also make it clear that the right has some extension to activities relating to marriage, *Loving* v. *Virginia* (1967) . . . ; procreation, *Skinner* v. *Oklahoma* (1942) . . . ; contraception, *Eisenstadt* v. *Baird* (1972). . . .

This right of privacy, whether it be founded in the Fourteenth Amendment's concept of personal liberty and restrictions upon state action, as we feel it is, or, as the District Court determined, in the Ninth Amendment's reservation of rights to the people, is broad enough to encompass a woman's decision whether or not to terminate her pregnancy. The detriment that the State would impose upon the pregnant woman by denying this choice altogether is apparent. Specific and direct harm medically diagnosable even in early pregnancy may be involved. Maternity, or additional offspring, may force upon the woman a distressful life and future. Psychological harm may be imminent. Mental and physical health may be taxed by child care. There is also the distress, for all concerned, associated with the unwanted child, and there is the problem of bringing a child into a family already unable, psychologically and otherwise, to care for it. In other cases, as in this one, the additional difficulties and continuing stigma of unwed motherhood may be involved. All these are factors the woman and her responsible physician necessarily will consider in consultation.

On the basis of elements such as these, appellant and some amici argue that the woman's right is absolute and that she is entitled to terminate her pregnancy at whatever time, in whatever way, and for whatever reason she alone chooses. With this we do not agree. Appellant's arguments that Texas either has no valid interest at all in regulating the abortion decision, or no interest strong enough to support any limitation upon the woman's sole determination, is unpersuasive. The Court's decisions recognizing a right of privacy also acknowledge that some state regulation in areas protected by that right is appropriate. As noted above, a State may properly assert important interests in safeguarding health, in maintaining medical standards, and in protecting potential life. At some point in pregnancy, these respective interests become sufficiently compelling to sustain regulation of the factors that govern the abortion decision. The privacy right involved, therefore, cannot be said to be absolute. In fact, it is not clear to us that the claim asserted by some amici that one has an unlimited right to do with one's body as one pleases bears a close relationship to the right of privacy previously articulated in the Court's decisions. The Court has refused to recognize an unlimited right of this kind in the past. *Jacobson* v. *Massachusetts* (1905) . . . (vaccination); *Buck* v. *Bell* (1927) . . . (sterilization).

We, therefore, conclude that the right of personal privacy includes the abortion decision, but that this right is not unqualified and must be considered against important state interests in regulation.

Where certain "fundamental rights" are involved, the Court has held that regulation limiting these rights may be justified only by a "compelling state interest," . . . and that legislative enactments must be narrowly drawn to express only the legitimate state interests at stake. . . .

The District Court held that the appellee failed to meet his burden of demonstrating that the Texas statute's infringement upon Roe's rights was necessary to support a compelling state interest. . . . Appellee argues that the State's determination to recognize and protect prenatal life from and after conception constitutes a compelling state interest. As noted above, we do not agree fully with either formulation.

A. The appellee and certain amici argue that the fetus is a "person" within the language and meaning of the Fourteenth Amendment. In support of this, they outline at length and in detail the well-known facts of fetal development. If this suggestion of personhood is established, the appellant's case, of course, collapses, for the fetus' right to life is then guaranteed specifically by the Amendment. The appellant conceded as much on reargument. On the other hand, the appellee conceded on reargument that no case could be cited that holds that a fetus is a person within the meaning of the Fourteenth Amendment.

The Constitution does not define "person" in so many words. Section 1 of the Fourteenth Amendment contains three references to "person." The first, in defining "citizens," speaks of "persons born or naturalized in the United States." The word also appears both in the Due Process Clause and in the Equal Protection Clause. "Person" is used in other places in the Constitution. . . . But in nearly all these instances, the use of the word is such that it has application only postnatally. None indicates, with any assurance, that it has any possible prenatal application.

All this, together with our observation, supra, that throughout the major portion of the 19th century prevailing legal abortion practices were far freer than they are today, persuades us that the word "person," as used in the Fourteenth Amendment, does not include the unborn. . . .

B. The pregnant woman cannot be isolated in her privacy. She carries an embryo and, later, a fetus, if one accepts the medical definitions of the developing young in the human uterus. . . . The situation therefore is inherently different from marital intimacy, or bedroom possession of obscene material, or marriage, or procreation, or education, with which *Eisenstadt, Griswold, Stanley, Loving, Skinner, Pierce,* and *Meyer* were respectively concerned. As we have intimated above, it is reasonable and appropriate for a State to decide that at some point in time another interest, that of health of the mother or that of potential human life, becomes significantly involved. The woman's privacy is no longer sole and any right of privacy she possesses must be measured accordingly.

Texas urges that, apart from the Fourteenth Amendment, life begins at conception and is present throughout pregnancy, and that, therefore, the State has a compelling interest in protecting that life from and after conception. We need not resolve the difficult question of when life begins. When those trained in the respective disciplines of medicine, philosophy, and theology are unable to arrive at any consensus, the judiciary, at this point in the development of man's knowledge, is not in a position to speculate as to the answer.

It should be sufficient to note briefly the wide divergence of thinking on this most sensitive and difficult question. . . .

In view of all this, we do not agree that, by adopting one theory of life, Texas may override the rights of the pregnant woman that are at stake. We repeat, however, that the State does have an important and legitimate interest in preserving and protecting the health of the pregnant woman, whether she be a resident of the State or a nonresident who seeks medical consultation and treatment there, and that it has still *another* important and legitimate interest in protecting the potentiality of human life. These interests are separate and distinct. Each grows in substantiality as the woman approaches term and, at a point during pregnancy, each becomes "compelling."

With respect to the State's important and legitimate interest in the health of the mother, the "compelling" point, in the light of present medical knowledge, is at approximately the end of the first trimester. This is so because of the now-established medical fact, referred to above . . . that until the end of the first trimester mortality in abortion may be less than mortality in normal childbirth. It follows that, from and after this point, a State may regulate the abortion procedure to the extent that the regulation reasonably relates to the preservation and protection of maternal health. Examples of permissible state regulation in this area are requirements as to the qualifications of the person who is to perform the abortion; as to the licensure of that person; as to the facility in which the procedure is to be performed, that is, whether it must be a hospital or may be a clinic or some other place of less-than-hospital status; as to the licensing of the facility; and the like.

This means, on the other hand, that, for the period of pregnancy prior to this "compelling" point, the attending physician, in consultation with his patient, is free to determine, without regulation by the State, that, in his medical judgment, the patient's pregnancy should be terminated. If that decision is reached, the judgment may be effectuated by an abortion free of interference by the State.

With respect to the State's important and legitimate interest in potential life, the "compelling" point is at viability. This is so because the fetus then presumably has the capability of meaningful life outside the mother's womb.

State regulation protective of fetal life after viability thus has both logical and biological justifications. If the State is interested in protecting fetal life after viability, it may go so far as to proscribe abortion during that period, except when it is necessary to preserve the life or health of the mother.

Measured against these standards, Art. 1196 of the Texas Penal Code, in restricting legal abortions to those "procured or attempted by medical advice for the purpose of saving the life of the mother," sweeps too broadly. The statute makes no distinction between abortions performed early in pregnancy and those performed later, and it limits to a single reason, "saving" the mother's life, the legal justification for the procedure. The statute, therefore, cannot survive the constitutional attack made upon it here. . . .

75

City of Akron v. Akron Center for Reproductive Health (1982)

Justice O'Connor, . . . dissenting.

. . . The trimester or "three-stage" approach adopted by the Court in *Roe,* and, in a modified form, employed by the Court to analyze the regulations in these cases, cannot be supported as a legitimate or useful framework for accommodating the woman's right and the State's interests. . . .

As the Court indicates today, the State's compelling interest in maternal health changes as medical technology changes, and any health regulation must not "depart from accepted medical practice." In applying this standard, the Court holds that "the safety of second-trimester abortions has increased dramatically" since 1973, when *Roe* was decided. Although a regulation such as one requiring that all second-trimester abortions be performed in hospitals "had strong support" in 1973 "as a reasonable health regulation," *ante,* at 435, this regulation can no longer stand because, according to the Court's diligent research into medical and scientific literature, the dilation and evacuation (D&E) procedure, used in 1973 only for first-trimester abortions, "is now widely and successfully used for second-trimester abortions." Further, the

From *City of Akron v. Arkon Center for Reproductive Health,* 462 U.S. 416 (1982).

medical literature relied on by the Court indicates that the D&E procedure may be performed in an appropriate nonhospital setting for "at least . . . the early weeks of the second trimester. . . ." The court then chooses the period of 16 weeks of gestation as that point at which D&E procedures may be performed safely in a nonhospital setting, and thereby invalidates the Akron hospitalization regulation.

It is not difficult to see that despite the Court's purported adherence to the trimester approach adopted in *Roe,* the lines drawn in that decision have now been "blurred" because of what the Court accepts as technological advancement in the safety of abortion procedure. The State may no longer rely on a "bright line" that separates permissible from impermissible regulation, and it is no longer free to consider the second trimester as a unit and weigh the risks posed by all abortion procedures throughout that trimester. Rather, the State must continuously and conscientiously study contemporary medical and scientific literature in order to determine whether the effect of a particular regulation is to "depart from accepted medical practice" insofar as particular procedures and particular periods within the trimester are concerned. Assuming that legislative bodies are able to engage in this exacting task, it is difficult to believe that our Constitution *requires* that they do it as a prelude to protecting the health of their citizens. . . .

Just as improvements in medical technology inevitably will move *forward* the point at which the State may regulate for reasons of maternal health, different technological improvements will move *backward* the point of viability at which the State may proscribe abortions except when necessary to preserve the life and health of the mother. . . .

. . . [R]ecent studies have demonstrated increasingly earlier fetal viability. It is certainly reasonable to believe that fetal viability in the first trimester of pregnancy may be possible in the not too distant future. . . .

The *Roe* framework, then, is clearly on a collision course with itself. As the medical risks of various abortion procedures decrease, the point at which the State may regulate for reasons of maternal health is moved further forward to actual childbirth. As medical science becomes better able to provide for the separate existence of the fetus, the point of viability is moved further back toward conception. . . .

Even assuming that there is a fundamental right to terminate pregnancy in some situations, there is no justification in law or logic for the trimester framework adopted in *Roe* and employed by the Court today on the basis of *stare decisis.* For the reasons stated above, that framework is clearly an unworkable means of balancing the fundamental right and the compelling state interests that are indisputably implicated.

The Court in *Roe* correctly realized that the State has important interests "in the areas of health and medical standards" and that "[t]he State has a legitimate interest in seeing to it that abortion, like any other medical procedure, is performed under circumstances that insure maximum safety for the patient." The Court also recognized that the State has "*another* important and legitimate interest in protecting the potentiality of human life." I agree completely that the State has these interests, but in my view, the point at which these interests become compelling does not depend on the trimester of pregnancy. Rather, these interests are present *throughout* pregnancy.

This Court has never failed to recognize that "a State may properly assert important interests in safeguarding health [and] in maintaining medical standards." It cannot be doubted that as long as a state statute is within "the bounds of reason and [does not] assum[e] the character of a merely arbitrary fiat . . . [then] [t]he State . . . must decide upon measures that are needful for the protection of its people." . . .

The fallacy inherent in the *Roe* framework is apparent: just because the State has a compelling interest in ensuring maternal safety once an abortion may be more dangerous than childbirth, it simply does not follow that the State has *no* interest before that point that justifies state regulation to ensure that first-trimester abortions are performed as safely as possible.

The state interest in potential human life is likewise extant throughout pregnancy. In *Roe,* the Court held that although the State had an important and legitimate interest in protecting potential life, that interest could not become compelling until the point at which the fetus was viable. The difficulty with this analysis is clear: *potential* life is no less potential in the first weeks of pregnancy than it is at viability or afterward. At any stage in pregnancy, there is the *potential* for human life. Although the Court refused to "resolve the difficult question of when life begins," *id.,* at 159, the Court chose the point of viability—when the fetus is *capable* of life independent of its mother—to permit the complete proscription of abortion. The choice of viability as the point at which the state interest in *potential* life becomes compelling is no less arbitrary than choosing any point before viability or any point afterward. Accordingly, I believe that the State's interest in protecting potential human life exists throughout the pregnancy. . . .

This Court has acknowledged that ". . . *Roe* did not declare an unqualified 'constitutional right to an abortion'. *Maher* (1977) Rather, the right protects the woman from unduly burdensome interference with her freedom to decide whether to terminate her pregnancy." . . .

The requirement that state interference "infringe substantially" or "heavily burden" a right before heightened scrutiny is applied is not novel in our fundamental-rights jurisprudence, or restricted to the abortion context. In *San Antonio Independent School District* v. *Rodriguez,* 411 U.S. 1, 37–38 (1973), we observed that we apply "strict judicial scrutiny" only when legislation may be said to have " 'deprived,' 'infringed,' or 'interfered' with the free exercise of some such fundamental personal right or liberty." If the impact of the regulation does not rise to the level appropriate for our strict scrutiny, then our inquiry is limited to whether the state law bears "some rational relationship to legitimate state purposes." . . .

For the reasons states above, I find no justification for the trimester approach used by the Court to analyze this restriction. I would apply the "unduly burdensome" test and find that the hospitalization requirement does not impose an undue burden on that decision. . . .

A health regulation, such as the hospitalization requirement, simply does not rise to the level of "official interference" with the abortion decision. . . .

76

Hodgson v. Minnesota (1990)

JUSTICE STEVENS announced the judgment of the Court and delivered the opinion of the Court with respect to [the unconstitutionality of the two-parent notification requirement], an opinion with respect to [the constitutionality of the 48 hour delay period], in which JUSTICE O'CONNOR joins, and a dissenting opinion with respect to [the constitutionality of the judicial bypass].

A Minnesota statute, Minn. Stat. (1988), provides, with certain exceptions, that no abortion shall be performed on a woman under 18 years of age until at least 48 hours after both of her parents have been notified. In subdivisions 2–4 of the statute the notice is mandatory unless (1) the attending physician certifies that an immediate abortion is necessary to prevent the woman's death and there is insufficient time to provide the required notice; (2) both of her parents have consented in writing; or (3) the woman declares that she is a victim of parental abuse or neglect, in which event notice of her declaration must be given to the proper authorities. . . . Subdivision 6 of the same statute provides that if a court enjoins the enforcement of subdivision 2, the same notice requirement shall be effective unless the pregnant woman obtains a court order permitting the abortion to proceed. . . .

For reasons that follow, we now conclude that the requirement of notice to both of the pregnant minor's parents is not reasonably related to legitimate state interests and that subdivision 2 is unconstitutional. A different majority of the Court, for reasons stated in separate opinions, concludes that subdivision 6 is constitutional.

From *Hodgson v. Minnesota,* 58 LW 4958 (1990).

We think it is clear that a requirement that a minor wait 48 hours after notifying a single parent of her intention to get an abortion would reasonably further the legitimate state interest in ensuring that the minor's decision is knowing and intelligent. We have held that when a parent or another person has assumed "primary responsibility" for a minor's well-being, the State may properly enact "laws designed to aid discharge of that responsibility." . . . The brief waiting period provides the parent the opportunity to consult with his or her spouse and a family physician, and it permits the parent to inquire into the competency of the doctor performing the abortion, discuss the religious or moral implications of the abortion decision, and provide the daughter needed guidance and counsel in evaluating the impact of the decision on her future. . . .

It is equally clear that the requirement that *both* parents be notified, whether or not both wish to be notified or have assumed responsibility for the upbringing of the child, does not reasonably further any legitimate state interest. The usual justification for a parental consent or notification provision is that it supports the authority of a parent who is presumed to act in the minor's best interest and thereby assures that the minor's decision to terminate her pregnancy is knowing, intelligent, and deliberate. To the extent that such an interest is legitimate, it would be fully served by a requirement that the minor notify one parent who can then seek the counsel of his or her mate or any other party, when such advice and support is deemed necessary to help the child make a difficult decision. In the ideal family setting, of course, notice to either parent would normally constitute notice to both. A statute requiring two-parent notification would not further any state interest in those instances. In many families, however, the parent notified by the child would not notify the other parent. In those cases the State has no legitimate interest in questioning one parent's judgment that notice to the other parent would not assist the minor or in presuming that the parent who has assumed parental duties is incompetent to make decisions regarding the health and welfare of the child.

Not only does two-parent notification fail to serve any state interest with respect to functioning families, it disserves the state interest in protecting and assisting the minor with respect to dysfunctional families. The record reveals that in the thousands of dysfunctional families affected by this statute, the two-parent notice requirement proved positively harmful to the minor and her family. The testimony at trial established that this requirement, ostensibly designed for the benefit of the minor, resulted in major trauma to the child, and often to a parent as well. In some cases, the parents were divorced and the second parent did not have custody or otherwise participate in the child's upbringing. . . .

We therefore hold that this requirement violates the Constitution.

The Court holds that the constitutional objection to the two-parent notice requirement is removed by the judicial bypass option provided in subdivision 6 of the Minnesota statute. I respectfully dissent from that holding.

A majority of the Court has previously held that a statute requiring one parent's consent to a minor's abortion will be upheld if the State provides an "alternate procedure whereby a pregnant minor may demonstrate that she is sufficiently mature to make the abortion decision herself or that, despite her immaturity, an abortion would be in her best interests." . . . [This] precedent should [not] control our decision today. . . .

For reasons already set forth at length, a rule requiring consent or notification of both parents is not reasonably related to the state interest in giving the pregnant minor the benefit of parental advice. . . .

A judicial bypass that is designed to handle exceptions from a reasonable general rule, and thereby preserve the constitutionality of that rule, is quite different from a requirement that a minor—or a minor and one of her parents—must apply to a court for permission to avoid the application of a rule that is not reasonably related to legitimate state goals. . . .

JUSTICE O'CONNOR, concurring in part and concurring in the judgment in part.

. . . I agree that the Court has characterized "[a] woman's decision to beget or to bear a child [as] a component of her liberty that is protected by the Due Process Clause of the Fourteenth Amendment to the Constitution." This Court extended that liberty interest to minors in *Bellotti v. Baird* (1979) (*Bellotti II*), and *Planned Parenthood of Central Missouri v. Danforth* (1976), albeit with some important limitations: "[P]arental notice and consent are qualifications that typically may be imposed by the State on a minor's right to make important decisions. As immature minors often lack the ability to make fully informed choices that take account of both immediate and long-range consequences, a State reasonably may determine that parental consultation often is desirable and in the best interest of the minor." Cf. *Thompson v. Oklahoma,* (1988) ("Inexperience, less education, and less intelligence make the teenager less able to evaluate the consequences of his or her conduct while at the same time he or she is much more apt to be motivated by mere emotion or peer pressure than is an adult"); *Stanford v. Kentucky* (1989) (BRENNAN, J., dissenting) ("[M]inors are treated differently from adults in our laws, which reflects the simple truth derived from communal experience, that juveniles as a class have not the level of maturation and responsibility that we presume in adults and consider desirable for full participation in the rights and duties of modern life").

It has been my understanding in this area that "[i]f the particular regulation does not 'unduly burde[n]' the fundamental right, . . . then our evaluation of that regulation is limited to our determination that the regulation rationally relates to a legitimate state purpose." It is with that understanding that I agree with JUSTICE STEVENS' statement that the "statute cannot be sustained if the obstacles it imposes are not reasonably related to legitimate state interests."

I agree with JUSTICE STEVENS that Minnesota has offered no sufficient justification for its interference with the family's decisionmaking processes created by subdivision 2—two-parent notification. Subdivision 2 is the most stringent notification statute in the country. . . .

The Minnesota exception to notification for minors who are victims of neglect or abuse is, in reality, a means of notifying the parents. As JUSTICE STEVENS points out, to avail herself of the neglect or abuse exception, the minor must report the abuse. A report requires the welfare agency to immediately "conduct an assessment." If the agency interviews the victim, it must notify the parent of the fact of the interview; if the parent is the subject of an investigation, he has a right of access to the record of the investigation. . . . The combination of the abused minor's reluctance to report sexual or physical abuse, with the likelihood that invoking the abuse exception for the purpose of avoiding notice will result in notice, makes the abuse exception less than effectual.

Minnesota's two-parent notice requirement is all the more unreasonable when one considers that only half of the minors in the State of Minnesota reside with both biological parents. A third live with only one parent. Given its broad sweep and its failure to serve the purposes asserted by the State in too many cases, I join the Court's striking of subdivision 2.

In a series of cases, this Court has explicitly approved judicial bypass as a means of tailoring a parental consent provision so as to avoid unduly burdening the minor's limited right to obtain an abortion. In *Danforth,* the Court stated that the

> "primary constitutional deficiency lies in [the notification statute's] imposition of an absolute limitation on the minor's right to obtain an abortion. . . . [A] materially different constitutional issue would be presented under a provision requiring parental consent or consultation in most cases but providing for prompt (i) judicial resolution of any disagreement between the parent and the minor, or (ii) judicial determination that the minor is mature enough to give an informed consent without parental concurrence or that abortion in any event is in the minor's best interest. Such a provision would not impose parental approval as an absolute condition upon the minor's right but would assure in most instances consultation between the parent and child."

Subdivision 6 passes constitutional muster because the interference with the internal operation of the family required by subdivision 2 simply does not exist where the minor can avoid notifying one or both parents by use of the bypass procedure.

JUSTICE MARSHALL, with whom JUSTICE BRENNAN and JUSTICE BLACKMUN join, concurring in part, concurring in the judgment in part, and dissenting in part.

. . . Although I do not believe that the Constitution permits a State to require a minor to notify or consult with a parent before obtaining an abortion,

I am in substantial agreement with the [Court's decision that] Minnesota's two-parent notification requirement is not even reasonably related to a legitimate state interest. Therefore, that requirement surely would not pass the strict scrutiny applicable to restrictions on a woman's fundamental right to have an abortion.

I dissent from the judgment of the Court, however, that the judicial bypass option renders the parental notification and 48-hour delay requirements constitutional. . . .

Neither the scope of a woman's privacy right nor the magnitude of a law's burden is diminished because a woman is a minor. Rather, a woman's minority status affects only the nature of the State's interests. . . .

A substantial proportion of pregnant minors voluntarily consult with a parent regardless of the existence of a notification requirement. . . . But for those young women who would choose not to inform their parents, the burden is evident: the notification requirement destroys their right to avoid disclosure of a deeply personal matter.

A notification requirement can also have severe physical and psychological effects on a young woman. First, forced notification of one parent, like forced notification of both parents, can be extremely traumatic for a young woman, depending on the nature of her relationship with her parents. The disclosure of a daughter's intention to have an abortion often leads to a family crisis, characterized by severe parental anger and rejection. . . .

Second, the prospect of having to notify a parent causes many young women to delay their abortions, thereby increasing the health risks of the procedure. . . .

In addition, a notification requirement compels many minors seeking an abortion to travel to a State without such a requirement to avoid notifying a parent. . . . Other women may resort to the horrors of self-abortion or illegal abortion rather than tell a parent. . . . Still others would forgo an abortion entirely and carry the fetus to term (9% of minors in family planning clinics said they would carry fetus to term rather than inform parents of decision to abort), subjecting themselves to the much greater health risks of pregnancy and childbirth and to the physical, psychological, and financial hardships of unwanted motherhood. . . . Clearly, then, requiring notification of one parent significantly burdens a young woman's right to terminate her pregnancy.

The 48-hour delay *after* notification further aggravates the harm caused by the *pre*-notification delay that may flow from a minor's fear of notifying a parent. Moreover, the 48-hour delay burdens the rights of all minors, including those who would voluntarily consult with one or both parents. JUSTICE STEVENS' assertion that the 48-hour delay "imposes only a minimal burden," ignores the increased health risks and costs that this delay entails. . . .

The State argues that the bypass procedure saves the notification and delay requirements because it provides an alternative way to obtain a legal abortion for minors who would be harmed by those requirements. This Court has upheld a one-parent consent requirement where the State provided an alternative judicial procedure "whereby a pregnant minor [could] demonstrate that she [was] sufficiently mature to make the abortion decision herself or that, despite her immaturity, an abortion would be in her best interests."

I continue to believe, however, that a judicial bypass procedure of this sort is itself unconstitutional because it effectively gives a judge "an absolute veto over the decision of the physician and his patient." See also *Bellotti II,* (STEVENS, J., concurring in judgment) ("The provision of an absolute veto to a judge . . . is to me particularly troubling. . . . It is inherent in the right to make the abortion decision that the right may be exercised without public scrutiny and in defiance of the contrary opinion of the sovereign or other third parties"); *Planned Parenthood of Central Mo.,* ("[T]he State does not have the constitutional authority to give a third party an absolute, and possibly arbitrary, veto over the decision of the physician and his patient to terminate the patient's pregnancy, regardless of the reason for withholding the consent"). No person may veto *any* minor's decision, made in consultation with her physician, to terminate her pregnancy. An "immature" minor has no less right to make decisions regarding her own body than a mature adult.

Minnesota's bypass provision allows a judge to authorize an abortion if he determines either that a woman is sufficiently mature to make the decision on her own or, if she is not sufficiently mature, that an abortion without parental notification would serve her best interests. Of course, if a judge refuses to authorize an abortion, a young woman can then reevaluate whether she wants to notify a parent. But many women will carry the fetus to term rather than notify a parent. Other women may decide to inform a parent but then confront parental pressure or abuse so severe as to obstruct the abortion. For these women, the judge's refusal to authorize an abortion effectively constitutes an absolute veto. . . .

A majority of the Court today strikes down an unreasonable and vastly overbroad requirement that a pregnant minor notify both her parents of her decision to obtain an abortion. With that decision I agree. At the same time, though, a different majority holds that a State may require a young woman to notify one or even both parents and then wait 48 hours before having an abortion, as long as the State provides a judicial bypass procedure. From that decision I vehemently dissent. This scheme forces a young woman in an already dire situation to choose between two fundamentally unacceptable alternatives: notifying a possibly dictatorial or even abusive parent and justifying her profoundly personal decision in an intimidating judicial proceeding to a black-robed stranger. For such a woman, this dilemma is more likely to result in trauma and pain than in an informed and voluntary decision.

JUSTICE SCALIA, concurring in the judgment in part and dissenting in part.

As I understand the various opinions today: One Justice holds that two-parent notification is unconstitutional (at least in the present circumstances) without judicial bypass, but constitutional with bypass (O'CONNOR, J., concurring in part and concurring in judgment); four Justices would hold that two-parent notification is constitutional with or without bypass (KENNEDY, J., concurring in judgment in part and dissenting in part); four Justices would hold that two-parent notification is unconstitutional with or without bypass, though the four apply two different standards, (opinion of STEVENS, J.), (MARSHALL, J., concurring in part and dissenting in part); six Justices hold that one-parent notification with bypass is constitutional, though for two different sets of reasons, *Ohio* v. *Akron Center for Reproductive Health* (STEVENS, J., concurring in judgment); and three Justices would hold that one-parent notification with bypass is unconstitutional (BLACKMUN, J., dissenting). One will search in vain the document we are supposed to be construing for text that provides the basis for the argument over these distinctions; and will find in our society's tradition regarding abortion no hint that the distinctions are constitutionally relevant, much less any indication how a constitutional argument about them ought to be resolved. The random and unpredictable results of our consequently unchanneled individual views make it increasingly evident, Term after Term, that the tools for this job are not to be found in the lawyer's—and hence not in the judge's—workbox. I continue to dissent from this enterprise of devising an Abortion Code, and from the illusion that we have authority to do so.

JUSTICE KENNEDY, with whom THE CHIEF JUSTICE, JUSTICE WHITE, and JUSTICE SCALIA join, concurring in the judgment in part and dissenting in part.

"There can be little doubt that the State furthers a constitutionally permissible end by encouraging an unmarried pregnant minor to seek the help and advice of her parents in making the very important decision whether or not to bear a child. That is a grave decision, and a girl of tender years, under emotional stress, may be ill-equipped to make it without mature advice and emotional support" (*Bellotti II*). Today, the Court holds that a statute requiring a minor to notify both parents that she plans to have an abortion is not a permissible means of furthering the interest described with such specificity in *Bellotti II*. This conclusion, which no doubt will come as a surprise to most parents, is incompatible with our constitutional tradition and any acceptable notion of judicial review of legislative enactments. I dissent from the portion of the Court's judgment affirming the Court of Appeal's conclusion that Minnesota['s] two-parent notice statute is unconstitutional.

The Minnesota statute also provides, however, that if the two-parent notice requirement is invalidated, the same notice requirement is effective unless the pregnant minor obtains a court order permitting the abortion to proceed. The Court of Appeals sustained this portion of the statute, in effect a two-parent notice requirement with a judicial bypass. Five Members of the Court, the four who join this opinion and JUSTICE O'CONNOR, agree with the Court of Appeals' decision on this aspect of the statute. As announced by JUSTICE STEVENS, who dissents from this part of the Court's decision, the Court of Appeals' judgment on this portion of the statute is therefore affirmed. . . .

The State identifies two interests served by the law. The first is the State's interest in the welfare of pregnant minors. The second is the State's interest in acknowledging and promoting the role of parents in the care and upbringing of their children. JUSTICE STEVENS, writing for two Members of the Court, acknowledges the legitimacy of the first interest, but decides that the second interest is somehow illegitimate, at least as to whichever parent a minor chooses not to notify. I cannot agree that the Constitution prevents a State from keeping both parents informed of the medical condition or medical treatment of their child under the terms and conditions of this statute.

The welfare of the child has always been the central concern of laws with regard to minors. The law does not give to children many rights given to adults, and provides, in general, that children can exercise the rights they do have only through and with parental consent. Legislatures historically have acted on the basis of the qualitative differences in maturity between children and adults, and not without reason. Age is a rough but fair approximation of maturity and judgment, and a State has an interest in seeing that a child, when confronted with serious decisions such as whether or not to abort a pregnancy, has the assistance of her parents in making the choice. If anything is settled by our previous cases dealing with parental notification and consent laws, it is this point.

Protection of the right of each parent to participate in the upbringing of her or his own children is a further discrete interest that the State recognizes by the statute. . . .

A State pursues a legitimate end under the Constitution when it attempts to foster and preserve the parent-child relation by giving all parents the opportunity to participate in the care and nurture of their children. We have held that parents have a liberty interest, protected by the Constitution, in having a reasonable opportunity to develop close relations with their children. We have recognized, of course, that there are limits to the constitutional right of parents to have custody of or to participate in decisions affecting their children. If a parent has relinquished the opportunity to develop a relation with the child, and his or her only link to the child is biological, the Constitution does not require a State to allow parental participation. But the fact that the Constitution does not protect the parent-child relationship in all circumstances does not mean that the State cannot attempt to foster parental participation where the Constitution does not demand that it do so. A State may seek to protect and facilitate the parent-child bond on the assumption that parents will act in their child's best interests. . . .

In this case, the Court rejects a legislature's judgment that parents should at least be aware of their daughter's intention to seek an abortion, even if the State does not empower the parents to control the child's decision. That judgment is rejected although it rests upon a tradition of a parental role in the care and upbringing of children that is as old as civilization itself. Our precedents do not permit this result.

It is true that for all too many young women the prospect of two parents, perhaps even one parent, sustaining her with support that is compassionate and committed is an illusion. Statistics on drug and alcohol abuse by parents and documentations of child neglect and mistreatment are but fragments of the evidence showing the tragic reality that becomes day-to-day life for thousands of minors. But the Court errs in serious degree when it commands its own solution to the cruel consequences of individual misconduct, parental failure, and social ills. The legislative authority is entitled to attempt to meet these wrongs by taking reasonable measures to recognize and promote the primacy of the family tie, a concept which this Court now seems intent on declaring a constitutional irrelevance.

77

Brown v. Board of Education (1954)

Mr. Chief Justice Warren *delivered the opinion of the Court:*

These cases come to us from the States of Kansas, South Carolina, Virginia, and Delaware. They are premised on different facts and different local conditions, but a common legal question justifies their consideration together in this consolidated opinion.

In each of the cases, minors of the Negro race, through their legal representatives, seek the aid of the courts in obtaining admission to the public schools of their community on a nonsegregated basis. In each instance, they have been denied admission to schools attended by white children under laws requiring or permitting segregation according to race. This segregation was alleged to deprive the plaintiffs of the equal protection of the laws under the Fourteenth Amendment. . . .

In the first cases in this Court construing the Fourteenth Amendment, decided shortly after its adoption, the Court interpreted it as proscribing all state-imposed discriminations against the Negro race. The doctrine of "separate but equal" did not make its appearance in this Court until 1896 in the case of Plessy v. Ferguson, supra, involving not education but transportation. American courts have since labored with the doctrine for over half a century. In this Court, there have been six cases involving the "separate but equal" doctrine in the field of public education. In Cumming v. Board of Education of Richmond County, and Gong Lum v. Rice, the validity of the doctrine itself was not challenged. In more recent cases, all on the graduate school level, inequality was found in that specific benefits enjoyed by white students were denied to Negro students of the same educational qualifications. In none of these cases was it necessary to reexamine the doctrine to grant relief to the Negro plaintiff. And in Sweatt v. Painter the Court expressly reserved decision on the question whether Plessy v. Ferguson should be held inapplicable to public education.

In approaching this problem, we cannot turn the clock back to 1868 when the Amendment was adopted, or even to 1896 when Plessy v. Ferguson was written. We must consider public education in the light of its full development and its present place in American life throughout the Na-

From *Brown v. Board of Education* 347 U.S. 483 (1954).

tion. Only in this way can it be determined if segregation in public schools deprives these plaintiffs of the equal protection of the laws.

Today, education is perhaps the most important function of state and local governments. Compulsory school attendance laws and the great expenditures for education both demonstrate our recognition of the importance of education to our democratic society. It is required in the performance of our most basic public responsibilities, even service in the armed forces. It is the very foundation of good citizenship. Today it is a principal instrument in awakening the child to cultural values, in preparing him for later professional training, and in helping him to adjust normally to his environment. In these days, it is doubtful that any child may reasonably be expected to succeed in life if he is denied the opportunity of an education. Such an opportunity, where the state has undertaken to provide it, is a right which must be made available to all on equal terms.

We come then to the question presented: Does segregation of children in public schools solely on the basis of race, even though the physical facilities and other "tangible" factors may be equal, deprive the children of the minority group of equal educational opportunities? We believe that it does.

In Sweatt v. Painter, in finding that a segregated law school for Negroes could not provide them equal educational opportunities, this Court relied in large part on "those qualities which are incapable of objective measurement but which make for greatness in a law school." In McLaurin v. Oklahoma State Regents, the Court, in requiring that a Negro admitted to a white graduate school be treated like all other students, again resorted to intangible considerations: ". . . his ability to study, to engage in discussions and exchange views with other students, and, in general, to learn his profession." Such considerations apply with added force to children in grade and high schools. To separate them from others of similar age and qualifications solely because of their race generates a feeling of inferiority as to their status in the community that may affect their hearts and minds in a way unlikely ever to be undone. The effect of this separation on their educational opportunities was well stated by a finding in the Kansas case by a court which nevertheless felt compelled to rule against the Negro plaintiffs:

> "Segregation of white and colored children in public schools has a detrimental effect upon the colored children. The impact is greater when it has the sanction of the law; for the policy of separating the races is usually interpreted as denoting the inferiority of the negro group. A sense of inferiority affects the motivation of a child to learn. Segregation with the sanction of law, therefore, has a tendency to [retard] the educational and mental development of Negro children and to deprive them of some of the benefits they would receive in a racial[ly] integrated school system."

Whatever may have been the extent of psychological knowledge at the time of Plessy v. Ferguson, this finding is amply supported by modern authority.* Any language in Plessy v. Ferguson contrary to this finding is rejected.

We conclude that in the field of public education the doctrine of "separate but equal" has no place. Separate educational facilities are inherently unequal. Therefore, we hold that the plaintiffs and others similarly situated for whom the actions have been brought are, by reason of the segregation complained of, deprived of the equal protection of the laws guaranteed by the Fourteenth Amendment. . . .

*K.B. Clark, Effect of Prejudice and Discrimination on Personality Development (Midcentury White House Conference on Children and Youth, 1950); Witmer and Kotinsky, Personality in the Making (1952), c. VI; Deutscher and Chen, The Psychological Effects of Enforced Segregation: A Survey of Social Science Opinion, 26 J. Psychol. 259 (1948); Chein, What are the Psychological Effects of Segregation Under Conditions of Equal Facilities?, 3 Int. J. Opinion and Attitude Res. 229 (1949); Brameld, Educational Costs, in Discrimination and National Welfare (MacIver, ed. 1949), 44-48; Frazier, the Negro in the United States (1949), 674-681. And see generally Myrdal, An American Dilemma (1944).

78

Plessy v. Ferguson (1896)

Mr. Justice Brown *delivered the opinion of the Court:*

This case turns upon the constitutionality of an act of the General Assembly of the State of Louisiana, passed in 1890, providing for separate railway carriages for the white and colored races.

The first section of the statute enacts "that all railway companies carrying passengers in their coaches in this State, shall provide equal but separate accommodations for the white, and colored races, by providing two or more passenger coaches for each passenger train, or by dividing the passenger coaches by a partition so as to secure separate accommodations: *Provided,* That this section shall not be construed to apply to street rail-

From *Plessy v. Ferguson* 163 U.S. 537 (1896).

roads. No person or persons shall be permitted to occupy seats in coaches other than the ones assigned to them, on account of the race they belong to." . . .

The information filed in the criminal district court charged in substance that Plessy, being a passenger between two stations within the state of Louisiana, was assigned by officers of the company to the coach used by the race to which he belonged, but he insisted upon going into a coach used by the race to which he did not belong. Neither in the information nor plea was his particular race or color averred. . . .

[Justice Brown summarized the provisions of the first section of the Fourteenth Amendment.]

The object of the amendment was undoubtedly to enforce the absolute equality of the two races before the law, but in the nature of things it could not have been intended to abolish distinctions based upon color, or to enforce social as distinguished from political equality, or a commingling of the two races upon terms unsatisfactory to either. Laws permitting, and even requiring, their separation in places where they are liable to be brought into contact do not necessarily imply the inferiority of either race to the other, and have been generally, if not universally, recognized as within the competency of the state legislatures in the exercise of their police power. The most common instance of this is connected with the establishment of separate schools for white and colored children, which has been held to be a valid exercise of the legislative power even by courts of States where the political rights of the colored race have been longest and most earnestly enforced. . . .

The distinction between laws interfering with the political equality of the negro and those requiring the separation of the two races in schools, theaters, and railway carriages, has been frequently drawn by this court. Thus, in Strauder v. West Virginia, it was held that a law of West Virginia limiting to white male persons, twenty-one years of age and citizens of the state, the right to sit upon juries, was a discrimination which implied a legal inferiority in civil society. . . . [The further discussion of the distinction between laws denying political equality and laws denying social equality is omitted.]

So far, then, as a conflict with the 14th Amendment is concerned, the case reduces itself to the question whether the statute of Louisiana is a reasonable regulation, and with respect to this there must necessarily be a large discretion on the part of the legislature. In determining the question of reasonableness it is at liberty to act with reference to the established usages, customs and traditions of the people, and with a view to the promotion of their comfort, and preservation of the public peace and good order. Gauged by this standard, we cannot say that a law which authorizes or even requires the separation of the two races in public conveyances is unreasonable, or more obnoxious to the 14th Amendment than the acts of Congress requiring separate schools for colored children in the District of Columbia, the constitutionality of which does not seem to have been questioned, or the corresponding acts of state legislatures.

We consider the underlying fallacy of the plaintiff's argument to consist in the assumption that the enforced separation of the two races stamps the colored race with a badge of inferiority. If this be so, it is not by reason of anything found in the act, but solely because the colored race chooses to put that construction upon it. The argument necessarily assumes that if as has been more than once the case, and is not unlikely to be so again, the colored race should become the dominant power in the state legislature, and should enact a law in precisely similar terms, it would thereby relegate the white race to an inferior position. We imagine that the white race, at least, would not acquiesce in this assumption. The argument also assumes that social prejudices may be overcome by legislation, and that equal rights cannot be secured to the negro except by an enforced commingling of the two races. We cannot accept this proposition. If the two races are to meet upon terms of social equality, it must be the result of natural affinities, a mutual appreciation of each other's merits and voluntary consent of individuals. As was said by the court of appeals of New York in People v. Gallagher, "this end can neither be accomplished nor promoted by laws which conflict with the general sentiment of the community upon whom they are designed to operate. When the government, therefore, has secured to each of its citizens equal rights before the law and equal opportunities for improvement and progress, it has accomplished the end for which it was organized and performed all of the functions respecting social advantages with which it is endowed." Legislation is powerless to eradicate racial instincts or to abolish distinctions based upon physical differences, and the attempt to do so can only result in accentuating the difficulties of the present situation. If the civil and political rights of both races are equal, one cannot be inferior to the other civilly or politically. If one race be inferior to the other socially, the Constitution of the United States cannot put them upon the same plane. . . .

Mr. Justice Harlan, dissenting.

 . . . It was said in argument that the statute of Louisiana does not discriminate against either race, but prescribes a rule applicable alike to white and colored citizens. But this argument does not meet the difficulty. Every one knows that the statute in question had its origin in the purpose, not so much to exclude white persons from railroad cars occupied by blacks, as to exclude colored people from coaches occupied by or assigned to white persons. Railroad corporations of Louisiana did not make discrimination among whites in the matter of accommodation for travelers. The thing to acoomplish was, under the guise of giving equal accommodation for whites and blacks, to compel the latter to keep to themselves while traveling in railroad passenger coaches. No one would be so wanting in candor as to assert the contrary. The fundamental objection, therefore, to the statute, is that it interferes with the personal freedom of citizens. . . .

The white race deems itself to be the dominant race in this country. And so it is, in prestige, in achievements, in education, in wealth, and in power. So, I doubt not, it will continue to be for all time, if it remains true to its great heritage, and holds fast to the principles of constitutional liberty. But in view of the constitution, in the eye of the law, there is in this country no superior, dominant, ruling class of citizens. There is no caste here. Our constitution is color-blind, and neither knows nor tolerates classes among citizens. In respect of civil rights, all citizens are equal before the law. The humblest is the peer of the most powerful. The law regards man as man, and takes no account of his surroundings or of his color when his civil rights as guaranteed by the supreme law of the land are involved. It is therefore to be regretted that this high tribunal, the final expositor of the fundamental law of the land, has reached the conclusion that it is competent for a state to regulate the enjoyment by citizens of their civil rights solely upon the basis of race. . . .

The arbitrary separation of citizens, on the basis of race, while they are on a public highway, is a badge of servitude wholly inconsistent with the civil freedom and the equality before the law established by the constitution. It cannot be justified upon any legal grounds.

If evils will result from the commingling of the two races upon public highways established for the benefit of all, they will be infinitely less than those that will surely come from state legislation regulating the enjoyment of civil rights upon the basis of race. We boast of the freedom enjoyed by our people above all other peoples. But it is difficult to reconcile that boast with a state of the law which, practically, puts the brand of servitude and degradation upon a large class of our fellow citizens,—our equals before the law. The thin disguise of "equal" accommodations for passengers in railroad coaches will not mislead anyone, nor atone for the wrong this day done. . . .

79

Eugene J. McCarthy

A Note on the New Equality (1977)

. . . Alexis de Tocqueville, in *Democracy in America,* wrote of the powerful appeal and danger of the idea of equality in a democratic society. He wrote also of its potential for demagoguery. I would be less concerned about the rise to popularity of the word, and the idea, if I thought it the result of conscious intention to elicit political support—that is, if those who made the appeal knew that they were being demagogic. I fear, however, that the use of the word is not intentionally demagogic. It seems to approach the automatic "It is good" justification that George Orwell described as characterizing the world order of 1984.

In his inaugural address President Carter said: "We have already found a high degree of personal liberty, and we are now struggling to enhance equality of opportunity." One may well question the President's language. Liberty was a goal of the American Revolution. We have it in this country not because we "found" it but rather as a result of our having declared it a political and social goal and then achieving it in some measure. As to the President's second point, that "we are now struggling to enhance equality of opportunity," such language does not clearly describe the concept of "equality" as it is applied today. Economic, educational, political, and cultural equality—and not equality of opportunity, "enhanced" or otherwise—is the goal in the new application.

Economic equality is in this new conception to be achieved primarily through equalizing income. Equalization of wealth—that is, of wealth already accumulated—may come later. Economic equality is not conceived as a base upon which differences may then build, but as an average. One state governor occasionally asks if it might be better if people doing unpleasant work were paid as much as or more than those whose work is culturally and physically preferable.

Political economists have developed the notion of a negative income tax as the basis for tax reform. Essentially the idea is this: that everyone should have enough income to pay taxes at the beginning or threshold rate,

Reprinted from *Commentary,* by permission; copyright © 1977 by the American Jewish Committee.

and that if one does not have enough income to reach that level, something should be done to make up for the deficiency. Where the idea came from, or how the taxable level of income was chosen as the absolute standard for relative judgments and adjustments, is not clear. It seems that the tax base is to be accepted as a first principle upon which we are to build. It is an axiom, rather like "I think, therefore I am." One could as well arbitrarily assert that everyone should, for the good of the commonwealth, pay $100 in income taxes, and then proceed through measures of redistribution to raise all incomes to the level at which everyone would have to pay $100 in taxes. . . .

The second area in which the new concept of equality is being applied is in politics and government. The principle of one-person-one-vote was formally recognized in a Supreme Court ruling affecting defined political jurisdictions. The court did not in its ruling extend the principle to relationships among jurisdictions. The ruling simply said that, within given units of government, each vote should be equal to every other vote. Thus, since the Constitution provides for direct election of the House of Representatives on the basis of population, the rule requires that each congressional district have roughly the same number of persons.

The Constitution also provides that each state, no matter what its size, shall have two Senators. Thus the citizen of a small state gets proportionally more of a vote than the resident of a large state. The Constitution further provides that the President shall be elected through the Electoral College, on a state-by-state basis, thus weighting the votes of smaller states favorably as against those cast in larger states. The drive now is to eliminate that weighting by abolishing the Electoral College and instituting direct popular election of the President. No proposal has yet been made to reduce senatorial representation to a strict population base.

The principle of equality is also applied through the Federal Election Campaign Act, which attempts to equalize the non-voting influence of citizens on candidates for political office. The present law limits the size of contributions to a political candidate in any one campaign to $1,000 per contributor. This is considered a transitional phase to a time when all campaigns will be publicly financed. The argument for the limitation is that the larger the contribution, the greater the influence a contributor has on the officeholder and the more time he gets to spend with the officeholder. Theoretically, with public financing, every taxpayer will have made an equal contribution and will be entitled to as much time with the officeholder as any other taxpayer. What time non-taxpayers will get has not yet been determined by the reformers. Despite the $1,000 limit on contributions in the last national elections, and the fact that the presidential campaigns were financed principally through federal grants, within a few days of the election President-elect Carter flew to St. Simon's Island, the domain of the Reynolds family, and President Ford went to Palm Springs—presumably to speak to the average citizens who dewll in those precincts.

It does not take much imagination to foresee a time when citizens might go to court, charging that they were discriminated against because their calls were not taken in presidential telethons and transmitted to the President for his attention. A full practical application of this principle would argue for an equal right to speak or otherwise communicate with all officeholders, even removing the personal screening of Walter Cronkite.

The objective of equalizing communications and influence on office-holders is also sought in efforts to control lobbyists. Proposals generally recommend more thorough regulation of lobbyists, limits on their expenditures, and public disclosure not only of expenditures but also of meetings and communications with officeholders.

It will not be surprising if someone suggests having lobbyists provided at government expense, so as to insulate them from the undue influence of their principals, in somewhat the same way that officeholders are to be insulated from their constituencies. Under this arrangement, anyone who had a case to make to the government would apply for a lobbyist who would be assigned from a pool in the way that public defenders are assigned by the courts. . . .

The new concept of equality is also applied in government and government-influenced employment practices, in what has been labeled the "quota system." The rationale of the quota system is that, since not every person can be hired, we should have within each employed group a representation or sampling of the total employable work force. Selection currently is on the basis of physiological characteristics of age, sex, and race. There are some obvious historical reasons as to why these standards are being tried. There are also some obvious difficulties in their application, especially if one attempts to extend the principle—as will surely be done—to other racial and ethnic groups, or to groups less easily defined in terms of psychological and cultural differences.

A similar drive to realize the new idea of equality has marked educational development in recent years. The standardized curriculum, quota admissions, open admissions, and free college education are all manifestations of this drive. Full application of the principle could lead to compulsory college education, with the level of education so reduced that all who enter do so with assurance of successful graduation. With no possible abandonment of hope at any point, they could look forward to something like the judgment of the Dodo after the caucus race in *Alice in Wonderland:* *"Everybody* has won, and *all* must have prizes."

What are the dangers in this drive to a newly conceived equality? I see a danger first in the inevitable weakening of those institutions that are expected to give form and direction to society, such as professional and educational institutions, and which have traditionally been treated as having an identity separate from politically-controlled areas of society.

I see it also as significantly affecting the individual's conception of his place in society. Most persons cannot stand either physical or cultural isolation, and will seek a base of some certainty in a community of persons and in a cultural complex. The cultural security of Americans traditionally has been found in a society of some tension, but a society in which a balance between individual freedom and liberty on the one side and the social good on the other could be achieved. The alternative now offered, the security of equalization, is depersonalizing. It is a deceptively angelistic conception of man in society. It is one which cannot be sustained. It will in all likelihood move persons in search of security, if not identity, to accept greater and greater socialization in politics, in economics, and in culture.

80

Kurt Vonnegut Jr.

Harrison Bergeron (1961)

The year was 2081, and everybody was finally equal. They weren't only equal before God and the law. They were equal every which way. Nobody was smarter than anybody else. Nobody was better looking than anybody else. Nobody was stronger or quicker than anybody else. All this equality was due to the 211th, 212th, and 213th Amendments to the Constitution, and to the unceasing vigilance of agents of the United States Handicapper General.

Some things about living still weren't quite right, though. April, for instance, still drove people crazy by not being springtime. And it was in that clammy month that the H-G men took George and Hazel Bergeron's fourteen-year-old son, Harrison, away.

It was tragic, all right, but George and Hazel couldn't think about it very hard. Hazel had a perfectly average intelligence, which meant she couldn't think about anything except in short bursts. And George, while his intelligence was way above normal, had a little mental handicap radio in his ear. He was required by law to wear it at all times. It was tuned to a government transmitter. Every twenty seconds or so, the transmitter would send out some sharp noise to keep people like George from taking unfair advantage of their brains.

George and Hazel were watching television. There were tears on Hazel's cheeks, but she'd forgotten for the moment what they were about.

On the television screen were ballerinas.

A buzzer sounded in George's head. His thoughts fled in panic, like bandits from a burglar alarm.

"That was a real pretty dance, that dance they just did," said Hazel.

"Huh?" said George.

"That dance—it was nice," said Hazel.

"Yup," said George. He tried to think a little about the ballerinas. They weren't really very good—no better than anybody else would have been, anyway. They were burdened with sashweights and bags of birdshot, and their faces were masked, so that no one, seeing a free and graceful gesture or a pretty face, would feel like something the cat drug in. George was toying with the vague notion that maybe dancers shouldn't be handicapped. But he didn't get very far with it before another noise in his ear radio scattered his thoughts.

George winced. So did two out of the eight ballerinas.

Hazel saw him wince. Having no mental handicap herself, she had to ask George what the latest sound had been.

"Sounded like somebody hitting a milk bottle with a ball peen hammer," said George.

"I'd think it would be real interesting, hearing all the different sounds," said Hazel, a little envious. "All the things they think up."

"Um," said George.

"Only, if I was Handicapper General, you know what I would do?" said Hazel. Hazel, as a matter of fact, bore a strong resemblance to the Handicapper General, a woman named Diana Moon Glampers. "If I was Diana Moon Glampers," said Hazel, "I'd have chimes on Sunday—just chimes. Kind of in honor of religion."

"I could think, if it was just chimes," said George.

"Well—maybe make 'em real loud," said Hazel. "I think I'd made a good Handicapper General."

"Good as anybody else," said George.

"Who knows bett'n I do what normal is?" said Hazel.

"Right," said George. He began to think glimmeringly about his abnormal son who was now in jail, about Harrison, but a twenty-one-gun salute in his head stopped that.

"Boy!" said Hazel, "that was a doozy, wasn't it?"

It was such a doozy that George was white and trembling, and tears stood on the rims of his red eyes. Two of the eight ballerinas had collapsed to the studio floor, were holding their temples.

"All of a sudden you look so tired," said Hazel. "Why don't you stretch out on the sofa, so's you can rest your handicap bag on the pillows, honeybunch." She was referring to the forty-seven pounds of birdshot in a canvas bag, which was padlocked around George's neck. "Go on and rest the bag for a little while," she said. "I don't care if your're not equal to me for a while."

George weighed the bag with his hands. "I don't mind it," he said. "I don't notice it any more. It's just a part of me."

"You been so tired lately—kind of wore out," said Hazel. "If there was just some way we could make a little hole in the bottom of the bag, and just take out a few of them lead balls. Just a few."

"Two years in prison and two thousand dollars fine for every ball I took out," said George. "I don't call that a bargain."

"If you could just take a few out when you came home from work," said Hazel. "I mean—you don't compete with anybody around here. You just set around."

"If I tried to get away with it," said George, "then other people'd get away with it—and pretty soon we'd be right back to the dark ages again, with everybody competing against everybody else. You wouldn't like that, would you?"

"I'd hate it," said Hazel.

"There you are," said George. "The minute people start cheating on laws, what do you think happens to society?"

If Hazel hadn't been able to come up with an answer to this question, George couldn't have supplied one. A siren was going off in his head.

"Reckon it'd fall all apart," said Hazel.

"What would?" said George blankly.

"Society," said Hazel uncertainly. "Wasn't that what you just said?"

"Who knows?" said George.

The television program was suddenly interrupted for a news bulletin. It wasn't clear at first as to what the bulletin was about, since the announcer, like all announcers, had a serious speech impediment. For about half a minute, and in a state of high excitement, the announcer tried to say, "Ladies and gentlemen—"

He finally gave up, handed the bulletin to a ballerina to read.

"That's all right—" Hazel said of the announcer, "he tried. That's the big thing. He tried to do the best he could with what God gave him. He should get a nice raise for trying so hard."

"Ladies and gentlemen—" said the ballerina, reading the bulletin. She must have been extraordinarily beautiful, because the mask she wore was hideous. And it was easy to see that she was the strongest and most graceful of all the dancers, for her handicap bags were as big as those worn by two-hundred-pound men.

And she had to apologize at once for her voice, which was a very unfair voice for a woman to use. Her voice was a warm, luminous, timeless melody. "Excuse me—" she said, and she began again, making her voice absolutely uncompetitive.

"Harrison Bergeron, age fourteen," she said in a grackle squawk, "has just escaped from jail, where he was held on suspicion of plotting to overthrow the government. He is a genius and an athlete, is underhandicapped, and should be regarded as extremely dangerous."

A police photograph of Harrison Bergeron was flashed on the screen upside down, then sideways, upside down again, then right side up. The picture showed the full length of Harrison against a background calibrated in feet and inches. He was exactly seven feet tall.

The rest of Harrison's appearance was Halloween and hardware. Nobody had ever born heavier handicaps. He had outgrown hindrances faster than the H-G men could think them up. Instead of a little ear radio for a mental handicap, he wore a tremendous pair of earphones, and spectacles with thick wavy lenses. The spectacles were intended to make him not only half blind, but to give him whanging headaches besides.

Scrap metal was hung all over him. Ordinarily, there was a certain symmetry, a military neatness to the handicaps issued to strong people, but Harrison looked like a walking junkyard. In the race of life, Harrison carried three hundred pounds.

And to offset his good looks, the H-G men required that he wear at all times a red rubber ball for a nose, keep his eyebrows shaved off, and cover his even white teeth with black caps at snaggle-tooth random.

"If you see this boy," said the ballerina, "do not—I repeat, do not— try to reason with him."

There was the shriek of a door being torn from its hinges.

Screams and barking cries of consternation came from the television set. The photograph of Harrison Bergeron on the screen jumped again and again, as though dancing to the tune of an earthquake.

George Bergeron correctly identified the earthquake, and well he might have—for many was the time his own home had danced to the same crashing tune. "My God—" said George, "that must be Harrison!"

The realization was blasted from his mind instantly by the sound of an automobile collision in his head.

When George could open his eyes again, the photograph of Harrison was gone. A living, breathing Harrison filled the screen.

Clanking, clownish, and huge, Harrison stood in the center of the studio. The knob of the uprooted studio door was still in his hand. Ballerinas, technicians, musicians, and announcers cowered on their knees before him, expecting to die.

"I am the Emperor!" cried Harrison. "Do you hear? I am the Emperor! Everybody must do what I say at once!" He stamped his foot and the studio shook.

"Even as I stand here—" he bellowed, "crippled, hobbled, sickened—I am a greater ruler than any man who ever lived! Now watch me become what I *can* become!"

Harrison tore the straps of his handicap harness like wet tissue paper, tore straps guaranteed to support five thousand pounds.

Harrison's scrap-iron handicaps crashed to the floor.

Harrison thrust his thumbs under the bar of the padlock that secured his head harness. The bar snapped like celery. Harrison smashed his headphones and spectacles against the wall.

He flung away his rubber-ball nose, revealed a man that would have awed Thor, the god of thunder.

"I shall now select my Empress!" he said, looking down on the cowering people. "Let the first woman who dares rise to her feet claim her mate and her throne!"

A moment passed, and then a ballerina arose, swaying like a willow.

Harrison plucked the mental handicap from her ear, snapped off her physical handicaps with marvelous delicacy. Last of all, he removed her mask.

She was blindingly beautiful.

"Now—" said Harrison, taking her hand, "shall we show the people the meaning of the word dance? Music!" he commanded.

The musicians scrambled back into their chairs, and Harrison stripped them of their handicaps, too. "Play your best," he told them, "and I'll make you barons and dukes and earls."

The music began. It was normal at first—cheap, silly, false. But Harrison snatched two musicians from their chairs, waved them like batons as he sang the music as he wanted it played. He slammed them back into their chairs.

The music began again and was much improved.

Harrison and his Empress merely listened to the music for a while— listened gravely, as though synchronizing their heartbeats with it.

They shifted their weights to their toes.

Harrison placed his big hands on the girl's tiny waist, letting her sense the weightlessness that would soon be hers.

And then, in an explosion of joy and grace, into the air they sprang!

Not only were the laws of the land abandoned, but the law of gravity and the laws of motion as well.

They reeled, whirled, swiveled, flounced, capered, gamboled, and spun.

They leaped like deer on the moon.

The studio ceiling was thirty feet high, but each leap brought the dancers nearer to it.

It became their obvious intention to kiss the ceiling.

They kissed it.

And then, neutralizing gravity with love and pure will, they remained suspended in air inches below the ceiling, and they kissed each other for a long, long time.

It was then that Diana Moon Glampers, the Handicapper General, came into the studio with a double-barreled ten-gauge shotgun. She fired twice, and the Emperor and the Empress were dead before they hit the floor.

Diana Moon Glampers loaded the gun again. She aimed it at the musicians and told them they had ten seconds to get their handicaps back on.

It was then that the Bergerons' television tube burned out.

Hazel turned to comment about the blackout to George. But George had gone ʻut into the kitchen for a can of beer.

George came back in with the beer, paused while a handicap signal shook him up. And then he sat down again. "You been crying?" he said to Hazel.

"Yup," she said.

"What about?" he said.

"I forget," she said. "Something real sad on television."

"What was it?" he said.

"It's all kind of mixed up in my mind," said Hazel.

"Forget sad things," said George.

"I always do," said Hazel.

"That's my girl," said George. He winced. There was the sound of a rivetting gun in his head.

"Gee—I could tell that one was a doozy," said Hazel.

"You can say that again," said George.

"Gee—" said Hazel, "I could tell that one was a doozy."

81

Thomas Jefferson

The Natural Aristocracy (1813)

Jefferson to Adams

. . . For I agree with you that there is a natural aristocracy among men. The grounds of this are virtue and talents. Formerly bodily powers gave place among the aristoi. But since the invention of gunpowder has armed the weak as well as the strong with missile death, bodily strength, like beauty, good humor, politeness and other accomplishments, has become but an auxiliary ground of distinction. There is also an artificial aristocracy founded on wealth and birth, without either virtue or talents; for with these it would belong to the first class. The natural aristocracy I consider as the most precious gift of nature for the instruction, the trusts, and government of society. And indeed it would have been inconsistent in creation to have formed man for the social state, and not to have provided virtue and wisdom enough to manage the concerns of the society. May we not even say that that form of government is the best which provides the most effectually for a pure selection of these natural aristoi into the offices of government? The artificial aristocracy is a mischievous ingredient in government, and provision should be made to prevent it's ascendancy. On the question, What is the best provision, you and I differ; but we differ as rational friends, using the free exercise of our own reason, and mutually indulging it's errors. *You* think it best to put the Pseudo-aristoi into a separate chamber of legislation where they may be hindered from doing mischief by their coordinate branches, and where also they may be a protection to wealth against the Agrarian and plundering enterprises of the Majority of the people. I think that to give them power in order to prevent them from doing mischief, is arming them for it, and increasing instead of remedying the evil. For if the coordinate branches can arrest their action, so may they that of the coordinates. Mischief may be done negatively as well as positively. Of this a cabal in the Senate of the U.S. has furnished many proofs. Nor do I believe them necessary to protect the wealthy; because enough of these will find their way into every branch of the legislation to protect

From *The Adams-Jefferson Letters*, Vol. II, Lester J. Cappon, ed., University of North Carolina Press, 1959.

themselves. From 15 to 20 legislatures of our own, in action for 30 years past, have proved that no fears of an equalisation of property are to be apprehended from them.

I think the best remedy is exactly that provided by all our constitutions, to leave to the citizens the free election and separation of the aristoi from the pseudo-aristoi, of the wheat from the chaff. In general they will elect the real good and wise. In some instances, wealth may corrupt, and birth blind them; but not in sufficient degree to endanger the society.

It is probable that our difference of opinion may in some measure be produced by a difference of character in those among whom we live. From what I have seen of Massachusetts and Connecticut myself, and still more from what I have heard and the character given of the former by yourself, who know them so much better, there seems to be in these two states a traditionary reverence for certain families, which has rendered the offices of the government nearly hereditary in those families. I presume that from an early period of your history, members of these families happening to possess virtue and talents, have honestly exercised them for the good of the people, and by their services have endeared their names to them. . . .

At the first session of our legislature after the Declaration of Independence, we passed a law abolishing entails. And this was followed by one abolishing the privilege of Primogeniture, and dividing the lands of intestates equally among all their children, or other representatives. These laws, drawn by myself, laid the axe to the root of Pseudo-aristocracy. And had another which I prepared been adopted by the legislature, our work would have been complete. It was a Bill for more general diffusion of learning. This proposed to divide every county into wards of 5 or 6 miles square, like your townships; to establish in each ward a free school for reading, writing and common arithmetic; to provide for the annual selection of the best subjects from these schools who might receive at the public expense a higher degree of education at a district school; and from these district schools to select a certain number of the most promising subjects to be completed at an University, where all the useful sciences should be taught. Worth and genius would thus have been sought out from every condition of life, and completely prepared by education for defeating the competition of wealth and birth for public trusts.

My proposition had for a further object to impart to these wards those portions of self-government for which they are best qualified, by confiding to them the care of their poor, their roads, police, elections, the nomination of jurors, administration of justice in small cases, elementary exercises of militia, in short, to have made them little republics, with a Warden at the head of each, for all those concerns which, being under their eye, they would better manage than the larger republics of the county or state. A general call of ward-meetings by their Wardens on the same day thro' the state would at any time produce the genuine sense of the people on any required point, and would enable the state to act in mass, as your people have so often done, and with so much effect, by their town meetings. The law for religious freedom, which made a part of this system, having put down the aristocracy of the clergy, and restored to the citizen the freedom of the mind, and those of entails and descents nurturing an equality of condition among them, this on Education would have raised the mass of the people to the high ground of moral respectability necessary to their own safety, and to orderly government; and would have completed the great object of qualifying them to select the veritable aristoi, for the trusts of government, to the exclusion of the Pseudalists: and the same Theognis who has furnished the epigraphs of your two letters assures us that ʽουδεμιαν πω Κυρν᾽ αγαθοι πολιν ὠλεσαν ανδρες ["Curnis, good men have never harmed any city"]᾽. Altho᾽ this law has not yet been acted on but in a small and inefficient degree, it is still considered as before the legislature, with other bills of the revised code, not yet taken up, and I have great hope that some patriotic spirit will, at a favorable moment, call it up, and make it the key-stone of the arch of our government.

With respect to Aristocracy, we should further consider that, before the establishment of the American states, nothing was known to History but the Man of the old world, crowded within limits either small or overcharged, and steeped in the vices which that situation generates. A government adapted to such men would be one thing; but a very different one than for the Man of these states. Here every one may have land to labor for himself if he chuses; or, preferring the exercise of any other industry, may exact for it such compensation as not only to afford a comfortable subsistence, but wherewith to provide for a cessation from labor in old age. Every one, by his property, or by his satisfactory situation, is interested in the support of law and order. And such men may safely and advantageously reserve to themselves a wholesome control over their public affairs, and a degree of freedom, which in the hands of the Canaille of the cities of Europe, would be instantly perverted to the demolition and destruction of every thing public and private. The history of the last 25 years of France, and of the last 40 years in America, nay of it's last 200 years, proves the truth of both parts of this observation.

But even in Europe a change has sensibly taken place in the mind of Man. Science had liberated the ideas of those who read and reflect, and the American example had kindled feelings of right in the people. An insurrection has consequently begun, of science, talents and courage against rank and birth, which have fallen into contempt. It has failed in it's first effort, because the mobs of the cities, the instrument used for it's accomplishment, debased by ignorance, poverty and vice, could not be restrained to rational action. But the world will recover from the panic of this first catastrophe.

Science is progressive, and talents and enterprize on the alert. Resort may be had to the people of the country, a more governable power from their principles and subordination; and rank, and birth, and tinsel-aristocracy will finally shrink into insignificance, even there. This however we have no right to meddle with. It suffices for us, if the moral and physical condition of our own citizens qualifies them to select the able and good for the direction of their government, with a recurrence of elections at such short periods as will enable them to displace an unfaithful servant before the mischief he meditates may be irremediable. . . .

82

Alexis de Tocqueville

Why So Many Ambitious Men and So Little Lofty Ambition Are To Be Found in the United States (1840)

The first thing that strikes a traveler in the United States is the innumerable multitude of those who seek to emerge from their original condition; and the second is the rarity of lofty ambition to be observed in the midst of the universally ambitious stir of society. No Americans are devoid of a yearning desire to rise, but hardly any appear to entertain hopes of great magnitude or to pursue very lofty aims. All are constantly seeking to acquire property, power, and reputation; few contemplate these things upon a great scale; and this is the more surprising as nothing is to be discerned in the manners or laws of America to limit desire or to prevent it from spreading its impulses in every direction. . . .

What chiefly diverts the men of democracies from lofty ambition is not the scantiness of their fortunes, but the vehemence of the exertions they daily make to improve them. They strain their faculties to the utmost to achieve paltry results, and this cannot fail speedily to limit their range of view and to circumscribe their powers. They might be much poorer and still be greater.

The small number of opulent citizens who are to be found in a democracy do not constitute an exception to this rule. A man who raises himself by degrees to wealth and power contracts, in the course of this protracted labor, habits of prudence and restraint which he cannot afterwards shake off. A man cannot gradually enlarge his mind as he does his house. . . .

In a democratic society, as well as elsewhere, there is only a certain number of great fortunes to be made; and as the paths that lead to them are indiscriminately open to all, the progress of all must necessarily be slackened. As the candidates appear to be nearly alike, and as it is difficult to make a selection without infringing the principle of equality, which is the supreme law of democratic societies, the first idea which suggests itself is to make them all advance at the same rate and submit to the same trials. . . . From hatred of privilege and from the embarrassment of choosing, all men are at last forced, whatever may be their standard, to pass the same ordeal; all are indiscriminately subjected to a multitude of petty preliminary exercises, in which their youth is wasted and their imagination quenched, so that they despair of ever fully attaining what is held out to them; and when at length they are in a condition to perform any extraordinary acts, the taste for such things has forsaken them.

In China, where the equality of conditions is very great and very ancient, no man passes from one public office to another without undergoing a competitive trial. This probation occurs afresh at every stage of his career; and the notion is now so rooted in the manners of the people that I remember to have read a Chinese novel in which the hero, after numberless vicissitudes, succeeds at length in touching the heart of his mistress by doing well on an examination. A lofty ambition breathes with difficulty in such an atmosphere. . . .

I confess that I apprehend much less for democratic society from the boldness that from the mediocrity of desires. What appears to me most to be dreaded is that in the midst of the small, incessant occupations of private life, ambition should lose its vigor and its greatness; that the passions of man should abate, but at the same time be lowered; so that the march of society should every day become more tranquil and less aspiring.

I think, then, that the leaders of modern society would be wrong to seek to lull the community by a state of too uniform and too peaceful happiness, and that it is well to expose it from time to time to matters of difficulty and danger in order to raise ambition and to give it a field of action.

Moralists are constantly complaining that the ruling vice of the present time is pride. This is true in one sense, for indeed everyone thinks that he is better than his neighbor or refuses to obey his superior; but it is extremely false in another, for the same man who cannot endure subordination or equality has so contemptible an opinion of himself that he thinks he is born only to indulge in vulgar pleasures. He willingly takes up with low desires without daring to embark on lofty enterprises, of which he scarcely dreams.

Thus, far from thinking that humility ought to be preached to our contemporaries, I would have endeavors made to give them a more enlarged idea of themselves and of their kind. Humility is unwholesome to them; what they most want is, in my opinion, pride. I would willingly exchange several of our small virtues for this one vice.

Appendix

The Constitution of the United States of America

We the People of the United States, in Order to form a more perfect Union, establish Justice, insure domestic Tranquillity, provide for the common defence, promote the general Welfare, and secure the Blessings of Liberty to ourselves and our Posterity, do ordain and establish this Constitution for the United States of America.

Article. I.

Section. 1. All legislative Powers herein granted shall be vested in a Congress of the United States, which shall consist of a Senate and House of Representatives.

Section. 2. The House of Representatives shall be composed of Members chosen every second Year by the People of the several States, and the Electors in each State shall have the Qualifications requisite for Electors of the most numerous Branch of the State Legislature.

No Person shall be a Representative who shall not have attained to the age of twenty-five Years, and been seven Years a Citizen of the United States, and who shall not, when elected, be an Inhabitant of that State in which he shall be chosen.

Representatives and direct Taxes shall be apportioned among the several States which may be included within this Union, according to their respective Numbers, which shall be determined by adding to the whole Number of free Persons, including those bound to Service for a Term of Years, and excluding Indians not taxed, three-fifths of all other Persons. The actual Enumeration shall be made within three Years after the first Meeting of the Congress of the United States, and within every subsequent Term of ten Years, in such Manner as they shall by Law direct. The Number of Representatives shall not exceed one for every thirty Thousand, but each State shall have at Least one Representative; and until such enumeration shall be made, the State of New Hampshire shall be entitled to chuse three, Massachusetts eight, Rhode-Island and Providence Plantations one, Connecticut five, New York six, New Jersey four, Pennsylvania eight, Delaware one, Maryland six, Virginia ten, North Carolina five, South Carolina five, and Georgia three.

When vacancies happen in the Representation from any State, the Executive Authority thereof shall issue Writs of Election to fill such Vacancies.

The House of Representatives shall chuse their Speaker and other Officers; and shall have the sole Power of Impeachment.

Section. 3. The Senate of the United States shall be composed of two Senators from each State, chosen by the Legislature thereof, for six Years; and each Senator shall have one Vote.

Immediately after they shall be assembled in Consequence of the first Election, they shall be divided as equally as may be into three Classes. The Seats of the Senators of the first Class shall be vacated at the Expiration of the second Year, of the second Class at the Expiration of the fourth Year, and of the third Class at the Expiration of the sixth Year, so that one third may be chosen every second Year; and if Vacancies happen by Resignation, or otherwise, during the Recess of the Legislature of any State, the Executive thereof may make temporary Appointments until the next Meeting of the Legislature, which shall then fill such Vacancies.

No Person shall be a Senator who shall not have attained to the Age of thirty Years, and been nine Years a Citizen of the United States, and who shall not, when elected, be an Inhabitant of that State for which he shall be chosen.

The Vice President of the United States shall be President of the Senate, but shall have no Vote, unless they be equally divided.

The Senate shall chuse their other Officers, and also a President pro tempore, in the Absence of the Vice President, or when he shall exercise the Office of President of the United States.

The Senate shall have the sole Power to try all Impeachments. When sitting for that Purpose, they shall be on Oath or Affirmation. When the President of the United States is tried the Chief Justice shall preside: And no Person shall be convicted without the Concurrence of two thirds of the Members present.

Judgment in Cases of Impeachment shall not extend further than to removal from Office, and disqualification to hold and enjoy any Office of honor, Trust or Profit under the United States: but the Party convicted shall nevertheless be liable and subject to Indictment, Trial, Judgment and Punishment, according to Law.

Section. 4. The Times, Places and Manner of holding Elections for Senators and Representatives, shall be prescribed in each State by the

Legislature thereof; but the Congress may at any time by Law make or alter such Regulations, except as to the Places of chusing Senators.

The Congress shall assemble at least once in every Year, and such Meeting shall be on the first Monday in December, unless they shall by Law appoint a different Day.

Section. 5. Each House shall be the Judge of the Elections, Returns and Qualifications of its own Members, and a Majority of each shall constitute a Quorum to do Business; but a smaller Number may adjourn from day to day, and may be authorized to compel the Attendance of absent Members, in such Manner, and under such Penalties as each House may provide.

Each House may determine the Rules of its Proceedings, punish its Members for disorderly Behaviour, and, with the Concurrence of two-thirds, expel a Member.

Each House shall keep a Journal of its Proceedings, and from time to time publish the same, excepting such Parts as may in their Judgment require Secrecy; and the Yeas and Nays of the Members of either House on any question shall, at the Desire of one-fifth of those Present, be entered on the Journal.

Neither House, during the Session of Congress, shall, without the Consent of the other, adjourn for more than three days, nor to any other Place than that in which the two Houses shall be sitting.

Section. 6. The Senators and Representatives shall receive a Compensation for their Services, to be ascertained by Law, and paid out of the Treasury of the United States. They shall in all Cases, except Treason, Felony and Breach of the Peace, be privileged from Arrest during their Attendance at the Session of their respective Houses, and in going to and returning from the same; and for any Speech or Debate in either House, they shall not be questioned in any other Place.

No Senator or Representative shall, during the Time for which he was elected, be appointed to any civil Office under the Authority of the United States, which shall have been created, or the Emoluments whereof shall have been encreased during such time; and no Person holding any Office under the United States, shall be a Member of either House during his Continuance in Office.

Section. 7. All Bills for raising Revenue shall originate in the House of Representatives; but the Senate may propose or concur with amendments as on other Bills.

Every Bill which shall have passed the House of Representatives and the Senate, shall, before it become a Law, be presented to the President of the United States; If he approve he shall sign it, but if not he shall return it, with his Objections to that House in which it shall have originated, who shall enter the Objections at large on their Journal, and proceed to reconsider it. If after such Reconsideration two thirds of that House shall agree to pass the Bill, it shall be sent, together with the Objections, to the other House, by which it shall likewise be reconsidered, and if approved by two thirds of that House, it shall become a Law. But in all such Cases the Votes of both Houses shall be determined by yeas and Nays, and the Names of the Persons voting for and against the Bill shall be entered on the Journal of each House respectively. If any Bill shall not be returned by the President within ten Days (Sunday excepted) after it shall have been presented to him, the Same shall be a Law, in like Manner as if he had signed it, unless the Congress by their Adjournment prevent its Return, in which Case it shall not be a Law.

Every Order, Resolution, or Vote to which the Concurrence of the Senate and House of Representatives may be necessary (except on a question of Adjournment) shall be presented to the President of the United States; and before the Same shall take Effect, shall be approved by him, or being disapproved by him, shall be repassed by two thirds of the Senate and House of Representatives, according to the Rules and Limitations prescribed in the Case of a Bill.

Section. 8. The Congress shall have Power To lay and collect Taxes, Duties, Imposts, and Excises, to pay the Debts and provide for the common Defence and general Welfare of the United States; but all Duties, Imposts and Excises shall be uniform throughout the United States;

To borrow Money on the credit of the United States;

To regulate Commerce with foreign Nations, and among the several States, and with the Indian Tribes;

To establish an uniform Rule of Naturalization, and uniform Laws on the subject of Bankruptcies throughout the United States;

To coin Money, regulate the Value thereof, and of foreign Coin, and fix the Standard of Weights and Measures;

To provide for the Punishment of counterfeiting the Securities and current Coin of the United States;

To establish Post Offices and post Roads;

To promote the Progress of Science and useful Arts, by securing for limited Times to Authors and Inventors the exclusive Right to their respective Writings and Discoveries;

To constitute Tribunals inferior to the supreme Court;

To define and punish Piracies and Felonies committed on the high Seas, and Offences against the Law of Nations;

To declare War, grant Letters of Marque and Reprisal, and make Rules concerning Captures on Land and Water;

To raise and support Armies, but no Appropriation of Money to that Use shall be for a longer Term than two Years;

To provide and maintain a Navy;

To make Rules for the Government and Regulation of the land and naval Forces;

To provide for calling forth the Militia to execute the Laws of the Union, suppress Insurrections and repel Invasions;

To provide for organizing, arming, and disciplining, the Militia, and for governing such Part of them as may be employed in the Service of the United States, reserving to the States respectively, the Appointment of the Officers, and the Authority of training the Militia according to the discipline prescribed by Congress;

To exercise exclusive Legislation in all Cases whatsoever, over such District (not exceeding ten Miles square) as may, by Cession of Particular States, and the Acceptance of Congress, become the Seat of the Government of the United States, and to exercise like Authority over all Places purchased by the Consent of the Legislature of the State in which the Same shall be, for the Erection of Forts, Magazines, Arsenals, dock-Yards, and other needful Buildings;—And

To make all Laws which shall be necessary and proper for carrying into Execution the foregoing Powers, and all other Powers vested by this Constitution in the Government of the United States, or in any Department or Officer thereof.

Section. 9. The Migration or Importation of such Persons as any of the States now existing shall think proper to admit, shall not be prohibited by the Congress prior to the Year one thousand eight hundred and eight, but a Tax or duty may be imposed on such Importation, not exceeding ten dollars for each Person.

The Privilege of the Writ of Habeas Corpus shall not be suspended, unless when in Cases of Rebellion or Invasion the public Safety may require it.

No Bill of Attainder or ex post facto Law shall be passed.

No Capitation, or other direct, Tax shall be laid, unless in Proportion to the Census of Enumeration herein before directed to be taken.

No Tax or Duty shall be laid on Articles exported from any State.

No Preference shall be given by any Regulation of Commerce or Revenue to the Ports of one State over those of another; nor shall Vessels bound to, or from, one State, be obliged to enter, clear or pay Duties in another.

No Money shall be drawn from the Treasury, but in Consequence of Appropriations made by Law; and a regular Statement and Account of the Receipts and Expenditures of all public Money shall be published from time to time.

No Title of Nobility shall be granted by the United States; And no Person holding any Office of Profit or Trust under them, shall, without the Consent of the Congress, accept of any present, Emolument, Office, or Title, of any kind whatever, from any King, Prince, or foreign State.

Section. 10. No State shall enter into any Treaty, Alliance, or Confederation; grant Letters of Marque and Reprisal; coin Money; emit Bills of Credit; make any Thing but gold and silver Coin a Tender in Payment of Debts; pass any Bill of Attainder, ex post facto Law, or Law impairing the Obligation of Contracts, or grant any Title of Nobility.

No State shall, without the Consent of the Congress, lay any Imposts or Duties on Imports or Exports, except what may be absolutely necessary for executing its inspection Laws; and the net Produce of all Duties and Imposts, laid by any State on Imports or Exports, shall be for the Use of the Treasury of the United States; and all such Laws shall be subject to the Revision and Controul of the Congress.

No State shall, without the Consent of Congress, lay any Duty of Tonnage, keep Troops, or Ships of War in time of Peace, enter into any Agreement or Compact with another State, or with a foreign Power, or engage in War, unless actually invaded, or in such imminent Danger as will not admit of delay.

Article. II.

Section. 1. The executive Power shall be vested in a President of the United States of America. He shall hold his Office during the Term of four Years, and, together with the Vice President, chosen for the same Term, be elected, as follows

Each State shall appoint, in such Manner as the Legislature thereof may direct, a Number of Electors, equal to the whole Number of Senators and Representatives to which the State may be entitled in the Congress: but no Senator or Representative, or Person holding an Office of Trust or Profit under the United States, shall be appointed an Elector.

The Electors shall meet in their respective States, and vote by Ballot for two Persons, of whom one at least shall not be an Inhabitant of the same State with themselves. And they shall make a List of all the Persons voted for, and of the Number of Votes for each; which List they shall sign and certify, and transmit sealed to the Seat of the Government of the United States, directed to the President of the Senate. The President of the Senate shall, in the Presence of the Senate and House of Representatives, open all the Certificates, and the Votes shall then be counted. The Person having the greatest Number of Votes shall be the President, if such Number be a Majority of the whole Number of Electors appointed; and if there be more than one who have such Majority, and have an equal Number of Votes, then the House of Representatives shall immediately chuse by Ballot one of them for President; and if no Person have a Majority, then from the five highest on the List the said House shall in like Manner chuse the President. But in chusing the President, the Votes shall be taken by States, the Representation from each State having one Vote; a quorum for this Purpose shall consist of a Member or Members from two thirds of the States, and a Majority of all the States shall be necessary to a Choice. In every Case, after the Choice of the President, the Person having the greatest Number of Votes of the Electors shall be the Vice President. But if there should remain two or more who have equal Votes, the Senate shall chose from them by Ballot the Vice President.

The Congress may determine the Time of chusing the Electors, and the Day on which they shall give their votes; which Day shall be the same throughout the United States.

No Person except a natural born Citizen, or a Citizen of the United States, at the time of the Adoption of this Constitution, shall be eligible to the Office of President; neither shall any person be eligible to that Office who shall not have attained to the Age of thirty five Years, and been fourteen Years a Resident within the United States.

In Case of the Removal of the President from Office, or of his Death, Resignation, or Inability to discharge the Powers and Duties of the said Office, the Same shall devolve on the Vice President, and the Congress may by Law provide for the Case of Removal, Death, Resignation or Inability, both of the President and Vice President, declaring what Officer shall then act as President, and such Officer shall act accordingly, until the Disability be removed, or a President shall be elected.

The President shall, at stated Times, receive for his Services, a Compensation, which shall neither be encreased nor diminished during the Period for which he shall have been elected, and he shall not receive within that Period any other Emolument from the United States, or any of them.

Before he enter on the Execution of his Office, he shall take the following Oath or Affirmation:—"I do solemnly swear (or affirm) that I will faithfully execute the Office of President of the United States, and will to the best of my Ability, preserve, protect and defend the Constitution of the United States."

Section. 2. The President shall be Commander in Chief of the Army and Navy of the United States, and of the Militia of the several States, when called into the actual Service of the United States; he may require the Opinion, in writing, of the principal Officer in each of the executive Departments, upon any Subject relating to the Duties of their respective Offices, and he shall have Power to grant Reprieves and Pardons for Offenses against the United States, except in Cases of Impeachment.

He shall have Power, by and with the Advice and Consent of the Senate, to make Treaties, provided two thirds of the Senators present concur; and he shall nominate, and by and with the Advice and Consent of the Senate, shall appoint Ambassadors, other public Ministers and Consuls, Judges of the supreme Court, and all other Officers of the United States, whose Appointments are not herein otherwise provided for, and which shall be established by Law; but the Congress may by Law vest the Appointment of such inferior Officers, as they think proper, in the President alone, in the Courts of Law, or in the Heads of Departments.

The President shall have Power to fill up all Vacancies that may happen during the Recess of the Senate, by granting Commissions which shall expire at the End of their next Session.

Section. 3. He shall from time to time give to the Congress Information of the State of the Union, and recommend to their Consideration such Measures as he shall judge necessary and expedient; he may, on extraordinary Occasions, convene both Houses, or either of them, and in Case of Disagreement between them, with Respect to the Time of Adjournment, he may adjourn them to such Time as he shall think proper; he shall receive Ambassadors and other public Ministers; he shall take Care that the Laws be faithfully executed, and shall Commission all the Officers of the United States.

Section. 4. The President, Vice President and all Civil Officers of the United States, shall be removed from Office on Impeachment for, and Conviction of, Treason, Bribery, or other high Crimes and Misdemeanors.

Article. III.

Section. 1. The judicial Power of the United States, shall be vested in one supreme Court, and in such inferior Courts as the Congress may from time to time ordain and establish. The Judges, both of the supreme and inferior Courts, shall hold their Offices during good Behaviour, and shall, at stated Times, receive for their Services, a Compensation, which shall not be diminished during their Continuance in Office.

Section. 2. The judicial Power shall extend to all Cases, in Law and Equity, arising under this Constitution, the Laws of the United States, and Treaties made, or which shall be made, under their Authority;—to all Cases affecting Ambassadors, other public Ministers and Consuls;—to all Cases of admiralty and maritime Jurisdiction;—to Controversies to which the

United States shall be a Party;—to Controversies between two or more States;—between a State and Citizens of another State;—between Citizens of different States;—between Citizens of the same State claiming Lands under Grants of different States, and between a State, or the Citizens thereof, and foreign States, Citizens or Subjects.

In all Cases affecting Ambassadors, other public Ministers and Consuls, and those in which a State shall be Party, the supreme Court shall have original Jurisdiction. In all the other Cases before mentioned, the supreme Court shall have appellate Jurisdiction, both as to Law and Fact, with such Exceptions, and under such Regulations as the Congress shall make.

The Trial of all Crimes, except in Cases of Impeachment, shall be by Jury; and such Trial shall be held in the State where the said Crimes shall have been committed; but when not committed within any State, the Trial shall be at such Place or Places as the Congress may by Law have directed.

Section. 3. Treason against the United States, shall consist only in levying War against them, or in adhering to their Enemies, giving them Aid and Comfort. No Person shall be convicted of Treason unless on the Testimony of two Witnesses to the same overt Act, or on Confession in open Court.

The Congress shall have Power to declare the Punishment of Treason, but no Attainder of Treason shall work Corruption of Blood, or Forfeiture except during the Life of the Person attainted.

Article. IV.

Section. 1. Full Faith and Credit shall be given in each State to the public Acts, Records, and judicial Proceedings of every other State. And the Congress may by general Laws prescribe the Manner in which such Acts, Records and Proceedings shall be proved, and the Effect thereof.

Section. 2. The Citizens of each State shall be entitled to all Privileges and Immunities of Citizens in the several States.

A Person charged in any State with Treason, Felony, or other Crime, who shall flee from Justice, and be found in another State, shall on Demand of the executive Authority of the State from which he fled, be delivered up, to be removed to the State having Jurisdiction of the Crime.

No Person held to Service or Labour in one State, under the Laws thereof, escaping into another, shall, in Consequence of any Law or Regulation therein, be discharged from such Service or Labour, but shall be delivered up on Claim of the Party to whom such Service or Labour may be due.

Section. 3. New States may be admitted by the Congress into this Union; but no new State shall be formed or erected within the Jurisdiction of any other State; nor any State be formed by the Junction of two or more States, or Parts of States, without the Consent of the Legislatures of the States concerned as well as of the Congress.

The Congress shall have Power to dispose of and make all needful Rules and Regulations respecting the Territory or other Property belonging to the United States; and nothing in this Constitution shall be so construed as to Prejudice any Claims of the United States, or of any particular State.

Section. 4. The United States shall guarantee to every State in this Union a Republican Form of Government, and shall protect each of them against Invasion; and on Application of the Legislature, or of the Executive (when the Legislature cannot be convened) against domestic Violence.

Article. V.

The Congress, whenever two thirds of both Houses shall deem it necessary, shall propose Amendments to this Constitution, or, on the Application of the Legislatures of two thirds of the several States, shall call a Convention for proposing Amendments, which, in either Case, shall be valid to all Intents and Purposes, as Part of this Constitution, when ratified by the Legislatures of three fourths of the several States, or by Conventions in three fourths thereof, as the one or the other Mode of Ratification may be proposed by the Congress; Provided that no Amendment which may be made prior to the Year One thousand eight hundred and eight shall in any Manner affect the first and fourth Clauses in the Ninth Section of the first Article; and that no State, without its Consent, shall be deprived of its equal Suffrage in the Senate.

Article. VI.

All Debts contracted and Engagements entered into, before the Adoption of this Constitution, shall be as valid against the United States under this Constitution, as under the Confederation.

This Constitution, and the Laws of the United States which shall be made in Pursuance thereof; and all Treaties made, or which shall be made, under the Authority of the United States, shall be the supreme Law of the Land; and the Judges in every State shall be bound thereby, any Thing in the Constitution or Laws of any State to the Contrary notwithstanding.

The Senators and Representatives before mentioned, and the Members of the several State Legislatures, and all executive and judicial Officers, both of the United States and of the several States, shall be bound by Oath or Affirmation, to support this Constitution; but no religious Test shall ever be required as a Qualification to any Office or public Trust under the United States.

Article. VII.

The Ratification of the Conventions of nine States, shall be sufficient for the Establishment of this Constitution between the States so ratifying the Same.

done in Convention by the Unanimous Consent of the States present the Seventeenth Day of September in the Year of our Lord one thousand seven hundred and Eighty seven and of the Independence of the United States of America the Twelfth In witness whereof We have hereunto subscribed our Names, Go. Washington—President. and deputy from Virginia

Amendments to the Constitution

Amendment [I.]*

Congress shall make no law respecting an establishment of religion, or prohibiting the free exercise thereof; or abridging the freedom of speech, or of the press; or the right of the People peaceably to assemble, and to petition the Government for a redress of grievances.
[Ratified December 15, 1791]

Amendment [II.]

A well regulated Militia, being necessary to the security of a free State, the right of the people to keep and bear Arms, shall not be infringed.
[Ratified December 15, 1791]

Amendment [III.]

No Soldier shall, in time of peace be quartered in any house, without the consent of the Owner, nor in time of war, but in a manner to be prescribed by law.
[Ratified December 15, 1791]

Amendment [IV.]

The right of the people to be secure in their persons, houses, papers, and effects, against unreasonable searches and seizures, shall not be

*Brackets enclosing an amendment number indicate that the number was not specifically assigned in the resolution proposing the amendment.

violated, and no Warrants shall issue, but upon probable cause, supported by Oath or affirmation, and particularly describing the place to be searched, and the persons or things to be seized.
[Ratified December 15, 1791]

Amendment [V.]

No person shall be held to answer for a capital, or otherwise infamous crime, unless on a presentment or indictment of a Grand Jury, except in cases arising in the land or naval forces, or in the Militia, when in actual service in time of War or public danger; nor shall any person be subject for the same offence to be twice put in jeopardy of life or limb; nor shall be compelled in any criminal case to be a witness against himself, nor be deprived of life, liberty, or property, without due process of law; nor shall private property be taken for public use, without just compensation.
[Ratified December 15, 1791]

Amendment [VI.]

In all criminal prosecutions, the accused shall enjoy the right to a speedy and public trial, by an impartial jury of the State and district wherein the crime shall have been committed, which district shall have been previously ascertained by law, and to be informed of the nature and cause of the accusation; to be confronted with the witnesses against him; to have compulsory process for obtaining witnesses in his favor, and to have the Assistance of Counsel for his defence.
[Ratified December 15, 1791]

Amendment [VII.]

In Suits at common law, where the value in controversy shall exceed twenty dollars, the right of trial by jury shall be preserved, and no fact tried by a jury, shall be otherwise re-examined in any Court of the United States, than according to the rules of the common law.
[Ratified December 15, 1791]

Amendment [VIII.]

Excessive bail shall not be required, nor excessive fines imposed, nor cruel and unusual punishments inflicted.
[Ratified December 15, 1791]

Amendment [IX.]

The enumeration in the Constitution, of certain rights, shall not be construed to deny or disparage others retained by the people.
[Ratified December 15, 1791]

Amendment [X.]

The powers not delegated to the United States by the Constitution, nor prohibited by it to the States, are reserved to the States respectively, or to the people.
[Ratified December 15, 1791]

Amendment [XI.]

The Judicial power of the United States shall not be construed to extend to any suit in law or equity, commenced or prosecuted against one of the United States by Citizens of another State, or by Citizens or Subjects of any Foreign State.
[Ratified January 23, 1798]

Amendment [XII.]

The Electors shall meet in their respective states and vote by ballot for President and Vice-President, one of whom, at least, shall not be an inhabitant of the same state with themselves; they shall name in their ballots the person voted for as President, and in distinct ballots the person voted for as Vice-President, and they shall make distinct lists of all persons voted for as President, and of all persons voted for as Vice-President, and of the number of votes for each, which lists they shall sign and certify, and transmit sealed to the seat of the government of the United States, directed to the President of the Senate;—The President of the Senate shall, in the presence of the Senate and House of Representatives, open all the certificates and the votes shall then be counted;—The person having the greatest number of votes for President, shall be the President, if such number be a majority of the whole number of Electors appointed; and if no person have such majority, then from the persons having the highest numbers not exceeding three on the list of those voted for as President, the House of Representatives shall choose immediately by ballot, the President. But in choosing the President, the votes shall be taken by states, the representation from each state having one vote; a quorum for this purpose shall consist of a member or members from two-thirds of the states, and a majority of all the states shall be necessary to a choice. And if the House of Representatives shall not choose a President whenever the right of choice shall devolve upon them, before the fourth day of March next following, then the Vice-President shall act as President, as in the case of the death or other constitutional disability of the President.— The person having the greatest number of votes as Vice-President, shall be the Vice-President, if such number be a majority of the whole number of Electors appointed, and if no person have a majority, then from the two highest numbers on the list, the Senate shall choose the Vice-President; a quorum for the purpose shall consist of two-thirds of the whole number of Senators, and a majority of the whole number shall be necessary to a

choice. But no person constitutionally ineligible to the office of President shall be eligible to that of Vice-President of the United States.
[Ratified June 15, 1804]

Amendment [XIII.]

Section 1. Neither slavery nor involuntary servitude, except as a punishment for crime whereof the party shall have been duly convicted, shall exist within the United States, or any place subject to their jurisdiction.

Section 2. Congress shall have power to enforce this article by appropriate legislation.
[Ratified December 6, 1865]

Amendment [XIV.]

Section 1. All persons born or naturalized in the United States and subject to the jurisdiction thereof, are citizens of the United States and of the State wherein they reside. No State shall make or enforce any law which shall abridge the privileges or immunities of citizens of the United States; nor shall any State deprive any person of life, liberty, or property, without due process of law; nor deny to any person within its jurisdiction the equal protection of the laws.

Section 2. Representatives shall be apportioned among the several States according to their respective numbers, counting the whole number of persons in each State, excluding Indians not taxed. But when the right to vote at any election for the choice of electors for President and Vice President of the United States, Representatives in Congress, the Executive and Judicial officers of a State, or the members of the Legislature thereof, is denied to any of the male inhabitants of such State, being twenty-one years of age, and citizens of the United States, or in any way abridged, except for participation in rebellion, or other crime, the basis of representation therein shall be reduced in the proportion which the number of such male citizens shall bear to the whole number of male citizens twenty-one years of age in such State.

Section 3. No person shall be a Senator or Representative in Congress, or elector of President and Vice President, or hold any office, civil or military, under the United States, or under any State, who, having previously taken an oath, as a member of Congress, or as an officer of the United States, or as a member of any State legislature, or as an executive or judicial officer of any State, to support the Constitution of the United States, shall have engaged in insurrection or rebellion against the same, or given aid or comfort to the enemies thereof. But Congress may by a vote of two-thirds of each House, remove such disability.

Section 4. The validity of the public debt of the United States, authorized by law, including debts incurred for payment of pensions and bounties for services in suppressing insurrection or rebellion, shall not be questioned. But neither the United States nor any State shall assume or pay any debt or obligation incurred in aid of insurrection or rebellion against the United States, or any claim for the loss or emancipation of any slave; but all such debts, obligations and claims shall be held illegal and void.

Section 5. The Congress shall have power to enforce, by appropriate legislation, the provisions of this article.
[Ratified July 9, 1868]

Amendment [XV.]

Section 1. The right of citizens of the United States to vote shall not be denied or abridged by the United States or by any State on account of race, color, or previous condition of servitude.

Section 2. The Congress shall have power to enforce this article by appropriate legislation.
[Ratified February 2, 1870]

Amendment [XVI.]

The Congress shall have power to lay and collect taxes on incomes, from whatever source derived, without apportionment among the several States, and without regard to any census or enumeration.
[Ratified February 3, 1913]

Amendment [XVII.]

The Senate of the United States shall be composed of two Senators from each State, elected by the people thereof, for six years; and each Senator shall have one vote. The electors in each State shall have the qualifications requisite for electors of the most numerous branch of the State legislatures.

When vacancies happen in the representation of any State in the Senate, the executive authority of such State shall issue writs of election to fill such vacancies; *Provided,* That the legislature of any State may empower the executive thereof to make temporary appointments until the people fill the vacancies by election as the legislature may direct.

This amendment shall not be so construed as to affect the election or term of any Senator chosen before it becomes valid as part of the Constitution.
[Ratified April 8, 1913]

Amendment [XVIII.]

Section 1. After one year from the ratification of this article the manufacture, sale, or transportation of intoxicating liquors within, the importation thereof into, or the exportation thereof from the United States and all territory subject to the jurisdiction thereof for beverage purposes is hereby prohibited.

Section 2. The Congress and the several States shall have concurrent power to enforce this article by appropriate legislation.

Section 3. This article shall be inoperative unless it shall have been ratified as an amendment to the Constitution by the legislatures of the several States, as provided in the Constitution, within seven years from the date of the submission hereof to the States by the Congress.
[Ratified January 16, 1919]

Amendment [XIX.]

The right of citizens of the United States to vote shall not be denied or abridged by the United States or by any State on account of sex.

Congress shall have power to enforce this article by appropriate legislation.
[Ratified August 18, 1920]

Amendment [XX.]

Section 1. The terms of the President and Vice President shall end at noon on the 20th day of January, and the terms of Senators and Representatives at noon on the 3d day of January, of the years in which such terms would have ended if this article had not been ratified; and the terms of their successors shall then begin.

Section 2. The Congress shall assemble at least once in every year, and such meeting shall begin at noon on the 3d day of January, unless they shall by law appoint a different day.

Section 3. If, at the time fixed for the beginning of the term of the President, the President elect shall have died, the Vice President elect shall become President. If a President shall not have been chosen before the time fixed for the beginning of his term, or if the President elect shall have failed to qualify, then the Vice President elect shall act as President until a President shall have qualified; and the Congress may by law provide for the case wherein neither a President elect nor a Vice President elect shall have qualified, declaring who shall then act as President, or the manner in which one who is to act shall be selected, and such person shall act accordingly until a President or Vice President shall have qualified.

Section 4. The Congress may by law provide for the case of the death of any of the persons for whom the House of Representatives may choose a President whenever the right of choice shall have devolved upon them, and for the case of the death of any of the persons from whom the Senate may choose a Vice President whenever the right of choice shall have devolved upon them.

Section 5. Sections 1 and 2 shall take effect on the 15th day of October following the ratification of this article.

Section 6. This article shall be inoperative unless it shall have been ratified as an amendment to the Constitution by the legislatures of three-fourths of the several States within seven years from the date of its submission.
[Ratified January 23, 1933]

Amendment [XXI.]

Section 1. The eighteenth article of amendment to the Constitution of the United States is hereby repealed.

Section 2. The transportation or importation into any State, Territory or possession of the United States for delivery or use therein of intoxicating liquors, in violation of the laws thereof, is hereby prohibited.

Section 3. This article shall be inoperative unless it shall have been ratified as an amendment to the Constitution by conventions in the several States, as provided in the Constitution, within seven years from the date of the submission thereof to the States by the Congress.
[Ratified December 5, 1933]

Amendment [XXII.]

Section 1. No person shall be elected to the office of the President more than twice, and no person who has held the office of President, or acted as President, for more than two years of a term to which some other person was elected President shall be elected to the office of the President more than once. But this Article shall not apply to any person holding the office of President when this Article was proposed by the Congress, and shall not prevent any person who may be holding the office of President, or acting as President, during the term within which this Article becomes operative from holding the office of President or acting as President during the remainder of such term.

Section 2. This Article shall be inoperative unless it shall have been ratified as an amendment to the Constitution by the legislatures of three-

fourths of the several States within seven years from the date of its submission to the States by the Congress.
[Ratified March 1, 1951]

Amendment [XXIII.]

Section 1. The District constituting the seat of Government of the United States shall appoint in such manner as the Congress may direct:

A number of electors of President and Vice President equal to the whole number of Senators and Representatives in Congress to which the District would be entitled if it were a State, but in no event more than the least populous State; they shall be in addition to those appointed by the States, but they shall be considered, for the purposes of the election of President and Vice President, to be electors appointed by a State; and they shall meet in the District and perform such duties as provided by the twelfth article of amendment.

Section 2. The Congress shall have power to enforce this article by appropriate legislation.
[Ratified April 3, 1961]

Amendment [XXIV.]

Section. 1. The right of citizens of the United States to vote in any primary or other election for President or Vice President, for electors for President or Vice President, or for Senator or Representative in Congress, shall not be denied or abridged by the United States or any State by reason of failure to pay any poll tax or other tax.

Section 2. The Congress shall have power to enforce this article by appropriate legislation.
[Ratified January 23, 1964]

Amendment [XXV.]

Section 1. In case of the removal of the President from office or his death or resignation, the Vice President shall become President.

Section 2. Whenever there is a vacancy in the office of the Vice President, the President shall nominate a Vice President who shall take office upon confirmation by a majority vote of both houses of Congress.

Section 3. Whenever the President transmits to the President pro tempore of the Senate and the Speaker of the House of Representatives his written declaration that he is unable to discharge the powers and duties of his office, and until he transmits to them a written declaration to the contrary, such powers and duties shall be discharged by the Vice President as Acting President.

Section 4. Whenever the Vice President and a majority of either the principal officers of the executive department or of such other body as Congress may by law provide, transmit to the President pro tempore of the Senate and the Speaker of the House of Representatives their written declaration that the President is unable to discharge the powers and duties of his office, the Vice President shall immediately assume the powers and duties of the office as Acting President.

Thereafter, when the President transmits to the President pro tempore of the Senate and the Speaker of the House of Representatives his written declaration that no inability exists, he shall resume the powers and duties of his office unless the Vice President and a majority of either the principal officers of the executive department or of such other body as Congress may by law provide, transmit within four days to the President pro tempore of the Senate and the Speaker of the House of Representatives their written declaration that the President is unable to discharge the powers and duties of his office. Thereupon Congress shall decide the issue, assembling within 48 hours for that purpose if not in session. If the Congress, within 21 days after receipt of the latter written declaration, or, if Congress is not in session, within 21 days after Congress is required to assemble, determines that the President is unable to discharge the powers and duties of his office, the Vice President shall continue to discharge the same as Acting President; otherwise, the President shall resume the powers and duties of his office.
[Ratified February 11, 1967]

Amendment [XXVI.]

Section 1. The right of citizens of the United States, who are 18 years of age or older, to vote shall not be denied or abridged by the United States or any state on account of age.

Section 2. The Congress shall have the power to enforce this article by appropriate legislation.
[Ratified July 5, 1971]